The Adolescent Brain

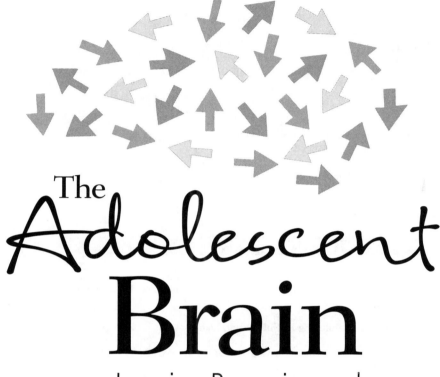

The Adolescent Brain

Learning, Reasoning, and Decision Making

Edited by
Valerie F. Reyna, Sandra B. Chapman,
Michael R. Dougherty, and Jere Confrey

American Psychological Association • Washington, DC

Published by
American Psychological Association
750 First Street, NE
Washington, DC 20002
www.apa.org

To order
APA Order Department
P.O. Box 92984
Washington, DC 20090-2984
Tel: (800) 374-2721; Direct: (202) 336-5510
Fax: (202) 336-5502; TDD/TTY: (202) 336-6123
Online: www.apa.org/books/
E-mail: order@apa.org

In the U.K., Europe, Africa, and the Middle East, copies may be ordered from
American Psychological Association
3 Henrietta Street
Covent Garden, London
WC2E 8LU England

Typeset in Goudy by Circle Graphics, Inc., Columbia, MD

Printer: Edwards Brothers, Inc., Ann Arbor, MI
Cover Designer: Naylor Design, Washington, DC

The opinions and statements published are the responsibility of the authors, and such opinions and statements do not necessarily represent the policies of the American Psychological Association.

Library of Congress Cataloging-in-Publication Data

The adolescent brain : learning, reasoning, and decision making / edited by Valerie F. Reyna . . . [et al.]. — 1st ed.
   p. cm.
 Includes index.
 ISBN-13: 978-1-4338-1070-1
 ISBN-10: 1-4338-1070-0
 1. Adolescent psychology. 2. Cognition in adolescence. I. Reyna, Valerie F., 1955-

 BF724.A274 2012
 155.5—dc23
                              2011025796

British Library Cataloguing-in-Publication Data

A CIP record is available from the British Library.

Printed in the United States of America
First Edition

DOI: 10.1037/13493-000

To my husband, Chuck, my partner in lab, love, and life;
and to my son, Bertrand, our best collaboration.
—*Valerie F. Reyna*

To my husband, Don, whose constant love and spirit of fun keep me
full of inspiration; to our amazing BrainHealth research team;
and to all the teenagers now and in the future.
—*Sandra B. Chapman*

To my wife, Jill, for her infinite patience and continued support,
and my two wonderful daughters, Emma and Eve,
for providing much-needed distractions.
—*Michael R. Dougherty*

To Ernst Von Glasersfeld (1917–2010), who taught all of us the
value of seeing the world through the eyes of children.
—*Jere Confrey*

CONTENTS

CONTRIBUTORS

Mark H. Ashcraft, PhD, Department of Psychology, University of Nevada, Las Vegas

Sharona M. Atkins, MA, Department of Psychology, University of Maryland, College Park

Kristen P. Blair, PhD, School of Education, Stanford University, Stanford, CA

Donald J. Bolger, PhD, Department of Human Development, University of Maryland, College Park

Michael F. Bunting, PhD, Center for Advanced Study of Language, University of Maryland, College Park

Christine M. Caffray, PhD, Children's Board of Hillsborough County, Tampa, FL

Sandra B. Chapman, PhD, Center for BrainHealth, Behavioral and Brain Sciences, The University of Texas at Dallas

Christina F. Chick, BA, Department of Human Development, Cornell University, Ithaca, NY

Jere Confrey, PhD, William and Ida Friday Institute for Educational Innovation, College of Education, North Carolina State University, Raleigh

Michael R. Dougherty, PhD, Department of Psychology, Program in Neuroscience and Cognition Science, University of Maryland, College Park

Amy Ellis, PhD, Department of Curriculum & Instruction, University of Wisconsin–Madison

Mathew D. Felton, PhD, Department of Mathematics, The University of Arizona, Tucson

Adriana Galván, PhD, Department of Psychology, Brain Research Institute, University of California, Los Angeles

Jacquelyn F. Gamino, PhD, Center for BrainHealth, The University of Texas at Dallas

Jay N. Giedd, MD, Child Psychiatry Branch, National Institute of Mental Health, National Institutes of Health, Bethesda, MD

Mary Hare, PhD, Department of Psychology, Bowling Green State University, Bowling Green, OH

Charles Kalish, PhD, Department of Educational Psychology, University of Wisconsin–Madison

Jennifer A. Kaminski, PhD, Center for Cognitive Science, The Ohio State University, Columbus

Saman Khalkhali, MSci, Department of Psychology, Social Science Centre, University of Western Ontario, London, Ontario, Canada

Eric Knuth, PhD, Department of Curriculum & Instruction, University of Wisconsin–Madison

Francois Lalonde, PhD, Child Psychiatry Branch, National Institute on Mental Health, National Institutes of Health, Bethesda, MD

Nancy Raitano Lee, PhD, Child Psychiatry Branch, National Institute on Mental Health, National Institutes of Health, Bethesda, MD

Rhoshel K. Lenroot, MD, Neuroscience Research Australia, Randwick, Sydney, Australia

Maria Liverpool, BA, Child Psychiatry Branch, National Institute on Mental Health, National Institutes of Health, Bethesda, MD

Ken McRae, PhD, Department of Psychology, University of Western Ontario, London, Ontario, Canada

Raksha Anand Mudar, PhD, Department of Speech and Hearing Science, University of Illinois at Urbana–Champaign

Valerie F. Reyna, PhD, Center for Behavioral Economics and Decision Research, Human Development, Psychology, Cognitive Science, and Neuroscience (IMAGINE Program), Cornell University, Ithaca, NY

Nathan O. Rudig, BA, Department of Psychology, University of Nevada, Las Vegas

Sandra L. Schneider, PhD, Department of Psychology, University of South Florida, Tampa

Daniel L. Schwartz, PhD, School of Education, Stanford University, Stanford, CA

Vladimir M. Sloutsky, PhD, Center for Cognitive Science, The Ohio State University, Columbus

Keith E. Stanovich, PhD, Department of Human Development and Applied Psychology, University of Toronto, Toronto, Ontario, Canada

Michael Stockman, BS, Child Psychiatry Branch, National Institute on Mental Health, National Institutes of Health, Bethesda, MD

Maggie E. Toplak, PhD, Department of Psychology, York University, Toronto, Ontario, Canada

Gregory L. Wallace, PhD, Child Psychiatry Branch, National Institute on Mental Health, National Institutes of Health, Bethesda, MD

Catherine Weddle, BA, Child Psychiatry Branch, National Institute on Mental Health, National Institutes of Health, Bethesda, MD

Richard F. West, PhD, Department of Graduate Psychology, James Madison University, Harrisonburg, VA

Caroline Williams, MA, Department of Curriculum & Instruction, University of Wisconsin–Madison

PREFACE

This book brings together the work of scientists with basic or foundational research expertise (e.g., cognitive, developmental, and social psychologists; neuroscientists) and those with an applied emphasis (e.g., on education; public health; applied economics and decision research; and science, technology, engineering, and mathematics, the so-called STEM fields) to address a critically understudied area in life-course learning: higher order cognition in adolescence and young adulthood. The purpose of integrating these scientific communities is twofold: (a) to advance the basic science of the developing brain by focusing scientists on key problems that are ripe for groundbreaking discoveries and (b) to apply cutting-edge theory and high-quality research methods to real-world problems of learning, cognition, and development, thereby enhancing the effectiveness of research and its immediate relevance to pressing societal needs.

A short time ago, such a book would have been impossible. Adolescence and emerging adulthood have become increasingly active areas of research in the past 30 years; the Society for Research on Adolescence was founded just 27 years ago. The pioneers in developmental neuroscience are contemporaries, cited heavily in the pages of this volume for their recent work. Only in the past decade have neuroimaging studies showing extensive brain development during adolescence through young adulthood debunked the myth that such development is complete in early childhood.[1] Especially pertinent to our focus on higher cognition, although brain areas corresponding to the basic functions of motor and sensory processing mature early, higher cognitive areas develop later during the teen years and even into the 20s. Brain areas that are involved in reasoning, planning, and decision making (e.g., the prefrontal cortex) change around the same time that activation of the "reward center" of the brain—the ventral striatum—also changes, and the connections between cognition- and emotion-related areas become strengthened. It is no wonder that interest in the adolescent brain has intensified, drawing in social, cognitive, developmental, and educational neuroscientists and clinical psychologists, among others.

The impetus for the book sprang from the Workshop on Higher Cognition in Adolescence and Young Adults: Social, Behavioral, and Biological Influences on Learning, sponsored by the National Science Foundation (NSF award BCS-0840111). The workshop was highly successful, attracting top scholars, encouraging interdisciplinary collaborations, and inspiring new research initiatives. Building on the fruits of that NSF workshop, but going far beyond it, this volume captures emerging science on the development of the brain in adolescence and young adulthood, particularly with respect to the advanced cognitive skills required in scientific and technical fields, but also in everyday life (e.g., skills involved in choosing to avoid unprotected sex).

Advanced cognitive skills, such as comprehension, reasoning, judgment, and decision making, are essential in a 21st-century knowledge-based economy. In this volume, we pay special attention to the acquisition of mathematical knowledge and skills and their application in reasoning (e.g., quantitative reasoning) and judgment (e.g., social and economic judgments). There are several reasons for this emphasis. First, the cognitive processes involved in learning mathematics are understudied relative to other educational skills, such as reading.[2] Second, difficulty in learning mathematics, notably algebra, but also ranging downward to fractions and upward to calculus, is a major cause of school failure and economic underachievement. In addition, understanding science, technology, and engineering requires mastery of the symbolic language of mathematics, a higher order cognitive skill.

---

[1]Dahl, R. E., & Spear, L. P. (2004). *Adolescent brain development: Vulnerabilities and opportunities*. Annals of the New York Academy of Science. New York, NY: New York Academy of Sciences. See Chapter 1 of this volume for an up-to-date review.
[2]National Mathematics Advisory Panel. (2008). *Foundations for success: The final report of the National Mathematics Advisory Panel*. Washington, DC: U.S. Department of Education.

Finally, life outcomes are linked to appreciating quantitative concepts, such as risk, probability, and expected value (the multiplicative integration of probability and reward to yield the "value" of gambles) and their cousins, such as expected utility (a version of expected value used by economists and decision researchers).[3]

The audience for this book includes researchers in all of the aforementioned disciplines and subdisciplines, as well as practitioners, educators, and policymakers. Clinical psychologists need to understand how higher cognition and emotion interrelate in high-risk behaviors and how development unfolds in the healthy brain. Those involved in the legal system, from social workers to judges, need to understand how cognitive control and decision making change across youth and influence crime and culpability. Educators need to understand how young people learn, especially how more students can transition to higher cognition and higher education; only 25% of the population currently completes college in the United States. This book is suitable for scholars as well as advanced undergraduates; graduate students in education, psychology, sociology, and neuroscience; and professional students in law and education. Although every effort was made to define technical terms, readers can also consult the *APA Dictionary of Psychology*[4] and the *APA College Dictionary of Psychology*[5] for useful explanations of terms, concepts, and theories.

Special thanks are due to Amy Sussman and Peter Vishton, Program Directors for Developmental and Learning Sciences at NSF; Karen Marrongelle, Program Director, Division of Research on Learning in Formal and Informal Settings at NSF, the Research and Evaluation on Education in Science and Engineering Program at NSF; and Michael Motes of the Center for BrainHealth. (Naturally, the views herein do not necessarily represent those of the NSF or its staff.) Thanks are also due to Karene Booker at Cornell University. Karene has been involved in every step, from conceptualization to constructing our website with free resources for the public and scholars (http://www.human.cornell.edu/hd/outreach-extension/nsfalw/index.cfm), to working with authors and advising regarding the cover art. Her contributions have been pivotal. Support from the National Cancer Institute, the National Institute on Aging, and the National Institutes of Health (Office of AIDS Research; American Recovery and Reinvestment Act) is also gratefully acknowledged.

---

[3]Reyna, V. F., Nelson, W., Han, P., & Dieckmann, N. F. (2009). How numeracy influences risk comprehension and medical decision making. *Psychological Bulletin, 135*, 943–973. doi:10.1037/a0017327

[4]VandenBos, G. R. (Ed.) (2007). *APA dictionary of psychology*. Washington, DC: American Psychological Association.

[5]*APA college dictionary of psychology* (2009). Washington, DC: American Psychological Association.

In closing, it is important to remember the ultimate reasons for understanding the adolescent brain: the 19-year-old college sophomore on the threshold of life, dead after alcohol intoxication; the 15-year-old who became homeless and 2 years later was admitted to Harvard University; and the 17-year-old high school dropout who became the U.S. Surgeon General. In these and many other instances, the pitfalls and possibilities of adolescence depend on developing the power of the human brain to learn, to reason, and to decide.

—Valerie F. Reyna

The Adolescent Brain

INTRODUCTION TO THE ADOLESCENT BRAIN: LEARNING, REASONING, AND DECISION MAKING

VALERIE F. REYNA, SANDRA B. CHAPMAN,
MICHAEL R. DOUGHERTY, AND JERE CONFREY

The period from adolescence through young adulthood is one of extraordinary promise and vulnerability (Santrock, 2010). Consistent with the World Health Organization and others, we define *adolescence* as roughly encompassing the second decade of life, which would include the proverbial college sophomore and other "emerging adults" (Arnett, 2000). The knowledge, skills, and habits of a lifetime are often established at this time of life, and they have disproportionate influence on the later economic productivity and health of individuals (Reyna & Farley, 2006).

To capture the relation between educational achievement and economic well-being, Chapman coined the term "brainomics" (Center for BrainHealth, n.d.; Chapman, 2011). Brainomics refers to the high economic cost of the failure of individuals to reach their cognitive potential. Economists have estimated that the benefit to the United States would amount to about $100 trillion if educational achievement were to match the levels of the highest performing countries, such as Finland and Canada, in mathematics, reasoning, and science (Hanushek & Woessmann, 2010). As Hanushek and Woessmann (2010) concluded, low educational achievement has a high economic cost (see also Reyna, Nelson, Han, & Dieckmann, 2009). Further, as the chapters in this volume attest, cognitively enriched lifestyles provide benefits beyond education, including effective regulation of emotion, avoidance of unhealthy or risky behaviors, and staving off of age-related cognitive decline.

In particular, the ability of young people to comprehend, imagine, reason, and decide sets a trajectory for their lives in education, careers, and patterns of behavior (Fischhoff, 2008). Research on brain development, reviewed in this volume, has documented the protracted and substantial changes in the brain that occur during the period from adolescence through the mid-20s. Areas underpinning higher cognition and cognitive control are among the latest areas to mature (e.g., Van Leijenhorst et al., 2010). Ergo, understanding the adolescent brain requires understanding the development of higher cognition and cognitive control and the interactions of these faculties with others via neural circuits (e.g., Somerville, Jones, & Casey, 2010).

Because of recent advances in functional brain imaging and other technologies over the past decade, we are experiencing a period of rapid discovery regarding the complex and asynchronous development of the adolescent brain. Ordinarily, there is a long lag time of approximately 20 to 30 years between discovery in basic research and implementation in the real world. However, we aim to accelerate this process of translation so that findings across areas of neuroscience can inform both public policy regarding investments in future research and educational practice regarding training the innovators and problem solvers of the future. We hope to further this aim of translation by including—under one cover—distinguished scientists from different disciplinary and subdisciplinary backgrounds. Thus, the contributions in this volume provide an overview of higher cognition in adolescents and young adults, with special emphasis on brain development and on learning of scientific reasoning and mathematical knowledge and skills that are relevant to real-world applications of comprehension, reasoning, judgment, and decision making.

A major implication of the research summarized in this book is the contrast between the advanced cognitive competence of adolescents and the failure to display that competence in socially important settings such as mathematics learning and everyday decision making. Historically, adolescence was viewed as the apogee of higher cognition, for instance, the period in which Piaget claimed that formal operational thought—the highest cognition—emerged. Later, information-processing theorists showed that cognition was efficient and accurate in adolescence, although subtle gaps in logic existed until late adolescence (Ricco & Overton, in press). However, the general intelligence that psychologists and economists have cited as humans' adaptive edge in negotiating the real world seems to be surprisingly absent among adolescents and young adults. The chapters in this volume confront this mystery with different approaches, some by pointing out effects of emotion on cognition, others by distinguishing intelligence from rationality, and still others by breaking higher cognition into separable components, such as verbatim-based versus gist-based reasoning or reward processing versus cognitive control, that are acquired at different rates by the developing brain (see also Chein, Albert, O'Brien, Uckert, & Steinberg, 2010).

Another major implication of the research, and a recurring theme across chapters, is that the adolescent brain is cognitively malleable, able to acquire advanced reasoning skills under the right conditions of training. This malleability is manifested by the ability to abstract and generalize learning principles across different content (e.g., science and mathematics, including logic) as well as to contexts requiring social reasoning (e.g., in risky decision making). As implicated in each part of this book, recent developments in research on the neural correlates of reasoning support the exciting possibility that fluid intelligence is trainable and that such intelligence can generalize to learning, social behavior, and occupational achievement (Sternberg, 2008). Our hope is that the evidenced-based principles delineated in these chapters will help inform educational practices to improve adolescent learning and achievement and to move teaching beyond rote learning to higher cognition. In a world in which information is changing rapidly, advancing higher cognition in adolescence requires that we take advantage of the developing capacity of adolescent brain to reason and to develop strategies, not simply train encoding and retrieval of discrete facts and knowledge that has been memorized. The ability to abstract principles through reasoning provides an advanced cognitive strategy to engage and build the rapidly developing frontal brain networks during this stage of life; to facilitate and enhance student learning across core content areas such as mathematics, social studies, science, and literature; and to improve the processes central to social reasoning in making healthy life choices. Therefore, this book concomitantly addresses advances in development, learning, social cognition, and cognitive neuroscience in practical ways, with specific ideas for advancing adolescents' life potential.

Specifically, the main body of the book is divided into three parts representing three areas of focus: Memory, Meaning, and Representation; Learning, Reasoning, and Problem Solving; and Judgment and Decision Making. These foci were selected to represent scholarly work that is exemplary and innovative in the area of higher cognition and the most practically relevant to applied concerns. Within each area, the chapter authors summarize research and discuss developmental differences in higher cognition between adolescents and either older adults or children; sometimes comparisons are made to both age groups. Authors also discuss how the expression of cognitive competence interacts with effects of emotion, inhibition, self-regulation, disabilities (e.g., attention deficits), and other individual and developmental differences (e.g., in intelligence). Although chapters have been allocated to these three parts, many of them defy narrow classification, spanning all or some of these areas. Thus, the reader will discover that some chapters in one part also discuss concepts examined in another.

The book begins with a part entitled "Foundations," containing a masterful overview of the development of the adolescent brain by Giedd and colleagues that touches on cognition, emotion, and behavior. They are able to draw on magnetic resonance imaging scans, neuropsychological testing, and genetic analysis from over 2,000 subjects, assessed longitudinally, to provide a comprehensive foundation for the chapters that follow.

McRae, Khalkhali, and Hare kick off "Memory, Meaning, and Representation" by discussing the preeminent role of meaning in semantic memory (the memory necessary for the use of language, or mental lexicon) and pointing out that there is significant development from adolescence to young adulthood in how word knowledge is mentally organized. This semantic organization, in turn, underlies such phenomena as memory for verbal materials and picture-word facilitation (or interference), which is relevant to the content and design of effective textbooks and other instructional materials. Because adolescents can define words and seem so cognitively advanced, this surprising growth in semantic organization is easily missed, despite its importance. In short, the adolescent brain becomes better organized around the meaning of concepts in memory.

"Memory, Meaning, and Representation" continues with a provocative chapter by Kaminski and Sloutsky on how providing concrete examples of abstract concepts can be less helpful for learning than providing decontextualized symbolic mathematics. In adolescence, students learn abstract concepts, such as those of algebra, with spotty success. Using a wide range of concepts from science and mathematics, Kaminski and Sloutsky explain how concrete examples can communicate irrelevant and superfluous information about an abstract concept, which students then mistakenly generalize to other superficially similar instances. The authors use rigorous evidence to challenge the pervasive assumption that abstract representations of information are harder to learn from than concrete examples.

In a counterpoint to Kaminski and Sloutsky, Blair and Schwartz ask whether there is still a place for concrete instructional materials in adolescence, despite the increased emphasis on abstract concepts in language and mathematics classes, compared with earlier grades. They propose a *co-evolution hypothesis*, which holds that the advantages of concrete and symbolic materials complement one another. They then apply this subtle hypothesis about interplay of representations to such topics as statistics, proportionality, and density. These authors also remind readers of the importance of meaning in external representations of concepts, noting that novices often misinterpret the meaning of presented materials and feedback.

This part closes with a chapter by Chapman, Gamino, and Mudar emphasizing the distinction between gist-based reasoning (i.e., reasoning using global, meaning-based memory representations) as opposed to using rote memorization and retrieval of facts to answer reasoning questions. Chapman et al. review evidence suggesting that gist-based reasoning entails frontally mediated, top-down cognitive control processes, which develop appreciably in adolescence. The work by Chapman and team illustrates that enhancing gist extraction—an advanced reasoning strategy—generalizes to other forms of learning, such as mathematical reasoning and nonverbal reasoning, that are not directly trained. They present further evidence that gist-based training is effective in reducing achievement gaps in normally developing adolescents and also in youth with brain injury and attention-deficit/hyperactivity disorder. Their general approach fits with others (see Chapters 8 and 12) who see potential benefits in training fluid intelligence as a way to increase the general capacity to think logically and solve problems in novel situations. This chapter provides a bridge between constructs of meaning, memory, and mental representation (gist vs. verbatim) and the following part, "Learning, Reasoning, and Problem Solving."

An expert in mathematics education, Confrey leads off the "Learning, Reasoning, and Problem Solving" part with an analysis of rational number processing from childhood to adolescence. Confrey explains how concepts of *a/b* (as fraction, ratio, and operator) can be derived from the more fundamental concept of equipartitioning. Poor understanding of these basic concepts has been identified as a major stumbling block in learning advanced concepts in algebra (National Mathematics Advisory Panel, 2008). Confrey describes different developmental trajectories in learning these basic concepts, based on her studies and those in the literature. She also presents a much-needed framework for corresponding diagnostic assessments that can be used with adolescent learners.

In the next chapter, Knuth, Kalish, Ellis, Williams, and Felton contrast the difficulty of mathematical reasoning, particularly proofs, with the relative ease of reasoning based on empirical evidence in nonmathematical domains (i.e., reasoning using concrete examples rather than abstract mathematical generalizations). In adolescence, students appear to have difficulty with the idea of mathematical truth, or deductive necessity, as opposed to inductive truth, in which generalizations are made based on examples. Middle schoolers progress in their justifications for such statements as "Adding any three odd numbers together gives an answer that is always odd." However, Knuth et al. report that less than half of the students produce appropriately general justifications by the end of middle school. Knuth et al. go on to compare performance of middle schoolers, college students, and science/technology/ engineering/mathematics, or STEM, experts on an array of problem types, with informative results for both theorists and practitioners.

Chapters in "Learning, Reasoning, and Problem Solving," such as Knuth et al.'s, characterize weaknesses in adolescent reasoning (as well as strengths), presenting a challenge to researchers and educators to find ways to improve such reasoning. Atkins, Bunting, Bolger, and Dougherty take up this challenge by offering a promising approach for improving adolescents' higher cognition. Atkins et al. turn the usual assumptions about cognitive development in adolescence on their heads. They argue that, far from being static, cognitive development and brain plasticity continue during adolescence, young adulthood, and beyond. Moreover, they present evidence that adaptive cognitive training can be used to remediate deficits and to improve cognitive abilities of adolescents. The premise of their approach is to train cognitive processes that are important for mental ability, including those that contribute to intelligence. They also review the associated neural circuits and their maturation in the adolescent brain and illustrate applications to dyslexia, attention–deficit disorder, and mathematical reasoning (among other topics). Like Chapman et al., Atkins et al. contradict the view of adolescence as "the culmination of cognitive development and the end of intellectual malleability" (p. 214, this volume).

The final contribution in the "Learning, Reasoning, and Problem Solving" part, by Ashcraft and Rudig, provides a bridge to the part that follows by discussing emotion and other noncognitive variables such as motivation, self-efficacy, and mathematics anxiety and their impact on adolescents' learning of mathematics in the classroom, also summarizing brain substrates for these functions. Experts on mathematics anxiety, Ashcraft and Rudig explain how such factors as stereotype threat (e.g., false beliefs that women are not competent at mathematics) and time pressure tax working memory resources, producing declines in mathematics performance, even when students are highly knowledgeable. As mathematics becomes more difficult in high school, the expected drop in performance due to anxiety becomes a greater problem. Ashcraft and Rudig remind readers that mathematics learning involves emotion, too, which clouds thinking and limits academic performance in adolescence. The research they present suggests that efforts to increase mathematics performance should target some of the straightforward and cost-effective strategies that have been developed to combat mathematics anxiety and stereotype threat (e.g., Cohen, Garcia, Apfel, & Master, 2006).

The effects of emotion are also central to the chapters under "Judgment and Decision Making." In the lead chapter in this part, Galván discusses some of the same brain areas implicated previously in the context of higher cognition and cognitive control. She describes research indicating that risk taking can be related to neurodevelopmental changes in brain regions critical for decision making, reward processing, and risky behavior, such as frontostriatal circuitry. In addition to the imbalance during adolescence of the developing prefrontal cognitive system (slower to develop) and the subcortical reward system (faster to develop), Galván introduces a critical third factor of environment, or the context of risk taking. Galván provides a comprehensive integration of evidence-based behavioral theories of risk taking and neurobiological evidence, with a focus on developmental changes in the brain.

Schneider and Caffray, in Chapter 11, take the study of risk taking further into the realm of health, examining emotional and motivational factors across a wide variety of behaviors. The period from adolescence to adulthood is the stage in which habits and lifestyles begin to crystallize, exerting lifelong influences on health. Although most scholars studying this period emphasize health-threatening behaviors (e.g., drinking alcohol, smoking cigarettes), Schneider and Caffray also examine health-enhancing behaviors (e.g., exercising, healthy eating). The authors integrate research on dual process theories, brain development, and individual differences, such as self-esteem and future orientation, with vivid insights into the daily affective promoters and deterrents of health behaviors in adolescence and emerging adulthood.

Whereas Schneider and Caffray describe how goals can differ across behaviors, Stanovich, West, and Toplak define *rationality* as the pursuit of appropriate goals. One might assume that intelligence is an asset in identifying and effectively pursuing goals and, thus, in behaving adaptively. However, smarter is not necessarily wiser. Stanovich et al. explain how rationality and intelligence differ conceptually and empirically. Research on developmental decreases in reasoning biases from childhood to adulthood (e.g., belief bias or reliance on statistical evidence) is juxtaposed with persistent or increasing biases across the same time period (e.g., myside bias, framing effects). These differing developmental trajectories converge with findings separating rationality from intelligence, including relations between IQ tests and judgment-and-decision-making biases. Stanovich et al. make sense of the paradox that modern technological societies, which promote consumption of all kinds, are hostile environments for intelligent young people.

In the fourth and final chapter in this part, Chick and Reyna describe a theory of adolescent learning, reasoning, and decision making that is grounded in experimental evidence as well as in surveys of adolescents' behaviors: fuzzy trace theory. They then use this theory to integrate and interpret evidence on neurodevelopment from adolescence to adulthood, explaining, for example, how massive pruning of gray matter coheres with assumptions about the growth of reliance on simpler representations and processes during this period. They also relate aspects of personality and motivation, such as reward

sensitivity and behavioral inhibition (self-control), to mental representations, retrieval of social and moral values, and application of these representations and values in real life, including discussing implications for behavioral
change in adolescence in a variety of domains of risky behavior.

Finally, in the Epilogue, Reyna and Dougherty describe the paradoxes
of the adolescent brain as illustrated in the aforementioned chapters: the
hyperrationality, which promotes risk taking (acting with thinking based on
cost-benefit analysis) versus impulsivity, which promotes a qualitatively different kind of risk taking (acting without thinking, which fits the stereotype
of adolescent irrationality). Reyna and Dougherty summarize the implications of developmental changes in higher cognition for important life outcomes, ranging from mathematics anxiety to unhealthy habits, concluding
that the way young people learn, reason, and decide *changes* and *can be changed*.
As all of these contributions illustrate, higher cognition continues to develop
substantially into adolescence and young adulthood, as reflected in studies of
brain development, with ramifications for education and health.

At a broader level, the relation between behavior and neuroscience is a
major crosscutting theme of the book. That is, the authors draw out implications of behavioral evidence, which are relevant for neuroscientific approaches,
as well as implications of neuroscientific evidence that are relevant for behavioral approaches. The methods of neuroscience have opened the door to new
questions about behavior and have uncovered surprising development in
the adolescent brain. However, much of this work has been descriptive and
correlational, rather than explanatory and predictive. As neuroscience continues to mature as an area of inquiry, it has already begun to focus increasingly on explanation and prediction, rather than merely description. Therefore,
the mechanisms tested in well-designed behavioral studies will provide crucial
constraints in understanding neurocircuitry and neurodevelopment. It is our
hope that this volume accelerates this process, furthering the essential exchange
among diverse scholars, to advance understanding of the adolescent brain.

REFERENCES

Arnett, J. J. (2000). Emerging adulthood: A theory of development from the late teens
through the twenties. *American Psychologist, 55,* 469–480. doi:10.1037/0003-
066X.55.5.469

Center for BrainHealth. (n.d.). In *Wikipedia.* Retrieved July 5, 2011, from http://en.
wikipedia.org/wiki/Center_for_BrainHealth

Chapman, S. (2011, June). Center for BrainHealth. *International Innovation,* 17–19.
Retrieved from http://www.researchmedia.eu

Chein, J., Albert, D., O'Brien, L., Uckert, K., & Steinberg, L. (2011). Peers increase adolescent risk taking by enhancing activity in the brain's reward circuitry. *Developmental Science, 14*, F1–F10.

Cohen, G. L., Garcia, J., Apfel, N., & Master, A. (2006, September 1). Reducing the racial achievement gap: A social-psychological intervention. *Science, 313*, 1307–1310. doi:10.1126/science.1128317

Fischhoff, B. (2008). Assessing adolescent decision-making competence. *Developmental Review, 28*, 12–28. doi:10.1016/j.dr.2007.08.001

Hanushek, E. A., & Woessmann, L. (2010). *The high cost of low educational performance: The long-run economic impact of improving PISA outcomes.* Paris, France: Organisation for Economic Cooperation and Development.

National Mathematics Advisory Panel. (2008). *Foundations for success: The final report of the National Mathematics Advisory Panel.* Washington, DC: U.S. Department of Education.

Reyna, V. F., & Farley, F. (2006). Risk and rationality in adolescent decision-making: Implications for theory, practice, and public policy. *Psychological Science in the Public Interest, 7*(1), 1–44.

Reyna, V. F., Nelson, W., Han, P., & Dieckmann, N. F. (2009). How numeracy influences risk comprehension and medical decision making. *Psychological Bulletin, 135*, 943–973. doi:10.1037/a0017327

Ricco, R. B., & Overton, W. F. (in press). Reasoning development and dual systems processing: Competence-procedural developmental systems theory. *Developmental Review.*

Santrock, J. W. (2010). *Adolescence* (13th ed.). New York, NY: McGraw-Hill Reyerson.

Somerville, L. H., Jones, R. M., & Casey, B. J. (2010). A time of change: Behavioral and neural correlates of adolescent sensitivity to appetitive and aversive environmental cues. *Brain and Cognition, 72*(1), 124–133. doi:10.1016/j.bandc.2009.07.003

Sternberg, R. J. (2008). Increasing fluid intelligence is possible after all. *Proceedings of the National Academy of Sciences, USA, 105*, 6791–6792.

Van Leijenhorst, L., Moor, B. G., Op de Macks, Z. A., Rombouts, S. A. R., Westenberg, P. M., & Crone, E. A. (2010). Adolescent risky decision-making: Neurocognitive development of reward and control regions. *NeuroImage, 51*(1), 345–355. doi:10.1016/j.neuroimage.2010.02.038

I
FOUNDATIONS

1

ANATOMIC MAGNETIC RESONANCE IMAGING OF THE DEVELOPING CHILD AND ADOLESCENT BRAIN

JAY N. GIEDD, MICHAEL STOCKMAN, CATHERINE WEDDLE,
MARIA LIVERPOOL, GREGORY L. WALLACE, NANCY RAITANO LEE,
FRANCOIS LALONDE, AND RHOSHEL K. LENROOT

Few parents of a teenager are surprised to hear that the brain of a 16-year-old is different from the brain of an 8-year-old. Yet pinning down these differences in a rigorous scientific way has been elusive. Magnetic resonance imaging, with the capacity to provide exquisitely accurate quantifications of brain anatomy and physiology without the use of ionizing radiation, has launched a new era of adolescent neuroscience. Longitudinal studies of subjects from the ages of 3 to 30 years demonstrate a general pattern of childhood peaks of gray matter followed by adolescent declines, functional and structural increases in connectivity and integrative processing, and a changing balance between limbic/subcortical and frontal lobe functions, extending well into young adulthood. Although overinterpretation and premature application of neuroimaging findings for diagnostic purposes remain risks, converging data from multiple imaging modalities are beginning to elucidate the implications of these brain changes for cognition, emotion, and behavior.

The brain is wrapped in a tough leathery membrane, surrounded by a cushioning moat of fluid, and completely encased in bone. This shielding has protected us well from falls and attacks by predators, but it has also created obstacles for scientists seeking to uncover its secrets. The advent of magnetic resonance imaging (MRI), which provides exquisitely accurate pictures of brain anatomy and physiology, has provided unprecedented access to the living, growing brain. It has been just over 20 years since the first MRI studies of healthy development were reported, using methods such as hand-drawing brain regions on paper prints of MRI scans to demonstrate age-related changes (Schaefer et al., 1990). Rapid improvements in MRI scanner technology and analysis methods have taken us to present-day studies, in which sophisticated mathematical models incorporating tens of thousands of high-resolution anatomical observations can be used to describe how complex systems of relationships between brain regions relate to maturing function (Dosenbach et al., 2010; Power, Fair, Schlaggar, & Petersen, 2010). One of the most important developments in the field has been the ability to begin mapping trajectories of brain maturation. Because MRI does not use ionizing radiation, it can be used not only to scan children but also to scan them repeatedly during the course of development. This capacity to safely acquire longitudinal brain maturation data has launched a new era of child and adolescent neuroscience.

Begun by Markus Krusei in 1989, our group at the Child Psychiatry Branch (CPB) of the National Institute of Mental Health (NIMH) has been conducting a study in which subjects between the ages of 3 and 30 years come to the campus in Bethesda, Maryland, at approximately 2-year intervals for MRI scans, neuropsychological testing, and genetic analysis. Currently, the database consists of over 6,000 scans from over 2,000 subjects, approximately half from clinical populations (e.g., subjects with conditions such as attention-deficit/hyperactivity disorder, autism, and childhood-onset schizophrenia) and half from typically developing people, including 800 scans from twins.

In this chapter, we summarize findings taken primarily from our work with typically developing subjects. The focus on MRI data from our lab is not meant to slight the excellent work done by many other groups but to provide an integrated overview from scans of subjects with the same inclusion/exclusion criteria acquired on the same scanner, using the same acquisition sequence and same methods of analysis. The organization of the chapter is to (a) describe developmental trajectories of brain anatomy during typical childhood and adolescence, (b) explore influences on the developmental trajectories, and (c) discuss implications of the neuroimaging findings.

MAPPING DEVELOPMENTAL ANATOMIC TRAJECTORIES DURING TYPICAL CHILDHOOD AND ADOLESCENCE

Longitudinal studies have made it possible to map how different parts of the brain change over time and to explore what factors may affect these trajectories. As described in this section, the path through development is different for males and females. The interaction between genetic and environmental factors shifts over the course of maturation, and specific genetic polymorphisms may affect the shape of the developmental curve in measurable ways. All of these findings, however, are dependent on precise and consistent methodology that allows the capture of subtle brain changes over time.

Methodological Considerations

MRI uses a powerful magnet, radio waves, and sophisticated computer software to discern signals from different types of brain tissue. These signal differences are driven mostly by the density of hydrogen atoms. Although in principle many different brain tissue classifications are feasible, the most common approach is to sort into (a) gray matter (GM); (b) white matter (WM); (c) cerebrospinal fluid; and (d) a miscellaneous category of "other," which may include vasculature, skin, bone, and so forth.

The smallest size of tissue that the MRI can measure is termed a *voxel*. The word *voxel* is a contraction of "volume element," and each voxel is assigned a single MRI signal value. For most studies in the literature, the cube-shaped voxel is around 1 cubic milliliter (ml), although with more powerful magnets and longer time in the scanner smaller voxel sizes are possible. The size of the voxel has important implications for what can be interpreted from the images, because within a 1-cubic-millimeter voxel there could be millions of neurons and trillions of synaptic connections.

Once anatomic MR images are acquired, they are processed with ever-evolving image analysis hardware and software tools. One fundamental objective is to classify every voxel of an individual's image as being of a certain tissue type and belonging to a predefined structure, lobe, or region of interest. Another fundamental goal of image analysis is to create a one-to-one correspondence between a given voxel in one brain to a corresponding voxel in the brains of other people or in the brain of the same person at a different point of development. If this one-to-one correspondence is reasonably well achieved, it opens the door to more powerful statistical approaches of comparing brains such as creating "average" brains of groups.

Total Cerebral Volume

In the CPB cohort, total cerebral volume follows an inverted-U-shaped trajectory peaking at age 10.5 in girls and 14.5 in boys (Lenroot et al., 2007). In both boys and girls, the brain is already at 95% of its peak size by age 6. A striking feature of brain size measures is the high variability across individuals. For example, as seen in Figure 1.1, two healthy 10-year-old boys can have a nearly twofold difference in total brain size. This high variability extends to measures of brain substructures as well, and it has important implications for the interpretation and utility of brain imaging results.

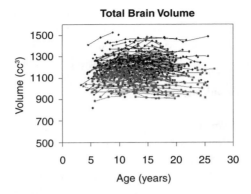

Total Brain Volume

Figure 1.1. Scatterplot of longitudinal measurements of total brain volume for males (*n* = 475 scans, shown in dark gray) and females (*n* = 354 scans, shown in light gray). Reprinted from "Sexual Dimorphism of Brain Developmental Trajectories During Childhood and Adolescence," by R. K. Lenroot, N. Gogtay, D. K. Greenstein, E. M. Wells, G. L. Wallace, L. S. Clasen, . . . J. N. Giedd, 2007, *NeuroImage, 36,* p. 1067. Figure in public domain.

Also noteworthy is that across these pediatric ages the group-average brain size for males is approximately 10% larger than for females (see Figure 1.2a). This 10% difference has also been found in hundreds of adult neuroimaging and post-mortem studies but is often explained as being related to the larger body size of males. However, in our pediatric subjects, the boys' bodies are not larger than girls' until after puberty. In fact, because of an earlier growth spurt, girls tend to be somewhat taller from ages 10 through 13, both in our sample and according to data from the Centers for Disease and Control and Prevention. Further evidence that brain size is not tightly linked to body size is the fundamental decoupling of brain- and body-size maturational trajectories, with body size increasing through approximately age 17.

One of the most important principles emerging from neuroimaging research is that differences in brain size should not be interpreted as necessarily imparting any sort of functional advantage or disadvantage. In the case of male/female differences, gross structural measures may not reflect sexually dimorphic differences in functionally relevant factors such as neuronal connectivity and receptor density.

Cerebellum

Cerebellum is Latin for "little brain," and in many ways this is an apt description. Although only about one ninth the volume of the cerebrum, the cerebellum actually contains more brain cells than the cerebrum. The function of the cerebellum has traditionally been described as related to motor control, but it is now commonly accepted that the cerebellum is also involved

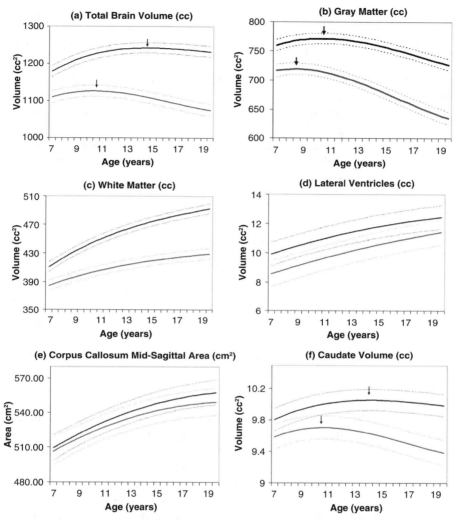

Figure 1.2. Mean volume by age in years for males (N = 475 scans) and females (N = 354 scans). Middle lines in each set of three lines represent mean values, and upper and lower lines represent upper and lower 95% confidence intervals. All curves differed significantly in height and shape with the exception of lateral ventricles, in which only height was different, and the mid-sagittal area of the corpus callosum, in which neither height nor shape was different. (a) Total brain volume, (b) gray matter volume, (c) white matter volume, (d) lateral ventricle volume, (e) mid-sagittal area of the corpus callosum, (f) caudate volume. Reprinted from "Sexual Dimorphism of Brain Developmental Trajectories During Childhood and Adolescence," by R. K. Lenroot, N. Gogtay, D. K. Greenstein, E. M. Wells, G. L. Wallace, L. S. Clasen, . . . J. N. Giedd, 2007, *NeuroImage, 36,* p. 1068. Figure in public domain.

in emotional processing and other higher cognitive functions that mature throughout adolescence (Riva & Giorgi, 2000; Schmahmann, 2004).

Similar to the cerebrum, developmental curves of total cerebellum size follow an inverted-U-shaped developmental trajectory with peak size occurring at age 11.3 in girls and age 15.6 in boys (Tiemeier et al., 2010). The cerebellum is not a unitary structure but is composed of functionally distinct subunits. In cross section, the anatomy of the cerebellum resembles a butterfly shape, with the central body part corresponding to the cerebellar vermis and the wings corresponding to the cerebellar hemispheric lobes. In contrast to the evolutionarily more recent cerebellar hemispheric lobes that followed the inverted-U-shaped developmental trajectory, cerebellar vermis size did not change across this age span.

Lateral Ventricles

The lateral ventricles are distinctive as a brain morphometry measure in that they are cerebrospinal fluid-filled compartments, not GM or WM. Lateral ventricle size measures are usually interpreted as an indirect assessment of loss of the tissue from neighboring structures, which define its borders. The increasing size of lateral ventricle volume is shown in Figure 1.2d. That ventricular volume increases so robustly during typical child and adolescent development should be considered when interpreting the many reports of increased ventricular volumes in a broad range of neuropsychiatric conditions.

White Matter

The "white" of white matter is from the color of myelin, a fatty insulating sheath from oligodendrocytes that wraps around axons and increases conduction velocity. The electrical insulating properties of myelin allow signals to travel at speeds up to 100 times faster than for unmyelinated axons. Also, in myelinated axons, the ion pumps need to reset the ion gradients only at nodes between sections of myelin, instead of along the entire expanse of the axons. This results in an up to a 30-fold increase in the frequency with which a given neuron can transmit information. The combination of increased speed ($100 \times$) and quicker recovery time ($30 \times$) can yield a 3,000-fold increase in the amount of information transmitted per second. This nonsubtle impact of myelin on the brain's ability to process information may underlie many of the cognitive abilities associated with our species.

WM volumes increased throughout childhood and adolescence in the CPB sample (Figure 1.2c). At lobar levels (i.e., frontal, temporal, and parietal lobes), the trajectories are roughly similar. However, for smaller regions the growth rates can be quite dynamic, with as much as a 50% change over a 2-year period (Thompson et al., 2000).

The corpus callosum (CC) is the most prominent WM structure and easily visualized on midsagittal MR images. The CC consists of approximately 200 million mostly myelinated axons connecting homologous areas of the left and right cerebral hemispheres. The functions of the CC can generally be thought of as integrating the activities of the left and right cerebral hemispheres, including functions related to the unification of sensory fields (Berlucchi, 1981; Shanks, Rockel, & Powel, 1975), memory storage and retrieval (Zaidel & Sperry, 1974), attention and arousal (Levy, 1985), and enhancement of language and auditory functions (Cook, 1986). In agreement with several studies that have indicated increasing CC size during adolescence (Allen, Richey, Chai, & Gorski, 1991; Cowell, Allen, Zalatimo, & Denenberg, 1992; Pujol, Vendrell, Junque, Marti-Vilalta, & Capdevila, 1993; Rauch & Jinkins, 1994; Thompson et al., 2000), total midsagittal CC area increased robustly from ages 4 through 20 years in the CPB sample (Figure 1.2e).

Increasing WM during childhood and adolescence allows for greater integration of disparate neural circuitry. This increased connectivity is the hallmark of many maturational changes in brain function. However, recent investigations into WM are revealing a much more nuanced role for myelin than a simple "pedal to the metal" increase in transmission speed. Neurons integrate information from other neurons by summing excitatory and inhibitory input. If excitatory input exceeds a certain threshold, the receiving neuron fires and initiates a series of molecular changes that strengthens the synapses, or connections, from the input neurons. Donald Hebb (1949) famously used the catchphrase "cells that fire together wire together" to describe the formation of cell assemblies through neuronal interactions. This process forms the basis for learning. For input from nearby and more distant neurons to arrive simultaneously, the transmission must be exquisitely timed. Myelin is intimately involved in the fine-tuning of this timing, which encodes the basis for thought, consciousness, and meaning in the brain. The dynamic activity of myelination during adolescence reflects how much new wiring is occurring. Myelination also plays a central role in developmental changes in the brain's ability to change in response to its environment by inhibiting axon sprouting and the creation of new synapses (Fields, 2008).

The centrality of WM in understanding brain development in health and illness has spurred the development of new imaging techniques, such as diffusion tensor imaging and magnetization transfer, which can be used to assess directionality and microstructure. These new techniques further confirm an increase in WM organization during adolescence, which correlates in specific brain regions with improvements in language (Nagy, Westerberg, & Klingberg, 2004), reading (Deutsch et al., 2005), ability to inhibit a response (Liston et al., 2006), and memory (Nagy et al., 2004).

Gray Matter

Tissue classified as GM by MRI consists mostly of cell bodies, dendrites, and dendritic processes but also includes axons, glia, blood vessels, and extracellular space (Braitenberg, 2001). Although GM and WM are bound by lifelong reciprocal relationships, they have different developmental trajectories (Figure 1.2b). Whereas WM increases throughout childhood and adolescence, GM developmental trajectories follow an inverted-U-shaped curve, with peak sizes occurring at different times in different regions. For instance, in the frontal lobes, peak cortical GM volume occurs at 9.5 years in girls and 10.5 years in boys; in the temporal lobes at 10.0 years in girls and 11.0 years in boys; and in the parietal lobes at 7.5 years in girls and 9 years in boys (Figure 1.3).

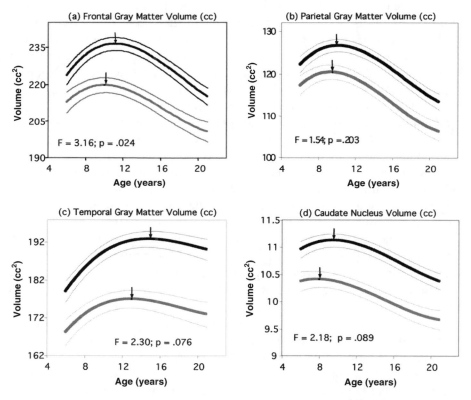

Figure 1.3. Gray matter subdivisions from same subjects as in Figure 1.2. (a) Frontal lobe, (b) parietal lobe, (c) temporal lobe, and (d) occipital lobe. Reprinted from "Sexual Dimorphism of Brain Developmental Trajectories During Childhood and Adolescence," by R. K. Lenroot, N. Gogtay, D. K. Greenstein, E. M. Wells, G. L. Wallace, L. S. Clasen, . . . J. N. Giedd, 2007, *NeuroImage, 36,* p.1069. Figure in public domain.

Cortical Gray Matter

Although some functional implications may be gleaned by examining GM at the lobar level, the capacity to quantify GM thickness at each of approximately 40,000 voxels on the brain surface provides a much more spatially nuanced approach. By analyzing scans acquired from the same individuals over the course of development, animations of cortical thickness change can be created. One such animation, derived from scans of 13 subjects who had each undergone scanning four times at approximately 2-year intervals between the ages of 4 and 22, is available online.[1] Still images of the animation at different ages are seen in Figure 1.3 (Gogtay et al., 2004).

The pattern of maturation is for GM to peak earliest in primary sensorimotor areas and latest in higher order association areas that integrate those primary functions such as the dorsolateral prefrontal cortex, inferior parietal, and superior temporal gyrus. Postmortem studies suggest that part of the GM changes may be related to synaptic proliferation and pruning (Huttenlocher, 1994). The connection between GM volume reductions, electroencephalography (EEG) changes, and synaptic pruning is also supported by an MRI/quantified EEG study of 138 healthy subjects from ages 10 to 30 years. Curvilinear reductions in frontal and parietal GM were matched by similar curvilinear reductions in EEG power of the corresponding regions (Whitford et al., 2007). Because EEG power reflects synaptic activity, the temporally linked EEG power and GM changes suggest that the GM volume reductions are accompanied by reductions in the number of synapses. Another consideration is that myelination may change classification of voxels along the interior cortical border from GM to WM, resulting in ostensible cortical thinning as assessed by MR volumetrics, but would not necessarily entail changes in the number of synapses (Sowell, Thompson, Tessner, & Toga, 2001). Knowledge of the degree to which these and other phenomena may be driving the MR changes has profound implications for interpreting the imaging results. Imaging of nonhuman primates with postmortem validation may help discern the cellular phenomenon underlying the MRI changes.

Subcortical Gray Matter—Basal Ganglia

The basal ganglia are a collection of subcortical nuclei (caudate, putamen, globus pallidus, subthalamic nucleus, and substantia nigra) that are involved in circuits mediating movement, higher cognitive functions, attention, and affective states. Basal ganglia anomalies have been reported for almost all neuropsychiatric disorders that have been investigated by neuroimaging (Giedd, Shaw, Wallace, Gogtay, & Lenroot, 2006). Because of the

---

[1]Retrieved from http://www.nimh.nih.gov/videos/press/prbrainmaturing.mpeg

small size and ambiguity of MR signal contrast of the borders defining the structures, only the caudate, putamen, and globus pallidus are readily quantifiable by MRI, and reliable automated techniques have been established only for the caudate. Like cortical GM, the caudate follows an inverted-U-shaped developmental trajectory, peaking at age 10.5 years in girls and 14.0 years in boys (see Figure 1.2f). The shape of the caudate developmental trajectory is more similar to that of frontal and parietal GM than temporal, supporting the notion that brain regions that share extensive connections also share similar developmental courses.

Subcortical Gray Matter—Amygdala and Hippocampus

The temporal lobes, amygdala, and hippocampus are integral players in the arenas of emotion, language, and memory (Nolte, 1993). Human capacity for these functions changes markedly between the ages of 4 and 18 years (Diener, Sandvik, & Larsen, 1985; Jerslid, 1963; Wechsler, 1974), although the relationship between the development of these capacities and morphological changes in the structures subserving these functions is poorly understood.

Valid quantification of amygdala and hippocampus volumes still requires manual tracing by expert raters and has not been completed for the longitudinal sample. In a previous report from a cross-sectional sample subset of the NIMH sample, amygdala volume increased significantly during adolescence only in males, and hippocampal volume increased significantly only in females (Giedd et al., 1996). This pattern of gender-specific maturational volumetric changes is consistent with nonhuman primate studies indicating a relatively higher number of androgen receptors in the amygdala (Clark, MacLusky, & Goldman-Rakic, 1988) and a relatively higher number of estrogen receptors in the hippocampus (Morse, Scheff, & DeKosky, 1986).

INFLUENCES ON DEVELOPMENTAL TRAJECTORIES OF BRAIN ANATOMY DURING CHILDHOOD AND ADOLESCENCE

The studies described thus far showed the overall course of brain development, opening the way to explore the effects of specific factors on the shape of the trajectory. This includes using statistical quantitative genetic methods such as twin studies to estimate relative effects of genes and environment, modeling effects of specific genes, and description of sex differences.

Genes and Environment

By comparing similarities between monozygotic (MZ) twins, who share approximately 100% of the same genes, and dizygotic (DZ) twins, who share approximately 50% of the same genes, we can estimate the relative contributions of genetic and nongenetic influences on trajectories of brain development. To pursue this question we are conducting a longitudinal neuroimaging study of twins and currently have acquired approximately 600 scans from 90 MZ and 60 DZ twin pairs.

The nature-versus-nurture question of biology has long been put to rest as a false dichotomy, as abundant evidence has made it clear that it is the developmentally sensitive interaction of genes and environment that leads to a person's unique phenotype. Sophisticated mathematical approaches, such as structural equation modeling (SEM), can be used to assess gene–environment interactions and other epistatic phenomena that challenge conventional interpretation of twin data. SEM describes the interacting effects as (A) additive genetic, (C) shared environmental, or (E) unique environmental factors (Neale, Cardon, & North Atlantic Treaty Organization, Scientific Affairs Division, 1992). For most brain structures examined, additive genetic effects (i.e., "heritability") are high and shared environmental effects are low (Wallace et al., 2006). Additive genetic effects for total cerebral and lobar volumes (including GM and WM subcompartments) ranged from 0.77 to 0.88; for the caudate, 0.80; and for the corpus callosum, 0.85. The cerebellum has a distinctive heritability profile with an additive genetic effect of only 0.49, although wide confidence intervals merit cautious interpretation. Highly heritable brain morphometric measures provide biologic markers for inherited traits and may serve as targets for genetic linkage and association studies (Gottesman & Gould, 2003).

Multivariate analyses allow assessment of the degree to which the same genetic or environmental factors contribute to multiple neuroanatomic structures. Like the univariate variables, these interstructure correlations can be parceled into relationships of either genetic or environmental origin. This knowledge is vitally important for interpretation of most of the twin data, including understanding the impact of genes that may affect distributed neural networks, as well as interventions that may have global brain impacts. Shared effects account for more of the variance than structure-specific effects, with a single genetic factor accounting for 60% of variability in cortical thickness (Schmitt et al., 2007). Six factors account for 58% of the remaining variance, with five groups of structures strongly influenced by the same underlying genetic factors. These findings are consistent with the radial unit hypothesis of neocortical expansion proposed by Rakic (1995) and with hypotheses that global, genetically mediated differences in cell division were the driving force behind interspecies differences in total brain volume (Darlington, Dunlop, & Finlay, 1999; Finlay & Darlington, 1995; Fishell, 1997). Expanding the entire brain when only specific functions might be selected for is metabolically costly, but the mutations required to affect cell division would be far fewer than those required to completely change cerebral organization.

Age-related changes in heritability may be linked to the timing of gene expression and related to the age of onset of disorders. In general, heritability increases with age for WM and decreases for GM volumes (Wallace et al., 2006), whereas heritability increases for cortical thickness in regions within the frontal cortex, parietal, and temporal lobes (Lenroot et al., 2009). Knowledge of when certain brain structures are particularly sensitive to genetic or environmental influences during development could have important educational and/or therapeutic implications.

Male/Female Differences

Given that nearly all neuropsychiatric disorders have different prevalence, age of onset, and symptomatology between males and females, sex differences in typical developmental brain trajectories are highly relevant for studies of pathology. As described under the section on individual areas of brain anatomy, above, the NIMH study found robust sex differences in developmental trajectories for nearly all structures, with GM volume peaks generally occurring 1 to 4 years earlier in females (Lenroot et al., 2007). Cortical thickness also showed different rates of development in males and females (Raznahan et al., 2010). In a subsample of the National Institutes of Health cohort studied between ages 9 and 22, overall cortical thickness was greater in males at age 9. Although cortical thinning occurred in both males and females over adolescence, rates of thinning were more rapid in males in several areas, particularly in the frontal lobes. Regions in the frontal lobes that had a relatively protracted maturational course in males are also those associated with functions such as self-regulation and impulse control, intriguingly consistent with the greater likelihood of risk-taking behaviors in males typically observed during adolescence.

The earlier peaking of brain volumes in females is similar to the earlier average female age of puberty, suggesting that the rising levels of pubertal hormones may be affecting the trajectory of development. Studies attempting to separate out effects of pubertal maturation from chronological age on brain development have begun to appear. For example, Bramen et al. (2011) compared volumes of GM in adolescent boys and girls matched on stage of pubertal maturation rather than age. As in the NIMH study, robust differences between males and females were found in hippocampal and amygdala volumes. The Bramen study was also able to show that differences increased with advancing sexual maturation, supporting sex-specific maturational trajectories as being related to pubertal influences in addition to age.

Recent work mapping the effects of androgen receptor (AR) polymorphisms further demonstrates the effects of sex steroids on brain maturation during adolescence. The X-linked gene encoding the AR receptor contains a functional trinucleotide (CAG)n repeat, whose length is related to the efficiency of the receptor's activity: Higher numbers of repeats are associated with lower levels of AR function, which has been linked in several studies to differences in sexually differentiated aspects of anatomy and function (Buchanan et al., 2004). In the NIH study of sex differences in cortical thickness described above, AR genotype (low vs. high numbers of CAG repeats) had a significant effect on the trajectory of cortical development. The more active form of AR was associated with a trajectory more similar to the overall masculine pattern than the less active form, consistent with a contribution of testosterone exposure in creating the sex differences seen during adolescence (Raznahan et al., 2010). Other groups have also shown effects of testosterone on adolescent GM and WM development and that the effects of testosterone are more pronounced in the presence of the more active form of the AR (Paus et al., 2010).

To assess the relative contributions of sex chromosomes and hormones, our group is studying subjects with anomalous sex chromosome variations (e.g., XXY, XXX, XXXY, XYY; Giedd et al., 2007), as well as subjects with anomalous hormone levels (seen as, e.g., congenital adrenal hyperplasia, familial male precocious puberty, and Cushing syndrome; Merke et al., 2003, 2005).

Specific Genes

As with any quantifiable behavioral or physical parameter, individuals can be categorized into groups on the basis of genotype. Brain images of individuals in the different genotype groups can then be averaged and compared statistically. In adult populations, one of the most frequently studied genes has been apolipoprotein E (*apoE*), which modulates risk for Alzheimer's disease. Carriers of the 4 allele of *apoE* have increased risk, whereas carriers of the 2 allele are possibly at decreased risk. To explore whether *apoE* alleles have distinct neuroanatomic signatures identifiable in childhood and adolescence, we examined 529 scans from 239 healthy subjects ages 4 to 20 years (Shaw et al., 2007). Although there were no significant IQ–genotype interactions, there was a stepwise effect on cortical thickness in the entorhinal and right hippocampal regions, with the 4 group exhibiting the thinnest, the 3 homozygotes in the middle range, and the 2 group the thickest cortices. These data suggest that pediatric assessments might one day be informative for adult-onset disorders.

SUMMARY AND DISCUSSION

Anatomic brain MRI measures show high individual variability. The high variability and substantial overlap of most measures for most groups being compared have profound implications for the diagnostic utility of psychiatric neuroimaging and the sensitivity and specificity in using neuroimaging to make predictions about behavior or ability in a particular individual. For example, although group average anatomic MRI differences have been reported for all major psychiatric disorders, MRI is not currently indicated for the routine diagnosis of any of them. Likewise, although, based on group averages, there are statistically robust differences between male and female brains, there is nothing on an individual MRI brain scan to confidently discern whether it is from a man or a woman. As an analogy, height for adult men is significantly greater than height for adult women. However, because there are so many women taller than many men, height alone would not be a very useful way to determine someone's sex. Male/female differences in height are larger in magnitude than neuroimaging or neuropsychological measures. Extrapolating from group average differences to individuals is one of the preeminent challenges of neuroimaging. A more immediate use of neuroimaging may be to provide endophenotypes, biologic markers that are intermediate between genes and behavior. Endophenotypes identified using neuroimaging methods have the potential to define biologically meaningful subtypes of disorders that may respond to different interventions.

Despite high individual variation, several statistically robust patterns of average maturational changes are evident. Specifically, WM volumes increase and GM volumes follow an inverted-U developmental trajectory, with peaks latest in high-association areas such as the dorsolateral prefrontal cortex.

These anatomic changes are consistent with electroencephalographic, functional MRI, postmortem, and neuropsychological studies indicating an increasing connectivity in the developing brain. *Connectivity* characterizes several neuroscience concepts. In anatomic studies, connectivity can mean a physical link between areas of the brain that share common developmental trajectories. In studies of brain function, connectivity describes the relationship between different parts of the brain that activate together during a task. In genetic studies, it refers to different regions that are influenced by the same genetic or environmental factors. All of these types of connectivity increase during adolescence (Power et al., 2010). A linguistic metaphor would be to consider the maturational changes not so much as adding new letters to the alphabet as combining existing letters into words, those words into sentences, and the sentences into paragraphs. Characterizing developing neural circuitry and the changing relationships among disparate brain components is one of the most active areas of neuroimaging research, using graph theory to quantify such things as small-world network properties of the brain (Hagmann et al., 2010).

Relatively late maturation of the dorsolateral prefrontal cortex, which is prominently involved in neural circuitry involved in judgment, decision making, and impulse control, has prominently entered discourse affecting the social, legislative, judicial, parenting, and educational realms. It is also consistent with a growing body of literature indicating a changing balance between earlier-maturing limbic system networks, the seat of emotion, and later-maturing frontal systems (Somerville, Jones, & Casey, 2010). The frontal/limbic relationship is highly dynamic. Appreciating the interplay between limbic and cognitive systems is imperative for understanding decision making during adolescence. Psychological tests are usually conducted under conditions of cold cognition—hypothetical, low-emotion situations. However, real-world decision making often occurs under conditions of hot cognition—high arousal, with peer pressure and real consequences. Neuroimaging investigations continue to discern the different biological circuitry involved in hot and cold cognition and are beginning to map how the parts of the brain involved in decision making mature (Van Leijenhorst et al., 2010).

In many ways, facilitating improved decision making is at the heart of interventions to help adolescent lives. At a time when many physical capacities are at their peak (e.g., strength, immunity, resistance to cancer), it is the decisions adolescents make that underlie most of the morbidity and mortality seen. Motor vehicle accidents, substance abuse, unwanted pregnancy, criminal actions, educational achievement, and development of skills preparing for the next stage of life can all be seen as directly related to the decisions adolescents make.

One aspect of decision making that is particularly relevant is the notion of temporal discounting, whereby younger people give less weight to future events. For instance, given a choice between a smaller immediate reward and a larger later reward, adolescents, more than adults, will require larger later rewards and shorter times of waiting before choosing against the immediate reward. Perhaps this is related to the protracted maturation of the frontal lobes, which allow us to "time travel" in the sense of imagining the future consequences of different courses of action without having to carry out the behaviors in the physical world. Appreciating adolescents' different weighing of long-term consequences has implications for understanding their decision making and guiding what interventions are likely to be most fruitful.

Another prominent challenge for linking brain-imaging findings to behavior, cognition, and emotion is that behaviors emanate from the integrated activity of distributed networks, not individual structures. Further complicating brain/behavior investigations is the growing realization that differences in the trajectories of development may in some cases be more informative than the final adult differences. For instance, in our longitudinal study looking at the relationship between cortical thickness and IQ differences, the shapes of the developmental curves of cortical thickness were more predictive of IQ than absolute differences in cortical thickness at age 20 years (Shaw et al., 2006). Trajectories are also more discriminating than static measures for sexual dimorphism and clinical investigations. The idea that in neuroimaging, as in life, the journey is often as important as the destination is becoming an accepted tenet of pediatric neuroimaging.

The "journey as well as destination" tenet also highlights the fundamentally dynamic nature of brain development. In fact, one of the most striking features of pediatric neuroimaging has been the ability to capture the phenomenal changeability of the human brain. The ability of our brains to adapt and change based on the demands of the environment is the hallmark of our species.

The dynamic brain changes during adolescence may be related to the emergence during this time of many types of psychopathology (Paus, Keshavan, & Giedd, 2008). However, it also confers an excellent opportunity for learning and adaptation. Understanding the mechanisms and influences may help us to harness the brain's plasticity, guiding interventions for clinical disorders and elucidating the path to optimal healthy development.

REFERENCES

Allen, L. S., Richey, M. F., Chai, Y. M., & Gorski, R. A. (1991). Sex differences in the corpus callosum of the living human being. *The Journal of Neuroscience, 11*, 933–942.

Berlucchi, G. (1981). Interhemispheric asymmetries in visual discrimination: A neurophysiological hypothesis. *Documenta Ophthalmologica. Proceedings Series, 30*, 87–93.

Braitenberg, V. (2001). Brain size and number of neurons: an exercise in synthetic neuroanatomy. *Journal of Computational Neuroscience, 10*(1), 71–77.

Bramen, J. E., Hranilovich, J. A., Dahl, R. E., Forbes, E. E., Chen, J., Toga, A. W., . . . Sowell, E. R. (2011). Puberty influences medial temporal lobe and cortical gray matter maturation differently in boys than girls matched for sexual maturity. *Cerebral Cortex, 21*, 636–646. doi:10.1093/cercor/bhq137

Buchanan, G., Yang, M., Cheong, A., Harris, J. M., Irvine, R. A., Lambert, P. F., . . . Tilley, W. D. (2004). Structural and functional consequences of glutamine tract variation in the androgen receptor. *Human Molecular Genetics, 13*, 1677–1692. doi:10.1093/hmg/ddh181

Clark, A. S., MacLusky, N. J., & Goldman-Rakic, P. S. (1988). Androgen binding and metabolism in the cerebral cortex of the deveoping rhesus monkey. *Endocrinology, 123,* 932–940. doi:10.1210/endo-123-2-932

Cook, N. D. (1986). *The brain code:Mechanisms of information transfer and the role of the corpus callosum.* London, England: Methuen.

Cowell, P. E., Allen, L. S., Zalatimo, N. S., & Denenberg, V. H. (1992). A developmental study of sex and age interactions in the human corpus callosum. *Developmental Brain Research, 66,* 187–192. doi:10.1016/0165-3806(92)90079-C

Darlington, R. B., Dunlop, S. A., & Finlay, B. L. (1999). Neural development in metatherian and eutherian mammals: Variation and constraint. *The Journal of Comparative Neurology, 411,* 359–368. doi:10.1002/(SICI)1096-9861(19990830) 411:3<359::AID-CNE1>3.0.CO;2-J

Deutsch, G. K., Dougherty, R. F., Bammer, R., Siok, W. T., Gabrieli, J. D., & Wandell, B. (2005). Children's reading performance is correlated with white matter structure measured by diffusion tensor imaging. *Cortex, 41,* 354–363. doi:10.1016/ S0010-9452(08)70272-7

Diener, E., Sandvik, E., & Larsen, R. F. (1985). Age and sex effects for affect intensity. *Developmental Psychology, 21,* 542–546. doi:10.1037/0012-1649. 21.3.542

Dosenbach, N. U., Nardos, B., Cohen, A. L., Fair, D. A., Power, J. D., . . . Schlaggar, B. L. (2010, September 10). Prediction of individual brain maturity using fMRI. *Science, 329,* 1358–1361. doi:10.1126/science.1194144

Fields, R. D. (2008). White matter in learning, cognition and psychiatric disorders. *Trends in Neurosciences, 31,* 361–370. doi:10.1016/j.tins.2008.04.001

Finlay, B. L., & Darlington, R. B. (1995, June 16). Linked regularities in the development and evolution of mammalian brains. *Science, 268,* 1578–1584. doi:10.1126/ science.7777856

Fishell, G. (1997). Regionalization in the mammalian telencephalon. *Current Opinion in Neurobiology, 7,* 62–69. doi:10.1016/S0959-4388(97)80121-3

Giedd, J. N., Clasen, L. S., Wallace, G. L., Lenroot, R. K., Lerch, J. P., Wells, E. M., . . . Samango-Sprouse, C. A. (2007). XXY (Klinefelter syndrome): A pediatric quantitative brain magnetic resonance imaging case-control study. *Pediatrics, 119,* e232–e240. doi:10.1542/peds.2005-2969

Giedd, J. N., Shaw, P., Wallace, G., Gogtay, N., & Lenroot, R. K. (2006). Anatomic brain imaging studies of normal and abnormal brain development in children and adolescents. In D. Cicchetti & D. J. Cohen (Eds.), *Developmental psychopathology* (2nd ed., Vol. 2, pp. 127–196). Hoboken, NJ: Wiley.

Giedd, J. N., Vaituzis, A. C., Hamburger, S. D., Lange, N., Rajapakse, J. C., Kaysen, D., . . . Rapoport, J. L. (1996). Quantitative MRI of the temporal lobe, amygdala, and hippocampus in normal human development: Ages 4–18 years. *The Journal of Comparative Neurology, 366,* 223–230. doi:10.1002/(SICI)1096- 9861(19960304)366:2<223::AID-CNE3>3.0.CO;2-7

Gogtay, N., Giedd, J. N., Lusk, L., Hayashi, K. M., Greenstein, D., Vaituzis, A. C., . . . Thompson, P. M. (2004). Dynamic mapping of human cortical development during childhood through early adulthood. *PNAS*, *101*, 8174–8179. doi:10.1073/pnas.0402680101

Gottesman, I. I., & Gould, T. D. (2003). The endophenotype concept in psychiatry: Etymology and strategic intentions. *The American Journal of Psychiatry*, *160*, 636–645. doi:10.1176/appi.ajp.160.4.636

Hagmann, P., Sporns, O., Madan, N., Cammoun, L., Pienaar, R., Wedeen, V. J., . . . Grant, P. E. (2010). White matter maturation reshapes structural connectivity in the late developing human brain. *PNAS, USA*, *107*, 19067–19072. doi:10.1073/pnas.1009073107

Hebb, D. O. (1949). *The organization of behavior*. New York, NY: Wiley.

Huttenlocher, P. R. (1994). Synaptogenesis in human cerebral cortex. In G. Dawson & K. Fischer (Eds.), *Human behavior and the developing brain* (pp. 137–152). New York, NY: Guilford Press.

Jerslid, A. T. (1963). *The psychology of adolescence* (2nd ed.). New York, NY: Macmillan.

Lenroot, R. K., Gogtay, N., Greenstein, D. K., Wells, E. M., Wallace, G. L., Clasen, L. S., . . . Giedd, J. N. (2007). Sexual dimorphism of brain developmental trajectories during childhood and adolescence. *NeuroImage*, *36*, 1065–1073. doi:10.1016/j.neuroimage.2007.03.053

Lenroot, R. K., Schmitt, J. E., Ordaz, S. J., Wallace, G. L., Neale, M. C., Lerch, J. P., . . . Giedd, J. N. (2009). Differences in genetic and environmental influences on the human cerebral cortex associated with development during childhood and adolescence. *Human Brain Mapping*, *30*, 163–174. doi:10.1002/hbm.20494

Levy, J. (1985). Interhemispheric collaboration: single mindedness in the asymmetric brain. In C. T. Best (Ed.), *Hemisphere function and collaboration in the child* (pp. 11–32). New York, NY: Academic Press.

Liston, C., Watts, R., Tottenham, N., Davidson, M. C., Niogi, S., Ulug, A. M., & Casey, B. J. (2006). Frontostriatal microstructure modulates efficient recruitment of cognitive control. *Cerebral Cortex*, *16*, 553–560. doi:10.1093/cercor/bhj003

Merke, D. P., Fields, J. D., Keil, M. F., Vaituzis, A. C., Chrousos, G. P., & Giedd, J. N. (2003). Children with classic congenital adrenal hyperplasia have decreased amygdala volume: Potential prenatal and postnatal hormonal effects. *The Journal of Clinical Endocrinology and Metabolism*, *88*, 1760–1765. doi:10.1210/jc.2002-021730

Merke, D. P., Giedd, J. N., Keil, M. F., Mehlinger, S. L., Wiggs, E. A., Holzer, S., . . . Chrousos, G. P. (2005). Children experience cognitive decline despite reversal of brain atrophy one year after resolution of Cushing syndrome. *The Journal of Clinical Endocrinology and Metabolism*, *90*, 2531–2536. doi:10.1210/jc.2004-2488

Morse, J. K., Scheff, S. W., & DeKosky, S. T. (1986). Gonadal steroids influence axonal sprouting in the hippocampal dentate gyrus: A sexually dimorphic response. *Experimental Neurology, 94,* 649–658. doi:10.1016/0014-4886 (86)90244-X

Nagy, Z., Westerberg, H., & Klingberg, T. (2004). Maturation of white matter is associated with the development of cognitive functions during childhood. *Journal of Cognitive Neuroscience, 16,* 1227–1233. doi:10.1162/0898929041920441

Neale, M. C., Cardon, L. R., & North Atlantic Treaty Organization, Scientific Affairs Division. (1992). *Methodology for genetic studies of twins and families.* Dordrecht, Netherlands; Boston, MA: Kluwer Academic.

Nolte, J. (1993). Olfactory and limbic systems. In R. Farrell (Ed.), *The human brain: An introduction to its functional anatomy* (3rd ed., pp. 397–413). St. Louis, MO: Mosby-Year Book.

Paus, T., Keshavan, M., & Giedd, J. N. (2008). Why do many disorders emerge during adolescence? *Nature Reviews Neuroscience, 9,* 947–957.

Paus, T., Nawaz-Khan, I., Leonard, G., Perron, M., Pike, G. B., Pitiot, A., . . . Pausova, Z. (2010). Sexual dimorphism in the adolescent brain: Role of testosterone and androgen receptor in global and local volumes of grey and white matter. *Hormones and Behavior, 57*(1), 63–75. doi:10.1016/j.yhbeh. 2009.08.004

Power, J. D., Fair, D. A., Schlaggar, B. L., & Petersen, S. E. (2010). The development of human functional brain networks. *Neuron, 67,* 735–748. doi:10.1016/ j.neuron.2010.08.017

Pujol, J., Vendrell, P., Junque, C., Marti-Vilalta, J. L., & Capdevila, A. (1993). When does human brain development end? Evidence of corpus callosum growth up to adulthood. *Annals of Neurology, 34,* 71–75. doi:10.1002/ana.410340113

Rakic, P. (1995). A small step for the cell, a giant leap for mankind: A hypothesis of neocortical expansion during evolution. *Trends in Neurosciences, 18,* 383–388. doi:10.1016/0166-2236(95)93934-P

Rauch, R. A., & Jinkins, J. R. (1994). Analysis of cross-sectional area measurements of the corpus callosum adjusted for brain size in male and female subjects from childhood to adulthood. *Behavioural Brain Research, 64,* 65–78. doi:10.1016/0166-4328 (94)90119-8

Raznahan, A., Lee, Y., Stidd, R., Long, R., Greenstein, D., Clasen, L., . . . Giedd, J. N. (2010). Longitudinally mapping the influence of sex and androgen signaling on the dynamics of cortical maturation in adolescence. *Proceedings of the National Academy of Sciences, USA, 107,* 16988–16993. doi:10.1073/pnas. 1006025107

Riva, D., & Giorgi, C. (2000). The cerebellum contributes to higher functions during development: Evidence from a series of children surgically treated for posterior fossa tumours. *Brain: A Journal of Neurology, 123*(5), 1051–1061. doi:10.1093/ brain/123.5.1051

Schaefer, G. B., Thompson, J. N., Bodensteiner, J. B., Hamza, M., Tucker, R. R., Marks, W., . . . Wilson, D. (1990). Quantitative morphometric analysis of brain growth using magnetic resonance imaging. *Journal of Child Neurology, 5,* 127–130.

Schmahmann, J. D. (2004). Disorders of the cerebellum: Ataxia, dysmetria of thought, and the cerebellar cognitive affective syndrome. *The Journal of Neuropsychiatry and Clinical Neurosciences, 16,* 367–378. doi:10.1176/appi.neuropsych.16.3.367

Schmitt, J. E., Wallace, G. L., Rosenthal, M. A., Molloy, E. A., Ordaz, S., Lenroot, R., . . . Giedd, J. N. (2007). A multivariate analysis of neuroanatomic relationships in a genetically informative pediatric sample. *NeuroImage, 35*(1), 70–82. doi:10.1016/j.neuroimage.2006.04.232

Shanks, M. F., Rockel, A. J., & Powel, T. P. S. (1975). The commissural fiber connections of the primary somatic sensory cortex. *Brain Research, 98,* 166–171. doi:10.1016/0006-8993(75)90516-8

Shaw, P., Greenstein, D., Lerch, J., Clasen, L., Lenroot, R., Gogtay, N., . . . Giedd, J. (2006, March 30). Intellectual ability and cortical development in children and adolescents. *Nature, 440,* 676–679. doi:10.1038/nature04513

Shaw, P., Lerch, J. P., Pruessner, J. C., Taylor, K. N., Rose, A. B., Greenstein, D., . . . Giedd, J. N. (2007). Cortical morphology in children and adolescents with different apolipoprotein E gene polymorphisms: An observational study. *Lancet Neurology, 6,* 494–500. doi:10.1016/S1474-4422(07)70106-0

Somerville, L. H., Jones, R. M., & Casey, B. J. (2010). A time of change: Behavioral and neural correlates of adolescent sensitivity to appetitive and aversive environmental cues. *Brain and Cognition, 72*(1), 124–133. doi:10.1016/j.bandc.2009.07.003

Sowell, E. R., Thompson, P. M., Tessner, K. D., & Toga, A. W. (2001). Mapping continued brain growth and gray matter density reduction in dorsal frontal cortex: Inverse relationships during postadolescent brain maturation. *The Journal of Neuroscience, 21,* 8819–8829.

Thompson, P. M., Giedd, J. N., Woods, R. P., MacDonald, D., Evans, A. C., & Toga, A. W. (2000, March 9). Growth patterns in the developing brain detected by using continuum mechanical tensor maps. *Nature, 404,* 190–193. doi:10.1038/35004593

Tiemeier, H., Lenroot, R. K., Greenstein, D. K., Tran, L., Pierson, R., & Giedd, J. N. (2010). Cerebellum development during childhood and adolescence. *NeuroImage, 49*(1), 63–70. doi:10.1016/j.neuroimage.2009.08.016

Van Leijenhorst, L., Moor, B. G., Op de Macks, Z. A., Rombouts, S. A. R. B., Westernberg, P. M., & Crone, E. A. (2010). Adolescent risky decision-making: Neurocognitive development of reward and control regions. *NeuroImage, 51*(1), 345–355. doi:10.1016/j.neuroimage.2010.02.038

Wallace, G. L., Schmitt, J. E., Lenroot, R., Viding, E., Ordaz, S., Rosenthal, M. A., . . . Giedd, J. N. (2006). A pediatric twin study of brain morphometry. *Journal of Child Psychology and Psychiatry, 47,* 987–993. doi:10.1111/j.1469-7610.2006.01676.x

Wechsler, D. (1974). *Wechsler intelligence scale for children—revised.* New York, NY: The Psychological Corporation.

Whitford, T. J., Rennie, C. J., Grieve, S. M., Clark, C. R., Gordon, E., & Williams, L. M. (2007). Brain maturation in adolescence: Concurrent changes in neuroanatomy and neurophysiology. *Human Brain Mapping, 28,* 228–237. doi:10.1002/hbm.20273

Zaidel, D., & Sperry, R. W. (1974). Memory impairment after commissurotomy in man. *Brain: A Journal of Neurology, 97,* 263–272. doi:10.1093/brain/97.1.263

II

MEMORY, MEANING, AND REPRESENTATION

2

SEMANTIC AND ASSOCIATIVE RELATIONS IN ADOLESCENTS AND YOUNG ADULTS: EXAMINING A TENUOUS DICHOTOMY

KEN McRAE, SAMAN KHALKHALI, AND MARY HARE

The constructs of semantic and associative relatedness have played a prominent role in research on semantic memory because researchers have historically drawn on the distinction between these two types of relations when formulating theories, creating experimental conditions, and explaining empirical results. We argue that the binary distinction between semantics and association is rooted in a fundamental problem in how the two are defined and contrasted. Whereas semantic relatedness has typically been limited to category coordinates, associative relatedness has most often been operationalized using the word-association task. We show that meaningful semantic relations between words/concepts certainly extend beyond category coordinates, that word association is driven primarily by meaningful semantic relations between cue and response words, and that nonmeaningful, purely associative relations between words generally are not retained in memory. To illustrate these points, we discuss research on semantic priming, picture naming, and the Deese–Roediger– McDermott false memory paradigm. Furthermore, we describe how research on the development of mnemonic skills in adolescents supports our view. That is, adolescents do not learn arbitrary associations between words but develop

This work was supported by National Institutes of Health grant HD053136 to Ken McRae and Mary Hare, and by Natural Sciences and Engineering Council Grant OGP0155704 to Ken McRae.

elaborative strategies for linking words by drawing on their rich knowledge of events and situations. In other words, adolescents use existing memories of meaningful relations to ground their memories for novel word pairs, even in an associative learning paradigm.

The term *semantic memory* refers to people's memory for concepts and word meanings. An important aspect of understanding semantic memory concerns delineating the ways in which knowledge of word meaning is organized, and a great deal of research has been aimed at providing insight into this issue. A key goal is to uncover the relations among concepts that are encoded in semantic memory. To this end, the constructs of semantic and associative relations have been central components of theories of the organization of semantic memory, and research comparing the two has provided a substantial amount of informative data that have furthered both theory development and empirical work. However, critical issues remain with regard to how semantic and associative relations have been defined and studied in semantic memory research and how they might best be defined and studied in future research.

In an influential paper on the organization of human memory, Tulving (1972) noted an increased interest among some of his contemporaries in the kind of memory that underlies the seemingly effortless execution of skills such as language processing and memory access. Tulving's definition of semantic memory still nicely captures some commonly held views:

> Semantic memory is the memory necessary for the use of language. It is a mental thesaurus, organized knowledge a person possesses about words and other verbal symbols, their meaning and referents, about relations among them, and about rules, formulas, and algorithms for the manipulation of these symbols, concepts, and relations. (p. 386)

Tulving also stated that "the relations among items in semantic memory are of much greater variety" (p. 388) than the relations among the contents of episodic memories, which he believed to be organized chiefly along spatiotemporal dimensions.

Since that time, a large number of theories and studies have focused on the contrast between semantic and associative relations because they are considered to be the two principal and distinguishable components of conceptual organization (Crutch & Warrington, 2010; Fischler, 1977; Hutchison, 2002; Shelton & Martin, 1992; Thompson-Schill, Kurtz, & Gabrieli, 1998; Yee, Overton, & Thompson-Schill, 2009). It has been a common working hypothesis in semantic memory research that these components are defined on orthogonal dimensions. Associative relatedness is defined typically in terms of stimulus–response combinations in a word-association task (e.g., *agony–pain*; Nelson, McEvoy, & Schreiber, 1998). In fact, Nelson et al.'s (1998) word-association norms, although not the sole source of word-association norms in the literature, have been the most often used operationalization of association in memory research for at least the past decade.

In contrast, *semantic relatedness* has typically been defined either as membership in the same superordinate category (e.g., *horse–dog*; Lupker, 1984), or as the degree to which the semantic features of two concepts overlap (*horse–cow*; Frenck-Mestre & Bueno, 1999). Often these two measures are treated as essentially the same, and indeed both are based on closeness in a representational structure, although featural overlap is more of a continuous dimension than is shared category.

In this chapter, we outline our position concerning the relationship between association and meaning. Association in its general sense—spatial and temporal co-occurrence in the world and language—is an important driving force in learning, and this includes the formation of semantic representations. Furthermore, word-association norms are an interesting and rich source of data. However, word associations on their own provide little if any insight into the relations that are encoded in semantic memory. Performance on word-association norms is driven by meaningful semantic relations, and these relations are identifiable and, in many cases, quantifiable. We also argue that it is not fruitful to attempt to understand semantic memory using a binary distinction between semantic similarity and word association (or even between semantic relatedness, broadly defined, vs. word association). On the one hand, the scope of semantic relations is much broader than similarity alone, and on the other hand, word associations are driven almost exclusively by semantic relations. Finally, a fruitful research strategy is to work toward understanding the relative importance or centrality of various types of semantic relations for various types of concepts. This approach, we believe, is the best path forward for understanding concepts and semantic memory.

To provide evidence for these ideas, and to couch our arguments, we focus on four areas of research in which the semantics–word association dichotomy has played a major role. In the section entitled "Research Relying on Differentiating Between Semantic and Associative Relations," the first subsection deals with experiments regarding picture–word facilitation and interference. The second subsection concerns the Deese–Roediger–McDermott false memory paradigm. The third subsection focuses on semantic priming. Finally, the fourth subsection describes research concerning how the ability to learn word pairs develops across adolescence and how this development hinges on semantic knowledge and the ability to employ that knowledge to make associations meaningful.

GOALS

Our goals in this chapter are as follows. First, we define the scope of what we mean by *semantically related*. We contend that lexical concepts are meaningfully related to each other in diverse ways and that an important aim of semantic memory research is to provide an empirical basis for the theoretical delineation of these semantic relations. Our second goal is to define *associatively related*. In general, an association between two concepts is due to their referents' spatial and/or temporal co-occurrence in the real world and/or in language. In cognitive psychology experiments, however, association typically is operationalized in terms of the word-association task. Over time, this empirical operationalization has become conflated with the theoretical notion of association. In this chapter, we generally distinguish between these two meanings by using *word association* when referring to the results from a word association task.

We argue, as others have before us (Anisfeld & Knapp, 1968; Brainerd, Yang, Reyna, Howe, & Mills, 2008; Grossman & Eagle, 1970) that word associations are best understood in terms of semantic relations. We contend that it is a fruitful research strategy to work toward understanding what drives responses in a word-association task. This requires detailed analyses of the types of semantic relations that underlie word-association performance. In our view, association, in terms of spatial and temporal co-occurrence, is a critical component of the process of acquiring lexical representations, but retained associations between concepts are almost always semantic in nature, and thus are encoded as semantic relations. A key task in investigating how lexical concepts are related to one another is to test what sorts of relations influence behavior of various types (see e.g., Estes, Golonka, & Jones, in press; Kalénine et al., 2009).

Although we distinguish between *association* and word-association norms, we do not argue that word-association norms are useless or irrelevant. We do argue, however, that because normative word associations are a product of semantic relations, one should explore the relations between a word and its strongest conceptual associates. Indeed, word-association norms provide a valuable metric for studying the relations between lexical concepts, but we do not believe they should be viewed as arising from undifferentiated associations of varying strengths. Thus, the goal should not be to construct theories that rely on undifferentiated word-association mechanisms.

The remainder of this chapter discusses implications of our view for existing and future research. A major point is that the practice of partitioning stimuli into associatively and semantically related sets of items is neither justified nor empirically fruitful in the long run. This argument has a number of implications. One is that many studies that have partitioned their stimuli in this way may need to be reconceptualized in terms of the types of information that was actually manipulated. This may not possible in many cases because studies using word-associated items typically intermingle heterogeneous semantic relations within their stimuli. Instead, then, we suggest a strategy for future research that emphasizes careful attention to the types of relation(s) being manipulated.

SEMANTIC RELATEDNESS

In a substantial amount of past research, semantic relatedness has been defined exclusively in terms of category coordinates, or featurally similar concepts, depending on the theoretical point of view (for reviews, see Hutchison, 2003; Lucas, 2000). Although shared category (or featural similarity) is important for many cognitive tasks, focusing exclusively on this relation has led to a rather narrow point of view when studying semantic relatedness. Indeed, it could be argued that it has hindered progress on understanding semantic relations and semantic memory.

In contrast, some researchers have studied a number of ways in which lexical concepts are related to one another. That is, many types of semantic relations are rooted in something other than membership in the same category. We present a taxonomy of the various dimensions of semantic relatedness in Table 2.1, to give an indication of the types of relations that might be studied. Given these numerous relation types, the task of researchers is to theoretically and empirically delineate among them. In the course of doing so, it may be found that some of them are accessed rapidly and automatically, even from single words, whereas others either are not encoded in semantic memory or are less strongly instantiated, thus requiring additional context (e.g., sentence, discourse, real-world context) for their influence to be observed. Studies involving a number of these relation types are described briefly in the section titled "Research Relying on Differentiating Between Semantic and Associative Relations."

ASSOCIATIVE RELATEDNESS

Association has a long history in psychology and an even longer one in philosophy. Lexical association is a construct that is often used to explain performance in memory and psycholinguistic studies. Bower (2000) defined *associations* as

> sensations that are experienced contiguously in time and/or space. The memory that sensory quality or event A was experienced together with, or immediately preceding, sensory quality or event B is recorded in the memory bank as an association from idea *a* to idea *b*. (p. 3)

TABLE 2.1
Semantic Relatedness Taxonomy

Relationship type	Subtype	Examples
Similar concepts	category coordinates	fox–wolf, hammer–pliers
	category exemplar pairs	vehicle–truck, dog–spaniel
	synonyms	car–automobile, dawn–daybreak
	antonyms	light–dark, good–evil
Entity	made-of	sink–enamel, pliers–metal
	entity behavior	clock–ticking
	external component	tricycle–pedals
	external surface property	apple–red
	internal component	cherry–pit
	internal surface property	fridge–cold, cake–sweet
	larger whole	ant–colony
	quantity	slippers–pair
	systemic feature	dolphin–intelligent
Situation	action/manner	screwdriver–turning
	situational	saucer–teacup
	function	drill–carpentry
	location	cupboard–kitchen
	origin	walnut–trees
	patient	mop–floor
	participant	wand–magician
	time	turkey–Thanksgiving
Introspective	affect emotion	wasp–annoyance, rattlesnake–fear
	contingency	car–gasoline
	evaluation	gown–fancy
Event	event-agent	lecture–professor
	event-patient	arrest–criminal
	event-instrument	cut–knife
	event-location	swim–lake

Deese (1965), a crucial bridge between the methods of behaviorism and cognitivism, noted that "almost all the basic propositions of current association theory derive from the sequential nature of events in human experience" (p. 1). Moss, Ostrin, Tyler, and Marslen-Wilson (1995) suggested that associations between words themselves are "built up through repeated co-occurrence of the two word forms." (p. 864). Fischler (1977) argued that associations between words could be formed from "accidents of contiguity," leading to the methodology, still used today, of separating stimuli into associated versus purely semantically related groups. Thus, the consensus regarding association appears to be that contiguity is key to forming a link between two concepts.

However, despite the consensus concerning the importance of contiguity, association in cognitive psychology typically is defined in terms of its operationalization, word-association norms. In a word-association task, a stimulus word is presented to a participant, who then produces the first word that comes to mind. Note that this operationalization is far removed from both the classical and modern definitions of association. Two words are now associated if one is given as a response to the other in a word-association task. There are a number of discontinuities between the definition of association and its operationalization. Association proper is learning-based; word association is retrieval or production-based. Association proper is based heavily on sensory information; word association is linguistically based. Association is based on contiguity, accidental or otherwise; word associations are, as we show, almost always meaningful.

Many researchers have used word *association*, often taken from Nelson et al.'s (1998) norms, to predict or explain performance on semantic and memory tasks. Typically, the responses are interpreted as being part of an associative network that predicts fast, automatic processing. However, much less research has attempted to determine the source of particular associative relations between two concepts (although doing so dates back at least to Jung, 1919). For instance, if *hammer* and *nail* are strong associates (Nelson et al., 1998), then why do participants respond *nail* to *hammer*? In an attempt to answer this question, Santos, Chaigneau, Simmons, and Barsalou (2011) classified word associations based on the relationship between the stimulus and response. Their classification taxonomy is presented in Table 2.2.

This taxonomy reveals the semantic nature of most word associations. Even those categories based on compound words or phrases can, in some sense, be considered as a semantic relationship. The first category is compound word continuation (*fruit–fly*, and *bus–boy*), with this type of item having been used to test for associative priming (Thompson-Schill et al., 1998; Yee et al., 2009). However, the fact that each of the words in the pair can stand on its

TABLE 2.2
A Taxonomy of Associative Relatedness

Type of association	Examples
1. Compound continuation forward	baseball–bat
2. Compound continuation backward	golf–miniature
3. Sound similarity	nature–nurture, roar–bore
4. Root similarity	convey–conveyance
5. Synonyms	car–automobile
6. Antonyms	light–heavy
7. Domain higher level	chair–furniture
8. Domain lower level	car–convertible
9. Domain same level	wolf–fox
10. Aspect of an object or situation	shark–teeth, restaurant–menu

Note. Data from Santos, Chaigneau, Simmons, & Barsalou (2011).

own as a separate word may be irrelevant; a fruit fly is a distinct semantic concept, different in representation from a *horsefly*, a *housefly*, a *butterfly*, and even just a *fly*, which as a noun usually refers to a housefly. Therefore, it is not an accident of contiguity that these two words are related; they are instead used in conjunction to refer to a specific concept. The second type of association in Santos et al.'s (2011) taxonomy is reversed compound words, such as *fly–fruit*. The third category is sound similarity. This is the least semantic of all the types of word associations. Root similarity is semantic (or at least morphological) because different linguistic forms of the same concepts comprise the two members of the word pair.

It is difficult to dispute the semantic character of the final six categories in Santos et al.'s (2011) taxonomy. Synonyms and antonyms are highly semantically similar concepts, with antonyms differing on a single dimension of meaning, such as *size* (*small–large*). The next three categories deal with category membership: superordinates, subordinates, and category coordinates. These three types of word association are the most frequently used as semantically related items in cognitive experiments. Superordinate (*chair–furniture*), subordinate (*insect–grasshopper*) and category coordinate relations (*robin–sparrow*) were incorporated as semantic relations in early models such as the hierarchical model (Collins & Quillian, 1969; but see O'Connor, Cree, & McRae, 2009). The last category, aspect of an object or situation, is overly broad, so it may be more useful to separate object features and scenes. Featural relations for objects (*bird–wing*) are a crucial aspect of semantics. Situational relations (*restaurant–menu*) rely on the participant generating a scene, script, schema, or otherwise using the common contexts of the two concepts in the pair.

From these examples, it is clear that at least six, and possibly as many as nine, of the 10 proposed categories in Santos et al.'s (2011) taxonomy of word associations are semantic. They are not based on accidental contiguity in space or time. They are likewise not solely based on perception-oriented associations. Instead, these word association categories can more easily be expressed in terms of semantic relations. The few that are not semantic may be better defined as linguistic relationships, with sound similarity representing phonological knowledge and root similarity arising from morphological information. Finally, another excellent example of classifying the semantic aspects of word association norms can be found in Guida and Lenci (2007), who focused on norms for Italian verbs.

Association has long been recognized as being crucial to the establishment of semantic representations (Nelson, McEvoy, & Dennis, 2000), but no consensus has been reached regarding the process by which this transformation from association to semantic relation occurs. Computational models have been introduced, based on large corpora of text and/or speech (Burgess & Lund, 1997; Jones, Kintsch, & Mewhort, 2006; Landauer & Dumais, 1997; Riordan

& Jones, 2011), but these theories have frequently met considerable opposition because of the purely linguistic nature of the associations involved in their computations, which is ironic considering the source of word association data. Nevertheless, issues remain concerning how the individual episodes that are associations become assimilated into semantic memory. In his 1959 article, Deese worried that the structural aspects of associative information were being lost in his contemporaries' concentration on temporal and spatial contiguity. In his 1965 book, Deese argued that associative *meaning* does not imply association in the behaviorist sense (i.e., focused on temporal contiguity). Rather, it is a natural distribution of responses to a particular stimulus. He described two main characteristics of associative meaning: (a) the limitation of these associations to verbal responses and (b) the minimization of contextual influence on these responses. Deese (1965) argued that the subsequent distribution of responses to a word stimulus thus defines the meaning of that word. This suggests that associative meaning is a subset of meaning proper, but it is the only analysis of meaning possible given the limitations of word association. Thus, whereas associations in similar experiments performed today are typically limited to just a few of the most frequent responses, Deese's framework for associative meaning incorporated all potential responses to a given stimulus.

Deese (1965) did not specify a transformation from association to semantic knowledge, but he did argue that the complete set of associations to a word comprises the semantics of that word. This is not dissimilar to the view of semantics proposed in this chapter. We argue that a sufficiently large set of associations, plus an understanding of the underlying semantic relations, minus relations such as phonological similarity, would likely result in a reasonable first-order approximation of a lexical concept. We have taken advantage of this proxy in past research. That is, semantic feature production norms, as collected by McRae, Cree, Seidenberg, and McNorgan (2005) or Vinson and Vigliocco (2008), can be viewed as a form of word association (this is another example of the fuzziness of the distinction between a semantic task and a typical word association task). However, in feature production norms, participants are directed to produce semantic relations of various sorts, and responses are classified into types of semantic relations.

One counterargument to the assertion that all retained associations are meaningful concerns experiments in which associations are learned between nonrelated concepts or nonsense words (Berry & Cole, 1973). Evidence of such learning would support the notion that even meaningless associations are retained, and therefore associations need not be semantic. However, it is unclear whether meaningless associations actually are retained. It appears that meaningless associations are in fact quite brittle and decay rapidly after the initial learning and testing phase unless an effort is made to make them systematic and meaningful, such as by incorporating them into a sentential context (Prior & Bentin, 2003, 2008). Furthermore, meaningless associations generalize in a limited fashion, only influencing processing if the testing phase and the learning phase present the associated stimuli in an identical or close-to-identical fashion (Goshen-Gottstein & Moscovitch, 1995; Pecher & Raaijmakers, 1999). Finally, even when detected, the effect seems to require extensive training over the course of several days (Schrijnemakers & Raaijmakers, 1997) or weeks (Dagenbach, Horst, & Carr, 1990), and several studies have failed to detect any effect (Carroll & Kirsner, 1982; Neely & Durgunoglu, 1985; Smith, MacLeod, Bain, & Hoppe, 1989). It appears then that meaningless associations are not retained precisely because they *are* meaningless. That is, these laboratory-learned associations are discarded because they are unimportant.

In summary, as a dependent variable, the distribution of responses in a word-association task is interesting and informative and has been used to account for findings in numerous experiments. However, the pattern of responses in a word association task does not inform researchers why some concepts are more or less associated with others. Certainly, investigations of word-association data show that the semantic relations between cue words and their respective associates are not randomly determined. Certain types of semantic relations appear to play a key role in determining people's responses. That is, there may be many reasons for the association of two lexical concepts, but word association by itself does not provide insight into this issue. As with semantic relations, a more nuanced notion of association emerges after examining the various ways in which words can co-occur in space and time. As Deese (1965) stated, "What is important about associations is not what follows what, but how sets of associations define structured patterns of relations among ideas" (p. vii).

RESEARCH RELYING ON DIFFERENTIATING BETWEEN SEMANTIC AND ASSOCIATIVE RELATIONS

In this section, we consider some areas of research that distinguish semantic from associative relations in several ways. We focus on word–picture facilitation and interference, false memories in the Deese–Roediger–McDermott paradigm, semantic priming, and association-based learning that develops during adolescence.

Picture–Word Facilitation and Interference

The role of context in lexical selection and production fluency has often been studied by testing the effect of a visually presented word on the time it takes to name a previously, simultaneously, or subsequently displayed picture.

For example, a picture of a cat might be presented for naming along with a word such as *dog* or *meow*. By altering the delay between presentation of the word and picture, researchers have investigated the time course of the influence of lexico-semantic processing of the word on semantic processing and subsequent naming of the picture.

Somewhat perplexingly, although some early experiments showed that the processing of semantically related words facilitates naming latencies for the target picture (Bajo, 1988; Sperber, McCauley, Ragain, & Weil, 1979), others showed interference (Glaser & Dungelhoff, 1984; Rosinski, 1977). To try to understand these inconsistent results, researchers have investigated the type of relation between the word and the picture. For example, La Heij, Dirkx, and Kramer (1990) suggested that categorical relations on their own do not cause facilitation. Rather, they argued that an additional associative relation exists between some category coordinates (*cat–dog*), and this is what yields priming. Their own experiments, which contrasted the effect of word primes that are both categorically and associatively related to the picture with the effect of categorically related but unassociated primes, supported this distinction between relations.

This point of view has been adopted by many other researchers. In the picture-naming literature, a common finding is that categorically related context words interfere with picture naming. For example, reading the word *dog* increases the time it takes to name a picture of a mouse. Conversely, words that are associatively but not categorically related to the target picture have generally been found to facilitate picture naming, as in the case of reading the word *cheese* and saying "mouse." Thus, born out of an effort to tease apart the sometimes subtle, sometimes obvious variations in the stimuli used to test picture–word facilitation and interference, the literature investigating this task appears to support a double dissociation between semantic and word associative relations. After describing two representative studies that are based on this distinction, we present arguments regarding the flaws inherent to such an approach.

As an illustrative example of how the semantics/association distinction is typically supported empirically, consider a study by Alario, Segui, and Ferrand (2000), who sought to clarify the role of semantic and associative processing in lexical production. The authors contrasted priming effects from semantically related word–picture pairs, such as *thread*–"rope," with effects from associatively related stimuli such as *carrot*–"rabbit." The authors used a number of stimulus onset asynchronies (SOA, the time between the presentation of the word and the picture) to test whether the influence of each relation on picture naming depends on the point in time at which the target picture is processed relative to the prime word. Crucially, Alario et al. claimed that they distinguished between the two relation types by ensuring that none of the category coordinate pairs were normatively associated and by choosing associatively related stimuli that were not category coordinates. When the onset of the word preceded the picture by 234 ms, no effect was obtained with category coordinates, whereas word associates facilitated picture naming. On the other hand, at a 114 ms SOA, category coordinates interfered with picture naming, but word associates had no effect. Note that the word and picture did not overlap in time in either case.

Alario et al. (2000) focused on addressing a particular debate in the literature on lexical selection, namely, whether there is competition between the lexical representations corresponding to the concept shown in the picture and similar concepts. That is, how does the (node corresponding to the) name of an object concept become uniquely selected for vocalization when naming a picture? Alario et al. concluded that interference effects are due to competition between semantically similar candidates, whereas associatively related words do not interfere with naming at any SOA because they are not lexical competitors of the picture name. That is, *carrot* does not compete with *rabbit* during production. The facilitation produced by word associates, on the other hand, was attributed to spreading activation from the word prime's lexical node to the node corresponding to the target picture in a localist production lexicon. In Alario et al.'s (2000) view, the separate loci of facilitation and interference effects constitute a dissociation between the mental processes that support each of the two types of relations.

Similar reasoning has been used to argue in favor of a semantic-associative distinction, using a variation of the conventional picture naming paradigm. In the picture–word interference paradigm, a word is displayed at a location on the screen overlapping with a picture at some time before, after, or at the same time as, the onset of the picture. The key difference between the picture–word interference task and the paradigm used in Alario et al. (2000) is that in the former case the distractor word stays on screen following its presentation, and so is superimposed on the picture. In a recent study employing this paradigm, category coordinate distractors such as *raisin*–"apple" interfered with picture naming when they were displayed 150 or 0 ms prior to onset of the picture (Sailor, Brooks, Bruening, Seiger-Gardner, and Guterman, 2009). In contrast, word associates such as *pie*–"apple" facilitated picture naming when presented between 450 and 0 ms prior to picture onset. Although they did not draw strong conclusions regarding a definite dissociation between associative and semantic relations, Sailor et al. (2009) suggested that "the facilitatory influence of associates occurs at a different stage of picture naming than the [interfering] influence of coordinates" (p. 797), in line with Alario et al.'s reasoning.

Although we certainly do not doubt the importance of using the picture-naming paradigm to probe the mental representations and processes underlying speech production and semantic memory, we suggest that the frequently proposed binary distinction between semantic and associative relatedness is not supported by empirical results. In particular, we argue that there is no basis for positing a double dissociation between associative and semantic priming effects. The fact that word associative and semantic relatedness are defined according to different operationalizations does not guarantee their independence.

The issue revolves around the architectural distinction between semantic and associative relatedness that seems overly narrow and ill-defined. As we have discussed, there is no clear consensus on where the boundary lies. Although category membership is the most frequently used operationalization of semantic relatedness, some researchers also recognize that other kinds of relations fall under this broad heading. Associative relatedness suffers from somewhat different problems. In some studies, associates were chosen using existing word association norms (Alario et al., 2000; Sailor et al., 2009), whereas in other studies participants rated the degree of association between two words (Bolte, Jorschick, & Zwitserlood, 2003).

We argue that distilling relatedness into associative and semantic components is not a viable strategy for attaining a deeper understanding of the processes involved in picture naming. Recent work shows the relationship to be more graded than that. With regard to semantic relations, priming between semantically similar concepts can be explained in terms of feature overlap. Indeed, Vigliocco, Vinson, Lewis, and Garrett (2004) tested the influence of degree of semantic similarity based on their Featural and Unitary Semantic System model, which incorporates feature-based representations of concepts. The research nicely illustrates the graded effects of semantic similarity on picture–word interference for both object nouns and action verbs. This type of research, in which a specific semantic relation was identified and tested, is precisely the type that we advocate. Nonetheless, there are many other types of semantic relations yet to be explored.

As for associative relations, priming between other kinds of meaningfully related words has not been adequately explained except by appealing to spreading activation. What appears to be needed is a taxonomy of the various ways in which primes/distractors can be meaningfully related to targets, to test and understand the microstructure of semantic interference/facilitation effects and their implications for the structure of semantic memory and for word production.

In fact, Costa, Alario, and Caramazza (2005) made arguments along these lines; as they stated, "It is unclear whether one can compare coordinate relationships to associative relationships. This is because associative relationships are heterogeneous: Whereas some associates are clearly semantically related, others are not" (p. 126). Using a picture–word interference task, they compared two types of semantic relations, "has a" relations (i.e., part–whole relations: *stinger*–"wasp"), and category coordinates (*bee*–"wasp"). Costa et al. found that parts facilitate picture naming, whereas category coordinates inhibit it. They based their interpretation on spreading activation networks. When the distractor is a semantically related part or category coordinate, spreading activation from the distractor to the semantically related target increases the activation of the target's lexical node (which by itself should cause facilitation). However, because the category coordinate belongs to the same superordinate category as the target, it is a possible candidate for selection in production, which causes interference in choosing the correct name. In contrast, activation of a "has a" distractor node is quickly disqualified as a possibility for selection because it belongs to a different type of relation. No interference occurs, and facilitation is observed because of initial activation of the target. Although we would not use this type of spreading activation metaphor to account for results such as these, we do believe that this type of research moves toward understanding the influence of specific types of semantic relations.

One could imagine probing more deeply into types of relations and other aspects of concepts. For example, would typical parts (*wheels–truck*), functions (*transportation–truck*), or locations (*garage–truck*) produce equivalent or different results? Perhaps aspects of concepts might show differential effects if the prime word denotes information from various modalities. Would distinctive features of concepts (*moos*–"cow") produce equivalent facilitation to that produced by features that are shared among multiple concepts (*chews*–"cow")? Studies such as these may be ultimately more informative about the structure and complexity of semantic memory than a simple (and somewhat artificial) bifurcation into semantic versus associative relations.

Deese–Roediger–McDermott False Memory Paradigm

The Deese–Roediger–McDermott (DRM) false memory paradigm has been used in numerous experiments to investigate representations and processes underlying false recall and recognition. In DRM experiments, participants typically are presented with a list of about 15 words and then are asked to recall them; they are possibly given a recognition task as well. The proportion of participants who falsely recall or recognize a critical nonpresented word is measured. For example, the list for the critical nonpresented word *doctor* consists of *nurse, sick, lawyer, medicine, health, hospital, dentist, physician, ill, patient, office, stethoscope, surgeon, clinic,* and *cure.*

The distinction between semantic and word associative relations has played a major role in this research for two reasons. First, word association explanations of DRM false memories enjoy a somewhat privileged position because, dating back to Deese (1959), DRM lists have been constructed using word association norms in the vast majority of studies. For example, many lists that have been used in DRM research, such as the *doctor* list presented above, consist of the 15 strongest word associates to the critical word. Second, the two major theories of false memories differ with respect to the centrality of associative and semantic relations. Activation/monitoring theory is based on spreading activation in a semantic network, and therefore the strength of normative association between list words and the non-presented critical word has played a major role in accounting for DRM false memories in this framework (Roediger, Watson, McDermott, & Gallo, 2001). For example, Roediger et al. (2001) presented word association and false recall and recognition data for a set of 55 commonly used DRM lists. Using regression analyses, they showed that the degree of association from the list words back to the critical word (backward associative strength, or BAS) strongly predicts the probability of false recall and recognition across those 55 lists.

The contrasting major framework is fuzzy trace theory (Brainerd & Reyna, 2002; Payne, Elie, Blackwell, & Neuschatz, 1996). The primary assumptions of this theory are that a verbatim trace and a gist trace are produced during encoding and that the corresponding processes operate in parallel. The verbatim trace represents the surface form of the presented list items, and the gist trace represents the semantic content, including the list words' meanings, and the semantic relations among items (Brainerd & Reyna, 2002). False recall is due to gist extraction during encoding, whereas veridical recall is due to verbatim traces. That is, in fuzzy trace theory, gist extraction (or episodic interpretation) of the semantic content of, and the semantic relations among, the list words serve as the primary source of false memories. Therefore, this theory leads researchers to investigate the semantic content of the associatively derived DRM lists.

One challenge for such semantic relations–based theories of false memories is to demonstrate that DRM effects that appear at first glance to be due to word associations are actually due to semantic relations. Brainerd et al. (2008) and Cann, McRae, and Katz (in press) have provided such evidence. Cann et al. used a knowledge type taxonomy developed by Wu and Barsalou (2009) to classify the relations found in the 55 commonly used DRM lists (Roediger et al., 2001). They classified list items into aspects of a situation in which the critical non-presented concept takes part (*music–concert*, with the first item being the critical concept, and the second a concept from the list), synonyms (*trash–garbage*), antonyms (*beautiful–ugly*), taxonomic relations (*fruit–apple*), entity relations (*window–glass*), and introspective relations (*needle–hurt*). Cann et al. found that virtually all of the words on DRM lists could be classified into these relations and that the number of items of certain relation types predicted mean backward association of the DRM lists. In particular, BAS was related to the number of situation relations, synonyms, antonyms, and taxonomic relations on a list. In addition, Cann et al. found that the number of situation relations, synonyms, entity relations, and taxonomic relations predict the probability of false recall. Finally, they demonstrated that lists of words that consist only of situation relations produce high rates of false recognition even though BAS is essentially zero. For example, their *breakfast* list had a mean BAS of only .03, and contained *bacon, cereal, food, coffee, eggs, fruit, juice, milk, pancakes, plate, muffin,* and *toast*.

Brainerd et al. (2008) presented an overlapping but more detailed investigation into the semantic content of DRM lists and of BAS in general. They investigated 16 semantic properties and found that DRM lists were exceptionally rich in meaning. These included the seven dimensions of Toglia and Battig's (1978) semantic word norms (familiarity, meaningfulness, concreteness, imagery, categorizability, number of attributes, pleasantness), the three dimensions of Bradley and Lang's (1999) emotion word norms (arousal, dominance, valence), the Wu and Barsalou (2009) knowledge types from Cann et al. (in press), and the nonsemantic predictors used by Roediger et al. (2001).

Brainerd et al. (2008) conducted factor analyses to investigate the factors on which these variables load. For the 55 DRM lists from Roediger et al. (2001), they found them to be rich in terms of the semantic variables, both those that measure aspects of single words (such as meaningfulness) and those that measure semantic relations. Furthermore, in a factor analysis using Roediger et al.'s data, they found false recall, false recognition, non-presented critical word familiarity, meaningfulness, and number of attributes, as well as mean BAS, all loaded on one factor. In an analysis using false recognition data from their study in which participants did not first recall the list, false recognition loaded on a factor with virtually the same semantic variables.

Brainerd et al. (2008) also constructed a stratified sample of 400 cue–target word pairs, using Nelson et al.'s (1998) norms to obviate any concerns regarding the manner in which DRM lists are constructed and constrained. Importantly, a number of the semantic variables varied by cue–target association strength. Considering the semantic properties of the target words, increases in cue–target association strength were accompanied by higher levels of categorizability, concreteness, familiarity, imagery, meaningfulness, number of attributes, and pleasantness and decreases in arousal and dominance. Considering the properties measured for cue words, increases in association strength were accompanied by increases in concreteness, imagery, and categorizability but decreases in valence and dominance. Finally, in terms of cue–target semantic relations, increases in association strength were accompanied by increases in synonyms, antonyms, and taxonomic relations, as well as decreases in introspective and situational relations.

In summary, research into the DRM false memory paradigm is an example of an area in which undifferentiated word associative relations has played a central role. However, recent research demonstrates that false memories can arise in the virtual absence of word association. Furthermore, the key associative variable, BAS, can be understood in terms of semantic variables and relations.

Semantic Priming

An asymmetry exists between the treatment of word association and semantic relations in the semantic priming literature. This is perhaps due to the assumed bottom-up nature of associations and the top-down nature of semantics, or perhaps to the fact that association has a much longer history. In semantic priming research, it is typical to remove associated pairs from semantically related stimuli but rare to strip semantic relatedness from associated pairs. However, this masks an even deeper asymmetry in the treatment of the two constructs; it has simply been assumed that associative priming exists. From the first attempts to remove association from semantic stimuli (Fischler, 1977) and the first models of semantic relatedness (Collins & Loftus, 1975; Collins & Quillian, 1969), there has been an implicit assumption that activation spreads through associative links, and, therefore, if one is to study true semantic connections between concepts, it is necessary to first negate or partial out word association. Thus, researchers have investigated "pure semantic priming without association" to discern semantic organization. Indeed, several authors (Hutchison, 2003; Lupker, 1984; Shelton & Martin, 1992) have argued that all so-called semantic priming is in fact associative. We believe that these researchers have come upon the same problem we discuss in this chapter, but from the opposite direction: the basic inability to distinguish what is considered associative from what is considered semantic.

The typical methodology for demonstrating priming based on semantic relations has been to omit all word pairs that are also associated according to word association norms (Fischler, 1977). On the assumption that associatively related items have been removed, a "pure" semantic category is left, with word pairs that are usually members of the same category (e.g., *bear–cow*). Although it has occasionally been found that this process eliminates priming (Lupker, 1984; Shelton & Martin, 1992), the consensus now appears to be that semantic priming remains intact (Chiarello et al., 1990; Hare, Jones, Thomson, Kelly, & McRae, 2009; Hines, Czerwinski, Sawyer, & Dwyer, 1986; Seidenberg, Waters, Sanders & Langer, 1984). Pure semantic priming has been found based on different types of relations (similar concepts, verb–patient relations, event-based relations) even when this type of item filtering is performed. Therefore, pure semantic priming does exist.

It is interesting that there has been no such conclusive demonstration in the opposite direction. Very few researchers have attempted to find a pure associative priming effect, one in which all traces of semantic relationships have been removed from the stimuli. The studies that have attempted to do so have demonstrated how difficult—or perhaps impossible—this is. Many authors have tried to limit the effect of semantics on associative word pairs, but because the definition of semantic relatedness in these studies has usually been limited to category membership, many other semantic relationships have intruded into associatively related stimuli. A few examples are listed in Table 2.3. Some earlier experiments (Fischler, 1977; Lupker, 1984) restricted their definition of semantics to category membership, which we argue is overly constrained. In those studies that did not, such as Thompson-Schill et al. (1998) and Yee et al. (2009), to remove semantic relations, they used compound-continuation forward items such as *bell–boy* and *book–worm* as their associatively related stimuli. However, they did not find priming for such items.

Experiment 3 of McKoon and Ratcliff (1992) is likely the most successful attempt to date at showing an associative priming effect in the absence of semantic relations. Rather than relying on word association norms (though these were included as a baseline), they used corpora co-occurrence statistics to measure contiguity. The assumption was that if the words co-occurred more than at chance in a six-million-word text corpus, then they should be "tagged" by the memory system as being associated through repeated contiguity. McKoon and Ratcliff found facilitation for high co-occurrence items, although the same was not true for lower (but still higher than chance) co-occurrence items. However, an examination of their stimuli reveals that many of the high co-occurrence items are, in fact, semantically related through scene

TABLE 2.3
Studies Examining Semantic and Associative Priming, Detailing Criteria
for Semantic Relatedness Decision and Typical Examples
of Nonsemantic Associated Stimuli

Study	Semantic relation	Examples of associated stimuli
Fischler (1977)	category coordinates	sugar–sweet, arm–leg, dream–sleep
Lupker (1984)	category coordinates	beet–red, ostrich–feather, sleep–bed
Chiarello et al. (1990)	category coordinates	cradle–baby, hammer–nail, rubber–tire
McKoon and Ratcliff (1992)	based on association and co-occurrence	kitchen–knife, apple–pie, officer–army
Shelton and Martin (1992)	category coordinates	hot–stove, day–night, cold–hot
Thomson-Schill et al. (1998)	Category coordinates and featural data	book–worm, bus–boy, fruit–fly
Hutchinson (2002)	No semantic, only condition	piano–key, engine–car, duck–water

relations (*kitchen–knife, hospital–baby*), category membership (*air–water*), or featural information (*young–kids, black–smoke*). Others were compound continuation forward relationships, as in Thompson-Schill et al. (1998), such as *movie–stars, apple–pie, heat–wave, fire–rucks,* and *power–plant.* There were very few semantically related items among their low-co-occurrence items (although some existed, e.g., *amputation–leg*), but this condition did not produce priming.

These data again illustrate one of the main points of this chapter, that concept pairs that produce behavioral consequences are related in meaningful ways. In McKoon and Ratcliff (1992), there are reasons why words co-occurred in a systematic manner, and the majority of their high co-occurrence items are semantically related in obvious ways. Again, we argue that this is not a coincidence. Higher than chance levels of co-occurrence between words are meaningful, and the semantic system takes advantage of this systematicity.

To date, no study has conclusively shown that pure associative priming exists, at least using preexisting knowledge tapped either by word association norms or local co-occurrence in corpora. Semantic priming in the absence of word association, in contrast, has been demonstrated many times (Ferretti, McRae, & Hatherell, 2001; Hare et al., 2009; McRae & Boisvert, 1998; see Lucas, 2000, for a review). Therefore, we conclude that it is much more likely that semantic relations are responsible for all of the results seen in 30 years of semantic priming experiments and that associative priming either simply does not exist or is so fragile that any associations that are not incorporated into the semantic system are quickly lost.

This conclusion leads to a number of recommendations. The first is our strong recommendation that items should not be removed from semantic priming tasks because the target was produced as a response to the prime in a word-association task. We have argued in this chapter that, because these associative responses are driven by semantic processes, the net effect of removing word associates from semantically related stimuli is to weaken semantic priming and make it more difficult to detect an effect if one is present. The primary consequence of omitting word associates is to remove the best items from a particular type of relationship. For example, in semantically similar priming stimuli used in McRae, de Sa, and Seidenberg (1997), the word-associated items had higher similarity ratings (5.4 on a 9-point scale) than did the nonassociated items (4.8). This is the case because semantic similarity is one factor that drives responses in a word association task.

Although researchers rarely talk about such experiences in print, we provide an illustrative anecdotal example regarding why it is illogical to remove associates from semantic stimuli. Ferretti et al. (2001) investigated priming between verbs and their typical agents (the entities performing an action: *arresting–cop*), patients (the entities or objects on which an action is performed: *interviewing–applicant*), instruments (the objects being used to perform an action: *stirred–spoon*), and locations (*skated–arena*). Such verb–noun pairs definitely should co-occur in sentences. We were aware that potential reviewers would likely demand removal of any items that were normatively associated. Therefore, we conducted analyses removing all word associates from our stimuli. The reviewers' comments were telling of the confusion that surrounds these issues. One reviewer essentially stated, "Responses in a word association task tend to come from the same major syntactic category as the stimulus, so your items are probably still associated." That is, even though they were not associated, the priming results were not valid because the items were probably still associated. However, another reviewer's comment was essentially that, "It seems silly to remove associated items according to word association norms. Of course *arrest* and *cop* or *eat* and *fork* are associated in the broad sense of the word, because they occur together in the world and in language. That's the point, isn't it?" We believe that this was exactly the point, in addition to Ferretti et al.'s (2001) goal of specifying the type of relationship in each condition and separately testing each type of relationship. That is, meaningful associations in the world and language are just that, and these associations are retained in memory as semantic knowledge.

In support of this position, we draw attention to Nelson et al.'s (1998) description of their instructions to participants in the word association task: "Participants were asked to write the first word that came to mind that was *meaningfully related or strongly associated* to the presented word on the blank shown next to each item" (our emphasis). Clearly, the manner in which word association norms have been used theoretically to draw a clear distinction between associative and semantic relations does not coincide with the actual instructions given to participants. That is, there exists no definitive line between word association and semantic relatedness.

Adolescents Use Meaning to Learn Associations

Throughout this chapter, we have argued for the intrinsically semantic nature of learned, retained associative relations. Arbitrary associations are rarely retained, because to do so requires at least some degree of meaningful relatedness. The ability to learn arbitrarily related word pairs increases across adolescence, suggesting that the ability to make them less arbitrary—to create or elaborate meaningful relations between them—develops across that period. Experimental findings, summarized next, are consistent with that suggestion.

Rohwer, Rabinowitz, and Dronkers (1982) were among the first to test this developmental trend. The authors created a set of word pairs that norming studies had shown to have either an "accessible" relationship (*ranch–cowboy*) or an inaccessible one (*ranch–floor*) and used them as stimuli in a cued-recall task. The participants were fifth- and 11th-grade students. These age groups bracket the adolescent years, as fifth graders are generally 10-year-old preadolescents and 11th graders are typically 17 years old.

In Rohwer et al. (1982), half of the participants in each age group were prompted to elaborate as they heard the word pairs, whereas the other half were not. Preadolescents' performance was strongly influenced by the prompt to elaborate but much more so in the inaccessible than in the accessible condition. The average number of correct responses to inaccessible items (*ranch–floor*) increased from 15 to 25 when the children had been prompted to elaborate during the study phase. In contrast, the average number of correct responses to accessible items (*ranch–cowboy*), which was relatively high to begin with, showed a more modest rise following the elaboration prompt.

Older adolescents, on the other hand, showed only an effect of accessibility. They made more correct responses to accessible than to inaccessible pairs in both prompt conditions, but their number of correct responses, even to the inaccessible pairs, was significantly higher than that of the younger children.

To account for these age-related differences across adolescence, Rohwer et al. (1982) argued that the children could learn the arbitrary pairs only if they made them less arbitrary—that is, if they elaborated a relationship between them. The authors noted that, to do this, the child must first develop sufficient knowledge of common events; otherwise he or she would have nothing on which to base a relationship. On this view, then, the developmental trend in paired-associate learning involves two factors. One is processing ability, or what the authors refer to as the propensity to elaborate. But as they point out, even with the highest ability, the child cannot elaborate an appropriate relationship unless she has developed a database of relevant events to use as a template. The younger children, then, were unable to learn the inaccessible pairs because they had insufficient knowledge of events to enable them to generate one that included both members of the pair.

Children also seem to develop more sophisticated learning strategies across the adolescent years. Beuhring and Kee (1987a, 1987b) asked fifth and 12th graders to talk through the strategies they used as they learned noun pairs. Fifth graders were much more likely to repeat the pairs to themselves than to elaborate them, whereas 12th-grade adolescents spontaneously preferred elaboration to simple rehearsal. The 12th graders also relied on an arsenal of other techniques that the younger children were much less likely to use. Many of these were meaning-based, creating, for example, events that integrated the pairs, "*I drank COFFEE while playing the HARP*," or relying on general event knowledge, "*A JANITOR wouldn't wear VELVET.*"

A regression analysis by Beuhring and Kee (1987b) showed that differential usage of elaboration and other associative strategies predicted the majority of the variance in the ability to recall word pairs. In other words, the greater success of the older children may be due not to an increase in memory ability itself but to increasingly effective semantic-based learning strategies. And indeed, when younger children were told to elaborate, their recall performance more than doubled. Such instructions had very little effect on the older adolescent, given that their performance was already high because they spontaneously used such elaborative strategies.

Finally, in a study that brought together false memories and adolescent word-pair memory strategies, Odegard, Holliday, Brainerd, and Reyna (2008) investigated the finding that false recall and recognition rates are lower for children than for adults. Odegard et al. compared the performance of 11-year-olds with that of young adults (with a mean age of 24) on a modified DRM task. Participants were shown items from a DRM list in a manner such that every item was paired with an associated word. Crucial to note, the associates were designed to either bias the list item's meaning toward the nonpresented critical word (the context-toward condition; presenting *shade–drapes* in the list related to *window*), or away from it (the context-away condition; presenting *shade–tree* in the *window* list). Consistent with fuzzy trace theory, Odegard et al. predicted that the children's false recognition rates would increase in the context-toward condition because they would be more likely to encode the appropriate gist under such learning conditions.

Although there is evidence that children over the age of 9 are better able to extract gist from a presented list of words than are younger children, the former are still not as adept at this skill as are adults (Brainerd, Forrest, Karibian, & Reyna, 2006). Thus, if false memories elicited by the DRM paradigm are due to efficient gist extraction, learning conditions that facilitate gist processing should increase the likelihood that critical items related to a list's gist trace will be falsely recognized. In fact, whereas Odegard et al. (2008) found that the type of encoding context did not alter false recognition rates for adults, false recognition of critical lures was more likely in the context-toward condition for 11-year-olds. Thus, consistent with Rohwer et al. (1982), the 11-year-olds significantly benefited from cues that facilitated the creation of meaningful connections between concepts, whereas such semantic processing took place without cuing in the older participants.

In summary, adolescents, like adults, do not learn arbitrary associations. Instead, even when tested in associative learning tasks, they show a developmental increase in the ability to semantically elaborate word pairs. That is, older adolescents possess the requisite generalized knowledge of events and situations, as well as the ability to bring this knowledge to bear even in a somewhat novel situation, allowing them to find or create meaningful relations between word pairs, rather than simply attempting to learn them as unrelated word associates. These abilities increase across adolescence, as the child becomes a more sophisticated learner, on the one hand, and develops richer and more sophisticated knowledge of events and situations, on the other.

CONCLUSION

In this chapter, we have put forth a number of arguments concerning the relationship between association and meaning. First, association in the sense of spatial and temporal co-occurrence in the world and language is an important driving force in learning and forming semantic representations. Second, word-association norms are an interesting and rich source of data. Third, word associations on their own do not provide insight into the relations that are encoded in semantic memory. Rather, word associations are driven by meaningful semantic relations. Furthermore, these relations are identifiable and, in many cases, quantifiable. Fourth, we have argued that it is not fruitful to attempt to understand semantic memory using a binary distinction between semantic similarity and word association (or even between semantic relatedness, broadly defined, vs. word association). On the one hand, the scope of semantic relations is much broader than similarity alone, and on the other, word associations are driven almost exclusively by semantic relations. Finally, a fruitful research strategy is to work toward understanding the relative importance or centrality of various types of semantic relations for various types of concepts. We have highlighted a few of many such investigations. This approach, we believe, is the best path forward for understanding concepts, semantic memory, and their development.

REFERENCES

Alario, F.-X., Segui, J., & Ferrand, L. (2000). Semantic and associative priming in picture naming. *The Quarterly Journal of Experimental Psychology A: Human Experimental Psychology, 53*, 741–764. doi:10.1080/027249800410535

Anisfeld, M., & Knapp, M. (1968). Association, synonymity, and directionality in false recognition. *Journal of Experimental Psychology, 77*, 171–179. doi:10.1037/h0025782

Bajo, M.-T. (1988). Semantic facilitation with pictures and words. *Journal of Experimental Psychology: Learning, Memory, and Cognition, 14*, 579–589. doi:10.1037/0278-7393.14.4.579

Berry, F. M., & Cole, S. R. (1973). Stimulus selection in paired-associated learning: Consonant-triad versus word-triad paradigms. *Journal of Experimental Psychology, 97*, 402–404. doi:10.1037/h0034097

Beuhring, T., & Kee, D. W. (1987a). Elaborative propensities during adolescence: The relationships between memory knowledge, strategy behavior, and memory performance. In M. A. McDaniel & M. Pressley (Eds.), *Imagery and related mnemonic processes* (pp. 257–273). New York, NY: Springer-Verlag.

Beuhring, T., & Kee, D. W. (1987b). Developmental relationships among metamemory, elaborative strategy use, and associative memory. *Journal of Experimental Child Psychology, 44*, 377–400. doi:10.1016/0022-0965(87)90041-5

Bolte, J., Jorschick, A., & Zwitserlood, P. (2003). Reading yellow speeds up naming a picture of a banana: Facilitation and inhibition in picture-word interference. In F. Schmalhofer, R. M. Young, & G. Katz (Eds.), *Proceedings of the European Cognitive Science Conference 2003* (pp. 55–60). Mahwah, NJ: Erlbaum.

Bower, G. H. (2000). A brief history of memory research. In E. Tulving & F. I. M. Craik (Eds.), *The Oxford handbook of memory* (pp. 3–32). New York, NY: Oxford University Press.

Bradley, M. M., & Lang, P. J. (1999). *Affective norms for English words (ANEW): Stimuli, instruction manual and affective ratings (Tech. Rep. No. C-1)*. Gainesville: The Center for Research in Psychophysiology, University of Florida.

Brainerd, C. J., Forrest, T. J., Karibian, D., & Reyna, V. F. (2006). Development of the false memory illusion. *Developmental Psychology, 42,* 962–979. doi:10.1037/0012-1649.42.5.962

Brainerd, C. J., & Reyna, V. F. (2002). Fuzzy-trace theory and false memory. *Current Directions in Psychological Science, 11,* 164–169. doi:10.1111/1467-8721.00192

Brainerd, C. J., Yang, Y., Reyna, V. F., Howe, M. L., & Mills, B. A. (2008). Semantic processing in "associative" false memory. *Psychonomic Bulletin & Review, 15,* 1035–1053. doi:10.3758/PBR.15.6.1035

Burgess, C., & Lund, K. (1997). Modelling parsing constraints with high-dimensional context space. *Language and Cognitive Processes, 12,* 177–210. doi:10.1080/016909697386844

Cann, D. R., McRae, K., & Katz, A. N. (in press). False recall in the Deese-Roediger-McDermott paradigm: The roles of gist and associative strength. *The Quarterly Journal of Experimental Psychology.*

Carroll, M., & Kirsner, K. (1982). Context and repetition effects in lexical decision and recognition memory. *Journal of Verbal Learning & Verbal Behavior, 21,* 55–69. doi:10.1016/S0022-5371(82)90445-5

Chiarello, C., Burgess, C., Richards, L., & Pollock, A. (1990). Semantic and associative priming in the cerebral hemispheres: Some words do, some words don't . . . sometimes, some places. *Brain and Language, 38,* 75–104. doi:10.1016/0093-934X(90)90103-N

Collins, A. M., & Loftus, E. F. (1975). A spreading activation theory of semantic processing. *Psychological Review, 82,* 407–428. doi:10.1037/0033-295X.82.6.407

Collins, A. M., & Quillian, M. R. (1969). Retrieval time from semantic memory. *Journal of Verbal Learning & Verbal Behavior, 8,* 240–247. doi:10.1016/S0022-5371(69)80069-1

Costa, A., Alario, F.-X., & Caramazza, A. (2005). On the categorical nature of the semantic interference effect in the picture-word interference paradigm. *Psychonomic Bulletin & Review, 12,* 125–131. doi:10.3758/BF03196357

Crutch, S. J., & Warrington, E. K. (2010). The differential dependence of abstract and concrete words upon associative and similarity-based information: Complementary semantic interference and facilitation effects. *Cognitive Neuropsychology, 27,* 46–71. doi:10.1080/02643294.2010.491359

Dagenbach, D., Horst, S., & Carr, T. H. (1990). Adding new information to semantic memory: How much learning is enough to produce automatic priming? *Journal of Experimental Psychology: Learning, Memory, and Cognition, 16*, 581–591. doi:10.1037/0278–7393.16.4.581

Deese, J. (1959). On the prediction of occurrence of particular verbal intrusions in immediate recall. *Journal of Experimental Psychology, 58*, 17–22. doi:10.1037/h0046671

Deese, J. (1965). *The structure of associations in language and thought.* Baltimore, MD: Johns Hopkins Press.

Estes, Z., Golonka, S., & Jones, L. L. (2011). Thematic thinking: The apprehension and consequences of thematic relations. In B. H. Ross (Ed.), *The psychology of learning and motivation: Advances in research and theory, Vol. 54* (pp. 249–294). San Diego, CA: Academic Press.

Ferretti, T. R., McRae, K., & Hatherell, A. (2001). Integrating verbs, situation schemas, and thematic role concepts. *Journal of Memory and Language, 44*, 516–547. doi:10.1006/jmla.2000.2728

Fischler, I. (1977). Semantic facilitation without association in a lexical decision task. *Memory & Cognition, 5*, 335–339. doi:10.3758/BF03197580

Frenck-Mestre, C., & Bueno, S. (1999). Semantic features and semantic categories: Differences in the rapid activation of the lexicon. *Brain and Language, 68*, 199–204. doi:10.1006/brln.1999.2079

Glaser, W. R., & Dungelhoff, F.-J. (1984). The time course of picture-word interference. *Journal of Experimental Psychology: Human Perception and Performance, 10*, 640–654. doi:10.1037/0096-1523.10.5.640

Goshen-Gottstein, Y., & Moscovitch, M. (1995). Repetition priming for newly formed and preexisting associations: Perceptual and conceptual influences. *Journal of Experimental Psychology. Learning, Memory, and Cognition, 21*, 1229–1248. doi:10.1037/0278-7393.21.5.1229

Grossman, L., & Eagle, M. (1970). Synonymity, antonymity, and association in false recognition responses. *Journal of Experimental Psychology, 83*, 244–248. doi:10.1037/h0028552

Guida, A., & Lenci, A. (2007). Semantic properties of word associations to Italian verbs. *Italian Journal of Linguistics, 19*, 293–326.

Hare, M., Jones, M., Thomson, C., Kelly, S., & McRae, K. (2009). Activating event knowledge. *Cognition, 111*, 151–167. doi:10.1016/j.cognition.2009.01.009

Hines, D., Czerwinski, M., Sawyer, P. K., & Dwyer, M. (1986). Automatic semantic priming: Effect of category exemplar level and word association level. *Journal of Experimental Psychology: Human Perception and Performance, 12*, 370–379. doi:10.1037/0096-1523.12.3.370

Hutchison, K. A. (2002). The effect of asymmetrical association on positive and negative semantic priming. *Memory & Cognition, 30*, 1263–1276. doi:10.3758/BF03213408

Hutchison, K. A. (2003). Is semantic priming due to association strength or feature overlap? A microanalytic review. *Psychonomic Bulletin & Review, 10,* 785–813. doi:10.3758/BF03196544

Jones, M. N., Kintsch, W., & Mewhort, D. J. K. (2006). High-dimensional semantic space accounts of priming. *Journal of Memory and Language, 55,* 534–552. doi:10.1016/j.jml.2006.07.003

Jung, C. G. (1919). *Studies in word-association* (M. D. Eder, Trans.). New York, NY: Moffatt, Yard & Company.

Kalénine, S., Peyrin, C., Pichat, C., Segebarth, C., Bonthoux, F., & Baciu, M. (2009). The sensory-motor specificity of taxonomic and thematic conceptual relations: A behavioral and fMRI study. *NeuroImage, 44,* 1152–1162. doi:10.1016/j.neuroimage.2008.09.043

La Heij, W., Dirkx, J., & Kramer, P. (1990). Categorical interference and associative priming in picture naming. *British Journal of Psychology, 81,* 511–525. doi:10.1111/j.2044-8295.1990.tb02376.x

Landauer, T. K., & Dumais, S. T. (1997). A solution to Plato's problem: The Latent Semantic Analysis theory of acquisition, induction, and representation of knowledge. *Psychological Review, 104,* 211–240. doi:10.1037/0033-295X.104.2.211

Lucas, M. (2000). Semantic priming without association: A meta-analytic review. *Psychonomic Bulletin & Review, 7,* 618–630. doi:10.3758/BF03212999

Lupker, S. J. (1984). Semantic priming without association: A second look. *Journal of Verbal Learning & Verbal Behavior, 23,* 709–733. doi:10.1016/S0022-5371(84)90434-1

McKoon, G., & Ratcliff, R. (1992). Spreading activation versus compound cue accounts of priming: Mediated priming revisited. *Journal of Experimental Psychology: Learning, Memory, and Cognition, 18,* 1155–1172. doi:10.1037/0278-7393.18.6.1155

McRae, K., & Boisvert, S. (1998). Automatic semantic similarity priming. *Journal of Experimental Psychology: Learning, Memory, and Cognition, 24,* 558–572. doi:10.1037/0278-7393.24.3.558

McRae, K., Cree, G. S., Seidenberg, M. S., & McNorgan, C. (2005). Semantic feature production norms for a large set of living and nonliving things. *Behavior Research Methods, 37,* 547–559. doi:10.3758/BF03192726

McRae, K., de Sa, V., & Seidenberg, M. S. (1997). On the nature and scope of featural representations of word meaning. *Journal of Experimental Psychology: General, 126,* 99–130. doi:10.1037/0096-3445.126.2.99

Moss, H. E., Ostrin, R. K., Tyler, L. K., & Marslen-Wilson, W. D. (1995). Accessing different types of lexical semantic information: Evidence from priming. *Journal of Experimental Psychology: Learning, Memory, and Cognition, 21,* 863–883. doi:10.1037/0278-7393.21.4.863

Neely, J. H., & Durgunoglu, A. Y. (1985). Dissociative episodic and semantic priming effects in episodic recognition and lexical decision tasks. *Journal of Memory and Language, 24,* 466–489. doi:10.1016/0749-596X(85)90040-3

Nelson, D. L., McEvoy, C. L., & Dennis, S. (2000). What is free association and what does it measure? *Memory & Cognition, 28*, 887–899. doi:10.3758/BF03209337

Nelson, D. L., McEvoy, C. L., & Schreiber, T. A. (1998). *The University of South Florida word association, rhyme, and word fragment norms.* Retrieved from http://web.usf.edu/FreeAssociation/

O'Connor, C. M., Cree, G. S., & McRae, K. (2009). Conceptual hierarchies in a flat attractor network: Dynamics of learning and computations. *Cognitive Science, 33*, 665–708. doi:10.1111/j.1551-6709.2009.01024.x

Odegard, T. N., Holliday, R. E., Brainerd, C. J., & Reyna, V. F. (2008). Attention to global gist processing eliminates age effects in false memories. *Journal of Experimental Child Psychology, 99*, 96–113. doi:10.1016/j.jecp.2007.08.007

Payne, D. G., Elie, C. J., Blackwell, J. M., & Neuschatz, J. S. (1996). Memory illusions: Recalling, recognizing, and recollecting events that never occurred. *Journal of Memory and Language, 35*, 261–285. doi:10.1006/jmla.1996.0015

Pecher, D., & Raaijmakers, J. G. W. (1999). Automatic priming for new associations in lexical decision and perceptual identification. *The Quarterly Journal of Experimental Psychology, 52*, 593–614. doi:10.1080/027249899390981

Prior, A., & Bentin, S. (2003). Incidental formation of episodic associations: The importance of sentential context. *Memory & Cognition, 31*, 306–316. doi:10.3758/BF03194389

Prior, A., & Bentin, S. (2008). Word associations are formed incidentally during sentential semantic integration. *Acta Psychologica, 127*, 57–71. doi:10.1016/j.actpsy.2007.01.002

Riordan, B., & Jones, M. N. (2011). Redundancy in perceptual and linguistic experience: Comparing feature-based and distributional models of semantic representation. *Topics in Cognitive Science, 3*, 303–345. doi:10.1111/j.1756-8765.2010.01111.x

Roediger, H. L., III, Watson, J. M., McDermott, K. B., & Gallo, D. A. (2001). Factors that determine false recall: A multiple regression analysis. *Psychonomic Bulletin & Review, 8*, 385–407. doi:10.3758/BF03196177

Rohwer, W. D., Jr., Rabinowitz, M., & Dronkers, N. F. (1982). Event knowledge, elaborative propensity, and the development of learning proficiency. *Journal of Experimental Child Psychology, 33*, 492–503. doi:10.1016/0022-0965(82)90061-3

Rosinski, R. R. (1977). Picture-word interference is semantically based. *Child Development, 48*, 643–647. doi:10.2307/1128667

Sailor, K., Brooks, P. J., Bruening, P. R., Seiger-Gardner, L., & Guterman, M. (2008). Exploring the time course of semantic interference and associative priming in the picture-word interference task. *The Quarterly Journal of Experimental Psychology, 62*, 789–801. doi:10.1080/17470210802254383

Santos, A., Chaigneau, S. E., Simmons, W. K., & Barsalou, L. W. (2011). Property generation reflects word association and situated simulation. *Language and Cognitive Processes, 3*, 83–199.

Schrijnemakers, J. M. C., & Raaijmakers, J. G. W. (1997). Adding new word associations to semantic memory: Evidence for two interactive learning components. *Acta Psychologica, 96,* 103–132. doi:10.1016/S0001-6918(96)00046-7

Seidenberg, M. S., Waters, G. S., Sanders, M., & Langer, P. (1984). Pre- and postlexical loci of contextual effects on word recognition. *Memory & Cognition, 12,* 315–328. doi:10.3758/BF03198291

Shelton, J. R., & Martin, R. C. (1992). How semantic is automatic semantic priming? *Journal of Experimental Psychology: Learning, Memory, and Cognition, 18,* 1191–1210. doi:10.1037/0278-7393.18.6.1191

Smith, M. C., MacLeod, C. M., Bain, J. D., & Hoppe, R. B. (1989). Lexical decision as an indirect test of memory: Repetition priming and list-wide priming as a function of type of encoding. *Journal of Experimental Psychology: Learning, Memory, and Cognition, 15,* 1109–1118. doi:10.1037/0278-7393.15.6.1109

Sperber, R. D., McCauley, C., Ragain, R. D., & Weil, C. M. (1979). Semantic priming effects on picture and word processing. *Memory & Cognition, 7,* 339–345. doi:10.3758/BF03196937

Thompson-Schill, S. L., Kurtz, K. J., & Gabrieli, J. D. E. (1998). Effects of semantic and associative relatedness on automatic priming. *Journal of Memory and Language, 38,* 440–458. doi:10.1006/jmla.1997.2559

Toglia, M. P., & Battig, W. F. (1978). *Handbook of semantic word norms.* Hillsdale, NJ: Erlbaum.

Tulving, E. (1972). Episodic and semantic memory. In E. Tulving & W. Donaldson (Eds.), *Organization of memory* (pp. 381–403). New York, NY: Academic Press.

Vigliocco, G., Vinson, D. P., Lewis, W., & Garrett, M. F. (2004). Representing the meanings of object and action words: The featural and unitary semantic space hypothesis. *Cognitive Psychology, 48,* 422–488. doi:10.1016/j.cogpsych.2003.09.001

Vinson, D. P., & Vigliocco, G. (2008). Semantic feature production norms for a large set of objects and events. *Behavior Research Methods, 40,* 183–190. doi:10.3758/BRM.40.1.183

Wu, L.-L., & Barsalou, L. W. (2009). Perceptual simulation in conceptual combination: Evidence from property generation. *Acta Psychologica, 132,* 173–189. doi:10.1016/j.actpsy.2009.02.002

Yee, E., Overton, E., & Thompson-Schill, S. L. (2009). Looking for meaning: Eye movements are sensitive to overlapping features, not association. *Psychonomic Bulletin & Review, 16,* 869–874. doi:10.3758/PBR.16.5.869

3

REPRESENTATION AND TRANSFER OF ABSTRACT MATHEMATICAL CONCEPTS IN ADOLESCENCE AND YOUNG ADULTHOOD

JENNIFER A. KAMINSKI AND VLADIMIR M. SLOUTSKY

By adolescence, students are learning more abstract and complex concepts, such as those of algebra and geometry. It is tempting to introduce these concepts through concrete, familiar instantiations that might deeply engage students in the learning process and possibly facilitate initial learning. However, a primary goal of acquiring mathematical concepts is the ability to apply structural knowledge outside the learning situation, and there is evidence that concrete instantiations can hinder transfer. This chapter addresses how successful analogical transfer is influenced by characteristics of the learning and target domains. We discuss results of a series of studies demonstrating that learners are more able to transfer mathematical structure from a learned generic instantiation than from a learned concrete instantiation. We suggest that concrete instantiations of abstract concepts communicate more extraneous information than their more abstract, generic counterparts. This extraneous information is retained in the learner's representation of the concept and hinders subsequent transfer. Implications for learning abstract concepts such as mathematical concepts in adolescence and young adulthood are discussed.

This research was supported by a grant from the Institute of Educational Sciences, U.S. Department of Education (#R305B070407).

The period from adolescence to young adulthood is a time when mathematical reasoning and problem solving become more sophisticated. In the preschool and elementary school years, much of children's mathematical knowledge concerns numbers and arithmetic. By adolescence, children are acquiring more abstract and complex concepts, such as those of algebra and geometry. For most students, the acquisition of this knowledge is not without its difficulties. How should mathematical concepts, such as probability theory, exponential growth, and rates of change, be introduced to students to ease these difficulties and best promote their acquisition and application to real-world problems? This chapter addresses how successful analogical transfer is influenced by characteristics of the learning and target domains. In particular, we discuss concepts featured in high school and college curricula, such as exponential growth, group theory, and rates of change (e.g., in physics).

One possibility is that such concepts are well acquired through concrete instantiations such as contextualized, real-world examples. Concrete approaches to learning have been advocated not only for very young children but also for older learners, such as adolescents and adults (for a review, see Anderson, Reder, & Simon, 1996). Support for such approaches often stems from the belief that because cognition is bound to specific situations, teaching abstractions is ineffective. Alternatively, students might learn more effectively through more abstract, generic instantiations of mathematics that present a minimal amount of extraneous information, such as traditional mathematical notation involving generic symbols not tied to specific situations. For example, *acceleration* is defined as the rate of change of velocity with respect to time. Students could learn the concept of acceleration through a concrete context of gravitational acceleration affecting falling objects or instead through the generic expression of $a = \dfrac{\Delta v}{\Delta t}$ where a is acceleration, Δv is change in velocity, and Δt is change in time.

To evaluate the effectiveness of concrete and generic instantiations, several questions should be considered. What is the definition of a concrete instantiation? What constitutes successful acquisition of a mathematical concept? How does learning a particular instantiation shape the internal representation of a mathematical concept and influence the learner's ability to transfer mathematical knowledge to novel analogous situations? In this chapter, we discuss the results of a series of studies conducted to address these questions. We begin by presenting an interpretation of concrete and abstract instantiations of mathematical concepts and an overview of previous findings on analogical transfer.

CONCRETENESS

In everyday practice, the term *concrete* is typically used in contrast to *abstract* often to differentiate what can and cannot be directly experienced by the senses. These terms can be used in seemingly different situations. For example, there would be little disagreement that the concept "cat" is more concrete than the concept "infinity." This is a comparison of the concreteness of two different concepts. Concreteness can also be compared between instantiations of the same concept; there would also be little disagreement that a real cat is a more concrete instantiation of the category "cat" than a schematic outline. Do these examples point to the same way of defining concreteness across different situations? We suggest that the answer is yes. In both cases, concreteness could be measured by the amount of information (or the amount of entropy reduction) communicated by a given concept or instantiation. Under this view, the concept "cat" communicates the presence of a feline animal and all the known facts associated with cats, assuming that one has prior knowledge of cats. The concept "infinity" communicates much less information (in fact, any set could potentially be infinite), thus leaving a great deal of uncertainty. Similarly, a real cat leaves less uncertainty than a schematic outline that does not communicate information such as color, size, or age. In both cases, therefore, the former is substantially more concrete than the latter.

For instantiations of a fixed concept such as "cat," if concreteness can be measured by the amount of communicated information, then *concrete* and *abstract* are not dichotomous; rather, they lie on a continuum over which the amount of communicated information varies. Specifically, for a given concept, instantiation A is more concrete than instantiation B, if A communicates more information than B. Furthermore, an instantiation of a concept (e.g., a particular cat) is often represented by a symbol that communicates information either perceptually, by the amount of detail in the physical stimuli, or verbally, by providing descriptions with different amounts of detail. Perceptually communicated concreteness often results in greater perceptual richness of an instance, which could be measured by physical properties such as contrast and spatial frequency.

To elaborate this point, consider the concept of "person" and how possible symbols can communicate different degrees of information. For example, images in Figure 3.1 communicate increasing amounts of information from left to right. Little could be said with certainty about the leftmost instantiation of a person; this most abstract, generic instantiation communicates only numerosity—the fact that there is a single individual. On the other hand, much could be said about the rightmost instantiation. Namely, this is a specific person, she is a young female, and she was born to an Asian parent. There would be even more information that could be retrieved from memory if the photograph depicts someone you know.

Increasing information/ Increasing concreteness

Figure 3.1. Possible symbols for the concept *person*.

It seems that a more abstract instantiation is often a better symbol of a given concept, to denote the entire group, than a more concrete instantiation. This is because a more concrete instantiation communicates much more information, part of which could be extraneous to the concept in question. For example, a stick figure can symbolize any person, yet a young schoolgirl may not well symbolize any person because it communicates additional information such as age and gender, which is nonessential to the concept of *person*. Similarly, a concrete instantiation may be a poor symbol for another concrete instantiation that does not share the same superficial features. Therefore, a schoolgirl is not a good symbol for a middle-aged man, and a middle-aged man is not a good symbol for a schoolgirl.

By the same reasoning, generic instantiations may serve as better symbols when attempting to communicate new, to-be-learned information about a given concept. For example, the lifetime risk of heart disease regardless of gender would probably be better communicated with a stick figure or generic example of the general population than with a picture of a young girl. Similarly, a photograph of a young girl would not make a good symbol when communicating information about a specific subset of the general population, such as the prevalence rate for prostate cancer in middle-aged men.

NATURE OF MATHEMATICAL CONCEPTS AND THEIR INSTANTIATIONS

Just as many everyday object concepts and their instantiations can vary in the amount of communicated information, mathematical concepts and their instantiations can also vary in the degree of communicated information.

However, there are critical differences between mathematical concepts and concepts such as "cat" or "person." Most everyday concepts are ill-defined (see Solomon, Medin, & Lynch, 1999) in the sense that their definitions can vary across cultures, individuals, and time. Furthermore, everyday concepts such as "cat" are grounded in perceptual similarity and acquired with little effort through encounters with instances of the concept (Kloos & Sloutsky, 2008). For example, most cats tend to have common observable features—similar size, four legs, whiskers, and pointed ears—and young children acquire this concept easily. Mathematical concepts, however, have precise definitions based on their relational structure. For example, exponential growth is defined as the change in quantity N according to the following formula:

$$N(t) = N_0 e^{\alpha t} \tag{1}$$

for a variable t and constant α, where e^x is the exponential function and N_0 is the initial value of N. Therefore, the concept of exponential growth is defined by the relational pattern between N_0, $N(1)$, $N(2)$, etc. Instances of mathematical concepts specify additional information beyond the defining relational structure. Instantiations of exponential growth would specify particular values of the constants α and N_0. More concrete instantiations would convey more information—perhaps growth of a particular population of wild eastern cottontail rabbits living in the midwestern United States.

Therefore, for mathematical concepts, instances can be vastly dissimilar, sharing few directly observable similarities. For example, in addition to describing populations of rabbits, exponential growth/decay can describe the metabolism of medication in the body and the temperature of a cooling cup of coffee. Because superficial features can vary widely, it is often difficult to spontaneously recognize instances of the same concept. As a result, the acquisition of such concepts is often difficult for both children and adults and typically requires some supervision (e.g., Kloos & Sloutsky, 2008), which may take the form of explicit instruction that begins with an initial instantiation.

One goal of learning mathematics is the ability to appropriately apply mathematical knowledge to novel situations. Therefore, an effective instantiation must promote two processes: learning of the instantiation and transfer of defining relational structure to a novel situation that is structurally analogous, or isomorphic. For example, successfully acquiring the concept of exponential growth from learning about growth of a rabbit population would imply that knowledge of exponential growth would be recognized and applied to (at least some) novel analogous situations, such as monetary growth of investments.

ANALOGICAL TRANSFER

How likely is it that structural knowledge will transfer outside of the learned situation? The past 20 years have produced a consensus on some aspects of analogical transfer. First, spontaneous analogical transfer is notoriously poor. This finding has been documented in numerous studies with both adults and children (e.g., Gick & Holyoak, 1980, 1983; Goswami, 1991; Novick, 1988; Reed, Dempster, & Ettinger, 1985; Reed, Ernst, & Banerji, 1974; Simon & Reed, 1976). Second, a factor that mediates transfer is similarity of the base and target domains. Transfer to similar instances, or near transfer, is more likely to occur than transfer to dissimilar instances, or far transfer (Holyoak & Koh, 1987; Holyoak & Thagard, 1997; Ross, 1987, 1989). High surface similarity between the base and the target domain can facilitate spontaneous retrieval of prior knowledge (Gentner, Ratterman, & Forbus, 1993). For example, college students who learned solutions to probability story problems were more likely to remember solution strategies and formulas when presented with novel isomorphic problems that involved similar story lines (e.g., both study and test problems involved mechanics randomly choosing cars to work on) rather than dissimilar story lines (e.g., the study problem involved mechanics choosing cars, and the test problem involved scientists choosing computers; Ross, 1987, 1989).

Finally, there is evidence that during successful analogical transfer, the reasoner aligns the learned and novel domains according to common structure (Gentner, 1983, 1988; Gentner & Holyoak, 1997; Holyoak & Thagard, 1989). Similarity can also affect transfer by affecting the process of structural alignment. Because similar elements are easier to align than dissimilar ones (Gentner, 1983, 1988; Gentner & Markman, 1997; Markman & Gentner, 1993), structural alignment is facilitated when similar elements play identical structural roles across the learning and transfer domains. As a result, transfer is more successful when similar elements hold analogous roles in both domains (e.g., for probability problems, both study and test problems involve mechanics choosing cars; Ross, 1987, 1989; for related findings, see Reed, 1987). However, when similar elements hold different structural roles across domains (e.g., the study problem involves mechanics choosing cars and the test question involves car owners choosing mechanics), learners tend to misalign structure by matching common elements (Ross, 1987, 1989), and consequently transfer fails.

Although surface features can affect both recall of previous domains and alignment between two domains, there is evidence that they can also influence the manner in which learners interpret the structure of a domain. In a series of studies involving algebra word problems, Bassok and her colleagues have demonstrated that students often interpret structure through the context in which it is presented (for summaries, see Bassok, 1996, 2003). When undergraduate students with no prior knowledge of probability theory were asked to solve permutation problems, their spontaneous solutions typically reflected semantic symmetry or asymmetry of the elements of the problem (Bassok, Wu, & Olseth, 1995). For example, some problems involved m secretaries assigned n computers. In everyday scenarios, secretaries and computers often play asymmetric semantic roles because they are different types of entities and secretaries may use computers. Participants generally placed them in asymmetric arithmetic roles, often involving m in the numerator and n in the denominator (e.g., $\frac{[m^3]}{[n!]}$). Students tended to generate categorically different solutions to isomorphic problems involving elements that are interpreted as semantically symmetric. For instance, when given problems involving m doctors working with n doctors, participants tended to place m and n in structurally symmetric roles (e.g., $\frac{[m+n]}{[mn]^3}$, here m and n appearing in both the numerator and denominator).

The behavior of interpreting structure through semantics of the context can often be a smart approach to problem solving because mathematics is often used to model the structure of real-world situations and therefore semantic structure often correlates with mathematical structure. For example, it is probably more expected to add a number of roses and a number of tulips than to divide a number of roses by a number of tulips. It is also probably more expected to divide a number of roses by a number of vases than to add a number of roses to a number of vases. The downside of using context to interpret structure occurs when attempting to transfer between two isomorphs that do not share a common structural interpretation. For example, when students learned solutions to permutation problems in a semantically asymmetric context (e.g., tulips to vases), they successfully transferred solution strategies to novel asymmetric problems but failed to do so to symmetric problems (e.g., tulips and roses; Bassok, Wu, & Olseth, 1995). Not only did participants fail to transfer, they were very confident that the two problems differed in their mathematical structure.

Transfer failure attributed to different structural interpretations has also been demonstrated between continuous and discrete models of change (Bassok & Olseth, 1995). For example, the change in the volume of water in a pool would be continuous (able to take on any real number within some range of numbers), whereas the change in people in a pool would be discrete (limited to only a subset of values within a range of numbers, in this case whole numbers). In one study, undergraduate students were taught solutions to word problems and then given novel problems in a different context. All the problems involved constant rates of change and could be solved by the same solution strategy. The contexts included populations, money, and basic physics. What differed between base and target domains was not only the cover story but also whether the change was interpreted as continuous or discrete. For example, some contexts involved the rate at which ice is melting from a glacier, while other contexts involved the rate at which ice is regularly delivered to a restaurant. When both base and target domains shared the type of change (continuous or discrete), transfer was much more likely than when the domains differed in type of change. Furthermore, an asymmetry was found in which transfer was more likely to occur from a discrete-change domain to a continuous-change domain than the reverse. These findings demonstrate that learners often interpret structure through context and that their interpretations can lead to transfer failure when novel isomorphs have contexts that appear to be structurally different.

One way of facilitating successful transfer from concrete instantiations is through explicit comparison of multiple instances. Several studies involving both children and adults have demonstrated better performance on relational tasks after comparing two instances than after learning only one instance or learning two instances sequentially (e.g., Catrambone & Holyoak, 1989; Gentner, Loewenstein, & Hung, 2007; Gentner, Loewenstein, & Thompson, 2003; Gentner & Namy, 2004; Gick & Holyoak, 1983). Adults who learned negotiation strategies (e.g., compromise on all issues vs. trade-off on specific issues between two parties) were more successful transferring learned strategies to novel situations when they first compared and noted similarities of two examples relative to those who only read and summarized the examples separately (Gentner et al., 2003). There is also some evidence of better conceptual and procedural knowledge of mathematical equation solving after middle school students compared two examples, particularly when the examples presented different solution methods, than after learning examples in succession (Rittle-Johnson, Star, & Durkin, 2009). The process of comparison can highlight common relational structure (Kotovsky & Gentner, 1996) and result in the construction of an abstract schematic representation of knowledge (Catrambone & Holyoak, 1989; Gick & Holyoak, 1983). Schematic knowledge representations can in turn promote subsequent transfer (Gick & Holyoak, 1983; Novick & Holyoak, 1991; Ross & Kennedy, 1990).

Taken together, prior research suggests that learners can form representations of abstract concepts, including mathematical concepts, through learning concrete instantiations, but these representations are far from purely abstract. A purely abstract representation, like mathematical definitions themselves, would contain nothing beyond the structural relations. However, internal representations contain considerable superficial information retained from the learning context. The existence of this information in a representation is not necessarily a bad thing per se. This information may be harmless in the case of a teacher being able to illustrate multiple examples of mathematical models of real-world phenomena. This information may, in some instances, be helpful because it may facilitate transfer to analogous, superficially similar situations. The negative impact occurs when nonessential information is interpreted as essential. The learner incorporates this information into the representation of the concept, and as a result transfer fails when potential transfer domains lack this extraneous information. Learning and comparing multiple instances can highlight common relational structure. The highlighting of common relations likely lessens the representational weight of any one set of superficial features and as a result a schematic representation is formed. However, an abstract schema does not appear to supplant mental representations of individual exemplars. As Medin and Ross (1989) suggested, abstract and specific knowledge coexist, with reasoning often case-based and induction often conservative.

SUPPORT FOR THE USE OF CONCRETE MATERIAL IN TEACHING

The previously discussed studies have investigated analogical transfer from a variety of concrete instantiations. In educational practice, the use of concrete instantiations to present mathematics is widespread. Several arguments support this practice (for discussions, see McNeil & Uttal, 2009; Uttal, Scudder, & DeLoache, 1997). First, some developmental theories posit that development proceeds from the concrete to the abstract (e.g., Bruner, 1966; Montessori, 1917; Piaget, 1970), and therefore teaching and learning should follow the same sequence (for a discussion, see McNeil & Uttal, 2009). Second, concrete instantiations may be more engaging for the learner than more abstract, generic instantiations; certainly, engagement in learning is necessary. Third, some concrete instantiations may tap prior knowledge and therefore facilitate initial learning.

There is some evidence that mathematical problem solving can be more accurate when presented in familiar, concrete contexts than when presented as decontextualized, symbolic mathematics. For example, adolescent Brazilian street vendors were able to solve arithmetic problems in the contexts of their sales but were unable to solve the same problems presented as symbolic mathematics (Carraher, Carraher, & Schliemann, 1985). Yet evidence of the effectiveness of concrete instantiations in teaching formal mathematics is not unequivocal (Sowell, 1989; Uttal, Liu, & DeLoache, 1999; Uttal, O'Doherty, Newland, Hand, & DeLoache, 2009). For example, Koedinger and Nathan (2004) demonstrated that algebra students were more successful in solving simple story problems than analogous mathematical equations, often using informal strategies such as guess-and-check to arrive at accurate solutions. However, for more complex problems, the reverse was the case: Students were more successful solving symbolic equations than solving word problems (Koedinger, Nathan, & Alibali, 2008). Therefore, concrete contexts may *sometimes* provide an advantage over decontextualized symbolic mathematics for problem solving. It is important to note that these findings were demonstrated for learning and problem solving in a single context (that of the individual problem). Nevertheless, for mathematical concepts, an important goal of learning is not only to acquire knowledge and problem-solving ability in a particular context but also to transfer the acquired mathematical knowledge to multiple novel contexts. Thus, while students may sometimes more accurately solve problems with concrete instantiations than analogous symbolic instantiations, the question remains: How likely is it that students will transfer the mathematical structure learned from concrete instantiations versus one learned from generic instantiations?

CONCRETENESS AS PERCEPTUAL RICHNESS

As discussed earlier, one dimension of concreteness is perceptual richness. Perceptual richness can hinder transfer of relations for both children and adults. One line of evidence comes from studies of young children's symbol use (DeLoache, 1991, 2000). Successful symbol use requires transfer of relations from one domain to another. For example, to effectively use a map as a symbol for a real location, one must recognize the common relations between entities on the map and their real-world analogs. In one study, children ages 2 and 3 years were shown the location of a toy in either a three-dimensional scale model or a two-dimensional picture and then asked to retrieve a real toy in an analogous location in a real room. Perhaps counterintuitively, those who were shown the picture were more successful than those who were shown the more realistic concrete model. A similar advantage for more generic material was found for prelinguistic infants, who were better able to extend labels from generic, perceptually sparse objects to perceptually rich objects than the reverse (Son, Smith, & Goldstone, 2008). Clearly, if young children benefit from generic instantiations of concepts, adolescents and young adults could be expected to do so, too.

As expected, not only does perceptual richness hinder young children's ability to transfer simple relations, it also can hinder adults' ability to transfer acquired knowledge of more complex structures. In one study (Goldstone & Sakamoto, 2003), undergraduate students learned the principle of competitive specialization, which explains how individual agents self-organize without a central plan. When students learned through a scenario of ants foraging for food, transfer to a novel isomorph was more successful when the ants and food were depicted more abstractly as dots and patches than when the depictions resembled ants and apples.

The studies discussed thus far varied the perceptual richness of the same instantiation. In contrast, we wanted to investigate the effect of concreteness, including perceptual richness, varied across different instantiations of the same mathematical structure. This is analogous to real-world scenarios in which mathematics may transfer between instantiations of different degrees of concreteness, such as generic symbolic notation and perceptually rich, scientific applications. In a series of studies, we varied the concreteness of the learning instantiation to consider its effect on transfer of mathematical structure. We chose a simple mathematical concept that we could instantiate in a variety of different ways that would appear novel to our study participants. The concept was that of a commutative mathematical group of order 3. This is a set of three elements, or equivalence classes, and an associated operation that has the properties of associativity and commutativity. In addition, the group has an identity element and inverses for each element (see Table 3.1 for properties). In our experiments, training was presented via computer and consisted of explicit presentation of the group rules using the elements of the given instantiation, questions with feedback, and examples. After training, participants received a multiple-choice test of novel complex questions.

In our first experiment, we considered concreteness as perceptual richness of the elements and context. Undergraduate students were trained and tested with an abstract, generic instantiation and a perceptually rich, concrete instantiation (Sloutsky, Kaminski, & Heckler, 2005). The generic instantiation was described as a written language involving three simple, monochromatic symbols in which combinations of two or more symbols yield a predictable resulting symbol. Statements were expressed as *symbol 1, symbol 2 → resulting symbol*. The concrete condition presented an artificial phenomenon involving images of three colorful, three-dimensional shapes. Participants watched movies of two or more shapes coming into contact, then

TABLE 3.1
Principles of Commutative Mathematical Group

A commutative group of order 3 is a closed set of three elements and a binary operation (denoted +) with the following properties:

Associative	For any elements x, y, z: $((x + y) + z) = (x + (y + z))$
Commutative	For any elements x, y: $x + y = y + x$
Identity	There is an element, I, such that for any element, x: $x + I = x$
Inverses	For any element, x, there exists another element, y, such that $x + y = I$

disappearing, and a resulting shape appearing. For both instantiations, the resulting symbol or shape was specified by the mathematical structure. After training and testing of one instantiation, participants were trained and tested with the other instantiation. We found that participants successfully learned both instantiations, with no difference in mean test score on the generic instantiation no matter which instantiation they learned first. However, there was a marked difference in mean test score on the concrete instantiation, with participants who were initially trained with the generic instantiation scoring higher on the concrete test than did participants who were initially trained with the concrete instantiation. In other words, learning the concrete instantiation resulted in no improved learning of the generic instantiation. On the other hand, learning the generic instantiation resulted in better performance on the concrete instantiation, suggesting that participants were able to transfer their knowledge from the generic to the concrete instantiation.

In a second experiment, we considered the effects of perceptual richness on initial learning. Participants learned an instantiation of a group that had different levels of concreteness: (a) generic black symbols; (b) colorful, patterned symbols; (c) classes of colorful, patterned symbols; or (d) classes of real objects. After training, participants were given a test of novel questions on the same instantiation. While all participants learned the rules, those who learned with the generic symbols scored significantly higher than did the other participants, with no differences across these three conditions (Sloutsky et al., 2005). Therefore, the mere addition of patterns and color lowered learning. Similar negative effects of perceptual richness were demonstrated in another recent study: Children ages 10 to 12 years made more errors on word problems involving money when they were given real bills and coins to help them solve the problems than children who were not given real money (McNeil, Uttal, Jarvin, & Sternberg, 2009).

The results of these experiments indicate that perceptual richness that is irrelevant to the to-be-learned concept hindered both learning and transfer. However, not all concreteness is irrelevant. Some concreteness may help to communicate relevant structure by tapping prior knowledge or by presenting perceptual information that is correlated with structure. This "relevant concreteness" would most likely facilitate learning of a novel concept, but its effect on transfer has not been clear.

RELEVANT CONCRETENESS

To investigate the effects of such relevant concreteness, we instantiated the concept of a mathematical group in a context involving familiar objects that might facilitate learning of the group rules (Kaminski, Sloutsky, & Heckler,

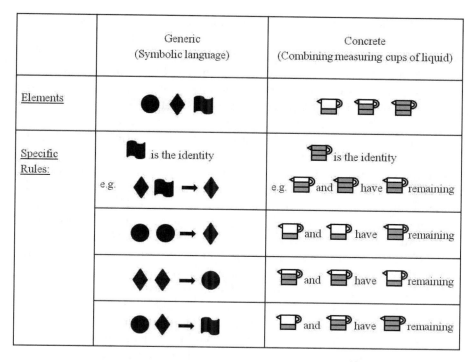

Figure 3.2. Generic and concrete instantiations of a mathematical group.

2005a). In this case, the elements of the group were three measuring cups (see Figure 3.2). Instead of learning arbitrary rules of symbol combinations, participants were told that they needed to determine a leftover amount of liquid when different measuring cups were combined. For example, combining and resulted in left over. We compared learning this instantiation with learning a generic instantiation. This generic instantiation was described, as in our earlier studies, as the rules of a symbolic language. Training consisted of explicit statements of the rules and one example. After training, participants answered a series of multiple-choice questions. The following are example questions from the generic learning condition.

1. What can go in the blanks to make a correct statement?

  ___ , ◆ , ___ , ● → ●

2. Find the resulting symbol:

  ◆ , ● , ● , ◪ → ___

The concrete condition presented the analogues of these questions. All training and testing was isomorphic across conditions. Participants in both conditions successfully learned the instantiation, but under the minimal training that they received (only one statement of the rules and one example), the relevantly concrete instantiation did have an advantage over the generic (81% vs. 63% correct, with chance = 38%).

To test whether this advantage would exist for transfer, we gave participants slightly more detailed training, including explicit examples and questions with feedback. Subsequently, as in the previous experiments, participants were tested and then presented with a novel isomorphic instantiation of mathematical group. This novel instantiation was intentionally concrete and contextually rich, as are many real-world instantiations of mathematics, and was described as a children's game from another country. Specifically, participants were asked to figure out the rules of the game. In the game, children point to a series of objects, then the child who is "it" points to a final object. This child wins if he or she points to the correct object according to the rules (see Figure 3.3). Participants were told that the rules of the game were like the rules of the system they had just learned (i.e., either the concrete or the generic instantiation). Then, participants were shown a series of examples from which the rules could be deduced. After seeing the examples, a multiple-choice test, isomorphic to the test of the learning

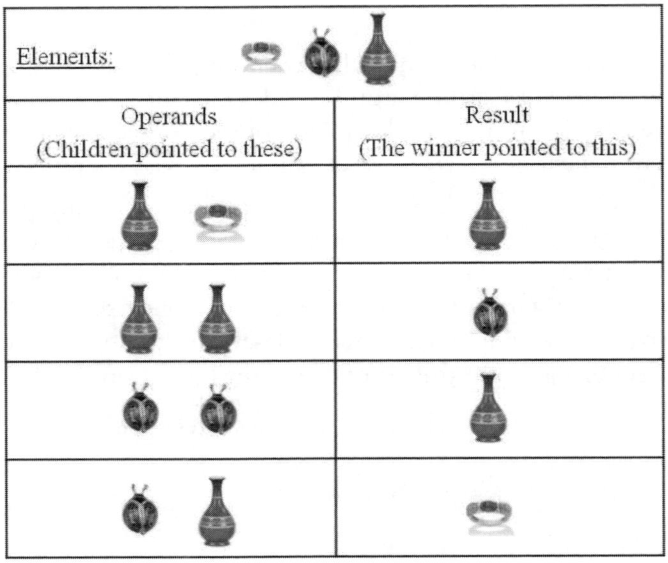

Figure 3.3. Instantiation of a commutative mathematical group used for the transfer domain.

domain, was given. The results revealed that with the slightly protracted training, there was no difference in learning scores across the two conditions (78% correct vs. 75% correct for the concrete and generic conditions, respectively). However, there was a striking difference in transfer. Participants in the concrete condition had an average test score of 54% correct, while the average score in the generic condition was 79% (with chance being 38%).

Because structural alignment is an essential component of successful analogical transfer, we wanted to know whether participants in each condition were able to align structure between the learning and transfer instantiations. As an indication of alignment, participants were asked to match analogous elements across domains. In the generic condition, 100% of participants were able to do so, whereas only 25% of participants in the concrete condition made the correct match. Because there were three elements, we would expect chance performance to result in 33% accuracy (Kaminski, Sloutsky, & Heckler, 2005b). Therefore, those who learned the concrete instantiation scored no better than guessing.

Why were participants in the concrete condition unable to align structure across the learning and transfer domains? There are two possibilities. First, perhaps learners in the concrete condition formed a representation of that instantiation that did not contain the relevant mathematical structure. It is possible that these participants were accurate on the test of the concrete instantiation because the familiar elements and context allowed them to "bootstrap" their way to correct answers without truly acquiring the mathematical structure. This possibility is reminiscent of Koedinger and Nathan's (2004) finding that algebra students often successfully solved simple story problems by using informal strategies without resorting to formal algebraic solutions. The second possibility is that the representation of the concrete instantiation did contain structure, but that structure was tightly tied to the elements and context such that learners were unable to recognize it in novel situations.

To test the possibility that failure to transfer from the concrete instantiation was due to difficulty in aligning structure and not due to failure to represent structure, we conducted another experiment that was identical to the previous one, with a single exception. Prior to the transfer test, we showed half of the participants the matching of analogous elements across domains. In the concrete condition, half were told 🍵 is like 🛞 , 🍵 is like 🌑 , 🍵 is like 🏺 . In the generic condition, half were told the analogous alignments between the generic elements and transfer elements. The goal was to assist learners with structural alignment by telling them the correspondence of analogous elements. We found that when learners in the concrete condition were given the correspondence, they transferred as successfully as the learners in the generic condition (85% accuracy for both condition). In the generic condition, there was no significant difference in transfer scores as a function of being given the element correspondence, suggesting that participants were able to spontaneously align structures between the learning and transfer domains (Kaminski, Sloutsky, & Heckler, 2006c). The fact that participants in the concrete condition were successful when assisted with structural alignment also indicates that structure was acquired during learning. If they had not actually learned the mathematical rules, it is highly unlikely that they would perform so well on difficult transfer questions by simply being given a matching of elements.

It seems that when acquiring a novel mathematical concept through a concrete context, structural knowledge is represented but tied to the learning context in a way that inhibits its spontaneous recognition in other situations. To consider this possibility more carefully, we tested whether learned structure could be recognized when instantiated with novel elements. Participants were trained with either the concrete or generic instantiation of the mathematical structure, as in the previous studies. After training, instead of being presented with the transfer domain and a test of complex questions, participants were given a structure discrimination task. On each trial, participants were presented with a set of three expressions. They were told that each set is from a new system and were asked whether the new system followed the same type of rules as the system they had previously learned. Four types of trials were used. Figure 3.4 shows examples of each type, as expressed for the concrete condition. For the generic conditions, the analogous state-

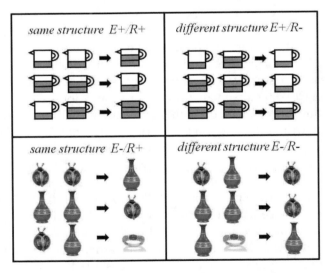

Figure 3.4. Example statements used for the structure discrimination task.

ments were expressed with the generic black symbols. Six trials involved the same elements as the learning phase and the same relational structure (E+/R+). Six trials involved the familiar elements but different relational structure (E+/R−). Six trials involved novel elements and the familiar relational structure (E−/R+). Another six trials involved both novel elements and novel relations (E−/R−). To measure discriminability, we calculated the number of correct "same structure" responses (on R+ trials) minus the number of incorrect "same structure" responses (on R− trials). We measured discriminability separately for familiar elements and novel elements. For familiar elements, participants in both conditions were highly accurate (90% correct). However, there were dramatic differences when it came to novel elements. Accuracy in the generic condition was 78%, while accuracy in the concrete condition was only 26% (Kaminski, Sloutsky, & Heckler, 2006a).

These findings suggest that although structure is represented when learning a concrete instantiation, the most salient aspect of the representation is the superficial, contextual information and not the important structural information. In a follow-up study, we asked participants, after they had learned either the concrete or the generic instantiation, to write down what they recalled about what they had learned. We then counted the number of statements

referring to structure such as reiteration of rules (e.g., ◆, ◆ ● ⟶

or combining 🝕 and 🝕 has 🝕 left over) and the number of statements referring to superficial elements such as "it was about the discovery of a symbolic language" or "it was about liquid in cups." We found that those who learned the generic instantiation made nearly 4 times as many structural comments as those who learned the concrete instantiation. The responses of the participants who learned the concrete instantiation contained approximately twice as many references to the superficial as references to structure. The opposite pattern was observed for participants in the generic condition: They made approximately 3 times as many references to structure as references to the superficial (Kaminski, Sloutsky, & Heckler, 2009). These results support the argument that the representation of the concrete instantiation was overwhelmed by superficial information. They also suggest that structure is salient in the representation of the generic instantiation. These findings parallel ideas of fuzzy trace theory, which posits that transfer succeeds when learners have formed "gist" knowledge representations that do not contain detailed information (Reyna & Brainerd, 1995; Wolfe, Reyna, & Brainerd, 2005). According to fuzzy trace theory, transfer fails when learners have formed detail-rich, verbatim knowledge representations. Because concrete instantiations communicate an abundance of extraneous information in comparison to more generic instantiations, presenting a learner with a concrete instantiation may encourage the inclusion of extraneous details in the representation, which hinders subsequent transfer.

As mentioned previously, one way of highlighting relational structure and improving transfer is through learning multiple instantiations of the same concept, particularly when learners compare instantiations. Given that a generic instantiation allows the learner to spontaneously recognize and transfer structure, we hypothesized that learning a generic instantiation may be a more efficient route to a representation that allows for successful transfer than learning multiple concrete instantiations. We tested this hypothesis by assigning learners to conditions in which they learned one, two, or three concrete instantiations or one generic instantiation (Kaminski, Sloutsky, & Heckler, 2008). We used the previously described concrete and generic instantiations and two other concrete instantiations. The two additional concrete instantiations involved pizzas and tennis balls and were designed, as was the measuring cup scenario, to tap everyday knowledge in familiar contexts. We equated the amount of training and testing across condition; all participants were presented with the same rules and the same number of examples, questions with feedback, and test questions. After learning, participants were given the same transfer task used in our previous experiments. We found a clear transfer advantage for learning a single generic instantiation. Participants in the generic condition had approximately 78% accuracy, while participants in the concrete conditions scored little or no better than chance, at 38%.

In two follow-up experiments, we attempted to highlight structure between learned instantiations (Kaminski et al., 2008). First, we considered whether giving participants the correspondence of analogous elements across two concrete learning instantiations would help integrate the representations of each and increase the salience of the common structure. This manipulation resulted in no improvement on transfer; scores were again no different than chance. Second, we asked participants, after they had learned two concrete instantiations, to compare them, match analogous elements, and write down any observed similarities. All participants correctly matched elements, but the distribution of transfer scores was bimodal. Approximately 44% of our participants scored high on the transfer test (mean score of 95% correct). The remaining 56% of participants did not do well (mean score of 51% correct). We concluded that the act of explicit comparison may help some learners transfer but may not help others. Moreover, although those who did transfer well scored very high on their initial test of learning, not all who scored high on learning succeeded in transferring after comparison. Therefore, successful learning is a necessary, but not sufficient, condition for successful transfer after comparison.

Given that concrete instantiations may have an advantage for initial learning and generic instantiations can have an advantage for subsequent transfer, we considered a possible "best of both worlds" scenario. We compared transfer after learning the concrete instantiation and then the generic instantiation to transfer when learning only the generic instantiation. Participants in both conditions successfully transferred, but those who learned only the generic significantly outperformed those who learned both (84% correct vs. 65% correct; Kaminski et al., 2008).

Taken together, these findings suggest that learning a generic instantiation of a mathematical concept can be an efficient, direct route to a schematic knowledge representation that can allow for successful transfer. Relational structure is the salient aspect, while elements and other superficial features can be interchanged with those of other instantiations. On the other hand, the course of forming such a representation from learning concrete instantiations is not as efficient, requiring learning more than one instantiation with less likelihood of subsequent transfer than after learning a single generic. When only one concrete instantiation is learned, superficial information dominates the representation and, in turn, interferes with transfer. Even when two and three concrete instantiations were learned in sequence, transfer failed, thus suggesting that these representations were stored independently of each other and not integrated. The fact that learning a concrete followed by a generic instantiation resulted in less transfer than learning a single generic one suggests that superficial information remained in the representation, interfering with successfully applying structural knowledge to the transfer domain.

THE PROBLEM WITH CONCRETENESS

Why is extraneous information in the learning context so damaging for transfer? We suggest that superficial information diverts attention from the relevant relational structure. Attentional resources are limited, and evidence suggests that superficial features and relational structure may compete for attention (DeLoache, 1991; Goldstone, Medin, & Gentner, 1991; Uttal et al., 1999). Goldstone, Medin, and Gentner (1991) suggested that in making similarity comparisons between two situations, attention is split into two separate pools, one for relational similarities and one for superficial similarities. As one pool gets larger, it pulls attention toward itself and away from the other pool.

For concrete instantiations, the superficial features are salient and attention grabbing. It is possible, then, that attention is allocated to these superficial features and diverted from relational structure, not only during similarity comparisons but also in the formation of representations of conceptual knowledge. When attempting to transfer, the learner needs to distinguish relevant from irrelevant information and inhibit the irrelevant. Generic instantiations have less superficial information and thus permit attention to be focused more easily on relevant relational structure.

The results we have discussed in this chapter involved undergraduate college students. It is possible that college students can successfully learn generic instantiations and transfer structural knowledge, but younger learners may need a concrete instantiation to begin to grasp an abstract concept. However, young children are less able than adults to control their focus of attention (Dempster & Corkill, 1999; Diamond, 2006; Napolitano & Sloutsky, 2004). Therefore, if the difficulty with concrete instantiations is due to extraneous information diverting attention from relevant structure, then concreteness may be at least as detrimental for younger children's transfer as it is for older students. To test this possibility, we taught 11-year-old children either the concrete or the generic instantiation and presented them with the transfer domain, as in our earlier experiments. Participants in both conditions successfully learned, but those who learned the concrete instantiation scored higher than those who learned the generic (82% vs. 66% correct). However, for the learners in the concrete condition, transfer scores were only marginally above the chance score of 38% (47% correct), whereas transfer scores in the generic condition were significantly above chance (61% correct; Kaminski, Sloutsky, & Heckler, 2006b). These results suggest that although the concrete instantiation was easily learned, it created an obstacle for children to align structure and successfully transfer. These findings further support the argument that concrete instantiations hinder transfer because the extraneous information diverts attention from relevant structure.

SUMMARY

Our research has compared learning of a novel mathematical concept through concrete instantiations or through a single generic instantiation. We found that relevant structure can be acquired from either concrete or generic instantiations, but the manner in which it is internally represented by the learner is categorically different in each case. Concrete instantiations communicate abundant extraneous information that may pull attention away from the relevant relational structure. The result is a representation in which the superficial is salient. This salient superficial information obfuscates the analogy between learned and novel isomorphs because the learner is unable to recognize structure in the novel situation. As a result, transfer fails. Successful transfer from concrete instantiations requires additional measures such as directly aligning structure for the learner across instantiations or asking the learner to compare multiple instantiations. However, potential transfer domains are not always known a priori, making direct alignment often impossible, and comparison may not always result in success.

Nevertheless, it seems that relational structure is the salient aspect of representations formed from generic instantiations. Consequently, learners spontaneously recognize structure and successfully transfer. Generic instantiations of mathematics, such as traditional symbolic notation, can be powerful educational tools providing efficient routes to portable knowledge representations. Knowledge gleaned from such instantiations can be applied to analogous situations that may appear on the surface to be quite dissimilar.

DISCUSSION

The appeal of concrete learning material is certainly understandable. Concrete instantiations of mathematical concepts are often perceptually rich and attractive. They can perhaps generate a level of initial engagement and interest for students that generic symbols may not. Some concrete instantiations may be familiar and tap prior knowledge to provide a leg up in the learning process. Yet the very aspects of concrete instantiations that make them engaging may also render them ineffective at promoting transfer. The complete story of how concreteness influences the learning, transfer, reasoning, and problem solving of mathematical knowledge over the lifetime of an individual is likely a complex one. The results of the research discussed here pinpoint some of the difficulties learners encounter with concrete instantiations of novel concepts.

In educational practice, concrete material such as base-10 blocks, Cuisenaire rods, and many real-world instantiations such as pizzas are commonly used. Many may wonder whether very young children may need concrete instantiations to begin to acquire mathematical concepts, such as place value or fractions. However, we are aware of no research that demonstrates an advantage of concrete material over more generic material with respect to transfer. If it is true that the difficulty in transferring mathematical knowledge from concrete instantiations stems from extraneous information diverting attention from the important underlying structure, then we would expect that younger children would also have difficulty with concrete instantiations. The ability to inhibit irrelevant information depends on components of executive function that improve through the course of development (Diamond, 2006). Therefore, we would expect a transfer advantage for generic instantiations over concrete instantiations for younger, preadolescent children as well.

Even so, as Blair and Schwartz discuss in Chapter 4 of this volume, educational learning activities often involve an integration of symbolic mathematics and concrete examples. As they illustrate, it is possible to design activities for some concepts in which students can benefit from interacting with concrete instantiations. Further research is needed into the benefits and costs of concrete material for learning and transfer of abstract concepts.

For pedagogical purposes, the possible advantages of choosing concrete learning material over more generic material need to be weighed carefully against the disadvantages, especially for adolescents and young adults who must acquire abstract concepts. In particular, two important questions should be addressed. First, what is the goal of the educational material at hand? If the goal is to learn a single domain, some concrete contextualization may not be a big obstacle. If the goal is to acquire knowledge that can be applied to a variety of superficially dissimilar situations, then the results of our studies suggest that generic material has a clear advantage. Second, what are the possible options for the learning material? In other words, concrete compared to what? For example, story problems about the acceleration of a thrown baseball are more concrete than analogous, strictly symbolic problems, but less concrete than actually measuring the acceleration of a real ball.

If the goal of learning is to acquire knowledge that can be broadly transferred, then generic instantiations are powerful. For mathematical concepts, an important aim of education is such broad transfer. Mathematics is expected to be successfully applied to many real-world situations. Some of these situations may be foreseeable, such as planning personal finances, and so it is reasonable to include such concrete instantiations in the course of formal learning. However, the manner in which mathematics can be applied to less understood situations is not necessarily foreseeable. For example, this is the challenge faced by many scientists as they venture into previously unexplored areas: to recognize consistent relational structure among elements and to transfer structural knowledge from a known analogous domain or model those situations with mathematical expressions. Those faced with the challenge of understanding the structure of unfamiliar domains may be well equipped by having acquired mathematical knowledge in adolescence and young adulthood through generic instantiations.

REFERENCES

Anderson, J. R., Reder, L. M., & Simon, H. A. (1996). Situated learning and education. *Educational Researcher, 25*(4), 5–11.

Bassok, M. (1996). Using content to interpret structure: Effects on analogical transfer. *Current Directions in Psychological Science, 5,* 54–58. doi:10.1111/1467-8721.ep10772723

Bassok, M. (2003). Analogical transfer in problem solving. In J. E. Davidson & R. J. Sternberg (Eds.), *The psychology of problem solving* (pp. 343–369). New York, NY: Cambridge University Press.

Bassok, M., & Olseth, K. L. (1995). Object-based representations: Transfer between cases of continuous and discrete models of change. *Journal of Experimental Psychology: Learning, Memory, and Cognition, 21,* 1522–1538. doi:10.1037/0278-7393.21.6.1522

Bassok, M., Wu, L., & Olseth, K. L. (1995). Judging a book by its cover: Interpretative effects of context on problem-solving transfer. *Memory & Cognition, 23,* 354–367. doi:10.3758/BF03197236

Bruner, J. S. (1966). *Toward a theory of instruction.* Cambridge, MA: Harvard University Press.

Carraher, T. N., Carraher, D. W., & Schliemann, A. D. (1985). Mathematics in the streets and in schools. *British Journal of Developmental Psychology, 3,* 21–29.

Catrambone, R., & Holyoak, K. J. (1989). Overcoming contextual limitations on problem-solving transfer. *Journal of Experimental Psychology: Learning, Memory, and Cognition, 15,* 1147–1156. doi:10.1037/0278-7393.15.6.1147

DeLoache, J. S. (1991). Symbolic functioning in very young children: Understanding of pictures and models. *Child Development, 62,* 736–752. doi:10.2307/1131174

DeLoache, J. S. (2000). Dual representation and young children's use of scale models. *Child Development, 71,* 329–338. doi:10.1111/1467-8624.00148

Dempster, F. N., & Corkill, A. J. (1999). Inference and inhibition in cognition and behavior: Unifying themes for educational psychology. *Educational Psychology Review, 11,* 1–88. doi:10.1023/A:1021992632168

Diamond, A. (2006). The early development of executive functions. In E. Bialystok & F. Craik (Eds.), *Lifespan cognition: Mechanisms of change* (pp. 70–95). New York, NY: Oxford University Press.

Gentner, D. (1983). Structure-mapping: A theoretical framework for analogy. *Cognitive Science, 7,* 155–170. doi:10.1207/s15516709cog0702_3

Gentner, D. (1988). Metaphor as structure mapping: The relational shift. *Child Development, 59,* 47–59. doi:10.2307/1130388

Gentner, D., & Holyoak, K. J. (1997). Reasoning and learning by analogy. *American Psychologist, 52,* 32–34. doi:10.1037/0003-066X.52.1.32

Gentner, D., Loewenstein, J., & Hung, B. (2007). Comparison facilitates children's learning of names for parts. *Journal of Cognition and Development, 8,* 285–307. doi:10.1080/15248370701446434

Gentner, D., Loewenstein, J., & Thompson, L. (2003). Learning and transfer: A general role for analogical encoding. *Journal of Educational Psychology, 95,* 393–405. doi:10.1037/0022-0663.95.2.393

Gentner, D., & Markman, A. B. (1997). Structure-mapping in analogy and similarity. *American Psychologist, 52,* 45–56. doi:10.1037/0003-066X.52.1.45

Gentner, D., & Namy, L. L. (2004). The role of comparison in children's early word learning. In S. R. Waxman & D. G. Hall (Eds.), *Weaving a lexicon* (pp. 533–568). Cambridge, MA: MIT Press.

Gentner, D., Ratterman, M. J., & Forbus, K. D. (1993). The roles of similarity in transfer: Separating retrievability from inferential soundness. *Cognitive Psychology*, *25*, 524–575. doi:10.1006/cogp.1993.1013

Gick, M. L., & Holyoak, K. J. (1980). Analogical problem solving. *Cognitive Psychology*, *12*, 306–355. doi:10.1016/0010-0285(80)90013-4

Gick, M. L., & Holyoak, K. J. (1983). Schema induction and analogical transfer. *Cognitive Psychology*, *15*, 1–38. doi:10.1016/0010-0285(83)90002-6

Goldstone, R. L., Medin, D. L., & Gentner, D. (1991). Relational similarity and the nonindependence of features in similarity judgments. *Cognitive Psychology*, *23*, 222–262. doi:10.1016/0010-0285(91)90010-L

Goldstone, R. L., & Sakamoto, Y. (2003). The transfer of abstract principles governing complex adaptive systems. *Cognitive Psychology*, *46*, 414–466. doi:10.1016/S0010-0285(02)00519-4

Goswami, U. (1991). Analogical reasoning: What develops? A review of research and theory. *Child Development*, *62*, 1–22. doi:10.2307/1130701

Holyoak, K. J., & Koh, K. (1987). Surface and structural similarity in analogical transfer. *Memory & Cognition*, *15*, 332–340. doi:10.3758/BF03197035

Holyoak, K. J. & Thagard, P. (1989). Analogical mapping by constraint satisfaction. *Cognitive Science*, *13*, 295–355.

Holyoak, K. J., & Thagard, P. (1997). The analogical mind. *American Psychologist*, *52*, 35–44. doi:10.1037/0003-066X.52.1.35

Kaminski, J. A., Sloutsky, V. M., & Heckler, A. F. (2005a). Relevant concreteness and its effects on learning and transfer. In B. Bara, L. Barsalou, & M. Bucciarelli (Eds.), *Proceedings of the XXVII Annual Conference of the Cognitive Science Society* (pp. 1090–1095). Mahwah, NJ: Erlbaum.

Kaminski, J. A., Sloutsky, V. M., & Heckler, A. F. (2005b). [Relevant concreteness and its effects on learning and transfer]. Unpublished raw data.

Kaminski, J. A., Sloutsky, V. M., & Heckler, A. F. (2006a). Effects of concreteness on representation: An explanation for differential transfer. In R. Sun & N. Miyake (Eds.), *Proceedings of the XXVIII Annual Conference of the Cognitive Science Society*. Mahwah, NJ: Erlbaum.

Kaminski, J. A., Sloutsky, V. M., & Heckler, A. F. (2006b). Do children need concrete instantiations to learn an abstract concept? In R. Sun & N. Miyake (Eds.), *Proceedings of the XXVIII Annual Conference of the Cognitive Science Society*. Mahwah, NJ: Erlbaum.

Kaminski, J. A., Sloutsky, V. M., & Heckler, A. F. (2006c). [Concreteness, transfer, and structural alignment]. Unpublished raw data.

Kaminski, J. A., Sloutsky, V. M., & Heckler, A. F. (2008, April 25). The advantage of abstract examples in learning math. *Science, 320*, 454–455. doi:10.1126/science. 1154659

Kaminski, J. A., Sloutsky, V. M., & Heckler, A. F. (2009). [Concreteness and representation of abstract knowledge]. Unpublished raw data.

Kloos, H., & Sloutsky, V. M. (2008). What's behind different kinds of kinds: Effects of statistical density on learning and representation of categories. *Journal of Experimental Psychology: General, 137*, 52–72. doi:10.1037/0096-3445.137.1.52

Koedinger, K. R., & Nathan, M. J. (2004). The real story behind story problems: Effects of representations on quantitative reasoning. *Journal of the Learning Sciences, 13*, 129–164. doi:10.1207/s15327809jls1302_1

Koedinger, K. R., Nathan, M. J., & Alibali, M. W. (2008). Trade-offs between grounded and abstract representations: Evidence from algebra problem solving. *Cognitive Science, 32*, 366–397. doi:10.1080/03640210701863933

Kotovsky, L., & Gentner, D. (1996). Comparison and categorization in the development of relational similarity. *Child Development, 67*, 2797–2822. doi:10.2307/ 1131753

Markman, A. B., & Gentner, D. (1993). Structural alignment during similarity comparisons. *Cognitive Psychology, 25*, 431–467. doi:10.1006/cogp.1993.1011

McNeil, N. M., & Uttal, D. H. (2009). Rethinking the use of concrete materials in learning: Perspectives from development and education. *Child Development Perspectives, 3*, 137–139. doi:10.1111/j.1750-8606.2009.00093.x

McNeil, N. M., Uttal, D. H., Jarvin, L., & Sternberg, R. J. (2009). Should you show me the money? Concrete objects both hurt and help performance on mathematics problems. *Learning and Instruction, 19*, 171–184. doi:10.1016/j.learn instruc.2008.03.005

Medin, D. L., & Ross, B. H. (1989). The specific character of abstract thought: Categorization, problem solving, and induction. In R. Sternberg (Ed.), *Advances in the psychology of human intelligence: Vol. 5* (pp. 189–223). Hillsdale, NJ: Erlbaum.

Montessori, M. (1917). *The advanced Montessori method.* New York, NY: Frederick A. Stokes.

Napolitano, A. C., & Sloutsky, V. M. (2004). Is a picture worth a thousand words? Part II: The flexible nature of modality dominance in young children. *Child Development, 75*, 1850–1870. doi:10.1111/j.1467-8624.2004.00821.x

Novick, L. R. (1988). Analogical transfer, problem similarity, and expertise. *Journal of Experimental Psychology: Learning, Memory, and Cognition, 14*, 510–520. doi:10.1037/0278-7393.14.3.510

Novick, L. R., & Holyoak, K. J. (1991). Mathematical problem solving by analogy. *Journal of Experimental Psychology: Learning, Memory, and Cognition, 17*, 398–415. doi:10.1037/0278-7393.17.3.398

Piaget, J. (1970). *Science of education and the psychology of the child*. New York, NY: Orion Press.

Reed, S. K. (1987). A structure-mapping model for word problems. *Journal of Experimental Psychology: Learning, Memory, and Cognition, 13,* 124–139. doi:10.1037/0278-7393.13.1.124

Reed, S. K., Dempster, A., & Ettinger, M. (1985). Usefulness of analogous solutions for solving algebra word problems. *Journal of Experimental Psychology: Learning, Memory, and Cognition, 11,* 106–125. doi:10.1037/0278-7393.11.1.106

Reed, S. K., Ernst, G. W., & Banerji, R. (1974). The role of analogy in transfer between similar problem states. *Cognitive Psychology, 6,* 436–450. doi:10.1016/0010-0285(74)90020-6

Reyna, V. F., & Brainerd, C. F. (1995). Fuzzy-trace theory: Some foundational issues. *Learning and Individual Differences, 7,* 145–162. doi:10.1016/1041-6080(95)90028-4

Rittle-Johnson, B., Star, J. R., & Durkin, K. (2009). The importance of prior knowledge when comparing examples: Influences on conceptual and procedural knowledge of equation solving. *Journal of Educational Psychology, 101,* 836–852. doi:10.1037/a0016026

Ross, B. H. (1987). This is like that: The use of earlier problems and the separation of similarity effects. *Journal of Experimental Psychology: Learning, Memory, and Cognition, 13,* 629–639. doi:10.1037/0278-7393.13.4.629

Ross, B. H. (1989). Distinguishing types of superficial similarities: Different effects on the access and use of earlier problems. *Journal of Experimental Psychology: Learning, Memory, and Cognition, 15,* 456–468. doi:10.1037/0278-7393.15.3.456

Ross, B. H., & Kennedy, P. T. (1990). Generalizing from the use of earlier examples in problem solving. *Journal of Experimental Psychology: Learning, Memory, and Cognition, 16,* 42–55. doi:10.1037/0278-7393.16.1.42

Simon, H. A., & Reed, S. K. (1976). Modeling strategy shifts in a problem solving task. *Cognitive Psychology, 8,* 86–97. doi:10.1016/0010-0285(76)90005-0

Sloutsky, V. M., Kaminski, J. A., & Heckler, A. F. (2005). The advantage of simple symbols for learning and transfer. *Psychonomic Bulletin & Review, 12,* 508–513. doi:10.3758/BF03193796

Solomon, K. O., Medin, D. L., & Lynch, E. (1999). Concepts do more than categorize. *Trends in Cognitive Sciences, 3,* 99–105. doi:10.1016/S1364-6613(99)01288-7

Son, J. Y., Smith, L. B., & Goldstone, R. L. (2008). Simplicity and generalization: Short-cutting abstraction in children's object categorizations. *Cognition, 108,* 626–638. doi:10.1016/j.cognition.2008.05.002

Sowell, E. (1989). Effects of manipulative materials in mathematics instruction. *Journal for Research in Mathematics Education, 20,* 498–505. doi:10.2307/749423

Uttal, D. H., Liu, L. L., & DeLoache, J. S. (1999). Taking a hard look at concreteness: Do concrete objects help young children learn symbolic relations? In

C. Tamis-LeMonda & L. Balter (Eds.), *Child psychology: A handbook of contemporary issues* (pp. 177–192). Philadelphia, PA: Psychology Press.

Uttal, D., O'Doherty, K., Newland, R., Hand, L., & DeLoache, J. (2009). Dual representation and the linking of concrete and symbolic representations. *Child Development Perspectives, 3*, 156–159. doi:10.1111/j.1750-8606.2009.00097.x

Uttal, D. H., Scudder, K. V., & DeLoache, J. S. (1997). Manipulatives as symbols: A new perspective on the use of concrete objects to teach mathematics. *Journal of Applied Developmental Psychology, 18*, 37–54. doi:10.1016/S0193-3973(97)90013-7

Wolfe, C. R., Reyna, V. F., & Brainerd, C. F. (2005). Fuzzy-trace theory: Implications for transfer in teaching and learning. In J. P. Mestre (Ed.), *Transfer of learning from a modern multidisciplinary perspective* (pp. 53–88). Greenwich, CT: Information Age Publishing.

4

A VALUE OF CONCRETE LEARNING MATERIALS IN ADOLESCENCE

KRISTEN P. BLAIR AND DANIEL L. SCHWARTZ

There are disagreements about the appropriate role of concrete materials for learning. We clarify the assumptions underlying different uses of concrete materials and abstract symbols in instruction for learning new mathematical ideas. We argue that despite the potential structural isomorphism of concrete materials and abstract representations, they engage different psychological processes. We describe several studies highlighting the unique psychological properties of concrete materials and abstract symbols for learning. We propose the coevolution hypothesis, in which concrete materials and symbols work together to help students discover the structure both in the world and in the abstract representations. In a classroom study with sixth-grade students learning about proportion and ratio, students who received instruction consistent with the coevolution hypothesis showed improved initial learning and greater transfer than students who first learned abstract symbols and mathematical principles and then applied them to concrete materials as practice.

Most parents of young children would testify to the value of concrete materials for learning. In a well-stocked home, children have hands-on educational toys, books with rich illustrations, and colorful interactive electronics. Even so, there is confusion among parents, teachers, policymakers, and instructional designers over the exact value of concrete materials for learning. For example, in California, the state's science curriculum commission proposed legislation that would limit hands-on learning to "no more than 20 to 25 percent" of instructional time. This resulted in an outcry from educators and business people, and the final legislation reversed the proposal to require that "*at least* 20 to 25 percent" of science instruction use hands-on material (California Science Teachers Association, 2004; emphasis added).

Confusion about concrete materials takes on special importance as children move into adolescence. Adolescents have begun to master the symbol systems of language and mathematics. These children can now learn in other ways besides directly interacting with concrete materials. Moreover, students need to increase fluency in the symbol systems that define adult life. Is there still a place for concrete materials, and, if so, how should an educator make decisions?

Ideally, an educator could look to the research literature to find answers. However, the literature is not as clarifying as one might hope. One reason is that there has been a tendency to pit concrete and symbolic materials against one another. Consider the case of mathematics learning, which is the focus of this chapter. Many of the mathematical ideas developed in early adolescence can be expressed both in concrete and symbolic form. For example, fraction addition can be accomplished by manipulating symbols or plastic wedges. This equivalence can naturally lead to an either–or mind-set and often generates the question of which is better for learning.

Rather than considering concrete and abstract as a dichotomy, we consider how they can work together to help students learn new mathematical concepts. While concrete and symbolic forms can achieve the same quantitative answers, they have different psychological properties for learning and problem solving. We propose a *coevolution hypothesis,* in which the understanding of concrete and symbolic materials develops in tandem by building on each other's psychological advantages. Of course, not just any combination of materials and activities will lead to optimal learning, and our burden is to help clarify when and how to use concrete materials. (Note that when we talk about concrete materials, we do not mean only physical materials. Our intent is to distinguish between symbolic notations and concrete instances, so that photographs, for example, would also count as concrete materials.)

We begin by briefly reviewing the conflicting research on the value of concrete materials for learning and transfer. We then consider some of the implicit assumptions that guide different uses of concrete materials. Many of these assumptions do not apply to our goal, which is to help students learn fundamentally new (to them) mathematical structures. To clarify this alternative goal and the coevolution hypothesis, we offer several examples, including an explicit instructional example that demonstrates the theoretical work in a successful classroom application.

All of the following examples focus on the grouping of quantities, as in the cases of statistical distributions, ratio, fractions, and place value. Learning to work with groups rather than just singletons is a precursor of rational number reasoning for younger students (Blair, 2009; Blair et al., 2008), and the ability to reason about proportion and ratio is one of the primary accomplishments of preadolescence to early adolescence and a cornerstone of algebra (Confrey, Chapter 6, this volume).

CONFUSIONS ABOUT CONCRETENESS

Learning from concrete materials has had four primary lines of investigation: motivation, development, transfer, and problem solving. We begin with motivation. Many teachers view concrete materials as engaging (Moyer, 2001). Whether it is the concreteness per se or the relief from more typical school tasks is unclear, but there is multistudy evidence that concrete materials improve student attitudes toward mathematics (Sowell, 1989). Surprisingly, to our knowledge, there is no theory of motivation that would predict the special motivation of concrete materials, though nearly all theories could presumably account for the effects after the fact.

In the context of development, the terms *concrete* and *abstract* often refer to mental structures and operations rather than external artifacts. Piaget (1941), as well as Bruner (1996), has proposed a developmental progression from concrete thought to more abstract understanding. For example, an adolescent can reason abstractly about physical materials, such as making decisions based on nonobservable properties or considering hypothetical actions. In contrast, the reasoning of a young child may be more tied to perceivable properties and physical manipulation of the materials.

More recently, theorists have argued that all mathematical ideas and operations, whether symbolic or not, and regardless of age, are grounded in conceptual metaphors that build from sensorimotor activities (e.g., Barsalou, 1999; Glenberg, Gutierrez, Levin, Japuntich, & Kaschak, 2004). From this "embodied cognition" perspective, the notion of a set is based on a metaphor of containership, which itself is grounded in the concrete experience of something being inside or outside one's own body (Lakoff & Núñez, 2000).

In contrast to learning progressions that build understanding primarily upon sensorimotor experiences, Vygotsky (1978) emphasized that culturally organized "scientific concepts" drive cognitive development. By scientific concepts, Vygotsky meant a culture's accumulated symbolic knowledge, which is passed from adults to children. Scientific concepts are differentiated from everyday concepts, which stem from concrete experience. From this, one might derive that children should receive cultural forms (e.g., symbolic organizations of thought) to propel learning. Here, we begin to see the theoretical complexity. From many contemporary theoretical perspectives, one might derive that children should receive concrete materials early in instruction. From Vygotsky, one recognizes the importance of culturally organized symbols in driving initial learning. We are left without a clear prescription of what the interaction should be between concrete and symbolic materials for development.

Transfer research has also yielded conflicting results and does not clarify the most appropriate use of concrete materials. Transfer research asks whether students can use their learning in new contexts that differ from the conditions of original learning. For example, if children learn about fractions using pie pieces, can they transfer this technique to solve problems with tiles? Some studies have found decreased transfer when learning occurs with concrete instances compared with only abstract symbols (e.g., Bassok & Holyoak, 1989; Kaminski, Sloutsky, & Heckler, 2008; see also Kaminski & Sloutsky, Chapter 3, this volume), while others have shown improved transfer for concrete materials over abstract ones (e.g., Goldstone & Son, 2005; Kellman, Massey, & Son, 2009; Schwartz, Chase, Oppezzo, & Chin, in press). In the final discussion, we attempt to reconcile some of the conflicting results from the transfer literature.

Another source of confusion about the value of concrete materials comes from the literature on problem solving. Effective problem solving is one of the main precursors to learning (Anderson, 1982). Ensuring that students can successfully engage in problem solving is an important part of enabling them to learn mathematics. Some scholars have proposed that concrete materials help students connect new ideas to their prior knowledge. In turn, students can make sense of complex mathematical problems that they simply could not handle as naked equations (Barron et al., 1998; Driscoll, 1983; Koedinger & Nathan, 2004; Resnick, 1983; Sowell, 1989). In contrast, some researchers have found that students focus on irrelevant aspects of the concrete materials (Harp & Mayer, 1998; Kaminski et al., 2009), and this pulls them away from the abstract mathematical structure. More generally, concrete materials are subject to multiple interpretations, and children may not find the designer's intent in the materials. For example, where the teacher sees groups of 10 being manipulated, the student may see only many individual items (Blair, 2009; Thompson, 1994). At an extreme, concrete materials may drive concrete ways of thinking instead of scaffolding more general symbolic interpretations (Schwartz & Moore, 1998; Uttal, Liu, & DeLoache, 1999).

CLARIFYING ASSUMPTIONS ON THE RELATION OF CONCRETE AND SYMBOLIC MATERIALS

The conflicting research and theories may be confusing for teachers and curriculum designers who try to decide whether and when to use concrete materials. It may be useful to consider the assumptions that drive different proposed relations between concrete and abstract materials. Often these assumptions are tacit, and educators and researchers may not be aware of making them. A key assumption involves what students already understand prior to using the materials. Table 4.1 lays out different possibilities of student understanding and their implications for the relation of concrete and symbolic materials in learning.

Practice

The upper left cell of Table 4.1 holds practice activities. The assumption is that students already understand the concrete materials and the symbols used to represent them. Using them together strengthens their association and the automaticity of mathematical thinking.

Concrete → Symbolic

The lower left cell of the table reflects a common assumption in the use of concrete materials, namely, that students already understand the concrete

TABLE 4.1
Assumptions About Student Understanding and the Relation of Concrete and Abstract Materials During Instruction

Assumptions about initial understanding	Concrete materials understood	Concrete materials not yet understood
Symbols understood	**Practice** *Example:* Student finds the means and standard deviations of familiar kinds of distributions.	**Symbols → Concrete** *Example:* Student finds the mean and standard deviation of a novel kind of distribution.
Symbols not yet understood	**Concrete → Symbols** *Example:* Instructor uses a concrete data distribution to explain the meaning of the standard deviation formula.	**Co-Evolution** *Example:* Student uses symbols to invent an index that will characterize the shape of a distribution.

materials and, through instruction, can use the concrete materials as meaningful anchors for more obscure symbolic representations. For example, students might be learning the term "1/4." To make this meaningful, one might have the students work with a circle made of four equal wedges. The students could pull out one wedge, and it would be labeled "1/4." The student could then pull out a second wedge, and the two wedges together would be labeled "2/4." From this perspective, students are not learning fundamentally new concepts through the use of concrete materials. The assumption is that they already understand what it means to have a physical whole split into parts and what it means to count up the parts of the whole. Instead, students are learning to ground symbolic operations and notations with physical materials that they already comprehend.

Using relatively familiar concrete materials and actions to ground symbolic terms and operations makes a good deal of sense. Getting to see a zebra surely helps one understand the word *zebra*. However, in the case of learning new concepts, the assumption that students can map from a known concrete instance to a novel symbolic representation does not always apply. This is because beginners often do not see the same structure in concrete instances as experts do (e.g., Gibson, 1969; Goodwin, 1994; Marton & Booth, 1997). Expert radiologists, for example, can see diagnostic details in X-rays overlooked by residents (Myles-Worsley, Johnston, & Simmons, 1988).

When learning new mathematical concepts, there is a risk that students will not see the intended structure in the concrete materials and, therefore, that the materials will not effectively ground the symbolic representations (e.g., Thompson, 1994). For example, in one class, we showed students a manipulative they had worked with for several days. The manipulative is intended to instantiate place-value notation in concrete form. We held up a single small cube and asked the students how many they saw. They said, "One!" We then held up a stick of 10 cubes, and they said, "Ten!" For a flat made of 10 sticks, they said, "A hundred." Finally, we held up a large cube consisting of 10 flats. Many said, "six hundred." Despite having handled the heavy cube before, they perceived that it had six sides of 100 flats. Asking students to map new symbolic structures to poorly encoded concrete materials will not yield much success for understanding.

Symbolic → Concrete

Scientists regularly use known symbolic procedures and structures to make sense of concrete instances. For example, given the problem of understanding the behavior of water in a tilting glass, scientists might try different integrals to see which provides the best model. Giving students opportunities to use symbolic mathematics to explain novel concrete instances is a good way to develop scientific sensibilities. However, it is important to distinguish the conditions of mature performance from those of early learning. In the example above, the scientists already understand the structure of the symbolic formulas used to characterize the phenomenon. Students learning a new concept may not yet have a deep understanding of the symbolic procedures they are taught.

The symbolic → concrete cell would suggest that students should memorize or derive symbolic procedures and structures first and then apply them to novel concrete instances. One argument in favor of this approach is that learning abstract symbolic procedures will lead to better transfer because learning will not be too heavily tied to particular concrete instances (e.g., Kaminski & Sloutsky, Chapter 3, this volume). However, the risk of this approach is that students will rely on the symbolic procedures and will never learn to see the structure in the concrete materials, leaving them with unstable symbolic rules (e.g., Hiebert & Wearne, 1996). In a later section, we provide an example of this problem. Students focus on the application of the formulas at the expense of learning the underlying contextual structures that make the formulas applicable in the first place. This hinders both initial learning and transfer.

Coevolution

In the preceding three cells of our analysis, the relations between symbols and concrete materials has been predicated on an isomorphic, one-to-one mapping between them (Post, 1981). As observed earlier, people can often manipulate physical objects and symbols to achieve the same answer. This leads to the assumption that learning involves mapping the correspondences between concrete and symbolic operations. However, the potential formal isomorphism between concrete and symbolic materials does not mean that there is a psychological isomorphism. Concrete and symbolic understandings have different properties, and learning new ideas depends on leveraging these properties in relation to each other to achieve a deeper understanding than either could achieve alone.

The coevolution cell of Table 4.1 proposes that concrete materials and symbols work together to help students discover the structure both in the world and in the abstract representations. We say more about this hypothesis below. But pending that elaboration, a concrete example of coevolution might help. We develop the example using a model of instruction called *inventing to prepare for learning* (IPL).

IPL asks students to invent symbolic accounts to characterize concrete instances. Our current example involves students learning about variance (for a representative collection of papers on learning variance, see Lajoie, 1998). The students who received the instruction had some vague intuitions about variability, but there was little precision. They also understood basic arithmetic, but they did not know how to compute variability. The IPL instruction encouraged students to coevolve both types of understanding.

In a series of studies, ninth-grade students learned statistical concepts and uses of variability (Schwartz & Martin, 2004). As a fairly prototypical activity, they used mathematics to invent a way to compute an "index" that could be applied to different pitching machines to let customers know the reliability of each machine. The narrative is that different companies produce baseball pitching machines. Figure 4.1 shows the results of testing the pitching machines. The black circles show where a ball landed when aimed at the

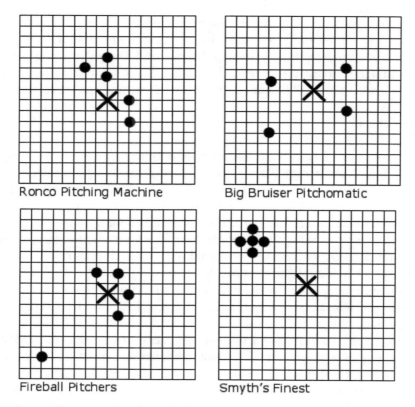

Figure 4.1. Students had to invent a way to compute a single number that could be used to compare the reliability of each baseball pitching machine. The black dots show where each machine pitched balls when aiming for the X in their respective grids. From "Inventing to Prepare for Learning: The Hidden Efficiency of Original Student Production in Statistics Instruction," by D. L. Schwartz and H. T. Martin, 2004, *Cognition & Instruction, 22,* p. 135. Copyright 2004 by Lawrence Erlbaum Associates, Inc. Reprinted with permission.

X in the center. Students had to invent a "consumer index" that indicates the relative "consistency" of the different pitching machines.

The grids were designed as contrasting cases (Bransford & Schwartz, 1999). Contrasting cases, much like wines side-by-side, can help novices perceive structure they might not already know. For example, in "Smyth's Finest," the balls are tightly clustered but far away from the target. This was intended to help students differentiate "inaccuracy" from "variability," which students often conflate. The students also had to invent an indexing procedure that would work across the cases. Here, the idea is that a demand for a precise symbolic, quantitative account leads them to look more carefully at the concrete instances and find the common structure across them. So, for example, students have to pay attention to the different numbers of balls used for the different pitching machines.

While doing the inventing activities, students made progress, but most did not come to a standard solution for capturing variability. However, after the inventing activities, students were more prepared to learn standard symbolic formulations and the situations they have been designed to describe. For example, the students received a short lecture on the mean deviation formula and practiced for a few minutes. A year later, these students were more capable of explaining why variance formulas divide by n (e.g., "To find the average") than were college students who had recently taken a semester of statistics (e.g., "Doesn't it have something to do with degrees of freedom?").

With respect to the coevolution hypothesis, students began with a vague, undifferentiated understanding of variability. In terms of concrete instances, they did not initially recognize a difference between inaccuracy and variability, and they did not consider the number of samples at all. In terms of symbolic understanding, the students did not initially have any knowledge of notations like Σ or the idea of variability as the average of the differences between the samples and the mean. Yet, by using symbols and concrete materials together, they developed an understanding of the concrete materials and symbolic operations. This prepared them to learn from subsequent direct instruction that introduced formal concepts of variability and their symbolic notations. In the coevolution process, the relationship between the concrete materials and symbolic formulas was not psychologically isomorphic; it was synergistic.

To unpack these ideas in the following sections, we first detail the psychological value of concrete activity for learning new ideas and the importance of learning to perceive mathematical structure in concrete materials. Then, we move to the psychological value of symbols for helping drive precise perception and generalization. Finally, we present a study, much like the preceding statistics study, that more directly highlights positive and negative possibilities for interactions between symbolic and concrete materials when learning new ideas.

THE VALUE OF CONCRETE ACTIVITY FOR LEARNING NEW MATHEMATICAL STRUCTURES

Perceiving mathematical structure in concrete instances is not automatic. It often needs to be learned. Interacting with concrete materials can help students move beyond a reliance on prior knowledge and enable them to notice new mathematical structure. Additionally, it can provide informative feedback about the results of taking mathematical actions.

Overcoming Prior Knowledge

We begin with two propositions: (a) A major challenge of learning to perceive new mathematical structure is that people will see what they already know rather than possibilities for what is new, and (b) interacting with concrete materials can help. The following example demonstrates these two propositions.

Martin and Schwartz (2005) worked with fourth-grade students who were at the cusp of understanding fraction operations. In the picture condition, the children saw a collection of pieces much like those shown in the left panel of Figure 4.2. Children had to circle a subset of the shapes to indicate their answers to problems such as, "What is 1/4 of these 8 pieces?" In the manipulate condition, the same children received the pieces rather than a picture, and they had to move the pieces to show the answer. Each child completed both conditions twice, using a variety of simple problems (e.g., 1/3 of 6 pieces). Regardless of order, the children were roughly three times more accurate in the manipulate condition than the picture condition.

What explains these results? In the picture condition, the children relied on their well-practiced, natural number schema. For example, they would

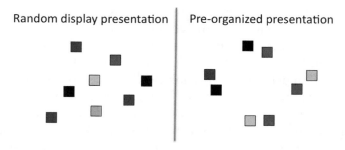

Random display presentation   Pre-organized presentation

Figure 4.2. Unstructured and pre-structured problem organization for 1/4 of 8. From "Physically Distributed Learning: Adapting and Reinterpreting Physical Environments in the Development of the Fraction Concept," by H. T. Martin and D. L. Schwartz, 2005, *Cognitive Science, 29*, p. 599. Copyright 2005 by Cognitive Science Society, Inc. Adapted with permission.

circle 1 chip, 4 chips, or both 1 and 4 chips. They interpreted the 1/4 as referring to the natural numbers, a 1 and a 4. This reliance on prior knowledge was quite strong in the picture condition. In fact, in a second study, the pieces were already pregrouped, as shown in the right panel of Figure 4.2. The students made the same mistake, circling 1 or 4 chips. The students simply did not see the intended meaning of this grouping organization.

In contrast, when the children had an opportunity to manipulate the pieces, they saw new possibilities emerge. For example, children moved several pieces at the same time, and this may have helped them recognize that pieces that moved together could be counted as one group. Once they started to perceive the relational possibility of grouping, they were on their way to solving the problem. For example, in a typical instance, children would start making separate piles of chips, and then they would stumble on the idea of making them equal groups. Once they had equal groups, they realized they could pick one of them as the answer. Manipulating the environment helped release the children from an overreliance on old interpretations to help them develop new ones (Martin, 2009).

Overcoming a Lack of Prior Knowledge

One of the compelling aspects of concrete materials is that they show the concrete outcome of an action. For example, if people do not throw a ball hard enough, it falls short of the target. In contrast, if people make a mistake with a physics equation, the erroneous outcome will become apparent only if people check their equations, get told they are wrong, or apply the equations to an actual instance. The ready availability of outcomes and feedback creates an intuitive argument for the value of concrete interactions during learning.

However, students may not have sufficient prior knowledge to interpret the feedback well. The feedback literature tacitly presupposes that informative feedback is readily perceived and that any problems that occur involve the internal processing of that information (Blair, 2009). We suggest, on the basis of our analysis of the difficulty of perceiving novel structure in concrete materials, that the same difficulty applies to concrete feedback. People may not perceive the feedback. They may rely on coarse aspects of feedback they already understand and miss more informative details. For example, a novice golfer may notice that his ball overshot the hole but fail to notice that the ball did not have enough backspin.

Given the potentially major omission in the feedback literature, Blair (2009) examined how children learn to pick up structural information in concrete feedback. Fourth-grade students used a computer game called *Spiderkid* to learn about iterated units (groups) in the context of bases and place value. We take some space here to explain the game, before describing the results.

The game was designed as a Teachable Agent (e.g., Chin et al., 2010), in which students learn by teaching a computer character. In this case, students taught Spiderkid how to use spiderwebs to make rescues from the city's skyscrapers (his Uncle Spiderman is planning on retiring). The floors of the city's buildings are designed with a recursive structure so that on different tries, the buildings could map into the bases of 3, 4, 5, or 6. For example, a base-3 building has special marks for each floor (3^0), for every third floor (3^1), and for every ninth floor (3^2).

Spiderkid has three kinds of webs, which can each be set to go a different distance. For example, to match the base-3 building, the student should set Spiderkid's webs to shoot 1, 3, and 9 floors, respectively. The goal is for children to choose the right size and numbers of webs for Spiderkid to rescue a cat trapped on one of the floors. The game proceeds through levels at which students solve increasingly difficult problems. At each level children get to see what Spiderkid does, based on what they have taught him.

As an example of how the feedback worked, Figure 4.3 shows a problem using a base-5 building. It is an early problem for the child, because it has been simplified to have floors marked at only 5^0 and 5^1, and the child is "training"

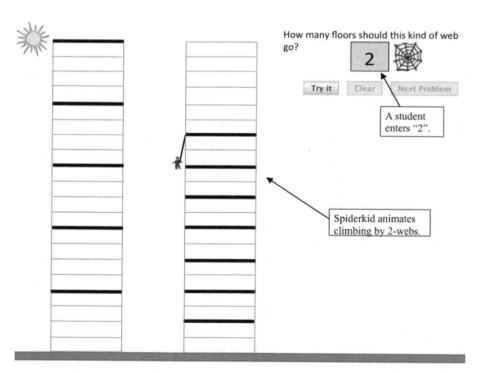

Figure 4.3. An early level of the *Spiderkid* game. The student's task is to match the building on the left. Spiderkid climbs the right building to provide feedback.

Spiderkid before he is ready to rescue cats. The child has entered the size of the web that she believes will get Spiderkid to land only on the floors indicated by the thicker lines in the left building. The child has incorrectly entered "2." The right building shows the outcome, where Spiderkid does as he was told. As feedback to the student, Spiderkid animates climbing the building using webs of size 2. As he climbs, Spiderkid leaves a trace for each floor he lands on. The child can then modify her answer in response to the feedback until Spiderkid matches the building on the left exactly. For this problem, the child repeats the same process of teaching Spiderkid for the place values of 5^0, 5^1, and 5^2. To get to the next level of the game, students have to get two consecutive problems correct on the first try.

At more advanced levels of the game, the children have to choose the sizes of all three webs. Finally, once Spiderkid has completed the training, the children are ready to rescue the cat. As shown in Figure 4.4, they have to indicate the length of each web and how many Spiderkid will need of each. For example, to rescue a cat on the 17th floor of a base-3 building, children should optimally choose one 9-floor web, two 3-floor webs, and two 1-floor webs

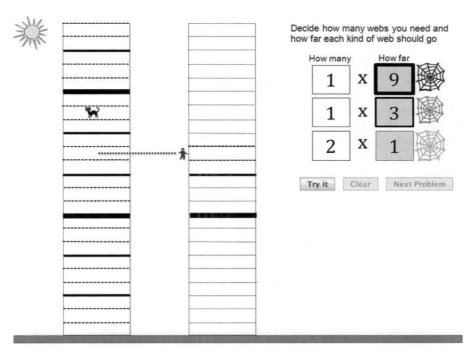

Figure 4.4. An adapted screen shot of a later level in the *Spiderkid* game. The student's task is to enter values for how far each kind of web should go, as well as how many of each kind of web are needed, to rescue Carl the Cat. Note that the environment used line color in place of line thickness.

(children learn that it is faster to use long webs first, so they do not just choose seventeen 1-floor webs). For the children, this corresponds to specifying the "place" and "face" values for a given quantity, and children do this for base-3, -4, -5, and -6 buildings.

In one study, 9- to 10-year-old children played Spiderkid for an hour, producing a log file of their actions and outcomes. A specially designed software tool (Blair, 2009) analyzed the log files by tracking student responses to feedback over time. Based on the students' postfeedback adjustments, the tool inferred what information the students extracted from the feedback. There were four levels of information:

1. *Correct/incorrect information*. Students only saw that Spiderkid was wrong. On their next turn, they changed their answer, but they actually made things worse by adjusting the wrong direction.
2. *Direction information*. Students saw whether Spiderkid had jumps that were too big or too small. On their next turn, children corrected the webs in the right direction, so they got closer by a bit.
3. *Approximate magnitude information*. Students saw both the direction of their mistake and whether it was a big or small mistake. On their next turn, children made a large correction in the right direction.
4. *Exact magnitude*. Students saw that they were off by a precise amount. On their next turn, children corrected their teaching by the exact amount of the discrepancy from the prior turn.

(There was also a "No Valid Information" coding, which occurred when the student did not appear to gain any information at all from the feedback, e.g., made no change in an incorrect response.)

Table 4.2 shows the percentage of times children transitioned between levels of feedback perception from one try to the next. For example, the 83%

TABLE 4.2
Percentage of Transitions Between Levels of Feedback
Within and Across Problems

	Next Level			
	Correct/ Incorrect	Direction	Approximate Magnitude	Exact Magnitude
Previous Level				
Correct/incorrect	39%	15%	21%	21%
Direction	11%	—	22%	44%
Approximate Magnitude	18%	—	18%	55%
Exact Magnitude	—	—	—	83%

Note. Columns do not sum to 100% because "No Valid Information" codes are omitted.

in the lower right corner indicates that once children learned to count the exact magnitude, they continued to do so for the next attempt 83% of the time. The table indicates that children generally increased the level of information they extracted from the feedback (i.e., larger percentages are above the diagonal).

Not all students followed this progression, however, and those who were unable to learn to see the information in their mistakes made little progress. For example, after playing the game, children were asked to draw what the buildings had looked like. Students who were characterized as being at lower levels of feedback perception failed to draw the equal interval grouping structure of the building in the redrawing task and instead drew floors haphazardly. These students did not appear to perceive the equal interval structure of Spiderkid's webs as he gave the student feedback, so they noticed only that they were wrong and nothing more.

A second study analyzed the pointing and speech of a new group of children as they interacted with the environment. The protocol data indicated that the children were learning to notice more precision in the feedback. For example, across several early trials, one student's comments referenced only approximate magnitude information as she watched the feedback: "Oh, that's too much," or "Too little." It was not until later that the student started to notice the exact amounts in the feedback, and then eventually found the base-structure with the exclamation, "I can multiply—it's 36!"

In summary, interacting with concrete materials can help students come to appreciate new (to them) quantitative structures. However, concrete materials are not simply "read off" by novices. Students must come to interpret the mathematical relations they involve, and interacting with the materials can help. In the case of learning fractions, children did better when they could manipulate the concrete materials. In the case of learning place values, children did not initially see the quantitative structure in the buildings or the feedback. Over time, they began to see the quantitative information more precisely. Still, some students did not find the mathematical structure in the concrete materials, even with Spiderkid, where the children received quantitative feedback that showed how their actions fell short of the outcome. Concrete materials can only achieve so much, and that is where symbols come in.

THE VALUE OF SYMBOLS FOR LEARNING NEW STRUCTURE

When learning with well-designed concrete materials, students can apply psychological processes that help them discern more structure in those materials. What learning processes do symbolic materials support? Abstract, symbolic notations are often taken as a way to compute an answer. However, they have other psychological properties that can help children learn to perceive structure in concrete instantiations, particularly relational structure.

Consider the case of the balance scales shown in Figure 4.5. In this classic developmental task (it has also been used with adults; e.g., Shen, 2006), children decide if the scale will balance, tilt left, or tilt right. The left side shows a scale with quantities that are very hard to count, whereas the right scale makes it much easier to count and to turn the physical quantities into discrete symbolic terms (e.g., "three" weights, "one" peg).

Ten- and 11-year-old students worked with several problems of either type (Schwartz, Martin, & Pfaffman, 2005). The hypothesis was that students working on the hard-to-count quantities would do quite poorly, because they could not enlist the aid of symbolic numbers. The hypothesis was supported. Almost 70% of the fifth-grade students in the hard-to-quantify condition performed at the level of sophistication generally associated with 5-year-olds when using a countable balance scale (Siegler, 1981). They reasoned exclusively about the weight of the beakers. They even failed to reason about the distances when weight of the beakers was held constant. For example, when two beakers were identically filled, they would say the scale would balance, even if the beaker on one side was at the very end and the other beaker was right next to the fulcrum. In contrast, only 30% of students in the countable materials condition performed like 5-year-olds. Instead, they performed at their age level.

Why did the easy-to-count condition help? These children did not have a firm grasp of the multiplicative relationship (Weight × Distance), as indicated by the performances of the otherwise similar children in the hard-to-count condition. There were at least three ways that using abstract mathematical symbols helped:

- Children could combine perceptually distinct dimensions, for example, weight and distance. A "3" can refer to a distance or a weight, and by representing weight and distance with digits, it made it possible to put them into a quantitative relationship that would be hard to do perceptually.

Figure 4.5. Balance Scale examples involving hard-to-count quantities (left) and easily countable quantities (right). From "How Mathematics Propels the Development of Physical Knowledge," by D. L. Schwartz, H. T. Martin, and J. Pfaffman, 2005, *Journal of Cognition and Development, 6*, p. 69. Copyright 2004 by Lawrence Erlbaum Associates, Inc. Adapted with permission.

- The symbols provided a compact representation that alleviated working memory burdens, at least compared to trying to maintain mental images of weight, distance, and the relation between them.
- Arithmetic provides a set of possibilities for generating possible explanations. Much as children's hands provided easy ways for children to manipulate the tile pieces in the fraction study above, simple arithmetic provides a set of candidate moves. For example, children can try adding values, multiplying values, and so forth. Different symbolic actions can help spark new interpretations.

A second set of studies more clearly demonstrates that the symbolic structure of math can propel the learning of proportional relations (Schwartz, Martin, & Pfaffman, 2005). Eight- and 10-year-olds worked with the easy-to-count balance problems in an online environment. Students received a series of problems that ranged in difficulty. For each problem, students predicted whether the scale would balance, tip right, or tip left, when it was released. Students were asked to justify their predictions in a little text box on the screen. In the invent-math condition, children had to use symbolic mathematics to justify their answers (e.g., "3 > 2"). In the words-only condition, children had to use words to justify their answer (e.g., "the left has more"). This was the sole difference between conditions. After answering, the children saw an animation of what actually happened when the scale was let go, and then they moved on to the next problem.

On a posttest with novel problems, children in the words-only condition performed at their age norms. They tended to focus their justifications on either weight or distance but not both. In contrast, students in the invent-math condition performed above their age norms. The 8-year-olds came up with answers that tried to integrate both weight and distance, and the 10-year-olds ended up solving the problems as well as adults by the posttest.

A fairly typical prototypical sequence in the invent-math condition comes from a girl who eventually found the multiplicative relation. What follows are her mathematical justifications typed into the textbox. (She did not label the values.)

(a) $3 > 2$
(b) $4 = 4$
(c) $3 + 1 > 2 - 2$
(d) $3 + 3 = 4 + 2$
(e) ???
(f) $2 \times 3 = 3 \times 2$.

For problems (a) and (b), she considered only one dimension (either weight or distance). At (c), she started to consider both the weight and distance dimensions in her explanation. At (d), she starts to use a single operation on both sides of the equation. Finally, by (f), she has tried multiplication to relate the two dimensions, and it worked. While this could appear to be blind symbol pushing, the symbols gave her a way to relate the dimensions of weight and distance and to test out mathematical relationships. This allowed her to discover the multiplicative relationship in the concrete materials.

The invent-math condition did not simply yield lucky trial-and-error success. It improved the children's qualitative understanding of the balance scale. On a transfer task that involved weights on three pegs, children in the invent-math condition could not solve the problems correctly, but they continued to reason with both the weight and distance dimensions simultaneously. And, as before, the words-only students focused on either weight or distance but not both. Consistent with fuzzy trace theory (Reyna & Brainerd, 2008), precise quantitative understanding predated qualitative intuitions.

CREATING EFFECTIVE INSTRUCTION FOR ADOLESCENTS

The coevolution hypothesis proposes that students ideally learn symbolic and concrete structures together. This differs from the one-to-one mapping approach, whereby students start with one or the other and then map back and forth between concrete and symbolic presentations of quantities. The preceding studies were designed to investigate basic psychological processes in learning, and they were not intended to teach students the best way possible. How do we apply the insights from these studies to design classroom learning?

The prescription is straightforward at a general level:

- *Focusing on big ideas.* Promote coevolution when students are learning new mathematical structures. Not all learning involves learning new concepts; however, for big ideas, it is important to have students develop a strong foundation early.
- *Using optimal concrete instances.* Provide concrete materials designed to help students come to perceive structure and interpret feedback. Our specific approach is to use contrasting cases. We carefully juxtapose concrete instances, where the differences and similarities can help students come to find structure. Plus, by having multiple cases, students can self-generate feedback by seeing if a solution for one instance applies to another.
- *Inventing mathematical structure.* Have students try to formulate symbolic organizations that can account for the structure (or processes) in the concrete materials. We have called this *inventing* to highlight the fact that students do not begin with a preformulated answer. Also, it is important to note that students do not need to actually discover the correct solution through

their inventing activity (Kapur, 2010). They simply need to start recognizing the key structures, which prepares them to understand subsequent formal explanations more deeply (Schwartz & Bransford, 1998).

Even if students invent incorrect solutions, they are more prepared to learn later than if they are told the correct solution at the outset (Schwartz & Martin, 2004). This latter point is particularly delicate. One might think that it is best to provide students with the symbolic formulation up front to help make sense of concrete materials, rather than have them invent their own (this would be the symbolic → concrete cell in Table 4.1). However, this approach runs into the problem that abstract representations can overshadow student learning of mathematical structure. In particular, students may come to rely on the symbolic procedures, and this reliance will interfere with their ability to find the structure in the concrete materials. The following study demonstrates this point.

To instantiate these high-level prescriptions for adolescent learning, Schwartz et al. (in press) worked with eighth graders learning physics. At this age, children learn about speed, density, and force. The three tenets were operationalized as follows:

- *Focusing on big ideas.* Density, speed, and force are separate big ideas in physics. Mathematically, however, they all depend on a single big idea—ratio and proportion. The formulas, $D = m/V$, $S = d/T$, and $F = ma$, all comprise intensive ratios among unlike physical quantities. Children of this age can procedurally solve problems involving ratios—they simply need to divide. But this does not mean they understand ratio structures. For example, they may not spontaneously notice the relevance of ratio in a new problem.

- *Using optimal concrete instances.* Figure 4.6a shows a "contrasting cases" worksheet that was specifically designed to help students perceive proportionate ratios while learning about the concept of density. The narrative of the worksheet is that each row represents a company that ships clowns to events. A company always packs its clowns into buses by the same amount, though it may use buses of different sizes. The meaning of "same amount" is what children need to come to understand (i.e., the same density). The degree to which the companies pack their clowns differs across the three companies.

  The contrasting cases are designed to include three levels of features. The first level is surface features. In the figure, two examples of surface features are the type of clown and the lines

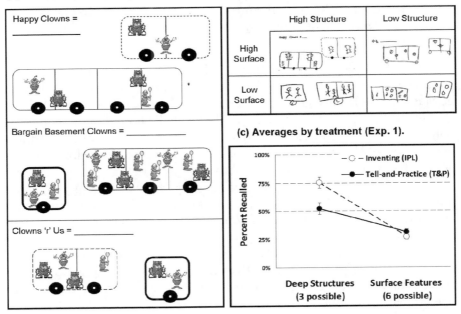

(a) Worksheet for learning density.

(b) Samples of recall 24 hrs later.

(c) Averages by treatment (Exp. 1).

Figure 4.6. Worksheet and students' subsequent recall of the worksheet. Adapted from "How Telling Too Soon Affects Transfer: Practicing vs. Inventing With Contrasting Cases," by D. L. Schwartz, C. Chase, D. B. Chin, and M. Oppezzo, 2011, *Journal of Educational Psychology, 103,* pp. 761–765. Copyright 2011 by the American Psychological Association.

defining the exterior of the buses. These incidental details are irrelevant to the concept of density, and they were included to examine the effect of surface features on learning as well as to make the tasks entertaining for the students. A second level of feature is the specific density used by a company for each of its buses. For example, the company shown in the first row has one bus that has four clowns and four bus compartments, and a second bus has two clowns and two compartments. The within-company density is a ratio of 1:1. The third and deepest level of structure is the general feature of ratio, which occurs *across* the paired cases or companies. While the specific values of the ratios differ for each company, all three use proportionate ratios. This last level of feature is termed the "invariant under transformation," or the deep structure. The invariant of ratio persists, despite changes in specific densities and surface features.

- *Inventing mathematical structure.* Students were told to make a "crowdedness index" that would enable comparison across the cases. Students had to make an index for three reasons. First, it is important for students to engage the structure across the cases, rather than to take each case one at a time. If students do not try to make an index that covers all the cases, they will be less likely to perceive the invariant under transformation. Therefore, they are asked to invent a single index procedure that works for all the cases. Second, working toward a compact and quantitatively precise index creates a simultaneous demand for precision when noticing the structure. For example, as demonstrated in the earlier studies with the Spiderkid game, it is not sufficient to just say and notice that one of the cases has "more" or "less" than another. Quantification requires identifying how much more or less. The third reason is that telling students the symbolic solution too soon shortcuts their search for the deep structure in the concrete materials. Inventing is one way to engage mathematical thinking without undermining the search for quantitative structure in the concrete instances.

The studies had two parts. In the first part, students in the invent condition tried to invent a crowdedness index for the clowns in Figure 4.6a. In the tell-and-practice condition, students were first taught the concept of density and its formula, and they received an abstract worked example of using the formula that highlighted the proportional structures without potentially distracting details. Their task was to use the formula to find the density of the clowns used by each company. The tell-and-practice instruction was meant to be a fair representation of the ubiquitous model of telling students the procedures first and then having them practice on a set of problems.

A day later, the students were asked to redraw the clown worksheet from memory. By looking at what the students remembered, it is possible to determine what structure they found in the contrasting cases. Students' drawings were coded for the number of surface features they recreated (e.g., dotted lines around buses). They were also coded for the pairs of buses that were recreated with the deep structure of a proportionate ratio. Figure 4.6b provides portions of student drawings that were high and low on surface and deep features. Figure 4.6c shows the results. Students in the tell-and-practice condition did not recreate the deep structure of the clown worksheet as frequently as did the invent students. This failure at encoding was not due to paying less attention to the task, because both conditions showed the same performance at recalling the surface features. Being told the symbolic method before working on the examples undercut the students' search for structure, because they could solve the problems symbolically without finding the structure in the concrete instances.

The second part of the research examined whether these differences in instruction and structural encoding had implications for learning physics. As before, the primary manipulation was whether students were told the symbolic formulas and then practiced applying them to concrete instances or whether they tried to invent symbolic procedures to capture the structure of the materials first, before being told the standard formulas.

After finishing the recall task, the tell-and-practice students received a lecture about ratio and the prevalence of ratio concepts in physics, including density, speed, and force. Then, over the next few days they completed tell-and-practice activities for three more sets of contrasting cases that covered density and speed. As before, they received brief explanations of the relevant concept, the formula, and an abstract worked example, and then they practiced applying the formula to sets of contrasting cases.

The invent condition worked with the same contrasting cases regarding density and speed that the tell-and-practice students received, but, as before, they had to invent an index. They were told about the standard formulas and concepts only after completing all the cases. This was done by giving them the same lecture that the tell-and-practice students had received. On the last day of instruction, both groups of students practiced on a set of standard word problems (e.g., find the density given two values).

Several weeks later, the students received two types of posttests. One posttest involved measuring whether students spontaneously transferred ratio to understand the spring constant. (The stiffness of a spring is the ratio of displacement by load.) They received a sheet similar to Figure 4.7. Students had to develop a way to describe the stiffness of the trampoline fabric, which is an instance of finding a spring constant. (The problem is a simplification of how trampolines work.) On the transfer problem, students in the invent condition were roughly 4 times as likely to use a ratio to describe the stiffness of the fabric for each of the trampolines. The tell-and-practice students were more likely to describe the stiffness of the fabric with a single number representing only one dimension, for example, the number of people or the number of rungs the fabric stretched, but not both. The strong advantage for the invent group was replicated, even when the posttest included only a single trampoline instead of four. Notably, the invent advantage was equally strong for both the high- and low-achieving students.

The second type of posttest included more traditional word problems. Students answered problems about density and speed. On this test, the students in both conditions performed equally well. Thus, the inventing activity did not diminish student learning of basic symbolic procedures, and it worked well for students at all levels of achievement.

In summary, the inventing activity helped students perceive the ratio structure of density and speed, which in turn helped them transfer the concept of ratio to understand new situations. In contrast, the tell-and-practice condition led to symbolic proficiency as measured by the word problems.

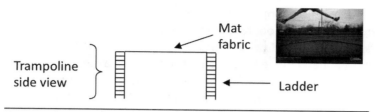

Figure 4.7. Delayed transfer problem. Students had to describe the stretchiness of the fabric used for each trampoline, which is the same as finding the spring constant. Adapted from "How Telling Too Soon Affects Transfer: Practicing vs. Inventing With Contrasting Cases," by D. L. Schwartz, C. Chase, D. B. Chin, and M. Oppezzo, 2011, *Journal of Educational Psychology, 103,* p. 765. Copyright 2011 by the American Psychological Association.

Given the symbolic formulation, these students focused on what they had been told rather than on the structure of the concrete situation. They did not see the ratio structure, neither during instruction nor at transfer. In short, being told too soon prevents the coevolution of concrete and symbolic understanding, and students do not learn the big ideas very well.

FINAL THOUGHTS

What role should symbols and concrete materials play in the learning of new concepts? The coevolution hypothesis suggests that symbolic actions can lead to new interpretations of concrete materials, which in turn can drive deeper understanding of the abstract symbols. However, not all relationships between symbols and concrete materials are optimal. We have argued that abstract symbols should be used in the service of trying to find and capture structure in concrete materials during the initial learning of new big ideas.

Our lead argument is that the psychological processes and benefits of handling symbolic and concrete materials are different, and they should be put in a complementary relation, and we provided specific examples to the point. This perspective differs from a view of mathematics learning that treats the abstraction of mathematical ideas as a process of subtraction. Confrey (1995) labeled this perspective *trahere*, the Latin term for "throw away." According to trahere, learning involves subtracting the nonessential surface features and properties of concrete materials. For example, Kaminski and Sloutsky (Chapter 3, this volume) found transfer benefits for presenting mathematical concepts abstractly rather than embedded in contextual examples. Researchers argue that if general principles become too deeply embedded in a particular context, students will not recognize the abstract mathematical structure and will not be able to apply their ideas to new concrete instances that differ on the surface (Bassock & Holyoak; Kaminski et al., 2008). The assumption appears to be that "real" mathematical understanding is independent of context, and, therefore, to accelerate learning, instruction should start with the abstraction to avoid problems with concrete materials.

From our perspective, a key aspect of mathematical learning involves coming to find the quantitative invariants within a concrete instance (Gibson, 1969). Invariants are those properties that generalize to new instances without losing their underlying structure. So, by this perspective, generalization does not depend on subtracting away concrete surface details to get to the essential abstraction. Rather, generalization depends on learning to perceive and account for structure in concrete instances (e.g., see Freudenthal, 1973; Greeno, Smith, & Moore, 1993).

To achieve this level of insight, students need to coordinate the psychological processes associated with symbolic and concrete materials.

The crucial question for novel learning is not the amount of superficial or contextual information contained in the concrete materials but, rather, how students interact with the materials. This may help explain some of the seemingly conflicting results between our studies and those of Kaminski and Sloutsky (Chapter 3, this volume). For example, Kaminski and Sloutsky found that people who learned from a concrete instantiation were more likely to reference superficial features and less likely to reference structure when recalling, compared with people who had learned from a more abstract instantiation. In contrast, in the clown density study, we found that students who had to invent a symbolic solution for concrete materials recalled the same level of surface detail and more structure than students who had been told the abstract formula first. We believe one reason for our results is the processing orientation taken by the inventing students. They had to integrate across instances to find the invariant structure within the concrete materials. By this interpretation, participants in the concrete condition of Kaminski and Sloutsky's study may have been able to use prior knowledge to solve each instance independently, shortcutting the need to seek general structure.

To test this hypothesis, Schwartz, Chase, and Bransford (in press) conducted a new study modeled after the clown density study. As before, students either had a tell-and-practice or invent processing orientation. The new, crossed factor was that half of the students in each condition worked with either abstract or concrete materials (abstract dots or clowns). Consistent with Kaminski and Sloutsky in the tell-and-practice condition, students who worked with abstract materials performed better than students who worked with the more concrete instantiation. However, in the invent condition, where students had to search for structure across the cases, the effect of concrete versus abstract materials disappeared. Moreover, the regardless of the concreteness of the materials, the invent students did twice as well as those in the abstract tell-and-practice condition.

Concrete materials support the discovery of new structure, and symbolic materials provide ways for students to account for the invariants in that structure. As the preceding studies have shown, these processes need to work in tandem. When teaching fundamentally new mathematical concepts, it does not work to assume that students already have a deep understanding of the symbols and that this understanding will be sufficient for them to make sense of new concrete instances. For example, in the final study, we demonstrated that teaching students the symbolic formulation too early actually shortcuts the search for structure in concrete materials. It also does not work to assume that students can "read off" novel structure from concrete instances. For example, without the support of symbolic activity, students will rely on vague prior knowledge. Thus, the challenge for developing mathematical understanding, in adolescence and at all ages, is an instructional problem of how to support coevolution. The inventing activity over contrasting cases provides one promising solution.

REFERENCES

Anderson, J. R. (1982). Acquisition of cognitive skill. *Psychological Review, 89*, 369–406. doi:10.1037/0033-295X.89.4.369

Barron, B. J., Schwartz, D. L., Vye, N. J., Moore, A., Petrosino, A., Zech, L., . . . The Cognition and Technology Group at Vanderbilt. (1998). Doing with understanding: Lessons from research on problem- and project-based learning. *Journal of the Learning Sciences, 7*, 271–311. doi:10.1207/s15327809jls0703&4_2

Barsalou, L. W. (1999). Perceptual symbol systems. *Behavioral and Brain Sciences, 22,* 577–660.

Bassok, M., & Holyoak, K. J. (1989). Interdomain transfer between isomorphic topics in algebra and physics. *Journal of Experimental Psychology: Learning, Memory, and Cognition, 15,* 153–166. doi:10.1037/0278-7393.15.1.153

Blair, K. P. (2009). *The neglected importance of feedback perception in learning: An analysis of children and adults' uptake of quantitative feedback in a mathematics simulation environment* (Doctoral dissertation). Stanford University, Stanford, CA.

Blair, K., Hartman, K., Martin, L., Hannula, M., Yun, C., McCandliss, B., & Schwartz, D. L. (2008, March). *Groupthink.* Symposium at the Annual Meeting of the American Educational Research Association, New York, NY.

Bransford, J. D., & Schwartz, D. L. (1999). Rethinking transfer: A simple proposal with multiple implications. *Review of Research in Education, 24,* 61–100.

Bruner, J. (1996). *The culture of education.* Cambridge, MA: Harvard University Press.

California Science Teachers Association. (2004). *K-8 instructional materials adoption.* Retrieved from http://www.cascience.org/csta/leg_criteria.asp

Chin, D. B., Dohmen, I. M., Cheng, B. H., Oppezzo, M. A., Chase, C. C., & Schwartz, D. L. (2010). Preparing students for future learning with Teachable Agents. *Educational Technology Research & Development, 58,* 649–669. doi 10.1007/s11423-010-9154-5

Confrey, J. (1995). A theory of intellectual development: Part III. *For the Learning of Mathematics, 15*(2), 36–45.

Driscoll, M. (1983). *Research within reach: Secondary school mathematics.* Reston, VA: National Council of Teachers of Mathematics.

Freudenthal, H. (1973). *Mathematics as an educational task.* Dordrecht, Netherlands: Reidel.

Gibson, E. (1969). *Principles of perceptual learning and development.* New York, NY: Appleton-Century-Crofts.

Glenberg, A. M., Gutierrez, T., Levin, J. R., Japuntich, S., & Kaschak, M. P. (2004). Activity and imagined activity can enhance young children's reading comprehension. *Journal of Educational Psychology, 96,* 424–436. doi:10.1037/0022-0663.96.3.424

Goldstone, R. L., & Son, J. Y. (2005). The transfer of scientific principles using concrete and idealized simulations. *Journal of the Learning Sciences, 14,* 69–110. doi:10.1207/s15327809jls1401_4

Goodwin, C. (1994). Professional vision. *American Anthropologist, 96,* 606–633. doi:10.1525/aa.1994.96.3.02a00100

Greeno, J., Smith, D. R., & Moore, J. L. (1993). Transfer of situated learning. In D. K. Detterman & R. J. Sternberg (Eds.), *Transfer on trial: Intelligence, cognition, and instruction* (pp. 99–167). Norwood, NJ: Ablex.

Harp, S. F., & Mayer, R. E. (1998). How seductive details do their damage: A theory of cognitive interest in science learning. *Journal of Educational Psychology, 90*, 414–434. doi:10.1037/0022-0663.90.3.414

Hiebert, J., & Wearne, D. (1996). Instruction, understanding, and skill in multidigit addition and subtraction. *Cognition and Instruction, 14*, 251–283. doi:10.1207/s1532690xci1403_1

Kaminski, J. A., Sloutsky, V. M., & Heckler, A. F. (2008, April 25). The advantage of abstract examples in learning math. *Science, 320*, 454–455. doi:10.1126/science.1154659

Kaminski, J., Sloutsky, V. M., & Heckler, A. (2009). Transfer of mathematical knowledge: The portability of generic instantiations. *Child Development Perspectives, 3*, 151–155. doi:10.1111/j.1750-8606.2009.00096.x

Kapur, M. (2010). Productive failure in mathematical problem solving. *Instructional Science, 38*, 523–550. doi:10.1007/s11251-009-9093-x

Kellman, P. J., Massey, C. M., & Son, J. Y. (2009). Perceptual learning modules in mathematics: Enhancing students' pattern recognition, structure extraction, and fluency. *Topics in Cognitive Science, 2*, 285–305. doi:10.1111/j.1756-8765.2009.01053.x

Koedinger, K.R. & Nathan, M.J. (2004). The real story behind story problems: Effects of representations on quantitative reasoning. *The Journal of the Learning Sciences, 13*(2), 129–164.

Lajoie, S. P. (1998). *Reflections on statistics.* Mahwah, NJ: Erlbaum.

Lakoff, G., & Núñez, R. (2000). *Where mathematics comes from: How the embodied mind brings mathematics into being.* New York, NY: Basic Books.

Martin, T. (2009). A theory of physically distributed learning: How external environments and internal states interact in mathematics learning. *Child Development Perspectives, 3*, 140–144. doi:10.1111/j.1750-8606.2009.00094.x

Martin, T., & Schwartz, D. L. (2005). Physically distributed learning: Adapting and reinterpreting physical environments in the development of the fraction concept. *Cognitive Science, 29*, 587–625. doi:10.1207/s15516709cog0000_15

Marton, F., & Booth, S. (1997). *Learning and awareness.* Mahwah, NJ: Lawrence Erlbaum.

Moyer, P. S. (2001). Are we having fun yet? How teachers use manipulatives to teach mathematics. *Educational Studies in Mathematics, 47*, 175–197. doi:10.1023/A:1014596316942

Myles-Worsley, M., Johnston, W. A., & Simons, M. A. (1988). The influence of expertise on X-ray image processing. *Journal of Experimental Psychology: Learning, Memory, and Cognition, 14*, 553–557. doi:10.1037/0278-7393.14.3.553

Piaget, J. (1941/1952). *The child's conception of number.* London, England: Routledge and Kegan Paul.

Post, T. R. (1981). Fractions: Results and implementation from national assessment. *The Arithmetic Teacher*, *28*, 26–31.

Resnick, L. B. (1983, April). Mathematics and science learning: A new conception. *Science*, *220*, 477–478. doi:10.1126/science.220.4596.477

Reyna, V. F., & Brainerd, C. J. (2008). Numeracy, ratio bias, and denominator neglect in judgments of risk and probability. *Learning and Individual Differences*, *18*, 89–107. doi:10.1016/j.lindif.2007.03.011

Schwartz, D. L., & Bransford, J. D. (1998). A time for telling. *Cognition and Instruction*, *16*, 475–522. doi:10.1207/s1532690xci1604_4

Schwartz, D. L., Chase, C., & Bransford, J. D. (in press). Adaptive transfer: The tension of routines and novelty. *Educational Psychologist*.

Schwartz, D. L., Chase, C. C., Oppezzo, M. A., & Chin, D. B. (in press). Practicing versus inventing with contrasting cases: The effects of telling first on learning and transfer. *Journal of Educational Psychology*.

Schwartz, D. L., & Martin, T. (2004). Inventing to prepare for learning: The hidden efficiency of original student production in statistics instruction. *Cognition and Instruction*, *22*, 129–184. doi:10.1207/s1532690xci2202_1

Schwartz, D. L., Martin, T., & Pfaffman, J. (2005). How mathematics propels the development of physical knowledge. *Journal of Cognition and Development*, *6*, 65–88. doi:10.1207/s15327647jcd0601_5

Schwartz, D. L., & Moore, J. L. (1998). The role of mathematics in explaining the material world: Mental models for proportional reasoning. *Cognitive Science*, *22*, 471–516. doi:10.1207/s15516709cog2204_3

Shen, J. (2006). Tools and task structures in modeling balance beam. *Proceedings of the 7th International Congress of the Learning Sciences*, 695–701.

Siegler, R. S. (1981). Developmental sequences within and between concepts. *Monographs of the Society for Research in Child Development*, *46*(2), 1–84. doi:10.2307/1165995

Sowell, E. J. (1989). Effects of manipulative materials in mathematics instruction. *Journal for Research in Mathematics Education*, *20*, 498–505. doi:10.2307/749423

Thompson, P. W. (1994). Concrete materials and teaching for mathematical understanding. *The Arithmetic Teacher*, *41*, 556–558.

Uttal, D. H., Liu, L. L., & DeLoache, J. S. (1999). Taking a hard look at concreteness: Do concrete objects help young children learn symbolic relations? In C. S. Tamis-LeMonda (Ed.), *Child psychology: A handbook of contemporary issues* (pp. 177–192). Philadelphia, PA: Psychology Press.

Vygotsky, L. (1978). *Mind in society: The development of higher psychological processes* (M. Cole, V. John-Steiner, S. Scribner, & E. Souberman, Eds.). Cambridge, MA: Harvard University Press.

5

HIGHER ORDER STRATEGIC GIST REASONING IN ADOLESCENCE

SANDRA B. CHAPMAN, JACQUELYN F. GAMINO,
AND RAKSHA ANAND MUDAR

Adolescents in the United States are falling behind those of other developed countries in advanced reasoning skills. In this chapter, we posit that the prevailing emphasis on rote fact learning, rather than on reasoned thinking, prevents our students from achieving a competitive level of cognitive potential. We put forth a theoretical and empirical case for focusing on the neglected fourth R of education, Reasoning. In particular, we focus on gist reasoning, defined as the ability to derive global meaning from explicit details, entailing frontally mediated, top-down cognitive control processes. Based on memory for gist, gist reasoning operates independently from and is superior to rote fact-based learning and memory. The independence of gist reasoning from fact learning is documented in studies of youth with brain injury and attention-deficit/hyperactivity disorder. This pattern is also documented in typically developing adolescents in whom the capacity to recall facts does not correspond with a capacity to engage in gist reasoning. We present evidence that gist reasoning training is optimal during adolescence, given that the brain is undergoing significant maturational

We would like to thank Lori Cook, PhD, for her help in editing this chapter. We also acknowledge the financial support of the National Institute of Neurological Disorders and Stroke (NINDS) Grant 2R01 NS21889-16, the Texas State Legislature, the AT&T Foundation, the Sparrow Foundation, the Hudson Foundation, the T. Boone Pickens Foundation, and the Meadows Foundation.

changes. Evidence for enhancing adolescent gist reasoning across a variety of populations, including typically developing adolescents, is demonstrated by a novel gist reasoning training program. Training strategic gist reasoning has direct applications to educational practice, with the ultimate goal of achieving advanced levels of critical thinking. In view of recent economic forecasts, every year we fail to teach advanced reasoning to youth, we fail to invest in the future of our human cognitive capital.

Adolescence represents one of the most optimal yet vulnerable stages for cognitive development of higher order thinking, reasoning, and problem solving (Dahl & Spear, 2004; Gamino, Chapman, Hull, & Lyon, 2010; Giedd et al., 2006). Theorists and educators recognize that higher order critical thinking skills typically undergo rapid expansion during adolescence and are refined in complexity and maturity throughout adulthood (Blakemore & Choudhury, 2006; Fischer et al., 2007; Piaget, 1972). With regard to vulnerability, the years when adolescents are in middle school (fifth through ninth grades) represent a period metaphorically referred to as a transitional "black hole" in education. The child moves out of the supportive and engaging learning environment of elementary school into a stage of increased personal choices, with greater risk for failure and dropping out and for developing some form of addictive behavior (Chambers, Taylor, & Potenza, 2003; Good, Aronoson, & Inzlicht, 2003; Langberg & Smith, 2006; Willis, 2009).

Educators, public policy experts, and cognitive neuroscientists are focusing on why a large number of adolescents stagnate cognitively and fail to thrive academically and personally as they transition from the elementary to the middle school years. In this chapter, we highlight core issues related to the impact of stagnating reasoning skills and offer an empirically and theoretically driven framework to enhance higher order reasoning and cognitive efficiency and perhaps strengthen frontal lobe development in the teen brain.

Two basic unanswered questions regarding adolescent development of higher order reasoning require consideration. The first question is whether higher order cognitive skills emerge on their own as the brain matures and adequate stimulation is provided or whether reasoning skills must be taught (Piaget, 1972; Steinberg, 2005). Basic trends suggest that higher order critical thinking skills may require training, since adolescents in the United States have failed to keep pace in these skills in the past decade as compared with the gains made by youth in other developed countries (Baldi, Jin, Skemer, Green, & Herget, 2007; Lemke et al., 2004). The causes for this downward trend in reasoning and critical thinking are multifactorial, with many pointing to the overemphasis on high-stakes standardized testing and "teaching to the test" that focuses largely on rote memorization of facts. In contrast, little testing has focused on how effectively students are able to reason, to synthesize meaning, and to solve new problems (Schwartz, 2009). Reasoning represents the neglected fourth *R* of education—reading, writing, 'rithmetic, and now *reasoning*.

The second question regarding development of higher order reasoning concerns the optimal age/timing for training higher order reasoning skills. We postulate that training the human mind to think critically is particularly opportune during the teen years, when the brain is undergoing dramatic maturational changes (Giedd et al., 2006; Gogtay et al., 2004). The most dramatic brain changes during adolescence take place in the frontal lobe networks, which have been associated with higher order learning, reasoning, and problem solving, extending into early adulthood (Blakemore & Choudhury, 2006; Bunge, Wendelken, Badre, & Wagner, 2004; Casey, Tottenham, Liston, & Durston, 2005; Gamino et al., 2010; Gogtay et al., 2004). Direct studies linking anatomical and functional brain changes to cognitive development are still in their infancy, particularly during the adolescent years. Nonetheless, evidence reveals that brain function becomes fine-tuned with cognitive development (Casey et al., 2005; Somerville, Jones, & Casey, 2010).

More American teens are dropping out of high school than at any time in history. It is estimated that one teen drops out every 26 seconds, resulting in an average one million dropouts each year (Herbert, 2009). Some have suggested that the increasing dropout rate is influenced by student boredom due to rote learning of facts and educators' failure to engage students in active inquiry and in-depth, thought-provoking discussions (Alberts, 2009). Overall, roughly two thirds of U.S. teenagers, including those who graduate from high school, are unprepared to master college-level work. No country can afford to underestimate the negative and lasting economic impact that follows when educational achievements are affected to such a large extent. As a forward-thinking society, we seek solutions as our country faces a growing sense of urgency to identify evidence-based educational practices to equip adolescents with the educational preparation and intellectual tools to become productive adults.

The educational environment plays a major role in "neuroengineering" the teen brain through ways in which students are taught to learn and how they are encouraged to think (Chapman, Gamino, & Anand, 2008; Ramsay, Sperling & Dornisch, 2010; Schwartz, 2009). Based on extant evidence that the brain changes according to how it is used, we would predict that students taught in a mechanistic rote style of learning facts would "build" brains very different from the brains of those trained to abstract, synthesize, connect, and apply meaning to their own world and other acquired knowledge. The first style emphasizes lower levels of thinking, whereas the second style capitalizes on higher order, more frontally mediated learning strategies (Brown & Day, 1983; Chapman et al., 2006; Gamino, Chapman & Cook, 2009; Gamino et al.,

2010). Thus, education, whether encountered in school, the home, or the community, provides a meaningful learning laboratory responsible, to a large extent, for modeling and building the adolescent brain and cognitive function, either promoting or neglecting higher order critical thinking (Gamino et al., 2010).

In the following sections, we present a theoretical framework and empirical evidence for a strategy-based approach to assess and promote higher order cognitive development in adolescents. We build on research showing that *gist reasoning,* defined as global meaning derived from connected language, supports advanced cognition (Reyna, Lloyd, & Brainerd, 2003). Growing evidence also supports the potential of strategy-based learning approaches to strengthen adolescents' ability to become independent learners (Bjorklund, Miller, Coyle, & Slawinski, 1997; Lawson, 1985; Sung, Chang, & Huang, 2008). Specifically, we propose that the cognitive construct of strategic gist reasoning may help enhance learning efficiency of complex verbal and written information during adolescence. A synthesized review is provided of the core research conducted by our BrainHealth team and other researchers who have used a form of abstract gist reasoning as a framework to assess and train higher order thinking skills. Evidence from both clinical populations and typically developing adolescents is presented regarding the ability to abstract meaning or construct generalized principles from complex information, similar to that encountered in the classroom. We propose that the years from middle school into high school offer a promising window of opportunity to identify, mitigate, and perhaps reverse the expanding prevalence of a delay in cognitive development of abstract reasoning in adolescence. Based on evidence linking timing of strategic gist-reasoning development to adolescence, it is timely to evaluate approaches that characterize and train the ability to extract generalized ideas and principles as well as to learn the fundamental facts during the teen years (Alberts, 2009).

STRATEGIC GIST REASONING: A FRAMEWORK TO PROMOTE LEARNING EFFICIENCY

In this section, we make a case for promoting learning efficiency and advancing innovative thinking at a critical stage of cognitive development in adolescents. One approach to enhancing higher order thinking is to train cognitive strategies to constantly synthesize novel meanings. Synthesizing novel meaning, achieved through the construct of gist reasoning, is a rich cognitive process that engages the complex frontal lobe networks that are undergoing rapid maturation during the teen years. This view is supported by cognitive neuroscience principles and evidenced-based studies.

Definition of Strategic Gist Reasoning

We define *strategic gist reasoning* as the ability to combine/bind details to form abstract gist meanings from different input sources, such as auditory, visual, and other sensory modalities (Chapman, Gamino, Cook, Hanten, Li, & Levin, 2006; Gabrieli, 2004; Reyna, 1996; van Dijk, 1995). One impressive feat that continues to evolve during human cognitive development is the expanding capacity to construct abstract gist meanings from the vast amount of incoming information and stimuli to which we are exposed daily, with new evidence that the capacity is primed to significantly expand during adolescence (Gamino et al., 2010). Brainerd and Reyna (1996) reported that meaning is rarely stored in its concrete/explicit form, but rather is quickly synthesized to a more generalized gist-based meaning. Gabrieli (2004), for example, noted that generalized/gist meanings are more robustly stored and retrieved than are specific concrete facts/details, which are rapidly lost. Constructing abstract gist meaning is a skill that applies to informal as well as formal learning activities, such as reading a school assignment, listening and taking notes from a lecture, writing a class report on a specific topic, watching a movie or television program, or listening to a friend's joke. In sum, remembering the abstracted gist meaning from class readings, for example, may be a more important indicator of depth and efficiency of learning than recalling the specific facts (Brown, Day, & Jones, 1983). Indeed, remembering exact wording has been found to be independent of remembering the meaning of text (Reyna & Kiernan, 1994).

Theoretical Framework of Processes Core to Strategic Gist Reasoning

We developed a theoretical framework consisting of three processes that represent the cognitive core capacities underlying the ability to engage in strategic gist reasoning (Chapman et al., 2008). These are strategic attention, integrated reasoning, and elaborated reasoning. The first, *strategic attention*, utilizes cognitive control to reduce the load of the incoming details by focusing on and encoding the important information while inhibiting less relevant information. By fifth grade, students are capable of condensing familiar information by deleting the trivial details and leaving only the most important facts (Brown & Day, 1983). When individuals attempt to attend to and retain all incoming information at the same level, working memory and other cognitive resources become overloaded and inefficient (Bjork, 1989; McNab & Klingberg, 2008). The second major process, *integrated reasoning*, combines explicit and important facts to form higher order abstracted meanings that are not explicitly stated in the stimuli/text. This capacity to abstract novel meanings is illustrated symbolically by $a + b = c$, where a and b are explicit facts, and *c* represents the cognitive–linguistic construction of a novel, unstated, generalized meaning that while derived from the facts, is not explicitly stated. Integrated reasoning is achieved by integrating the explicit content in the context of one's own concepts by conveying the ideas into one's own words, combining these ideas with preexisting knowledge to form more global, gist-based representations. This construction of gist meaning is captured by "the whole is more than the sum of its parts." The third key process, *elaborated reasoning*, draws on the fluency and fluidity of thinking to derive multiple abstract interpretations and/or generalized applications beyond the explicit content to other contexts.

Figure 5.1 provides a schematic of the dynamic, bidirectional flow in the three key processes just outlined, by which gist-based meanings from texts or verbal talks/lectures are derived from the incoming details. At the initial stage (see *a*, Figure 5.1), the incoming explicit details are processed with reference to preexisting knowledge. Once sufficient initial details are encoded and comprehended from the input information, an initial gist representation (*b*, Figure 5.1) is generated. This initial gist representation (*b*, Figure 5.1) is generated in a bottom-up approach by strategically attending to and combining important details while inhibiting trivial details. In the intermediate stage, the initial gist is further refined when combined with world knowledge through integrated

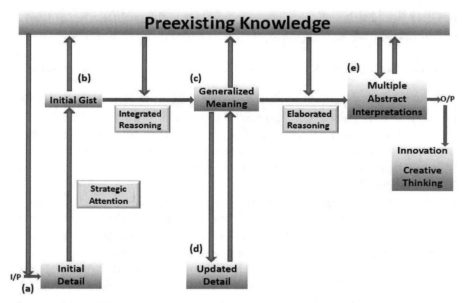

Figure 5.1. Schematic of the use and dynamic flow of the three core cognitive processes, strategic attention, integrated reasoning, and elaborated reasoning, that we propose are essential to engaging strategic gist reasoning.

reasoning to generate a novel generalized meaning (*c*, Figure 5.1). This generalized meaning is not explicitly stated but rather is derived by updating incoming facts (*d*, Figure 5.1) in the context of world knowledge. The generalized meaning (*c*, Figure 5.1) is used in a top-down fashion to verify and update the details of the incoming information (*d*, Figure 5.1) that is being processed. Similarly, the updated details (*d*, Figure 5.1) will influence generalized meaning in a bottom-up approach as long as the incoming information stream continues. In the later stage, the novel generalized meaning (*c*, Figure 5.1) is further generalized to derive multiple abstract interpretations (*e*, Figure 5.1) that are relevant to new contexts through the use of elaborated reasoning.

DEVELOPMENT OF HIGHER ORDER CRITICAL THINKING AND STRATEGIC GIST REASONING

Cognitive Development Associated With Gist Reasoning

Adolescence has long been thought of as the stage of life when the ability to engage in higher order reasoning begins to emerge (Jacobs & Klaczynski, 2005; Piaget, 1972). Piaget termed the stage commencing at approximately 11 years of age extending into early adulthood the *formal operational stage*. During this stage of development, adolescents were thought to show a shift from concrete thinking to developing a capacity to think abstractly, to engage in logical reasoning, and to devise plans to solve problems. Prior to this formal operational stage, in the concrete operational stage, children were thought to be able to understand concrete facts but have difficulty constructing abstract meanings and extracting generalized principles. Although reasoning has turned out to be remarkably variable across age, these distinctions between more versus less advanced reasoning remain instructive. For example, some conceptual knowledge during an earlier stage may be prerequisite for executive control processes that allow construction of higher order meanings at later stages.

The ability to benefit from training and to actively engage in strategic reasoning (e.g., synthesize meaning) may be optimal during adolescence and young adulthood (Brown & Day, 1983; Gamino et al., 2010). In particular, the mastery of strategic gist reasoning improves during the middle school years, with continued refinement throughout early adulthood (Brown & Day, 1983). Students as early as the first grade begin to condense complex information in the form of summaries by restating/selecting the important content while omitting the less important or trivial details, well before they develop the ability to use abstract gist reasoning (Johnson, 1983; Malone & Mastropieri, 1991; Torgesen, 1980). Student sensitivity to the most important information to retain in summaries continues to evolve into fifth grade (Brown & Day,

1983). The ability to effectively engage in strategic gist reasoning, as reflected by the ability to construct novel meaning, emerges in the fifth grade but with only rare usage, approximately 14% of the time. Strategic gist reasoning production increases to 28% in seventh grade, to approximately 36% in 10th grade, and to around 50% in the first year of college (Brown & Day, 1983). It is important to note that these levels of constructing novel and abstract meaning are not equivalent to the competency levels that are apparent in mature learners (85%).

For the most part, cognitive development theory is considered as "domain general," implying that formal reasoning may have a generalized application, whether considering how concepts and principles are abstracted in science, language arts, history, or mathematics. Some theorists, however, have challenged this notion, suggesting a domain-specific ability such that a different type of reasoning may be required across core knowledge areas (Gigerenzer & Hug, 1992). Whether competencies in verbal reasoning, for example, are associated with nonverbal reasoning, social reasoning, or mathematics reasoning, to mention a few, remains unanswered. The possibility that different forms of reasoning may partially share brain networks suggests that there may be some overlap in types of reasoning and that training one form of reasoning could potentially generalize to others (Fischer et al., 2007).

Neurobiological Evidence Linking Frontal Networks to Gist Processing

With regard to brain networks subserving gist reasoning, a handful of brain imaging studies have attempted to examine underlying neural differences in the complex processing of gist versus detail information. These studies have implicated the role of frontal regions in processing gist. For instance, in a functional magnetic resonance imaging (fMRI) study, Robertson et al. (2000) asked participants to attend to meaning-related (gist-based) and -unrelated (nongist) sentences. Comprehension of gist was associated with right inferior frontal activation, whereas comprehension of details was associated with left anterior temporal activation. Similar results of activation in the right prefrontal cortex were found in a positron emission tomography study during abstraction of gist-based meaning from discourse (Nichelli et al., 1995). In a resting-state single photon emission computerized tomography (SPECT) study, Wong et al. (2006) found a positive correlation between perfusion in right frontal regions and higher gist abstraction abilities in eight children 3 years after sustaining a brain injury. Chapman et al. (2005) found a similar relationship between gist scores and regional cerebral perfusion in the right frontal regions in a resting-state SPECT study involving individuals with frontotemporal lobar degeneration.

In more recent studies, we have examined the underlying neural basis of processing gist versus details in two separate studies, one using event-related potentials (ERPs) and the other using fMRI in young adults (Anand, 2008; Anand et al., 2009). Participants in both studies judged whether a given statement corresponded to gist or details conveyed in complex digital pictures while either ERP or fMRI data were collected. Each picture was paired with statements that conveyed congruent gist or described details that were present in the picture and foil statements that conveyed incongruent gist or described details that were not present. For example, we showed participants a digital image of a Norman Rockwell painting that depicts a tough-looking young girl sitting on a bench. She has a black eye and has presumably been sent to the principal's office for fighting. Through the cracked door, we can see two adults inside, apparently discussing the girl. Participants were asked to judge whether each of the following statements matched the painting by pushing the yes/no button on the response box: (a) "Stand up for what you believe" (a congruent gist), (b) "Home is where the heart is" (an incongruent gist), (c) Two adults are in the next room (a congruent detail), and (d) "The boy is looking into a book" (an incongruent detail). For the purpose of counterbalancing, the congruent gist and detail statements of one picture were used as foil statements for others. The ERP study revealed differences between gist and detail processing between 690 ms and 1070 ms over bilateral frontal regions (see Figure 5.2). In

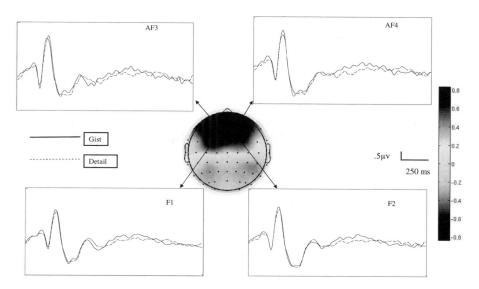

Figure 5.2. Topographical map and event-related potential waveforms showing differences in bilateral frontal regions (at electrodes F1, F2, AF3, and AF4) between gist versus detail processing during 690–1070 ms.

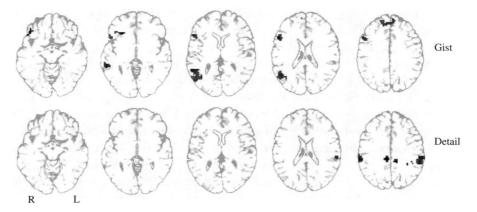

R　　L

Figure 5.3. Contrast maps showing areas of significantly greater activation when hemodynamic responses elicited by processing of gist and detail were statistically compared with baseline ($p < .05$, FDR Corrected).

Gist

Detail

the fMRI study, greater activation for the gist condition was observed primarily in medial frontal, left inferior frontal, and left temporal regions. Greater activation for details was observed primarily in bilateral superior parietal regions (see Figure 5.3). Overall, the results suggested that gist processing engages different brain regions than does identifying details, with the greatest differences being in frontal regions during gist processing.

In sum, although the research examining the neural networks of gist processing is only in its infancy, the early work points to the pivotal role of frontal lobe regions and their reciprocal connections. The fact that the frontal lobes are undergoing extensive remodeling and growth during adolescence motivates research to explore the correspondence between development of strategic gist reasoning and adolescent brain development, specifically related to frontal networks and their elaborate connections across brain regions. Future studies are needed to examine those who fail to develop gist reasoning, as well as those who develop average to high performance on gist reasoning tasks.

ASSESSMENT OF STRATEGIC GIST REASONING SKILLS

A major void exists in objectively measuring the capacity to synthesize novel and abstract meanings from complex information. In the sections that follow, we outline studies that informed a major effort directed at developing a systematic measure of gist reasoning capacity. As indicated, measuring gist reasoning may provide an informative index of a wide variety of teaching effectiveness programs across subject content areas.

Summarization: A Promising Paradigm to Measure Strategic Gist Reasoning

Over the past 20 years, we have developed cognitive paradigms to explore differences in how individuals process gist-based and detail-based information. We adopted the task of summarizing text information as a cognitive paradigm to assess and guide training of strategic gist reasoning. Our team developed a new measure, of how youth approach understanding and conveying the central meaning of complex texts, the Test of Strategic Learning (TOSL; Chapman, Hart, Levin, Cook, & Gamino, 2010). The test was based on prior theoretical frameworks and empirical research on gist processing (Brown & Day, 1983; Brown, Day, & Jones, 1983; Chapman, Nasits, Challas, & Billinger, 1999; Chapman et al., 2004; 2006; Jenkins, Heliotis, Stein, & Haynes, 1987; Johnson, 1983; Kintsch, 1998; Kintsch & van Dijk, 1978; Malone & Mastropieri, 1991; Reyna & Brainerd, 1995). Specifically, the TOSL was designed to measure the ability to process information at two levels: (a) At a lower level, the TOSL measures the student's ability to learn the important facts/details conveyed by the text; (b) at a higher level, the TOSL measures the student's ability to engage in strategic gist-level reasoning, represented by combining the facts to construct abstract meanings that are not explicitly stated in the text.

Disparity Between Two Levels: Gist Versus Detail

Some intriguing patterns of disparity between strategic gist and detail level processing first emerged from our research in clinical populations, including youth with traumatic brain injury (TBI), stroke, attention-deficit/hyperactivity disorder (ADHD), and language impairment and typical public school adolescents (Chapman, Levin, Wanek, Weyrauch, & Kufera, 1998; Chapman, Max, Gamino, McGlothlin, & Cliff, 2003; Chapman et al., 1997, 2001, 2004, 2006, 2008; Gamino & Chapman, 2009; Gamino, Chapman, & Cook, 2009; Gamino, Chapman, Cook, Burkhalter, & Vanegas, 2008; Gamino, Chapman, Hull, Vanegas, & Cook, 2009; Gamino & Hull, 2009). For the purposes of this chapter, we highlight the results from populations with TBI or ADHD, although a similar pattern of findings has been reported in the stroke and language-impaired populations. In our research, we have focused on elucidating the paradox of relatively intact ability for straightforward learning of details/facts versus the marked gap in competence to construct higher order gist meaning in clinical populations. In characterizing the discrepancy between strategic gist reasoning and good performance on discrete fact learning, we postulated that higher order cognitive skills involving top-down processing may be more vulnerable than bottom-up skills to a compromised brain after a traumatic brain injury or in disorders such as ADHD.

Traumatic Brain Injury

Some of the first evidence of a marked disparity between adolescent development in the ability to engage in higher order critical thinking versus a relative competence in remembering the concrete facts came from longitudinal and retrospective studies of youth who had a history of TBI (Chapman, 2006; Chapman et al., 1998, 2001, 2004, 2006; Gamino, Chapman, & Cook, 2009). Recent studies have documented a marked disparity in how preadolescents and adolescents who suffered a TBI subsequently developed the ability to encode mental representations at two different levels—lower level rote/verbatim level of learning versus a higher order abstracted gist meaning level—years after injury, especially during adolescent developmental stages. Specifically, we identified a stall in higher order cognitive development in strategic gist reasoning as compared with control groups in a series of studies investigating children and teens with earlier TBI (Chapman, 2006; Chapman et al., 2004; Gamino, Chapman, & Cook, 2009). Children and adolescents with severe TBI exhibited marked deficits when asked to summarize complex textual information and to give interpretations of the global meaning/gist meanings. The most frequently occurring pattern of the youth with TBI was a condensed version of the original text that contained pieces of explicit information, with only rare occurrence of statements that conveyed global/gist-based concepts. That is, the youth with TBI predominantly used an immature strategy of information reduction manifested by conveying explicit facts and deleting information, as contrasted with the criterion behavior of typically developing adolescents, who used strategic gist reasoning manifested by constructing abstract meanings (Brown & Day, 1983). Interestingly, the youth with TBI condensed or omitted the same amount of information (quantity) as their age-matched control peers when asked to produce a synthesized summary of information. However, the youth with TBI failed to exhibit the ability to use strategic gist reasoning; instead, they engaged in lower level cognitive processing. They copied rote facts from the original text without combining ideas to form higher order gist-based concepts, similar to behavior observed in younger, elementary-grade children.

Moreover, we found that the earlier the age at injury, the more guarded the prognosis in developing later-emerging higher order cognitive skills such as strategic gist reasoning (Cook, Chapman, & Gamino, 2007). Thus, children injured prior to 2 years of age performed lower than those injured after 5 years of age in terms of strategic gist reasoning when assessed during adolescence, years after the brain injury (Chapman, 2006). One of the presumptive key factors that contribute to a failure to develop gist reasoning is a disruption in subsequent development of the frontal brain networks, which undergo dramatic remodeling and growth during adolescence (Chapman et al., 2001, 2004; Gamino, Chapman, & Cook, 2009). Extant evidence reveals that a moderate to severe TBI damages the axonal connections between frontal and posterior brain regions in the majority of cases (Levin et al., 1993; Mendelsohn et al., 1992). Thus, the cognitive consequences of earlier disruption of subcortical connections/networks may not be apparent until later developmental stages during adolescence when higher order cognitive skills fail to emerge.

The neurocognitive stall in higher order cognitive skills such as strategic gist reasoning stands in sharp contrast to evidence across studies that suggest that the majority of youth with TBI recover their basic intellectual function and show normal development in their ability to learn concrete facts when followed years after the earlier brain injury (see Cook et al., 2007). The pattern of relatively intact encoding and retrieval of the important facts indicated that youth with TBI process and encode concrete details at a level comparable with that of typically developing adolescents. Thus, the ability to learn concrete and explicit facts from information comparable with what appears in textbooks or is conveyed in lectures typically improves to a normal range of performance in students with TBI when evaluated years after their injury.

The principal reason to bring to the forefront the disparity between detail versus strategic gist reasoning in pediatric TBI is that few may realize this potential linkage. Prevalence data suggest that TBI, the number one cause of acquired disability in childhood, may have affected an estimated 15% to 20% of students per classroom (Langlois, Rutland-Brown, & Thomas, 2006). Unfortunately, by the time these students enter middle school or high school, the history of an earlier brain injury is often no longer documented or deemed relevant (Chapman, 2006). For the most part, doctors, families, students, and teachers do not understand that higher order deficits may be associated with a brain injury sustained years ago. Only recently has evidence documented that later-emerging deficits may arise from earlier brain injuries. Because these children typically regain basic intellectual function and the ability to learn facts by rote, they are seldom identified as eligible to receive specialized training during later stages of development (Chapman, 2006; Gamino, Chapman, & Cook 2009).

Attention-Deficit/Hyperactivity Disorder

In more recent work, we examined the ability of preadolescents and adolescents to synthesize details into higher level gist meanings as well as their ability to learn explicit facts from the texts. Similar to the pattern in youth with TBI, we identified a disparity between strategic gist reasoning ability and learning explicit facts in youth with ADHD (Gamino et al., 2008; Gamino, Chapman, Hull, et al., 2009). The preadolescents and adolescents

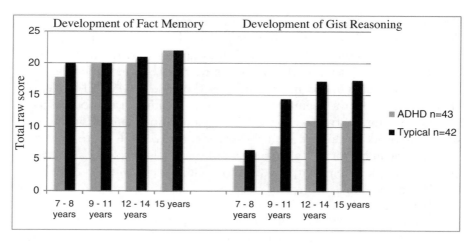

Figure 5.4. This figure demonstrates the development trajectory of students with ADHD. The light gray bar signifies the students with ADHD, and the dark gray bar represents the typically developing mid- to upper socioeconomic status students. This figure demonstrates that memory for explicit information is similar in typically developing youth. The differences in strategic learning are somewhat minimal in the early years, but as students with ADHD reach adolescence, reasoning appears to plateau as compared with high-performing typically developing students. From "Effects of Higher-Order Cognitive Strategy Training on Gist Reasoning and Fact Learning in Adolescents," by J. F. Gamino, S. B. Chapman, E. Hull, and G. R. Lyon, 2010, *Frontiers in Psychology, 1*, p. 188. Copyright 2010 by the authors. Reprinted with permission.

with ADHD showed significantly lower strategic gist reasoning ability on summarization tasks, failing to condense, synthesize, and chunk details into abstracted gist meanings when compared to typically developing peers (Figure 5.4; Gamino et al. 2008). The youth with ADHD demonstrated a lower level cognitive strategy of "copy/delete" of explicit facts rather than integrating information into higher level ideas. Moreover, the ability of students with ADHD to learn and recall the important details from the text was similar to that of typically developing peers and of youth with brain injury (Figure 5.5; Gamino et al., 2008).

We postulated that the delay or stall in strategic gist reasoning may reflect inefficient learning strategies whereby the student with ADHD over-relies on learning explicit details at the cost of consolidating and synthesizing details into abstract gist meanings. As implicated in pediatric brain injury, we believe that children and adolescents with ADHD may have a tendency to strengthen posterior neural networks through detail-focused learning rather than frontally mediated networks necessary for strategic gist reasoning (Chapman et al., 2006). This possible explanation warrants careful future study using brain connectivity analyses.

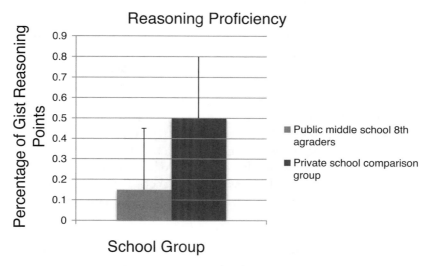

<figure>

Reasoning Proficiency

Percentage of Gist Reasoning Points (y-axis: 0, 0.1, 0.2, 0.3, 0.4, 0.5, 0.6, 0.7, 0.8, 0.9)

School Group (x-axis)

■ Public middle school 8th agraders

■ Private school comparison group
</figure>

Figure 5.5. This graph demonstrates the delay in strategic reasoning proficiency found in public school students when compared to private school peers (public school eighth-grade students are represented by the light gray bar and private school control eighth-grade students are represented by the dark bar). From "Effects of Higher-Order Cognitive Strategy Training on Gist Reasoning and Fact Learning in Adolescents," by J. F. Gamino, S. B. Chapman, E. Hull, and G. R. Lyon, 2010, *Frontiers in Psychology, 1* , p. 188. Copyright 2010 by the authors. Reprinted with permission.

TYPICALLY DEVELOPING ADOLESCENTS: NEUROCOGNITIVE DELAY IN GIST REASONING

New evidence suggests that competence in abstracting gist meaning may be failing to fully develop in normally developing teens despite relatively strong recall of details and facts (Chapman et al., 2008; Gamino et al., 2010). We questioned whether an educational approach focused on verbatim learning could impede the acquisition of higher order abstraction and problem solving skills. On the basis of prior evidence, we postulated that encouraging a cognitive style of learning concrete facts may strengthen posterior brain regions (e.g., hippocampal dependent neural networks) at the cost of frontally mediated cognitive systems, such as those supporting strategic gist reasoning (Chapman et al., 2006).

As mentioned in the introduction, there is growing concern regarding stagnating reasoning and higher order cognitive skills in typically developing adolescents. Reliance on high-stakes standardized tests across the nation continues to emphasize the "regurgitation" of information rather than a focus on reasoning and critical thinking. The need for metrics that inform the learning of basic content is important; nonetheless, teaching to such tests may strengthen lower level bottom-up cognitive processes rather than top-down processing. The reported stagnation of reasoning in adolescents across the United States and the cognitive stall of higher order cognition in both TBI and ADHD populations suggested that reasoning deficits were a potential problem for typically developing middle school students (Baldi et al., 2007; Lemke et al., 2004).

In a recent study, we examined the utilization of strategic gist reasoning skills in a typically developing group of eighth-grade students from an urban Texas public middle school (Gamino et al., 2010). The students who participated were in Advancement via Individual Determination (AVID) classes. AVID is a nationwide program that is offered to bolster students who are neither low performers nor identified as gifted in school. AVID students are chosen for the program on the basis of their potential for college and to offer support for average students who might otherwise "slip through the cracks" of the educational system and be at risk for dropping out of school. Thus, while capable, these students are considered average rather than high achieving.

Using the TOSL, we assessed the ability to abstract gist-based meaning in 54 eighth graders and found that strategic reasoning was significantly impaired when compared with our age-based criterion level. We determined the age-based criterion from the work of Brown and Day (1983) and our control groups of students, in which proficient gist reasoning was attained through production of 60% or more of the gist concepts that could be gleaned from the texts. More specifically, results revealed that 84% of the urban middle school eighth-grade students failed to reach preestablished criteria for gist reasoning. Our findings suggest that typically developing, urban public school eighth-grade students do not develop abstract reasoning skills at the same trajectory as their private school peers (Figure 5.5). More evidence is needed to determine if the developmental delays in using abstract gist meanings during summarization are due to teaching methods, environmental factors, or the need to specifically train abstraction of meaning to advance development of higher order strategic reasoning skills. Based on our randomized study (results summarized below), it appears that the potential to enhance strategic gist reasoning is promising in public school eighth-graders, given intensive training over a relatively short interval.

TRAINING TO MITIGATE STALL IN STRATEGIC GIST REASONING

Adolescence appears to be an optimal time to intervene to create a cognitive shift away from straightforward learning of facts to a more active strategic learning style, such as gist reasoning. Given the large scope of the problem and recent declines, educators, cognitive scientists, and policymakers are asking whether specific training can promote effective reasoning, critical thinking and active use of learning strategies.

Does Reasoning Need to be Taught?

There has long been interest in improving students' ability to actively use strategies to enhance higher order reasoning and learning. Much of the work has evolved out of training students with learning disabilities and reading problems (Graves, 1986; Jenkins et al., 1987; Malone & Mastropieri, 1991; Torgesen, 1980). Whereas research continues to show that tangible rewards improve learning, the reinforcement alone may not be sufficient to achieve lasting learning gains when basic reasoning skills are missing (Jenkins, Barksdale & Clinton, 1978; Roberts & Smith, 1980). Instead, specific strategy training may be required.

Synthesizing Meaning Improves Learning

As discussed earlier, summarization tasks provide an informative cognitive-linguistic paradigm to measure whether a child relies primarily on a verbatim/rote learning style or on a gist representation, constructing meaning at a more abstract level (Brown & Day, 1983; Chapman et al., 2004, 2006). Now, we want to consider the use of summarization strategies to improve gist reasoning. Given proper instruction, youth can be trained to effectively synthesize details into gist-based meaning, with precursor skills emerging as young as age 7 to 8 and with more reliable and greater sophistication during adolescence (Brown & Day, 1983; Johnson, 1983). For example, in a randomized study of middle school students with learning differences, Malone and Mastropieri (1991) compared three reading-comprehension training conditions, with two including summarization training of narrative texts (one involving summarization alone and the other summarizing plus a self-monitoring checklist for students to mark off completed steps) and one a teaching-as-usual-condition in which the focus emphasized identifying key vocabulary in the passages. The summarization training asked the student to identify the core information regarding (a) who or what the paragraph was about and (b) what was happening to the characters in the narrative. Their results revealed that students with learning disabilities benefited the most from summarization training (i.e., they were trained to use a paragraph-restatement strategy), especially when accompanied by a self-monitoring checklist to make sure they answered the summary probes. The self-monitoring checklist simply consisted of a 3 × 5-in. index card with the summary probes of "who or what," "what happened," and "summary sentence" written across the top and a place to put a check where the students indicated they had completed the steps for each paragraph. Moreover, the researchers found that the benefits from the summarization strategy, combined with self-monitoring, generalized from summarizing narrative text to employing the strategies with expository social studies texts.

These studies added important foundational data that summarization could provide beneficial ways to enhance learning in middle school students with learning differences or reading problems. What was not apparent from these earlier studies was the *degree to which* the students were able to abstract meaning from the paragraphs. The approaches did not incorporate metrics of gist abstraction performance. Rather, the metrics primarily consisted of scoring points for including the most important but nonetheless explicitly stated (verbatim) information. In the following section, we present recent empirical evidence that supports the informative potential of strategic gist reasoning to guide training of higher order cognitive skills in adolescence.

STRATEGIC MEMORY AND REASONING TRAINING (SMART)

We developed the Strategic Memory and Reasoning Training (SMART) program to determine the efficacy of teaching cognitive strategies that support abstraction of meaning in response to our findings that students with ADHD and students with TBI demonstrated impaired gist reasoning ability (SMART; Chapman & Gamino, 2008). The SMART program trains students to abstract generalized meanings/principles through gist reasoning with less direct emphasis on learning rote facts. The SMART program encompasses a dynamic engagement of both strategic gist reasoning to abstract concepts and important detail meanings, as shown in our model (Figure 5.1).

For experimental purposes, we evaluated the SMART program delivered in approximately 10 hr over 1 month. The program is not content driven but, rather, trains adolescents to use a set of hierarchical cognitive strategies to abstract and convey meaning by incorporating world knowledge with new information conveyed by text. The strategies are taught in the first six sessions, with application and generalization built into the last four sessions. The emphasis of the training is *how* to learn rather than *what* to learn. The SMART program reinforces the student's ability to derive multiple abstract interpretations and to apply the generalized meanings to multiple contexts. The students are encouraged to use the SMART strategies while doing classroom and homework assignments.

We have examined and continue to explore whether adolescents, whether typically developing or diagnosed with ADHD or even brain injury, can be trained to use higher order cognitive skills to abstract meanings and principles from the component details across various types of classroom texts, ranging from language arts and social studies through science and history. The focus on abstracting meaning and principles has never been more relevant given the rapid change and instant access to facts now driven by technology. In a generation where information overload is the norm, students may require specific instruction to enable them to synthesize and condense relevant facts.

Strategic Memory and Reasoning Training (SMART) in Youth With ADHD

As reviewed above, new evidence reveals that preadolescents and adolescents with ADHD perform limited online synthesis and integration of information. They experience difficulty in converting details to abstract meanings in their summarization and interpretation responses (Gamino et al., 2008). In a recent study based on earlier work, we wanted to determine whether higher order strategic gist reasoning could be trained and would replace the use of a copy/delete style of condensing information in students with ADHD (i.e., after participating in the SMART program; Chapman & McKinnon, 2000; Chapman et al., 2004).

We randomized 40 students diagnosed with ADHD into one of two interventions (Gamino, Chapman, Hull, et al., 2009). Prior to randomization, the students were assessed for reasoning ability using the TOSL. At baseline, there were no significant differences between the two groups' gist reasoning ability. One group received the SMART program individually in ten 45-min sessions. The other group received training to focus attention, one of the core deficits of ADHD, individually in fifteen 45-min sessions. The attention training group learned focus by playing games that required selective attention, such as Jenga and various card games, while disregarding controlled distracters, such as background noise of a baby crying. After completing the separate interventions, both groups were reassessed with the TOSL. The group who received SMART significantly improved their gist reasoning performance compared with baseline testing. However, the students from the attention training group did not show significant improvement on the gist-based reasoning measure. This evidence suggests that despite the students' impaired ability to abstract gist meaning, training can ameliorate and reduce strategic gist reasoning deficits in students with ADHD after 10 training sessions. Moreover, the lack of improvement in reasoning from the attention training group suggests that training or medication to improve attention alone may be insufficient to develop higher order cognitive skills, even though it may increase attention and concentration in students with ADHD. A number of important questions from this line motivate future research. For one, how lasting are the gist reasoning training benefits, and do the benefits generalize to classroom performance? Second, do students show incremental benefits when training modules are combined? That is, do students exhibit a larger gain when they are given combined gist reasoning and attention training? Another important issue to consider is whether there is a bidirectional benefit of either strategic gist reasoning training or other types of executive functioning training, for example, in working memory. For example, it would be informative to elucidate whether frontally mediated cognitive processes show a synergistic or crossover training effect, such as where working memory training benefits gist-reasoning skills or vice versa.

Strategic Gist Reasoning in Typically Developing Public Middle School Students

The evidence for the efficacy of training reasoning ability in students with ADHD motivated our team to examine the efficacy of strategic gist reasoning training (i.e., SMART) in typically developing students. We conducted a controlled study in the eighth-grade AVID class mentioned previously (Gamino et al., 2010). We randomized 54 students into one of three groups: the experimental SMART group (training described earlier); a Memory group that was trained to use rote memory strategies; and a Teen Brain group that learned about the dynamic learning potential of the adolescent brain and developmental risk factors, such as substance abuse, concussion, sleep deprivation, and stress. The students and their instructor were blinded to the group status, as they were told they were going to be taught strategies to improve their learning potential.

After nine 45-min small-group training sessions over the course of 1 month, the students were reassessed using the TOSL. We found that the students in the SMART group significantly improved their gist abstraction ability by spontaneously producing a greater number of gist-based concepts during the summarization task, whereas the students in the other two groups did not demonstrate significant gist reasoning improvement (Gamino et al., 2010; Figure 5.6). With regard to fact learning, it is not surprising that the Memory group showed the greatest gains after training (Figure 5.6). Nonetheless, the gains in the SMART-trained group were also significant, despite no specific training focused on memory for details. We postulate that chunking important details into abstract ideas bolsters memory for important details, perhaps also allowing the individual a more efficient search process to retrieve the facts. Furthermore, the students in the SMART group significantly increased their performance on state-mandated standardized reading tests, whereas the students trained to memorize facts and those who learned about the teen brain did not.

In summary, the promising findings of benefits from short-term, intensive training in strategic gist reasoning, for both typically developing public school adolescents and those with ADHD, provide support for the use of

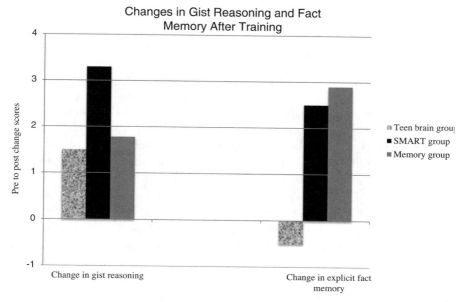

Figure 5.6. This graph represents the change in strategic reasoning scores after the randomized control study. The light gray bar indicates the nonsignificant change scores for rote memory strategy group. The black bar represents the significant change in scores for the students in the SMART group. The mottled gray bar represents a nonsignificant change in reasoning scores for the Teen Brain group. The right side of the graph represents the change in memory for explicit facts after the intervention. The rote memory strategy group, represented by the light gray bar, demonstrated a significant change in scores. The black bar represents a change approaching significance for the SMART group. The mottled gray bar represents the Teen Brain group's nonsignificant change in scores. From "Effects of Higher-Order Cognitive Strategy Training on Gist Reasoning and Fact Learning in Adolescents," by J. F. Gamino, S. B. Chapman, E. Hull, and G. R. Lyon, 2010, *Frontiers in Psychology, 1*, p. 188. Copyright 2010 by the authors. Reprinted with permission.

training to enhance development of higher order reasoning in adolescence. Research is just beginning to emerge from randomized studies evaluating the potential benefits of linking cognitive neuroscience frameworks of higher order reasoning to develop training protocols that are being evaluated in the classroom. Whereas considerable research exists in elementary schools regarding learning development, few investigations have considered the informative aspects of cognitive neuroscience frameworks in adolescence, with a few notable exceptions (e.g., Kaminski, Sloutsky, & Heckler, 2008; Ramsay et al., 2010). Furthermore, recent research provides hope for facilitating educational directives aimed at improving reasoning abilities in adolescents across the country.

CONCLUSIONS

We offer three major conclusions based on the evidence presented in this chapter. First, given the current state of our society, with rapid access to massive amounts of information and educational emphasis on standardized tests that require detail-based learning, formal training is useful for ameliorating underdeveloped reasoning and critical thinking skills. Many typically developing teens as well as youth from at-risk clinical populations (e.g., ADHD, TBI, dyslexia, likely to comprise a relatively large proportion of students in middle school and high school classes) are failing to develop adequate higher order reasoning skills. Second, emerging cognitive neuroscience evidence indicates that adolescence may be a pivotal stage of brain development wherein the brain is primed to develop higher order thinking skills, given appropriate cognitive training/stimulation. Third, early evidence lends support to training benefits for strategic gist reasoning, at least in the short term.

Whereas considerably more research is needed from a multitude of perspectives and reasoning domains (e.g., scientific reasoning, nonverbal reasoning as required for playing chess), evidenced-based protocols are emerging as promising tools to elevate higher order reasoning skills in adolescence. Beyond demonstrating that strategic gist reasoning can be enhanced with specialized training, it is also critically important that research evaluate the effectiveness of training paradigms to promote learning efficiency in adolescents across academic subjects and curriculum objectives. We propose that training benefits should increase *learning efficiency*, defined as the cognitive ability to engage in resilient (longer lasting) learning (Chapman et al., 2008). Enhancing gist reasoning and learning efficiency may secondarily be associated with improvements in performance on other executive function measures (Jaeggi, Buschkuehl, Jonides, & Perrig, 2008; Sternberg, 2008).

To achieve optimal learning potential in adolescence, we propose that the following four objectives should be met in future research to establish whether training protocols enhance higher order critical thinking: (a) promote appropriate levels of cognitive development based on academic readiness (Lawson, 1985), (b) enhance knowledge that is stable over time as opposed to transient learning of isolated facts (Brown, Day, & Jones, 1983), (c) generalize to novel contexts/contents beyond the specific material taught (Malone & Mastropieri, 1991), and (d) transfer to the real world, that is, from educational to occupational performance/achievement (Sternberg, 2008).

Emerging brain studies suggest that training adolescents in how to engage higher order critical thinking will serve as a catalyst to promote frontal lobe development, foundational to achieving adult-level reasoning, judgment, and problem-solving skills (Casey et al., 2005; Chapman et al., 2008;

Gamino et al., 2010, Giedd et al., 2006). Although systematic studies are needed to follow youth longitudinally, the inadequate development of higher order reasoning appears to be long lasting, with patterns apparent in young adults as well. For example, a number of large corporations with which we work report that young adults in their 20s and 30s manifest poor critical thinking skills even though they made good grades in college. Teaching a teen to absorb facts does little more than impart isolated information rather than contributing to deeper knowledge and understanding. Not to underemphasize the importance of fundamental facts, core facts can be used to build abstract meaning and generalized principles as a student realizes the need to synthesize and process information at an abstract, more meaningful level. Moreover, rote learning is less crucial as facts are revised and altered with new discoveries, and it may work against the ability to synthesize information to form innovative ideas and approaches. As a final comment, we insist that it is imperative to recognize the larger economic impact of a failure to train adolescents in how to become critical and independent thinkers. The research on critical thinking and higher order reasoning in adolescence reveals an impending loss of human cognitive capital that has been linked to national economic performance (Hanushek & Woessmann, 2010). A report prepared for the Organization for Economic Co-operation and Development suggests that adding 1 year of schooling to the education of youth would boost the Gross Domestic Product per capita of OECD countries by billions of dollars over the ensuing years.

Adolescents may be more likely to remain in school and reach graduation when they are actively engaged in abstract reasoning and in-depth classroom discussion as well as encouraged to participate in inquiry (Alberts, 2009). With dropout rates as high as 50% in urban public schools, every 5 years that we delay in making substantial changes in building higher order critical thinking skills, we lose another cohort of students who fail to complete high school with adequate reasoning ability. Businesses, law firms, medical institutes, engineering firms, and industry, to mention a few, have urged that educational practices move away from memorization of facts and rewarding simplistic answers towards problem solving, reasoning, and decision making. Corporate America reports that high school and college graduates are ill-prepared to excel in the workforce and to solve challenging problems (Alberts, 2009). This change will require the successful integration of collaborative efforts across federal and statewide funding agencies, research, education and its leadership, cognitive neuroscience, and public policy to discover evidenced-based teaching practices to better promote the growth of higher order critical thinking skills in adolescents. This chapter, in combination with others in this book, will help accelerate the cause for training the fourth R—reasoning.

REFERENCES

Alberts, B. (2009, December 18). The breakthroughs of 2009. *Science, 326,* 1589. doi:10.1126/science.1185821

Anand, R. (2008). *Differences between gist and detail processing.* Available from ProQuest Dissertations and Theses database. (UMI No. 3305835).

Anand, R., Motes, M. A., Maguire, M. J., Moore, P. S., Chapman, S. B., & Hart, J. (2009, October). *Neural basis of abstracted meaning.* Poster presented at Neurobiology of Language, Chicago, IL.

Baldi, S., Jin, Y., Skemer, M., Green, P. J., & Herget, D. (2007). *Highlights from PISA 2006: Performance of U.S. 15-year-old students in science and mathematics literacy in an international context* (NCES 2008–016). Washington, DC: National Center for Education Statistics, Institute of Education Sciences, U.S. Department of Education.

Bjork, R. A. (1989). Retrieval inhibition as an adaptive mechanism in human memory. In H. L. Roediger & F. I. M. Craik (Eds.), *Varieties of memory and consciousness: Essays in honour of Endel Tulving* (pp. 309–330). Mahwah, NJ: Erlbaum.

Bjorklund, D. F., Miller, P. H., Coyle, T. R., & Slawinski, J. L. (1997). Instructing children to use memory strategies: Evidence of utilization deficiencies in memory training studies. *Developmental Review, 17,* 411–441. doi:10.1006/drev.1997.0440

Blakemore, S. J., & Choudhury, S. (2006). Development of the adolescent brain: Implications for executive function and social cognition. *Journal of Child Psychology and Psychiatry, 47,* 296–312. doi:10.1111/j.1469-7610.2006.01611.x

Brainerd, C. J., & Reyna, V. F. (1996). Mere memory testing creates false memories in children. *Developmental Psychology, 32,* 467–478. doi:10.1037/0012-1649.32.3.467

Brown, A. L., & Day, J. D. (1983). Macrorules for summarizing texts: The development of expertise. *Journal of Verbal Learning & Verbal Behavior, 22,* 1–14. doi:10.1016/S0022-5371(83)80002-4

Brown, A. L., Day, J. D., & Jones, R. S. (1983). The development of plans for summarizing texts. *Child Development, 54,* 968–979. doi:10.2307/1129901

Bunge, S. A., Wendelken, C., Badre, D., & Wagner, A. D. (2004). Analogical reasoning and prefrontal cortex: Evidence for separable retrieval and integration mechanisms. *Cerebral Cortex, 15,* 239–249. doi:10.1093/cercor/bhh126

Casey, B. J., Tottenham, N., Liston, C., & Durston, S. (2005). Imaging the developing brain: What have we learned about cognitive development? *Trends in Cognitive Sciences, 9,* 104–110. doi:10.1016/j.tics.2005.01.011

Chambers, R. A., Taylor, J. R., & Potenza, M. N. (2003). Developmental neurocircuitry of motivation in adolescence: A critical period of addiction vulnerability. *The American Journal of Psychiatry, 160,* 1041–1052. doi:10.1176/appi.ajp.160.6.1041

Chapman, S. B. (2006). Neurocognitive stall: A paradox in long term recovery from pediatric brain injury. *Brain Injury Professional, 3,* 10–13.

Chapman, S. B., Bonte, F. J., Wong, S. B., Zientz, J. N., Hynan, L. S., Harris, T. S., & Lipton, A. M. (2005). Convergence of connected language and SPECT in variants of frontotemporal lobar degeneration. *Alzheimer Disease and Associated Disorders, 19,* 1–12. doi:10.1097/01.wad.0000189050.41064.03

Chapman, S. B., Gamino, J. F., & Anand, R. (2008, March). *Strategic memory and reasoning in teens: Implications for cognitive efficiency, development, and learning theory.* Proceedings of National Science Foundation Conference on Adolescent and Young Adult Reasoning, Washington, D. C.

Chapman, S. B., Gamino, J. F., Cook, L. G., Hanten, G., Li, X., & Levin, H. S. (2006). Impaired discourse gist and working memory in children after brain injury. *Brain and Language, 97,* 178–188. doi:10.1016/j.bandl.2005.10.002

Chapman, S. B., Hart, J. M., Levin, H. S., Cook, L. G., & Gamino, J. F. (2010). *The test of strategic learning.* Manuscript submitted for publication.

Chapman, S. B., Levin, H. S., Wanek, A., Weyrauch, J., & Kufera, J. (1998). Discourse after closed head injury in young children. *Brain and Language, 61,* 420–449. doi:10.1006/brln.1997.1885

Chapman, S. B., Max, J. E., Gamino, J. F., McGlothlin, J. H., & Cliff, S. N. (2003). Discourse plasticity in children after stroke: Age at injury and lesion effects. *Pediatric Neurology, 29,* 34–41. doi:10.1016/S0887-8994(03)00012-2

Chapman, S. B., & McKinnon, L. (2000). Discussion of developmental plasticity: Factors affecting cognitive outcome after pediatric traumatic brain injury. *Journal of Communication Disorders, 33,* 333–344. doi:10.1016/S0021-9924(00) 00029-0

Chapman, S. B., McKinnon, L., Levin, H. S., Song, J., Meier, M. C., & Chiu, S. (2001). Longitudinal outcome of verbal discourse in children with traumatic brain injury: Three-year follow-up. *The Journal of Head Trauma Rehabilitation, 16,* 441–455. doi:10.1097/00001199-200110000-00004

Chapman, S. B., Nasits, J., Challas, J. D., & Billinger, A. P. (1999). Long-term recovery in paediatric head injury: Overcoming the hurdles. *Advances in Speech Language Pathology, 1,* 19–30. doi:10.3109/14417049909167150

Chapman, S. B., Sparks, G., Levin, H. S., Dennis, M., Roncadin, C., Zhang, L., & Song, J. (2004). Discourse macrolevel processing after severe pediatric traumatic brain injury. *Developmental Neuropsychology, 25,* 37–60. doi:10.1207/ s15326942dn2501&2_4

Chapman, S. B., Watkins, R., Gustafson, C., Moore, S., Levin, H. S., & Kufera, J. A. (1997). Narrative discourse in children with closed head injury, children with language impairment and typically developing children. *American Journal of Speech-Language Pathology, 6,* 66–76.

Cook, L. G., Chapman, S. B., & Gamino, J. F. (2007). Impaired discourse gist in pediatric brain injury: Missing the forest for the trees. In K. Cain & J. Oakhill (Eds.), *Children's comprehension problems in oral and written language: A cognitive perspective* (pp. 218–243). New York, NY: Guilford.

Dahl, R. E., & Spear, L. P. (2004). Adolescent brain development: Vulnerabilities and opportunities. *Annals of the New York Academy of Sciences, 1021*, 1–22. doi:10.1196/annals.1308.001

Fischer, K. W., Daniel, D. B., Immordino-Yang, M. H., Stern, E., Battro, A., & Koizumi, H. (2007). Why *Mind, Brain, and Education?* Why now? *Mind, Brain, and Education, 1*, 1–2. doi:10.1111/j.1751-228X.2007.00006.x

Gabrieli, J. D. (2004). Memory: Pandora's hippocampus? *Cerebrum, 6*(4), 39–48.

Gamino, J. F., & Chapman, S. B. (2009). Reasoning in children with attention deficit hyperactivity disorder: A review of current research. *Advances in ADHD, 3*, 82–88.

Gamino, J. F., Chapman, S. B., & Cook, L. G. (2009). Strategic learning in youth with traumatic brain injury: Evidence for stall in higher-order cognition. *Topics in Language Disorders, 29*, 224–235. doi:10.1097/TLD.0b013e3181b531da

Gamino, J. F., Chapman, S. B., Cook, L. G., Burkhalter, M., & Vanegas, S. (2008, February). *Strategic learning in children with attention deficit hyperactivity disorder.* Abstract presented at the International Neuropsychological Society Annual Meeting, Waikoloa, HI.

Gamino, J. F., Chapman, S. B., Hull, E., & Lyon, G. R. (2010). Effects of higher-order cognitive strategy training on gist reasoning and fact learning in adolescents. *Frontiers in Psychology, 1*, 188. doi:10.3389/fpsyg.2010.00188

Gamino, J. F., Chapman, S. B., Hull, E., Vanegas, S. B., & Cook, L. G. (2009, March). *New hope for executive function and reasoning remediation in children with ADHD: Strategic Memory and Reasoning Training, SMART©* [Abstract]. Presented at Cognitive Neuroscience Society Annual Meeting, Symposium on Executive Function, San Francisco, CA.

Gamino, J. F., & Hull, E. (2009, May). *Get SMART©: The evolution of an adolescent reasoning program.* Poster session presented at International Mind, Brain, and Education Society Conference, Philadelphia, PA.

Gigerenzer, G., & Hug, K. (1992). Domain-specific reasoning: Social contracts, cheating, and perspective change. *Cognition, 43*, 127–171. doi:10.1016/0010-0277(92)90060-U

Giedd, J. N., Clasen, L. S., Lenroot, R., Greenstein, D., Wallace, G. L., Ordaz, S., & Chrousos, G. P. (2006). Puberty-related influences on brain development. *Molecular and Cellular Endocrinology, 254–255*, 154–162. doi:10.1016/j.mce.2006.04.016

Gogtay, N., Giedd, J. N., Lusk, L., Hayashi, K. M., Greenstein, D., Vaituzis, A. C., & Thompson, P. M. (2004). Dynamic mapping of human cortical development during childhood through early adulthood. *Proceedings of the National Academy of Sciences, USA, 101*, 8174–8179. doi:10.1073/pnas.0402680101

Good, C., Aronoson, J., & Inzlicht, M. (2003). Improving adolescents' standardized test performance: An intervention to reduce the effects of stereotype threat. *Journal of Applied Developmental Psychology, 24*, 645–662. doi:10.1016/j.appdev.2003.09.002

Graves, A. (1986). Effects of direct instruction and metacomprehension training on finding main ideas. *Learning Disabilities Research, 1*, 90–100.

Hanushek, E. A., & Woessmann, L. (2010). *The high cost of low educational performance: The long-run economic impact of improving PISA outcomes*. Paris, France: Organisation for Economic Co-operation and Development.

Herbert, B. (2009, September 28). Peering at the future. *The New York Times*. Retrieved from http://www.nytimes.com

Jacobs, J., & Klaczynski, P. (Eds.). (2005). *The development of decision making in children and adolescents*. Mahwah, NJ: Erlbaum.

Jaeggi, S. M., Buschkuehl, M., Jonides, J., & Perrig, W. J. (2008). Improving fluid intelligence with training on working memory. *Proceedings of the National Academy of Sciences of the United States of America, 105*, 6829–6833. doi:10.1073/pnas.0801268105

Jenkins, J. R., Barksdale, A., & Clinton, L. (1978). Improving reading comprehension and oral reading: Generalization across behaviors, settings, and time. *Journal of Learning Disabilities, 11*, 607–617. doi:10.1177/002221947801101002

Jenkins, J. R., Heliotis, J. D., Stein, M. L., & Haynes, M. C. (1987). Improving reading comprehension by using paragraph restatements. *Exceptional Children, 54*, 54–59.

Johnson, N. S. (1983). What do you do if you can tell the whole story? The development of summarization skills. In K. E. Nelson (Ed.), *Children's language* (pp. 314–383). New York: Gardner Press.

Kaminski, J. A., Sloutsky, V. M., & Heckler, A. F. (2008, April 25). The advantage of abstract examples in learning math. *Science, 320*, 454–455.

Kintsch, W. (1998). *Comprehension: A paradigm for cognition*. New York, NY: Cambridge University Press.

Kintsch, W., & van Dijk, T. (1978). Toward a model of text comprehension and production. *Psychological Review, 85*, 363–394. doi:10.1037/0033-295X.85.5.363

Langberg, J. M., & Smith, B. H. (2006). Developing evidence-based interventions for deployment into school settings: A case example highlighting key issues of efficacy and effectiveness. *Evaluation and Program Planning, 29*, 323–334. doi:10.1016/j.evalprogplan.2006.02.002

Langlois, J. A., Rutland-Brown, W., & Thomas, K. E. (2006). *Traumatic brain injury in the United States: Emergency department visits, hospitalizations, and deaths*. Atlanta, GA: Centers for Disease Control and Prevention, National Center for Injury Prevention and Control.

Lawson, A. (1985). A review of research on formal reasoning and science teaching. *Journal of Research in Science Teaching, 22*, 569–617. doi:10.1002/tea.3660220702

Lemke, M., Sen, A., Pahlke, E., Partelow, L., Miller, D., Williams, T., . . . Jocelyn, L. (2004). *International outcomes of learning in mathematics literacy and problem solving: PISA 2003 results from the U.S. perspective* (NCES 2005-003). Washington, DC: National Center for Education Statistics, Institute of Education Sciences, U.S. Department of Education.

Levin, H. S., Culhane, K. A., Mendelsohn, D., Lilly, M. A., Bruce, D., Fletcher, J. M., . . . Eisenberg, H. M. (1993). Cognition in relation to magnetic resonance imaging in head-injured children and adolescents. *Archives of Neurology, 50,* 897–905.

Malone, L. D., & Mastropieri, M. A. (1991). Reading comprehension instruction: Summarization and self-monitoring training for students with learning disabilities. *Exceptional Children, 58,* 270–279.

McNab, F., & Klingberg, T. (2008). Prefrontal cortex and basal ganglia control access to working memory. *Nature Neuroscience, 11,* 103–107. doi:10.1038/nn2024

Mendelsohn, D., Levin, H. S., Bruce, D., Lilly, M., Harward, H., Culhane, K. A., & Eisenberg, H. M. (1992). Late MRI after head injury in children: Relationship to clinical features and outcome. *Child's Nervous System, 8,* 445–452. doi:10.1007/BF00274405

Nichelli, P., Grafman, J., Pietrini, P., Clark, K., Lee, K. Y., & Miletich, R. (1995). Where the brain appreciates the moral of a story. *Neuroreport, 6,* 2309–2313. doi:10.1097/00001756-199511270-00010

Piaget, J. (1972). Intellectual evolution from adolescence to adulthood. *Human Development, 15,* 1–12. doi:10.1159/000271225

Ramsay, C. M., Sperling, R. A., & Dornisch, M. M. (2010). A comparison of the effects of students' expository text comprehension strategies [published online]. *Instructional Science.* doi:10.1007/s11251-008-9081-6

Reyna, V. F. (1996). Conceptions of memory development, with implications for reasoning and decision making. *Annals of Child Development, 12,* 87–118.

Reyna, V. F., & Brainerd, C. J. (1995). Fuzzy-trace theory: An interim synthesis. *Learning and Individual Differences, 7,* 1–75. doi:10.1016/1041-6080(95)90031-4

Reyna, V. F., & Kiernan, B. (1994). The development of gist versus verbatim memory in sentence recognition: Effects of lexical familiarity, semantic content, encoding instruction, and retention interval. *Developmental Psychology, 30,* 178–191. doi:10.1037/0012-1649.30.2.178

Reyna, V. F., Lloyd, F. J., & Brainerd, C. J. (2003). Memory, development, and rationality: An integrative theory of judgment and decision-making. In S. Schneider & J. Shanteau (Eds.), *Emerging perspectives on judgment and decision research* (pp. 201–245). New York, NY: Cambridge University Press.

Roberts, M., & Smith, D. D. (1980). The relationship among correct and error oral reading rates and comprehension. *Learning Disability Quarterly, 3,* 54–64. doi:10.2307/1510426

Robertson, D. A., Gernsbacher, M. A., Guidotti, S. J., Robertson, R. R. W., Irwin, W., Mock, B. J., & Campana, M. E. (2000). Functional neuroanatomy of the cognitive process of mapping during discourse comprehension. *Psychological Science, 11,* 255–260. doi:10.1111/1467-9280.00251

Schwartz, M. (2009). Cognitive development and learning: Analyzing the building of skills in classrooms. *Mind, Brain, and Education, 3,* 198–208. doi:10.1111/j.1751-228X.2009.01070.x

Somerville, L. H., Jones, R. M., & Casey, B. J. (2010). A time of change: Behavioral and neural correlates of adolescent sensitivity to appetitive and aversive environmental cues. *Brain and Cognition, 72*, 124–133. doi:10.1016/j.bandc.2009.07.003

Steinberg, L. (2005). Cognitive and affective development in adolescence. *Trends in Cognitive Sciences, 9*, 69–74. doi:10.1016/j.tics.2004.12.005

Sternberg, R. J. (2008). Increasing fluid intelligence is possible after all. *Proceedings of the National Academy of Sciences, USA, 105*, 6791–6792. doi:10.1073/pnas.0803396105

Strategic Memory and Reasoning Training (SMART). (n.d.) Provisional patent application 61/237,525 entitled "System for Strategic Memory and Reasoning Training (SMART)" was filed on 8/27/2009 and Patent Cooperation Treaty (PCT) patent application PCT/US2010/046849 entitled "Systems for Strategic Memory and Reasoning Training (SMART)" was filed on 8/26/2010.

Sung, Y. T., Chang, K. E., & Huang, J. S. (2008). Improving children's reading comprehension and use of strategies through computer-based strategy training. *Computers in Human Behavior, 24*, 1552–1571. doi:10.1016/j.chb.2007.05.009

Torgesen, J. K. (1980). Conceptual and educational implications of the use of efficient task strategies by learning disabled children. *Journal of Learning Disabilities, 13*, 19–26. doi:10.1177/002221948001300704

van Dijk, T. A. (1995). On macrostructure mental models and other inventions: A brief personal history of the Kintsch-van Dijk Theory. In C. A. Weaver, S. Mannes, & C. R. Fletcher (Eds.), *Discourse comprehension* (pp. 383–410). Hillsdale, NJ: Erlbaum.

Willis, C. (2009). *Creating inclusive learning environments for young children: What to do on Monday morning.* Thousand Oaks, CA: Corwin Press.

Wong, S., Chapman, S. B., Cook, L. G., Anand, R., Gamino, J. F., & Devous, M. D. (2006). A SPECT study of language and brain reorganization three years after pediatric brain injury. *Progress in Brain Research, 157*, 173–185.

III

LEARNING, REASONING, AND PROBLEM SOLVING

6

BETTER MEASUREMENT OF HIGHER COGNITIVE PROCESSES THROUGH LEARNING TRAJECTORIES AND DIAGNOSTIC ASSESSMENTS IN MATHEMATICS: THE CHALLENGE IN ADOLESCENCE

JERE CONFREY

Many students' failure to succeed in algebra can be traced to a failure to reason with variables representing underlying arithmetic relations. This failure often rests on student weakness with rational number reasoning (RNR). RNR develops gradually through elementary school and into middle school, and it revolves around the meaning of a/b (as fraction, ratio, and operator) situated within the operations of multiplication, division, addition, and subtraction. RNR culminates in the generalization linking division (as a divided by b) to ratios and fractions (as a:b or a/b). Successfully addressing student weakness in RNR depends on first developing better measures to assess its essential landmarks and obstacles in students' development of key concepts over time. Mathematics education researchers are identifying learning trajectories as a means to address learning over time and, from these, to build diagnostic assessments to help teachers address students' instructional needs. In this chapter, a learning trajectory for equipartitioning, the sharing of collections or wholes into equal-sized groups or parts, is described as a foundation for RNR, and shown to evolve gradually from kindergarten to eighth grade.

Adolescence is the period in which foundational concepts and skills acquired in elementary school must be deepened in order for higher order cognition to mature. For example, facility with multiplication, division, and elementary fractions must be deepened and interconnected with reasoning, problem solving, and decision making to solve complex problems involving ratio, proportion decimals, and percentage. Although higher order cognition can and should be part of education at all levels, by adolescence the shift to higher cognition is imperative. Unfortunately, progress toward this goal has been impeded by inadequate measurement of higher order cognition, particularly when concepts develop gradually over time. Typical measures of conceptual knowledge in mathematics capture only a snapshot of what a student knows; as such, school assessments exert a detrimental effect on instruction (Shepard, 1996; Pellegrino, 2004). Overreliance on rote multiple-choice testing and the predictable sampling of easily measured standards and objectives have contributed to tendencies to game the test rather than strengthen student achievement (Brosnan et al., 2003; Confrey & Carrejo, 2002).

A fundamental aspect of creating better measures and assessments is an understanding of the higher order cognitive processes themselves. In the field of mathematics, for a particular cluster of topics, this requires careful attention to (a) sets of related mathematical ideas, (b) forms of reasoning characteristic of the discipline, and (c) the evolution of learning from naïve to sophisticated ideas in relation to student thinking. Once this understanding is in place, one can move to build new forms of assessment for the clusters of concepts. Such assessments—to inform teachers of the progress made by their students, over time, at a fine-grained level—can usher in a new meaning for diagnostic assessments, one based not on descriptions of deficits but on identifying the key constructs necessary for supporting the development of advanced reasoning. In this chapter, I select one cluster of topics that is critical to success in advanced mathematics and show how the emerging construct of learning trajectories can lead to the development of more sophisticated assessments.

Specifically, I argue for strengthening higher cognitive processes of adolescents in *rational number reasoning* (RNR). RNR includes the topics of multiplication, division, fraction, ratio, rate, decimals, percentages, similarity, and scaling. Failure to gain competence in RNR represents a critical barrier to successful entrance to algebra (National Mathematics Advisory Panel, 2008) and the learning of advanced mathematics (Hiebert & Behr, 1988) for many students. Proficiency in RNR underlies a variety of applied skills across multiple disciplines both in and out of school (Nunes Schliemann, & Carraher, 1993; Schliemann et al., 1998). Early adolescence is the critical time for securing proficiency in these skills, though their initial development should begin much earlier (Harel & Confrey, 1994; Nunes et al., 1993).

A synthesis of the RNR literature establishes the three distinct meanings and use of the symbolic expression a/b: fraction, ratio, and operator. Proficiency with each of these three meanings, and in distinguishing among them, is essential for success in mastering algebra and advanced mathematical concepts

(Hiebert & Behr, 1988). Having most students successfully acquire that proficiency depends in part on developing better assessments that measure key aspects of higher cognitive thinking. Such assessments matter because they provide feedback to teachers and school systems regarding the extent to which the goals of higher cognition have been achieved by individual students.

In this chapter, the idea of a *learning trajectory* is introduced as a means to describe characteristics of the path of progressive understanding that emerges as a child encounters these ideas—over time and through instruction—and moves toward more complex understanding. *Equipartitioning,* a newly synthesized construct, is then introduced as the foundation of these three key concepts. A learning trajectory for equipartitioning is introduced, along with an accompanying process to develop assessments associated with this trajectory. This process of developing cognitively valid assessments for measuring student progress on key mathematics concepts is suggested as a means to support better student preparation for the study of algebra and advanced mathematics in adolescence.

LEARNING TRAJECTORIES

Learning trajectories can be envisioned as potential paths through a "conceptual corridor" (Brown, 1992; Confrey, 2006; Lehrer & Schauble, 2004), in which certain landmarks and obstacles must be properly negotiated (Figure 6.1). Local (district), state, and common core standards could serve as the boundary constraints (banks-of-a-stream metaphor shown in Figure 6.1) for the conceptual corridor, implemented through the periodic administration of associated valid diagnostic assessments.

To be useful across learning, instructional, and assessment contexts, however, learning trajectories must be based on evidence of student learning. A learning trajectory is defined as

> an empirically-supported description of the ordered network of constructs a student encounters through instruction (i.e. activities, tasks, tools, forms of interaction and methods of evaluation), in order to move from informal ideas, through successive refinements of representation, articulation, and reflection, towards increasingly complex concepts over time. (Confrey, 2008)

A number of features of learning trajectories separate this approach from others:

- "Learning trajectories" are models of students' likely paths.
- "Empirically supported" refers to a three-step process: reviewing and synthesizing the relevant literature, asking outside experts to review our syntheses, and conducting further empirical studies.

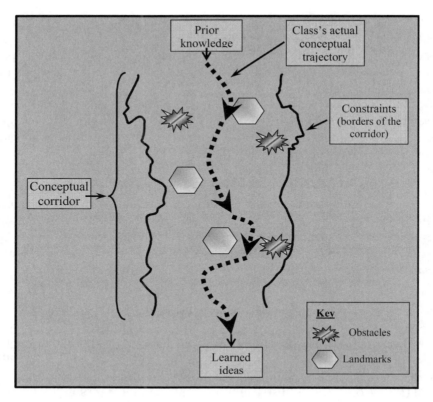

Figure 6.1. A learning trajectory within a conceptual corridor. From *The Cambridge Handbook of the Learning Sciences* (p. 146), by R. K. Sawyer, 2006, New York, NY: Cambridge University Press. Copyright 2006 Cambridge University Press. Reprinted with permission.

- "Through instruction" involves the recognition that students will progress only if given appropriate opportunities to learn the material and that these opportunities are carefully sequenced to intentionally support the trajectory (which does not imply "direct instruction").
- "Through successive refinements" is included to emphasize the need for students' active involvement in the learning process and their engagement in cycles of problem-solving behavior. This overall approach involves supporting constructivist practices such as building on experience, using student language as a bridge to technical vocabulary, supporting discourse that advances learning, using contextual problems to enhance learning, and so forth. Further, choices of curriculum and technology influence the course of the learning trajectory.

To account at least in part for movement within the trajectories toward increasingly higher cognitive reasoning, it has proven useful to distinguish a variety of cognitive behaviors.

- Strategies, used to solve the problems, are typically seen at the lower levels as students simply try to solve the tasks (e.g., dealing as a means to share a collection).
- Mathematical reasoning practices are used to explain the strategies and solutions, including naming and justifying, and must be discussed with children as conventions of mathematical practice (e.g., showing the equivalent height of stacks of coins to establish equality).
- Emergent properties and relations of the mathematics, which act as local generalizations to guide future approaches, occur as students coordinate the strategies and the practices to begin to anticipate solutions and propose classifications of tasks and regularities in approaches (e.g., if more people share, then each person's share will be smaller).
- Systematic tendencies toward certain errors or misconceptions and their resolutions are noted as likely or compelling alternative ways to operate, that need to be addressed (e.g., cutting a circle with horizontal cuts is not an effective way to make fair shares, even though it works for rectangles).
- Generalizations of increasing power slowly emerge as the categories and cases merge (e.g., sharing m things among n people results in shares of size m/n).

SYNTHESIS: THREE KEY CONSTRUCTS FOR A/B IN RATIONAL NUMBER REASONING

To synthesize the research on RNR, we examined the theoretical claims and the empirical evidence on children's thinking, strategies, and methods, and developed a framework to compare and contrast results. Syntheses are not simply literature reviews. As Cooper (1998) wrote, "The investigator must propose overarching schemes that help make sense of many related but not identical studies" (p. 12). Our aim in constructing these syntheses is to identify areas of consensus about children's thinking. As a result, "the cumulative results are more complex than any single study, because they have to explain higher-order relations" (p. 13). Not everything in the synthesis has to come directly from the reviewed articles themselves. As stated by Cooper, "Perhaps the most challenging circumstance in the social sciences occurs when a new concept is introduced to explain old findings" (p. 17). Finding

EXHIBIT 6.1
Publications Grouped by Rational Number Reasoning Topic

Partitioning (30)	Multiplication and Division (93)
Area and Volume (56)	Fractions (137)
Ratio, Proportion, and Rate (129)	Decimals and Percentages (30)
Similarity and Scaling (30)	Probability (23)

Note. Each publication was designated with a single topic, though the content of many publications applies to more than one topic.

the construct for equipartitioning and recognizing its importance represented this kind of synthetic activity.

In initially reviewing the RNR literature, we identified six topical or conceptual subareas: (a) equipartitioning/splitting; (b) multiplication and division, (c) fractions, ratio, and rate; (d) area and volume; (e) similarity and scaling; and (f) decimals and percentages. In constructing the syntheses, we reviewed major journals (in English), books and monographs, and refereed conference proceedings; we also solicited contributions directly from researchers in the field. We built a database (Confrey et al., 2008) for the studies, recording the following information for each study: title, author, source type, theoretical/empirical nature of the study, topic, grade level, assessment items, the study demographics, analysis, and abstract. Exhibit 6.1 shows the number of articles in each topic.

The synthesis work produced a number of key findings. First, the six constructs for a/b, proposed in the seminal work of the Rational Number Project[1] were simplified to three major meanings: a/b as a fraction, as a ratio, and as an operator. The construct a/b as a fraction (in which a and b are integers) refers to measuring a quantity whose magnitude is either a whole unit of that quantity or lies between two whole units of that quantity. This version of a/b can refer to lengths, areas, volumes, any continuous quantity, or even a discontinuous quantity that can be treated as continuous (e.g., numbers of apples, assuming each apple can be partitioned into equal sections). The essential characteristic of a/b as a fraction is that its meaning is defined in relation to a specified unit of one. Thus, if two fractional quantities are to be compared, for instance 1/2 and 2/3, or even 1/4 and 6/5, they are assumed to share a common-sized unit of one.

In contrast, a/b as a ratio refers to the relative size of a and b. While a and b are defined in terms of some unit, those units may relate to *different* types of quantities (e.g., 35 miles per 1 hour). The meaning of equivalence in the case of ratios is described in terms of an invariance among the relative size of

---

[1]http://www.cehd.umn.edu/rationalnumberproject

a and *b*, such that that relationship is preserved when *a* and *b* are changed by the same factor (known as a scale factor). Based on this, if *a* and *b* happen to share the same unit, then the ratio *a/b* can also be regarded as a fraction. Thus, fractions are ratios, with the numerator and denominator sharing the same unit of one, but ratios are not always fractions.

Finally, *a/b* as an operator refers to situations in which one multiplies *a/b* × *m* to produce *am/b*. There are two instances to consider with such multiplication: referent-preserving and referent-transforming (Schwartz, 1988). In the *referent-preserving* instance, such as in the problem, "If two thirds of the 12 apple trees were blighted, how many trees were blighted?" the 2/3 refers to two trees out of every three trees. Thus, the meaning of the operator can be understood as a composition of factors. Instead of multiplication by a simple scale factor, *m* (e.g., twice as many trees), the problem incorporates a composition of two scale factors: $1/b^{th}$ of (equivalent to dividing by *b*, and often viewed as a "shrink," if *b* > 1), followed by a "stretch" by a factor *a*.

In contrast, in the *referent-transforming* instance, the operator acts as a ratio, acting on another ratio to transform the quantities. For example, if the price per ticket is $3 per two tickets and one sells 36 tickets (for a performance), then the result is that one divides the set of tickets into groups of two (18) and multiples by the price per group of two (18 × $3), to get a total amount of $54 (for the performance). Both instances are examples of *a/b* as an operator.

A second critical result of the synthesis work concerned the identification of the primitive construct that has been named *equipartitioning* (Confrey, Maloney, Nguyen, Mojica, & Myers, 2009; Confrey, Maloney, Nguyen, & Wilson, in press) or *splitting* (Confrey, 1988). Equipartitioning/splitting refers to cognitive behaviors that have the goal of producing equal-sized groups (from collections) or pieces (from continuous wholes). This construct, discussed at greater length below, derived from recognizing the centrality of fair sharing in young children's lives. Overall, the literature described three cases of fair sharing, but those cases were employed in various individual studies, and no other researchers had tried to follow the development of children systematically across all three cases:

- Case A: sharing a collection of *mn* objects fairly among *n* children, where *m* and *n* are natural numbers;
- Case B: sharing a single whole among *n* children; and
- Case C: sharing multiple wholes, *m*, among *n* children where *n* is not a factor of *m*, producing fractional shares (proper and improper fractions).

Based on study of the development of children in solving a sequence of these problems, in a set of clinical interviews ($N = 52$; grades K–6), an underlying learning trajectory was proposed. The underlying conjecture of the work is that equipartitioning acts as the foundation for rational number reasoning and the development of the related constructs.

The third critical recognition in the synthesis work was the role of dimensionality[2] in the approach. When children share a collection of mn objects among n people, the result can be described as many-to-one (m objects per child) or as many-as-one, a group of m objects. Our research suggested that these two descriptions lead differentially to (a) a ratio construct and (b) representation of single-dimensional quantities—"extensive quantities" (Schwartz, 1988) and fractions-as-numbers.

When children maintain awareness of both dimensions (many objects per person or many-to-one, as opposed to many-as-one), they are prepared to preserve the relation and to develop a new notion of equivalence. This equivalence is exemplified by 12 objects for three children being *the same as* four objects *per one child*, that is, the equivalence of the relation between two quantities (objects and children), instead of the number of either quantity. Visually, this can be illustrated by a two-dimensional coordinate plane in which one axis represents the number of objects (x) and the other axis represents the number of children among whom the objects are shared (y). The coordinate point $(12, 3)$ lies on the same vector as the point $(4, 1)$ because the relationship between objects and people is the same but is not positioned on the same point in the plane. This is distinct from the case in which two quantities are named relative to the same unit and are represented as equivalent fractions located on the same point on a number line.

Now, if children were to think of the problem as 12 objects partitioned equally into three groups of four and disregard the fixity of the relationship between objects and people, they are more likely to be setting up the idea that 12 objects divided by 3 (split into three piles) equals 4 or, more precisely, four objects. This idea leads readily toward what is known as *partitive division* and thence to its inverse, *multiplication*, as "times as many." There is only one salient dimension here, namely, objects. The splitting operation in this instance establishes the foundation of the ideas of a scalar (a dimensionless number possessing only magnitude) and a scaling factor.

Likewise, if in sharing a single whole among n people, children see the result not as $1/n^{\text{th}}$ *per child*, but instead simply as a "part," then fractional parts are produced within the construct many-as-one. Based on Case A, children

---

[2]Dimension and quantity are distinguished here. *Quantity* refers to the amount or magnitude of something one has, and it is measured in units of some kind. For instance, a quantity of honey can be measured in tablespoonfuls. Quantity of people can be measured simply in numbers of people. When the units of a quantity are discrete, it is typical to measure them in numbers (though not always; for instance, one may have potatoes as discrete objects, but one may also measure them as continuous, by weight, with the units being grams or pounds). If a situation involves two distinct quantities, we refer to it as *two-dimensional*. Each dimension can be used to represent a quantity. Dimensions can also be enumerated, and identified as representing a quantity.

can develop an understanding of the other meaning of equivalence by (a) sharing one whole into three equal parts by equipartitioning and giving each recipient one part (1/3) or (b) equipartitioning the whole into six equal parts and giving each participant two parts (2/6). These two solutions are equivalent, in the sense of equal quantities or amounts within a single dimension; this can be physically demonstrated by the way the parts coincide when placed on top of each other. It is important to keep in mind, however, that since fractions are ratios, they also carry the other meaning of equivalence, that is, they express an equivalent relation such that 3:1::6:2.

Because the operations of division and multiplication can be either referent preserving or referent transforming, thus applying both to many-to-one and many-as one relations, they are building on equipartitioning as a foundation.

A conceptual map (see Figure 6.2) was devised to represent the evolution of each of these three major constructs over time and their interrelationships. Ideally, the map would probably be better viewed as a cylinder, so that the ratio construct would be linked to the fractional construct as well, but this is not feasible in the context of display in two dimensions.

Equipartitioning is represented by the concepts displayed as black rectangles with white type. With fair sharing as its initial concept, it serves as the foundation for RNR. The left side of the map (gray, oval boxes) represents the development of the ratio concept, maintaining "many-to-one" relationships established in equipartitioning. It evolves into a concept of equal distribution, explicated by Streefland (1991) in his studies of young children's ideas of how a group of people could be distributed among tables so that each subgroup would receive equal proportions of pizza. This extends to proto-ratio (Resnick & Singer, 1993) and to the subsequent evolution of ratio tables and ratio units (Confrey & Scarano, 1995), graphing ratios as vectors in two dimensions (Confrey & Scarano, 1995; Kaput & West, 1994), and on to a fuller concept of ratio. Vergnaud (1988, 1994) explains simple ratio and proportion in relation to two measures M_1 and M_2 with values a, b, c, and d, for which a and c are values of M_1 and b and d are values of M_2.

In contrast, the right side of the map contains the development of length, area, and volume as quantity and of fractions as extensions of whole numbers. After addressing comparison and equivalence of fractions, the introduction of operations on fractions parallels the conventional approaches with whole numbers, ordered as addition, subtraction, multiplication, and division.

Within the RNR map, however, multiplication and division (and ratios) are derived directly from equipartitioning—because equipartitioning leads to partitive division and to multiplication as reassembly (Confrey et al., 2009; Confrey et al., in press). Only later is division as repeated subtraction introduced, as is multiplication as repeated addition. The distributive law forms a critical bridge between the operations of multiplication and addition.

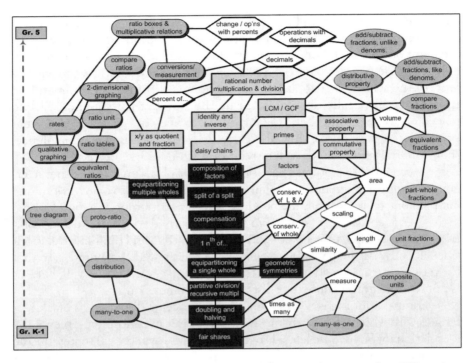

Figure 6.2. Learning trajectories approach to rational number reasoning. Different learning trajectories are represented by different shape and shading combinations. Learning trajectories are: Equipartitioning (dark rectangles), Multiplication and Division (light rectangles), Ratio and Proportion (gray ovals), Fraction (gray ellipses), Length and Area (pentagons), Similarity and Scaling (diamonds), and Decimals and Percent (hexagons). change/op'ns with percents = change and operations with percents; conserv. of whole = conservation of the whole; conserv. of L&A = conservation of length and area.

The map illustrates the foundational position of equipartitioning in rational number reasoning. The map of the RNR topics also illustrates the interrelationships among the various ideas in a rich and flexible way. It visually distinguishes the three distinct meanings of *a/b*—as ratio (left side), fraction (right side), and operator (middle). Finally, it demonstrates how a rich and complex set of interrelationships can be analyzed as strands of concepts, a learning trajectory approach.

Further, the map supports two interpretations for the overall sequencing of the development of RNR reasoning. In traditional programs, multiplication and division are developed as outgrowths of counting, addition, and subtraction. Fractions are sequenced by applying concepts of equivalent fractions, after which the operations of addition and subtraction are developed. Multiplication and division of fractions are taught last, and fractions are then extended to decimals and percentages. Ratio and proportion are typically delayed until middle grades.

In contrast to the traditional approach, a broader base for RNR is proposed. Equipartitioning is used to develop multiplication and division. Ratio and proportion are simultaneously developed in parallel with fractions. On the basis of this parallel structure, students would gradually develop complex reasoning through interplay among the concepts, rather than learning them in a linear series. Confrey introduced children to the ideas in parallel during a 3-year teaching experiment that resulted in children entering middle school with robust ideas of ratio and with strong interrelationships among multiplication, division, and fractions (Confrey & Scarano, 1995).

ELABORATING EQUIPARTITIONING/SPLITTING AS A LEARNING TRAJECTORY

The most notable context for equipartitoining or splitting—producing equal-sized groups (from collections) or pieces (from continuous wholes) is *fair sharing,* in which a collection, a whole, or multiple wholes are to be equally distributed among a set of individuals. It is important to explicitly emphasize that equipartitioning/splitting is not breaking, fracturing, fragmenting, or segmenting in which unequal parts can results. In the following sections, the levels of proficiency in the learning trajectory are characterized in terms of students' behaviors, utterances, and explanations.

The literature on equipartitioning suggests that very young children show competence at Case A (defined in the previous section), sharing a collection fairly by dealing out equal portions, as one would deal cards (Frydman & Bryant, 1988; Pepper, 1991). Children do this systematically by establishing a one-to-one correspondence between the objects and each recipient in each "round" of dealing. They typically express confidence in the equivalence of the results, sometimes checking by counting. Pepper (1991) and Pepper and Hunting (1998) provided evidence that children's competence in splitting collections does not depend on their ability to count. More sophisticated responses include dealing using composite units (dealing two or three objects at once) and even shifts in unit size as students approach the termination of the count. In the learning trajectory matrix, Case A is listed at the bottom (Figure 6.3), indicating it is the most elementary level.

Case B, sharing a whole, incorporates more complexity and variation in children's activities and varied levels of success. When sharing a rectangular or circular whole, the two-split (i.e., splitting into two equal parts) is foundational. The four- and eight-splits are next easiest, as children often learn these as splits of splits (to get four equal parts) and splits-of-splits-of-splits (eight),

Equipartitioning Learning Trajectory Matrix (grades K–8)

Task Classes→

Proficiency Levels	A Collections	B 2-split (Rect/Circle)	C 2^n split (Rect)	D 2^n split (Circle)	E Even split (Rect)	F Odd split (Rect)	G Even split (Circle)	H Odd split (Circle)	I Arbitrary integer split	J $p = n + 1$; $p = n-1$	K p is odd, and $n = 2^i$	L $p \gg n$, p close to n	M all p, all n (integers)
16 *Generalize*: a among $b = a/b$													
15 *Distributive property*, multiple wholes													
14 *Direct-, inverse- and co-variation*													
13 *Compositions* of splits, multiple wholes													
12 Equipartition *multiple wholes*													
11 Assert *continuity principle*													
10 *Transitivity* arguments													
9 Redistribution of shares (*quantitative*)													
8 Factor-based changes (*quantitative*)													
7 *Compositions* of splits; *factor-pairs*													
6 *Qualitative compensation*													
5 *Re-assemble*: n times as much													
4 *Name* a share w.r.t. the referent unit													
3 *Justify* the results of equipartitioning													
2 *Equipartition single wholes*													
1 *Equipartition collections*													

Figure 6.3. Equipartitioning learning trajectory. Proficiency levels comprise the vertical dimension. Task classes (problem contexts) comprise the horizontal dimension. w.r.t. = with respect to.

showing the power of recursively applying the two-split. In the case of the rectangle, many children will discover that they can make $n-1$ parallel cuts to produce n splits vertically or horizontally. Even-numbered splits tend to be easier than splits to produce odd numbers of parts, because for even splits, children can use the binary split as a subgoal and starting point. Surprisingly, children repeatedly showed that they found it easier on a circle to construct a six-split than a three-split (unless a child had previously been explicitly taught the three-split). They typically bisected a circle first, and then made three-splits on each of the circle halves. The resulting straight edge of the semicircle seems to support the development of the radial cut (from the center of the circle but not completely through the diameter), whereas the full circle does not. Recognition of the varied difficulty of tasks in different contexts led to the vertical levels of the trajectory, with a horizontal dimension that specifies a variety of task classes (Figure 6.3).

Children learn far more than to simply generate correct solutions to these problems. The physical action of sharing, including how it is accomplished, is an important element of what and how children learn. Folding a piece a paper is different from cutting or marking it, and the different types of activities produce different insights (Empson & Turner, 2006; Lamon, 1996). For instance, with cutting it is not uncommon to witness children using the congruence of the parts by stacking one piece on top of the other. When folding, congruence is built directly into the activity through symmetries, but the result of the action is hidden until the paper is unfolded, providing opportunities to examine one's predictions. These kinds of insights, which involve both the "strategies" children use to solve a problem and the "representations" or inscriptions produced by children as part of the solution, are used to increase students' repertoires of approaches to novel tasks.

A second class of cognitive behaviors involves social aspects of mathematics: describing, naming, and justifying to others (all aspects of communicating their thinking to others, as well as attempting to secure their own mathematical language). For instance, when children are asked to justify the equality of shares, they may (a) count, (b) stack pieces or parts, (c) spontaneously create arrays of the number of shares by the number of objects and show the correspondences, or (d) form similar patterns of sets in clusters. Naming is another mathematical practice fundamental to RNR proficiency. For instance, children may name the result of a collection of 10 objects shared fairly between two people as (a) five objects, (b) one half of the collection, (c) five objects per person, or (d) one half of the collection per person. The differences in naming rest in the *many-to-one* and *many-as-one* distinctions and in the choice of reference unit, what is considered as the unit whole of the problem. As one examines the trajectory levels, and the practices of justifying (level 3) and naming (level 4) come after the initial activities of demonstrating the process of fair sharing.

In the equipartitioning learning trajectory, the next level is that of "reassembly," often expressed as "times as many" or "times as much." Piaget (1970) stressed the importance of reversibility in the development of operations. Children need to understand that they can reverse equipartitioning to reconstruct the whole. The reversal of equipartitioning is reassembly, not counting. This reassembly is the foundation of multiplication, just as equipartitioning is the foundation of partitive division. In a collection, the whole collection, mn, is n times as many as the fair share m, because there are n groups of m objects. It is also true that the collection equals $m + m + m \ldots$ (n times, as repeated addition), but what is significant is that the size of the collection or of the whole is n times as large as the result or the part. A consequence of the distinction between the collection or whole as m times n vs. $m + m + m \ldots$ will become more apparent at proficiency level 7, "composition of splits," at which students engage with splitting a split and its reassembly.

Proficiency levels 6 through 11 express another critical element of learning trajectory, namely, "emergent properties." Emergent properties are mathematical ideas that may eventually transform into critical elements of the "rules of arithmetic" or formal properties of mathematics. From a students' point of view, these comprise intermediate levels of generalization, guide student solutions to solve more complex tasks, and provide access to more sophisticated ideas. The equipartitioning learning trajectory includes the following emergent properties:

- *Qualitative (level 6) and then quantitative (level 8, factor-based changes) compensation.* At the qualitative level, young children understand that if more or fewer children share, the fair shares will be smaller or larger, respectively. When this becomes quantitative compensation, they understand that these changes in number of persons imply factor-based changes in the size of the shares. That is, if twice as many people must share, a resulting fair share will be half as large as for the original number of persons, but if just one more person shares, a fair share is not simply one less item of a collection.

- *Composition of splits (level 7).* A critical recognition is the idea of composition of splits, which entails splitting the results of a previous split. The earliest or most accessible version of this is cutting a rectangle both vertically and then horizontally. When initially presented with this situation, children often predict that, for instance, a two-split followed by a three-split (in the orthogonal direction), will produce five equal shares. However, recognizing that the three-split acts *on* the two-split as a composition (resulting in six equal shares, or 2×3) allows a child to turn an additive misconception into a multiplicative conception, which is critical in understanding multiplication and repeated multiplication. In the context of repeated splits and their reassembly, the recursive action of equipartitioning becomes differentiated from the iterative actions of addition and subtraction.

- *Redistribution of shares (level 9).* For a single continuous whole or a collection of objects, either of which has already been equipartitioned, changing the number of persons sharing may involve redistributing one or more of the shares (if reducing the number of persons), or distributing parts of each existing share until equivalence of shares is achieved (increasing the number of persons). Thus, equipartitioning a collection can be accomplished either by equipartitioning the entire collection directly or by breaking the collection into unequal portions, equipartitioning each of the portions, and adding the fair shares together.

- *Transitivity arguments (level 10).* Laying the foundation for transitive properties, students recognize the equivalence of fair shares of identical continuous wholes, even when the wholes are split in noncongruent ways into the same number of fair shares. For instance, a rectangular whole might be split for two persons either by a horizontal cut or by a diagonal cut. The resulting fair shares are not congruent, but, regardless of the way the fair split is made, the result is still halves of the original whole. When students learn to claim that, for example, the triangular half is equal to the rectangular half, either by decomposing one shape into the other, or by reasoning based on the equivalence of their being halves of the same sized whole, they are applying an emergent transitive property of equivalence. In using transitivity arguments, students build on earlier proficiency levels, including naming, and explicitly assert equivalence of shares based on the process of the equipartitioning itself.

- *Continuity arguments (level 11).* As students extend their strategies to a variety of different values for splits, they become prepared to assert that any whole could be shared fairly among any number of people.

The upper levels (12 through 16) of the equipartitioning learning trajectory extend the ideas into Case C, sharing of multiple wholes among multiple people to produce fractional parts as fair shares (proper and improper fractions and mixed numbers). Researchers using instances of this case have documented that students employ a variety of strategies to solve these problems (Charles & Nason, 2000; Lamon, 1996; Toluk & Middleton, 2004). However, as students encountered more complex or challenging versions of these problems, they reverted to more primitive methods and demonstrated considerable context sensitivity and instability of approaches. For instance, students asked to share multiple cookies among multiple people would resist splitting the cookies (too crumbly), but if asked the same question involving multiple pizzas (and with multiple types of toppings), many students would equipartition individual pizzas to give each person an equal amount of each type of pizza. Overall, three major strategies were documented:

- With more objects to share (m) than people (n), students would first reduce the problem to $m = r + jn$, in which j was the largest multiple of n that fit into the number of items m. Then, they would solve the problem of sharing the remaining r wholes among n people; the answer would be a mixed number, $j + r/n$. In particular, if $m = 1 + jn$, students could use this strategy to solve the problem as a Case A (collections) problem combined with a Case B (single continuous whole) problem.
- With fewer objects than people ($m < n$), students would frequently partition the m objects into benchmark parts (halves, quarters, eighths), creating a collection of mp parts ($p = 2, 4,$ or 8), and hope that this collection of parts could be fairly shared among the n people by dealing.
- Regardless of the size of m or n, some students would equipartition each whole into n fair shares and recognize that each person would receive m $1/n^{\text{th}}$ parts, or m/n wholes.

The first two strategies constitute a way to shift the problem to a Case A (collections) problem involving different units. However, students often exhibited difficulty in naming the results due to the presence of mixed or new units or a lack of confidence in what unit to use as the reference unit in relation to the shares. For instance, students might experience difficulty in determining whether the result of sharing five parts among seven people should be called one seventh (of the five wholes) or five sevenths (of one whole). Full understanding of this level (12) produces facility with both names. At level 15 (distributivity), students can explain the equivalence of the different methods and of the names in relation to different referent units.

In level 14 (direct- inverse- and covariation), students recognize that another way to preserve fair shares is to partition the number of objects and the number of persons sharing with the same split. This results in a form of covariation often captured by a table of values and can produce a single fair share as a unit ratio (the number of items per person; Confrey, 1995; Neuman, 1993; Streefland, 1991).

Thus, the culmination of the learning trajectory produces the broadest possible generalization, *a* shared among *b* equals *a/b* per person. It is important to stress that although students are often taught this generalization as an assertion, without the underlying proficiencies such a generalization is merely a form of "pseudoconcept" (Vygotsky, 1986). Without experiencing a full range of strategies, representations, mathematical practices, emergent properties, and reconciliation of misconceptions, students are unlikely to gain the necessary proficiencies required for more complex applications of rational number reasoning.

In fact, data collected via clinical interviews and field testing of assessment items suggest that if the concepts of equipartitioning are not learned in the early grades, they continue to impede students' performance in the higher grades. Middle school students fail to solve related problems if they have not engaged with the range of concepts to build up knowledge of the strategies, representations, practices, properties, and generalizations. The misconceptions arise again and again under pressure as the problems become even more difficult during high school. Hence, one of the most important challenges in adolescence is to achieve deeper understanding of mathematical concepts such as rational numbers in order to robustly extend this understanding to novel and complex problems.

BUILDING DIAGNOSTIC ASSESSMENTS FOR HIGHER COGNITIVE PROCESSES

Assessments drive instructional practice. There is a clear need for better assessment measures that drive instruction to support students' improved cognitive proficiency. In mathematics, better assessments come from selecting topics of critical importance to advancement in mathematical study, such as RNR. In addition, those measures must tap into documented patterns of student reasoning that are associated with the discipline and which provide evidence of steady movement toward increased proficiency in the topics.

The identification of the critical proficiency levels in a learning trajectory such as equipartitioning is the foundation for building such new assessments. To do this, items are constructed to match proficiency levels and task classes. In the example shown in Figures 6.4 and 6.5, the item assesses level 12 on equipartitioning multiple wholes among multiple people.

Based on clinical interviews, an outcome space is defined for each level. Items are designed and then field-tested with a broad spectrum of students—across geographic region, socioeconomic status, cultural backgrounds, and

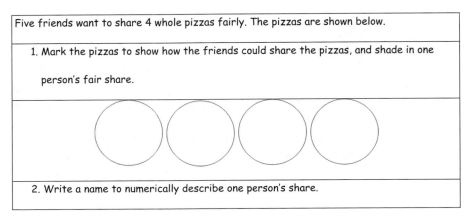

Five friends want to share 4 whole pizzas fairly. The pizzas are shown below.

1. Mark the pizzas to show how the friends could share the pizzas, and shade in one

person's fair share.

2. Write a name to numerically describe one person's share.

Figure 6.4. Item pertaining to level 12 (Equipartition multiple wholes), task class J
($p = n + 1$; $p = n - 1$)

grades—to ascertain whether the item captures varied student solutions. In the example (Figure 6.4), students are asked to share four pizzas among five people. The rubric (Figure 6.5) displays a variety of responses and how they are scored. Full credit is given for equipartitioning each pizza into five equal parts, sharing one part of each pizza, and then naming the result: 4/5 of a pizza. Partial credit is given for correctly representing equipartitioning but failing to identify or to correctly name one person's fair share: for example (second row, Figure 6.5), the student should have specified, verbally or by drawing and labeling, that a single piece is 1/20 of the four pizzas and that each person would receive four of these pieces, or 4/5 of one pizza, and 4/20 or 1/5 of all of the pizza. Partial credit is also assigned for correctly recognizing that one person's share is 20% of the total pizza but drawing horizontal—and unequal— uts on the pizzas (third row, Figure 6.5). Zero points are given for completely incorrect responses, such as equipartitioning each pizza into four parts. Note that none of the written responses shows clear evidence of knowledge of describing the reference unit, resulting in ambiguity for both the responses "4/5" and "20%."

These assessments are designed to inform teachers of their students' progress over time at a fine-grained level and therefore to provide a new approach to diagnostic assessment. Developing such assessments based on definitive evidence of patterns of student thinking over time is a time-consuming, resource-intensive process. If it results in valid diagnostics that can inform educators of both student progress and student needs across a range of ages, proficiency levels, and backgrounds, it will propel the field forward.

Level	Description	Exemplar
2	For #1, creates accurate equipartitions and shades one person's share AND For #2, names the share as one of the following: • 4/5 of one pizza (or equivalent fraction) • 1/5 of all pizza • 1/5 of each pizza • 4 of the 20 slices (or equivalent) • other correct rational number (Note: a count of pizza slices without a referent unit is not awarded credit)	1. Mark the pizzas to show how the friends could share the pizzas, and shade in one person's fair share. 2. Write a name to numerically describe one person's share. $\frac{4}{5}$
1	A. For #1, creates accurate equipartitions and shades one person's share AND For #2, does not name the share as one of the following: • 4/5 of one pizza (or equivalent fraction) • 1/5 of all pizza • 1/5 of each pizza • 4 of the 20 slices (or equivalent) • other correct rational number	1. Mark the pizzas to show how the friends could share the pizzas, and shade in one person's fair share. 2. Write a name to numerically describe one person's share. $\frac{1}{20}$

(continues)

Figure 6.5. Scoring rubric for item in Figure 6.4.

		Five friends want to share 4 whole pizzas fairly. The pizzas are shown below.
	B. For #1, <u>does not</u> create accurate equipartitions and shades one person's share AND For #2, names the share as one of the following: • 4/5 of one pizza (or equivalent fraction) • 1/5 of all pizza • 1/5 of each pizza • 4 of the 20 slices (or equivalent) • other correct rational number (Note: a count of pizza slices without a referent unit is not awarded credit)	1. Mark the pizzas to show how the friends could share the pizzas, and shade in one person's fair share. 2. Write a name to numerically describe one person's share. 20 percent
0	Incorrect or unintelligible	1. Mark the pizzas to show how the friends could share the pizzas, and shade in one person's fair share. 2. Write a name to numerically describe one person's share. I D ¼
	I. Insufficient Evidence	
8	No Response	

Figure 6.5. Scoring rubric for item in Figure 6.4.

JERE CONFREY

174

Additionally, responses on this item should be coded with the following, if applicable.

Code	Exemplar
O: Creates *n+1* parts instead of *n* parts (# of cuts versus # of parts)	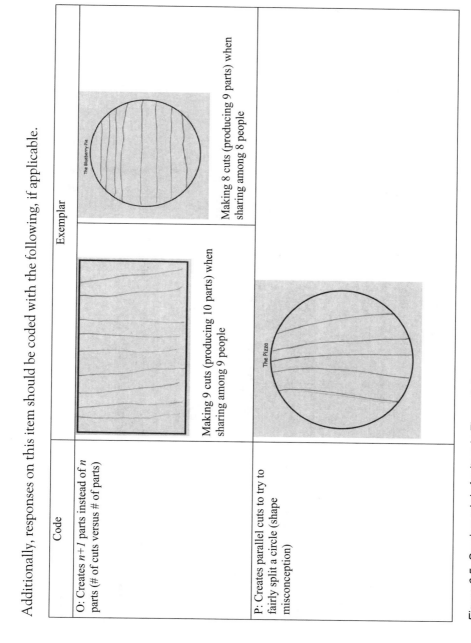 Making 9 cuts (producing 10 parts) when sharing among 9 people
	Making 8 cuts (producing 9 parts) when sharing among 8 people
P: Creates parallel cuts to try to fairly split a circle (shape misconception)	

Figure 6.5. Scoring rubric for item in Figure 6.4.

(continues)

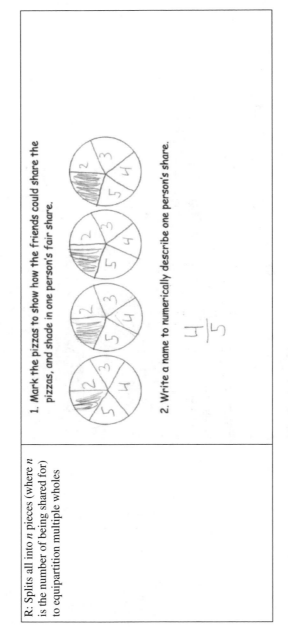

R: Splits all into *n* pieces (where *n* is the number of being shared for) to equipartition multiple wholes

1. Mark the pizzas to show how the friends could share the pizzas, and shade in one person's fair share.

2. Write a name to numerically describe one person's share.

$$\frac{4}{5}$$

Figure 6.5. Scoring rubric for item in Figure 6.4.

S: Creates benchmarks to equipartition multiple wholes	
U: Uses coordinated splitting to equipartition multiple wholes	No exemplar
W: Names as m/nth of one whole (improper fraction)	2. Write a name to numerically describe one person's share.
X: Names as 1/nth of all wholes	⁹⁄₆ of 7 pizzas

Figure 6.5. Scoring rubric for item in Figure 6.4.

(continues)

| Y: Names as 1/nth of each whole | 2. Write a name to numerically describe one person's share.

1 person = $\frac{1}{6}$ of each pizza |
| Z: Names as a count of parts | 2. Write a name to numerically describe one person's share.

Each get 7 slices |

Figure 6.5. Scoring rubric for item in Figure 6.4.

SUMMARY AND CONCLUSIONS

Understanding how the complex and interrelated ideas in RNR develop gradually over many years is key to building better assessments to support teachers in helping students develop higher cognitive reasoning abilities for algebra and advanced mathematics. Learning trajectories are proposed as a means to characterize this gradual development. However, they must be based on careful empirical study of the development of student reasoning and not simply delineated as a logical analysis of mathematical topics.

The chapter demonstrated how a synthesis of the field can produce a comprehensive conceptual map and reduce to three the multiple meanings of a/b, simplifying the target for mature understanding. Then the equipartitioning was proposed as a critical foundation for this map.

The learning trajectory for equipartitioning specifies levels of proficiency across student strategies and representations, fluency in key mathematical practices, recognition and understanding of emergent properties, avoidance of misconceptions, and, finally, acquisition of broad generalizations. Once a learning trajectory is validated in relation to the literature, it requires further validation in relation to items, rubrics, and measures (Maloney & Confrey, 2010). That process was illustrated here for one item on sharing multiple wholes among multiple people.

Much research remains to be done to implement diagnostic assessments for RNR. It requires the completion of the same type of synthesis and analysis work for related constructs. In addition, models for such diagnostics must include methods for accumulating and interpreting data and then executing appropriate instructional actions in light of those data. Before diagnostic assessments can be successfully implemented at scale, their validity must be established in relation to instructional guidance and consequential validity for diverse groups of students under various instructional conditions.

REFERENCES

Brosnan, W., Chapman, S., Cizek, G., DiPasqua, F., Giordano, A., Gonzalez, L., . . . Tucker, A. (2003). *Final report to New York State Board of Regents and New York Commissioner of Education: Independent panel on Math A*. Retrieved from http://www.regents.nysed.gov/meetings/2003Meetings/October2003/1003brd3.htm

Brown, A. L. (1992). Design experiments: Theoretical and methodological challenges in creating complex interventions in classroom settings. *Journal of the Learning Sciences, 2*, 141–178. doi:10.1207/s15327809jls0202_2

Charles, K., & Nason, R. (2000). Young children's partitioning strategies. *Educational Studies in Mathematics, 43*, 191–221. doi:10.1023/A:1017513716026

Confrey, J. (1988). Multiplication and splitting: Their role in understanding exponential functions. In M. J. Behr, C. LaCompagne, & M. Wheeler (Eds.), *Proceedings of the tenth annual meeting of the North American Chapter of the International Group for the Psychology of Mathematics Education* (pp. 250–259). DeKalb, IL.

Confrey, J. (1995). Student voice in examining "splitting" as an approach to ratio, proportions and fractions. *Proceedings of the 19th Annual Meeting of the International Group for the Psychology of Mathematics Education* (Vol. 1, pp. 3–29). Recife, Brazil: Universidade Federal de Pernambuco.

Confrey, J. (2006). The evolution of design studies as methodology. In R. K. Sawyer (Ed.), *The Cambridge handbook of the learning sciences* (pp. 135–151). New York, NY: Cambridge University Press.

Confrey, J. (2008, July). *A synthesis of the research on rational number reasoning: A learning progressions approach to synthesis.* Paper presented at the 11th International Congress of Mathematics Instruction, Monterrey, Mexico.

Confrey, J., & Carrejo, D. (2002). A content analysis of exit level mathematics on the Texas assessment of academic skills: Addressing the issue of instructional decision-making in Texas. In D. S. Mewborn, P. Sztajn, D. Y. White, H. G. Wiegel, R. L. Bryant, & K. Nooney, K. (Eds.), *Proceedings of the Twenty-Fourth Annual Meeting of the North American Chapter of the International Group for the Psychology of Mathematics Education: Vol. 2* (pp. 539–550). Athens, GA.

Confrey, J., & Maloney, A. P. (in press). Next generation digital classroom assessment based on learning trajectories in mathematics. In C. Dede and J. Richards (Ed.), *Steps toward a digital teaching platform*. New York, NY: Teachers College Press.

Confrey, J., Maloney, A. P., & Nguyen, K. H. (2008). *Rational number reasoning database*. Retrieved from http://gismo.fi.ncsu.edu/database

Confrey, J., Maloney, A., Nguyen, K., Mojica, G., & Myers, M. (2009, July). *Equipartitioning/splitting as a foundation of rational number reasoning using learning trajectories.* Paper presented at the 33rd Conference of the International Group for the Psychology of Mathematics Education, Thessaloniki, Greece.

Confrey, J., Maloney, A. P., Nguyen, K. H., and Wilson, P. H. (in press). Equipartitioning, a foundation for rational number reasoning: Elucidation of a learning trajectory. In J. Confrey, A. P. Maloney, & K. H. Nguyen (Eds.), *Learning Over Time: Learning Trajectories in Mathematics Education*. Charlotte, NC: Information Age.

Confrey, J., & Scarano, G. H. (1995, October). *Splitting reexamined: Results from a three-year longitudinal study of children in grades three to five.* Paper presented at the Annual Meeting of the North American Chapter of the International Group for the Psychology of Mathematics Education, Columbus, OH.

Cooper, H. (1998). *Synthesizing research*. Thousand Oaks, California: Sage.

Empson, S. B., & Turner, E. (2006). The emergence of multiplicative thinking in children's solutions to paper folding tasks. *The Journal of Mathematical Behavior, 25*, 46–56. doi:10.1016/j.jmathb.2005.11.001

Frydman, O., & Bryant, P. (1988). Sharing and the understanding of number equivalence by young children. *Cognitive Development, 3,* 323–339. doi:10.1016/0885-2014(88)90019-6

Harel, G., & Confrey, J. (1994). *The development of multiplicative reasoning in the learning of mathematics.* Albany, NY: State University of New York Press.

Hiebert, J., & Behr, M. (Eds.). (1988). *Number concepts and operations in the middle grades.* Reston, VA: National Council of Mathematics Teachers.

Kaput, J., & West, M. M. (1994). Missing-value proportional reasoning problems: Factors affecting informal reasoning patterns. In G. Harel & J. Confrey (Eds.), *The development of multiplicative reasoning in the learning of mathematics* (pp. 235–287). Albany, NY: State University of New York Press.

Lamon, S. J. (1996). The development of unitizing: Its role in children's partitioning strategies. *Journal for Research in Mathematics Education, 27,* 170–193. doi:10.2307/749599

Lehrer, R., & Schauble, L. (2004). Modeling natural variation through distribution. *American Educational Research Journal, 41,* 635–679. doi:10.3102/00028312041003635

Maloney, A. P., & Confrey, J. (2010, July). *The construction, refinement, and early validation of the equipartitioning learning trajectory.* Paper presented at the 9th International Conference of the Learning Sciences, Chicago, IL.

National Mathematics Advisory Panel. (2008). *Foundations for success: The final report of the National Mathematics Advisory Panel.* Washington, DC: U.S. Department of Education.

Neuman, D. (1993). Early conceptions of fractions: A phenomenographic approach. *Proceedings of the 17th International Conference for the Psychology of Mathematics Education* (pp. 170–77). Tsukuba, Japan.

Nunes, T., Schliemann, A. D., & Carraher, D. W. (1993). *Street mathematics and school mathematics.* London, England: Cambridge University Press.

Pellegrino, J. W. (2004). *The evolution of educational assessment: Considering the past and imagining the future.* Sixth William H. Angoff Memorial Lecture. Princeton, NJ: Educational Testing Service.

Pepper, K. L. (1991). Preschoolers knowledge of counting and sharing in discrete quantity settings. In R. P. Hunting & G. Davis (Eds.), *Early fraction learning* (pp. 103–129). New York, NY: Springer-Verlag.

Pepper, K. L., & Hunting, R. P. (1998). Preschoolers' counting and sharing. *Journal for Research in Mathematics Education, 29,* 164–183. doi:10.2307/749897

Piaget, J. (1970). *Genetic epistemology.* New York, NY: Norton.

Resnick, L. B., & Singer, J. A. (1993). Protoquantitative origins of ratio reasoning. In T. P. Carpenter, E. Fennema, & T. A. Romberg (Eds.), *Rational numbers: An integration of research* (pp. 107–130). Hillsdale, NJ: Erlbaum.

Schliemann, A. D., Araujo, C., Cassunde, M. A., Macedo, S., & Niceas, L. (1998). Use of multiplicative commutativity by school children and street sellers. *Journal for Research in Mathematics Education, 29,* 422–435. doi:10.2307/749859

Schwartz, J. (1988). Intensive quantity and referent transforming arithmetic operations. In J. Hiebert & M. Behr (Eds.), *Number concepts and operations in the middle grades* (pp. 41–52). Reston, VA: Erlbaum/NCTM.

Shepard, L. A. (1996, September). *Measuring achievement: What does it mean to test for robust understanding?* Paper presented at the Third Annual William H. Angoff Memorial Lecture Series, Princeton, New Jersey.

Streefland, L. (1991). *Fractions in realistic mathematics education: A paradigm of developmental research.* Dordrecht, Netherlands: Kluwer. doi:10.1007/978-94-011-3168-1

Toluk, Z., & Middleton, J. A. (2004). The development of children's understanding of the quotient: A teaching experiment. *International Journal for Mathematics Teaching and Learning.* Retrieved from http://www.cimt.plymouth.ac.uk/journal/middleton.pdf

Vergnaud, G. (1988). Multiplicative structures. In J. Hiebert & M. J. Behr (Eds.), *Number concepts and operations in the middle grades* (pp. 141–161). Mahwah, NJ: Erlbaum.

Vergnaud, G. (1994). Multiplicative conceptual field: What and why? In G. Harel & J. Confrey (Eds.), *The development of multiplicative reasoning in the learning of mathematics* (pp. 41–59). Albany, NY: State University of New York Press.

Vygotsky, L. S. (1986). *Thought and language* (A. Kozulin, Trans.). Cambridge, MA: MIT Press.

7

ADOLESCENT REASONING IN MATHEMATICAL AND NONMATHEMATICAL DOMAINS: EXPLORING THE PARADOX

ERIC KNUTH, CHARLES KALISH, AMY ELLIS, CAROLINE WILLIAMS, AND MATHEW D. FELTON

Mathematics education and cognitive science research paint differing portrayals of adolescents' reasoning. A perennial concern in mathematics education is that students fail to understand the nature of evidence and justification in mathematics. In particular, students rely overwhelmingly on examples-based (inductive) reasoning to justify the truth of mathematical statements, and they often fail to successfully navigate the transition from inductive to deductive reasoning. In contrast, cognitive science research has demonstrated that children often rely quite successfully on inductive inference strategies to make sense of the natural world. In fact, by the time children reach middle school, they have had countless experiences successfully employing empirical, inductive reasoning in domains outside of mathematics. In this chapter, we explore this seeming paradox and, in particular, explore the question of whether the skills or knowledge that underlie adolescents' abilities to reason in nonmathematical domains can be leveraged to foster the development of increasingly more sophisticated ways of reasoning in mathematical domains.

This research is supported in part by the National Science Foundation under grant DRL-0814710. The opinions expressed herein are those of the authors and do not necessarily reflect the views of the National Science Foundation.

A perennial concern in mathematics education is that students fail to understand the nature of evidence and justification in mathematics (Kloosterman & Lester, 2004). Consequently, mathematical reasoning—proof, in particular—has been receiving increased attention in the mathematics education community, with researchers and reform initiatives alike advocating that proof should play a central role in the mathematics education of students at all grade levels (e.g., Ball, Hoyles, Jahnke, & Movshovitz-Hadar, 2002; Knuth, 2002a, 2002b; National Council of Teachers of Mathematics, 2000; RAND Mathematics Study Panel, 2002; Sowder & Harel, 1998; Yackel & Hanna, 2003). Proof plays a critical role in promoting deep learning in mathematics (Hanna, 2000); as Stylianides (2007) noted, "Proof and proving are fundamental to doing and knowing mathematics; they are the basis of mathematical understanding and essential in developing, establishing, and communicating mathematical knowledge" (p. 289). Yet, despite its importance to learning as well as the growing emphasis being placed on proof in school mathematics, research continues to paint a bleak picture of students' abilities to reason mathematically (e.g., Dreyfus, 1999; Healy & Hoyles, 2000; Knuth, Choppin, & Bieda, 2009; Martin, McCrone, Bower, & Dindyal, 2005).

In contrast, cognitive science research has revealed surprising strengths in children's abilities to reason inferentially in nonmathematical domains (e.g., Gelman & Kalish, 2006; Gopnik et al., 2004). Although more traditional (Piagetian) views posit children as limited to understanding obvious relations among observable properties, there is growing evidence that children are capable of developing sophisticated causal theories and of using powerful strategies of inductive inference when reasoning about the natural world (for a review, see Gelman & Kalish, 2006). In the former case, for example, children can integrate statistical patterns to form representations of underlying causal mechanisms (Gopnik & Schulz, 2007). In the latter case, for example, children often organize their knowledge of living things in ways that reflect theoretical principles rather than superficial appearances (Gelman, 2003). Thus, this raises something of a paradox: Why do children appear so capable when reasoning in nonmathematical domains, yet seemingly appear so incapable when reasoning in mathematical domains?

In this chapter, we explore the paradox by considering the research on adolescents' reasoning capabilities within mathematics education as well as within cognitive science. In particular, we briefly consider research that provides a portrayal of adolescents' reasoning in mathematical and nonmathematical domains. Next, we present preliminary results from the first phase of our multiyear research effort to better understand the relationships between adolescents' reasoning in mathematical and nonmathematical domains. We view such relationships as a means for potentially leveraging the strengths adolescents demonstrate when reasoning in nonmathematical domains to foster the development of their mathematical ways of reasoning. Finally, we discuss the implications of our research as well as its future directions.

SITUATING THE PARADOX

Mathematics education and cognitive science research paint differing portrayals of adolescents' reasoning, particularly with respect to the nature of their reasoning strategies. In the world outside the mathematics classroom, children typically rely quite successfully on inductive inference strategies—empirical generalizations and causal theories—to make sense of the natural world. For example, preschool-age children are able to interpret and construct interventions to identify causal mechanisms in simple systems (Gopnik et al., 2004). Young children also have rich knowledge structures supporting explanation and predictions of physical, biological, and social phenomena (Gelman & Kalish, 2006). In fact, by the time children reach middle school, they have had countless experiences successfully employing empirical, inductive reasoning in domains outside of mathematics.[1] Not surprisingly, many students also employ similar reasoning strategies as they encounter ideas and problems in mathematics (Recio & Godino, 2001); however, they often fail to successfully navigate the transition from inductive to deductive reasoning—the latter being the essence of reasoning in mathematics. As Bretscher (2003) noted, "Proof in everyday life tends to take the form of evidence used to back up a statement. Mathematical proof is something quite distinct: evidence alone might support a conjecture but would not be sufficient to be called a proof" (p. 3).

Adolescent Reasoning in Mathematical Domains

It is generally accepted that students' understandings of mathematical justification are "likely to proceed from inductive toward deductive and toward greater generality" (Simon & Blume, 1996, p. 9). Indeed, various mathematical reasoning hierarchies have been proposed that reflect this expected progression (e.g., Balacheff, 1987; Bell, 1976; van Dormolen, 1977; Waring, 2000); yet research continues to show that many students fail to successfully make the transition from inductive to deductive reasoning.[2] One of

---

[1]Unfortunately, children's experiences in successfully employing empirical, inductive reasoning in elementary school also tend to engender the belief that such reasoning suffices as proof in mathematical domains.
[2]The hierarchies that have been proposed, although based on empirical data, do not provide accounts regarding the actual transition from inductive to deductive reasoning. Rather, the hierarchies primarily note differences in the nature of students' inductive reasoning (e.g., justifications that rely on several "typical" cases vs. those that rely on "extreme" cases) with deductive reasoning being at the "upper end" of the hierarchies, and not how (or if) such inductive reasoning strategies can develop into deductive reasoning strategies.

the primary challenges students face in developing an understanding of deductive proof is overcoming their reliance on empirical evidence (Fischbein, 1982). In fact, the wealth of studies investigating students' proving competencies demonstrates that students overwhelmingly rely on examples to justify the truth of statements (e.g., Healy & Hoyles, 2000; Knuth, Choppin, & Bieda, 2009; Porteous, 1990).[3]

As a means of illustrating adolescent reasoning in mathematics, we briefly present results from our prior work concerning middle school students' proving and justifying competencies. The following longitudinal data are from 78 middle school students who completed a written assessment at the beginning of Grades 6 and 7 and at the end of Grade 8; the assessment focused on students' production of justifications as well as on their comprehension of justifications.[4] In the narrative that follows, we present a representative sample of the assessment items and corresponding student responses. Justifications in which examples were used to support the truth of a statement were categorized as *empirical,* justifications in which there was an attempt to treat the general case (i.e., demonstrate that the statement is true for all members of the set) were categorized as *general,* and justifications that did not fit either of these two aforementioned categories were categorized as *other.*[5]

As an example, students were asked to provide a justification to the following item: "If you add any three odd numbers together, is your answer always odd?" The following two student responses are representative of empirical justifications:

- "Yes because $7 + 7 + 7 = 21$; $3 + 3 + 3 = 9$; $13 + 13 + 13 = 39$. Those problems are proof that it is true." (Grade 6 student)
- "$1 + 3 + 3 = 7$. $3 + 11 + 1 = 15$. Yes it would be but you will have to do it a 100 times just to make sure." (Grade 7 student)

In contrast, the following two responses are representative of general justifications:

- "If you add two odds, the result is even. An even plus one more odd is odd. So three odds added together always results in odd." (Grade 6 student)

---

[3]For the purposes of this chapter, we define *inductive reasoning* as reasoning that is based on the use of empirical evidence, and by *empirical evidence* we mean the use of examples to justify statements or conjectures. Moreover, inductive reasoning is not to be confused with mathematical induction—a mathematically valid method of proving.

[4]The assessment items presented below were the same for each administration of the assessment, and the same group of students completed the assessment at all three time points.

[5]We have simplified the categorizations described in this chapter, as we are primarily interested in highlighting the differences between empirically based justifications and more general, deductive justifications. See Knuth, Choppin, and Bieda (2009) and Knuth, Bieda, and Choppin (2011) for more detail about the study's results.

TABLE 7.1
Categories of Student Justifications to the *Three Odd Numbers Sum* Item

Grade	Empirical	General	Other
6	37%	21%	42%
7	42%	36%	22%
8	40%	46%	14%

- "We know that odd and odd equals even. So even (2 odds) added together with odd equals odd. This shows us that no matter what three odd numbers you add together, the sum will always be an odd number." (Grade 8 student)

Responses categorized as *other* (see footnote 2) were often restatements of the question (without further justification) or nonsensical responses (e.g., "It is not always odd because some problems are even like $1 + 2 + 3 = 6, 3 + 4 + 5 = 12$"). Table 7.1 displays the overall results of students' justifications for this item. As the table illustrates, a significant number of students relied on examples as their means of justification, with very little change occurring across the middle grades. We also see an increase in the number of students attempting to produce more general, deductive justifications from Grade 6 to Grade 8; yet still less than half the students produce such justifications even by the end of their middle school mathematics education.

As a second example, consider students' responses to the following assessment item:

Sarah discovers a cool number trick. She thinks of a number between 1 and 10, she adds 3 to the number, doubles the result, and then she writes this answer down. She goes back to the number she first thought of, she doubles it, she adds 6 to the result, and then she writes this answer down. [A worked-out example, including the computations, followed the preceding text.] Will Sarah's two answers always be equal to each other for any number between 1 and 10?

In this case, it is also worth noting that students could use examples to prove that the statement is always true by testing the entire set of possible numbers (i.e., numbers between 1 and 10). Table 7.2 presents the results for this item;

TABLE 7.2
Categories of Student Justifications to the *Number Trick* Item

Grade	Empirical	General	Other
6	30%	28%	42%
7	28%	32%	40%
8	22%	42%	36%

justifications based on proof-by-exhaustion are also included in the *general* category (only approximately 5% of students in each grade level used this method). Given the significant proportion of students whose responses were categorized as *other*, it is worth briefly discussing potential reasons underlying their responses. The majority of these responses were either a result of (a) students misinterpreting the problem, thinking that the end result must always be 20 (the result that was provided in the worked-out example that accompanied the problem); or (b) students not being able to articulate a general argument—students could "see" what was going on but were unable to provide an adequate justification. In the former case, the following response is representative: "No, because the number comes out differently if you chose a number like 11. It does not come out as 20" (Grade 8 student). In the latter case, the following response is representative: "The answers will always be equal because you're just doing the same thing" (Grade 7 student). Although the percentage of students who relied on empirically based justifications decreased relative to the previous example, the grade-level trend regarding the number of students providing general, deductive justifications remained about the same (again, less than 50% of the students at any grade level provided this type of justification).

As a final example, consider the following item in which students were asked to compare an empirically based justification with a general, deductive justification:

> The teacher says the following is a mathematical fact: When you add any two consecutive numbers, the answer is always odd. Two students offer their explanations to show that this fact is true [Note: an empirical-based justification and a general, deductive justification are then presented for the students]. Whose response proves that if we were to add <u>any</u> two consecutive numbers we would get an answer that is an odd number?

As Table 7.3 suggests, for many middle school students, an empirically based justification seems to suffice as proof. We see a slight grade-level increase in viewing the general, deductive justification as proving the claim and, interesting, we see a substantial decrease by Grade 7 in students who think both justifications prove the claim.

TABLE 7.3
Categories of Student Responses to the Consecutive *Numbers Sum* Item

Grade	Empirical	General	Both	Other
6	37%	32%	20%	11%
7	40%	39%	3%	18%
8	36%	49%	7%	8%

In summary, the snapshot of adolescents' mathematical reasoning illustrated above is typical of the findings from much of the research: Adolescents are limited in their understanding of what constitutes evidence and justification in mathematics. Moreover, they demonstrate a proclivity for empirically based, inductive reasoning rather than more general, deductive reasoning. Although most studies have focused on adolescents in a particular grade level or across grade levels (i.e., cross-sectional studies), the research discussed above provides a longitudinal view into the development of adolescents' mathematical reasoning. And given this longitudinal view, we see very little development as adolescents progress through their middle school years, and what development we do see falls far short of desired outcomes.

Adolescent Reasoning in Nonmathematical Domains

The difficulties that adolescents show with regard to mathematical reasoning, including the apparent lack of development as they progress through middle school, raise the question of whether there is some developmental constraint that limits adolescents' mathematical reasoning. The most likely candidate would be abilities to do and understand deductive inference. The emergence of deductive inference has been a central focus of research on adolescent cognitive development, spurred in part by Piaget's theory of formal operations (Overton, 1990). Although there is considerable debate within this literature, a plausible reading suggests there is nothing special about adolescence in terms of acquiring deduction. Younger children, for example, have been shown to appreciate that deductive inference leads to certain conclusions and is stronger than inductive inference (Pillow, 2002). However, even adults struggle to reason formally and deductively.[6] Thus, deductive inference seems neither impossible before adolescence nor guaranteed after. Rather than review the literature on the development of deductive inference in nonmathematical domains (see Falmagne & Gonsalves, 1995), we take a slightly different approach here. Similar to the mathematics education research on proof discussed above, researchers in psychology have often argued that people rely on empirical solutions to deductive problems. An interesting difference with the literature in mathematics education, however, is that these empirically based solutions are typically evaluated quite positively in nonmathematical domains. That is, the kind of performance that makes people look like poor deductive reasoners is actually consistent with their being quite good inductive reasoners.

Deductive and inductive arguments have very different qualities. On the one hand, in making a deductive argument, one endeavors to show that

---

[6]Note that in this literature, as in almost all work in psychology, *adult* means college-age.

the hypothesized conjecture must be true as a logical consequence of the premises (i.e., axioms, theorems). On the other hand, in making an inductive argument, one seeks supporting evidence as the means for justifying that the conjecture is likely to be true. We will refer to arguments based on accumulation of evidence as *empirical*. Often the empirical support in inductive arguments is provided by examples. The conclusion "All ravens are black" is supported by encounters with black ravens (and the absence of nonblack ones).[7] The critical point is that deductive arguments prove their conclusions though logic, whereas inductive arguments provide evidence that conclusions are likely. Again, though there is strong debate, one influential view is that people often seek evidence (make inductive arguments based on examples from a class) when asked to evaluate logical validity (make deductive arguments).

One of the clearest examples of inductive approaches to a deductive problem is Oaksford and Chater's (1994) analysis of performance on the Wason selection task. The selection task is a classic test of logical argumentation. A participant is asked to evaluate a conjecture about a conditional relation, such as "If there is a p on one side of a card, then there is a q on the other side." The participant is presented with four cards: one each showing p, not-p, q, and not-q. The task is to select just the cards necessary to validate the conjecture. The logical solution is to ensure that the cards are consistent with the conjecture: that there are no p and not-q cards. To confirm this involves checking that there is a q on the back of the p card, and checking that there is a not-p on the back of the not-q card. In practice, most people do check the p card, but very few examine the not-q card. Rather, most people opt to explore the q card, which is logically irrelevant (both p and q and not-p and not-q are consistent with the conjecture). This behavior is often interpreted as akin to the logical fallacy of affirming the consequent (if p then q, q, therefore p). Oaksford and Chater argued that selecting the p and the q cards is actually a reasonable strategy for assessing the evidential support for the conjecture. Though the details are quite complex, they show that, given reasonable assumptions about the relative frequencies of p and q, the cards selected are the most informative tests. That is, people's behavior conforms to a normative standard of hypothesis testing (e.g., optimal experiment design).

The distinction turns on two different ways of construing the task. Interpreting the problem as a deductive one (the way experimenters intend it) can be glossed something like this: Is the statement logically consistent with the features of the four cards on the table? The inductive construal is something like the following: Is the statement likely to be true of cards in general?

---

[7]There are many other sources of inductive support. For example, that one's teacher says "All ravens are black" provides some reason for adopting the belief.

Although the deductive problem can be solved conclusively, it is not really that interesting or important (who cares about these four cards?). The inductive problem can never be truly solved (absent investigation of every card in the world); however, it is just the kind of problem that people really care about and face in their everyday lives. How can past experience (the four cards) help in the future (expectations about new cards)?

The idea that people often employ inductive—evidential support—strategies to solve deductive problems is part of a general approach to cognition and cognitive development that emphasizes probabilistic reasoning (Chater & Oaksford, 2008). From this perspective, most of the cognitive challenges people face involve estimating probabilities from evidence. This is straightforward for processes of categorization and property projection. Learning that barking things tend to be dogs, and that dogs tend to bark, seems to involve learning some conditional probabilities. Influential accounts of language acquisition suggest that children are not learning formal grammars (deductive rewrite rules) but rather patterns of probabilities in word co-occurrences and transitions. Even vision has been analyzed as Bayesian inference about structures likely to have generated a given perceptual experience. The general perspective is that inductive inference is ubiquitous; we are continually engaged in the task of evaluating and seeking evidential support. Given the centrality of inductive inference, it should not be surprising that many psychologists argue that we are surprisingly good at it, and good at it from a surprisingly young age (Xu & Tenenbaum, 2007a, 2007b).

Several lines of research are potentially relevant to understanding adolescents' reasoning strategies in mathematics. Perhaps the most direct connection is with research on evaluations of inductive arguments. In contrast to deductive arguments, which are either valid or invalid, inductive arguments can vary in strength. If people are good at reasoning inductively, then they ought to be able to distinguish better and poorer arguments, and stronger and weaker evidence, for conclusions. This work has both a descriptive focus—How do people distinguish stronger and weaker evidence?—and a normative focus—Do people's strategies conform to normative standards for evidence evaluation?

Most work on adolescent inductive inference has focused on the problem of identifying causal relations in multivariate domains (for a review, see Kuhn, 2002). Questions center on children's abilities to construct and recognize unconfounded experiments, to distinguish between hypotheses and evidence, and generally to adopt systematic investigation strategies. Similar to the literature on deductive inference, the conclusions are generally that young children show some important abilities but are quite limited; adults are better, but far from perfect; and adolescents are somewhere in the middle. Other forms or elements of inductive reasoning show a significantly different

TABLE 7. 4
Some Examples of Criteria for Evidential Strength

Principle	Description: Arguments with . . .	Example for conclusions concerning "all birds" have X
Amount	More examples are stronger than fewer	(robins, sparrows, and cardinals have X) > (robins have X)
Diversity	Dissimilar examples are stronger than similar	(robins, hawks, and penguins have X) > (robins, sparrows, and cardinals have X)
Typicality	Typical examples are stronger than atypical	(robins have X) > (penguins have X)
Contrast	Negative examples are stronger than those without	(robins have X, cats lack X) > (robins have X)

profile: Even young children are skilled at inductive inference (see Gopnik & Schulz, 2007). Adolescents have not been the direct focus of research, but there seems to be no reason to believe that inductive inference skills should decline from early childhood to adolescence.

Research on evidential support explores how people respond to or generate evidence. Evidence in this work consists of different kinds of examples or instances.[8] The task is to make or evaluate a conclusion based on that evidence. For example, given that robins are known to have a certain property (e.g., hollow bones), how likely is it that owls also have the property? The evidence consists of examples known to have the property in question. These examples can be understood as premises in an argument about the conclusion: The strength of the argument is confidence in the conclusion conditional on the evidence. Osherson, Smith, Wilkie, Lopez, and Shafir (1990) developed one of the first models and described several criteria for evidential strength. Subsequent research has explored the development and application of these and other criteria (Heit & Hahn, 2001; Lopez, Gelman, Gutheil, & Smith, 1992; Rhodes, Gelman, & Brickman, 2010). Table 7.4 lists proposed criteria; note that some of these criteria are more normatively defensible than others.

Although there remains some debate about preschool-age children, most researchers would agree that by middle childhood children use the criteria in Table 7.4 to evaluate examples as evidence. Thus, children judge that many examples are more convincing than are fewer, that a diverse set of examples is better than a set of very similar examples, and that an argument based on a typical example is stronger than an argument based on an atypical example. Research continues on other principles of example-based arguments, such as

---

[8]In much of this work, the "examples" are categories of animals. It is unclear whether category-to-category inferences ("robins" to "owls") is different from individual-to-individual inferences ("these three robins" to "these three owls").

the role of contrasting cases (e.g., nonbirds that do not have hollow bones; Kalish & Lawson, 2007) and children's appreciation of the importance of sampling. The general conclusion is that children, including adolescents, are similar to adults in their evaluations of evidence. Moreover, children's evaluations accord quite well with normative standards of evidence.

Adolescent Reasoning in Mathematical and Nonmathematical Domains

The preceding discussion highlights some important differences between adolescent reasoning in mathematical and nonmathematical domains. In mathematics education, inductive strategies are typically treated as a stumbling block to overcome rather than as an object of study. Moreover, mathematics education research has focused primarily on distinctions between empirical/inductive and formal/deductive justifications, and questions such as what makes one empirical justification better than another or what constitutes better/stronger evidence have not been well addressed.[9] Christou and Papageorgiou (2007) argued that the skills involved in induction, such as "comparing" or "distinguishing," were similar in mathematical and nonmathematical domains. Christou and Papageorgiou's work showed that students can identify similarities among numbers, distinguish nonconforming examples, and extend a pattern to include new instances. Thus, identifying how adolescents use such abilities to evaluate both mathematical and nonmathematical conjectures and how they think about the nature of evidence used to support conjectures may suggest a means for leveraging their inductive reasoning skills to foster the development of more sophisticated (deductive) ways of reasoning in mathematical domains.

EXPLORING THE PARADOX

What kinds of skills or knowledge underlie adolescents' abilities to reason in nonmathematical domains, and might such skills or knowledge have any relevance to reasoning in mathematical domains? There are many different accounts of inductive inference, but one fairly consistent component is a representation of relevant similarity in the domain. To make or evaluate empirically based, inductive inferences, one must have a sense of the significant relations among the examples or objects. For example, if the task is to

---

[9]Although mathematics education researchers have noted differences in the nature of empirical justifications—checking a few "random" cases, systematically checking a few cases (e.g., even and odd numbers), and checking extreme cases (e.g., Balacheff, 1987)—they have not engaged in any deeper study of empirical justifications.

decide whether birds have hemoglobin in their blood or not, the most inform-ative examples will be objects similar to birds. The argument that since spi-ders lack hemoglobin birds must lack it as well is not particularly convincing because spiders and birds seem very different. In contrast, knowing that rep-tiles have hemoglobin seems quite relevant if we believe birds and reptiles are relevantly similar. The critical question, then, is, What makes two things rel-evantly similar? Other principles of inductive inference described earlier also depend on similarity relations (e.g., typical examples are better because they are similar to many other examples). The relevant similarity relations are, in part, knowledge dependent. Airplanes are similar to birds and may be useful examples to use when making inferences about aerodynamics; however, the question about hemoglobin calls for a biological sense of similarity. Getting the right similarity relations is a critical part of expertise. For example, experts tend to see "deep" similarities (e.g., evolutionary history), whereas novices often rely on shallow, domain-general similarities (e.g., appearances; Bedard & Chi, 1992). Put another way, reasoning from similar cases will be successful only if one's representation of "similar" really does capture important relations in the domain.

Assessing Similarity in Nonmathematical Domains

A considerable amount of research and debate in the cognitive devel-opmental literature involves just what kinds of similarity relations children recognize and how such relations are acquired. Some have argued, for exam-ple, that evolution has equipped us to be sensitive to significant similarities (Quine, 1969; Spelke, 2000). Others have argued that domain-general learn-ing principles allow children to home in on the important relations (Rogers & McClelland, 2004). Regardless, the general finding is that quite young chil-dren seem to display useful and productive intuitions about similarity in the empirical domains studied. Even preschoolers recognize that reptiles are more like birds than are airplanes when biological questions are involved, but that airplanes may be more informative about birds when the questions involve aerodynamics (e.g., Kalish & Gelman, 1992). Unfortunately, the mecha-nisms that have been hypothesized to underlie the development of similarity in empirical domains may fail to support a sense of mathematical similarity useful for evaluating mathematical conjectures.

The nativist view of similarity suggests that evolutionary pressures have shaped the human cognitive system to focus on important relations. For example, snakes often look like sticks, but an organism that focused on these similarities would find itself in significant peril. Clearly, quantitative relations have adaptive significance and a long enough history to suggest that our species could have evolved specific cognitive dispositions to represent such relations. Indeed, there are important claims of just such a "number sense" involving representations of approximate magnitude (see Dehaene, 1999). Beyond the early grades, however, such relations are generally not important parts of mathematical thinking or reasoning. A sense of numerical similarity based on approximate magnitude is a limited basis for evaluating or making inferences about mathematical relations. The principles of mathematical relations depend on a formal system, which is too recent an invention to have had any significant selective pressure on the human cognitive system (see Geary, 1995). In geometry, basic mechanisms for representing shape provide a natural organization to the domain. It seems possible that this sense of similarity may be more productive, more related to mathematically significant properties, than representations of number.

Empiricist views of the development of similarity also suggest pessimism about a mathematical sense of similarity. The empiricist idea is that children form representations in a domain by tracking statistical patterns. In the natural world, objects tend to form clusters: There are natural discontinuities (Rosch, Mervis, Gray, Johnson, & Boyes-Braem, 1976). The features that are important for representing animals tend to come in groups, with high intragroup correlations among features and low intergroup correlations. For example, birds tend to fly, have wings, and have feathers. These features co-occur and tend to be distinctive from the features of mammals that walk, have legs, and have fur. These patterns in the distributions of observed features allow people to pick out informative features and represent kinds or categories that reflect those distributions. A sense of mathematical similarity will also be dependent on the kinds of relations and distributions of properties observed in experience. Again, it seems likely that many of the most significant relations among mathematical objects in children's experiences at school and elsewhere may not be particularly well correlated with mathematically significant relations. A tendency to notice similarity in appearance does lead one toward a fairly useful notion of similarity among animals, because biological properties tend to be correlated with appearance. In contrast, a tendency to notice frequency or magnitude among numbers does not typically lead to a mathematically useful notion of similarity of numbers. Moreover, mathematical objects, at least numbers, have a network organization: There are many crosscutting dimensions of similarity. In contrast, there is one, taxonomic, way of representing similarity relations among living things that seems primary (but see Ross, Medin, & Cox, 2007, on significance of ecological relations). Again, geometric objects, with a strong hierarchical organization and a closer tie to psychological mechanisms of shape perception, may be somewhat different from numbers in this regard.

Thus, an important first step toward developing a deeper understanding of students' inductive reasoning in the domain of mathematics is to explore their representations of similarity relations among mathematical objects.[10] Successful inductive reasoning depends on seeing objects as similar to the degree that they really do share important features or characteristics. How do students make judgments about whether two numbers or two geometric shapes are similar? What features or characteristics do students attend to when considering the similarity of numbers or geometric shapes? How do students' similarity judgments compare with experts' similarity judgments? Answers to such questions may provide insight into students' choices for the empirical evidence they use to justify mathematical conjectures, which, in turn, may provide insight into means to foster their transition to more deductive ways of reasoning.[11]

Assessing Similarity in Mathematical Domains

The first phase of our current research was to determine which features and characteristics individuals attend to when considering whole numbers and common geometric shapes. In particular, on what features might individuals base their decisions when determining whether a particular number or shape is typical? We conducted semistructured interviews with 14 middle school students and 14 undergraduates, as well as 14 doctoral students in mathematics and engineering fields (hereinafter, STEM experts). Participants examined various numbers and shapes on individual cards and then sorted and re-sorted them into groups according to whatever principles they chose (Medin et al., 1997). The numbers and shapes presented to participants for inclusion are shown in Figures 7.1 and 7.2.

Participants engaged in three types of sorts: an open sort, a prompted sort, and a constrained sort. For the open sort, participants grouped and regrouped numbers or shapes into categories of their own choosing until they had exhausted the types of categories they deemed relevant. For the prompted sort, the interviewer grouped some numbers (or shapes) according to a characteristic and asked participants to place additional numbers (or shapes) into the group. For instance, the interviewer might place the numbers 4, 25, and 81 (all perfect squares) into a group and ask the participant to include other numbers in the group. For the constrained sort, the interviewer provided a group of numbers (e.g., 4, 25, and 81) and then included an additional set of

---

[10]Note that our use of similarity refers to conceptual similarity unless we explicitly write mathematical similarity.

[11]Mathematics education research has revealed very little insight into students' thinking regarding their choices of empirical evidence, yet such insight is critical in helping students develop more sophisticated ways of reasoning. For example, selecting examples that provide insight into the structure underlying why a conjecture is true can offer a potential means for generating a general, deductive justification (e.g., Yopp, 2009).

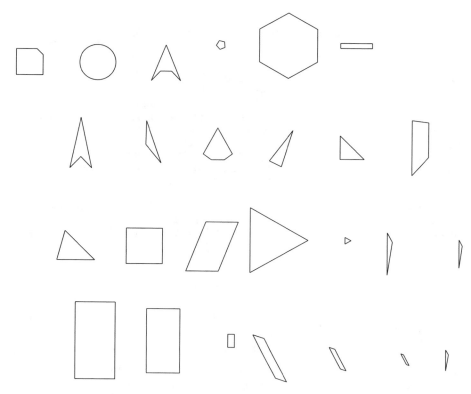

Figure 7.1. Geometric shapes in the sorting task.

numbers (e.g., 23, 36, 51, and 100) and asked the participants which, if any, of the additional numbers should be included in the group. The prompted and constrained sorts allowed us to determine whether participants would sort by particular features deemed mathematically interesting, such as a number being a perfect square, versus other noticeable, yet mathematically uninteresting features, such as the number of digits of a number or the value of one of its digits.

0	1	2	3	4	5	9	11
14	15	17	21	23	25	20	30
35	36	51	60	81	90	100	

Figure 7.2. Numbers in the sorting task.

TABLE 7.5
Number Categories and Their Meanings

Category	Meaning
Parity	Even vs. odd
Multiples	3, 9, 36, 81, and 90 are all multiples of 3
Factors	3, 9, 15, 30, and 90 all go into 90 evenly
Prime	2, 5, 11, and 17 go together because they're prime
Composite	25, 30, and 60 are all composite numbers
Squared	4, 25, and 81 are perfect squares
Sequence	3, 9, and 15 go together because they go up by 6
Value of digit	1, 11, 21, and 81 all have a "1" at the same spot
Intervals	11, 14, 15, and 17 are all between 10 and 20
Number of digits	1, 2, 3, 5, and 9 are all one-digit numbers
Contains a digit	5, 15, and 51 all contain a 5, so they belong together
Arithmetic	2, 3, and 5 are a group because $2 + 3 = 5$
Relational	100, 25, 36, and 9 because $100/25 = 4$ and $36/9 = 4$

The participants' responses to the sorting interview yielded 13 number categories and 13 shape categories denoting features deemed relevant in each domain. Table 7.5 presents the number categories and their meanings. One of the more salient results from the number-sorting task was the number of similarities between the middle school students and the STEM experts in terms of which features they noticed. For instance, consider the parity category. Figure 7.3 shows the percentage of participants from each group who sorted according to parity in the three sorts. The "Parity 1st" part of the graph shows the percentage of participants who sorted by parity as their first-choice sort in the open sort. The "Parity Open" part shows the percentage of participants who sorted by parity in the open sort, but not as their first sort, and the "Parity Prompt" section shows the percentage of participants who were able to sort according to parity only in the prompted or constrained sorts. In this case it is clear that parity was a particularly salient feature for all three groups.

The similarities between the middle school students and the STEM experts led us to wonder: Were there any features that one group attended to but the other did not? The *factors* category was the only category that appeared to be salient to the middle school students but not to the undergraduates or the STEM experts. Just over 20% of the middle school students sorted according to factors in the open sort, whereas none of the undergraduates or STEM experts sorted according to factors. There was also just one category that the STEM experts could sort by more readily than the middle school students, and this was the *squared* category, referring to numbers that are perfect squares. Figure 7.4 shows the percentage of participants in each group who were able to sort by perfect squares.

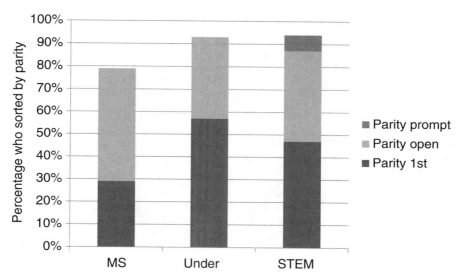

Figure 7.3. Percentage of participants in each group who sorted by parity. Parity 1st = percentage of participants who sorted by parity as their first-choice sort in the open sort; Parity Open = percentage of participants who sorted by parity in the open sort, but not as their first sort; Parity Prompt = percentage of participants who were able to sort according to parity only in the prompted or constrained sorts; MS = middle school students; Under = undergraduate students; STEM = science, technology, engineering, or mathematics students.

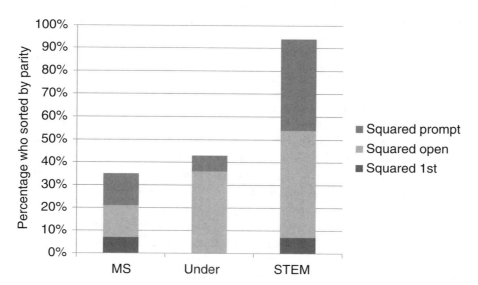

Figure 7.4. Percentage of participants in each group who sorted by squares. Parity 1st = percentage of participants who sorted by parity as their first-choice sort in the open sort; Parity Open = percentage of participants who sorted by parity in the open sort, but not as their first sort; Parity Prompt = percentage of participants who were able to sort according to parity only in the prompted or constrained sorts; MS = middle school students; Under = undergraduate students; STEM = science, technology, engineering, or mathematics students.

TABLE 7.6
Number Categories Sorted According to Salience

Principle	Middle school	Undergrad	STEM
Multiples	86% (1)	93% (2)	93% (1)
Parity	79% (2)	93% (1)	87% (2)
Prime	50% (3)	71% (3)	80% (3)
Value of digit	50% (3)	29% (9)	47% (6)
No. of digits	43% (5)	36% (6)	20% (8)
Intervals	36% (6)	50% (4)	53% (4)
Contains digit	29% (7)	43% (5)	13% (8)
Squared	21% (8)	36% (6)	53% (4)
Sequence	21% (8)	14% (11)	20% (8)
Factors	21% (8)	0% (12)	0% (13)
Arithmetic	14% (11)	36% (6)	40% (7)
Composite	14% (11)	21% (10)	20% (8)
Relational	7% (13)	0% (12)	13% (8)

Note. STEM = science, technology, engineering, mathematics

The *prime* category was the other category of number we expected to be more salient to STEM experts, but this turned out not to be the case. Almost 90% of the STEM experts could sort according to primes, but 70% of the middle school students and the undergraduates could sort according to primes as well. Additionally, there were some mathematically uninteresting features that we expected the middle school students to attend to more than the experts, such as *intervals, value of the digits, number of digits, contains a digit,* and *arithmetic*. But of those five categories, differences emerged only for *contains a digit* and *number of digits*, and the differences were not large: 36% of the middle school students versus 21% of the experts sorted according to *contains a digit*, and 43% and 29%, respectively, sorted according to *number of digits*.

Table 7.6 presents the categories for the number sort organized by the features to which each group of participants attended, in order from the most salient to the least. The middle school students and undergraduates were somewhat more attentive to common digits and number of digits than were the STEM experts, whereas the STEM experts were more attentive to perfect squares and arithmetical relationships.

Table 7.7 presents the categories of shape that the participants identified in the sorting task. The most salient category across all three groups was the number of sides, which all of the participants in each group used for grouping in either the first sort or the open sort. The other two categories that were also salient across all three groups were *shape* and *size*.

The only category that was more salient for the STEM experts than for the other participants was the *regular* category. Of the STEM experts, 43% grouped shapes according to whether they were regular, but only 14% of the

TABLE 7.7
Shape Categories and Their Meanings

Category	What it means
No. of sides	Grouping shapes with the same number of sides
Angles	Grouping shapes on angle size (all have an obtuse angle)
Equal sides	Two or more equal sides
Regular	Grouping regular shapes together
Shape	Resemblance to a shape (e.g., "arrows," "sharp")
Familiar	Common shapes you see in school
Size	Grouping large or small shapes together
Orientation	Grouping according to orientation on paper
Compose	A group of shapes that can be made from others
Tessellate	Grouping shapes that would tessellate
Similar	Grouping similar shapes together
Symmetry	Grouping symmetric shapes together
Convex/concave	Grouping according to concavity

middle school students sorted according to this principle, and those students did so only in a prompted sort. None of the undergraduates sorted according to regularity. We anticipated that three more categories would be more salient for the STEM experts: *similar*, *symmetry*, and *tessellate*. This turned out to be the case only for symmetry (see Figure 7.5): STEM experts sorted according to symmetry more often than did middle school students (47% vs. 21% for both the middle school students and the undergraduate students). Contrary to our expectations, as shown in Figure 7.5, middle school students attended to similarity slightly more than STEM experts did (50% vs. 40%). Only one participant across the three groups attended to tessellations, and this participant was a middle school student.

We anticipated that categories such as *size*, *familiar*, and *orientation* would be ones that would be more salient for middle school students, particularly because we consider these categories to denote principles of shape that are not mathematically important. However, orientation and size were actually slightly more salient for the STEM experts, and the *familiar* category was equally salient across all three groups (36% of each group sorted according familiarity of shape). Of the STEM experts, 27% grouped according to orientation, whereas only 14% of the middle school students and 7% of the undergraduates sorted by orientation. All of the STEM experts sorted according to size, versus 78% of middle school students and 85% of the undergraduates.

Table 7.8 presents the categories of shape sorted by which features each group of participants attended to, in order from the most salient to the least. We found that STEM experts noticed symmetry and regularity more than did

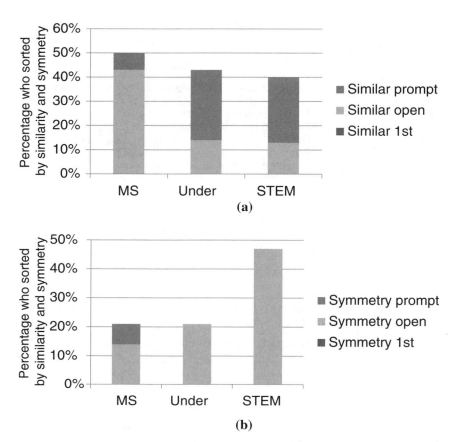

Figure 7.5. Percentage of participants in each group who sorted by similarity and symmetry. Parity 1st = percentage of participants who sorted by parity as their first-choice sort in the open sort; Parity Open = percentage of participants who sorted by parity in the open sort, but not as their first sort; Parity Prompt = percentage of participants who were able to sort according to parity only in the prompted or constrained sorts; MS = middle school students; Under = undergraduate students; STEM = science, technology, engineering, or mathematics students.

TABLE 7.8
Shape Categories Sorted According to Salience

Principle	Middle school	Undergrad	STEM
Size	78% (2)	85% (3)	100% (3)
Shape	64% (2)	78% (4)	93% (2)
Angles	64% (2)	85% (2)	80% (4)
Similar	50% (5)	43% (8)	40% (11)
Concavity	43% (5)	14% (8)	40% (7)
Equal Sides	36% (5)	21% (6)	26% (11)
Composition	36% (10)	43% (9)	27% (8)
Familiar	35% (5)	43% (5)	34% (8)
Symmetry	21% (8)	21% (6)	47% (5)
Orientation	14% (8)	7% (9)	27% (8)
Regular	14% (11)	0% (11)	53% (6)
Tessellate	7% (11)	0% (11)	0% (12)
No. of sides	100% (1)	100% (1)	100% (1)

Note. STEM = science, technology, engineering, mathematics

middle school students, whereas middle school students attended to similarity and equal sides more readily.

Findings from the sorting study showed that, in general, there were not many differences among the middle school students, the undergraduates, and the STEM experts in terms of the characteristics of number and shape that they attended to. Furthermore, we found that some of the most salient features of number included multiples, parity, primes, and intervals (i.e., the relative size of numbers). Several of the more salient features of shape included the number of sides, the shape's size, recognizable features of a shape, and the size of its angles. These findings are important in that they reveal particular characteristics that participants find noticeable, such as a number's relative size or a shape's size—characteristics that matter to students but are not mathematically important from our perspective.

DISCUSSION AND CONCLUDING REMARKS

The results from our initial study suggest that adolescents and experts have very similar representations of similarity among (some) mathematical objects. In particular, adolescents did notice mathematically significant relations among the objects; part of what makes two numbers or shapes similar is that they share properties relevant to mathematical theorems and conjectures. Of course, participants did notice less significant properties as well, for example, shared digits of numbers and shared orientation of shapes. There was some evidence that these less significant properties played a larger role in adolescents' representations of number and shape; however, such properties also showed up in the STEM experts' sorts. One possible explanation for this result, at least in part, is the extremely open-ended, unconstrained nature of our similarity measures. For example, participants were not instructed to focus on "mathematical" similarity. As noted, expertise includes being able to select an appropriate similarity metric for the task at hand. We suspect that experts would tend to ignore irrelevant features (e.g., orientation) in the context of evaluating mathematical conjectures. It is less clear whether adolescents would show the same selectivity; exploring the significance of contextual variations (e.g., mathematics class) is one aspect included in the next steps for this research program. The importance of the current findings, though, is that adolescents do represent mathematically significant similarity relations. The pressing question for future research, however, is how they use such relations to evaluate conjectures.

In this chapter, we have taken a relatively new perspective (in mathematics education research) on adolescents' use of empirical strategies for evaluating mathematical conjectures. Rather than seeing such strategies as limited or as failures to adopt deductive strategies, we suggest that there may be value in such inductive strategies. The argument so far has been that inductive inference is a powerful and useful form of reasoning, and one that people (especially adolescents) seem both disposed to use and use relatively successfully. Our proposal is to consider inductive inference about mathematical conjectures as an object of study in and of itself. To that end, we seek to better understand the adolescents' inductive reasoning in the domain of mathematics. The empirical work presented in this chapter is a first step in a larger project of exploring just how adolescents use empirical examples and inductive methods to reason about mathematical objects. In short, we believe that inductive inference strategies should play an important role in mathematics and that understanding adolescents' inductive reasoning may provide important insight into helping adolescents transition to more sophisticated, deductive ways of reasoning in mathematics.

In closing, we want to make a more extended argument in favor of our perspective that inductive inference can and should play a productive role in school mathematics. Can this kind of reasoning support the transition to more general, deductive ways of reasoning? We began the chapter by noting that inductive arguments are commonplace in mathematics classrooms among middle school adolescents and that more general, deductive reasoning is relatively rare. In contrast, we also noted that inductive arguments are important outside of mathematics and that adolescents often employ quite sophisticated inductive strategies on many tasks that seem to call for deductive inference. The perspective from cognitive science is that people are not so much poor deductive reasoners as they are reluctant deductive reasoners. One reason for this reluctance may be that (outside of mathematics) we rarely care about the deductive implications of some set of facts or propositions. Invariably, it is the empirical significance that people seem to care about in most aspects of their lives. Yet mathematics is different precisely because of the demand to attend to deductive relations. To the question of the proper place of inductive inference in mathematics education we offer three responses.

Although induction is not the accepted form of mathematical inference, it is a form of inference. Inductive reasoning can help students develop a feel for a mathematical situation and can aid in the formation of conjectures (Polya, 1954). It also provides a means of testing the validity of a general proof, especially where students are uncertain about the scope and logic of their argument (Jahnke, 2005). A major challenge in mathematics education, however, lies in moving students from reasoning based on empirical cases to making inferences and deductions from a basis of mathematical structures. By using more accessible inductive inference strategies, at least as an intermediate step, students may begin to appreciate that mathematics is a body of knowledge that can be reasoned about, explained, and justified. A concern with justification and explanation, even if inductively based, may support, rather than undermine, acquisition of more formal proof strategies.

Inductive inferences are important mathematical strategies in their own right. Mathematical problems do not always demand formal solution approaches. This point is very much akin to the value of estimation in relation to exact computation. For example, it is very useful to be able to guess whether a novel problem will be like some familiar problem; perhaps the same solution strategies will work in both cases. One does not need a formal proof that the two problems are isomorphic. Of course, the induction may be false and the apparent similarities misleading. However, developing better inductive strategies, such as recognizing which dimensions of similarity are important, is an important mathematical skill. Even in the context of theorem proving, inductive strategies are invaluable because they can often be used to provide evidence suggesting that a conjecture may be true (or false). Second, the process of producing a proof depends on intuitions about the likely value of different steps or transformations. Intuitions that certain problems are related, or that some problems are more difficult, are expectations derived from experience. The critical point is that some intuitions and perceptions of similarities will be more useful than others. If students employ inappropriate inductive strategies, they will not develop adequate mathematical reasoning skills.

Although empirical induction is not an accepted form of proof within mathematics, it is *a* form of justification (and, as previously discussed, a very common form among students). If students are encouraged to reason in more familiar ways, inductively, they may come to recognize the limitations of such reasoning with regard to proof as well as the power (in terms of proving) of deductive methods. Moreover, reflecting on the strengths and limitations of inductive argumentation may be an excellent bridge to introduce deductive methods. For example, empirical methods cannot conclusively prove conjectures, but they can conclusively disprove them (by exposing counterexamples). The idea of proof by contradiction could flow naturally from discussion of this feature of inductive reasoning. A similar trajectory might work for introducing mathematical induction as a kind of systemization or grounding of empirical induction. For example, students could be prompted to consider the limits of empirical induction and challenged to identify how (or if) mathematical induction overcomes those limits.

We argue that inductive strategies are an important and valuable part of mathematical reasoning. Yet, even from the perspective that inductive strategies have shortcomings in the long run, there is overwhelming evidence that students do rely on them. Understanding inductive strategies is critical to understanding what students are taking from mathematics instruction. For example, teachers illustrate mathematical concepts with specific instances, but what do students infer from these particular instances? In such cases, are students led to believe that examples suffice as proof?

The overwhelming message from mathematics education and cognitive science is that students do use empirical, inductive strategies to reason about their world (including mathematics). Mathematics education can either ignore such strategies by treating them as "errors" to be overcome, or it can ask whether there is some value, as instructional tools or as important mathematical content, to supporting inductive approaches. The perspective from cognitive science emphasizes the value of induction; to be a good reasoner is largely to be a good inductive reasoner. Mathematics may be different, but that difference does not obviate the need for or value of inductive reasoning. The study of adolescents' inductive reasoning in the domain of mathematics is at a very early stage. If the literature on nonmathematical domains is any guide, we should expect to see powerful and sophisticated strategies of inference in the domain of mathematics. Inductive inference is likely a real source of strength upon which mathematics education can build.

REFERENCES

Balacheff, N. (1987). Treatment of refutations: Aspects of the complexity of a constructivist approach to mathematics learning. In E. von Glasersfeld (Ed.), *Radical constructivism in mathematics education* (pp. 89–110). Dordrecht, Netherlands: Kluwer Academic.

Ball, D., Hoyles, C., Jahnke, H., & Movshovitz-Hadar, N. (2002, August,). *The teaching of proof.* Paper presented at the International Congress of Mathematicians, Beijing, China.

Bédard, J., & Chi, M. T. (1992). Expertise. *Current Directions in Psychological Science, 1*, 135–139. doi:10.1111/1467-8721.ep10769799

Bell, A. (1976). A study of pupils' proof-explanations in mathematical situations. *Educational Studies in Mathematics, 7*, 23–40. doi:10.1007/BF00144356

Bretscher, N. (2003). The spirit of the subject. *Mathematics Teacher, 184*, 1–7.

Chater, N., & Oaksford, M. (2008). *The probabilistic mind: Prospects for Bayesian cognitive science.* Oxford, England: Oxford University Press.

Christou, C., & Papageorgiou, E. (2007). A framework of mathematics inductive reasoning. *Learning and Instruction, 17*, 55–66. doi:10.1016/j.learninstruc.2006.11.009

Dehaene, S. (1999). *The number sense.* New York, NY: Oxford University Press.

Dreyfus, T. (1999). Why Johnny can't prove. *Educational Studies in Mathematics, 38*(1), 85–109. doi:10.1023/A:1003660018579

Falmagne, R. J., & Gonsalves, J. (1995). Deductive inference. *Annual Review of Psychology, 46*, 525–559. doi:10.1146/annurev.ps.46.020195.002521

Fischbein, E. (1982). Intuition and proof. *For the Learning of Mathematics, 3*(2), 9–24.

Geary, D. C. (1995). Reflections of evolution and culture in children's cognition: Implications for mathematical development and instruction. *American Psychologist, 50*, 24–37. doi:10.1037/0003-066X.50.1.24

Gelman, S. A., & Kalish, C. W. (2006). Conceptual development. In D. Kuhn, R. S. Siegler, W. Damon & R. M. Lerner (Eds.), *Handbook of child psychology: Vol 2. Cognition, perception, and language* (6th ed., pp. 687–733). Hoboken, NJ: Wiley.

Gelman, S. A. (2003). *The essential child: Origins of essentialism in everyday thought.* New York, NY: Oxford University Press.

Gopnik, A., Glymour, C., Sobel, D. M., Schulz, L. E., Kushnir, T., & Danks, D. (2004). A theory of causal learning in children: Causal maps and Bayes nets. *Psychological Review, 111*, 3–32. doi:10.1037/0033-295X.111.1.3

Gopnik, A., & Schulz, L. (2007). *Causal learning: Psychology, philosophy, and computation.* New York, NY: Oxford University Press.

Hanna, G. (2000). A critical examination of three factors in the decline of proof. *Interchange, 31*(1), 21–33. doi:10.1023/A:1007630729662

Healy, L., & Hoyles, C. (2000). A study of proof conceptions in algebra. *Journal for Research in Mathematics Education, 31*, 396–428. doi:10.2307/749651

Heit, E., & Hahn, U. (2001). Diversity-based reasoning in children. *Cognitive Psychology, 43*, 243–273. doi:10.1006/cogp.2001.0757

Jahnke, H. N. (2005, February). A genetic approach to proof. In M. Bosch (Ed.), *Proceedings of the Fourth Congress of the European Society for Research in Mathematics Education* (pp. 428–437). Sant Feliu de Guíxols, Spain.

Kalish, C. W., & Gelman, S. A. (1992). On wooden pillows: Multiple classification and children's category-based inductions. *Child Development, 63*, 1536-1557.

Kalish, C. W., & Lawson, C. A. (2007). Negative evidence and inductive generalization. *Thinking & Reasoning, 13*, 394–425.

Kloosterman, P., & Lester, F. (2004). *Results and interpretations of the 1990 through 2000 mathematics assessments of the National Assessment of Educational Progress.* Reston, VA: National Council of Teachers of Mathematics.

Knuth, E. (2002a). Secondary school mathematics teachers' conceptions of proof. *Journal for Research in Mathematics Education, 33*, 379–405. doi:10.2307/4149959

Knuth, E. (2002b). Teachers' conceptions of proof in the context of secondary school mathematics. *Journal of Mathematics Teacher Education, 5*(1), 61–88. doi:10.1023/A:1013838713648

Knuth, E., Bieda, K., & Choppin, J. (2011). *The longitudinal development of middle school students' justifying and proving competencies.* Manuscript in preparation.

Knuth, E., Choppin, J., & Bieda, K. (2009). Middle school students' production of mathematical justifications. In D. Stylianou, M. Blanton, & E. Knuth (Eds.), *Teaching and learning proof across the grades: A K-16 perspective* (pp. 153–170). New York, NY: Routledge.

Kuhn, D. (2002). What is scientific thinking, and how does it develop? In U. Goswami (Ed.), *Blackwell handbook of childhood cognitive development* (p. 371–393). Malden, MA: Blackwell. doi:10.1002/9780470996652.ch17

López, A., Gelman, S. A., Gutheil, G., & Smith, E. E. (1992). The development of category-based induction. *Child Development, 63,* 1070–1090. doi:10.2307/1131519

Martin, T. S., McCrone, S. M. S., Bower, M. L., & Dindyal, J. (2005). The interplay of teacher and student actions in the teaching and learning of geometric proof. *Educational Studies in Mathematics, 60*(1), 95–124. doi:10.1007/s10649-005-6698-0

Medin, D. L., Lynch, E. B., Coley, J. D., & Atran, S. (1997). Categorization and reasoning among tree experts: Do all roads lead to Rome? *Cognitive Psychology, 32,* 49–96. doi:10.1006/cogp.1997.0645

National Council of Teachers of Mathematics. (2000). *Principles and standards for school mathematics.* Reston, VA: Author.

Oaksford, M., & Chater, N. (1994). A rational analysis of the selection task as optimal data selection. *Psychological Review, 101,* 608–631. doi:10.1037/0033-295X.101.4.608

Osherson, D. N., Smith, E. E., Wilkie, O., Lopez, A., & Shafir, E. (1990). Category-based induction. *Psychological Review, 97,* 185–200. doi:10.1037/0033-295X.97.2.185

Overton, W. (Ed.). (1990). *Reasoning, necessity, and logic: Developmental perspectives.* Hillsdale, NJ: Erlbaum

Pillow, B. H. (2002). Children's and adults' evaluation of the certainty of deductive inferences, inductive inferences, and guesses. *Child Development, 73,* 779–792. doi:10.1111/1467-8624.00438

Polya, G. (1954). *Induction and analogy in mathematics.* Princeton, NJ: Princeton University Press.

Porteous, K. (1990). What do children really believe? *Educational Studies in Mathematics, 21,* 589–598. doi:10.1007/BF00315946

Quine, W. (1969). Natural kinds. In C. Hempel, D. Davidson, & N. Rescher, (Eds.), *Essays in honor of Carl G. Hempel* (pp. 5–23). Dordrecht, Netherlands: Reidel.

RAND Mathematics Study Panel. (2002). *Mathematical proficiency for all students: A strategic research and development program in mathematics education.* Washington, DC: U.S. Department of Education.

Recio, A. M., & Godino, J. D. (2001). Institutional and personal meanings of mathematical proof. *Educational Studies in Mathematics, 48*(1), 83–99. doi:10.1023/A:1015553100103

Rhodes, M., Gelman, S. A., & Brickman, D. (2010). Children's attention to sample composition in learning, teaching, and discovery. *Developmental Science, 13,* 421–429. doi:10.1111/j.1467-7687.2009.0896.x

Rogers, T. T., & McClelland, J. L. (2004). *Semantic cognition: A parallel distributed processing approach.* Cambridge, MA: MIT Press.

Rosch, E., Mervis, C. B., Gray, W. D., Johnson, D. M., & Boyes-Braem, P. (1976). Basic objects in natural categories. *Cognitive Psychology, 8*, 382–439. doi:10.1016/0010-0285(76)90013-X

Ross, N., Medin, D., & Cox, D. (2007). Epistemological models and culture conflict: Menominee and Euro-American hunters in Wisconsin. *Ethos, 35*, 478–515. doi:10.1525/eth.2007.35.4.478

Simon, M., & Blume, G. (1996). Justification in the mathematics classroom: A study of prospective elementary teachers. *The Journal of Mathematical Behavior, 15*, 3–31. doi:10.1016/S0732-3123(96)90036-X

Sowder, L., & Harel, G. (1998). Types of students' justifications. *Mathematics Teacher, 91*, 670–675.

Spelke, E. (2000). Core knowledge. *American Psychologist, 55*, 1233–1243. doi:10.1037/0003-066X.55.11.1233

Stylianides, A. (2007). Proof and proving in school mathematics. *Journal for Research in Mathematics Education, 38*, 289–321.

van Dormolen, J. (1977). Learning to understand what giving a proof really means. *Educational Studies in Mathematics, 8*, 27–34. doi:10.1007/BF00302502

Waring, S. (2000). *Can you prove it? Developing concepts of proof in primary and secondary schools.* Leicester, England: The Mathematical Association.

Xu, F., & Tenenbaum, J. B. (2007a). Word learning as Bayesian inference. *Psychological Review, 114*, 245–272. doi:10.1037/0033-295X.114.2.245

Xu, F., & Tenenbaum, J. B. (2007b). Sensitivity to sampling in Bayesian word learning. *Developmental Science, 10*, 288–297. doi:10.1111/j.1467-7687.2007.00590.x

Yackel, E., & Hanna, G. (2003). Reasoning and proof. In J. Kilpatrick, W. G. Martin, & D. Schifter (Eds.), *A research companion to the* Principles and standards for school mathematics (pp. 227–236). Reston, VA: National Council of Teachers of Mathematics.

Yopp, D. (2009). From inductive reasoning to proof. *Mathematics teaching in the middle school, 15*(5), 286–291.

8

TRAINING THE ADOLESCENT BRAIN: NEURAL PLASTICITY AND THE ACQUISITION OF COGNITIVE ABILITIES

SHARONA M. ATKINS, MICHAEL F. BUNTING,
DONALD J. BOLGER, AND MICHAEL R. DOUGHERTY

The human brain develops throughout childhood and adolescence and reaches maturity in early adulthood. Previously, brain plasticity, the brain's ability to change in response to internal or external stimuli, was thought to be limited to developing brains: a thought that was also held with regard to cognitive abilities. Recent research has challenged these beliefs and shown that mature brains are plastic and that even elderly adults have the ability to remediate cognitive decline through adaptive plasticity-based training. This chapter examines the neurological basis of cognitive abilities in the developing adolescent brain and addresses the issue of using adaptive cognitive training to remediate deficits and to improve cognitive abilities of adolescents.

Few topics in the psychological study of human behavior have garnered as much interest, acclaim, and contentious debate as the topic of intelligence. In this volume alone, chapters by Stanovich, West, and Toplak; Galván; and Kaminski and Sloutsky all touch upon topics intimately tied to the nature of human intelligence. These authors discuss topics ranging from the underlying neurological architecture of cognitive abilities to the specific abilities needed for problem solving and rational thought. In many ways, these chapters are representative of the broad interest in intelligence by researchers in psychology, education, and neuroscience. The nature of intelligence and its role in higher order thought are of particular relevance to understanding the adolescent brain, as it is during adolescence that individuals experience tremendous opportunity to apply their developing intellectual and cognitive abilities in both academic and social contexts. It is also during this period that many higher order cognitive processes inextricably linked to intelligence, such as logical reasoning, reach a high level of performance (Overton, 1990). Indeed, research indicates that performance on complex analogical reasoning tasks that require overcoming perceptual distractions draw heavily on cognitive processes linked to intelligence, such as working memory and inhibition (Richland, Morrison, & Holyoak, 2006), that continue to develop throughout adolescence and into early adulthood (Casey, Tottenham, Liston, & Durston, 2005; Gogtay et al., 2004).

In this chapter, we explore the fundamental basis of human intellectual and cognitive abilities in terms of their neurocognitive underpinnings, and we address the question of how these basic cognitive abilities might be propelled toward positive change. Drawing on recent work in cognitive neuroscience, we review contemporary cognitive and biological models of intelligence and argue that the processes responsible for intelligence can be modified through progressive brain plasticity training—training procedures that help build and maintain the cortical structures responsible for human cognitive abilities. The potential of these training procedures for improving everything from academic achievement to daily functioning is only now beginning to be realized, but many promising results have already emerged in work on dyslexia (Temple et al., 2003), attention-deficit disorders (Klingberg et al., 2005), and age-related declines in mental functioning (Mahncke et al., 2006).

BACKGROUND

Methods for analyzing human intelligence have existed for at least 2 millennia, beginning when the Chinese developed a civil service exam for classifying individuals based on intellectual abilities (French & Hale, 1990). Even after more than a century of formal psychometric assessment, many fundamental issues are still heavily contested, including the nature and organization of intelligence, its heritability, and its amenability to change (Sternberg, Lautrey, & Lubart, 2004). Heredity and environment are operative in the development of any trait, but the delineation of their respective contributions to cognitive ability has remained particularly elusive. Petrill (2004), among others (Barrett & Eysenck, 1992; Haier, Siegel, Tang, Abel, & Buchsbaum, 1992; Matarazzo, 1992; Pedersen, Plomin, & McClearn, 1994), made a compelling case for the partial heritability of cognitive abilities, suggesting that at least the general ability facet of intelligence[1] has a substantial heritable component. Equally compelling, but to the contrary, Flynn (1998; Dickens & Flynn, 2001) demonstrated a steady increase in intelligence test scores over the 20th century, suggesting the impact of ecological factors on the development of intelligence. Known as the *Flynn effect*, this shows the potential for improving intelligence, or at least some aspect of it, through environmental intervention. The mechanism underlying the Flynn effect is not fully understood, though Dickens and Flynn (2001) suggested it may be driven by an increasingly complex society that places more and more demands on individuals' cognitive system.

The idea that intelligence can be modified by environmental demands has been of interest for years (see Garlick, 2002, 2003). However, exactly how the environment shapes intelligence and whether such environmental influences can be replicated in the lab were poorly understood until just recently. Specifically, it is now known that the brain possesses an incredible ability to adapt to the demands placed upon it by the environment—a property often referred to as *brain plasticity*. The basic premise of brain plasticity is that the specific neural processes necessary for carrying out a particular mental task are refined through experience. In short, the brain reshapes itself to meet the recurring processing demands faced by the individual. In recent years, researchers have begun developing cognitive training procedures that exploit the plastic nature of the brain, thereby enabling individuals to rapidly improve their intellectual and cognitive abilities (Atkins et al., 2011; Chein & Morrison, 2010; Jaeggi, Buschkuel, Jondies, & Perrig, 2008; Klingberg et al., 2005; Mahncke et al., 2006; Olesen, Westerberg, & Klingberg, 2004; Temple et al., 2003).

The premise of the cognitive training approach is to study the trainability of cognitive processes that are important for mental ability, including those abilities that contribute to mathematics, reading and language, and more generally, intelligence. Cognitive training methods, like all educational approaches, are focused on mental development and the enhancement of intelligence. However, cognitive training methods target the development of general thought processes, rather than the acquisition of knowledge specific to a given area or discipline. Therefore, cognitive training aims not only to improve performance of a single task, or performance within a restricted domain, but also to improve all related cognitive tasks broadly construed. Thus, researchers

---

[1]Most contemporary theories of intelligence suggest that intelligence is multifaceted and discretely organized. Cattell (1941, 1987) maintained that there were two separate general intelligence factors: fluid intelligence (denoted Gf) and crystallized intelligence (denoted Gc). Gf refers to the ability to think and reason abstractly and solve new problems irrespective of skills or knowledge. Gc refers to the general intelligence factor that draws on experience, including the ability to retrieve experiential information from memory.

using this methodology are interested both in producing gains on a single task over training and in showing the durability of the training over time and its transfer to other tasks that have not been trained but rely on the same process(es). In other words, the goal is not to train task-specific strategies per se but, rather, general cognitive processes that are more widely applicable.

To be sure, early work on cognitive training throughout the 1980s and early 1990s met with a modicum of success (see Loarer, 2003, for a review). However, rigid beliefs about the heritability and constancy of intelligence have held back more widespread adoption of this approach, the prevailing view being that only children and, to a lesser extent, adolescents had the cognitive flexibility to benefit from training, and therefore slowed progress in developing effective training methodologies (cf. Herrnstein & Murray, 1994; Jensen, 1998, 2000). Although this may cast doubt on the utility of the approach with adults, recent advances in cognitive psychology and cognitive neuroscience have shed new light on the functioning of the brain and have led to insights in how best to construct cognitive-training methodologies that work across the life span. For example, research in cognitive psychology over the past 2 decades (Conway, Cowan, Bunting, Therriault, & Minkoff, 2002; Engle, Tuholski, Laughlin, & Conway, 1999; Kyllonen & Christal, 1990) has identified the specific cognitive processes that underlie intelligence, particularly fluid intelligence but also mathematical and reading abilities. At the same time, work within cognitive neuroscience has begun to identify the neural and biological architecture of these cognitive processes (see Ferrer, O'Hare, & Bunge, 2009, for a review) and the mutability of these structures. By drawing on this work, researchers can now identify the specific neurocognitive structures responsible for intelligence and can construct cognitive training methodologies that target and enhance these structures and pathways. The maturation of the prefrontal cortex, the area largely responsible for fluid intelligence, during adolescence presents an ideal time to introduce such targeted cognitive training procedures that can accelerate and shape its development. Hence, rather than adolescence being viewed as the culmination of cognitive development and the end of intellectual malleability, it can instead be viewed as the beginning of a second phase of life in which cognitive training can improve the cognitive abilities necessary for the acquisition and use of knowledge acquired throughout one's life span.

NATURE OF GENERAL COGNITIVE ABILITIES

Although the construct of intelligence has been widely studied, there is considerable disagreement regarding its fundamental basis. French and colleagues (Ekstrom, French, Harman, & Dermen, 1976; French, Ekstrom, &

Price, 1963) identified over 20 facets of human intelligence. In contrast, Engle et al. (1999; also Conway et al., 2002) proposed that fluid intelligence was best defined as an individual's capacity for controlled attention, whereas Vernon (1983) suggested that processing speed is a core feature. Despite these differences, most contemporary models of intelligence recognize the central role of the *working memory* system—the system dedicated to the temporary processing, maintenance, and integration of task-relevant information and other knowledge during the performance of everyday cognitive tasks (Baddeley & Hitch, 1974; Cowan, 1995, 2005). Working memory is responsible for processing verbal and spatial information from auditory, visual, and other sensory modalities.

There are many diverse theoretical descriptions of the working memory system (cf. the 12 unique perspectives in Miyake & Shah, 1999). Working memory is classically discussed in terms of two different subsystems or components: visual-spatial working memory, which represents, manipulates, and briefly maintains information in the spatial domain; and verbal working memory, which handles verbally mediated representations and processing (Baddeley & Hitch, 1974; Baddeley & Logie, 1999). More recent theories of working memory are process-oriented rather than structural. Probably the most influential model in this regard is Cowan's (1995, 2005) model. Cowan (1995, 2005) proposed a two-tier structure for working memory, distinguishing a zone of privileged and immediate access—the focus of attention—from activated but not immediately accessible long-term memory. Memory in the focus of attention is highly accessible and available,[2] but the focus of attention is capacity limited to a fixed number of items, or chunks (but see Reyna & Brainerd, 1995). The activated portion of long-term memory is not capacity limited, but memory in this state is prone to forgetting due to interference and/or decay. Attentional control is responsible for manipulating the contents of working memory. Among other things, attentional control helps to activate, focus, update, switch, and inhibit memory during information processing.

Working memory is clearly a multifaceted system, with the control and maintenance functions serving as the source of important individual differences that affect performance on a variety of cognitive tasks. In fact, it is now widely believed that individual components within the broader working memory system may be more or less important for performance on individual tasks. For example, evidence suggests that phonological rehearsal and verbal rehearsal draw on storage and underlying neurological mechanisms that are different from those of visual-spatial rehearsal (Baddeley, 2003b; D'Esposito, 2007; Repovs & Baddeley, 2006). Thus, verbally mediated processing tasks (e.g., reading and comprehending a sentence) may tap subprocesses that are

---

[2]The accessibility of activated memory is defined by the time needed to retrieve it, while availability is defined by the probability for accurate retrieval (McElree, 2001).

different from spatially mediated processing tasks (e.g., processing non-symbolic numeric quantities or geometric configurations), whereas general-purpose, attention-controlled executive functions moderate the operation of these and other subprocesses and regulate the dynamics of human cognition (Kane, Conway, Hambrick, & Engle, 2007; Miyake et al., 2000). The best defined and most clearly distinguishable executive functions are task switching and the operations of memory updating and inhibition.

Task Switching

Real-world situations often require multiple tasks to be completed in tandem. These situations require that attention be quickly and efficiently allocated to the processing of different stimuli competing for attention. Task-switching ability appears to reach its zenith in adolescence and young adulthood (Cepeda, Kramer, & Gonzalez de Sather, 2001). In some cases, attention may be divided between two competing sources, which are processed simultaneously. However, in a great many cases, attention is not shared concurrently by both tasks but switches back-and-forth between the tasks dynamically. Task switching concerns shifting back-and-forth between multiple tasks, operations, or mental sets (Monsell & Driver, 2000). It is one of many general-purpose, attention-controlled executive functions that moderate the operation of various cognitive subprocesses and regulate the dynamics of human cognition (Miyake et al., 2000).

Theoretical accounts vary in attempting to explain why dual-task performance is more difficult than single-task performance. Proponents of structural bottleneck theories (e.g., Pashler's, 1998, "response selection bottleneck") have argued that some processing is necessarily serial, thus attention has to be selectively applied. Capacity theories (e.g., Kahneman, 1973) permit parallel processing, but because attentional capacity resources are finite, assume that sharing capacity diminishes processing speed and efficiency. Multiple resource theories are variations on these accounts (cf. Gopher, 1993; Wickens, 1984).

There are significant individual differences in task-switching ability. Some individuals are markedly better at doing two or three things at once than others, controlling for the extent of prior practice and background knowledge drawn on in the task situation. Task-switching ability also deteriorates with aging; young adults are typically better at dual-task performance than older and elderly adults (Salthouse, Friscoe, McGuthery, & Hambrick, 1998). Salthouse et al. (1998) found that switching from one task to another produced meaningful and reliable switch costs,[3] both in the time and error

---

[3]*Switch costs* are the measurable decrements in task accuracy and reaction time that are associated with performing two tasks simultaneously rather than separately.

measures. Furthermore, the measures of task switching were positively and significantly related to measures of reasoning ability, speeded pattern matching, and problem solving (i.e., faster switchers had higher levels of cognitive performance).

Updating and Inhibition

The process of *updating* the contents of working memory requires monitoring and coding incoming information for relevance to the task at hand and then appropriately revising the items held in working memory by replacing older, no longer relevant information with newer, more relevant information (Morris & Jones, 1990). Updating is more than a simple maintenance function. That is, the essence of updating lies in the requirement to manipulate relevant information actively in working memory, rather than passively to store information.

Inhibition is a highly related, maybe even integral, process of updating; it is one's ability to deliberately inhibit dominant, automatic, or prepotent responses when necessary. The color-naming Stroop task is a prototypical inhibition task. In computerized versions of this task, participants are asked to name, quickly and accurately, the color in which objects, words, and nonwords appear. On critical trials, the word is the name of a color (e.g., the word *red*) appearing in another color (e.g., written in blue). One needs to inhibit or override the tendency to produce a more dominant or automatic response (i.e., name the word) in order to do the task correct (i.e., say the color). Whereas inhibition and task (or set) switching appear to reach adult levels by about age 12 (e.g., Crone, Ridderinkhof, Worm, Somsen, & Van der Molen, 2004), set-maintenance abilities continue to develop into adolescence (see also Huizinga & Van der Molen, 2007).

In everyday cognition, students engage in multiple tasks with competing goals, and, even when they limit their attention to a single, important task, they often need to ignore outside distractions and their own intruding thoughts. Updating and inhibition functions make this possible. For example, the ability to update the contents of working memory with new information is important for reading and language comprehension, as well as for mathematics. Working memory capacity is important for language use and comprehension when there is a need to retain a specific word or phrase until disambiguating information comes later in the sentence or paragraph. Consider the following sentence: "While Anna dressed the baby spit up on the bed." Readers tend to initially commit to a particular interpretation (Anna dressed the baby), but must revise this interpretation (i.e., Anna dressed) in light of later occurring information (the baby spit up on the bed). Inhibition processes are important for suppressing inappropriate interpretations and for allowing readers to recover correct interpretations from ambiguous sentences (Novick, Trueswell, & Thompson-Schill, 2005).

Neurobiology of Cognitive Abilities

The multitude of functions involved in working memory are subserved by a broad network of neurological structures, which includes portions of the dorsal- and ventral-lateral prefrontal, parietal, and temporal cortices, among other areas. Returning to the classic model of working memory proposed by Baddeley and Hitch (1974), various components of working memory can be localized anatomically. For example, the cognitive control system is widely believed to involve portions of the dorsal- and ventral-lateral prefrontal cortex (DLPFC and VLPFC, respectively), whereas visual-spatial and verbal working memory subprocesses are assumed to engage structures localized in the parietal and temporal regions (Baddeley, 2003a). Ridderinkhof, Ullsperger, Crone, and Nieuwenhuis (2004) proposed that the medial frontal and dorsolateral prefrontal cortex, including the anterior cingulate cortex, serve important regulatory functions in monitoring rewards and implementing performance adjustments (MacDonald, Cohen, Stenger, & Carter, 2000). These functions are part of a larger cognitive control network that also includes processes in the superior and inferior portions of the parietal lobe (SPL and IPL, respectively), the anterior cingulate cortex (ACC), and medial frontal gyrus (MeFG), as well as subcortical regions of the striatum including the basal ganglia and hypothalamus (Cole, Pathak, & Schneider, 2010; Cole & Schneider, 2007).

The cognitive control system is itself nonunitary, as differential working memory control processes are subserved by separate neural substrates. Working memory storage processes, more directly impacted by load, appear to implicate regions of parietal cortex, whereas the prefrontal regions (namely, DLPFC) appear to be more directly involved in the rehearsal and maintenance functions of working memory (Cohen et al., 1997; D'Esposito, 2007; Jonides et al., 2008; Klingberg, 2000). One point of separation for spatial and verbal working memory processing may be localized to the modality-specific storage mechanisms in parietal cortex as opposed to prefrontal cortex (Dehaene, Piazza, Pinel, & Cohen, 2003; Delazer et al., 2003; Ischebeck et al., 2006; Ischebeck, Zamarian, Schocke, & Delazer, 2009). More specifically, the intraparietal sulcus (IPS) and regions bordering MT/V5 may be more directly involved in spatial processing, whereas more anterior regions of angular and supramarginal gyrus are more involved in verbal processing (Chochon, Cohen, van de Moortele, & Dehaene, 1999). Despite the separation of modalities, both verbal and visual-spatial working memory processes are subserved by developing frontoparietal and frontostriatal networks (McNab & Klingberg, 2008; Wright, Matlen, Baym, Ferrer, & Bunge, 2008).

Developmentally, the set of functions referred to as *executive function*—such as working memory, task switching, and inhibition—are thought to improve from childhood to adolescence as a result of increasingly focused prefrontal cortical activity (Bunge & Wright, 2007; Casey, Tottenham, Liston, & Durston, 2005; Finn, Sheridan, Hudson Kam, Hinshaw & D'Esposito, 2010). The trajectory of development for these executive functions reveals increasingly segregated computational regions that communicate via highly integrated neural "hubs" as characterized by graph theory analyses of correlated activity while the brain is at rest (Fair et al., 2007, 2009). This neural communication across the networks relies on the structure of fiber tracts (the brain's white matter) between these regions, which appear to vary according to ability (Klingberg et al., 2000; Niogi & McCandliss, 2006). In addition, the neurological regions underlying working memory are among the last to fully mature with respect to measures of gray matter density (Gogtay et al., 2004; Lenroot & Giedd, 2006). In fact, these studies in conjunction with postmortem studies of synapse formation suggest that the developmental time course of the prefrontal cortex plateaus between mid-adolescence and early adulthood (Huttenlocher, 1979; Huttenlocher & Dabholkar, 1997). These findings demonstrate that although the development of gray matter has largely leveled off after a period of neural pruning between early childhood and adolescence, white matter fiber tracks (myelin sheaths) that form the thick insulation around axons connecting various regions of cortex continue to develop into adulthood (see Paus, 2005, for a review).

It is important to emphasize that areas of the prefrontal cortex are implicated in a variety of functions related to decision making, such as reward sensitivity and monitoring and response inhibition (see Chapter 10, this volume). The regulatory role of the prefrontal cortex over the limbic structures that produce the surges of neurochemicals such as dopamine and norepinephrine, which lead to arousal and reward, is limited by the slowly developing myelin fibers and the remodeling of the dopaminergic system during adolescence (Crone, 2009; Wahlstrom, Collins, White & Luciana, 2010). In fact, the decreasing response to negative feedback and increasing response to positive feedback as a function of development peaks in adolescence are reflected in variations in the brain's reward centers in the striatal regions that directly project to prefrontal cortex (van Duijvenvoorde, Zanolie, Rombouts, Raijmakers, & Crone, 2008). Because adolescence is a period characterized by an increased opportunity for risk taking, the late developmental time course of the frontal regions and their connective pathways across cortex may be a particularly important factor underlying the increased tendency toward risk-taking behaviors among teens, such as risky sexual behavior and substance abuse (Steinberg, 2004, 2008, 2010). Findings from gambling tasks (Van Leijenhorst et al., 2010) have revealed an increasing response to reward in prefrontal cortex from childhood to adolescence, whereas the conflict-monitoring region, the ACC, shows decreases during this time period, providing a neural marker for increasing valuation of potential reward and a diminishing potency of consequences.

TRAINING THE ADOLESCENT BRAIN

The network of abilities involved with working memory and cognitive control appear to develop throughout adolescence and, in some cases, into early adulthood, and recent work has suggested that the functioning of these abilities can be accelerated through progressive cognitive training exercise. Recent research has demonstrated that the neurological structures underlying cognitive abilities remain plastic throughout adolescence and in adulthood and can be improved via adaptive cognitive training (Chein & Schneider, 2005; Draganski et al, 2006; Maguire et al., 2000; May et al., 2007; Mercado, 2008; Takeuchi, Taki, & Kawashima, 2010; Thomas, 2003).

In a recent study by Jaeggi et al. (2008), young adults underwent 20 hours of training on an adaptive cognitive training task, the n-back task. In this task, participants were presented streams of visual block arrays and auditory letters. For instance, participants might be presented with the letters X, B, M, N, K, B, K, sequentially (and one at a time) and asked to indicated when the current stimulus matched the one presented n items back. In this example, if $n = 4$, the participant should respond when the second B is shown, but not otherwise. Jaeggi et al. (2008) used an adaptive dual n-back task that involved monitoring both the visual-spatial location (in a 4×4 grid) of the letter and the letters themselves. Thus, participants were to respond if the spatial location or the letter matched n items back. Not surprisingly, participants' performance on the n-back task improved as a function of training. However, the more striking result was that participants also showed performance gains on a non-trained measure of general fluid abilities, the Raven's progressive matrices task—a standardized multiple-choice test that measures spatial reasoning abilities.

How can training on the n-back task lead to improvements in fluid intelligence? The n-back task requires the maintenance and updating of information in working memory, and appropriately designed n-back tasks (as used by Jaeggi et al., 2010, 2008; Schneiders, Opitz, Krick, & Mecklinger, 2011) also require inhibition processes. Neurophysiologically, this task is known to engage cortical regions associated with the cognitive control network in the prefrontal region, with spatial versions of the task also recruiting spatial attention processes in the IPS. Training on the adaptive n-back task is assumed to improve the processing efficiency or capacity of the neurocognitive processes responsible for cognitive control and spatial attention. It is important to note that the Raven's progressive matrices task shares no similarity with the n-back task in terms of the task requirements but presumably relies on some of the same underlying neurocognitive mechanisms.

The assertion that the success of cognitive training is driven by brain-based changes in frontal and parietal regions is supported by a number of recent neuroimaging results (Erickson et al., 2007; Olesen et al., 2004; Takeuchi, Taki, & Kawashima, 2010). Olesen et al. (2004) used functional magnetic resonance imaging (fMRI) to examine differences in the brain function of healthy young adults following 5 weeks of visual-spatial working memory training. As in the Jaeggi (2008) study, Olesen et al. (2004) observed improvement in the training task. However, they also found pre/post increases in brain activity, as measured with fMRI, in the MeFG and the superior and inferior parietal areas immediately after training. As we just discussed, the MeFG is known to subserve general cognitive control, whereas the superior and inferior parietal areas are assumed to subserve visual-spatial attention (Erickson et al., 2007; Klingberg, 2006; Klingberg, Forssberg, & Westerberg, 2002b; Smith & Jonides, 1998). Thus, the Olesen et al. (2004) study indicates that cognitive training on a visual-spatial working memory task can lead to changes in the neurological structures responsible for fluid abilities.

The brain areas that exhibit enhanced activity following cognitive training are those mostly related to executive control and working memory. Cognitive training also results in enhancement of brain function in task-specific locations, such as the IPL following visual-spatial training (Klingberg, Forssberg, & Westerberg, 2002a; Olesen et al., 2004; Westerberg & Klingberg, 2007) and the left inferior frontal gyrus following phonological temporal training (Temple et al., 2003). Those task-specific areas are reported in addition to the brain circuitry involved in executive and working memory processes (prefrontal and parietal area; Olesen et al., 2004) and the middle and inferior temporal lobe (Westerberg & Klingberg, 2007).

Other work has shown important evidence of structural changes in cortex following cognitive training. For example, Haier, Karama, Leyba, and Jung (2009) showed that extensive practice on a visual-spatial task led to changes in gray-matter density, as well as changes in activation patterns. Keller and Just (2009) implemented a reading-strategies training program and showed that the cortical connectivity of white-matter fiber tracks was altered following 100 hours of training. Finally, Takeuchi, Sekiguchi, et al. (2010) showed that the training on a working memory task (an n-back task consisting of mathematics operations) led to enhancements of the white-matter microstructures connecting parietal and frontal cortex. It is interesting that the observed behavioral changes in cognitive performance are not always limited to the corresponding changes in cortical activity or structure (e.g., Haier et al., 2009). This suggests that particular training methodologies may have widespread impact on cortex in ways that improve the targeted skills (e.g., executive functioning) as well as the implicit perceptual abilities necessary for the particular training task.

The neurotransmitter dopamine is widely believed to play a critical role in the functioning of working memory (Cools, Gibbs, Miyakawa, Jagust, & D'Esposito, 2008), and one may question if, and how, cognitive training might impact the dopaminergic system. McNab et al. (2009) addressed this question by measuring D1 receptor density (the receptors responsible for uptake of dopamine) in the prefrontal cortex both prior to and after 5 weeks of cognitive training. They found the binding potential of the cortical D1 receptors decreased following the cognitive training; more specifically, larger decreases in DP-1 binding potential were associated with larger improvements on behavioral measures of working memory. This result suggests that cognitive training has an impact at the cellular level. Moreover, Rueda, Rothbart, McCandliss, Saccomanno, and Posner (2005) showed neural and behavioral differences in performance on the "flankers" tasks between children with the long versus short allele on the *DAT1* gene, a dopamine transporter. These findings are particularly important because they identify a close correspondence between the biological mechanisms of brain functioning and cognitive abilities. These findings may inform the development of cognitive interventions that can be used in place of pharmacological interventions when treating disorders characterized by a lack of cognitive control, such as attention-deficit/hyperactivity disorder (ADHD).

DRIVING POSITIVE CHANGE BEYOND THE LABORATORY

Accelerating cognitive changes in adolescence could have implications for academic achievement in high school, enrollment in and graduation from college, and workforce development more generally. An important question regarding cognitive training concerns the nature of training procedures that yield positive change and how these training procedures yield improvements that generalize outside the laboratory. Lövdén, Backman, Lindenberger, Schaefer, and Schmiedek (2010) suggested that alterations in the functional capacity of one's cognitive system are driven by a mismatch between the environmental demands placed on the individual's cognitive system and his or her current cognitive flexibility. *Cognitive flexibility* is one's ability to adapt to the functional demands of any particular task. The idea is that the brain flexibly allocates the amount of cognitive resources needed to perform the task at hand if the resources are available, but the range of flexibility is restricted by an individual's functional resource supply. From this perspective, students with poor cognitive abilities have a narrower range of adaptability (less flexibility). Therefore, increases in task difficulty can quickly outstrip the available cognitive resources needed for engaging in the task. In contrast, students with higher cognitive abilities have a larger range of adaptability and can flexibly allocate cognitive resources across a range of easy and difficult tasks.

The supply-mismatch model proposed by Lövdén et al. (2010) implies that a primary goal of cognitive training is to increase capacity for flexible change by increasing the supply of cognitive resources. Operationally, this means that cognitive training tasks need to adapt to current maximal proficiency levels, in which the difficulty of the task increases to maintain a constant level of proficiency at the highest possible level of difficulty adapted for that individual; the task must become more challenging as the students' skill on the task increases.

The need for adaptive training suggests that adaptive computer games may well induce changes in cognitive performance. Green and Bavelier (2003) showed just this. Green and Bavelier had healthy young adults play challenging action computer games and observed both changes in game performance and generalized changes in measures of spatial and attentional abilities. They observed that performance improved, not surprisingly, as a function of time spent playing. The computer games that the participants played were single-person shooter games, in which the participants' avatars had to navigate a maze and attend to threatening targets popping out at them. According to Green and Bavelier's (2003) analysis, their game and other games in this class target visual-spatial attentional processes. The progressive increase in task difficulty trained the visual-spatial attentional processes, as evident in the participants' performance in the game and participants' improvement on the cognitive assessments.

Obviously, an important characteristic of any successful training, whether cognitive, educational, or vocational, is that improvements on the training tasks generalize to nontrained tasks. Here we distinguish between two forms of generalization: knowledge generalization versus process generalization. *Knowledge generalization* occurs when the information, procedures, or rules one learns for one task can be directly applied to another task. For example, mnemonic strategies learned for the purposes of memorizing a list of random words can be generalized to memorizing grocery lists, names of new acquaintances, or even speeches, but they will be of limited use for engaging in mental arithmetic or solving an analogy. Typical educational interventions generally focus on improving knowledge, with the idea that the knowledge can be flexibly applied and generalized to novel situations.

Process generalization, in contrast, refers to the degree to which a particular set of cognitive or neurological abilities (e.g., working memory, vision attention, temporal processing) can be used by different tasks. Thus, any two tasks that require the same neurological structures and functions will benefit from process generalization, regardless of the content. For example, both the acquisition (learning) of verbal material and continuous mental arithmetic may benefit from improvements in attentional control. We argue that process generalization is key to successful cognitive training procedures. Indeed, its importance has already been observed in whole class interventions designed to promote the development of executive functioning (Diamond, Barnett, Thomas, & Munro, 2007).

To understand the idea of process generalization, it is useful to draw an analogy with performance domains in which individuals undergo extensive training—namely, athletics. In most athletic domains, individuals typically engage in a host of training exercises. Many of these exercises are directed at the specific skills needed for the athletic event, such as throwing motion for perfecting a curveball or a spiral or the coordinated motion involved in shooting a basketball. The motor coordination involved in each of these activities is highly specialized, and gaining high levels of performance in one skill does not guarantee high performance levels in another. In other words, these skills are highly domain specific and akin to proceduralized knowledge representations. However, in addition to their specialized skills training, athletes also engage in other forms of training, such as strength training and cardiovascular training. Strength training and conditioning of this sort extend beyond the individual sport and apply to any other domain in which strength or cardiovascular fitness is necessary. In other words, these "skills" are domain general. Successful cognitive training methods are akin to strength and conditioning training—they aim to improve the neurological processes that are of general use. In this way, cognitive training that focuses on increasing the functional capacity of specific processes, as opposed to knowledge, holds promise of having a number of implications beyond merely improving the functioning of healthy students. We discuss a few of these implications here.

The Aging Brain

Cognitive functioning peaks around age 30 (Mahncke, Bronstone, & Merzenich, 2006) and slowly declines as individuals age, as a consequence of age-related disorders (mild cognitive impairment [MCI], Alzheimer's disease, and Parkinson's disease) as well as part of the normal aging process, commonly known as *age-related cognitive decline*. Mahncke, Connor, et al. (2006) administered a cognitive training intervention designed to reduce age-related cognitive decline and, in a three-group controlled trial, found that only the cognitive training group (compared to an active control and a no-contact control group) showed increased performance on memory measures. These improvements manifested both immediately following the training and at the

3-month follow-up assessment. With average expected life span increasing, the potential economic costs of treating age-related cognitive deficits, as well as the social and familial demands of coping with aging family members, will continue to rise. Treating age-related declines in cognitive functioning through the use of cognitive training methodologies may help to offset some of these costs and positively benefit elderly adults (Borella, Carretti, Riboldi, & De Beni, 2010).

Developmental Dyslexia

Developmental dyslexia is characterized by a language-based learning impairment in reading and writing. Merzenich, Tallal, and colleagues (Merzenich et al., 1996; Tallal et al., 1996) devised cognitive training that manipulated temporal processing, to provide remediation for students with language-based learning impairments. They administered the training to dyslexic students. After approximately a month of training, the students improved in their ability to recognize fast and brief sequences of non-speech and speech stimuli, their speech discrimination, and their language comprehension abilities.

Using a similar phonological-temporal training method, Temple et al. (2003) trained dyslexic and normal children for 100 minutes a day, 5 days a week for an average of 27.9 days. The dyslexic children, who had exhibited below-normal standardized reading and language assessments prior to training, improved to normal levels on the subsequent reading and language assessments. These improvements also manifested as better grades in school, as well as increased activity in the brain. Following the adaptive training, the children with developmental dyslexia displayed increased activity in multiple brain regions, such as the left inferior frontal gyrus, the right temporal and parietal regions and the anterior cingulated gyrus, bringing the brain's activity closer to the level displayed by normal children. This increase in brain function correlated with the improvement in oral language and reading performance.

Similarly, Horowitz-Kraus and Breznitz (2009) found that dyslexic college students benefited more from cognitive training than did nondyslexic college students. Both the dyslexic and the nondyslexic students participated in 24 training sessions (6–8 total hours). Although both groups showed improvement after training, the dyslexic group showed significantly greater improvement on behavioral measures of working memory (digit span) and reading ability (numbers of words per minute), when measured 6 months after training. Brain changes following training, measured via event-related potentials from electrodes placed over the ACC, showed enhanced error-related-negativity following training. As in Temple et al.'s (2003) research, the increase in the amplitude of the error-related-negativity correlated with the increase in working memory.

Attention-Deficit/Hyperactivity Disorder

Another population that has benefited from cognitive training research has been children with ADHD (Beck, Hanson, Puffenberger, Benninger, & Benninger, 2010; Holmes et al., 2010; Klingberg et al., 2002a, 2005). ADHD is characterized by inattention, impulsivity, and hyperactivity, as well as working memory impairments. Klingberg et al. (2005) devised a cognitive training procedure to aid children with ADHD, which included visual-spatial and verbal working memory tasks. They recruited nonmedicated ADHD children and had them undergo 90 trials daily (on average 40 minutes of training) for at least 20 days (mean hours trained, 16.67). Children in the adaptive training group had the trial difficulty increase on the basis of each child's performance, as opposed to the control group, whose trial difficulty remained at the lowest level. Following 20 days of training, children in the training group showed improvements on non-trained executive function tasks, such as the Span Board Task, Digit Span Task, Raven's Matrices, and Stroop Interference Task. In addition, children in the training group exhibited reduced inattention symptoms, as measured by the Conners Rating Scale for parents' ratings of behavioral ADHD symptoms. Children in the control group did not exhibit these improvements in behavioral or executive function measures. It is important to note that these cognitive and behavioral improvements were maintained in the training group, when the children were examined at a 3-month follow-up. These findings suggest long-lasting and even potentially permanent changes following cognitive training.

Mathematical Reasoning

The demonstrated improvements following cognitive training in dyslexics and children with ADHD, as well as those in healthy adults, lead us to believe that cognitive training also holds promise for improving achievement in quantitative reasoning and language comprehension. Therefore, such training may help address achievement gaps. Recent longitudinal research has shown the predictive relationship between mathematical achievement and executive function, in particular visual-spatial working memory (Bull, Espy, & Wiebe, 2008; D'Amico & Guarnera, 2005; Geary, Byrd-Craven, Hoard, Nugent, & Numtee, 2007; Swanson, Jerman, & Zheng, 2008). Bull et al. (2008) administered cognitive assessments, including measures of executive function (Shape School, Tower of London), verbal (digit span forward and backward) and visual-spatial working memory (Corsi blocks forward and backward), and assessments of number, phonetic, and reading skills (PIPS: Performance Indicators in Primary School), to children at age 4 and examined their performance at ages 5 and 7. They found that executive function measures were predictive of general learning, whereas visual-spatial working memory measures specifically predicted mathematical performance.

Dehaene (2009) and others (Booth & Siegler, 2006; Siegler, 2009) have argued that the ability to understand and process numeric quantities, a process referred to as *numerosity* or *number sense*, is one of the core building blocks for the development of math abilities. Recent work indicates that the horizontal segment of the bilateral intraparietal sulcus (hIPS) is responsible for the coding of numeric information. Dehaene, Molko, Cohen, and Wilson (2004) argued that the hIPS plays a central role in the representation and manipulation of numeric quantity and magnitudes and that prefrontal regions are largely responsible for managing sequential operations in working memory. Evidence for the role of the hIPS comes from neurophysiological studies of humans and monkeys. Functional MRI studies on humans indicate that the hIPS is activated by both symbolic (e.g., Arabic numerals) and nonsymbolic (e.g., random dot arrays) numeric stimuli, above and beyond activation due to spatial attention, attention movements, and saccades (Dehaene et al., 2004; Libertus, Brannon, & Pelphrey, 2009). In monkeys, intracranial recording revealed that specific neurons in the hIPS uniquely code for numeric quantities (Nieder & Miller, 2003). Finally, some subpopulations of adolescents diagnosed with dyscalcia (a developmental deficit in basic number processing) show structural and functional deficits in the IPS: Those with developmental dyscalcia show reduced gray matter and reduced activation levels in regions of the IPS that were activated during mental arithmetic in IQ-matched controls (Isaacs, Edmonds, Lucas, Gadian, 2001). Similar results of arithmetic ability and IPS were found in adolescents suffering from velo-cardiofacial syndrome, a genetic disorder resulting from the depletion in 22q11.2. Barnea-Goraly, Eliex, Menon, Bammer and Reiss (2005) found the fractional anisotropy of the white-matter tracks in the left supramarginal and angular gyri and the left IPS to be positively correlated to arithmetic ability. The wealth of evidence indicates that the hIPS is one (if not the) core neurological region for numeric processing.

While portions of the IPS appear to be specifically tuned to the processing of numbers, adjacent areas of the IPS appear to be important for processing ordinal relations (e.g., 4 < 7; Franklin & Jonides, 2009) and for visual-spatial short-term memory (vsSTM; Todd & Marois, 2004; Vogel & Machizawa, 2004; Xu & Chun, 2006). The juxtaposition of vsSTM and numeric processing within the IPS may explain the finding that mathematical ability often correlates with visual-spatial ability (McLean & Hitch, 1999; Rourke,

1993): "The fact that brain regions sensitive to number lie within the dorsal visual processing stream suggests that numerical quantity may be derived from the visual-spatial representations processed in this cortical pathway" (Roitman, Brannon, & Platt, 2007, p. 1672). The representation and estimation of quantities in the hIPS are important components of the development of number sense (Dehaene et al., 2004).

However, quantitative ability per se likely requires the coordinated operation of multiple areas of the brain. Indeed, regions of the posterior superior parietal lobule and the frontal and prefrontal cortex (Dehaene, 2009), which are part of the larger cognitive control network involved with working memory, are also implicated in mathematics. All of the regions implicated in mathematical cognition have been shown to undergo plastic changes as a result of cognitive training (Olesen et al., 2004). This suggests that cognitive training methodologies may be useful for accelerating the acquisition of skills necessary for mathematics (see D'Amico, 2006; Holmes, Gathercole, & Dunning, 2009).

The Risky Brain

Some of the brain areas that have been implicated in quantitative ability and in cognitive training have also been implicated in cognitive control of risk taking. Behaviorally, adolescence is marked by an increased rate of risk-taking behavior. During adolescence, individuals are prone to increased rates of vehicle accidents, unintentional injuries, driving without seatbelts, carrying weapons, using illicit drugs, and engaging in unprotected sex (Eaton et al., 2006; Lejuez et al.,2007; Reynolds, Magidson, Mayes, & Lejuez, 2009). Recent theoretical work on the emergence of risky behavior throughout adolescence has focused on the development of two neurological systems (Casey, Getz, & Galván, 2008; see also Chapter 10, this volume). One system is the limbic system, which is subserved by subcortical regions of accumbens and amygdala, which are responsible for the processing of reward, pleasure, and affect. The second system is the executive control system, which is subserved by neurological structures in the MeFG of the DLPFC, as well as the IPL. Although both of these systems develop throughout childhood and adolescence, their developmental trajectories are quite different. For example, the cortical structures responsible for processing rewards are believed to be fully developed by middle adolescence, whereas the cognitive control network does not fully develop until the middle 20s. This asymmetrical development leads to an imbalance between the processing of rewards and the ability to override impulsive tendencies. Thus, when confronted with a potential socially rewarding context (e.g., becoming popular by drinking alcohol), adolescents may lack the cognitive control to inhibit a potentially risky behavior.

Imbalance theory proposes that the increased tendency to engage in risky behavior is due to an underdeveloped cognitive control system, coupled with an overly sensitive reward system (Casey et al., 2008). Given this as the case, we hypothesize that cognitive plasticity training may be able to serve as a prophylactic against engaging in risky behavior by accelerating the neuro-cognitive development of the cognitive control system. Although there is no direct evidence that such an approach may be successful, the work reviewed above on ADHD, which is largely characterized by a lack of impulse/cognitive control, suggests that it is promising.

CONCLUSION

Cognitive abilities, which previously had been thought to stabilize during adolescence, have instead been shown to be plastic and to maintain the potential to adapt throughout adulthood. This cognitive plasticity has been established in the context of intense individualized cognitive training. Cognitive training can have a profound impact on youth who are at the threshold of establishing their educational and economic foundations for adulthood. Arguments for early intervention, such as Head Start, often assume that adolescents and young adults cannot be transformed intellectually. However, generalized benefits from training have been shown to improve cognitive and achievement abilities, remediate known deficits, and improve daily interaction. Not all cognitive training generalizes beyond the trained task, but many training procedures have shown generalized improvements to visual attention abilities, general fluid intelligence, reading and oral language abilities, and memory. Neurological imaging studies have also shown changes in activation patterns, and even structural changes in gray and white matter, in areas related to working memory and executive functions, following cognitive training. These neuronal changes have been found to correlate with the behavioral improvements following cognitive training. Although these neuronal changes have not been proven to be permanent long-lasting effects, behavioral benefits have been shown at least 3 months after cognitive training. Cognitive training regimes need to be carefully constructed to capitalize upon the plastic nature of the brain processes to remediate deficits such as the achievement gap, to aid students with dyscalculia, dyslexia, or ADHD.

The success of cognitive training for improving cognitive performance in healthy individuals and remediating deficits in students with neurocognitive deficits has been independently established in a number of research groups (Ball, Edwards, & Ross, 2007; Hayes, Warrier, & Nicol, 2003; Klingberg et al., 2002b; Mahncke, Connor, et al., 2006; Merzenich et al., 1996; Thorell, Lindqvist, Bergman, Bohlin, & Klingberg, 2009). Collectively, these studies indicate that cognitive training improves cognitive functioning in adolescence and young adulthood, remediates known deficits in functionality, leads to improvements on untrained tasks, and has beneficial implications for day-to-day functioning. Moreover, there is good reason to believe that the behavioral improvement observed after cognitive training stems from the still-maturing adolescent brain (Erickson et al., 2007; Olesen et al., 2004; Temple et al., 2003).

REFERENCES

Atkins, S. M., Dougherty, M. R., Harbison, J. I., Novick, J. M., Weems, S. A., Chrabaszcz, J. S., & Bunting, M. F. (2012). *Persistence and transferability of working memory-training over time.* Manuscript submitted for publication.

Baddeley, A. (2003a). Working memory and language: An overview. *Journal of Communication Disorders, 36,* 189–208. doi:10.1016/S0021-9924(03)00019-4

Baddeley, A. (2003b). Working memory: Looking back and looking forward. *Nature Reviews Neuroscience, 4,* 829–839. doi:10.1038/nrn1201

Baddeley, A. D., & Hitch, G. (1974). Working memory. In G. H. Bower (Ed.), *The psychology of learning and motivation: Advances in research and theory: Vol. 8* (pp. 47–89). New York, NY: Academic Press.

Baddeley, A. D., & Logie, R. H. (1999). The multiple component model. In A. Miyake & P. Shah (Eds.), *Models of working memory: Mechanisms of active maintenance and executive control* (pp. 28–61). New York, NY: Cambridge University Press.

Ball, K., Edwards, J. D., & Ross, L. A. (2007). The impact of speed of processing training on cognitive and everyday functions. *The Journals of Gerontology. Series B, Psychological Sciences and Social Sciences, 62,* 19–31.

Barnea-Goraly, N., Eliez, S., Menon, V., Bammer, R., & Reiss, A. L. (2005). Arithmetic ability and parietal alterations: a diffusion tensor imaging study in velo-cardiofacial syndrome. *Cognitive Brain Research, 25,* 735–740. doi:10.1016/j.cogbrainres.2005.09.013

Barrett, P. T., & Eysenck, H. J. (1992). Brain evoked potentials and intelligence: The Hendrickson paradigm. *Intelligence, 16,* 361–381. doi:10.1016/0160-2896(92)90015-J

Beck, S. J., Hanson, C. A., Puffenberger, S. S., Benninger, K. L., & Benninger, W. B. (2010). A controlled trial of working memory training for children and adolescents with ADHD. *Journal of Clinical Child and Adolescent Psychology, 39,* 825–836. doi:10.1080/15374416.2010.517162

Booth, J. L., & Siegler, R. S. (2006). Developmental and individual differences in pure numerical estimation. *Developmental Psychology, 42,* 189–201. doi:10.1037/0012-1649.41.6.189

Borella, E., Carretti, B., Riboldi, F., & De Beni, R. (2010). Working memory training in older adults: Evidence of transfer and maintenance effects. *Psychology and Aging, 25*, 767–778. doi:10.1037/a0020683

Bull, R., Espy, K. A., & Wiebe, S. A. (2008). Short-term memory, working memory, and executive functioning in preschoolers: Longitudinal predictors of mathematical achievement at age 7 years. *Developmental Neuropsychology, 33*, 205–228. doi:10.1080/87565640801982312

Bunge, S. A., & Wright, S. B. (2007). Neurodevelopmental changes in working memory and cognitive control. *Current Opinion in Neurobiology, 17*, 243–250. doi:10.1016/j.conb.2007.02.005

Casey, B. J., Getz, S., & Galván, A. (2008). The adolescent brain and risky decisions. *Developmental Review, 28*, 62–77.

Casey, B. J., Tottenham, N., Liston, C., & Durston, S. (2005). Imaging the developing brain: what have we learned about cognitive development? *Trends in Cognitive Sciences, 9*, 104–110. doi:10.1016/j.tics.2005.01.011

Cattell, R. B. (1941). Some theoretical issues in adult intelligence testing. *Psychological Bulletin, 38*, 592.

Cattell, R. B. (1987). *Intelligence: Its structure, growth, and action*. Boston, MA: Houghton Mifflin.

Cepeda, N. J., Kramer, A. F., & Gonzalez de Sather, J. C. M. (2001). Changes in executive control across the life-span: Examination of task switching performance. *Developmental Psychology, 37*, 715–730. doi:10.1037/0012-1649.37.5.715

Chein, J. M., & Morrison, A. B. (2010). Expanding the mind's workspace: Training and transfer effects with a complex working memory span task. *Psychonomic Bulletin & Review, 17*, 193–199. doi:10.3758/PBR.17.2.193

Chein, J. M., & Schneider, W. (2005). Neuroimaging studies of practice related change: fMRI and meta analytic evidence of a domain general control network for learning. *Cognitive Brain Research, 25*, 607–623. doi:10.1016/j.cogbrainres.2005.08.013

Chochon, F., Cohen, L., van de Moortele, P. F., & Dehaene, S. (1999). Differential contributions of the left and right inferior parietal lobules to number processing. *Journal of Cognitive Neuroscience, 11*, 617–630. doi:10.1162/089892999563689

Cohen, J. D., Perlstein, W. M., Braver, T. S., Nystrom, L. E., Noll, D. C., Jonides, J., & Smith, E. E. (1997, April). Temporal dynamics of brain activation during a working memory task. *Nature, 386*, 604–608. doi:10.1038/386604a0

Cole, M. W., Pathak, S., & Schneider, W. (2010). Identifying the brain's most globally connected regions. *NeuroImage, 49*, 3132–3148. doi:10.1016/j.neuroimage.2009.11.001

Cole, M. W., & Schneider, W. (2007). The cognitive control network: Integrated cortical regions with dissociable functions. *NeuroImage, 37*, 343–360. doi:10.1016/j.neuroimage.2007.03.071

Conway, A. R. A., Cowan, N., Bunting, M. F., Therriault, D. J., & Minkoff, S. R. B. (2002). A latent variable analysis of working memory capacity, short-term memory capacity, processing speed, and general fluid intelligence. *Intelligence, 30*, 163–184. doi:10.1016/S0160-2896(01)00096-4

Cools, R., Gibbs, S. E., Miyakawa, A., Jagust, W., & D'Esposito, M. (2008). Working memory capacity predicts dopamine synthesis capacity in the human striatum. *The Journal of Neuroscience, 28*, 1208–1212. doi:10.1523/JNEUROSCI.4475-07.2008

Cowan, N. (1995). Attention and memory: An integrated framework. *Oxford Psychology Series, No. 26*. New York, NY: Oxford University Press.

Cowan, N. (2005). *Working memory capacity*. Hove, East Sussex, England: Psychology Press. doi:10.4324/9780203342398

Crone, E. A. (2009). Executive functions in adolescence: inferences from brain and behavior. *Developmental Science, 12*, 825–830. doi:10.1111/j.1467-7687.2009.00918.x

Crone, E. A., Ridderinkhof, K. R., Worm, M., Somsen, R. J. M., & Van der Molen, M. W. (2004). Switching between spatial stimulus-response mappings: A developmental study of cognitive flexibility. *Developmental Science, 7*, 443–455. doi:10.1111/j.1467-7687.2004.00365.x

D'Amico, A. (2006). Potenziare la memoria di lavoro per prevenire l'insuccesso in matematica. [Training of working memory for preventing mathematical difficulties]. *Età Evolutiva, 83*, 90–99.

D'Amico, A., & Guarnera, M. (2005). Exploring working memory in children with low arithmetical achievement. *Learning and Individual Differences, 15*, 189–202. doi:10.1016/j.lindif.2005.01.002

D'Esposito, M. (2007). From cognitive to neural models of working memory. *Philosophical transactions of the Royal Society B: Biological Sciences, 362*, 761–772. doi:10.1098/rtsb.2007.2086

Dehaene, S. (2009). Origins of mathematical intuitions: The case of arithmetic. *Annals of the New York Academy of Sciences, 1156*, 232–259. doi:10.1111/j.1749-6632.2009.04469.x

Dehaene, S., Molko, N., Cohen, L., & Wilson, A. J. (2004). Arithmetic and the brain. *Current Opinion in Neurobiology, 14*, 218–224. doi:10.1016/j.conb.2004.03.008

Dehaene, S., Piazza, M., Pinel, P., & Cohen, L. (2003). Three parietal circuits for number processing. *Cognitive Neuropsychology, 20*, 487–506. doi:10.1080/02643290244000239

Delazer, M., Domahs, F., Bartha, L., Brenneis, C., Lochy, A., Trieb, T., & Benke, T. (2003). Learning complex arithmetic—an fMRI study. *Cognitive Brain Research, 18*(1), 76–88. doi:10.1016/j.cogbrainres.2003.09.005

Diamond, A., Barnett, W. S., Thomas, J., & Munro, S. (2007, November 30). Preschool program improves cognitive control. *Science, 318*, 1387–1388. doi:10.1126/science.1151148

Dickens, W. T., & Flynn, J. R. (2001). Heritability estimates versus large environmental effects: The IQ paradox resolved. *Psychological Review, 108*, 346–369. doi:10.1037/0033-295X.108.2.346

Draganski, B., Gaser, C., Kempermann, G., Kuhn, H. G., Winkler, J., Büchel, C., & May, A. (2006). Temporal and spatial dynamics of brain structure changes during extensive learning. *The Journal of Neuroscience, 26,* 6314–6317. doi:10.1523/JNEUROSCI.4628-05.2006

Eaton, I. M., Kann, L., Kinchen, S., Ross, J., Hawkins, J., Harris, W. A., . . . Weschler, H. (2006). Youth risk behavior surveillance—United States, 2005, CDC Surveillance summaries. *Morbidity and Mortality Weekly Report, 55*(SS-5), 1–108.

Ekstrom, R. B., French, J. W., Harman, M. H., & Dermen, D. (1976). *Manual for kit of factor-referenced cognitive tests.* Princeton, NJ: Educational Testing Service.

Engle, R. W., Tuholski, S. W., Laughlin, J. E., & Conway, A. R. A. (1999). Working memory, short-term memory, and general fluid intelligence: A latent-variable approach. *Journal of Experimental Psychology: General, 128,* 309–331. doi:10.1037/0096-3445.128.3.309

Erickson, K. I., Colcombe, S. J., Wadhwa, R., Bherer, L., Peterson, M. S., Scalf, P. E., . . . Kramer, A. F. (2007). Training-induced functional activation changes in dual-task processing: An fMRI Study. *Cerebral Cortex, 17,* 192–204. doi:10.1093/cercor/bhj137

Fair, D. A., Cohen, A. L., Power, J. D., Dosenbach, N. U. F., Church, J. A., Miezin, F. M., . . . Petersen, S. E. (2009). Functional brain networks develop from a "local to distributed" organization. *PLoS Computational Biology 5*(5): e1000381. doi:10.1371/journal.pcbi.1000381 (PMC2671306)

Fair, D. A., Dosenbach, N. U. F., Church, J. A., Cohen, A. L., Miezin, F. M., Barch, D., . . . Schlaggar, B. L. (2007) Development of distinct task control networks through segregation and integration. *Proceedings of the National Academy of Sciences, USA, 104,* 13507–13512. (PMC1940033)

Ferrer, E., O'Hare, E. D., & Bunge, S. A. (2009). Fluid reasoning and the developing brain. *Frontiers in Neuroscience, 3,* 46–51. doi:10.3389/neuro.01.003.2009

Finn, A. S., Sheridan, M. A., Hudson Kam, C. L., Hinshaw, S., & D'Esposito, M. (2010). Longitudinal evidence for functional specialization of the neural circuit supporting working memory in the human brain. *The Journal of Neuroscience, 30,* 11062–11067. doi:10.1523/JNEUROSCI.6266-09.2010

Flynn, J. R. (1998). IQ gains over time: Toward finding the causes. In U. Neisser (Ed.), *The rising curve: Long-term gains in IQ and related measures* (pp. 25–66). Washington, DC: American Psychological Association. doi:10.1037/10270-001

Franklin, M., & Jonides, J. (2009). Order and magnitiude share a common representation in parietal cortex. *Journal of Cognitive Neuroscience, 21,* 2114–2120. doi:10.1162/jocn.2008.21181

French, J. L., & Hale, R. L. (1990). A history of the development of psychological and educational testing. In C. R. Reynolds & R. W. Kamphaus (Eds.), *Handbook of psychological and educational assessment of children* (pp. 3–28). New York, NY: Guilford Press.

French, J. W., Ekstrom, R. B., & Price, L. A. (1963). *Manual and kit of reference tests for cognitive factors.* Princeton, NJ: Educational Testing Services.

Garlick, D. (2002). Understanding the nature of the general factor of intelligence: The role of individual differences in neural plasticity as an explanatory mechanism. *Psychological Review, 109,* 116–136. doi:10.1037/0033-295X.109.1.116

Garlick, D. (2003). Integrating brain science research with intelligence research. *Current Directions in Psychological Science, 12,* 185–189. doi:10.1111/1467-8721.01257

Geary, D. C., Byrd-Craven, J., Hoard, M. K., Nugent, L., & Numtee, C. (2007). Cognitive mechanisms underlying achievement deficits in children with mathematical learning disability. *Child Development, 78,* 1343–1359. doi:10.1111/j.1467-8624.2007.01069.x

Gogtay, N., Giedd, J. N., Lusk, L., Hayashi, K. M., Greenstein, D., Vaituzis, A. C., & Nugent, T. F., . . . Thompson, P.M. (2004) Dynamic mapping of human cortical development during childhood through early adulthood. *Proceedings of the National Academy of Sciences, USA, 101,* 8174–8179.

Gopher, D. (1993). The skill of attention control: Acquisition and execution of attention strategies. In D. E. Meyer & S. Kornblum (Eds.), *Attention and performance XIV* (pp. 299–322). Cambridge, MA: MIT Press.

Green, C. S., & Bavelier, D. (2003, April 20). Action video game modifies visual selective attention. *Nature, 423,* 534–537. doi:10.1038/nature01647

Haier, R. J., Karama, S., Leyba, L., & Jung, R. E. (2009). MRI assessment of cortical thickness and functional activity changes in adolescent girls following three months of practice on a visual-spatial task. *BMC Research Notes, 2,* 174. doi:10.1186/1756-0500-2-174

Haier, R. J., Siegel, B., Tang, C., Abel, L., & Buchsbaum, M. S. (1992). Intelligence and changes in regional cerebral glucose metabolic rate following learning. *Intelligence, 16,* 415–426. doi:10.1016/0160-2896(92)90018-M

Hayes, E. A., Warrier, C. M., & Nicol, T. G. (2003). Neural plasticity following auditory training in children with learning problems. *Clinical Neurophysiology, 114,* 673–684. doi:10.1016/S1388-2457(02)00414-5

Herrnstein, R. J., & Murray, C. (1994). *The bell curve: Intelligence and class structure in American life.* New York, NY: Simon & Schuster.

Holmes, J., Gathercole, S. E., & Dunning, D. L. (2009). Adaptive training leads to sustained enhancement of poor working memory in children. *Developmental Science, 12*(4), F9–F15. doi:10.1111/j.1467-7687.2009.00848.x

Holmes, J., Gathercole, S. E., Place, M., Dunning, D. L., Hilton, K. A., & Elliot, J. G. (2010). Working memory deficits can be overcome: Impacts of training and medication on working memory in children with ADHD. *Applied Cognitive Psychology, 24,* 827–836. doi:10.1002/acp.1589

Horowitz-Kraus, T., & Breznitz, Z. (2009). Can the error detection mechanism benefit from training the working memory? A comparison between dyslexics and controls—An ERP sstudy. *PLoS ONE, 4*(9), e7141. doi:10.1371/journal. pone.0007141

Huizinga, M., & Van der Molen, M. W. (2007). Age-group differences in set-switching and set-maintenance on the Wisconsin Card Sorting Task. *Developmental Neuropsychology, 31,* 193–215.

Huttenlocher, P. R. (1979). Synaptic density in human frontal cortex—developmental changes and effects of aging. *Brain Research, 163,* 195–205. doi:10.1016/0006-8993(79)90349-4

Huttenlocher, P. R., & Dabholkar, A. S. (1997). Regional differences in synapto-genesis in human cerebral cortex. *The Journal of Comparative Neurology, 387,* 167–178. doi:10.1002/(SICI)1096-9861(19971020)387:2<167::AID-CNE1>3.0.CO;2-Z

Isaacs, E. B., Edmonds, C. J., Lucas, A., & Gadian, D. G. (2001). Calculation difficulties in children with very low birthweight: A neural correlate. *Brain: A Journal of Neurology, 124,* 1701–1707. doi:10.1093/brain/124.9.1701

Ischebeck, A., Zamarian, L., Schocke, M., & Delazer, M. (2009). Flexible transfer of knowledge in mental arithmetic: An fMRI study. *NeuroImage, 44,* 1103–1112. doi:10.1016/j.neuroimage.2008.10.025

Ischebeck, A., Zamarian, L., Siedentopf, C., Koppelstätter, F., Benke, T., Felber, S., & Delazer, M. (2006). How specifically do we learn? Imaging the learning of multiplication and subtraction. *NeuroImage, 30,* 1365–1375. doi:10.1016/j.neuro image.2005.11.016

Jaeggi, S. M., Buschkuehl, M., Jonides, J., & Perrig, W. J. (2008). Improving fluid intelligence with training on working memory. *Proceedings of the National Academy of Sciences, USA, 105,* 6829–6833. doi:10.1073/pnas.0801268105

Jaeggi, S. M., Studer-Luethi, B., Buschkuehl, M., Su, Y., Jonides, J., & Perrig, W. J. (2010). The relationship between n-back performance and matrix reasoning—implications for training and transfer. *Intelligence, 38,* 625–635. doi:10.1016/j.intell.2010.09.001

Jensen, A. R. (1998). *The G factor: The science of mental ability.* Westport, CT: Praeger.

Jensen, A. R. (2000). Testing: The dilemma of group differences. *Psychology, Public Policy, and Law, 6,* 121–128. doi:10.1037/1076-8971.6.1.121

Jonides, J., Lewis, R. L., Nee, D. E., Lustig, C. A., Berman, M. G., & Moore, K. S. (2008). The mind and brain of short-term memory. *Annual Review of Psychology, 59,* 193–224. doi:10.1146/annurev.psych.59.103006.093615

Kahneman, D. (1973). *Attention and effort.* Englewood Cliffs, NJ: Prentice-Hall.

Kane, M. J., Conway, A. R. A., Hambrick, D. Z., & Engle, R. W. (2007). Variation in working memory capacity as variation in executive attention and control. In A. R. A. Conway, C. Jarrold, M. J. Kane, A. Miyake, & J. N. Towse (Eds.), *Variation in working memory* (pp. 21–46). New York, NY: Oxford University Press.

Keller, T. A., & Just, M. A. (2009). Altering cortical connectivity: Remediation-induced changes in the white matter of poor readers. *Neuron, 64*, 624–631. doi:10.1016/j.neuron.2009.10.018

Klingberg, T. (2000). Limitations in information processing in the human brain: Neuroimaging of dual task performance and working memory tasks. *Progress in Brain Research, 126*, 95–102. doi:10.1016/S0079-6123(00)26009-3

Klingberg, T. (2006). Development of a superior frontal-intraparietal network for visuo-spatial working memory. *Neuropsychologia, 44*, 2171–2177. doi:10.1016/j.neuro psychologia.2005.11.019

Klingberg, T., Fernell, E., Olesen, P., Johnson, M., Gustafsson, P., Dahlström, K., . . . Westerberg, H. (2005). Computerized training of working memory in children with ADHD—a randomized, controlled trial. *Journal of the American Academy of Child & Adolescent Psychiatry, 44*, 177–186. doi:10.1097/00004583-200502000-00010

Klingberg, T., Forssberg, H., & Westerberg, H. (2002a). Training of working memory in children with ADHD. *Journal of Clinical and Experimental Neuropsychology, 24*, 781–791. doi:10.1076/jcen.24.6.781.8395

Klingberg, T., Forssberg, H., & Westerberg, H. (2002b). Increased brain activity in frontal and parietal cortex underlies the development of visuospatial working memory. *Journal of Cognitive Neuroscience, 14*, 1–10. doi:10.1162/089892902317205276

Klingberg, T., Hedehus, M., Temple, E., Salz, T., Gabrieli, J. D. E., Moseley, M. E., & Poldrack, R. A. (2000). Microstructure of temporo-parietal white matter as a basis for reading ability: Evidence from diffusion tensor magnetic resonance imaging. *Neuron, 25*, 493–500. doi:10.1016/S0896-6273(00)80911-3

Kyllonen, P. C., & Christal, R. E. (1990). Reasoning ability is (little more than) working-memory capacity?! *Intelligence, 14*, 389–433. doi:10.1016/S0160-2896(05)80012-1

Lejuez, C. W., Aklin, W. M., Daughters, S. B., Zvolensky, M. J., Kahler, C. W., & Gwadz, M. (2007). Reliability and validity of the youth version of the Balloon Analogue Risk Task (BART-Y) in the assessment of risk-taking behavior among inner-city adolescents. *Journal of Clinical Child and Adolescent Psychology, 36*, 106–111. doi:10.1207/s15374424jccp3601_11

Lenroot, R. K., & Giedd, J. N. (2006). Brain development in children and adolescents: Insights from anatomical magnetic resonance imaging. *Neuroscience and Biobehavioral Reviews, 30*, 718–729. doi:10.1016/j.neubiorev.2006.06.001

Libertus, M. E., Brannon, E. M., & Pelphrey, K. A. (2009). Developmental changes in category-specific responses to numbers and letters in a working memory task. *NeuroImage, 44*, 1404–1414. doi:10.1016/j.neuroimage.2008.10.027

Loarer, E. (2003). Cognitive training for individuals with deficits. In R. J. Sternberg, J. Lautrey, & T. I. Lubart (Eds.), *Models of Intelligence: International Perspectives* (pp. 243–260). Washington, DC: American Psychological Association.

Lövdén, M., Bäckman, L., Lindenberger, U., Schaefer, S., & Schmiedek, F. (2010). A theoretical framework for the study of adult cognitive plasticity. *Psychological Bulletin, 136*, 659–676. doi:10.1037/a0020080

MacDonald, A. W., Cohen, J. D., Stenger, V. A., & Carter, C. S. (2000, June 9). Dissociating the role of dorsolateral prefrontal and anterior cingulate cortex in cognitive control. *Science, 288,* 1835–1838. doi:10.1126/science.288.5472.1835

Maguire, E. A., Gadian, D. G., Johnsrude, I. S., Good, C. D., Ashburner, J., Frackowiak, R. S. J., & Frith, C. D. (2000). Navigation-related structural change in the hippocampi of taxi drivers. *Proceedings of the National Academy of Sciences, USA, 97,* 4398–4403. doi:10.1073/pnas.070039597

Mahncke, H. W., Bronstone, A., & Merzenich, M. M. (2006). Brain plasticity and functional losses in the aged: Scientific bases for a novel intervention. In A. R. Møller (Ed.), *Reprogramming the brain* (pp. 81–109). Amsterdam, Netherlands: Elsevier. doi:10.1016/S0079-6123(06)57006-2

Mahncke, H. W., Connor, B. B., Appelman, J., Ahsanuddin, O. N., Hardy, J. L., Wood, R. A., . . . Merzenich, M. M. (2006). Memory enhancement in healthy older adults using a brain plasticity-based training program: A randomized, controlled study. *Proceedings of the National Academy of Sciences, USA, 103,* 12523–12528. doi:10.1073/pnas.0605194103

Matarazzo, J. D. (1992). Psychological testing and assessment in the 21st century. *American Psychologist, 47,* 1007–1018. doi:10.1037/0003-066X.47.8.1007

May, A., Hajak, G., Gänßbauer, S., Steffens, T., Langguth, B., Kleinjung, T., & Eichhammer, P. (2006). Structural brain alterations following 5 days of intervention: Dynamic aspects of neuroplasticity. *Cerebral Cortex, 17,* 205–210. doi:10.1093/cercor/bhj138

McElree, B. (2001). Working memory and focal attention. *Journal of Experimental Psychology: Learning, Memory, and Cognition, 27,* 817–835. doi:10.1037/0278-7393.27.3.817

McLean, J. F., & Hitch, G. J. (1999). Working memory impairments in children with specific arithmetic learning difficulties. *Journal of Experimental Child Psychology, 74,* 240–260. doi:10.1006/jecp.1999.2516

McNab, F., & Klingberg, T. (2008). Prefrontal cortex and basal ganglia control access to working memory. *Nature Neuroscience, 11,* 103–107. doi:10.1038/nn2024

McNab, F., Varrone, A., Farde, L., Jucaite, A., Bystritsky, P., Forssberg, H., & Klingberg, T. (2009, February 6). Changes in cortical dopamine D1 receptor binding associated with cognitive training. *Science, 323,* 800–802. doi:10.1126/science.1166102

Mercado, E. (2008). Neural and cognitive plasticity: from maps to minds. *Psychological Bulletin, 134,* 109–137. doi:10.1037/0033-2909.134.1.109

Merzenich, M. M., Jenkins, W. M., Johnston, P., Schreiner, C., Miller, S. L., & Tallal, P. (1996, January 5). Temporal processing deficits of language-learning impaired children ameliorated by training. *Science, 271,* 77–81. doi:10.1126/science.271.5245.77

Miyake, A., & Shah, P. (Eds.). (1999). *Models of working memory: Mechanisms of active maintenance and executive control.* New York, NY: Cambridge University Press.

Miyake, A., Friedman, N. P., Emerson, M. J., Witzki, A. H., Howerter, A., & Wager, T. (2000). The unity and diversity of executive functions and their contributions to complex "frontal lobe" tasks: A latent variable analysis. *Cognitive Psychology, 41*, 49–100. doi:10.1006/cogp.1999.0734

Monsell, S., & Driver, J. (2000). *Control of cognitive processes.* Cambridge, MA: MIT Press.

Morris, N., & Jones, D. M. (1990). Memory updating in working memory: The role of central executive. *British Journal of Psychology, 81*, 111–121. doi:10.1111/j.2044-8295.1990.tb02349.x

Morrison, A. B., & Chein, J. M. (2011). Does working memory training work? The promise and challenges of enhancing cognition by training working memory. *Psychonomic Bulletin & Review, 18*(1), 46–60. doi:10.3758/s13423-010-0034-0

Nieder, A., & Miller, E. K. (2003). Coding of cognitive magnitude: Compressed scaling of numerical information in the primate prefrontal cortex. *Neuron, 37*, 149–157. doi:10.1016/S0896-6273(02)01144-3

Niogi, S. N., & McCandliss, B. D. (2006). Left lateralized white matter microstructure accounts for individual differences in reading ability and disability. *Neuropsychologia, 44*, 2178–2188. doi:10.1016/j.neuropsychologia.2006.01.011

Novick, J. M., Trueswell, J. C., & Thompson-Schill, S. L. (2005). Cognitive control and parsing: Reexamining the role of Broca's area in sentence comprehension. *Cognitive, Affective & Behavioral Neuroscience, 5*, 263–281. doi:10.3758/CABN.5.3.263

Olesen, P. J., Westerberg, H., & Klingberg, T. (2004). Increased prefrontal and parietal activity after training of working memory. *Nature Neuroscience, 7*, 75–79. doi:10.1038/nn1165

Overton, W. F. (Ed.). (1990). *Reasoning, necessity, and logic: Developmental perspectives.* Hillsdale, NJ: Erlbaum.

Paus, T. (2005). Mapping brain maturation and cognitive development during adolescence. *Trends in Cognitive Sciences, 9*, 60–68. doi:10.1016/j.tics.2004.12.008

Pashler, H. (1998). *The psychology of attention.* Cambridge, MA: MIT Press.

Pedersen, N. L., Plomin, R., & McClearn, G. E. (1994). Is there G beyond g? (Is there genetic influence on specific cognitive abilities independent of genetic influences on general cognitive ability?). *Intelligence, 18*, 133–143. doi:10.1016/0160-2896(94)90024-8

Petrill, S. A. (2004). The development of intelligence: Behavioral genetic approaches. In R. J. Sternberg, J. Lautrey, & T. I. Lubart (Eds.), *Models of intelligence: International perspectives* (pp. 81–90). Washington, DC: American Psychological Association.

Repovs, G., & Baddeley, A. (2006). The multi-component model of working memory: Exploration in experimental cognitive psychology. *Neuroscience, 139*, 5–21. doi:10.1016/j.neuroscience.2005.12.061

Reyna, V. F., & Brainerd, C. J. (1995). Fuzzy-trace theory: An interim synthesis. *Learning and Individual Differences, 7*(1), 1–75. doi:10.1016/1041-6080(95)90031-4

Reynolds, E. K., Magidson, J., Mayes, L., & Lejuez, C. W. (2009). Risk-taking behaviors across the transition from adolescence to young adulthood. In J. E. Grant and M. N. Potenza (Eds.), *Young adult mental health.* New York, NY: Oxford University Press

Richland, L. E., Morrison, R. G., & Holyoak, K. J. (2006). Children's development of analogical reasoning: Insights from scene analogy problems. *Journal of Experimental Child Psychology, 94,* 249–273. doi:10.1016/j.jecp.2006.02.002

Ridderinkhof, K. R., Ullsperger, M., Crone, E. A., & Nieuwenhuis, S. (2004, October 15). The role of the medial frontal cortex in cognitive control. *Science, 306,* 443–447. doi:10.1126/science.1100301

Roitman, J. D., Brannon, E. M., & Platt, M. L. (2007). Monotonic coding of numerosity in macaque lateral intraparietal area. *PLoS Biology, 5*(8), e208. doi:10.1371/journal.pbio.0050208

Rourke, B. P. (1993). Arithmetic disabilities, specific and otherwise: A neuropsychological perspective. *Journal of Learning Disabilities, 26,* 214–226. doi:10.1177/002221949302600402

Rueda, M. R., Rothbart, R. K., McCandliss, B. D., Saccomanno, L., & Posner, M. I. (2005). Training, maturation, and genetic influences on the development of executive attention. *Proceedings of the National Academy of Sciences, USA, 102,* 14931–14936. doi:10.1073/pnas.0506897102

Salthouse, T. A., Friscoe, N., McGuthery, K. E., & Hambrick, D. Z. (1998). Relation of task switching to speed, age, and fluid intelligence. *Psychology and Aging, 13,* 445–461. doi:10.1037/0882-7974.13.3.445

Schneiders, J. A., Opitz, B., Krick, C. M., & Mecklinger, A. (2011). Separating intramodal and across-modal training effects in visual working memory fMRI investigation. *Cerebral Cortex.* Advance online publication. doi:10.1093/cercor/bhr037.

Siegler, R. S. (2009). Improving the numerical understanding of children from low-income families. *Child Development Perspectives, 3,* 118–124. doi:10.1111/j.1750-8606.2009.00090.x

Smith, E. E., & Jonides, J. (1998). Neuroimaging analyses of human working memory. *Proceedings of the National Academy of Sciences, USA, 95,* 12061–12068. doi:10.1073/pnas.95.20.12061

Steinberg, L. (2004). Risk taking in adolescence: What changes and why? *Annals of the New York Academy of Sciences, 1021,* 51–58. doi:10.1196/annals.1308.005

Steinberg, L. (2008). A social neuroscience perspective on adolescent risk taking. *Developmental Review, 28,* 78–106. doi:10.1016/j.dr.2007.08.002

Steinberg, L. (2010). A dual system model of adolescent risk taking. *Developmental Psychobiology, 52,* 216–224.

Sternberg, R. J., Lautrey, J., & Lubart, T. I. (2004). Where are we in the field of intelligence, how did we get here, and where are we going? In R. J. Sternberg, J. Lautrey, & T. I. Lubart (Eds.), *Models of intelligence: International perspectives* (pp. 3–25). Washington, DC: American Psychological Association.

Swanson, H. L., Jerman, O., & Zheng, X. (2008). Growth in working memory and mathematical problem solving in children at risk and not at risk for serious math difficulties. *Journal of Educational Psychology, 100,* 343–379. doi:10.1037/0022-0663.100.2.343

Takeuchi, H., Sekiguchi, A., Taki, Y., Yokoyama, S., Yomogida, Y., Komuro, N., . . . Kawashima, R. (2010). Training of working memory impacts structural connectivity. *The Journal of Neuroscience, 30,* 3297–3303. doi:10.1523/JNEUROSCI.4611-09.2010

Takeuchi, H., Taki, Y., & Kawashima, R. (2010). Effect of working memory training on cognitive functions and neural systems. *Reviews in the Neurosciences, 21,* 427–449.

Tallal, P., Miller, S. L., Bedi, G., Byma, G., Wang, X., Nagarajan, S., . . . Merzenich, M. M. (1996, January 5). Language comprehension in language learning impaired children improved with acoustically modified speech. *Science, 271,* 81–84. doi:10.1126/science.271.5245.81

Temple, E., Deutsch, G. K., Poldrack, R. A., Miller, S. L., Tallal, P., Merzenich, M. M., & Gabrieli, J. D. (2003). Neural deficits in children with dyslexia ameliorated by behavioral remediation: Evidence from functional MRI. *Proceedings of the National Academy of Sciences, USA, 100,* 2860–2865. doi:10.1073/pnas.0030098100

Thomas, M. S. C. (2003). Limits on plasticity. *Journal of Cognition and Development, 4,* 99–125. doi:10.1207/S15327647JCD4,1-04

Thorell, L. B., Lindqvist, S., Bergman, S., Bohlin, G., & Klingberg, T. (2009). Training and transfer effects of executive functions in preschool children. *Developmental Science, 12,* 106–113. doi:10.1111/j.1467-7687.2008.00745.x

Todd, J. J., & Marois, R. (2004, April 15). Capacity limit of visual short-term memory in human posterior parietal cortex. *Nature, 428,* 751–754. doi:10.1038/nature02466

van Duijvenvoorde, A., Zanolie, K., Rombouts, S. A. R. B., Raijmakers, M., & Crone, E. A. (2008). Evaluating the negative or valuing the positive? Neural mechanisms supporting feedback-based learning across development. *The Journal of Neuroscience, 28,* 9495–9503. doi:10.1523/JNEUROSCI.1485-08.2008

Van Leijenhorst, L., Gunther Moor, B., Op de Macks, Z. A., Rombouts, S. A. R. B., Westenberg, P. M., & Crone, E. A. (2010). Adolescent risky decision making: Neurocognitive development of reward and control regions. *NeuroImage,* 345–355. doi:10.1016/j.neuroimage.2010.02.038

Vernon, P. A. (1983). Speed of information processing and general intelligence. *Intelligence, 7,* 53–70. doi:10.1016/0160-2896(83)90006-5

Vogel, E. K., & Machizawa, M. G. (2004, April 15). Neural activity predicts individual differences in visual working memory capacity. *Nature, 428,* 748–751. doi:10.1038/nature02447

Wahlstrom, D., Collins, P., White, T., & Luciana, M. (2010). Developmental changes in dopamine neurotransmission in adolescence: Behavioral implications and issues in assessment. *Brain and Cognition, 72,* 146–159. doi:10.1016/j.bandc.2009.10.013

Westerberg, H., & Klingberg, T. (2007). Changes in cortical activity after training of working memory: A single-subject analysis. *Physiology & Behavior, 92*, 186–192. doi:10.1016/j.physbeh.2007.05.041

Wickens, C. D. (1984). Processing resources in attention. In R. Parasuraman & D. R. Davies (Eds.), *Varieties of attention* (pp. 63–102). New York, NY: Academic Press.

Wright, S. B., Matlen, B. J., Baym, C. L., Ferrer, E., & Bunge, S. A. (2008). Neural correlates of fluid reasoning in children and adults. *Frontiers in Human Neuroscience, 1*(8), 1–8.

Xu, Y., & Chun, M. M. (2006, March 2. Dissociable neural mechanisms supporting visual short term memory for objects. *Nature, 440*, 91–95. doi:10.1038/nature04262

9

HIGHER COGNITION IS ALTERED BY NONCOGNITIVE FACTORS: HOW AFFECT ENHANCES AND DISRUPTS MATHEMATICS PERFORMANCE IN ADOLESCENCE AND YOUNG ADULTHOOD

MARK H. ASHCRAFT AND NATHAN O. RUDIG

Mainstream research in cognition neglects the influence of individual differences related to personal variables, by default taking the stand that such variables are tangential or will have negligible effects on performance. This is a dangerous stance when learning and performance in mathematics are considered. In fact, a substantive literature has identified important predictive relationships among noncognitive variables such as motivation, self-efficacy, and mathematics anxiety and their impact on adolescents' learning and pursuit of mathematics in the classroom. Likewise, there have been reports of immediate or online declines in cognitive performance due to the effects of mathematics anxiety, stereotype threat, and pressure, all of which appear to tax working memory resources. When such resources are taxed, mathematics performance declines, in spite of skills and knowledge. Because these noncognitive factors have both global effects on learning and local effects on performance, theories of mathematical cognition and efforts concerned with mathematics achievement and curriculum design must acknowledge their importance and impact.

We begin with an anecdote, originally told in Ashcraft (2002), to set the stage for this chapter. A young college student was being tested on a straightforward laboratory test of mental subtraction, asked to state out loud the answer to problems like $34 - 19 = ?$. She struggled with the task, becoming increasingly nervous throughout the session, and eventually burst into tears. The graduate assistant who reported this story remarked that many of the participants he was testing showed unease or apprehension during testing and often made stray comments concerning their nervousness or poor performance (or even their low intelligence; e.g., "I've always been dumb at math").

Such unprompted confessions are telling, we feel, and represent a neglected factor in ongoing recent attempts to improve mathematics education and achievement, not to mention current theories of mental representation of number knowledge. Ask yourself the following questions about the student who wept in response to subtraction with borrowing. Is this young woman confident in her mathematical abilities and motivated to do well at mathematics? Did she master the mathematics curriculum she was exposed to prior to college? Is she likely to pursue further mathematics in college, or a mathematics-oriented career? Was her performance on the laboratory task fluent and skilled?[1]

One of the major themes of this book is that adolescents and young adults are, in many respects, at their intellectual zenith, but their behavior often does not reflect their intellectual potential. One reason for this "achievement gap" is that adolescence can be a time of heightened emotion and stress (Casey et al., 2010). In this chapter, we present evidence concerning how emotion—specifically, anxiety—hinders mathematics learning and performance, and, hence, mathematics achievement.

We examine the influence of noncognitive factors—like the young woman's emotional reaction—in two broad realms related to mathematics. First, we focus on the basic learning and mastery of mathematics in the classroom. What do students learn about mathematics, say, in middle and high school, how much do they master, and how are these things influenced by such noncognitive factors as motivation, self-efficacy, and mathematics anxiety? As it happens, there is an important literature on these topics, although it is largely neglected when reforms in mathematics education are being considered. Second, we turn to immediate, online effects of noncognitive factors: How do influences like mathematics anxiety impact cognitive processing

---

[1] Conventional terminology for a problem like $34 - 19 = ?$ refers to subtraction with *borrowing*, where 10 is borrowed from 30, added to the 4, then 9 is subtracted from 14, etc. In the mathematical education community, the borrowing function is termed *regrouping*; the 10 is regrouped into 10 ones, added to the 4, and so forth (likewise, carrying in addition is also regrouping). The point we develop later in this chapter is that the mental operations involved, regardless of the term being used, are demanding of working memory resources. Similarly, some individuals solve the above problem by rounding 19 up to 20, subtracting without borrowing, then correcting the answer for the initial rounding. Such a transformation solution, we suggest, also involves multiple steps and a nontrivial load on working memory (e.g., LeFevre, Sadesky, & Bisanz, 1996).

when an individual is actually doing mathematics? Again, there is a growing literature on such effects, with some important results that need to be integrated into discussions of adolescent and adult cognition and into mathematics education and reform.

THE COGNITIVE APPROACH TO NONCOGNITIVE FACTORS

The question being posed here is, How do noncognitive factors impact higher cognition related to mathematics?—or, more basically, Do noncognitive factors have an important impact on mathematical cognition? It is a bit curious to pose such questions from the standpoint of mainstream cognitive psychology. In the 50 or so years since the beginning of the cognitive revolution (Gardner, 1985), cognitive psychology and cognitive science have attained something like dominant or majority status in experimental approaches to understanding behavior and the mind. Likewise, it has been roughly 40 years since the first published reports appeared in the area now known as *mathematical cognition,* studies on the cognitive psychology of mathematics (e.g., Suppes & Groen, 1967). (Earlier efforts, such as those by Thorndike, 1922, were mainly behaviorist rather than cognitive; but see Wertheimer, 1959.) Cognitive psychology has achieved tremendous insights into issues of mental representation and processing and has seen its influence spread to important studies of the organization, development, and plasticity of the brain. The same can be said, on a smaller scale, of the area of mathematical cognition, from its initial infatuation with computationally feasible models based on counting algorithms (Groen & Parkman, 1972; Suppes & Groen, 1967) to current models based on retrieval and use of strategies (e.g., Campbell, 1987; Campbell & Epp, 2005) and the underlying neural circuitry involved in number processing (Dehaene, Piazza, Pinel, & Cohen, 2005).

While cognitive psychologists do not typically investigate questions involving noncognitive, personal factors, the field of mathematics education has cast a broader net, encompassing affect, motivation, and individual differences (e.g., McLeod, 1994). Stated another way, mainstream cognitive psychology does not customarily deal with individual differences, certainly not those pertaining to person-related factors normally relegated to fields such as personality or social psychology. A search of the cognitive literature will result in few, if any, "hits" on topics like the effects of motivation on cognitive processing, for example (but for a recent step in this direction, see Maddox & Markman, 2010). Likewise, there are few, if any, research reports on the influence of other personal factors such as self-efficacy, need achievement, introversion versus extroversion—or even gender—on tasks such as word recognition, semantic priming, text comprehension, and so on. For the most part, cognitive psychology treats participants as neutral with respect to such affective or personal variables, on fairly plausible grounds: Aside from needing to have some adequate level of motivation to perform in an experiment, a participant's "motivation to read" or "feelings of self-efficacy in text comprehension," and so forth are probably irrelevant to performance and to theory. In any event, we reason that variations in such factors will simply be part of error variance.

The one clear exception to this generalization—cognitive psychology's indifference to individual differences—is its focus on working memory. Since the early work on the construct (Baddeley & Hitch, 1974), research has shown repeatedly how far ranging the influence of working memory capacity truly is, with important effects from basic attentional phenomena up through reading comprehension and fluid intelligence (for reviews, see Engle, 2001; and Miyake & Shah, 1999). A typical experiment tests participants on a working memory span task, separates participants into high- versus low-capacity groups, then tests the groups on a working memory–intensive task to see the outcome of processing differences. Such studies often show the clear advantages of higher capacity in terms of additional working memory resources that can be devoted to some taxing mental task.

Note that even in this exception, the individual difference is derived from a cognitive construct, the capacity of working memory, rather than a personal variable such as motivation. And even in this case, the experimental stimuli given to participants in the task, whether words to be heard or sentences to be comprehended, are chosen to be equally known and understandable by all participants using widely available norms. Such an assumption is likely safe enough in studies with robust and consistent effects, but it is not necessarily warranted in the topic we cover in this chapter, that is, arithmetic and other mathematical problems being solved by adolescents and young college adults. Indeed, the major point of the next section is that affective and other noncognitive factors have an impact on what adolescents learn when they take mathematics in school, both positive and negative. Regardless of the root causes of these factors, many of them can yield the kind of unfortunate educational effect that our society is now experiencing: substandard or deficient mathematics achievement, widespread at a national level. For example, only 23% of U.S. 12th graders are proficient in mathematics (National Mathematics Advisory Panel, 2008). The point we are making is not complex, of course; indeed, it seems all too obvious. But it is important, possibly as important as our concerns over improving mathematics curricula and teacher education. The point is simply that noncognitive factors compromise the learning and doing of mathematics.

NONCOGNITIVE FACTORS AND THEIR EFFECTS ON MATHEMATICS LEARNING

Separate from the main currents of cognitive research, there has been a consistent stream of work in psychology on noncognitive factors and their relation to general issues of individual mathematics achievement. (It is surprising how little impact this literature has had on issues of curriculum reform or debates about plummeting levels of mathematics achievement at the national level.) The most commonly examined variables are interest, motivation, self-efficacy, and mathematics anxiety, tested almost invariably—and not surprisingly, of course—in correlational designs, and almost universally measured by self-report questionnaires. A consequence of these designs and of the inherent nature of the factors themselves is that very little is clear with respect to causal relationships: Is low self-efficacy a cause, a consequence, or merely a correlate of high mathematics anxiety? Despite this uncertainty, the impact of the constellation of factors is clear on the outcome measure of interest, which is the individual's learning and achievement in mathematics.

Interest and Motivation

We begin with interest, the "curious" emotion in Silvia's (2008) description, and the role it plays in mathematics learning. Are children and adolescents interested in mathematics and in learning mathematics? The few relevant studies that exist indicate that young children in fact view mathematics rather positively when they begin formal education. In Stevenson et al.'s (1990a) study, 72% of first and fifth graders expressed positive attitudes toward mathematics. In our own data, 87% of first graders said that they felt "very good" when doing arithmetic and other mathematics, and 74% rated themselves as "very good" at arithmetic and other mathematics; these favorable attitudes declined, but only moderately, by fifth grade (Moore & Ashcraft, 2010). Unfortunately, self-rated interest and its close neighbor, motivation, show sharp declines during adolescence, when students report their attitudes about mathematics.

One possible reason for the decline in interest and motivation is that students encounter more stumbling blocks as they enter middle school, in the form of more difficult and more intellectually challenging mathematics, especially algebra. Furthermore, middle school students also begin to experience greater pressure to obtain passing grades, to prepare for proficiency and other high-stakes tests, and the like. Note also that different tracks also begin to appear at these grade levels, and then come the choices of mathematics courses beyond the graduation requirement.

Several large-scale correlational studies on interest and motivation have tested middle school and high school students and have revealed rather consistent findings. As an example, Köller, Baumert, and Schnabel (2001) tested 600 students in Grades 7 through 12, assessing their interest in mathematics, administering a standardized mathematics test, and keeping track of their enrollment in mathematics courses completed by Grade 12. Although interest in mathematics declined somewhat across the years because of competing nonscholastic interests, there was still a strong positive relationship between students' self-rated interest and their completion of the mathematics curriculum; students with the highest levels of interest selected and completed the highest level mathematics classes. In a similar vein, Simpkins, Davis-Kean, and Eccles (2006) used longitudinal data from the Michigan Childhood and Beyond study, which sampled students from Grades 5 through 12. Students who had participated in out-of-school mathematics activities in Grade 5 showed higher interest and self-concepts in mathematics and rated mathematics as more important at Grades 6 and 10. Furthermore, at a general level, the data revealed that students who took more mathematics courses had higher self-concepts and interest in mathematics, rated mathematics as more important, and achieved higher grades.

Zakaria and Nordin (2008) examined motivation, mathematics anxiety, and mathematics achievement in a sample of high school seniors. The motivation to continue studying mathematics or involve oneself in mathematics-related tasks was positively correlated with mathematics achievement scores ($r = .31$) and strongly negatively associated with mathematics anxiety ($r = -.72$). In other words, as motivation to study mathematics increased, mathematics achievement increased, but as mathematics anxiety increased, motivation and math achievement both decreased. Naturally, because these are correlations, causation could flow in either direction.

An important distinction should be made here between intrinsic and extrinsic motivation, since differing outcomes have been observed. Students who are intrinsically motivated in mathematics ("task focused") express the desire to increase their understanding, insight, and skill at mathematics; take more elective courses; and perceive an intrinsic importance in learning mathematics. In most contexts, intrinsically motivated students persevere in pursuing mathematics. In contrast, students who adopt an extrinsic motivation seek to gain rewards such as grades or praise from peers, teachers, and parents while avoiding negative consequences; for example, they are less likely to seek help from teachers because that would only provide additional opportunities for negative judgments. They seek tasks in which they already excel and focus on outperforming other students. When faced with negative feedback, they disengage or discontinue their pursuit of mathematics (e.g., National Mathematics Advisory Panel, 2008; Ryan & Pintrich, 1997).

Self-Efficacy

To paraphrase Bandura's (1977) definition and shape it to the topic of mathematics, *self-efficacy* is an individual's confidence in his or her ability to perform mathematics and is thought to directly impact the choice to engage in, expend effort on, and persist in pursuing mathematics, such as taking further mathematics classes and excelling in them. (Self-efficacy is a self-assessment of competence to perform a specific task, whereas self-esteem or self-concept are more general notions involving self-worth; Pajares, 1997.) Upon reflection, there appear to be elements both of prior success and positive motivation in the definition of self-efficacy. That is, it seems that an adolescent's confidence in doing well at mathematics results, at least in part, from prior success at mathematics. Likewise, if one continues to be engaged in mathematics, and if one persists in taking mathematics courses, these behaviors seem to exemplify standard definitions of motivation.

Despite definitional issues, the literature on self-efficacy and mathematics yields much the same kind of conclusion as is found with factors such as interest and motivation: Higher self-efficacy is also positively related to higher mathematics performance and lower mathematics anxiety. Three representative studies will suffice to illustrate.

Pietsch, Walker, and Chapman (2003) tested over 400 ninth and 10th graders, evaluating their mathematics self-concept, their mathematics self-efficacy, and their performance on an end-of-year comprehensive exam. Mathematics self-efficacy was evaluated both at a general level and separately for specific content areas (e.g., "How confident are you at computing percentages?"). Self-efficacy was found to be a better predictor of end-of-year performance than self-concept overall, and the topic-specific measure of self-efficacy was a better predictor of topic-specific performance than general self-efficacy was for overall performance. In a similar study, Lee (2009) examined mathematics self-concept, self-efficacy, mathematics anxiety, and mathematics performance of 250,000 fifteen-year-olds from 41 countries. Overall, there was a significant relationship ($r = .42$) between self-efficacy and mathematics performance; correlations within each participating country ranged from .15 to .59, and all were significant. Likewise, the relationship between mathematics anxiety and performance was negative, $r = -.65$ (and, as in Pietsch et al., 2003, self-efficacy was a better predictor than self-concept). And finally, Cooper and Robinson (1991) tested incoming university students on mathematics self-efficacy, mathematics anxiety, and two standardized mathematics performance tests. Mathematics self-efficacy and mathematics anxiety correlated negatively ($-.41$) as expected, and, also as expected, self-efficacy showed a positive relationship to the two performance tests, $r = .22$ for a state placement test and $r = .25$ for the ACT-Quantitative test. (For recent work on self-efficacy in math, the perceived classroom environment, and math performance, see Fast et al., 2010.)

Mathematics Anxiety

In essentially all respects, the effects of mathematics anxiety are exactly the opposite of those for interest, motivation, and self-efficacy. For the "positive" personal variables, high levels of interest, motivation, and self-efficacy are predictors of positive outcomes—taking more mathematics classes, getting better grades in mathematics, expressing more favorable attitudes about mathematics, scoring higher on performance tests, and indicating greater intention to pursue mathematics courses and career paths involving mathematics. Just the reverse outcomes are observed in the case of the "negative" variable of mathematics anxiety.

Hembree's (1990) meta-analysis is the convenient repository of results for the largely correlational literature on mathematics anxiety and the variables it is associated with; see Figure 9.1 for an illustration of some important correlations (for a more complete summary, see Ashcraft, Krause, & Hopko, 2007). As indicated, those high in mathematics anxiety take fewer mathematics courses, both in high school and college (i.e., fewer elective courses), and they get lower grades in the (required) mathematics courses they do take. Their scores on standardized tests are lower. They express dislike of mathematics, intend to avoid taking additional mathematics courses if possible, and avoid college majors and career paths that involve mathematics. On a partic-

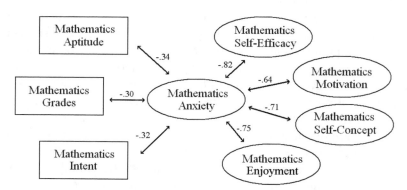

Figure 9.1. Representative correlations between mathematics anxiety and three mathematics-related behaviors (rectangles), performance on aptitude/achievement tests, grades in mathematics courses, and intent to enroll in mathematics courses (college), and four mathematics-related attitudes (ovals), self-efficacy, motivation in mathematics, self-concept in mathematics, and enjoyment of mathematics. All correlations are taken from Hembree (1990) and are significant beyond $p < .01$.

ularly depressing note, of the college majors surveyed, the students highest in mathematics anxiety were those preparing to be elementary school teachers. Of special importance here, data analyzed in Hembree's review clearly show an increase in mathematics anxiety, for both genders, during adolescence (i.e., from Grades 6 through 10); scores leveled off beyond that point, although scores from college samples are of course affected by attrition relative to scores from high school samples (i.e., attrition of high school students who do not pursue college).

Beliefs About Mathematics and Mathematical Abilities

A final note on an affective factor concerns students' beliefs about mathematics and their own learning and intelligence. Some students believe that intelligence and the ability to learn and do well in mathematics are largely due to fixed attributes or qualities that are not malleable (i.e., innate factors). They tend to do worse than students who believe that intelligence and learning are largely due to effort and persistence. As an example, Blackwell, Trzesniewski, and Dweck (2007) found that students who viewed intelligence as a fixed trait declined in their performance across the first semester of seventh grade and continued to decline across the next 2 years. In accordance with their beliefs about the importance of immutable attributes, this "fixed" group devoted less and less effort to mathematics when faced with the more difficult demands of seventh-grade mathematics. In contrast, the group that viewed intelligence and mathematics learning as due to effort did not show a performance decline during the same time period. This "malleable" group, with its greater belief in the importance of effort and more mastery-oriented reactions to setbacks, simply showed more persistence and effort as the seventh-grade mathematics curriculum made more difficult demands. Unfortunately, the belief in a fixed or innate capacity for mathematics learning and intelligence tends to be far more characteristic of Western attitudes, especially those in the United States, than Asian attitudes (e.g., Stevenson et al., 1990b). However, Blackwell et al. (2007) showed in a randomized trial design that these beliefs about intelligence can be changed, and those changes produced increases in mathematics achievement.

Summary

As we have noted, most of the results just described are correlational in nature, and only experimental or careful longitudinal research can truly disentangle the factors of interest, motivation, self-efficacy, anxiety, and beliefs in order to draw cause-and-effect conclusions (for promising work in the area of test anxiety, see Lang & Lang, 2010). But the weight of the correlational evidence should not be ignored, given the associations with a variety of important outcome measures. Students with low interest and motivation for mathematics, low self-efficacy, or high mathematics anxiety take fewer mathematics courses and learn less mathematics in the courses they take. Their mathematics achievement is lower than those with higher motivation and self-efficacy, or those with lower mathematics anxiety. Students who have these problems but nevertheless manage to enter college are very likely the ones to need more remedial coursework in mathematics, to avoid mathematics-related majors and careers, and to struggle more with the required mathematics they do take. Taken together, these affective reactions correlate with a general tendency to avoid mathematics, affording students even fewer opportunities to learn. Contrast this with the positive outcomes associated with high interest and motivation, high self-efficacy, low mathematics anxiety, and the belief that intelligence and mathematics learning are due to effort and persistence. These positive outcomes can be generally called approach outcomes, a general tendency to approach mathematics and excel at it.

There are clear consequences of approach versus avoidance behavioral patterns during formal education, especially for adolescence, including the middle school years, when algebra is taught. Putting it in stark terms, with the approach constellation of personal factors we get adolescents who are more likely to learn and master mathematics in middle school and high school and be interested in pursuing mathematics further in their education; there is an "affective boost" to their learning. We get just the opposite pattern with the avoidance constellation, adolescents who have not mastered mathematics, adolescents who need remedial work if they pursue college, and adolescents who shun further mathematics in their education—an "affective drop" in learning.

NONCOGNITIVE FACTORS AND THEIR EFFECT ON MATHEMATICS PROCESSING

We turn now to a discussion of the effects that noncognitive factors have on cognitive processing while individuals are actually doing mathematics in a laboratory setting. Although there is not a great deal of this research in the literature, what does exist is quite consistent in its conclusions, in terms of the cognitive processing that is affected, and in its implications. To foreshadow the general conclusion of this work, all signs indicate that these noncognitive factors exert their influence on the working memory system, typically by depleting working memory of the resources that are necessary for proficient mathematical problem solving.

Mathematics Anxiety

We conducted several early studies on the possible effects that mathematics anxiety might have on cognitive process during arithmetic problem solving. These were exploratory studies, apparently the first to examine the possibility that mathematics anxiety might compromise online mathematics processing (Ashcraft & Faust, 1994; Faust, Ashcraft, & Fleck, 1996). We presented arithmetic problems to college students in a timed task, comparing the results to the large existing literature that had accrued on cognitive processing on such tasks (for a review, see Ashcraft, 1992). There were minimal effects of mathematics anxiety on the simple one-digit "basic facts" of addition and multiplication (e.g., $3 + 5$, 4×6) in terms of latency or accuracy of responses, but larger effects on more complex arithmetic problems.

In particular, highly mathematics-anxious participants often responded quite rapidly on complex problems (e.g., division problems) with especially high error rates, as compared to performance by low-anxiety participants. This suggested that our high mathematics-anxious groups were using a speed–accuracy tradeoff rather strategically, sacrificing accuracy simply in order to hurry the testing session along to its conclusion; we termed this "local avoidance," in contrast to the general avoidance of mathematics-anxious individuals noted above. Second, our high mathematics-anxious participants, especially on two-column addition and subtraction problems, were typically much slower and more error prone than our low mathematics-anxious participants, particularly when the problems involved carrying or borrowing.

This latter finding, the particular disruption of processing when carrying or borrowing (regrouping) was involved, suggested strongly that there might be a connection between mathematics anxiety and working memory. That is, problems such as $27 + 39 = ?$ or $43 - 17 = ?$ involve not only the retrieval of basic fact information, column by column, but also regrouping (or transformations, or some other compensatory process, e.g., solving $27 + 39$ as $27 + 40 - 1$) and various keeping-track processes. And to the extent that even the basic facts ($7 + 9$, $13 - 7$) are solved via some nonretrieval process, even by college students (e.g., LeFevre et al., 1996), the load on working memory would increase substantially more (for a thorough review of the importance of working memory to mathematics processing, see LeFevre, DeStefano, Coleman, & Shanahan, 2005).

A second, more theoretically driven reason suggested that working memory might be involved in the mathematics anxiety effect as well. As our early mathematics-anxiety studies were being conducted, Eysenck was beginning to articulate his important theoretical views on the general effects of anxiety on cognition (e.g., Eysenck, 1992; Eysenck & Calvo, 1992). In this approach, anxiety is expected to degrade or interfere with performance efficiency

(i.e., speed or accuracy) whenever processing taps working memory to a significant degree. Eysenck's explanation is based on the general notion that
anxiety is a state that leads to internal, mental rumination and negative, pre-
occupying thoughts about the anxiety itself and that those thoughts consume
some of the resources of working memory. For any task that requires substantial working memory resources, therefore, there will be a shortage; hence,
those high in anxiety will show performance deficits.

Eysenck's (1992) formulation seemed to make clear predictions for mathematics anxiety, to the degree that mathematics anxiety functions like general
or state anxiety (the correlation with general anxiety is .35, and with state anxiety is .42). We reasoned that the more working memory was involved in problem solving, the greater disadvantage mathematics-anxious individuals would
show during problem solving, whereas in conditions of low working-memory
involvement, group differences should be minimal or nonexistent. A series of
studies by Ashcraft and Kirk (2001) confirmed these predictions. First, participants were classified, by means of a standard mathematics-anxiety survey, into
low, medium, and high mathematics-anxiety groups. In an untimed prepara-
tory testing session, the groups demonstrated preexperimental equivalence on
the addition problems to be tested in the main experiment, a necessary step to
eliminate mathematics ability as a potential confound in any difference found
among mathematics-anxiety groups. (In other words, the groups were equated
for mathematical ability but differed in mathematics anxiety.) Then, in the
main study, they were given the same addition problems again, in a dual-task
procedure: On one block, of trials, they merely had to perform arithmetic; on
another block, they performed a letter-recall task with either two or six letters
as the working memory load; and, in the dual task, they performed both arithmetic and the letter-recall task together. The logic here is that the dual task
condition, combining difficult arithmetic and a six-letter load on working
memory, should tax working memory capacity. If high mathematics anxiety
also drains working memory resources, then performance for this group should
be especially disrupted.

The results were very straightforward and confirmed our predictions.
Both in the control conditions and in the minimal memory-load condition,
there were essentially no anxiety group differences in performance, either in
terms of latencies or errors. To be sure, errors increased in the higher load
conditions and were higher for carry problems, but these were not differentially affected by the mathematics-anxiety factor. But in the most difficult
condition, in which the memory load was high and the arithmetic problem
involved a carry, the mathematics-anxiety effect was quite prominent. High
mathematics-anxious participants committed far more errors in this condition (39% on the letter-recall task) than they did in the low memory-load
(14%) or control (15%) condition. The low- and medium-anxiety groups

committed only 20% and 25% errors in the difficult condition, by comparison. In other words, the additional burden of mathematics anxiety while processing these difficult trials had led to the marked increase in errors—or, in Eysenck's (1992) terms, the marked decrease in processing efficiency. This pattern of results has recently been replicated by Krause, Rudig, and Ashcraft (2009), using two-column subtraction problems. In parallel fashion, borrowing in a high memory-load condition yielded the highest error rates, especially for high mathematics-anxious individuals.

Although we are confident of the conclusion that mathematics anxiety has a major impact on cognitive processing via its disruption of working memory, recent evidence suggests that this impact is not limited to situations involving lengthy or complex arithmetic and mathematics. Maloney, Risko, Ansari, and Fugelsang (2010) tested low versus high mathematics-anxious individuals on the venerable subitizing task, asking their participants merely to state how many objects were shown in briefly presented displays of 1 to 8 dots. They found the standard subitizing result of a nearly flat latency function up to set size 3, and a more sharply increasing function from 4 to 8 items, where the sharply increasing function is indicative of counting as opposed to rapid, automatic apprehension of small numerosities in the 1 to 3 range. What was interesting about the results, however, was that high mathematics-anxious individuals showed a significantly steeper slope for the counting function from 4 to 8, compared with the low-anxiety group. Apparently, even dealing with the low-level processing involved in counting dots was sufficient to arouse enough anxiety to interfere with performance.

Stereotype Threat

A variable that is related to mathematics anxiety, stereotype threat, has also been investigated with respect to mathematics performance. A classic series of studies done by Steele (e.g., Aronson et al., 1999; Steele & Aronson, 1995) examined the overall effects of stereotype threat with respect to race and ethnic group. When a group of participants is exposed to a self-relevant, negative stereotype concerning performance on a task, individuals perform more poorly on that task than would otherwise be the case. For example, African Americans exposed to a negative stereotype about their race's performance on intelligence testing (Steele & Aronson, 1995) did more poorly on the test than those not exposed to the stereotype. In Aronson et al. (1999), Caucasian men exposed to a negative stereotype about white men doing poorly on mathematics tests in fact did more poorly on the test. It appears that members of virtually any group, if exposed to a plausible negative stereotype about the group, will suffer in performance from exposure to the stereotype (or conceivably, if the stereotype is positive, will experience a boost in performance).

Given these effects, Beilock, Rydell, and McConnell (2007) examined the possible cognitive underpinnings of the stereotype threat effect across several experiments. They gave their participants easy and more difficult modular arithmetic problems, a novel type of multistep arithmetic problem.[2] Some of the female participants were exposed to a standard stereotype threat, which stated that the purpose of the study was to understand why males consistently score higher on standardized mathematics tests than females do. In the first study, the women exposed to gender stereotype performed worse on high-demand problems but not on low-demand problems, presumably because high-demand problems required more working memory resources. A follow-up study confirmed this interpretation: Female participants' performance was compromised only on the difficult modular arithmetic problems that were novel, that is, those that had not been repeated across blocks of practice within the experiment. In other words, only those problems that still required substantial levels of working memory involvement were affected by the manipulation of stereotype threat (see also Schmader & Johns, 2003; interestingly, Johns, Schmader, & Martens, 2005, eliminated the stereotype threat effect by informing women about it). And in a dramatic demonstration, Krendl, Richeson, Kelley, and Heatherton (2008) demonstrated with functional magnetic resonance imaging techniques that participants exposed to stereotype threat in a mathematics task showed activation in emotion-regulation regions of the neocortex (ventral anterior cingulate cortex) during processing. Those who performed under normal conditions (no stereotype threat) showed activations consistent with typical mathematics learning (angular gyrus and left parietal and prefrontal cortex).

Pressure

Pressure, as typically conceptualized in cognitive psychology, represents an external factor that induces a performance criterion or expectation in a task. Manipulations of generalized pressure have historically been used in paradigms such as deadline or speed–accuracy tradeoff procedures, in which a participant must respond within a certain time period or under instructions that emphasize either rapid or accurate performance. A small but important group of studies in the mathematics cognition area has implemented an exter-

---

[2]Modular arithmetic, introduced by Gauss in 1801, involves integer arithmetic problems of the form $a \equiv b \pmod n$, for example $51 \equiv 19 \pmod 4$. The problem is said to be "congruent modulo," or "true," if the difference $a - b$ is evenly divisible by n; in the example, $51 - 19 = 32$, and since 32 is evenly divisible by 4 the problem is true. Equivalently, if both a and b have the same remainder when divided by n, the problem is true. In Beilock et al. (2007), low demand (easy) problems used small numbers for a and b, for example, $8 \equiv 4 \pmod 2$.

nal pressure manipulation in the context of mathematics problem solving, specifically designed to induce a personal impact. Important, the pressure manipulation is intended to mimic the kinds of pressure experienced in high-stakes testing situations that students encounter in school.

Consider as representative a study by Beilock and Carr (2005; see also Beilock & DeCaro, 2007; Beilock, Kulp, Holt, & Carr, 2004). Participants were first categorized according to their working memory capacity and were then tested on a set of easy and difficult modular arithmetic problems. Problems were tested under two pressure conditions, low and high. In the low-pressure condition, participants were simply told that they were receiving yet another block of practice trials and that they should continue to respond as they had been doing. In the high-pressure condition, they were exposed to a multipronged pressure manipulation, involving monetary incentive, peer pressure, and social evaluation. They were told that both they and an unseen partner needed to improve their performance by 20% over the first block of trials in order to receive a monetary reward, that the partner had already done so, and that a video of their performance would be viewed by professors and mathematics teachers.

Faced with such pressure, the group that tested for high working memory capacity experienced a significant decline in performance but only on the difficult problems, that is, only on those problems that were most reliant on working memory. Problems that required only minimal working memory involvement were unaffected by the pressure manipulation, not surprisingly, and the performance of low-capacity participants, fairly low even with low pressure, was essentially unchanged by the pressure manipulation. One clear implication of this work, replicated several times, is particularly disturbing: Those most capable of high-level performance are the most vulnerable to performance decrements under conditions of high pressure, such as high-stakes or high-pressure testing represented by proficiency tests or college entrance (e.g., SAT, ACT) tests. Such results do not imply that testing should be eliminated, but they further underline the need to understand how individual differences interact with the pressure-to-performance relationship.

Summary

The overall message of online testing with respect to anxiety, mathematics anxiety, stereotype threat, and manipulations of pressure is very clear: All of these variables appear to compromise the resources available to working memory, resources needed for normal problem solving. Thus, when mathematics coursework grows more difficult, the "affective drop" in performance becomes more pronounced. To our knowledge, no comparable research has demonstrated an "affective boost" in mathematics performance.

CONCLUSION

In terms of scientific understanding and educational interventions, it would be desirable to know which personal variables are primary and which are secondary: Does initial lower ability in mathematics lead to lower motivation and lower self-efficacy, which in turn yield mathematics anxiety and performance decrements, or does mathematics anxiety appear first, leading to lower performance through a different set of pathways? Very little is known about the causal mechanisms involved in these factors, although there are some strong hints. For example, Turner et al. (2002) found that various forms of avoidance in math classes were associated with teachers who conveyed a high demand for correctness but provided little cognitive or motivational support during lessons. And recent work has shown that female teachers' mathematics anxiety has an impact on young girls' levels of mathematics achievement and gender stereotyping (i.e., the belief that girls are not as good at mathematics as boys; Beilock, Gunderson, Ramirez, & Levine, 2010). Thus, teachers may be a vector through which cultural stereotypes, as well as mathematics anxiety, are transmitted.

Although definitive causal evidence is not yet available, extant evidence points to the conclusion that mathematics anxiety, motivation, self-efficacy, and teacher's (and society's) attitudes toward mathematics undermine students' learning and mastery of mathematics. These noncognitive factors appear to have global effects on the learning of mathematics in school, the pursuit of further mathematics training, and the selection of mathematics-related career paths. They also have local, online effects, when participants are tested in the laboratory and when students are given achievement tests. These effects, centered on disruption of the working memory system, are anything but trivial. Even two-column addition with carrying or regrouping, a topic in the second-grade curriculum, involves a substantial working memory load. Thus, higher level mathematics—for example, solving algebra problems with two unknowns—clearly involves even more of this critical processing resource.

Given the research that we have reviewed, it is insufficient merely to warn researchers to be vigilant about personal factors when conducting studies on mathematics performance. Variations in personal factors appear to influence not just the mastery of mathematics (the basic representation of underlying knowledge) but also online performance during testing: Mathematics achievement scores are lowered by mathematics anxiety, by stereotype threat, and by pressure, as are performance measures in the laboratory. A theory about the representation of algebraic knowledge, for example, must consider not only the representation of that knowledge and how well it was originally learned but also how it is retrieved and applied and how all our assessments and measurements have been filtered through a system coping with affective reactions. A theory of higher level mathematical processing that neglects the noncognitive factors that determine such retrieval and application will be incomplete or even misleading.

Likewise, given the research base, educational practice needs to be mindful of personal factors in at least two ways. First, students harbor attitudes and beliefs that can have a profound influence on their learning. The influence can be desirable, if those attitudes and beliefs lead to the approach constellation discussed earlier, or unfortunate, in the case of the avoidance constellation. But it's possible that the avoidance beliefs and attitudes are more malleable than has been assumed; Blackwell et al. (2007), for example, demonstrated that "fixed intelligence" beliefs can be changed. Second, it is likely that teacher attitudes and beliefs need to be addressed as well, both for noncognitive factors discussed here (e.g., a teacher's mathematics anxiety) and for matters of classroom style and the learning environment constructed for students (e.g., the demanding, nonsupportive math teacher). After all, even a well-designed curriculum will yield poor results if affective factors—whether on the part of the student or the teacher—prevent the learner from engaging in the topic.

REFERENCES

Aronson, J., Lustina, M. J., Good, C., Keough, K., Steele, C. M., & Brown, J. (1999). When white men can't do math: Necessary and sufficient factors in stereotype threat. *Journal of Experimental Social Psychology, 35*, 29–46. doi:10.1006/jesp.1998.1371

Ashcraft, M. H. (1992). Cognitive arithmetic: A review of data and theory. *Cognition, 44*, 75–106. doi:10.1016/0010-0277(92)90051-I

Ashcraft, M. H. (2002). Math anxiety: Personal, educational, and cognitive consequences. *Current Directions in Psychological Science, 11*, 181–185. doi:10.1111/1467-8721.00196

Ashcraft, M. H., & Faust, M. W. (1994). Mathematics anxiety and mental arithmetic performance: An exploratory investigation. *Cognition and Emotion, 8*, 97–125. doi:10.1080/02699939408408931

Ashcraft, M. H., & Kirk, E. P. (2001). The relationships among working memory, math anxiety, and performance. *Journal of Experimental Psychology: General, 130*, 224–237. doi:10.1037/0096-3445.130.2.224

Ashcraft, M. H., Krause, J. A., & Hopko, D. R. (2007). Is math anxiety a mathematical learning disability? In D. B. Berch & M. M. M. Mazzocco (Eds.), *Why is math so hard for some children? The nature and origins of mathematical learning difficulties and disabilities* (pp. 329–348). Baltimore, MD: Paul H. Brookes.

Baddeley, A. D., & Hitch, G. (1974). Working memory. In G. H. Bower (Ed.), *The psychology of learning and motivation: Vol. 8* (pp. 47–89). New York, NY: Academic Press.

Bandura, A. (1977). Self-efficacy: Toward a unifying theory of behavioral change. *Psychological Review, 84,* 191–215. doi:10.1037/0033-295X.84.2.191

Beilock, S. L., & Carr, T. H. (2005). When high-powered people fail: Working memory and "choking under pressure" in math. *Psychological Science, 16,* 101–105. doi:10.1111/j.0956-7976.2005.00789.x

Beilock, S. L., & DeCaro, M. S. (2007). From poor performance to success under stress: Working memory, strategy selection, and mathematical problem solving under pressure. *Journal of Experimental Psychology: Learning, Memory, and Cognition, 33,* 983–998. doi:10.1037/0278-7393.33.6.983

Beilock, S. L., Gunderson, E. A., Ramirez, G., & Levine, S. C. (2010). Female teachers' math anxiety affects girls' math achievement. *Proceedings of the National Academy of Sciences Early Edition.* Retrieved from http://www.pnas.org/cgi/doi/10.1073.pnas.0910967107

Beilock, S. L., Kulp, C. A., Holt, L. E., & Carr, T. H. (2004). More on the fragility of performance: Choking under pressure in mathematical problem solving. *Journal of Experimental Psychology: General, 133,* 584–600. doi:10.1037/0096-3445.133.4.584

Beilock, S. L., Rydell, R. J., & McConnell, A. R. (2007). Stereotype threat and working memory: Mechanisms, alleviation, and spillover. *Journal of Experimental Psychology: General, 136,* 256–276. doi:10.1037/0096-3445.136.2.256

Blackwell, L. S., Trzesniewski, K., & Dweck, C. S. (2007). Implicit theories of intelligence predict achievement across an adolescent transition: A longitudinal study and an intervention. *Child Development, 78,* 246–263. doi:10.1111/j.1467-8624.2007.00995.x

Campbell, J. I. D. (1987). Network interference and mental multiplication. *Journal of Experimental Psychology: Learning, Memory, and Cognition, 13,* 109–123. doi:10.1037/0278-7393.13.1.109

Campbell, J. I. D., & Epp, L. J. (2005). Architectures for arithmetic. In J. I. D. Campbell (Ed.), *Handbook of mathematical cognition* (pp. 347–360). New York, NY: Psychology Press.

Casey, B. J., Jones, R. M., Levita, L., Libby, V., Pattwell, S., Ruberry, E., . . . Somerville, L. H. (2010). The storm and stress of adolescence: Insights from human imaging and mouse genetics. *Developmental Psychobiology, 52,* 225–235.

Cooper, S. E., & Robinson, D. A. (1991). The relationship of mathematics self-efficacy beliefs to mathematics anxiety and performance. *Measurement and Evaluation in Counseling & Development, 24,* 4–11.

Dehaene, S., Piazza, M., Pinel, P., & Cohen, L. (2005). Three parietal circuits for number processing. In J. I. D. Campbell (Ed.), *Handbook of mathematical cognition* (pp. 433–453). New York, NY: Psychology Press.

Engle, R. W. (2001). What is working memory capacity? In H. L. Roediger, J. S. Nairne, I. Neath, & A. M. Superant (Eds.), *The nature of remembering: Essays in honor of Robert G. Crowder* (pp. 297–314). Washington, DC: American Psychological Association.

Eysenck, M. W. (1992). *Anxiety: The cognitive perspective.* Hove, England: Erlbaum.

Eysenck, M. W., & Calvo, M. G. (1992). Anxiety and performance: The processing efficiency theory. *Cognition and Emotion, 6,* 409–434. doi:10.1080/02699939208409696

Fast, L. A., Lewis, J. L., Bryant, M. J., Bocian, K. A., Cardullo, R. A., Rettig, M., & Hammond, K. A. (2010). Does math self-efficacy mediate the effect of the perceived classroom environment on standardized math test performance? *Journal of Educational Psychology, 102,* 729–740. doi:10.1037/a0018863

Faust, M. W., Ashcraft, M. H., & Fleck, D. E. (1996). Mathematics anxiety effects in simple and complex addition. *Mathematical Cognition, 2,* 25–62. doi:10.1080/135467996387534

Gardner, H. (1985). *The mind's new science: A history of the cognitive revolution.* New York, NY: Basic Books.

Groen, G. J., & Parkman, J. M. (1972). A chronometric analysis of simple addition. *Psychological Review, 79,* 329–343. doi:10.1037/h0032950

Hembree, R. (1990). The nature, effects, and relief of mathematics anxiety. *Journal for Research in Mathematics Education, 21,* 33–46. doi:10.2307/749455

Johns, M., Schmader, T., & Martens, A. (2005). Knowing is half the battle: Teaching stereotype threat as a means of improving women's math performance. *Psychological Science, 16,* 175–179. doi:10.1111/j.0956-7976.2005.00799.x

Köller, O., Baumert, J., & Schnabel, K. (2001). Does interest matter? The relationship between academic interest and achievement in mathematics. *Journal for Research in Mathematics Education, 32,* 448–470. doi:10.2307/749801

Krause, J. A., Rudig, N. O., & Ashcraft, M. H. (2009, November). *Math, working memory, and math anxiety effects.* Poster presented at the meetings of the Psychonomic Society, Boston.

Krendl, A. C., Richeson, J. A., Kelley, W. M., & Heatherton, T. F. (2008). The negative consequences of threat: A functional magnetic resonance imaging investigation of the neural mechanisms underlying women's underperformance in math. *Psychological Science, 19,* 168–175. doi:10.1111/j.1467-9280.2008.02063.x

Lang, J. W. B., & Lang, J. (2010). Priming competence diminishes the link between cognitive test anxiety and test performance: Implications for the interpretation of test scores. *Psychological Science, 21,* 811–819. doi:10.1177/0956797610369492

Lee, J. (2009). Universals and specifics of math self-concept, math self-efficacy, and math anxiety across 41 PISA 2003 participating countries. *Learning and Individual Differences, 19,* 355–365. doi:10.1016/j.lindif.2008.10.009

LeFevre, J., DeStefano, D., Coleman, B., & Shanahan, T. (2005). Mathematical cognition and working memory. In J. I. D. Campbell (Ed.), *Handbook of Mathematical Cognition* (pp. 361–377). New York, NY: Psychology Press.

LeFevre, J., Sadesky, G. S., & Bisanz, J. (1996). Selection of procedures in mental addition: Reassessing the problem-size effect in adults. *Journal of Experimental Psychology: Learning, Memory, and Cognition, 22,* 216–230. doi:10.1037/0278-7393.22.1.216

Maddox, W. T., & Markman, A. B. (2010). The motivation–cognition interface in learning and decision making. *Current Directions in Psychological Science, 19,* 106–110. doi:10.1177/0963721410364008

Maloney, E. A., Risko, E. F., Ansari, D., & Fugelsang, J. (2010). Mathematics anxiety affects counting but not subitizing during visual enumeration. *Cognition, 114,* 293–297. doi:10.1016/j.cognition.2009.09.013

McLeod, D. (1994). Research on affect and mathematics learning in JRME: 1970 to the present. *Journal for Research in Mathematics Education, 25,* 637–647. doi:10.2307/749576

Miyake, A., & Shah, P. (Eds.). (1999). *Models of working memory: Mechanisms of active maintenance and executive control.* New York, NY: Cambridge University Press.

Moore, A. M., & Ashcraft, M. H. (2010). Relationships across mathematics tasks in elementary school children. Unpublished manuscript, University of Nevada, Las Vegas.

National Mathematics Advisory Panel. (2008). *Foundations for success.* Reports of the Task Groups and Subcommittees. Washington, DC: U.S. Department of Education. Retrieved from http://edpubs.ed.gov

Pajares, F. (1997). Current directions in self-efficacy research. In M. L. Maehr & P. R. Pintrich (Eds.), *Advances in motivation and achievement: Vol. 10* (pp. 1–49). Greenwich, CT: JAI Press.

Pietsch, J., Walker, R., & Chapman, E. (2003). The relationship among self-concept, self-efficacy, and performance in mathematics during secondary school. *Journal of Educational Psychology, 95,* 589–603. doi:10.1037/0022-0663.95.3.589

Ryan, A. M., & Pintrich, P. R. (1997). "Should I ask for help?" The role of motivation and attitudes in adolescents' help seeking in math class. *Journal of Educational Psychology, 89,* 329–341. doi:10.1037/0022-0663.89.2.329

Schmader, T., & Johns, M. (2003). Converging evidence that stereotype threat reduces working memory capacity. *Journal of Personality and Social Psychology, 85,* 440–452. doi:10.1037/0022-3514.85.3.440

Silvia, P. J. (2008). Interest: The curious emotion. *Current Directions in Psychological Science, 17,* 57–60. doi:10.1111/j.1467-8721.2008.00548.x

Simpkins, S. D., Davis-Kean, P. E., & Eccles, J. S. (2006). Math and science motivation: A longitudinal examination of the links between choices and beliefs. *Developmental Psychology, 42,* 70–83. doi:10.1037/0012-1649.42.1.70

Steele, C. M., & Aronson, J. (1995). Stereotype threat and the intellectual test performance of African Americans. *Journal of Personality and Social Psychology, 69*, 797–811. doi:10.1037/0022-3514.69.5.797

Stevenson, H. W., Lee, S., Chen, C., Lummis, M., Stigler, J., Fan, L., & Ge, F. (1990a). Mathematics achievement of children in China and the United States. *Child Development, 61*, 1053–1066. doi:10.2307/1130875

Stevenson, H. W., Lee, S., Chen, C., Stigler, J. W., Hsu, C., Kitamura, S., & Hatano, G. (1990b). Contexts of achievement: A study of American, Chinese, and Japanese children. *Monographs of the Society for Research in Child Development, 55* (1–2), Serial no. 221.

Suppes, P., & Groen, G. J. (1967). Some counting models for first grade performance on simple addition facts. In J. M. Scandura (Ed.), *Research in mathematics education*. Washington, DC: National Council of Teachers of Mathematics.

Thorndike, E. (1922). *The psychology of arithmetic*. New York, NY: Macmillan. doi:10.1037/11080-000

Turner, J. C., Midgley, C., Meyer, D. K., Gheen, M., Anderman, E. M., Kang, Y., & Patrick, H. (2002). The classroom environment and students' reports of avoidance strategies in mathematics: A multimethod study. *Journal of Educational Psychology, 94*, 88–106. doi:10.1037/0022-0663.94.1.88

Wertheimer, M. (1959). *Productive thinking*. New York, NY: Harper & Row.

Zakaria, E., & Nordin, N. M. (2008). The effects of math anxiety on matriculation students as related to motivation and achievement. *Eurasia Journal of Mathematics, Science & Technology Education, 4*, 27–30.

IV

JUDGMENT AND
DECISION MAKING

10

RISKY BEHAVIOR IN ADOLESCENTS: THE ROLE OF THE DEVELOPING BRAIN

ADRIANA GALVÁN

Adolescence and young adulthood are characterized by increased risk-taking behavior. Coincident with these behavioral alterations are significant neuro-developmental changes in brain regions critical for decision making, reward processing, and risky behavior, namely, frontostriatal circuitry. This chapter begins by describing a neurobiological model designed to capture developmental changes in this circuitry as they may relate to risk-taking behavior, examines the role of context in magnifying these effects, and outlines recent studies that provide a biological basis for the model. The chapter concludes with some speculative remarks that integrate the proposed models as they may generalize to real-life adolescent behavior.

The developmental period of adolescence is fascinating. In recent years, researchers from a broad spectrum of scientific disciplines have shown significant interest in this period of the life span due to its intense physical, behavioral, social, and neurological changes (Somerville, Jones, & Casey, 2010). Numerous reviews, chapters, and empirical studies have documented the rise and fall of risk-taking behaviors that characterize adolescence (Boyer, 2006; Reyna & Farley, 2006; Steinberg, 2008). Not only does this period confer a conspicuous behavioral change, but it also marks a significant time in neurodevelopment. In particular, two key neural systems, the prefrontal cortex and the striatal system, show developmental changes that likely contribute to the risky behavior that often characterizes adolescence and young adulthood. The developmental relationship between these neural systems has been characterized in the imbalance model (Casey, Getz, & Galván, 2008; Casey, Hare, & Galván, in press). This chapter begins by outlining this model and subsequently proposes that, in addition to the two factors it describes (the prefrontal cognitive system and subcortical reward system), a critical third factor is environment, or context. The remainder of the chapter outlines empirical evidence to support the model and concludes with some speculative remarks.

NEUROBIOLOGY OF RISK IN ADOLESCENCE: A TALE OF TWO SYSTEMS

As reviewed in greater detail below, converging evidence suggests that two key cognitive and neural changes are occurring in adolescence. First, there is improved cognitive control with maturation of the prefrontal cortex (e.g., Bunge, Dudukovic, Thomason, Vaidya, & Gabrieli, 2002; Casey et al., 1997). Second, there is heightened proclivity toward reward-seeking behaviors, with exaggerated neural activation in dopamine-rich neural regions (Ernst et al., 2005; Galván et al., 2006; Geier, Terwilliger, Teslovich, Velanova, & Luna, 2010). Both of these changes undoubtedly influence risky behavior. While the adolescent may experience greater neural activation following rewards, which subsequently biases him or her to engage in further reward-seeking and risky behavior, the prefrontal cortex is not yet ready to regulate this reward-driven behavior. This notion is akin to numerous dual process theories put forth previously (e.g., Casey et al., 2008; Gerrard, Gibbons, & Gano, 2003; Gibbons, Gerrard, & Lane, 2003; Rivers, Reyna, & Mills, 2008; Steinberg, 2008). These theories posit that humans are dual processors. In this sense, people are capable of controlled, analytic, rational processes but often rely on more automatic, intuitive, heuristic processes (Epstein, 1998; Evans, 1984; Evans, Venn, & Feeney, 2002; Kirkpatrick & Epstein, 1992; Metcalfe & Mischel, 1999; Reyna, 2004; Reyna & Brainerd, 1995; Sloman, 1996). In neurobiological terms, the controlled, analytic component is subserved by the prefrontal cortex, whereas the automatic and intuitive process is mediated by the subcortical, affect-related systems.

In our own version of this notion, we propose the imbalance model (Casey et al., 2008; Casey et al., in press; see Figure 10.1). This neurobiological model of adolescent development evolved within the dual process framework and built on rodent models (Adriani & Laviola, 2004; Laviola, Macri, Morley-Fletcher, & Adriani, 2003; Spear, 2000) and imaging studies of

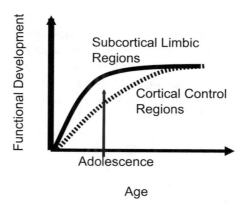

Figure 10.1. Imbalance model of neurobiological development in adolescence.

adolescence (Ernst et al., 2005; Galván, Hare, Voss, Glover, & Casey, 2007; Hare et al., 2008) and is corroborated by more recent evidence in animal studies (Robinson, Zitzman, Smith, & Spear, 2011; Toledo-Rodriguez & Sandi, 2011; Wilmouth & Spear, 2009) and human studies (Cohen et al., 2010; Geier et al., 2010; Van Leijenhorst et al., 2010). This characterization of adolescence goes beyond exclusive association of risky behavior to the immaturity of the prefrontal cortex. Instead, the proposed neurobiological model illustrates how limbic subcortical and prefrontal top-down control regions must be considered together. Figure 10.1 shows different developmental trajectories for these systems, with limbic systems developing earlier than prefrontal control regions. According to this model, the individual is biased more by functionally mature limbic regions during adolescence (i.e., imbalance of limbic relative to prefrontal control), compared with children, for whom these systems (i.e., both limbic and prefrontal) are still developing, and compared with adults, for whom these systems are fully mature. This perspective provides a basis for nonlinear shifts in behavior across development, due to earlier maturation of the limbic relative to the less mature top-down prefrontal control region (Colby, Van Horn, & Sowell, 2011; Galván et al., 2006).

While this theory is most consonant with a dual-systems approach, it is worth noting that other theoretical perspectives on risk taking are equally valuable in tackling this question in the context of development. These other approaches will only briefly be mentioned here, but the reader is encouraged to refer to a summary (Reyna & Rivers, 2008b) in an excellent special issue of *Developmental Review* (Reyna & Rivers, 2008a). The behavioral decision-making framework (Fischhoff, 2008) emphasizes the need to consider decision-making competence in models of adolescent risky decision making. Given the critical role of the prefrontal cortex in cognitive competence and sophisticated problem solving, it is impossible to ignore the importance of assessing competence, questioning it, and integrating it into these models. This integration is particularly relevant when examining the ways in which researchers assess competence (e.g., What is the best way to assess probabilities or risk in adolescents? Does protracted development of the prefrontal cortex throughout adolescence preclude adultlike estimates of risk and probability?).

Consonant with the subcortical systems development component described in the imbalance model is the fuzzy trace theory, because it highlights the intuitive, "gist-based" element of decision-making that is often driven by affect and emotion as indexed by valence, arousal, and feeling states/moods (for more detail, see Rivers et al., 2008), which are all neurobiologically rooted in subcortical systems. As adolescents mature into adults, they gain greater traction in using gist-based instinct to avoid unhealthy risks, rather than allowing emotion-laden environments of adolescence to interfere with the ability to recognize the gist that danger is present (Rivers et al., 2008). In sum, all the models described here recognize the importance of emotion and affect, in addition to cognitive competence, in evaluating adolescent decision-making. What has been less emphasized is the role that the environment has on risky choice during adolescence. In the following section, I argue for the inclusion of a contextual component to the existing imbalance model.

RISKY BEHAVIOR: THE ROLE OF CONTEXT

Risk-taking behavior does not occur in a vacuum. Rather, risky choices are largely influenced by the context in which they are presented. This phenomenon has been demonstrated in numerous psychological and economic studies (e.g., Tversky & Kahneman, 1986), showing that the frame (De Martino, Kumaran, Seymour, & Dolan, 2006; Hardin, Pine, & Ernst, 2009; Tversky & Kahneman, 1981), social context (Ary, Duncan, Duncan, & Hops, 1999; Gardner & Steinberg, 2005), and circumstances (Porcelli & Delgado, 2009) in which a risky choice is presented largely influence whether an individual will subsequently make a risky (or nonrisky) decision. For instance, Chien, Lin, and Worthley (1996) used an adaptation of Tversky and Kahneman's (1981) vaccination problem to show that adolescents shift preference as a function of problem wording and therefore are quite susceptible to framing effects. Like adults, adolescents tended to prefer a riskier option when choices were presented with loss frames, and they preferred less risky options when choices were presented with gain frames. This finding was in contrast to framing effects (or lack thereof) in children, as Reyna and Ellis (1994) first reported. They presented participants (preschoolers, second graders, and fifth graders) with a choice between a gamble and a sure thing, framed either in terms of gains or losses. In the gain-framed condition, children were asked to choose between automatically winning a small prize (a sure thing, probability = 1.0) and a gamble that involved the prize's expected value (i.e., a larger prize, with probability = .5, .67, or .75, as determined by the colored portions of a spinner). In the loss-framed condition, children were asked to choose between automatically losing a small prize and losing its riskier expected value (i.e., a larger prize, with lesser probability). Across frames, participants preferred risk over certainty; however, unlike older children and adults, younger children tended to make choices relatively uniformly across frames, and in this sense, they exhibited less susceptibility to framing effects (Reyna & Ellis, 1994). Collectively, these studies suggest that adolescence is a critical point in development during which framing, or *context*, begins to show a particularly influential role in risky decision making and behavior. As Boyer (2006) noted,

> This line of research is important in that it emphasizes the role of the environment on risk-taking; that is, if problem frame can be generalized as representative of environmental variability, and it influences risk preference, the implicit suggestion is that risk taking, at least from a purely cognitive standpoint, may be the product of a contextual–developmental interaction. (p. 298)

Arnett's (1992) theory of broad and narrow socialization (BNS) also draws very direct links between social developmental and risk-taking research. The major claim of the BNS model is that adolescents' abilities to engage in reckless behaviors are bound by the sociocultural context in which they develop. Rather, risk taking occurs, in part, because the social landscape in which decisions are made changes dramatically. Classic developmental research demonstrates that, as children become adolescents, they spend less time with adults and more time with similar-age peers (Brown, 2004). It is popularly acknowledged that peer influence of risk-taking behaviors occurs though direct (overt peer pressure) and indirect (socialization) mechanisms (Brechwald & Prinstein, 2011; Maxwell, 2002), and many self-report studies have consistently demonstrated that children and adolescents who associate with risk-taking peers are themselves more likely to engage in risky behaviors (Allen, Porter, & McFarland, 2006; Benthin, Slovic, & Severson, 1993; Cohen & Prinstein, 2006; Dishion, Nelson, & Yasui, 2005; Dishion & Owen, 2002; Jaccard, Blanton, & Dodge, 2005; Santor, Messervey, & Kusumaker, 2000). For instance, youth who engage in prototypical risk-taking behaviors (e.g., drinking alcohol, smoking cigarettes, interpersonal aggression, drug use) are more likely to have friends who engage in similar behaviors (Kobus, 2003), and numerous studies have shown that the higher teens' estimates of the number of schoolmates who drink alcohol, the more likely they themselves are to drink (Ferguson & Meehan, 2011; Trucco, Colder, & Wieczorek, 2011). In sum, the peer context is notorious for the facilitation of risk-taking behaviors.

Why do peers influence risk taking? Mounting evidence suggests that social interactions and the presence of peers elicit emotions that subsequently engage the affect neural systems described above (e.g., the striatum). Given the lower threshold with which rewards yield exaggerated neural signals in adolescents compared to adults or children, peers are conditioned stimuli that engage the reward-sensitive striatum. Research suggests that changes in brain development during adolescence orient teens toward the social world (Blakemore, 2008) and heighten neural sensitivity to peers (Guyer, McClure-Tone, Shiffrin, Pine, & Nelson, 2009). Further, recent work suggests that there is a relationship between resistance to peer influence, risky behavior, and ventral striatal activity (Pfeifer et al., 2011). Activation in this region is predictive of subsequent risk-taking behavior (e.g., Galván et al., 2007; Kuhnen & Knutson, 2005). Thus, peers induce significant contextual changes at both the behavioral and neurobiological levels. Chein, Albert, O'Brien, Uckert, and Steinberg (2011) provided convincing functional magnetic resonance imaging (fMRI) evidence in support of this hypothesis. Building on work by the same group showing that adolescents took more risks on a computer-simulated driving game than adults did (Gardner & Steinberg, 2005), Chein et al. demonstrated that the presence of peers increases teen risk-taking by enhancing activity in the brain striatal (reward) circuitry. These compelling findings lend further support for the notion that context (in this case, peers) can alter the relative contribution of neural mechanisms underlying reward seeking and risk taking.

The important work reviewed in this section convincingly argues for an influential role of context in adolescent risky behavior. Borrowing from aspects of the prototype-willingness model (Gerrard, Gibbons, Houlihan, Stock, & Pomery, 2008), which encompasses internal (e.g., willingness to engage in a particular behavior) as well as external (e.g., media exposure, peer group norms) factors, I propose the addition of an environmental/contextual component to the imbalance model that will move beyond the existing two-factor conceptualization. Although consideration of context in adolescent risk-taking is not new in general, it has not formally been incorporated into neurobiological models, largely because of inherent limitations in the ability to examine context in the scanner. However, the addition of this factor will complement the two existing prefrontal and striatal system factors and represents the ecologically important component of availability and/or opportunity (as described in the prototype-willingness model; Gerrard et al., 2003, 2008) that largely drives risk taking in the real world. There are many examples one could imagine in which the existing two-factor model only encapsulates neurobiological development but fails to capture the socially relevant world in which adolescents make decisions. For instance, a socially isolated teen with minimal exposure to potentially risky situations but who is neurodevelopmentally in sync with peers will probably engage in less risky behaviors than one who has increased opportunity for risk taking. Conversely, a teen who has not yet reached the reward-related "striatal peak" reported in numerous studies (for a review, see Galván, 2010) but who affiliates with risk-seeking peers may be neurodevelopmentally "scaffolded" (i.e. exhibit behaviors that are suggestive of a characteristic adolescent neuro-development pattern) to take more risks.

The integration of all three factors of the revised imbalance model accounts for the bidirectional influence of neurobiological and contextual factors. For instance, in the peer context, adolescents may be more inclined to engage in risky behavior because affect- and reward-related neural regions (e.g., striatum) may respond with greater activation in this context, and subsequently, greater risky behavior (Chein et al., 2011). However, another possibility is that emotional context may not only act to further engage the subcortical systems but that the prefrontal cortical systems may be *less* engaged. The study by Chein and colleagues (2011) also provides evidence for this hypothesis. Rather, similar to the way in which individuals are influenced by context, neural systems also act and are influenced by neural context; this means that increased subcortical activation may lead to decreased cortical engagement and, with increasing maturation, the opposite may be true. Somerville, Hare, and Casey (2010) provided insight into the contextual neural balance that occurs during adolescence. Specifically, they showed exaggerated ventral striatal representation of appetitive cues in adolescents relative to an intermediary cognitive control response that was not observed in children or adults. Additional empirical evidence to probe this phenomenon will be of utmost importance in future work.

ROLE OF REWARD IN RISKY DECISION MAKING

Why do individuals engage in risky behavior? Economic, computational, and experimental theorists have provided sophisticated explanations for this phenomenon, but in real life, in the heat of the moment, individuals engage in risky behavior because it is rewarding and fun. This notion is perhaps most true during adolescence, when risky behavior extends beyond gambling or other financial risks that adults undertake. Instead, adolescent risk-taking includes the rewarding value captured by novelty and social interactions. Given that observation, understanding the development of neural regions sensitive to reward has generated a substantial amount of research interest in recent years. In the adult literature, several groups have shown that, in fact, neural systems that underlie reward are also those that precede risky decision making (Kuhnen & Knutson 2005; Matthews, Simmons, Lane, & Paulus, 2004), suggesting a neural link between reward sensitivity and risk taking.

DEVELOPMENT OF THE DOPAMINE SYSTEM

Dopamine has been implicated in diverse cognitive operations and behaviors, including but not limited to learning, reward sensitivity, addiction, decision making, motor skills, and plasticity. From a human developmental standpoint, it has been linked to dramatic behavioral changes that are characteristic of adolescence (Spear, 2000). A plethora of research has shown that dopamine is intimately tied to reward and risk. They have shown that the neural regions that are rich in dopamine are highly responsive to all types of rewards, including monetary, social, novel, and primary rewards (e.g., Schultz, 2007). A central tenet in adolescent research is that changes in dopamine systems underlie reward-motivated behaviors during this developmental window.

Investigations using diverse methods have mapped out dopamine projections in the brain (see Figure 10.2). Most cell bodies of dopamine neurons are located in the midbrain (substantia nigra [SN] and ventral tegmental area [VTA]). Axons from these regions project in a topographic order to the striatum (SN to the caudate nucleus and putamen and VTA to the nucleus accumbens) and the prefrontal cortex (e.g., Haber, 2003). The nucleus accumbens (NAcc) can be further subdivided by histology and connectional patterns into core and shell regions; it is within this latter region that dopamine

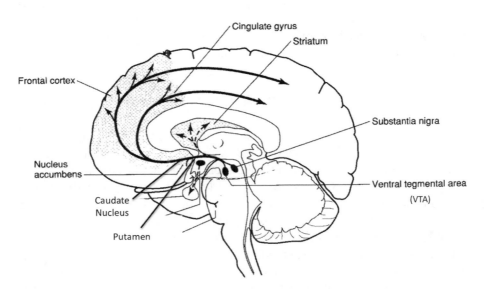

Figure 10.2. Dopamine projections from the midbrain (SN and VTA). From "Neural Mechanisms of Addiction: The Role of Reward-Related Learning and Memory" by S. E. Hyman, R. C. Malenka, and E. J. Nestler, 2006, *Annual Review of Neuroscience, 29,* p. 571. Copyright 2006 by Annual Reviews. Adapted with permission.

influences responses to novel reward stimuli (Hyman, Malenka, & Nestler, 2006; Ito, Robbins, & Everitt, 2004).

There are significant alterations in the dopamine system across development and in particular during adolescence, as demonstrated in animal models. Dopamine levels increase in the striatum during adolescence (Andersen, Dumont, & Teicher, 1997; Teicher, Andersen, & Hostetter, 1995). However, other reports have shown that young adolescent rats also display lower estimates of dopamine synthesis in the NAcc relative to older adolescent animals and lower NAcc dopamine turnover rates relative to adults. Stamford's (1989) work showed an apparent resolution to these different results by reporting a reduced basal rate of dopamine release but a larger dopamine storage pool in periadolescent, relative to adult, rats (Stamford, 1989). In fact, dopaminergic neurons in the adolescent, despite reduced dopamine release in basal conditions (Andersen & Gazzara, 1993; Stamford, 1989), are actually able to release more dopamine, if stimulated by environmental and/or pharmacological challenges (Laviola et al., 2001, 2003). Robinson et al. (2011) recently showed that while dopamine release habituated to social interactions in adult rats, the adolescent rats failed to do so, suggesting that the adolescent dopamine system is not only more reactive but more persistent as well. However, Bolaños, Barrot, Berton, Wallace-Black, and Nestler (2003) showed that chronic exposure to stimulants (i.e., methylphenidate) leads to decreased sensitivity to rewarding stimuli in adulthood. Taken together, these data suggest that during adolescence, rewarding events may result in larger dopamine release, when compared with adults (Laviola et al., 2003). So, if indeed it is the case that adolescent animals have lower basal rates of dopamine release, then perhaps adolescents initially seek out more stimulation (rewards) that will increase dopamine release; once stimulated, however, the adolescent will show greater dopamine release that subsequently contributes to a reinforcing feedback cycle that motivates additional reward-seeking behavior. In sum, the dopamine system in adolescence may predispose individuals in this age group to greater reward sensitivity. The neuroimaging studies outlined below have built on these animal models to identify the similar developmental patterns of change in humans.

THEORIES OF REWARD-DRIVEN BEHAVIOR IN ADOLESCENCE

Two primary theories about adolescent reward behavior center on two opposing possibilities: Is the neural reward system hyper- or hyporesponsive to rewards during adolescence? Adolescents may be more (or less) sensitive to available rewards in the environment than children and adults. Some theorists have proposed that adolescent reward seeking and risk taking might result from a relative deficit in the activity of motivational circuitry (Bjork et al., 2004; Bjork, Smith, Chen, & Hommer, 2010; Blum et al., 2000; Blum, Cull, Braverman, & Comings, 1996) such that more intense or more frequent rewarding stimuli are necessary to achieve the same neural engagement as adults. Support for this theory comes from data showing differences between adolescents and other ages in the perception of pleasure. For instance, some reports suggest human adolescents exhibit an increase in negative affect and depressed mood relative to older and younger adults (Larson & Asmussen, 1991) and also appear to experience the same positive situations as less pleasurable than adults do (as based on self-reports; Watson & Clark, 1984). Adolescents also find sweetness (sugar) less pleasant than children do (De Graff & Zandstra, 1999). Based on these data, some speculate that adolescents may generally attain less positive feeling from rewarding stimuli, which drives them to pursue new appetitive reinforcers (e.g., risky behavior) through increases in reward seeking that increase activity in dopamine-related circuitry (Spear, 2000).

An opposing theory postulates that disproportionately increased activation of the ventral striatal dopamine circuit (i.e., the increased dopaminergic release in response to rewarding events) underlies adolescent reward-related behavior (Chambers, Taylor, & Potenza, 2003). This view arises from extensive studies of dopamine and its principal role in the translation of encoded motivational drives into action (Panksepp, 1998). Further, rodent work shows that adolescent rats exhibit greater sucrose reactivity than adult rats (Willmouth & Spear, 2009). This theory posits that adolescent behavior is driven by reward-related appetitive systems. Although there are data to support both hypotheses, the latter theory (that adolescents are motivated to engage in high reward behaviors because of developmental changes in the striatum that confer hypersensitivity to reward; e.g., Ernst & Mueller, 2008; Galván, 2010) has disproportionately greater support (as reviewed in the following section). This high reward-seeking behavior is, thus, what subsequently leads to engagement in high-risk behaviors, given the link between hedonic experience and risk.

STRIATAL AND REWARD-RELATED NEURAL DEVELOPMENT IN ADOLESCENTS: INSIGHTS FROM FMRI

Developmental fMRI studies of reward have yielded two main findings that directly map onto the two hypotheses outlined above. The first suggests that adolescents, relative to adults, show less engagement of the ventral striatum in anticipation of reward (Bjork et al., 2004, 2010). Bjork and colleagues compared 13- to 18-year-olds with a group of adults on the monetary incentive delay (MID) task, which was designed for and has been widely used in adult samples (e.g., Knutson, Fong, Adams, Varner, & Hommer, 2001). In the MID task, participants were first presented with one of seven cues. After a delay, they were asked to press the target; finally, feedback was presented to notify participants whether they had won or lost money during the trial. Despite similar behavioral performance, the authors found significant neural differences between age groups, such that adolescents showed less ventral striatal activation in anticipation of reward, compared to adults. Bjork and colleagues interpreted these data as support for the hypothesis that adolescents have a ventral striatal activation deficit. That is, that adolescents engage in extreme incentives (e.g., risky behaviors) as a way of compensating for low ventral striatal activity (Bjork et al., 2004).

Although Bjork and colleagues have more recently replicated these findings in a doubled sample size and using an improved headcoil (Bjork, Smith, Chen, & Hommer, 2010), a plethora of papers have reported the opposite results (Cohen et al., 2010; Ernst et al., 2005; Galván et al., 2006; May et al., 2004; Van Leijenhorst et al., 2010). These studies have shown that relative to other age groups, adolescents show greater activation in the ventral striatum in response to reward. For instance, in our work, children, adolescents, and adults were asked to perform a simple, youth-friendly task in the scanner in which different reward values were delivered following correct responses (Galván et al., 2006). Relative to children and adults, the adolescent group showed heightened ventral striatal activation in anticipation of reward. In another example, Ernst et al. (2005) used a probabilistic monetary reward task to show that adolescents recruited significantly greater left nucleus accumbens activity than adults during winning trials. These findings directly contrast with the findings reported by Bjork et al. (2004, 2010) and lend support for the hypothesis that disproportionately increased activation of the ventral striatal motivational circuit characterizes adolescent neurodevelopment and behavior (Chambers et al., 2003). Additional support for this finding was found in a study in which we examined whether the neural activation in response to rewards was related to real-life risk taking. Indeed, greater striatal activation in response to rewards was associated with greater self-reported risk-taking behavior (Galván, Hare, Voss, Glover, & Casey, 2007). Recent work by other labs supports the hyperresponsive view as well. In contrast to the majority of similar work, Van Leijenhorst and colleagues (2010) used an fMRI paradigm that was not dependent on behavior. That is, participants passively viewed stimuli that either certainly or uncertainly predicted subsequent reward. This approach is particularly important because previous studies may have been confounded by the behavioral component of the tasks. Their main finding is that adolescents show greater striatal activation than children or adults in response to reward receipt (Van Leijenhorst et al., 2010), suggesting that even when reward is not contingent on behavior and thus there are no differences in motivation, adolescents show a hyperactive striatal response to reward. Geier et al. (2010) also demonstrated that, compared to adults, adolescents showed heightened ventral striatal activity in anticipation of reward.

These opposing findings further fuel the debate about *how* the dopamine system is altered during adolescence and mirror the seemingly contrasting findings of basal versus stimulated dopamine release in rodents. There are several possible explanations for the striking differences between studies (for more detail, see Galván, 2010). First, the studies differ greatly in the developmental stages and ages of participants. Second, studies differ in the comparison groups. Last, differences in task design, analysis, and baseline conditions can lead to significant differences in interpretation.

PROLONGED NEURAL DEVELOPMENT OF THE PREFRONTAL CORTEX

The prefrontal cortex is critical for higher cognition, including reasoning, judgment, risk evaluation, and inhibitory control (Fuster, 2001). Relative to other brain regions, the prefrontal cortex undergoes a prolonged developmental trajectory that persists into the adolescent and postadolescent years (e.g., Gogtay et al., 2004; see also Chapter 1, this volume). Given the vast improvements in higher cognitive abilities that adolescents exhibit, numerous adolescent researchers have postulated that cognitive development through the adolescent years is associated with progressively greater efficiency of cognitive control capacities (e.g., Yurgelun-Todd, 2007). This efficiency is described as dependent on maturation of the prefrontal cortex, which subsequently plays a significant role in improved decision making and goal-oriented choice behavior (Casey, Tottenham, & Fossella 2002; Casey et al., 1997).

Many tasks have been used together with fMRI to assess the neurobiological basis of these abilities, including go/no-go, flanker, stop signal, and antisaccade tasks (Bunge et al., 2002; Casey et al., 1997; Casey, Giedd, & Thomas, 2000; Luna et al. 2001). Collectively, these studies show that children recruit distinct but often larger, more diffuse prefrontal regions when performing these tasks than do adults. The pattern of activity within brain regions central to task performance (i.e., that correlate with cognitive performance) become more focal or fine-tuned with age, whereas regions not correlated with task performance diminish in activity with age. This pattern has been observed across both cross-sectional (Brown et al., 2005) and longitudinal (Durston et al., 2006) studies and across a variety of paradigms.

Although neuroimaging studies cannot definitively characterize the mechanism of such developmental changes (e.g., dendritic arborization, synaptic pruning), the findings reflect development within, and refinement of, projections to and from, activated brain regions with maturation and suggest that these changes occur over a protracted period of time (Brown et al., 2005; Bunge et al., 2002; Casey et al., 1997, 2002; Crone, Donohue, Honomichl, Wendelken, & Bunge, 2006; Luna et al., 2001; Moses et al., 2002; Schlaggar et al., 2002; Tamm, Menon, & Reiss, 2002; Thomas et al., 2004). In our own work, adolescents showed a neural recruitment pattern of the orbitofrontal cortex (OFC), a component of the prefrontal cortex that receives dense dopaminergic innervation (Wallis, 2007), that was more similar to children than to adults (Galván et al., 2006) during a reward task. Rather, while adolescents are transitioning from childhood to adulthood, their OFC is representing reward more similarly to children's activation pattern, suggesting that, relative to adults, the adolescent OFC is immature. Aberrant, or immature, activation patterns in the OFC have previously been linked to risky choice. For instance, Eshel, Nelson, Blair, Pine, and Ernst (2007) showed that immature activity in the OFC correlated with more risk-taking performance, compared with that of adults. Further, damage to this region impairs decision making and judgment (Fellows & Farah, 2007) and impairs contingency learning (Fellows, 2007). In sum, converging evidence suggests that, indeed, risky behavior, decision making, and judgment in adolescence may be partially influenced by the delayed development of the prefrontal cortex.

IS ADOLESCENT RISK TAKING PARADOXICAL?

As highlighted in several chapters in this volume, adolescents show vast maturational superiority in terms of physical capabilities, concrete reasoning, mathematical ability, and overall intelligence as compared with younger children. In most laboratory measures, adolescents have the same reasoning capabilities as adults (Reyna & Farley, 2006; Steinberg & Morris, 2001). In addition, they are physically stronger, more agile, and better coordinated. In many domains, adolescence is a developmental period of robust cognitive and physical ability.

However, overall risk-taking behavior associated with increased mortality, health-compromising behaviors, and harmful outcomes *increases* during this time. Of the approximately 13,000 adolescent deaths recorded in the United States each year by the National Center for Health Statistics, the leading causes are all preventable: motor vehicle crashes, unintentional injuries, homicide, and suicide (Eaton et al., 2006). Teens, like everyone else, increase their likelihood of an adverse outcome, including death, when they decide to drive a vehicle after drinking or without a seat belt, to carry a weapon, to use an illegal substance, and to engage in unprotected sex, which could result in unintended pregnancies and sexually transmitted diseases, including HIV infection (2005 National Youth Risk Behavior Survey; Eaton et al., 2006). Because such decisions are seen as arbitrary, the damage they produce among adolescents is often seen as preventable.

Notably, most of these decisions are rooted in emotionally driven behaviors. Further, decisions made during adolescence have large implications for future health-compromising behavior in adulthood. For instance, 80% of adult smokers become addicted to nicotine by age 18 (Centers for Disease Control, 2008) and an estimated 25 million people will die prematurely as adults from smoking-related illness, including 5 million people under 18 years of age (Centers for Disease Control, 2008). Research has suggested that if people do not start smoking as children or teenagers, it is unlikely that they will ever do so (Sussman, 2002).

Herein lies the paradox: Despite rapid increases in mental and physical abilities during adolescence, a substantial number of adolescents are notoriously poor decision makers. Why? The revised imbalance model described here offers a neurobiological explanation to suggest that the significant changes that occur during adolescence in neural systems critical for risky choice, rewards, and cognitive control can explain this phenomenon. Whereas previous theories postulated that risky behavior in adolescence was the manifestation of prolonged development of the prefrontal cortex, which is critical for cognitive control, more recent work has suggested that regions responsive to affect and emotion are equally influential in adolescence (for a review, see Galván, 2010). This notion is in accord with the affect-related decisions mentioned earlier. Both of these neural systems show substantial development during adolescence (e.g., Giedd et al., 1999; Sowell et al., 2003). Perhaps it is no coincidence that both are also critically involved in decision making and risky behavior. However, to make this link, it is important to understand *why* and *how* developmental change in these regions during adolescence leads to characteristic adolescent risky behavior.

The revised imbalance model attempts to reconcile the adolescent paradox. Adolescents are quite capable of rational decisions and understanding the risks of behaviors in which they engage (Reyna & Farley, 2006). However, in emotionally salient situations, the subcortical limbic system will perhaps win out over control systems, given its maturity relative to the prefrontal control system. Further, the context under which potentially risky decisions are made may tip the scale toward engaging in risky behavior or not.

CONCLUSION

The findings synthesized here indicate that increased risk-taking behavior in adolescence is associated with different developmental trajectories of subcortical pleasure and cortical control regions. However, this is not to say that adolescents are not capable of making rational decisions. Rather, in emotionally charged contexts, the more engaged limbic system may win over the prefrontal control system in deciding on a choice. The findings reviewed here provide crucial groundwork toward better understanding of risk taking in adolescence.

REFERENCES

Adriani, W., & Laviola, G. (2004). Windows of vulnerability to psychopathology and therapeutic strategy in the adolescent rodent model. *Behavioural Pharmacology*, *15*, 341–352. doi:10.1097/00008877-200409000-00005

Allen, J. P., Porter, M. R., & McFarland, F. C. (2006). Leaders and followers in adolescent close friendships: Susceptibility to peer influence as a predictor of risky behavior, friendship instability, and depression. *Development and Psychopathology*, *18*, 155–172. doi:10.1017/S0954579406060093

Andersen, S. L., Dumont, N. L., & Teicher, M. H. (1997). Developmental differences in dopamine synthesis inhibition by 7-OH-DPAT. *Naunyn-Schmiedeberg's Archives of Pharmacology*, *356*, 173–181. doi:10.1007/PL00005038

Andersen, S. L., & Gazzara, R. S. (1993). The ontogeny of apomorphine-induced alterations of neostriatal dopamine release: Effects of spontaneous release. *Journal of Neurochemistry*, *61*, 2247–2255. doi:10.1111/j.1471-4159.1993.tb07466.x

Arnett, J. J. (1992). Reckless behavior in adolescence: A developmental perspective. *Developmental Review*, *12*, 339–373. doi:10.1016/0273-2297(92)90013-R

Ary, D. V., Duncan, T. E., Duncan, S. C., & Hops, H. (1999). Adolescent problem behavior: The influence of parents and peers. *Behaviour Research and Therapy*, *37*, 217–230. doi:10.1016/S0005-7967(98)00133-8

Benthin, A., Slovic, P., & Severson, H. (1993). A psychometric study of risk perception. *Journal of Adolescence*, *16*, 153–168. doi:10.1006/jado.1993.1014

Blakemore, S. J. (2008). The social brain in adolescence. *Nature Reviews Neuroscience*, *9*, 267–277. doi:10.1038/nrn2353

Bjork, J. M., Knutson, B., Fong, G. W., Caggiano, D. M., Bennett, S. M., & Hommer, D. W. (2004). Incentive-elicited brain activation in adolescents: Similarities and differences from young adults. *The Journal of Neuroscience*, *24*, 1793–1802. doi:10.1523/JNEUROSCI.4862-03.2004

Bjork, J. M., Smith, A., Chen, G., & Hommer, D. W. (2010). Adolescents, adults and rewards: Comparing motivational neurocircuitry recruitment using fMRI. *PLoS ONE, 5*, e11440. doi:10.1371/journal.pone.0011440

Blum, K., Braverman, E., Holder, J., Lubar, J., Monastra, V., Miller, D., . . . Comings, D. (2000). Reward deficiency syndrome: A biogenetic model for the diagnosis and treatment of impulsive, addictive and compulsive behaviors. *Journal of Psychoactive Drugs, 32*, 1–112.

Blum, K., Cull, J. G., Braverman, E. R., & Comings, D. E. (1996). Reward deficiency syndrome. *American Scientist, 84*, 132–145.

Bolaños, C. A., Barrot, M., Berton, O., Wallace-Black, D., & Nestler, E. J. (2003). Methylphenidate treatment during pre- and periadolescence alters behavioral responses to emotional stimuli in adulthood. *Biological Psychiatry, 54*, 1317–1329. doi:10.1016/S0006-3223(03)00570-5

Boyer, T. W. (2006). The development of risk-taking: A multi-perspective review. *Developmental Review, 26*, 291–345. doi:10.1016/j.dr.2006.05.002

Brechwald, W. A., & Prinstein, M. J. (2011). Beyond homophily: A decade of advances in understanding peer influence processes. *Journal of Research on Adolescence, 21*, 166–179. doi:10.1111/j.1532-7795.2010.00721.x

Brown, B. B. (2004). Adolescents' relationship with peers. In R. Lerner & L. Steinberg (Eds.), *Handbook of Adolescent Psychology* (pp. 363–394). Hoboken, NJ: Wiley.

Brown, T. T., Lugar, H. M., Coalson, R. S., Miezin, F. M., Petersen, S. E., & Schlaggar, B. L. (2005). Developmental changes in human cerebral functional organization for word generation. *Cerebral Cortex, 15*, 275–290. doi:10.1093/cercor/bhh129

Bunge, S. A., Dudukovic, N. M., Thomason, M. E., Vaidya, C. J., & Gabrieli, J. D. (2002). Immature frontal lobe contributions to cognitive control in children: Evidence from fMRI. *Neuron, 33*, 301–311. doi:10.1016/S0896-6273(01)00583-9

Casey, B. J., Getz, S., & Galván, A. (2008). The adolescent brain. *Developmental Review, 28*, 62–77.

Casey, B. J., Giedd, J. N., & Thomas, K. M. (2000). Structural and functional brain development and its relation to cognitive development. *Biological Psychology, 54*, 241–257. doi:10.1016/S0301-0511(00)00058-2

Casey, B. J., Hare, T. A., & Galván, A. (in press). Risky and impulsive components of adolescent decision-making. In M. R. Delgado, E. A. Phelps, & T. W. Robbins (Eds.), *Attention and performance XXIII: Decision making, affect, and learning*. New York, NY: Oxford University Press.

Casey, B. J., Tottenham, N., & Fossella, J. (2002). Clinical, imaging, lesion and genetic approaches toward a model of cognitive control. *Developmental Psychobiology, 40*, 237–254. doi:10.1002/dev.10030

Casey, B. J., Trainor, R. J., Orendi, J. L., Schubert, A. B., Nystrom, L. E., Giedd, J. N., . . . Rapaport, J. L. (1997). A developmental functional MRI study of prefrontal activation during performance of a go-no-go task. *Journal of Cognitive Neuroscience, 9,* 835–847. doi:10.1162/jocn.1997.9.6.835

Centers for Disease Control and Prevention. (2008). Cigarette smoking among adults—United States, 2006. *MMWR Morbidity & Mortality Weekly Report, 56,* 1157–1161.

Chambers, R. A., Taylor, J. R., & Potenza, M. N. (2003). Developmental neuro-circuitry of motivation in adolescence: A critical period of addiction vulner-ability. *The American Journal of Psychiatry, 160,* 1041–1052. doi:10.1176/appi.ajp.160.6.1041

Chein, J., Albert, D., O'Brien, L., Uckert, K., & Steinberg, L. (2011). Peers increase adolescent risk taking by enhancing activity in the brain's reward circuitry. *Developmental Science, 14,* F1–F10.

Chien, Y. C., Lin, C., & Worthley, J. (1996). Effect of framing on adolescents' decision making. *Perceptual and Motor Skills, 83,* 811–819.

Cohen, G. L., & Prinstein, M. J. (2006). Peer contagion of aggression and health risk behavior among adolescent males: An experimental investigation of effects on public conduct and private attitudes. *Child Development, 77,* 967–983. doi:10.1111/j.1467-8624.2006.00913.x

Cohen, J. R., Asarnow, R. F., Sabb, F. W., Bilder, R. M., Bookheimer, S. Y., Knowlton, B. J., & Poldrack, R. A. (2010). A unique adolescent response to reward predic-tion errors. *Nature Neuroscience, 13,* 669–671. doi:10.1038/nn.2558

Colby, J. B., Van Horn, J. D., & Sowell, E. R. (2011). Quantitative in vivo evidence for broad regional gradients in the timing of white matter maturation during adolescence. *NeuroImage, 54,* 25–31. doi:10.1016/j.neuroimage.2010.08.014

Crone, E. A., Donohue, S., Honomichl, R., Wendelken, C., & Bunge, S. (2006). Brain regions mediating flexible rule use during development. *The Journal of Neuroscience, 26,* 11239–11247. doi:10.1523/JNEUROSCI.2165-06.2006

DeGraaf, C., & Zandstra, E. (1999). Sweetness intensity and pleasantness in chil-dren, adolescents and adults. *Physiology & Behavior, 67,* 513–520. doi:10.1016/S0031-9384(99)00090-6

De Martino, B., Kumaran, D., Seymour, B., & Dolan, R. J. (2006, August 4). Frames, biases, and rational decision-making in the human brain. *Science, 313,* 684–687. doi:10.1126/science.1128356

Dishion, T. J., Nelson, S. E., & Yasui, M. (2005). Predicting early adolescent gang involvement from middle school adaptation. *Journal of Clinical Child and Ado-lescent Psychology, 34,* 62–73. doi:10.1207/s15374424jccp3401_6

Dishion, T. J., & Owen, L. D. (2002). A longitudinal analysis of friendships and sub-stance use: Bidirectional influence from adolescence to adulthood. *Developmental Psychology, 38,* 480–491. doi:10.1037/0012-1649.38.4.480

Durston, S., Davidson, M. C., Tottenham, N., Galván, A., Spicer, J., Fossell, J., & Casey, B. J. (2006). A shift from diffuse to focal cortical activity with develop-ment. *Developmental Science, 9,* 18–20. doi:10.1111/j.1467-7687.2005.00458.x

Eaton, L. K., Kinchen, S., Ross, J., Hawkins, J., Harris, W. A., Lowry, R., . . . Wechsler, H. (2006). Youth Risk Behavior Surveillance—United States, 2005, Surveillance Summaries. *MMWR Surveillance Summaries, 55,* 1–5.

Epstein, S. (1998). Cognitive-experiential self-theory. In D. F. Barone & M. Herser (Eds.), *Advanced personality* (pp. 45–47). New York, NY: Plenum Press.

Ernst, M., Nelson, E. E., Jazbec, S. P., McClure, E. B., Monk, C. S., Leibenluft, E., . . . Pine, D. S. (2005). Amygdala and nucleus accumbens in responses to receipt and omission of gains in adults and adolescents. *NeuroImage, 25,* 1279–1291. doi:10.1016/j.neuroimage.2004.12.038

Ernst, M., & Mueller, S. C. (2008). The adolescent brain: Insights from functional neuroimaging research. *Developmental Neurobiology, 68,* 729–743. doi:10.1002/dneu.20615

Eshel, N., Nelson, E. E., Blair, R. J., Pine, D. S., & Ernst, M. (2007). Neural substrates of choice selection in adults and adolescents: Development of the ventrolateral prefrontal and anterior cingulated cortices. *Neuropsychologia, 45,* 1270–1279. doi:10.1016/j.neuropsychologia.2006.10.004

Evans, J. S. B. T. (1984). Heuristic and analytic processes in reasoning. *British Journal of Psychology, 75,* 451–468. doi:10.1111/j.2044-8295.1984.tb01915.x

Evans, J. S. B. T., Venn, S., & Feeney, A. (2002). Implicit and explicit processes in a hypothesis testing task. *British Journal of Psychology, 93,* 31–46. doi:10.1348/000712602162436

Fellows, L. K. (2007). The role of the orbitofrontal cortex in decision making: A component process account. *Annals of the New York Academy of Sciences, 1121,* 421–430. doi:10.1196/annals.1401.023

Fellows, L. K., & Farah, M. J. (2007). The role the ventromedial prefrontal cortex in decision making: Judgment under uncertainty or judgment per se? *Cerebral Cortex, 17,* 2669–2674. doi:10.1093/cercor/bhl176

Ferguson, C. J., & Meehan, D. C. (2011). With friends like these . . . : Peer delinquency influences across age cohorts on smoking, alcohol and illegal substance use. *European Psychiatry, 26,* 6–12. doi:10.1016/j.eurpsy.2010.09.002

Fischhoff, B (2008). Assessing adolescent decision-making competence. *Developmental Review, 28*(1), 12–28.

Fuster, J. M. (2001). The prefrontal cortex—an update: Time is of the essence. *Neuron, 30,* 319–333. doi:10.1016/S0896-6273(01)00285-9

Galván, A. (2010). Adolescent development of the reward system. *Frontiers in Human Neuroscience, 12,* 4:6. doi:10.3389/neuro.09.006.2010

Galván, A. (in press). Adolescent development of the reward system. *Frontiers in Neuroscience.*

Galván, A., Hare, T. A., Parra, C. E., Penn, J., Voss, H., Glover, G., & Casey, B. J. (2006). Earlier development of the accumbens relative to orbitofrontal cortex might underlie risk-taking behavior in adolescents. *The Journal of Neuroscience, 26,* 6885–6892. doi:10.1523/JNEUROSCI.1062-06.2006

Galván, A., Hare, T. A., Voss, H., Glover, G., & Casey, B. J. (2007). Risk-taking and the adolescent brain: Who is at risk? *Developmental Science, 10*, F8–F14. doi:10.1111/j.1467-7687.2006.00579.x

Gardner, M., & Steinberg, L. (2005). Peer influence on risk taking, risk preference, and risky decision making in adolescence and adulthood: an experimental study. *Developmental Psychology, 41*, 625–635. doi:10.1037/0012-1649.41.4.625

Geier, C. F., Terwilliger, R., Teslovich, T., Velanova, K., & Luna, B. (2010). Immaturities in reward processing and its influence on inhibitory control in adolescence. *Cerebral Cortex, 20*, 1613–1629. doi:10.1093/cercor/bhp225

Gerrard, M., Gibbons, F. X., & Gano, M. L. (2003). Adolescents' risk perceptions and behavioral willingness: Implications for intervention. In D. Romer (Ed.), *Reducing adolescent risk: Toward and integrated approach* (pp. 75–81). Newbury, CA: Sage.

Gerrard, M., Gibbons, F. X., Houlihan, A. E., Stock, M. L., & Pomery, E. A. (2008). A dual-process approach to health risk decision making: The prototype willingness model. *Developmental Review, 28*, 29–61. doi:10.1016/j.dr.2007.10.001

Gibbons, F. X., Gerrard, M., & Lane, D. J. (2003). A social reaction model of adolescent health risk. In J. M. Suls & K. Wallston (Eds.), *Social psychological foundations of health and illness* (pp. 28–31). Oxford, England: Blackwell. doi:10.1002/9780470753552.ch5

Giedd, J. N., Blumenthal, J., Jeffries, N. O., Castellanos, F. X., Liu, H., Zijdenbos, A., . . . Rapoport, J. L. (1999). Brain development during childhood and adolescence: A longitudinal MRI study. *Nature Neuroscience, 2*, 861–863. doi:10.1038/13158

Gogtay, N., Giedd, J. N., Lusk, L., Hayashi, K. M., Greenstein, D., & Vaituzis, A. C., . . . Thompson, P.M. (2004). Dynamic mapping of human cortical development during childhood through early adulthood. *Proceedings of the National Academy of Sciences, USA, 101*, 8174–8179.

Guyer, A. E., McClure-Tone, E. B., Shiffrin, N. D., Pine, D. S., & Nelson, E. E. (2009). Probing the neural correlates of anticipated peer evaluation in adolescence. *Child Development, 80*, 1000–1015. doi:10.1111/j.1467-8624.2009.01313.x

Haber, S. N. (2003). The primate basal ganglia: Parallel and integrative networks. *Journal of Chemical Neuroanatomy, 26*, 317–330. doi:10.1016/j.jchemneu.2003.10.003

Hardin, M. G., Pine, D. S., & Ernst, M. (2009). The influence of context valence in the neural coding of monetary outcomes. *NeuroImage, 48*, 249–257. doi:10.1016/j.neuroimage.2009.06.050

Hare, T. A., Tottenham, N., Galván, A., Voss, H. U., Glover, G. H., & Casey, B. J. (2008). Biological substrates of emotional reactivity and regulation in adolescence during an emotional go-nogo task. *Biological Psychiatry, 63*, 927–934. doi:10.1016/j.biopsych.2008.03.015

Hyman, S. E., Malenka, R. C., & Nestler, E. J. (2006). Neural mechanisms of addiction: The role of reward-related learning and memory. *Annual Review of Neuroscience, 29*, 565–598. doi:10.1146/annurev.neuro.29.051605.113009

Ito, R., Robbins, T. W., & Everitt, B. J. (2004). Differential control over cocaine-seeking behavior by nucleus accumbens core and shell. *Nature Neuroscience, 7*, 389–397. doi:10.1038/nn1217

Jaccard, J., Blanton, H., & Dodge, T. (2005). Peer influences on risk behavior: An analysis of the effects of a close friend. *Developmental Psychology, 41*, 135–147. doi:10.1037/0012-1649.41.1.135

Kirkpatrick, L. A., & Epstein, S. (1992). Cognitive-experiential self-theory and subjective probability: Further evidence for two conceptual systems. *Journal of Personality and Social Psychology, 63*, 534–544. doi:10.1037/0022-3514.63.4.534

Kobus, K. (2003). Peers and adolescent smoking. *Addiction, 98*, 37–55. doi:10.1046/j.1360-0443.98.s1.4.x

Knutson, B., Fong, G. W., Adams, C. M., Varner, J. L., & Hommer, D. (2001). Dissociation of reward anticipation and outcome with event-related fMRI. *NeuroReport, 12*, 3683–3687. doi:10.1097/00001756-200112040-00016

Kuhnen, C. M., & Knutson, B. (2005). The neural basis of financial risk taking. *Neuron, 47*, 763–770. doi:10.1016/j.neuron.2005.08.008

Larson, R., & Asmussen, L. (1991). *Anger, worry, and hurt in early adolescence: an enlarging world of negative emotions.* New York, NY: Aldine de Gruyter.

Laviola, G., Pascucci, T., & Pieretti, S. (2001). Striatal dopamine sensitization to D-amphetamine in periadolescent but not in adult rats. *Pharmacology, Biochemistry and Behavior, 68*, 115–124. doi:10.1016/S0091-3057(00)00430-5

Laviola, G., Macri, S., Morley-Fletcher, S., & Adriani, W. (2003). Risk-taking behavior in adolescent mice: Psychobiological determinants and early epigenetic influence. *Neuroscience and Biobehavioral Reviews, 27*, 19–31. doi:10.1016/S0149-7634(03)00006-X

Luna, B., Thulborn, K. R., Munoz, D. P., Merriam, E. P., Garver, K. E., Minshew, N. J., . . . Sweeney, J. A. (2001). Maturation of widely distributed brain function subserves cognitive development. *NeuroImage, 13*, 786–793. doi:10.1006/nimg.2000.0743

Matthews, S. C., Simmons, A. N., Lane, S. D., & Paulus, M. P. (2004). Selective activation of the nucleus accumbens during risk-taking decision making. *NeuroReport, 15*, 2123–2127. doi:10.1097/00001756-200409150-00025

Maxwell, K. A. (2002). Friends: The role of peer influence across adolescent risk behaviors. *Journal of Youth and Adolescence, 31*, 267–277. doi:10.1023/A:1015493316865

May, J. C., Delgado, M. R., Dahl, R. E., Stenger, V. A., Ryan, N. D., Fiez, J. A., & Carter, C. S. (2004). Event-related functional magnetic resonance imaging of reward-related brain circuitry in children and adolescents. *Biological Psychiatry, 55*, 359–366. doi:10.1016/j.biopsych.2003.11.008

Metcalfe, J., & Mischel, W. (1999). A hot/cool-system analysis of delay of gratification: Dynamics of willpower. *Psychological Review, 106*, 3–19. doi:10.1037/0033-295X.106.1.3

Moses, P., Roe, K., Buxton, R. B., Wong, E. C., Frank, L. R., & Stiles, J. (2002). Functional MRI of global and local processing in children. *NeuroImage, 16,* 415–424. doi:10.1006/nimg.2002.1064

Panksepp, J. (1998). *Affective neuroscience.* New York, NY: Oxford University Press.

Pfeifer, J. H., Masten, C. L., Moore, W. E., III, Oswald, T. M., Mazziotta, J. C., Iacoboni, M., & Dapretto, M. (2011). Entering adolescence: Resistance to peer influence, risky behavior, and neural changes in emotion reactivity. *Neuron, 69,* 1029–1036. doi:10.1016/j.neuron.2011.02.019

Porcelli, A. J., & Delgado, M. R. (2009). Acute stress modulates risk taking in financial decision making. *Psychological Science, 20,* 278–283. doi:10.1111/j.1467-9280.2009.02288.x

Prinstein, M. J., Boergers, J., & Spirito, A. (2001). Adolescents' and their friends' health-risk behavior: Factors that alter or add to peer influence. *Journal of Pediatric Psychology, 26,* 287–298. doi:10.1093/jpepsy/26.5.287

Reyna, V. F. (2004). How people make decisions that involve risk: A dual-process approach. *Current Directions in Psychological Science, 13,* 60–66. doi:10.1111/j.0963-7214.2004.00275.x

Reyna, V. F., & Brainerd, C. J. (1995). Fuzzy-trace theory: An interim synthesis. *Learning and Individual Differences, 7,* 1–75. doi:10.1016/1041-6080(95)90031-4

Reyna, V. F., & Ellis, S. C. (1994). Fuzzy-trace theory and framing effects in children's risky decision making. *Psychological Science, 5,* 275–279. doi:10.1111/j.1467-9280.1994.tb00625.x

Reyna, V. F., & Farley, F. (2006). Risk and rationality in adolescent decision making: Implications for theory, practice, and public policy. *Psychological Science in the Public Interest, 7,* 1–44.

Reyna, V., & Rivers, S. (Eds.). (2008a). Current directions in risk and decision making [Special issue]. *Developmental Review, 28*(1).

Reyna, V. F., & Rivers, S. E. (2008b). Current theories of risk and rational decision making. *Developmental Review, 28,* 1–11. doi:10.1016/j.dr.2008.01.002

Rivers, S. E., Reyna, V. F., & Mills, B. (2008). Risk taking under the influence: A fuzzy-trace theory of emotion in adolescence. *Developmental Review, 28,* 107–144. doi:10.1016/j.dr.2007.11.002

Robinson, D. L., Zitzman, D. L., Smith, K. J., & Spear, L. P. (2011). Fast dopamine release events in the nucleus accumbens of early adolescent rats. *Neuroscience, 176,* 296–307. doi:10.1016/j.neuroscience.2010.12.016

Santor, D. A., Messervey, D., & Kusumaker, V. (2000). Measuring peer pressure, popularity, and conformity in adolescent boys and girls: Predicting school performance, sexual attitudes, and substance abuse. *Journal of Youth and Adolescence, 29,* 163–182. doi:10.1023/A:1005152515264

Schlaggar, B. L., Brown, T. T., Lugar, H. M., Visscher, K. M., Miezin, F. M., & Petersen, S. E. (2002, May 24). Functional neuroanatomical differences between adults and school-age children in the processing of single words. *Science, 296,* 1476–1479. doi:10.1126/science.1069464

Schultz, W. (2007). Multiple dopamine functions at different time courses. *Annual Review of Neuroscience, 30,* 259–288.

Sloman, S. A. (1996). The empirical case for two systems of reasoning. *Psychological Bulletin, 119,* 3–22. doi:10.1037/0033-2909.119.1.3

Somerville, L. H., Hare, T., & Casey, B. J. (2010). Frontostriatal maturation predicts cognitive control failure to appetitive cues in adolescents. *Journal of Cognitive Neuroscience, 23,* 2123–2134. doi:10.1162/jocn.2010.21572

Somerville, L. H., Jones, R. M., & Casey, B. J. (2010). A time of change: Behavioral and neural correlates of adolescent sensitivity to appetitive and aversive environmental cues. *Brain and Cognition, 72,* 124–133. doi:10.1016/j.bandc.2009.07.003

Sowell, E. R., Peterson, B. S., Thompson, P. M., Welcome, S. E., Henkenius, A. L., & Toga, A. W. (2003). Mapping cortical change across the human life span. *Nature Neuroscience, 6,* 309–315. doi:10.1038/nn1008

Spear, L. P. (2000). The adolescent brain and age-related behavioral manifestations. *Neuroscience and Biobehavioral Reviews, 24,* 417–463. doi:10.1016/S0149-7634(00)00014-2

Stamford, J. A. (1989). Development and ageing of the rat nigrostriatal dopamine system studied with fast cyclic voltammetry. *Journal of Neurochemistry, 52,* 1582–1589. doi:10.1111/j.1471-4159.1989.tb09212.x

Steinberg, L. (2008). A social neuroscience perspective on adolescent risk-taking. *Developmental Review, 28,* 78–106. doi:10.1016/j.dr.2007.08.002

Steinberg, L., & Morris, A. S. (2001). Adolescent development. *Annual Review of Psychology, 52,* 83–110. doi:10.1146/annurev.psych.52.1.83

Sussman, S. (2002). Tobacco industry youth tobacco prevention programming: A review. *Prevention Science, 3,* 57–67. doi:10.1023/A:1014623426877

Tamm, L., Menon, V., & Reiss, A. L. (2002). Maturation of brain function associated with response inhibition. *Journal of the American Academy of Child & Adolescent Psychiatry, 41,* 1231–1238. doi:10.1097/00004583-200210000-00013

Teicher, M. H., Andersen, S. L., & Hostetter, J. C., Jr. (1995). Evidence for dopamine receptor pruning between adolescence and adulthood in striatum but not nucleus accumbens. *Developmental Brain Research, 89,* 167–172. doi:10.1016/0165-3806(95)00109-Q

Thomas, K. M., Hunt, R. H., Vizueta, N., Sommer, T., Durston, S., Yang, Y., . . . Worden, M. S. (2004). Evidence of developmental differences in implicit sequence learning: An fMRI study of children and adults. *Journal of Cognitive Neuroscience, 16,* 1339–1351. doi:10.1162/0898929042304688

Toledo-Rodriguez, M., & Sandi, C. (2011). Stress during adolescence increases novelty seeking and risk-taking behavior in male and female rats. *Frontiers in Behavioral Neuroscience, 5,* 17–19. doi:10.3389/fnbeh.2011.00017

Trucco, E. M., Colder, C. R., & Wieczorek, W. F. (2011). Vulnerability to peer influence: A moderated mediation study of early adolescent alcohol use initiation. *Addictive Behaviors, 36,* 729–736. doi:10.1016/j.addbeh.2011.02.008

Tversky, A., & Kahneman, D. (1981, January 30). The framing of decisions and the psychology of choice. *Science, 211,* 453–458. doi:10.1126/science.7455683

Tversky, A., & Kahneman, D. (1986). Rational choice and the framing of decisions. *The Journal of Business, 59,* S251–278. doi:10.1086/296365

Van Leijenhorst, L., Zanolie, K., van Meel, C. S., Westenberg, P. M., Rombouts, S. A., & Crone, E. A. (2010). What motivates the adolescent? Brain regions mediating reward sensitivity across adolescence. *Cerebral Cortex, 20,* 61–69. doi:10.1093/cercor/bhp078

Wallis, J. D. (2007). Orbitofrontal cortex and its contribution to decision-making. *Annual Review of Neuroscience, 30,* 31–56. doi:10.1146/annurev.neuro.30.051606.094334

Watson, D., & Clark, L. (1984). Negative affectivity: The disposition to experience aversive emotional states. *Psychological Bulletin, 96,* 465–490. doi:10.1037/0033-2909.96.3.465

Wilmouth, C. E., & Spear, L. P. (2009). Hedonic sensitivity in adolescent and adult rats: Taste reactivity and voluntary sucrose consumption. *Pharmacology, Biochemistry and Behavior, 92,* 566–573. doi:10.1016/j.pbb.2009.02.009

Yurgelun-Todd, D. (2007). Emotional and cognitive changes during adolescence. *Current Opinion in Neurobiology, 17,* 251–257. doi:10.1016/j.conb.2007.03.009

11

AFFECTIVE MOTIVATORS AND EXPERIENCE IN ADOLESCENTS' DEVELOPMENT OF HEALTH-RELATED BEHAVIOR PATTERNS

SANDRA L. SCHNEIDER AND CHRISTINE M. CAFFRAY

Recognition of the role of affect in adolescent decisions has increased through studies of adolescent risk taking, advances in neuroscience research, and growing attention to dual process models of decision making. This chapter explores relationships between adolescents' affective motives and their participation in both health-threatening (drinking alcohol, smoking cigarettes) and health-enhancing (exercising, "eating healthy") behaviors. In addition to summarizing recent literature, we provide an empirical demonstration of the perceived impact of affective motives on adolescents' decisions to engage in behaviors that influence their health. For health-threatening behaviors, results confirm the perceived importance of anticipatory regret in discouraging drinking and smoking and the differential importance of various promoters (e.g., feeling stressed, having a good time) in encouraging them. Results are less clear-cut for the health-enhancing behaviors, suggesting possible roles for anticipated regret, self-esteem/efficacy, and social/emotional goals in promoting exercising and healthy eating. The direction of influence for some motivators (e.g., feeling sad or stressed) may vary with experience, encouraging healthy behaviors among those with more experience and discouraging healthy behaviors among those with less experience. The discussion focuses on the likely role of social context and social meaning in shaping affective motivators. The authors speculate that affective motivators may be more likely to encourage healthy lifestyles when adolescents view their behaviors within the larger context of the future and longer term goals. Implications of this work are discussed with respect to interactions between affective and cognitive processes in adolescent decision making.

Some of the most important decisions we make on a daily basis are those that can influence our long-term health. Many of our choices in this area may hardly even seem like decisions, as we have developed tendencies over time to behave in certain ways as part of our daily routine. Nevertheless, our everyday choices, such as what we decide to eat and drink and what activities we pursue, have a profound impact on our continuing health status.

In this chapter, we explore how goals and beliefs related to affective states are likely to influence the development of health-related tendencies in those who are just approaching adulthood. In particular, we summarize the literature and provide an empirical demonstration of how previous experience may shape expectations about the affective determinants and consequences of behavior. Based on a dual process approach coupled with recent advances in neuroscience, we then suggest potentially fruitful avenues to explore in the development of interventions to discourage risky behaviors and encourage healthy practices among adolescents.

DUAL PROCESSES IN DECISION MAKING

Over the past 2 decades, there has been a remarkable increase in research and theorizing focused on the importance of affective processes in decision making. Although the study of decision making has historically emphasized perceived benefits as a primary influence on decisions to take risks, only recently has this influence been characterized as more than a cognitive appraisal. In their review of the most recent decade of decision research, Weber and Johnson (2009) described the "emotions revolution which has put affective processes on a footing equal to cognitive ones" (p. 53) in explaining judgment and decision making.

Much of this interest in affective processes can be traced to the increase in evidence that dual systems are involved in our evaluations of situations, such that our eventual decisions represent an interaction of more thoughtful analytic processes and more experience-based affective, heuristic, or motivational processes (Damasio, 1994; Epstein, 1994; Evans, 2008; Finucane, Peters, & Slovic, 2003; Gerrard et al., 2008; Hogarth, 2001; Kahneman, 2003; Klein, 1998; Lerner & Keltner, 2000; Lieberman, 2000; Loewenstein, 1996; Mellers & McGraw, 2001; Reyna, 2004; Stanovich & West, 2000; see also Simon, 1967).

Traditionally, the influence of nonanalytic or affective processes was assumed to be detrimental to the quality of decision making (e.g., Baron,

1998; Gilovich, 1991). More recently, however, it has become clear that affect plays a vital role in guiding behavior, particularly when the affective state directly or indirectly reflects expectations based on experience of the likely consequences of actions. Indeed, some have hypothesized that intuitive, gist-based or simplified representations that capture emotion may in some situations be more important for high-quality decisions than analytic approaches to decision making (e.g., Gigerenzer, 2000; Rivers, Reyna, & Mills, 2008; Steinberg, 2008, 2010).

Damasio (1994; see also Bechara, Damasio, Damasio, & Anderson, 1994) provided a particularly compelling example of the behavioral problems that result from a disruption of affective input to decision-making processes. Damasio described how the brain damage experienced by railroad worker Phineas Gage left intact the cognitive processes typically associated with rationality but resulted in any number of behavioral anomalies and poor social and personal decisions, presumably because the normal affective input into higher order processing was no longer possible. Damasio hypothesized that affective inputs from experience act as "somatic markers," building intuitions about the likely valence of consequences (i.e., good or bad) associated with behaviors. Under normal conditions, these markers help guide us through experience to automatically shy away from behaviors associated with bad outcomes and approach behaviors associated with good outcomes.

There is now considerable research and theory to support the role of affect-laden intuitions in judgment. Finucane, Peters, and Slovic (2003; Slovic, Finucane, Peters, & MacGregor, 2004, 2007) provided demonstrations suggesting that affect acts as a judgment heuristic, rapidly and automatically signaling whether stimuli in the environment are positive or negative. Gigerenzer (2000) included emotion as a potential "fast and frugal heuristic" for quickly and efficiently coming to satisfactory decisions. Stanovich and West (2000) included emotion-regulated behaviors among the autonomous processes that characterize cognitive "System 1," and Rivers et al. (2008) considered affect a key component of gist-based representations that summarize the meaning of behaviors in simplified form. Recent neuroscientific findings suggest that emotions are a fundamental influence in risk processing and risky decision making (Mohr, Biele, & Heekeren, 2010).

Despite the growing consensus of the role of affect in decision making, most researchers recognize that affective inputs to decision making are not always helpful. There are numerous demonstrations that affect can interfere with more cognitive or analytic inputs into decision making, sometimes influencing decisions in undesirable ways (e.g., Denes-Raj & Epstein, 1994; Loewenstein, 1996; Loewenstein, Weber, Hsee, & Welch, 2001; Slovic et al., 2004, 2007). Whether affect facilitates or interferes with good decision making is likely to vary as a function of the situation. Slovic et al. (2007) hypothesized that affect is more likely to facilitate decision making when the consequences of the decision are more immediate. This is because the affective or intuitive system can function to internalize the valence of behavioral outcomes, but only when the contingency between the behaviors and the outcomes are readily apparent and close in time. Longer term outcomes must be inferred, and thus they must of necessity be relegated to interpretation through the more analytic side of decision processes.

Decisions about health-related behaviors, as a class, tend to create a competition between immediate and longer term outcomes (e.g., Herrnstein & Prelec, 1992). The high experienced through drugs or alcohol, for instance, may provide an immediate positive state that often comes at the expense of longer term cognitive, economic, legal, or health-related negative consequences. Loewenstein (1996) provided a variety of demonstrations of the ability of intense emotions and visceral urges (e.g., sexual arousal) to overwhelm cognitive appraisals of longer term consequences, resulting in behaviors with potentially undesirable long-term health consequences (e.g., sexually transmitted diseases, AIDS).

Many have hypothesized that the overwhelming nature of immediate emotional states and visceral urges may be especially problematic among adolescents, who have not yet developed or honed skills in emotion regulation (e.g., Steinberg, 2005, 2007; see also Galván, Chapter 10, this volume). Based on recent advances in neuroscientific evidence, Steinberg (2005, 2007, 2008, 2010) has suggested that pubertal changes in the socioemotional brain system (i.e., changes in dopaminergic pathways) lead to greater reward and sensation seeking but that the prefrontal cognitive control system does not fully mature until later and so is not capable of curbing these tendencies until sometime in early adulthood (see also Casey, Jones, & Hare, 2008). Recent studies have continued to provide supporting evidence of the differential development rates of the reward and control systems (e.g., Somerville, Jones, & Casey, 2010; Van Leijenhorst et al., 2010). Due to unchecked emotional reactivity, feeling states are more likely to drive adolescent decision making than contravening knowledge about long-term consequences. So, for instance, adolescents who decide to start smoking cigarettes think predominantly about the positive emotions associated with smoking and very little about the long-term consequences (Slovic, 2001). Early neuroscientific evidence has suggested that adolescent substance abuse may actually disrupt the processing of risk but not reward (Nasrallah et al., 2011). In their summary of the literature, Reyna and Farley (2006) pointed out,

> In the heat of passion, in the presence of peers, on the spur of the moment, in unfamiliar situations, when trading off risk and benefits favors bad long-term outcomes and when behavioral inhibition is required for good outcomes, adolescents are likely to reason more poorly than adults. (p. 1)

ADOLESCENCE AND DECISIONS THAT ESTABLISH BEHAVIOR PATTERNS

Despite these challenges, the transition phase from adolescence to adulthood has been identified as the life stage in which behavioral choices are most likely to influence one's health and well-being (Baranowski, et al., 1997; Chassin, Presson, Rose & Sherman, 2001; Graber, Brooks-Gunn, & Galen, 1998; Elders, Perry, Eriksen, & Giovino, 1994; Hedberg, Bracken, & Stashwick, 1999; Jessor, Turbin, & Costa, 1998; Kandel, 1998, 2002; Maggs, Schulenberg, & Hurrelmann, 1997; Millstein, Petersen, & Nightingale, 1993). This developmental period is credited as being the one most responsible for the formation and adoption of health-related practices and behaviors. Health-related decisions made during adolescence and young adulthood tend to persist throughout all or a large part of one's lifetime, as they typically support a general pattern of behaviors or the development of a lifestyle.

Although adolescent vulnerabilities with respect to engaging in risky, health-threatening behaviors have received more attention, adolescents' decisions to engage in health-enhancing behaviors are also far-reaching. Such adolescent decisions influence future outcomes primarily by encouraging more healthy lifestyles. Decisions to engage in regular physical exercise, eat a proper diet, and get adequate sleep, for instance, may result in additional long-term benefits such as enhanced energy levels, improved cognitive functioning, and greater resistance to disease (e.g., Millstein et al., 1993). Thus, the potential for experiencing a variety of health gains, as well as possible losses, is highly contingent on the particular health-related behaviors adolescents choose to adopt during this formative life stage.

Historically, theories to explain health-related decisions in adolescence often represent a search for those factors that influence adolescents to engage in risky behaviors. Hosts of potential factors, including biological, economic, psychosocial, emotional/motivational, and societal variables, have been targeted as comprising the underlying etiological explanations for risk taking (e.g., Hawkins et al., 1992; Petraitis, Flay, & Miller, 1995). Most of these theoretical approaches implicate affective states as primary motivators in adolescent decisions. Studies of adolescents have repeatedly shown that goals associated with achieving or eliminating particular affective states contribute to decisions to engage in risky behaviors (Agrawal et al., 2008; Brown, Christiansen, & Goldman, 1987; Caffray & Schneider, 2000; Cooper, 1994; Cooper, Agocha, & Sheldon, 2000; Cooper, Wood, Orcutt, & Albino, 2003; Goldman, Brown, Christiansen, & Smith, 1991; Jessor & Jessor, 1977; Leigh, 1989; Leigh & Stacy, 1993; Newcomb, Chou, Bentler, & Huba, 1988; Parsons, Halkitis, Bimbi, & Borkowski, 2000; Slovic, 2001; Stacy, Newcomb, & Bentler, 1991). Moreover, affective motives have been implicated as some of the most proximal determinants or triggers in the pathway to participation in specific health-threatening behaviors (e.g., alcohol, drug use, risky sex; Agrawal et al., 2008; Baranowski et al., 1997; Cooper, 1994; Cooper et al., 2000; Cooper, Frone, Russell, & Mudar, 1995; Cooper et al., 2003; Cox & Klinger, 1988; Langer, 1996; Leigh, 1989).

More recently, approaches emanating from cognitive and decision sciences have been converging with neuroscientific advances to integrate many of the existing findings (see, e.g., Reyna & Farley, 2006; Reyna & Rivers, 2008; Steinberg, 2005, 2007, 2008, 2010). Both perspectives adopt dual-process approaches in which affective motivators are conceptualized as central to adolescent decision making. Both behavioral and neuroscientific research studies suggest that adolescents will be especially sensitive to intuitive, "gut-level," affective motivators because cognitive control processes have not yet fully matured to provide a more "reasoned" balance in decision making. Moreover, these affective motivators can function in different ways. They have the potential to serve as sources of temptation and vulnerability or as adaptive cues, depending on the type of motivation, the situation, and previous experience. Thus, studying affective motivators may help elucidate these relationships so that specific vulnerabilities can be identified and avoided, while adaptive tendencies can be nurtured and strengthened as adolescents navigate through the transition into adulthood.

AFFECTIVE MOTIVATIONS: CAUSAL PATHWAYS TO HEALTH-RELATED BEHAVIORS

Although it is now commonplace to find discussions of the powerful influence that emotions may have on adolescent decision making, the dual-process approach typically emphasizes only the approach or avoidance valence of affective states. Nevertheless, the developmental literature has uncovered numerous more subtle influences of different kinds of affective motivators in adolescent behavior.

Much of the work on differentiating the causal role of affective motivators has stemmed from the motivational model of alcohol use originally proposed by Cox and Klinger (1988). Their framework for alcohol motives comprises two dimensions, which represent the valence (i.e., positive or negative) and source (i.e., internal or external) of outcomes to be achieved by drinking. Variants of this model have been shown to capture substantial variance (up to 65%) in adolescent reports of the quantity and frequency of drinking (Cooper, 1994; Cooper et al., 1995). In the most successful variant of the model, Cooper et al. (1995; see also Caffray & Schneider, 2000) showed that three coping motives (i.e., tension reduction, negative emotions, and avoidance coping) and three enhancement motives (i.e., social/emotional, positive emotions, and sensation seeking) were especially important in predicting alcohol use. Social or enhancement motives have been more strongly associated with low to moderate drinking, whereas coping or avoidance motives have been more predictive of heavy, problem drinking (Agrawal et al., 2008; Cooper, 1994; Cooper et al., 2003; Farber, Khavari, & Douglas, et al., 1980; Reese, Chassin, & Molina, 1994). Similar trends have been identified for smoking cigarettes and having sex, with related motivational patterns being observed in using drugs and skipping school (Brandon et al., 1999; Caffray & Schneider, 2000; Cooper et al., 2003; Newcomb, Chou, Bentler & Huba, 1988). Results based on related expectancy/motivational models have established that the relationship between these kinds of affective motives and health-threatening behaviors is both causal and reciprocal in nature (Agrawal et al., 2008; Cooper et al., 1995, 2003; Del Boca, Darkes, Goldman & Smith, 2002; Goldman, Darkes, & Del Boca, 1999; Stacy, 1997).

Though these studies tell us a great deal about particular motivational factors that encourage health-threatening behaviors, motivations for avoiding participation in behaviors have rarely been systematically examined (Leigh, 1989; Newcomb et al., 1988). One exception is a study by Caffray and Schneider (2000) that assessed not only promoters of but also deterrents to five health-threatening behaviors. Taking an individual-differences approach, they explored differences in the potency of various affective motivators among adolescents who were either high or low in experience with a variety of health-threatening behaviors. In addition to exploring enhancement and coping motivators that might promote these behaviors, they included an additional group of "anticipated regret" motivators that they hypothesized might deter those risky behaviors. Based on the decision-making literature (e.g., Richard, van der Pligt, & de Vries, 1995, 1996; Roese & Olson, 1995), they predicted that anticipated regret would motivate some adolescents to avoid the negative feelings associated with behavioral choices that could eventuate in bad outcomes. This prediction was overwhelmingly supported in adolescents with less experience with engaging in each behavior. They consistently reported being motivated to avoid the health-threatening behavior based on anticipated bad outcomes. In contrast, adolescents with more experience in the behaviors paid little attention to anticipated regrets, reporting instead that they were motivated to engage in health-threatening behaviors in order to both enhance positive and reduce negative affective states, with differential patterns for different behaviors (e.g., tension reduction was more important for smoking).

Like others, Caffray and Schneider (2000) speculated that experience itself changes the way that affective motivators influence decision making. Once exposed to a health-threatening behavior, the lack of immediate negative consequences may lull adolescents into focusing on the positive aspects of the behavior. For adolescents who have not yet tried a particular risky behavior, affective deterrents such as anticipatory regret may prove useful in preventing them from ever starting. If adolescents experience this immediate and intuitive negative reaction to the idea of a health-threatening behavior, they may be in a better position to negotiate this period of potentially weak emotional regulation. In this way, anticipatory regret[1] may evoke an affective state that is protective, in that it brings a quick-reflex warning to stay away from trouble situations. This possibility is consistent with recommendations of Reyna and Farley (2006) and Rivers et al. (2008) that risk taking might be reduced if adolescents were able to develop intuitive reactions to environmental triggers that capture risk-avoidant values.

Affective motivators are no less relevant to questions concerning reinforcement of healthy behaviors, as emotional vulnerabilities may predominate here as well. In this case, greater experience with healthy behaviors may strengthen intuitive associations with the (more immediate) positive aspects of these behaviors, whereas less familiarity with health-enhancing behaviors may leave some adolescents with weak or possibly negative impressions of these behaviors. Anticipated regret may also hold promise in promoting health-enhancing behaviors by bringing to mind longer term goals that can only be met by creating healthy routines.

Assessing these possibilities has been difficult because substantially less empirical attention has been given to the proximal factors associated with participation in health-enhancing behaviors (Johnson, Blum, & Giedd, 2009; Millstein et al., 1993; Neumark-Sztainer et al., 1997), though better health practices have been generally linked to higher socioeconomic status (for reviews, see Bradley & Corwyn, 2002; Hanson & Chen, 2007). Despite the media's preoccupation with health-threatening behaviors (Maggs et al., 1997), practitioners and researchers are gradually beginning to focus more attention on processes that support participation in health-enhancing behaviors (e.g., Hedberg et al., 1999; Juszczak & Sadler, 1999; Larson, 2000; Millstein et al., 1993; Nelson et al., 2006; Story & Neumark-Sztainer, 1999; Youngblade et al., 2007). In the following empirical demonstration, we contribute to this effort by identifying connections between affective motivators and day-to-day behaviors, focusing not only on risky practices but also on those that improve health.

---

[1]Loewenstein, Weber, Hsee, and Welch (2001) differentiated anticipated and anticipatory emotions. They argued that anticipated emotion is a relatively "cold" acknowledgment of a predicted emotion, whereas anticipatory emotion is the "hot" experience of an emotion in anticipation of a decision outcome. Caffray and Schneider (2000) asked participants about their perceptions of what they would experience, so they asked about anticipated regret. Nevertheless, they hypothesize that it would be the actual experience of anticipatory regret that would protect the adolescent when confronted with an opportunity to engage in a health-threatening behavior.

A STUDY OF EXPERIENCE AND AFFECTIVE MOTIVATORS IN ADOLESCENT BEHAVIORS

Although the role of experience is considered key to the functioning of the intuitive system within dual process models, there has been little empirical evidence to date demonstrating how different levels of experience may be associated with different roles for affect in decision processes. In the following study, six categories of affective goals were explored to identify systematic differences as a function of amount of experience with four health-related behaviors. Based on previous research, we anticipated a highly differentiated role for affect in the decision process.

This study was aimed at gaining a better understanding of how different affective motives (e.g., desires to obtain or avoid different affective states) may be involved in decisions to participate in various health-related behaviors. In particular, the study was designed to explore how previous experience with given behaviors may be associated with different expectations concerning affective goals and may support differences in the development of routine health-related practices. Because of our interest in the development of these practices, we limited participants to those in the period of late adolescence (ages 18–20), in which these daily behavioral patterns are likely to still be emerging (e.g., Kandel, 1998; Kypri, McCarthy, Coe, & Brown, 2004; Millstein et al., 1993; Parsons et al., 2000). To maintain a relatively homogenous sample, we included only females in this study, as there is evidence that the dynamics associated with choices about health-related behaviors may be qualitatively different between males and females, with especially pronounced differences during adolescent developmental stages (e.g., Cusatis & Shannon, 1996; Douglas, et al., 1997; Waldron, 1997; Zweig, Lindberg, & McGinley, 2001).

This study broadened the scope of previous investigations by incorporating both health-threatening and health-enhancing behaviors. The two health-threatening behaviors were drinking alcohol and smoking cigarettes, and the two health-enhancing behaviors were exercising and eating healthy. All of these behaviors involve decisions that are associated with routine patterns of behavior. The two health-threatening behaviors were selected for inclusion as they pose critical public health risks and are among the primary behaviors characterized as major causes of mortality and morbidity for adolescents (e.g., Douglas et al., 1997; Hingson, Heeren, Winter, & Wechsler, 2005; Hingson, Zha, & Weitzman, 2009; Moskal, Dziuban, & West, 1999; Rivara, Park, & Irwin, 2009). The two health-enhancing behaviors were selected for playing important roles in preventing obesity and other health problems that can lead to the onset of chronic diseases (e.g., Cashman, 2007; Haberman & Luffey, 1998; Ortega, Ruiz, Castillo, & Sjostrom, 2008; Story & Neumark-Sztainer, 1999).

Unlike most previous studies, this study incorporated a wide array of affective states, including both sides of the motivational continuum with affective goals likely to promote the behaviors as well as other affective goals likely to deter participation in the behaviors. Based on the role of immediate reinforcement, it was anticipated that individuals with more behavioral experience would more strongly endorse promoters (desires to engage in a behavior, e.g., to have a good time). For those with less experience, deterrent motivators (desires to stay away from a behavior, e.g., to avoid regret) were expected to be viewed as more important, particularly for the health-threatening behaviors. It was also expected that some of the motives would be differentially influential for specific behaviors, consistent with previous studies. These more specific hypotheses are detailed below. We also explored the possibility that some affective states might be capable of either promoting *or* deterring decisions depending on participants' experience with health-enhancing behaviors.

METHOD

Participants and Procedure

The test instrument was administered individually in a laboratory setting to 262 female undergraduate students, 250 of whom met the required criteria of being between the ages of 18 and 20 years old and being native English speakers according to their self-reports. Of these participants, 36% were 18 years of age, 39% were 19 years old, and 25% were 20 years old. In addition to age and native language, participants also reported on their race or ethnicity. Seventy percent of the participants indicated that they were White or White/Hispanic, 15% reported being Black/African American or Black/Hispanic, 9% said they were Hispanic, 4% indicated Asian as their race, and 2% did not report on their race or ethnicity. Participants received extra credit toward their undergraduate psychology classes. (After completing this study, participants engaged in a second computerized study concerning memory processes that will not be discussed further.)

Measures

In this study, four health-related behaviors were examined in the same session. The two health-threatening behaviors were drinking alcohol and smoking cigarettes, and the two health-enhancing behaviors were exercising and "eating healthy," that is, making healthful food choices. The study included both promoter and deterrent affective states as motivators. Promoters included affective states that encourage participation in a behavior, and deterrents included affective states that motivate avoidance of a behavior. Each affective state represented either a desired state to be achieved or an undesired state to be avoided or eliminated. Table 11.1 presents the 13 affective motivators, organized into six different affective categories. Five of the categories corresponded to those proposed by Caffray and Schneider (2000; see also Cooper et al., 1995) in their revised emotional-motivational framework. These included (a) anticipated regret, (b) negative emotions, (c) tension reduction, (d) social/emotional, and (e) sensation seeking. The new category of self-esteem/efficacy represented an extension to the model to permit an assessment of the effectiveness of incorporating ego-related goals as promising motivational pathways for participation in health-enhancing behaviors. These types of goals have been cited previously as being important in adolescents' decisions about participating in behaviors such as physical exercise and making healthy food choices (e.g., Dutta & Youn, 1999; Schwarzer & Luszczynska, 2006; Story & Neumark-Sztainer, 1999; Trzesniewski et al., 2006). Although it is not entirely clear that ego-related goals represent a distinct form of affect, conventional wisdom suggests a close association.

The test instrument had two parts. The first part focused on previous experience, and the second consisted of the focal sentence-rating task assessing degree of endorsement of affective motivators. As part of the experience questionnaire, participants first completed a series of open-ended questions inquiring about their demographic characteristics (e.g., age, race, native language). Next, participants responded about their current experience with each of the four health-related behaviors, answering a series of questions about both the frequency of participation and their level of involvement (e.g., "During the past 7 days, on how many days did you exercise or participate in

TABLE 11.1
Affective Motivator Stimuli Categorized by Affect Type

Affective motivators	Affect type
Harm my future	Anticipated regret
Disappoint someone I care about	Anticipated regret
Might regret it	Anticipated regret
Feel lonely	Negative emotion
Feel sad	Negative emotion
Feel stressed	Tension reduction
Feel relaxed	Tension reduction
Have a good time	Social/emotional
Impress someone I like	Social/emotional
Feel bored	Sensation seeking
Have a little excitement	Sensation seeking
Feel confident	Self-esteem/efficacy
Feel unattractive	Self-esteem/efficacy

a physical activity that made you sweat or breathe hard such as walking, jogging, biking, aerobics, swimming, or team sports?"; "On the days that you exercised or participated in a physical activity, how much time on average {# minutes per day} did you spend doing this?"). Because of the complexity in assessing eating behavior, participants responded to weekly eating patterns for 14 different food categories (e.g., lean meats or fish, milk/yogurt/other dairy products). Additional follow-up questions were also included to assess the intensity or types of experience (e.g., binge drinking—five or more drinks of alcohol in a row within a couple of hours; smoking cigars, cigarillos, or little cigars in addition to cigarettes). Participants were instructed when responding that if the specific time period in question (e.g., past 7 days) was for some reason atypical, then they should respond according to a more normal or typical time period.

Experience questions were modeled after items used in the Youth Risk Behavior Survey, which is a comprehensive national health behavior surveillance study of over 15,000 adolescents conducted biennially by the Centers for Disease Control. (See Brener et al., 2004, for background and methodological details of the survey.) To achieve greater precision in reported levels of experience and to remove potential biases related to scaling or anchoring effects, items were modified from the prescribed response categories used in the Youth Risk Behavior Survey (e.g., six to 10 cigarettes per day, 11 to 20 cigarettes per day) to open-ended responses within a specified time frame (e.g., number of times in 7 days, number of minutes per day).

In addition to the more structured behavioral assessment questions, four completely open-ended questions were developed to give participants an opportunity to elaborate on their past experiences by providing a written description of their "policy" or regular routines for each of the behaviors (e.g., "I regularly smoke a pack of cigarettes daily"; "I never eat breakfast"; "I typically have a glass of wine with dinner"). These items were designed to yield additional information and clarity regarding participants' past experiences with each of the behaviors.

Although the participants' responses relied on retrospective self-reports, which may be subject to memory heuristics or recall biases, research has shown high correlations between retrospective reports and other more costly, less efficient methods such as daily reports (e.g., Leigh, 2000). Because our intent was only to capture broad distinctions in experience with these behaviors, the previously validated questionnaire approach was deemed sufficient.

The second part of the test instrument involved the completion of the sentence-rating task, which assessed the extent to which participants associated the affective motivators with each of the four health behaviors. A total of 68 sentences were to be rated, each of which paired one of the affective motivators with one of the four health behaviors. Fifty-two of the sentences

(13 affective motivators × 4 health behaviors) presented the affective motivators in their originally predicted direction of influence. For the health-threatening behaviors, sentences associated with anticipated regrets were phrased as discouraging the behavior (deterrent motives). For the remaining items, all of the sentences were phrased as encouraging participation in the behavior (i.e., promoter motives). An example of a deterrent sentence was "I would not want to drink alcohol because it might harm my future" and promoter sentences included "Feeling stressed makes me want to smoke a cigarette," "I would want to exercise to avoid disappointing someone I care about," and "Feeling unattractive would make me want to eat healthy." Participants rated how true they believed each of the sentences was for them using a 5-point scale from 1 = *never true* to 5 = *almost always true*. These ratings assessed the extent to which each of the affective motivators was expected to influence their participation in or avoidance of each of the behaviors.

Another 16 sentences were added to the test instrument to test the hypothesis that some affective states might fluctuate in their direction of influence and so might, in some cases, promote participation in health-enhancing behaviors but, in other cases, might deter the very same behaviors. Eight of the affective states (i.e., the three anticipated regret motives along with feeling sad, stressed, lonely, bored, and having a good time) were assessed in both directions of the motivational continuum. That is, in addition to the original sentences with affective motivators cast as promoters, a second set of sentences was created using the same affective motivators cast as potential deterrents of the behaviors of healthy eating and exercising. For example, the initial promoter sentence concerning "feeling bored" (e.g., "Feeling bored makes me want to exercise") was also paired with a deterrent sentence (e.g., "If I were feeling bored, I would not want to exercise"), and the promoter motive of feeling sad (e.g., "Feeling sad makes me want to eat healthy") was also tested as a deterrent (e.g., "If I were feeling sad, I would not want to eat healthy").

Four different orders of the sentence-rating task were developed. Random counterbalancing procedures were used to assign one of the four orders to each participant.

RESULTS

The overriding goal of the analyses was to examine the affective motivations associated with each of the four health-related behaviors (i.e., drinking alcohol, smoking cigarettes, exercising, and eating healthy) as a function of the amount of experience the participants had in engaging in each of the behaviors. To accomplish this, participants' experiences were first broadly categorized into high and low levels of experience with each of the behaviors separately. Next, differences in the perceived strength of the affective motivators were examined, first for the health-threatening behaviors and then for the health-enhancing behaviors. For both types of behavior, analyses involved a descriptive assessment of the general profiles of perceived affective influences for the low- and high experience groups, respectively, followed by a comparative analysis to determine whether the motivational patterns differed significantly between the groups.

For the health-threatening behaviors, we expected to replicate Caffray and Schneider (2000) by showing that the low experience groups would be predominantly influenced by the anticipated regret motives to refrain from smoking and drinking, but that the high experience groups would be predominantly influenced by more immediate desires to achieve or avoid affective states associated with using these substances. For the health-enhancing behaviors, we also hypothesized that there would be pronounced differences across the experience groups in the perceived strength of anticipated regrets. In this case, we expected that desires to avoid feelings of self-recrimination (e.g., regret) would figure more prominently in guiding the behavior of those who regularly engage in healthy behaviors and would be less important for those with relatively little experience with engaging in healthy practices. We also predicted that self-esteem/efficacy motives would be more important for those who regularly engage in health-enhancing behaviors than those who rarely do (Dutta & Youn, 1999; Schwarzer & Luszczynska, 2006; Story & Neumark-Sztainer, 1999; Trzesniewski et al., 2006). For the remaining affective motivators, we did not have sufficient data on which to base particular predictions, given the dearth of research on particular motivators of health-enhancing behaviors.

In some cases, it seemed possible that the different affective motivators might be capable of operating in either direction for the health-enhancing behaviors. To assess this possibility, a set of analyses was conducted on a subset of affective states to examine whether particular affective states might be capable at times of exerting an impact on both sides of the motivational continuum, that is, in both promoter and deterrent roles, depending on the level of previous experience with the health-enhancing behavior.

Analysis of variance (ANOVA) techniques were employed throughout to investigate the nature of these relationships. For two critical reasons, the four health-related behaviors were always examined separately. First, theoretical considerations made it likely that the impact of affective motivations would differ for each of the health-related behaviors, depending on their specific nature (i.e., either health-threatening or health-enhancing) or other associated characteristic features (e.g., outcome expectancies, pharmacological/physiological reactions). Second, many of the participants differed in the amount of experience they had with each of the four behaviors. Therefore, by isolating each behavior, the relationships between the affective motivators and each individual's experience level for that particular behavior could be independently evaluated.

Previous Experiences With Health-Related Behaviors

The amount of previous experience participants had with each of the four health-related behaviors was determined by examining their responses to the sets of experience questions, primarily those items that assessed the frequency and intensity of their involvement, and to the qualitative reports regarding their "policy" or routines about each behavior. Participants' detailed responses were assessed to create higher and lower experience dichotomies for each behavior.[2] As indicated earlier, this categorization process was conducted separately for each behavior, given that participants' experience with each of the four health-related behaviors varied. Thus, it was possible that participants were classified into high experience groups for some behaviors and low experience groups for others.

Smoking cigarettes resulted in the "purest" experience groups of those with virtually no experience with smoking ($n = 165$) versus some experience ($n = 85$). For drinking alcohol, the two experience groups were less extreme than for smoking, but the categorization process resulted in fairly balanced groups in which the high experience group comprised just under half of the participants ($n = 112$). This group included participants who reported consuming alcohol more than 3 days in the past month and/or consuming three or more drinks on at least one occasion. For exercising, high experience ($n = 146$) was defined as more than 30 minutes or more than 3 days (for any duration) of exercise in the past week or routinely, consistent with recommendations of the International Consensus Conference on Physical Activity Guidelines for Adolescents (Sallis & Patrick, 1994) and the Surgeon General's report on physical activity and health (U.S. Department of Health and Human Services, 1996).

The most difficult categorization involved healthful eating. Following an approach similar to that of Neumark-Stzainer et al. (1997), the low experience group (i.e., unhealthy eaters, $n = 152$) included individuals who indicated three or more instances (days) of (a) less than five servings of dairy foods; (b) less than five servings of fruit or fruit juices; (c) less than five servings of salads or vegetables; (d) more than five servings of sweets, coffee, snack chips, or fast food; (e) regularly skipping meals; or (f) any instance of risky dieting behavior in the past month.

---

[2]Although a regression approach might also have been considered, we opted for a categorical approach because of the difficulty in assigning more finely grained differences in experience to clearly defined quantitative scales.

Affective Motivators and Experience

Each of the affective motivators was paired with each of the four health behaviors in sentences, and participants rated how true they believed each of the sentences to be for them. These ratings represented the perceived motivational influence of each of the affective states on participants' decisions to engage in or avoid the health behaviors. The analyses were designed as an attempt to replicate the findings of Caffray and Schneider (2000) in a homogeneous group of late-adolescent girls. We also hoped to extend this work by examining affective motivational patterns driving two health-enhancing behaviors, as well as potential differences in the direction of motivational influence for several of the affective states.

Assessing the Consistency of the Affective Categories Between Behavior Types

Based on our previous work with combining affective motivators into theoretical categories (e.g., anticipated regret, sensation seeking; see Table 11.1), we again anticipated reliable internal consistency for the categories of motivators with respect to the health-threatening behaviors. Of interest was how well the affective motivators for the health-enhancing behaviors would conform to these same affect categories.

Although the categories consisted of only two or three items, the coefficient alphas were, as expected, fairly high for the health-threatening behaviors, ranging from .63 to .91. However, the results for the health-enhancing behaviors were considerably less stable, with alpha values ranging from .32 to .79. These less reliable findings for the affective categories motivating the health-enhancing behaviors may be attributable to the potential dual motivational role of some of the affective states in influencing these behaviors, which we discuss later. However, they may also suggest finer distinctions or subtleties in the affective states that promote or discourage participation in health-enhancing behaviors as compared to health-threatening behaviors. Regardless, for ease of interpretation, we periodically refer to the affective categories, but given the range of consistency of the categories, particularly with the health-enhancing behaviors, results by individual affective states are provided.

Comparing the Relative Strength of the Affective States as Motivators

Based on our previous work, it was anticipated that within each experience group, it was likely that patterns of differential affective influence would emerge for each of the health-related behaviors. To assess this, we first qualitatively extracted the general patterns of perceived impact for each group and, as needed, we confirmed visual impressions with sets of pairwise comparisons across the motivators to statistically test these distinctions. In these cases, a more stringent alpha criterion of .01 was adopted to help control for family-wise error given the number of pairwise combinations to be tested. Only statistically significant patterns are discussed below. Once these general patterns of differential affective influence were identified within each of the experience groups, they were compared across the groups to assess whether these motivational patterns differed between the high- and low experience groups.

Consistent with our previous research, the anticipated regret motives for both of the health-threatening behaviors were worded as deterrent influences, discouraging participation in the behavior, and all other motives were presented as promoters encouraging participation. For the health-enhancing behaviors, all items were presented as promoter influences and then a subset of motivators were explored in the deterrent motivational role.

Health-Threatening Behaviors and Low Experience Groups

For both of the health-threatening behaviors, the patterns of perceived strength of affective influence among the motivators were easily extracted. As seen in Figure 11.1, consistent with predictions, it was visibly apparent that the low experience groups' desires to avoid anticipated regret (i.e., the three deterrent motives) represented the strongest influences in their decisions to refrain from engaging in these behaviors. Not only did these low experience participants strongly endorse all of the anticipated regret motivators, they indicated that almost none of the other affective states were effective in promoting these behaviors except for a slight suggestion that alcohol consumption could possibly be influenced by desires to have a good time.

Health-Threatening Behaviors and High Experience Groups

Examining the patterns among the high experience groups for the health-threatening behaviors revealed differential impacts among the perceived relative strength of the motivators for each of these behaviors. Participants who reported that they regularly drank alcohol indicated that desires to have a good time and needs for experiencing some excitement were perceived as having the greatest influence on their decisions to drink, thereby replicating the previous findings from Caffray and Schneider (2000).

Among the smokers, the predominance of the affective motivation of stress was replicated from previous findings. Feelings of stress had the strongest perceived impact on cigarette smoking behavior among the promoter motives. It is also noteworthy that despite their participation, the smokers also reported that beliefs about avoiding harm to their future health were of considerable concern to them. Although we did not anticipate this

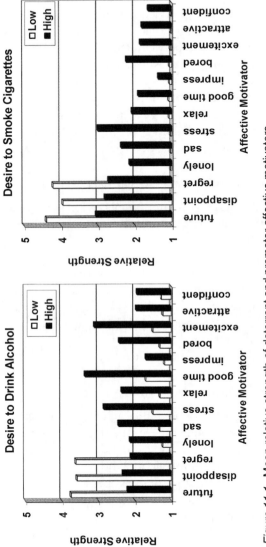

Figure 11.1. Mean relative strength of deterrent and promoter affective motivators.

finding, it is consistent with Slovic's (2001) data showing that as adolescent smokers become "regulars" during their transition into adulthood, they begin to become concerned about the longer term consequences of smoking, though the powerful nicotine addiction often thwarts attempts to stop.

Health-Threatening Behaviors: Comparing Affective Motivational Patterns Between Experience Groups

To examine whether differences existed in the patterns of affective influence between the high and low experience groups, multivariate analyses of variance (MANOVA) were employed for each health-threatening behavior separately. For both behaviors, the MANOVA results indicated significant differences between the experience groups across the sets of 13 affective motivators (see Table 11.2). Large effect sizes were observed for both of these behaviors, mirroring the Caffray and Schneider (2000) results. To assess the specific differential perceived impacts of the affective motivators between the groups, a set of 13 univariate ANOVA follow-up tests were conducted for each behavior. These results are also summarized in Table 11.2.

As shown in the table, the experience groups significantly differed in their perceptions about the motivating strength of each of the affective states in all cases for both of the health-threatening behaviors (i.e., all p values < .001). These pronounced results replicate the previous study's findings and provide strong evidence for the robustness of experience-related differences in these affect-behavior relationships.

Figure 11.1 graphically depicts these differential impressions of the affective motivators between the groups for the health-threatening behaviors. Consistent with predictions, there were large differences for both behaviors in the perceived influence of the deterrent anticipated-regret motivators across groups. The low experience group was significantly more influenced by these motives to avoid participation than was the high experience group. In contrast, the high experience group showed significantly more endorsement than the low group did for all of the promoter motives encouraging participation in the behaviors. This was particularly evident for smoking cigarettes; the low experience group reported virtually no desire to smoke cigarettes regardless of the affective state that might be achieved or avoided.

Health-Enhancing Behaviors and Low Experience Groups

Given the lack of prior research examining these relationships for the health-enhancing behaviors, it was difficult to make specific predictions regarding the perceived impact of affective states on decisions to participate in these behaviors. Nevertheless, we speculated that the low experience groups would report relatively low perceived impact from any of the promotional

TABLE 11.2
Analysis Results and Estimated Effect Sizes of the Between Group Differences on the Sentence Rating Task by Behavior and Motivators

Affective motivator	Alcohol		Smoking		Exercising		Eating	
	$F(13,229)$ ***	(η^2) **.54**	$F(13,230)$ ***	(η^2) **.56**	$F(13,228)$ ***	(η^2) **.20**	$F(13,228)$ ***	(η^2) .14
Univariate	$F(1,241)$ ***	(R^2)	$F(1,242)$ ***	(R^2)	$F(1,240)$ **	(R^2)	$F(1,240)$ ***	(R^2) .05
Future	***	.31	***	.20		.03		–
Disappoint	***	.20	***	.13		–	***	.05
Regret	***	.29	***	.21	***	.09	*	.02
Lonely	***	.23	***	.32	***	.07	**	.03
Sad	***	.26	***	.33	***	.15	*	.02
Stress	***	.31	***	.51	***	.06	**	.03
Relax	***	.30	***	.28	***	.06	**	.06
Good Time	***	.41	***	.22	*	.02	***	
Impress	***	.10	***	.06		.07		–
Bored	***	.29	***	.28	***	.08		–
Excite	***	.44	***	.25	***	–	**	.04
Unattractive	***	.18	***	.20		.12		–
Confident	***	.16	***	.21	***		**	.04

Note. Boldface indicates that at least 4% of the variance in responses is accounted for by the finding. Underlined text indicates that at least 15% of the variance in responses is accounted for.

* $p < .05.$ ** $p < .01.$ *** $p < .001.$

affective states, given their previous tendencies not to engage in health-enhancing behaviors.

As shown in Figure 11.2, the patterns of perceived affective influence were fairly similar for both exercising and eating behaviors but were not necessarily those that were expected. Despite participants' reports of little previous experience with these behaviors, several of the affective promoters were moderately to highly endorsed. This was particularly evident for participants' desires to avoid harming their future, their aspirations about self-esteem/efficacy (i.e., wanting to feel attractive and confident), and wanting to have a good time.

Health-Enhancing Behaviors and High Experience Groups

Again, because less was known about what might motivate involvement in these behaviors, we could not predict a particular pattern of perceived affective influences, beyond the expectation that avoiding anticipated regrets and attaining self-esteem/efficacy goals were likely to be fairly strong motivators of healthy behavior. Upon examination of the results, the patterns of endorsement that emerged for the high experience groups were almost identical to those seen for the low experience groups, although the perceived strength of motivations appeared greater for those with more involvement in the health-enhancing behavior. As expected, high experience participants indicated that their decisions to engage in both exercising and eating healthy were driven mostly by desires to avoid anticipated regrets and to succeed in self-esteem/efficacy motives (i.e., feeling confident, not feeling unattractive). The desire to have a good time was also a strong motivator encouraging healthy behaviors. In addition, exercising was perceived as strongly motivated by feelings of stress.

Health-Enhancing Behaviors: Comparing Affective Motivational Patterns Between Experience Groups

Given the observed similarities in the patterns of perceived influence between the experience groups, we were interested in statistically assessing the potential differences in relative strength. Similar to the between-group analyses used for the health-threatening behaviors, two MANOVAs were conducted to discern group differences among the sets of 13 promoter affective motivators. For both exercising and healthy eating, the MANOVA results indicated significant differences between the experience groups at $p < .0001$ (see Table 11.2). Follow-up univariate ANOVAs were conducted to isolate the specific between-group differences among the motivators. Results for these analyses are presented in Table 11.2. Although the findings were slightly less robust than found for the health-threatening behaviors, the

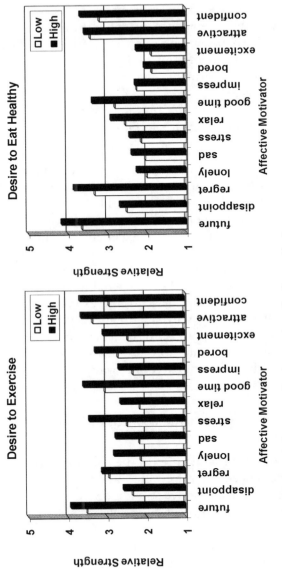

Figure 11.2. Mean relative strength of promoter affective motivators.

majority of experience-group differences in perceived affective motivational influence were significant.

All of the affective motivators were more influential in motivating exercising among the high experience group compared with the low experience group, with the possible exception of two of the anticipated regret motives (i.e., disappointing someone, regret) and feeling unattractive, in which the differences were in the expected direction but of questionable reliability. Effect sizes were generally modest, and strongest for feelings of stress and confidence. There were fewer instances of significant differences in endorsement of motives between the high- and low experience groups for healthy eating, but again the patterns always reflected the expected direction (i.e., greater influence for the high experience group). Effect sizes were generally small, especially in comparison to experience-based differences observed for health-threatening behaviors.

Health-Enhancing Behaviors: Reversing the Direction of Motivational Influence

Based on our speculation that affective states might fluctuate in motivational valence for the health-enhancing behaviors, we compared promoter and deterrent motivational strength for eight of the affective motivators. For the three anticipated regret motives (i.e., harm future, disappoint someone, regret) and five other motives (i.e., sad, lonely, stress, good time, bored), participants were asked about the extent to which each encouraged or discouraged participation in exercise and healthy eating. For example, the promoter affective state of feeling stressed ("Feeling stressed would make me want to eat healthy") was also presented as a possible deterrent for these behaviors (i.e., "If I were feeling stressed, I would not want to eat healthy"). Likewise, the three anticipated regret motives were also explored as deterrents, similar to pairing them with the health-threatening behaviors. However, when paired with the health-enhancing behaviors, these relationships seemed considerably less plausible (e.g., "I would not want to exercise because it might harm my future").

As a result of the counterintuitive direction for the anticipated regret motives, it was predicted that neither of the experience groups would strongly endorse these motivators as impacting decisions to avoid exercising or healthy eating. However, for the remainder of items, it was anticipated that the low experience groups would indicate that some of the affective states were likely to discourage healthy behavior. We also predicted that the low experience group would claim greater impact from these deterrent affective states in their decisions to avoid these behaviors, relative to the high experience groups. Two sets of eight univariate ANOVAs were employed to explore these predictions.

For the anticipated regret motives, the differential patterns of perceived influence depicted in Figure 11.3 descriptively corresponded to the expected results, in that neither group was concerned that exercising or healthy eating

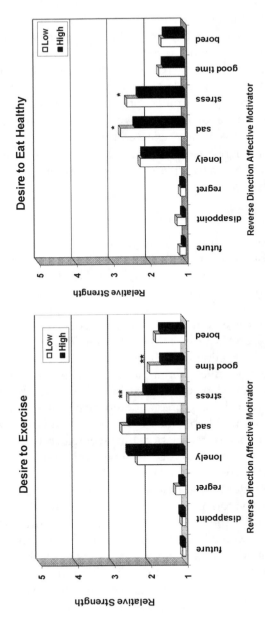

Figure 11.3. Mean relative strength of promoter versus deterrent affective motivators.
*p < .05. ** p < .01.

might be linked to regrettable consequences. (This essentially functioned as a manipulation check and added to our confidence that participants were carefully considering each of the motivator-behavior relationships in the sentence-rating task.) The ANOVA results did not suggest the presence of any significant differences between the experience groups for these deterrent motives.

For the other items, consistent with predictions, the affective motivators were seen as sometimes discouraging healthy behaviors, especially among the low experience groups. In particular, the more sedentary group reported significantly greater motivation than the high-exercise group to avoid exercising in response to feelings of stress, $F(1,239) = 9.12$, $p < .01$, and to beliefs that they would not have a good time, $F(1,239) = 8.04$, $p < .01$. Regarding food, those with poorer eating habits were more discouraged than others from healthy eating by feelings of sadness, $F(1,242) = 5.97$, $p < .05$, and stress, $F(1,239) = 4.46$, $p <. 05$. There were no other reliable differences shown between the experience groups.

Health-Enhancing Behaviors: Comparing the Direction of Motivational Influence

Given that the subset of eight affective motivators was assessed in both directions of motivational influence (i.e., as both promoters and deterrents), it was possible to compare the relative strength of each of these motivational roles. To do this, for each behavior, sets of exploratory pairwise comparisons were conducted, comparing the perceived strength of each affective state in their promoter and deterrent roles separately for each of the experience groups. A more stringent alpha criterion of .01 was adopted to reduce the likelihood of Type I errors, given the number of pairwise combinations to be tested.

As shown in Table 11.3, for many of the affective states, there was a more effective direction of influence as indicated by the significant differences in the perceived relative strength of the promoter versus deterrent motivational roles. For example, the anticipated regret motives were clearly more influential in promoting participation in both of the health-enhancing behaviors for both experience groups. Similarly, having a good time was also significantly more effective in promoting than deterring exercise and healthy eating for both experience groups. In contrast, there were no reliable differences in the impact of motivational roles associated with loneliness for either of the groups.

This analysis also revealed that many motivators could reliably serve as either a promoter or a deterrent and that the likely direction of influence often varied as a function of an individual's previous experiences with the behavior. For example, in the low experience groups, feeling sad was more likely to discourage rather than promote exercising and healthy eating, and feeling stressed was more likely to undermine healthy eating. In contrast, both feeling stressed and feeling bored were more influential as promoters than deterrents for those who routinely exercise.

TABLE 11.3
Mean Comparisons for Endorsements of Affective Motivators in Roles That Promote Versus Deter Engagement in Health-Enhancing Behaviors

Affective motivator	Exercising Low Prom.	Low Det.		High Prom.	High Det.		Healthy eating Low Prom.	Low Det.		High Prom.	High Det.	
Harm future	**3.51**	1.09	***	**3.91**	1.10	***	**3.64**	1.17	***	**4.15**	1.08	***
Disappoint	**2.34**	1.10	***	**2.57**	1.13	***	**2.51**	1.24	***	**2.68**	1.09	***
Regret	**2.94**	1.27	***	**3.13**	1.13	***	**3.31**	1.14	***	**3.84**	1.11	***
Lonely	2.13	2.32		2.81	2.57		1.99	2.23		2.25	2.16	
Sad	2.17	**2.73**	***	2.77	2.55		2.03	2.76	***	2.37	2.37	
Stress	2.48	2.54		**3.44**	2.11	***	2.13	2.58	***	2.42	2.27	
Good time	**3.04**	1.97	***	**3.59**	1.64	***	**2.79**	1.71	***	**3.37**	1.58	***
Bored	**2.71**	1.80	***	**3.29**	1.66	***	1.86	1.64		**2.05**	1.55	***

Note. Low and high refer to experience groups. Prom and Det refer to motivational roles as promoters or deterrents. Ratings range from 1 = *Never true* to 5 = *Almost always true.* Boldface indicates that the direction of the affective motivator (promotion or deferrence) is significantly stronger.
*** $p < .001$.

In sum, the bidirectional measure of motivational roles not only provided insight into the relative strength of each of the affective states as promoters and deterrents of exercising and eating healthy but also permitted comparisons to be made between these roles. These findings revealed that some of the affective states consistently operated in only one motivational direction, regardless of experience with either behavior (e.g., anticipated regrets in promoter role). Other affective states (e.g., feeling stressed or sad) could operate in either direction to impact decisions about these behaviors and, in these cases, experience was often the key to the most likely direction of perceived influence.

DISCUSSION

The results of this empirical demonstration contribute to the fast-growing literature on the role of affect in decision making. Overall, the findings suggest a critical role for affective motivators in decisions that determine the development and maintenance of health-related behavior patterns. As in Caffray and Schneider (2000; see also Slovic, 2001), the results confirm the perceived strength of anticipatory regret in the prevention of health-threatening behavior patterns and the increasing importance of immediate affective goals, such as relieving stress and having a good time, as experience increases. When the assessment is extended to health-enhancing behaviors, the results show promise for protective roles of anticipated regret as well as self-esteem/efficacy affective motivators, though the results also demonstrate that past experiences affect the intensity of motive–behavior relationships and, in some cases, the direction of motivational influence. In what follows, the potential implications of the findings are addressed and suggestions for future investigations are proposed.

Affect, Experience, and Intuitions

This study provides a novel demonstration of the interaction between experience and the perceived role of affect in decisions. With the growing popularity of dual process models, the role of more intuitive, experience-based, and affective processes is being recognized as essential to understanding decision making and to improving decisions. This is likely to be especially so in the case of adolescents, given recent neuroscientific findings suggesting that affective systems may develop more rapidly than the complementary cognitive control systems that regulate emotions (Casey et al., 2008; Steinberg, 2005, 2007, 2008, 2010; Van Leijenhorst et al., 2010).

Whether the role of affect is best described in terms of *somatic markers* (Damasio, 1994), *affect heuristics* (e.g., Slovic et al., 2007), *risk as feelings* (e.g.,

Loewenstein et al., 2001), or *gist-based feeling states* (Rivers et al., 2008), our results suggest that affect-based responses are likely to involve a complex combination of processes to produce what feels like an intuitive "gut reaction." These intuitive reactions are often assumed to be "simpler" than analytic contributors to decisions, but this characterization may only be accurate with respect to the immediacy of the response from the decision maker's perspective. The underlying complexity of the intuitive response is likely to be found in the mechanisms that aggregate and integrate the wide variety of affective reactions to previous experiences and related opportunities for learning. Rivers et al. (2008) argued that gist-based feeling states often embody values and beliefs derived from learning and experience. They suggested that interventions to reduce risk taking in adolescence can take advantage of this by "inculcat[ing] stable gist representations, enabling adolescents to identify [danger] quickly and automatically . . . even when experiencing emotion, which differs sharply from traditional approaches emphasizing deliberation and precise analysis" (p. 107).

Consistent with this view, our study suggests that some affective states may be especially suited to help in establishing and maintaining values supporting healthier choices during adolescence and beyond. The results also provide hints about the course of development of affect-laden intuitions through experience. Understanding this development process may be especially important in designing successful interventions.

Anticipatory Regret and Self-Esteem/Efficacy as Protective Motivators

Although it is often difficult to characterize the nature of affect and the fundamental differences among types of affect, our results suggest that tying affective states to their motivational underpinnings may help identify useful functional groupings. Four of our affective categories were based on the large amounts of previous developmental research supporting the creation of Cooper et al.'s (1995; see also Cooper et al., 2003) motivational model of adolescent decision making. Cooper and colleagues empirically validated four clusters of affect associated with behavioral goals in teenage alcohol drinking. Although some of these map onto standard affect categories (e.g., negative emotions, feeling sad), others are less routine but easily recognizable. Having a good time (social/emotional), feeling stressed (tension reduction), and feeling bored (sensation seeking) are the kinds of everyday affective experiences that decision makers are likely to associate with their actions. Our results provided additional support for Cooper et al.'s motivational model and provided a replication of Caffray and Schneider (2000), once again confirming the perceived importance of these affective motivators in a variety of common health-related behaviors.

Our results have also empirically validated two additional functional affect groups to be included in the list of useful categories for predicting general behavior patterns. These are anticipated regrets (e.g., not wanting to harm your future) and feelings of self-esteem/efficacy (e.g., wanting to feel confident and attractive). Just as in Caffray and Schneider (2000), our results have captured the powerful perceived influence of anticipated regret in the avoidance of health-threatening behaviors. In this study, we have extended earlier findings to show that anticipated regret can also work to encourage engagement in health-enhancing behaviors. In addition, we have corroborated evidence that feelings of self-esteem/efficacy may be especially important in establishing and maintaining healthy behavior patterns (e.g., Dutta & Youn, 1999; Schwarzer & Luszczynska, 2006; Story & Neumark-Sztainer, 1999; Trzesniewski et al., 2006). Future investigations with a broader sampling of different populations of adolescents will be vital to establish the generalizability of these influences.

The potential role of anticipated regret as a protective motivator seems especially promising, given the burgeoning interest in adolescents' future orientation (see, e.g., Nurmi, 1991; Seginer, 2009). Although differences in definitions of future orientation create some difficulties in interpretation (Steinberg et al., 2009), there is growing consensus that making plans for the future and having a positive orientation toward the future in adolescence can serve protective functions by decreasing the tendency to engage in high-risk behaviors. Nurmi (1991) argued that a normal part of adolescent development includes anticipating and planning for the future and that adolescents who are lacking in future orientation "may manifest other types of problem behaviors . . . such as delinquency, problems in school and drug use" (p. 45).

Having a positive attitude toward the future and planning for the future (not just fantasizing about the future; Oettingen & Mayer, 2002) have been associated with better behavioral outcomes. Keough, Zimbardo, and Boyd (1999), using the Zimbardo Time Perspective Inventory (Zimbardo & Boyd, 1999), reported that college students who were less focused exclusively on the present and at least somewhat interested in the future were less likely to report using alcohol, drugs, and tobacco (see also Trommsdorff & Lamm, 1980). Similarly, adjudicated adolescents who reported a positive attitude toward the future (including a sense of control) were less likely to show impulsive sensation-seeking tendencies and less likely to use alcohol or drugs (Robbins & Bryan, 2004). Even among junior high and high school students, a positive orientation regarding future career opportunities reduced the likelihood of engaging in high-risk behaviors during the following year (Skorikov & Vondracek, 2007). The ability to delay gratification, a behavioral measure associated with future orientation, has also been found to be stronger among adolescents who do not use alcohol, drugs, or tobacco (Romer et al., 2010).

Anticipatory regret, especially when operationalized in terms of "not wanting to harm my future," may represent a key proximal affective state that serves in-the-moment as the gist or intuition that protects against potentially risky behavior. In all of our analyses, "not wanting to harm my future" stands out as one of the most potent differences among those with high and low experience levels. Although especially salient with respect to health-threatening behaviors, interest in the future was also strongly associated with motivation to engage in health-enhancing behaviors. Thus, this affective response may help adolescents guide their experiences by approaching situations with rewards that will last into the future and by avoiding (perhaps entirely) the kinds of situations that tend to evoke strong visceral emotions supportive of risky behaviors (i.e., similar to what Reyna & Farley, 2006, referred to as *self-binding*).

Self-esteem/efficacy motivations may also play a crucial protective role, especially with respect to health-enhancing behaviors. Although the data from the current study are less decisive, there is growing evidence that feelings about one's own value and one's capabilities shape the development of health behavior patterns in adolescence (cf. Baumeister, Campbell, Krueger, & Vohs, 2003). Low self-esteem has been linked to alcohol use, cigarette smoking, and poorer mental and physical health (Boden, Fergusson, & Horwood, 2008; Dielman et al., 1987; Murphy & Price, 1988; Trzesniewski et al., 2006; Wild et al., 2004), and higher self-esteem and self-efficacy have been linked to better eating habits (French et al., 2001) and greater involvement in school-related activities, including athletics (Covington, 2000; Larson, 1994).

What is noticeably absent, however, is a view of self-esteem/efficacy that takes into account the strong affective states that may accompany these assessments. Anecdotally, it is easy to empathize with the negative emotions associated with not feeling up to a given task, or the rush of positive emotion from succeeding at a challenge, especially during the adolescent years. This study may be one of the early steps in linking emotion states and the potential impact of self-esteem/efficacy on health-related decision making in adolescence. Emotions related to one's self-view might be protective, for example, if they make risky behaviors unattractive through feelings associated with ideas like "Smoking makes you smell bad," or "Drinking and drugs mess with your brain," or "People who do drugs are going nowhere," and so forth.

Indirect evidence of this possibility can be found in related work by Gibbons, Gerrard, and colleagues on the role of social images and prototypes in adolescent decision making (Andrews et al., 2008; Gibbons & Gerrard, 1995; Gibbons, Houlihan, & Gerrard, 2009). Although their focus has been on the impact of developing cognitive representations on later behavioral choices, there are likely to be affective correlates of these images that can more proximally predict behavioral choices. Greater focus on the connection between these types of adolescent beliefs and affective motivations may bring clearer insights into the kinds of interventions most likely to prevent high-risk behaviors among adolescents.

Promotion, Deterrence, and the Affect-Motivation Link

This study also reveals a rather surprising characteristic of the functioning of affect in decision making. Affective motives may possess the ability to sometimes promote and sometimes deter a particular behavioral response. We identified several affective motivators that could either promote or discourage participation in the same health-enhancing behavior. Feeling stressed, for instance, might make one person want to exercise but make another person feel resistant to exercising. This difference in the direction of the effect of an affective state was often tied to level of experience with the behavior, but this difference might also vary as a function of the decision situation.

At the outset of this study, there seemed little reason to question the direction of influence for the affective motivators in health-threatening behaviors, given the striking differences between the experience groups in the deterrent effects of anticipated regret motives and the promoter effects of the other affective states. In retrospect, it now seems plausible that some of these affective motivators may also have the potential for reverse effects. As noted earlier, feelings associated with confidence and attractiveness, for instance, may encourage some people to drink, smoke, or use drugs while discouraging others from doing so. This possibility emphasizes the need to better understand the social meanings that adolescents attach to various behaviors (see, e.g., Sunstein, 2008).

Social meaning, social images, and the affective reactions that they generate are essential in determining whether doing drugs, exercising, and so on seem likely to heighten or diminish one's confidence or attractiveness (e.g., Andrews et al., 2008; Crosnoe, Muller, & Frank, 2004). Sometimes it may also be necessary to consider the context. Juvonen and Murdock (1995), for instance, found that preadolescents want both teachers and peers to see them as exerting substantial effort toward achievement. In contrast, young adolescents want to portray themselves as effortful only to teachers, and not to peers, for fear of reducing their popularity. From the standpoint of improving health decisions—and understanding how affect influences and is influenced by related intuitions—it is not sufficient to know the types of affective goals that may influence behavior. It is also necessary to be able to differentially predict how and on what basis these motivators will impact health-related decisions.

Promising Avenues for the Study of Affective Motivators in Decision Making

The current study provides substantial information about which affective motivators may be involved in health-related decisions and how the strength and direction of these influences may vary as a function of experience. An important next step is to go beyond these general patterns to understand the underlying processes. How do affective motivators develop and change over time and with experience? Anticipatory regret, for instance, seems especially promising as a tool in the prevention of health-threatening behaviors. Given the cross-sectional nature of this study's design, it was not possible to determine whether anticipatory regrets were at some point equally influential for all participants as young adolescents but then declined in impact for some, or whether possible regrets were never especially important for those participants who had come to regularly participate in risky behaviors. Preliminary research on future orientation suggests that one's social surroundings, including parents, teachers, and peers, are likely to be especially influential in determining what kinds of anticipatory regrets, if any, develop as one progresses from childhood through adolescence (Nurmi, 1987; Seginer, 2003; Somers & Gizzi, 2001).

Of course, longitudinal studies are necessary to provide a window into this developmental progression and possible predispositions for the establishment of relationships between particular affective motivators and behavior. Because the strength of affective motivators such as anticipatory regrets appears to be directly tied to participants' past experiences, there may be critical periods in which their influence may be especially effective in impacting health promotion. As the social context changes over time, the strength and direction of affective motivators are also likely to change. Throughout the period from childhood through young adulthood, evidence continues to grow regarding the importance of family and school ties in shaping beliefs and health behavior patterns (e.g., Boden et al., 2008; Resnick et al., 1997; Youngblade et al., 2007).

Adolescents tend to picture their future as being similar to that of their parents in terms of social status (Trommsdorff, 1983). As it turns out, their cognitive development, emotional health, and overall fitness *are* likely to be predicted by the socioeconomic status of their parents (Hanson & Chen, 2007; Najmen et al. 2004). Although the differences in opportunities between those of different socioeconomic status should not be discounted, there remain several aspects of health-related behaviors that are a matter of personal choice. The messages that parents are—or are not—sending to their children, whether verbally or through example, are likely to inform what motivates their children's choices about health-related behaviors. Aspects of family narratives, which are co-constructed through daily interactions, shape an adolescent's sense of identity and predict his or her sense of well-being (Fivush, Bohanek, & Marin, 2010). Similarly, family interactions, as well as interactions with teachers and peers, are likely to shape social meanings and the affective motivational strength of potential behaviors (Umberson & Montez, 2010).

This study was concerned with the development of behavior patterns in those approaching adulthood, but it is also important to consider the role of affective motivators in bringing about changes to already existing behavior patterns. Although speculative, our results may suggest which affective motives are likely to introduce qualitative changes in behavior patterns. Those who had little experience with health-threatening behaviors did not endorse any of the promoter affective states, except a mild response to the desire to have a good time. For someone who does not currently engage in health-threatening behaviors, it may be this desire to have a good time that could ultimately tempt the individual to explore drinking or smoking behaviors, only then to be confronted with more of the experience-based cravings that drive others to continue engaging in these risky behaviors (e.g., Slovic et al., 2004). Similarly, a gradual building of concerns about anticipated regret in the future might eventually motivate a smoker or heavy drinker to go through the effort of trying to break the health-threatening habit (Plummer et al., 2001; Prochaska et al., 1994). It is noteworthy that we found much higher levels of concern by smokers over harming their future in this study of older adolescents than we did in our earlier study of younger adolescents (Caffray & Schneider, 2000).

Future research will also be needed to clarify the sources of differences in the motivational patterns between health-threatening and health-enhancing behaviors. Unlike the clear-cut differences in motivational patterns for the health-threatening behaviors, our preliminary evidence suggests that the patterns of motivators for health-enhancing behaviors may be similar across low- and high experience groups. This similarity may be attributable to the greater accumulated knowledge that the participants had regarding the affective benefits that might ensue as a result of participating in the behaviors. For example, the low experience group would have had some level of direct experience with the health-enhancing behaviors, as some amount of exercise and healthy eating seems unavoidable in everyday living (e.g., walking to class, climbing stairs, eating some fruits or vegetables). Everyone has experience with eating fried foods or sweets—and receiving immediate gratification. What is it that pushes an adolescent into acting on one or another motivator? For some, the addictive quality of sweets may be involved in choices, or it may be quicker and easier to get unhealthy foods, or perhaps there is little access to healthy options (even with today's public school system offerings).

Similarly, most adolescents have exposure to the fun of sedentary activities like watching a movie or playing a video game, but they also have exposure to the fun of energetic activities like dancing, playing ball, or riding a bike. How might affective patterns develop to differentially sway behavior patterns toward relatively healthy or unhealthy routines? Our evidence suggests that the proximal motivators may not differ qualitatively in terms of the kinds of affect experienced. Again, the importance of social context suggests that family practices and selected peer groups are likely to exert substantial influence over how those affective motivators impact behavioral choices.

Healthy behavior of parents is likely to be modeled by their children (Youngblade et al., 2010; Umberson & Montez, 2010). The health behavior of friends is also likely to influence choices, and under the right circumstances, may encourage healthy behaviors (Larson, 1994, 2000). Boredom and convenience may also be important culprits in low levels of healthy behaviors. Often, it may simply be easier to engage in less healthy eating habits and more sedentary activities, so it may be more a question of how to convince adolescents (and their caregivers) to invest the energy in themselves to enhance their own well-being across the longer term. Larson (2000), for instance, suggested that many adolescents fail to learn the value of initiative because they have few opportunities to engage in structured voluntary activities such as sports, camps, or bands. These activities provide developmental opportunities to combine intrinsic motivation and concentration to support extended effort over time, contingency thinking, and other skills that contribute to the series of processes necessary for achieving longer term goals. Without this insight into each individual behavior as part of a larger goal, it may be more difficult for the isolated behaviors to become reliably associated with positive affective motivators.

On Developing a Healthy Lifestyle

Experience may provide feedback about behavioral outcomes, but experience alone cannot be counted on to properly develop affective motivators. Without an appreciation of behaviors within the larger context of the future and longer term goals, it is not especially surprising that behaviors could become dominated by activities associated with immediate gratification. Building toward a healthy lifestyle and avoiding opportunities for temptation require the development of affective reactions based on future outcomes. As Reyna and Farley (2006) recommended, it is best to engender "intuitive all-or-none categorical avoidance of dangerous risks" (p. 35). Encouraging an adolescent to develop a self-image that is engaged in the moment but also oriented toward the future may facilitate the development of anticipatory regret toward health-threatening behaviors. For health-enhancing behaviors, like exercising and healthy eating, this strategy may need to be expanded. Here there may be a need to deliberately trade active for sedentary behaviors and balance indulgence with moderation. Affective reinforcers associated with self-esteem/efficacy, including feelings of confidence and attractiveness, and potentially others such as pride and satisfaction, may prove instrumental. Improving our ability to differentiate these affective motivators, along with their causes and consequences, is an essential direction for future research.

Although dual process models tend to separate affect and cognition into two different systems, our results make salient how meaningful behavior requires an ongoing interdependence between the two systems. An explicit focus on the nature of the interactions between the two systems will be necessary to understand the motivational and goal-directed processes that underlie adolescent decision making. More finely grained affective states are largely meaningless unless they are connected with their cognitive context. The affect-based concepts of regret, confidence, and stress, for instance, are each inextricably tied to reasoned processes. People anticipate regret when thinking about the future, they experience confidence as a function of their evaluation of performance on some tasks, and they define stress on the basis of an assessment of the reasonableness of perceived demands. Even basic emotions such as sadness and happiness are typically defined as a function of the evaluation of the meaning of events (e.g., Schneider, 2001; Schneider & Barnes, 2003; Sunstein, 2008). To the extent that affect communicates motivational tendencies (e.g., goals to avoid negative affect and approach positive affect, or to value future outcomes), the interface between cognition and affect becomes the focal point for understanding the goal-directed nature of human behavior.

Our ability to improve decision making in a wide variety of contexts may depend on efforts to better understand and integrate the developmental or experiential progression of affective motivators within paradigms that have traditionally emphasized only cognitive processes. The current study provides evidence of how this kind of research may help us develop strategies to channel the protective capacity of affective motivators into decisions that will help adolescents maintain healthier lifestyles.

REFERENCES

Agrawal, A., Dick, D. M., Bucholz, K. K., Madden, P. A. F., Cooper, M. L., Sher, K. J., & Heath, A. C. (2008). Drinking expectancies and motives: A genetic study of young adult women. *Addiction, 103*, 194–204. doi:10.1111/j.1360-0443.2007.02074.x

Andrews, J. A., Hampson, S. E., Barckley, M., Gerrard, M., & Gibbons, F. X. (2008). The effect of early cognitions on cigarette and alcohol use during adolescence. *Psychology of Addictive Behaviors, 22*, 96–106. doi:10.1037/0893-164X.22.1.96

Baranowski, T., Cullen, K. W., Basen-Engquist, K., Wetter, D. W., Cummings, S., Martineau, D. S., . . . Hergenroeder, A. C. (1997). Transitions out of high school: Time of increased cancer risk? *Preventive Medicine, 26*, 694–703. doi:10.1006/pmed.1997.0193

Baron, J. (1998). *Judgment misguided: Intuition and error in public decision making.* New York, NY: Oxford University Press.

Baumeister, R. F., Campbell, J. D., Krueger, J. I., & Vohs, K. E. (2003). Does high self-esteem cause better performance, interpersonal success, happiness, or healthier lifestyles? *Psychological Science in the Public Interest, 4,* 1–44. doi:10.1111/1529-1006.01431

Bechara, A., Damasio, A., Damasio, H., & Anderson, S. (1994). Insensitivity to future consequences following damage to human prefrontal cortex. *Cognition, 50,* 7–15. doi:10.1016/0010-0277(94)90018-3

Boden, J. M., Fergusson, D. M., & Horwood, L. J. (2008). Does adolescent self-esteem predict later life outcomes? A test of the causal role of self-esteem. *Development and Psychopathology, 20,* 319–339. doi:10.1017/S0954579408000151

Bradley, R. H., & Corwyn, R. F. (2002). Socioeconomic status and child development. *Annual Review of Psychology, 53,* 371–399. doi:10.1146/annurev.psych.53.100901.135233

Brandon, T. H., Juliano, L. M., & Copeland, A. L. (1999). Expectancies for tobacco smoking. In I. Kirsch (Ed.), *How expectancies shape experience* (pp. 263–299). Washington, DC: American Psychological Association. doi:10.1037/10332-011

Brener, N. D., Kann, L., Kinchen, S. A., Grunbaum, J. A., Whalen, L., Eaton, D., . . . Ross, J. G. (2004). Methodology of the Youth Risk Behavior Surveillance System. *Morbidity and Mortality Weekly Report, 53*(RR-12), 1–13.

Brown, S. A., Christiansen, B. A. & Goldman, M. S. (1987). The alcohol expectancy questionnaire: An instrument for the assessment of adolescent and adult alcohol expectancies. *Journal of Studies on Alcohol, 48,* 483–491.

Caffray, C. M., & Schneider, S. L. (2000). Why do they do it? Affective motivators in adolescents' decisions to participate in risky behaviors. *Cognition and Emotion, 14,* 543–576. doi:10.1080/026999300402790

Casey, B. J., Jones, R. M., & Hare, T. A. (2008). The adolescent brain. *Annals of the New York Academy of Sciences, 1124,* 111–126. doi:10.1196/annals.1440.010

Cashman, K. D. (2007). Diet, nutrition, and bone health. *The Journal of Nutrition, 137,* 2507S–2512S.

Chassin, L., Presson, C. C., Rose, J. S., & Sherman, S. J. (2001). From adolescence to adulthood: Age-related changes in beliefs about cigarette smoking in a Midwestern community sample. *Health Psychology, 20,* 377–386. doi:10.1037/0278-6133.20.5.377

Cooper, M. L. (1994). Motivations for alcohol use among adolescents: Development and validation of a four-factor model. *Psychological Assessment, 6,* 117–128. doi:10.1037/1040-3590.6.2.117

Cooper, M. L., Agocha, V. B., & Sheldon, M. S. (2000). A motivational perspective on risky behaviors: The role of personality and affect regulatory processes. *Journal of Personality, 68,* 1059–1088. doi:10.1111/1467-6494.00126

Cooper, M. L., Frone, M. R., Russell, M., & Mudar, P. (1995). Drinking to regulate positive and negative emotions: A motivational model of alcohol use. *Journal of Personality and Social Psychology, 69,* 990–1005. doi:10.1037/0022-3514.69.5.990

Cooper, M. L., Wood, P. K., Orcutt, H. K., & Albino, A. (2003). Personality and the predisposition to engage in risky or problem behaviors during adolescence. *Jour-*

nal of Personality and Social Psychology, 84, 390–410. doi:10.1037/0022-3514.84.2.390

Covington, M. V. (1992). Making the grade: A self-worth perspective on motivation and school reform. New York, NY: Cambridge University Press.

Covington, M. V. (2000). Goal theory, motivation, and school achievement: An integrative review. Annual Review of Psychology, 51, 171–200.

Cox, W. M., & Klinger, E. (1988). A motivational model of alcohol use. Journal of Abnormal Psychology, 97, 168–180. doi:10.1037/0021-843X.97.2.168

Crosnoe, R., Muller, C., & Frank, K. (2004). Peer context and the consequences of adolescent drinking. Social Problems, 51, 288–304. doi:10.1525/sp.2004.51.2.288

Cusatis, D. C., & Shannon, B. M. (1996). Influences on adolescent eating behavior. The Journal of Adolescent Health, 18, 27–34. doi:10.1016/1054-139X(95)00125-C

Damasio, A. R. (1994). Descartes' error: Emotion, reason, and the human brain. New York, NY: Putnam.

Del Boca, F. K., Darkes, J., Goldman, M. S., & Smith, G. T. (2002). Advancing the expectancy concept via the interplay between theory and research. Alcoholism: Clinical and Experimental Research, 26, 926–935. doi:10.1111/j.1530-0277.2002.tb02623.x

Denes-Raj, V., & Epstein, S. (1994). Conflict between intuitive and rational processing: When people behave against their better judgment. Journal of Personality and Social Psychology, 66, 819–829. doi:10.1037/0022-3514.66.5.819

DeSteno, D., Petty, R. E., Wegener, D. T., & Rucker, D. D. (2000). Beyond valence in the perception of likelihood: The role of emotion specificity. Journal of Personality and Social Psychology, 78, 397–416. doi:10.1037/0022-3514.78.3.397

Dielman, T. E., Campanelli, P. C., Shope, J. T., & Butchart, A. T. (1987). Susceptibility to peer pressure, self-esteem, and health locus of control as correlates of adolescent substance abuse. Health Education Quarterly, 14, 207–221.

Douglas, K. A., Collins, J. L., Warren, C., Kann, L., Gold, R., Clayton, S., . . . Kolbe, L. J. (1997). Results from the 1995 National College Health Risk Behavior Survey. Journal of American College Health, 46, 55. doi:10.1080/07448489709595589

Dutta, M. J., & Youn, S. (1999). Profiling healthy eating consumers: A psychographic approach to social marketing. Social Marketing Quarterly, 4, 4–21. doi:10.1080/15245004.1999.9961078

Elders, M. J., Perry, C. L., Eriksen, M. P., & Giovino, G. A. (1994). The report of the Surgeon General: Preventing tobacco use among young people. American Journal of Public Health, 84, 543–547. doi:10.2105/AJPH.84.4.543

Epstein, S. (1994). Integration of the cognitive and psychodynamic unconscious. American Psychologist, 49, 709–724. doi:10.1037/0003-066X.49.8.709

Evans, J. S. B. T. (2008). Dual-processing accounts of reasoning, judgment, and social cognition. Annual Review of Psychology, 59, 255–278. doi:10.1146/annurev.psych.59.103006.093629

Farber, P. D., Khavari, K. A., & Douglas , F. M, (1980). A factor analytic study of reasons for drinking: Empirical validation of positive and negative reinforcement dimensions. *Journal of Consulting and Clinical Psychology, 48*, 780–781.

Finucane, M. L., Peters, E., & Slovic, P. (2003). Judgment and decision making: The dance of affect and reason. In S. L. Schneider & J. Shanteau (Eds.), *Emerging perspectives on judgment and decision research, Part III* (pp. 327–364). New York, NY: Cambridge University Press.

Fivush, R., Bohanek, J. G., & Marin, K. (2010). Patterns of family narrative co-construction in relation to adolescent identity and well-being. In K. C. McLean & M. Pasupathi (Eds.), *Narrative development in adolescence: Advancing responsible adolescent development*. New York, NY: Springer.

French, S. A., Leffert, N., Story, M., Neumark-Sztainer D., Hannan P. & Benson P. L. (2001). Adolescent binge/purge and weight loss behaviors: Associations with developmental assets. *Journal of Adolescent Health, 28*, 211–221. doi:10.1016/S1054-139X(00)00166-X

Gerrard, M., Gibbons, F. X., Houlihan, A. E., Stock, M. L., & Pomery, E. A. (2008). A dual process approach to health risk decision making: The prototype willingness model. *Developmental Review, 28*, 29–61. doi:10.1016/j.dr.2007.10.001

Gibbons, F. X., & Gerrard, M. (1995). Predicting young adults' health-risk behavior. *Journal of Personality and Social Psychology, 69*, 505–517. doi:10.1037/0022-3514.69.3.505

Gibbons, F. X., Houlihan, A. E., & Gerrard, M. (2009). Reason and reaction: The utility of a dual-focus, dual-processing perspective on promotion and prevention of adolescent health risk behaviour. *British Journal of Health Psychology, 14*, 231–248. doi:10.1348/135910708X376640

Gigerenzer, G. (2000). *Adaptive thinking: Rationality in the real world*. Oxford, England: Oxford University Press.

Gilovich, T. (1991). *How we know what isn't so*. New York, NY: Free Press.

Goldman, M. S., Brown, S. A., Christiansen, B. A., & Smith, G. T. (1991). Alcoholism and memory: Broadening the scope of alcohol expectancy research. *Psychological Bulletin, 110*, 137–146.

Goldman, M. S., Darkes, J., & Del Boca, F. K. (1999). Expectancy mediation of biopsychosocial risk for alcohol use and alcoholism. In I. Kirsch (Ed.), *How expectancies shape experience* (pp. 233–262). Washington, DC: American Psychological Association. doi:10.1037/10332-010

Graber, J. A., Brooks-Gunn, J., & Galen, B. R. (1998). Betwixt and between: Sexuality in the context of adolescent transitions. In R. Jessor (Ed.), *New perspectives on adolescent risk behavior* (pp. 270–316). New York, NY: Cambridge University Press. doi:10.1017/CBO9780511571138.010

Haberman, S., & Luffey, D. (1998). Weighing in college students' diet and exercise behaviors. *Journal of American College Health, 46*, 189. doi:10.1080/07448489809595610

Hanson, M. D., & Chen, E. (2007). Socioeconomic status and health behaviours in adolescence: A review of the literature. *Journal of Behavioral Medicine*, 30, 263–285.

Hawkins, J. D., Catalano, R. F., & Miller, J. Y. (1992). Risk and protective factors for alcohol and other drug problems in adolescence and early adulthood: Implications for substance abuse prevention. *Psychological Bulletin*, 112, 64–105. doi:10.1037/0033-2909.112.1.64

Hedberg, V. A., Bracken, A. C., & Stashwick, C. A. (1999). Long-term consequences of adolescent health behaviors: Implications for adolescent health services. *Adolescent Medicine*, 10, 137–151.

Herrnstein, R. J., & Prelec, D. (1992). A theory of addiction. In G. Loewenstein & J. Elster (Eds.), *Choice over time* (pp. 331–361). New York, NY: Russell Sage.

Hingson, R., Heeren, T., Winter, M., & Wechsler, H. (2005). Magnitude of alcohol-related mortality and morbidity among U.S. college students ages 18–24: Changes from 1998 to 2001. *Annual Review of Public Health*, 26, 259–279. doi:10.1146/annurev.publhealth.26.021304.144652

Hingson, R. W., Zha, W., & Weitzman, E. R. (2009). Magnitude of and trends in alcohol-related mortality and morbidity among U.S. college students ages 18–24, 1998–2005. *Journal of the Study of Alcohol and Drugs [Supplement]*, 16, 12–20.

Hogarth, R. M. (2001). *Educating intuition*. Chicago, IL: University of Chicago.

Jessor, R., & Jessor, S. L. (1977). *Problem behavior and psychosocial development: A longitudinal study of youth*. New York, NY: Academic Press.

Jessor, R., Turbin, M. S., & Costa, F. M. (1998). Protective factors in adolescent health behavior. *Journal of Personality and Social Psychology*, 75, 788–800. doi:10.1037/0022-3514.75.3.788

Johnson, S. B., Blum, R. W., & Giedd, J. N. (2009). Adolescent maturity and the brain: The promise and pitfalls of neuroscience research in adolescent health policy. *Journal of Adolescent Health*, 45, 216–221. doi:10.1016/j.jadohealth.2009.05.016

Juszczak, L., & Sadler, L. (1999). Adolescent development: Setting the stage for influencing health behaviors. *Adolescent Medicine*, 10, 1–11.

Juvonen, J., & Murdock, T. B. (1995). Grade-level differences in the social value of effort: Implications for self-presentation tactics of early adolescents. *Child Development*, 66, 1694–1705. doi:10.2307/1131904

Kandel, D. B. (1998). Persistent themes and new perspectives on adolescent substance use: A lifespan perspective. In R. Jessor (Ed.), *New perspectives on adolescent risk behavior* (pp. 43–89). New York, NY: Cambridge University Press. doi:10.1017/CBO9780511571138.004

Kandel, D. B. (2002). *Stages and pathways of drug involvement: Examining the gateway hypothesis*. New York, NY: Cambridge University Press. doi:10.1017/CBO9780511499777

Kahneman, D. (2003). A perspective on judgment and choice: Mapping bounded rationality. *American Psychologist*, 58, 697–720. doi:10.1037/0003-066X.58.9.697

Keough, K. A., Zimbardo, P. G., & Boyd, J. N. (1999). Who's smoking, drinking, and using drugs? Time perspective as a predictor of substance use. *Basic and Applied Social Psychology, 21*, 149–164.

Klein, G. (1998). *Sources of power: How people make decisions.* Cambridge, MA: MIT Press.

Kypri, K., McCarthy, D. M., Coe, M. T., & Brown, S. A. (2004). Transition to independent living and substance involvement of treated and high risk youth. *Journal of Child & Adolescent Substance Abuse, 13*, 85–100. doi:10.1300/J029v13n03_05

Langer, L. (1996). Modeling adolescent health behavior: The preadult health decision-making model. In C. B. McCoy, L. R. Metsch, & J. A. Inciardi (Eds.), *Intervening with drug-involved youth* (pp. 45–78). Thousand Oaks, CA: Sage.

Larson, R. W. (1994). Youth organizations, hobbies, and sports as developmental contexts. In R. K. Silbereisen & E. Todt (Eds.), *Adolescence in context: The interplay of family, school, peers, and work in adjustment* (pp. 46–65). New York, NY: Springer-Verlag.

Larson, R. W. (2000). Toward a psychology of positive youth development. *American Psychologist, 55*, 170–183. doi:10.1037/0003-066X.55.1.170

Leigh, B. C. (1989). In search of the seven dwarves: Issues of measurement and meaning in alcohol expectancy research. *Psychological Bulletin, 105*, 361–373. doi:10.1037/0033-2909.105.3.361

Leigh, B. C. (2000). Using daily reports to measure drinking and drinking patterns. *Journal of Substance Abuse, 12*, 51–65. doi:10.1016/S0899-3289(00)00040-7

Leigh, B. C., & Stacy, A. W. (1993). Alcohol outcome expectancies: Scale construction and predictive utility in higher order confirmatory models. *Psychological Assessment, 5*, 216–229.

Lerner, J. S., & Keltner, D. (2000). Beyond valence: Toward a model of emotion-specific influences on judgment and choice. *Cognition and Emotion, 14*, 473–493. doi:10.1080/026999300402763

Lieberman, M. D. (2000). Intuition: A social cognitive neuroscience approach. *Psychological Bulletin, 126*, 109–137. doi:10.1037/0033-2909.126.1.109

Loewenstein, G. (1996). Out of control: Visceral influences on behavior. *Organizational Behavior and Human Decision Processes, 65*, 272–292. doi:10.1006/obhd.1996.0028

Loewenstein, G. F., Weber, E. U., Hsee, C. K., & Welch, N. (2001). Risk as feelings. *Psychological Bulletin, 127*, 267–286. doi:10.1037/0033-2909.127.2.267

Maggs, J. L., Schulenberg, J., & Hurrelmann, K. (1997). Developmental transitions during adolescence: Health promotion implications. In J. Schulenberg, J. L. Maggs, & K. Hurrelmann (Eds.), *Health risks and developmental transitions during adolescence* (pp. 522–546). New York, NY: Cambridge University Press.

Mellers, B., & McGraw, A. P. (2001). Anticipated emotions as guides to choice. *Current Directions in Psychological Science, 10*, 210–214. doi:10.1111/1467-8721.00151

Millstein, S. G., Petersen, A. C., & Nightingale, E. O. (Eds.). (1993). *Promoting the health of adolescents: New directions for the twenty-first century* (pp. 3–10). New York, NY: Oxford University Press.

Mohr, P. N. C., Biele, G., & Heekeren, H. R. (2010). Neural processing of risk. *The Journal of Neuroscience, 30,* 6613–6619. doi:10.1523/JNEUROSCI.0003-10.2010

Moskal, P. D., Dziuban, C. D., & West, G. B. (1999). Examining the use of tobacco on college campuses. *Journal of American College Health, 47,* 260. doi:10.1080/07448489909595657

Murphy, N. T., & Price, C. J. (1988). The influence of self-esteem, parental smoking, and living in a tobacco production region on adolescent smoking behaviors. *The Journal of School Health, 58,* 401–405. doi:10.1111/j.1746-1561.1988.tb05814.x

Najman, J. M., Aird, R., Bor, W., O'Callaghan, M., Williams, G. M., & Shuttlewood, G. J. (2004). The generational transmission of socioeconomic inequalities in child cognitive development and emotional health. *Social Science & Medicine, 58,* 1147–1158. doi:10.1016/S0277-9536(03)00286-7

Nasrallah, N. A., Clark, J. J., Collins, A. L., Akers, C. A., Phillips, P. E., & Bernstein, I. L. (2011). Risk preference following adolescent alcohol use is associated with corrupted encoding of costs but not rewards by mesolimbic dopamine. *Proceedings of the National Academy of Sciences, USA, 108,* 5466–5471. doi:10.1073/pnas.1017732108

Nelson, M. C., & Gordon-Larsen, P. (2006). Physical activity and sedentary behavior patterns are associated with selected adolescent health risk behaviors. *Pediatrics, 117,* 1281–1290. doi:10.1542/peds.2005-1692

Nelson, M. C., Neumark-Stzainer, D., Hannan, P. J., Sirard, J. R., & Story, M. (2006). Longitudinal and secular trends in physical activity and sedentary behavior during adolescence. *Pediatrics, 118,* e1627–e1634.

Neumark-Sztainer, D., Story, M., Toporoff, E., Himes, J. H., Resnick, M. D., & Blum, R. W. (1997). Covariations of eating behaviors with other health-related behaviors among adolescents. *Journal of Adolescent Health, 20,* 450–458. doi:10.1016/S1054-139X(96)00279-0

Newcomb, M. D., Chou, C. P., Bentler, P. M., & Huba, G. J. (1988). Cognitive motivations for drug use among adolescents: Longitudinal tests of gender differences and predictors of change in drug use. *Journal of Counseling Psychology, 35,* 426–438. doi:10.1037/0022-0167.35.4.426

Nurmi, J.-E. (1987). Age, sex, social class, and quality of family interaction as determinants of adolescents' future orientation: A developmental task interpretation. *Adolescence, 22,* 977–991.

Nurmi, J.-E. (1991). How do adolescents see their future? A review of the development of future orientation and planning. *Developmental Review, 11,* 1–59. doi:10.1016/0273-2297(91)90002-6

Oettingen, G., & Mayer, D. (2002). The motivating function of thinking about the future: Expectations versus fantasies. *Journal of Personality and Social Psychology, 83,* 1198–1212. doi:10.1037/0022-3514.83.5.1198

Ortega, F. B., Ruiz, J. R., Castillo, M. J., & Sjostrom, M. (2008). Physical fitness in childhood and adolescence: A powerful marker of health. *International Journal of Obesity, 32,* 1–11. doi:10.1038/sj.ijo.0803774

Parsons, J. T., Halkitis, P. N., Bimbi, D., & Borkowski, T. (2000). Perceptions of the benefits and costs associated with condom use and unprotected sex among late adolescent college students. *Journal of Adolescence, 23,* 377–391. doi:10.1006/jado.2000.0326

Petraitis, J., Flay, B. R., & Miller, T. Q. (1995). Reviewing theories of adolescent substance use: Organizing pieces in the puzzle. *Psychological Bulletin, 117,* 67–86. doi:10.1037/0033-2909.117.1.67

Plummer, B. A., Velicer, W. F., Redding, C. A., Prochaska, J. O., Rossi, J. S., Pallonen, U. E., & Meier, K. S. (2001). Stage of change, decisional balance, and temptations for smoking: Measurement and validation in a large, school-based population of adolescents. *Addictive Behaviors, 26,* 551–571. doi:10.1016/S0306-4603(00)00144-1

Prochaska, J. O., Velicer, W. F., Rossi, J. S., Goldstein, M. G., Marcus, B. H., Rakowski, . . . Rossi, S. R. (1994). Stages of change and decisional balance for 12 problem behaviors. *Health Psychology, 13,* 39–46. doi:10.1037/0278-6133.13.1.39

Reese, F. L., Chassin, L., & Molina, B. S. G. (1994). Alcohol expectancies in early adolescents: Predicting drinking behavior from alcohol expectancies and parental alcoholism. *Journal of Studies on Alcohol, 55,* 276–284.

Resnick, M. D., Bearman, P. S., Blum, R. W., Bauman, K. E., Harris, K. M., Jones, J., . . . Udry, J. R. (1997). Protecting adolescents from harm: findings from the National Longitudinal Study on Adolescent Health. *JAMA, 278,* 823–832. doi:10.1001/jama.1997.03550100049038

Reyna, V. F. (2004). How people make decisions that involve risk: A dual-processes approach. *Current Directions in Psychological Science, 13,* 60–66. doi:10.1111/j.0963-7214.2004.00275.x

Reyna, V. F., & Farley, F. (2006). Risk and rationality in adolescent decision making: Implications for theory, practice, and public policy. *Psychological Science in the Public Interest, 7*(1), 1–44.

Richard, R., van der Pligt, J., & de Vries, N. (1995). Anticipated affective reactions and prevention of AIDS. *The British Journal of Social Psychology, 34,* 9–21. doi:10.1111/j.2044-8309.1995.tb01045.x

Richard, R., van der Pligt, J., & de Vries, N. (1996). Anticipated regret and time perspective: Changing sexual risk-taking behavior. *Journal of Behavioral Decision Making, 9,* 185–199. doi:10.1002/(SICI)1099-0771(199609)9:3<185::AID-BDM228>3.0.CO;2-5

Rivara, F. P., Park, M. J., & Irwin, C. E. (2009). Trends in adolescent and young adult morbidity and mortality. In R. J. Di Clemente, J. S. Santelli, & R. A. Crosby (Eds.), *Adolescent health: Understanding and preventing risk behaviors* (pp. 7–29). San Francisco, CA: Wiley.

Rivers, S. E., Reyna, V. F., & Mills, B. (2008). Risk taking under the influence: A fuzzy-trace theory of emotion in adolescence. *Developmental Review, 28,* 107–144. doi:10.1016/j.dr.2007.11.002

Robbins, R. N., & Bryan, A. (2004). Relationships between future orientation, impulsive sensation seeking, and risk behavior among adjudicated adolescents. *Journal of Adolescent Research, 19,* 428–445. doi:10.1177/074355 8403258860

Roese, N. J., & Olson, J. M. (Eds.). (1995). *What might have been: The social psychology of counterfactual thinking.* Mahwah, NJ: Erlbaum.

Romer, D., Duckworth, A. L., Sznitman, S., & Park, S. (2010). Can adolescents learn self-control? Delay of gratification in the development of control over risk taking. *Prevention Science, 11,* 319–330. doi:10.1007/s11121-010-0171-8

Sallis, J. F., & Patrick, K. (1994). Physical activity guidelines for adolescents: Consensus statement. *Pediatric Exercise Science, 6,* 302–314.

Schneider, S. L. (2001). In search of realistic optimism: Meaning, knowledge, and warm fuzziness. *American Psychologist, 56,* 250–263. doi:10.1037/0003-066X.56.3.250

Schneider, S. L., & Barnes, M. D. (2003). What do people really want? Goals and context in decision making. In S. L. Schneider & J. Shanteau (Eds.), *Emerging perspectives on judgment and decision research* (pp. 394–430). New York, NY: Cambridge University Press.

Schwarzer, R., & Luszczynska, A. (2006). Self-efficacy, adolescent's risk-taking behaviors, and health. In F. Pajares & T. Urdan (Eds.), *Self-efficacy beliefs of adolescents* (pp. 139–159). Greenwich, CT: Information Age.

Seginer, R. (2003). Adolescent future orientation in culture and family settings. In W. Friedlmeier, P. Chakkarath, & B. Schwarz (Eds.), *Culture and human development: The importance of cross-cultural research to social sciences.* Lisse, Netherlands: Swets & Zeitlinger.

Seginer, R. (2009). *Future orientation: Developmental and ecological perspectives.* New York, NY: Springer.

Simon, H. A. (1967). Motivational and emotional controls of cognition. *Psychological Review, 74,* 29–39. doi:10.1037/h0024127

Skorikov, V., & Vondracek, F. W. (2007). Positive career orientation as an inhibitor of adolescent problem behavior. *Journal of Adolescence, 30,* 131–146. doi:10.1016/j.adolescence.2006.02.004

Slovic, P. (2001). Cigarette smokers: Rational actors or rational fools? In P. Slovic (Ed.), *Smoking: Risk, perception, and policy* (pp. 97–124). Thousand Oaks, CA: Sage.

Slovic, P., Finucane, M. L., Peters, E., & MacGregor, D. G. (2004). Risk as analysis and risk as feelings: Some thoughts about affect, reason, risk, and rationality. *Risk Analysis, 24,* 311–322. doi:10.1111/j.0272-4332.2004.00433.x

Slovic, P., Finucane, M. L., Peters, E., & MacGregor, D. G. (2007). The affect heuristic. *European Journal of Operational Research, 177,* 1333–1352. doi:10.1016/j.ejor.2005.04.006

Somers, C., & Gizzi, T. (2001). Predicting adolescents' risky behaviors: The influence of future orientation, school involvement, and school attachment. *Adolescent & Family Health, 2*, 3–11.

Somerville, L. H., Jones, R. M., & Casey, B. J. (2010). A time of change: Behavioral and neural correlates of adolescent sensitivity to appetitive and aversive environmental cues. *Brain and Cognition, 72*, 124–133. doi:10.1016/j.bandc.2009.07.003

Stacy, A. W. (1997). Memory activation and expectancy as prospective predictors of alcohol and marijuana use. *Journal of Abnormal Psychology, 106*, 61–73. doi:10.1037/0021-843X.106.1.61

Stacy, A. W., Newcomb, M. D., & Bentler, P. M. (1991). Cognitive motivation and problem drug use: A nine-year longitudinal study. *Journal of Abnormal Psychology, 100*, 502–515.

Stanovich, K. E., & West, R. F. (2000). Individual differences in reasoning: Implications for the rationality debate? *Behavioral and Brain Sciences, 23*, 645–665. doi:10.1017/S0140525X00003435

Steinberg, L. (2005). Cognitive and affective development in adolescence. *Trends in Cognitive Sciences, 9*, 69–74. doi:10.1016/j.tics.2004.12.005

Steinberg, L. (2007). Risk taking in adolescence: New perspectives from brain and behavioral science. *Current Directions in Psychological Science, 16*, 55–59. doi:10.1111/j.1467-8721.2007.00475.x

Steinberg, L. (2008). A social neuroscience perspective on adolescent risk-taking. *Developmental Review, 28*, 78–106. doi:10.1016/j.dr.2007.08.002

Steinberg, L. (2010). A dual systems model of adolescent risk-taking. *Developmental Psychobiology, 52*, 216–224.

Steinberg, L., Graham, S., O'Brien, L., Woolard, J., Cauffman, E., & Banich, M. (2009). Age differences in future orientation and delay discounting. *Child Development, 80*, 28–44. doi:10.1111/j.1467-8624.2008.01244.x

Story, M., & Neumark-Sztainer, D. (1999). Promoting healthy eating and physical activity in adolescents. *Adolescent Medicine, 10*, 109–123.

Sunstein, C. R. (2008). Adolescent risk-taking and social meaning: A commentary. *Developmental Review, 28*, 145–152. doi:10.1016/j.dr.2007.11.003

Tiedens, L. Z., & Linton, S. (2001). Judgment under emotional certainty and uncertainty: The effects of specific emotions on information processing. *Journal of Personality and Social Psychology, 81*, 973–988. doi:10.1037/0022-3514.81.6.973

Trommsdorff, G. (1983). Future orientation and socialization. *International Journal of Psychology, 18*, 381–406. doi:10.1080/00207598308247489

Trommsdorff, G., & Lamm, H. (1980). Future orientation of institutionalized and noninstitutionalized delinquents and nondelinquents. *European Journal of Social Psychology, 10*, 247–278. doi:10.1002/ejsp.2420100304

Trzesniewski, K. H., Donnellan, M. B., Caspi, A., Moffitt, T. E., Robins, R. W., & Poultin, R. (2006). Adolescent low self-esteem is a risk factor for adult poor health, criminal behavior, and limited economic prospects. *Developmental Psychology, 42,* 381–390. doi:10.1037/0012-1649.42.2.381

Umberson, D., & Montez, J. K. (2010). Social relationships and health: A flashpoint for health policy. *Journal of Health and Social Behavior, 51,* S54–S66. doi:10.1177/0022146510383501

U.S. Department of Health and Human Services. (1996). *Physical activity and health: A report of the Surgeon General.* Atlanta, GA: Centers for Disease Control and Prevention, National Center for Chronic Disease Prevention and Health Promotion.

Van Leijenhorst, L., Moor, B. G., Op de Macks, Z. A., Rombouts, S. A. R. B., Westenberg, P. M., & Crone, E. A. (2010). Adolescent risky decision-making: Neurocognitive development of reward and control regions. *NeuroImage, 51,* 345–355. doi:10.1016/j.neuroimage.2010.02.038

Wagenaar, W. A. (1969). Note on the construction of digram-balanced Latin squares. *Psychological Bulletin, 72,* 384–386. doi:10.1037/h0028329

Waldron, I. (1997). Changing gender roles and gender differences in health behavior. In D. S. Gochman (Ed.), *Handbook of health research I: Personal and social determinants* (pp. 303–328). NY: Plenum Press.

Weber, E. U., & Johnson, E. J. (2009). Mindful judgment and decision making. *Annual Review of Psychology, 60,* 53–85. doi:10.1146/annurev.psych.60.110707.163633

Wild, L. G., Flisher, A. J., Bhana, A., & Lombard, C. (2004). Associations among adolescent risk behaviours and self-esteem in six domains. *Journal of Child Psychology and Psychiatry, and Allied Disciplines, 45,* 1454–1467. doi:10.1111/j.1469-7610.2004.00330.x

Youngblade, L. M., Theokas, C., Schulenberg, J., Curry, L., Huang, I. C., & Novak, M. (2007). Risk and promotive factors in families, schools, and communities: A contextual model of positive youth development in adolescence. *Pediatrics, 119,* S47–S53. doi:10.1542/peds.2006-2089H

Zimbardo, P. G., and Boyd, J. N. (1999) Putting time in perspective: A valid, reliable individual-differences metric. *Journal of Personality and Social Psychology, 77,* 1271–1288.

Zweig, J. M., Lindberg, L. D., & McGinley, K. A. (2001). Adolescent health risk profiles: The co-occurrence of health risks among females and males. *Journal of Youth and Adolescence, 30,* 707–728. doi:10.1023/A:1012281628792

12

JUDGMENT AND DECISION MAKING IN ADOLESCENCE: SEPARATING INTELLIGENCE FROM RATIONALITY

KEITH E. STANOVICH, RICHARD F. WEST, AND MAGGIE E. TOPLAK

Rational thinking involves adopting appropriate goals, taking the appropriate action given one's goals and beliefs, and holding beliefs that are commensurate with available evidence. Traditional tests of intelligence are not good proxies for rational thinking skills because rational thought and intelligence are conceptually and empirically separable. Thus, the developmental trajectories of the former must be studied in their own right. Research has shown unequivocally that children do show the biases that have been displayed in the adult literature, but the developmental trends have been quite varied. Across the age ranges studied, there appear to be developmental increases in the avoidance of belief bias, analytic responding in the selection task, probabilistic reasoning, and reliance on statistical information in the face of conflicting personal testimonials. All of these trends are in the direction of increasingly rational thought, at least according to the most commonly employed normative standards. These findings contrast, however, with findings from developmental studies of myside bias and framing effects. Neither of these biases was attenuated by development. The lack of developmental decreases in these two biases is interestingly convergent with findings that neither bias displays much of a correlation with intelligence.

Reasoning skills have developmental trajectories that have been the subject of a moderate amount of research (Bjorklund, 2004; Goswami, 2004;

Markovits, 2004; Reyna, Lloyd, & Brainerd, 2003). Because assessments of intelligence (and similar tests of cognitive ability) are taken to be the sine qua non of good thinking, it might be thought that such measures would serve as proxies for the developmental trajectories for judgment and decision-making skills. We argue in this chapter that such an assumption is misplaced. Traditional tests of intelligence are not good proxies for judgment and decision-making skills, and thus the developmental trajectories of the latter must be studied in their own right. Judgment and decision making are more properly regarded as components of rational thought, and it is often not recognized that rationality and intelligence (as traditionally defined) are two different things, conceptually and empirically.

Distinguishing between rationality and intelligence helps explain how adolescents can be, at the same time, intelligent *and* irrational. In the mid 1990s one of us coined the term *dysrationalia* (an analogue of *dyslexia*) to refer to the existence of irrational thought and action in intelligent individuals (Stanovich, 1993). Dysrationalia occurs in adults as well as adolescents, and we tend to be surprised by it. We tend to be surprised when a physician loses all his pension funds in a speculative financial venture or when an educated professional ignores proven medical treatments and goes to Mexico for a quack therapy. Likewise, we are baffled when highly intelligent adolescents display poor decision making and subject themselves to such obvious risk factors as substance abuse, sexually transmitted diseases, and unsafe driving (Reyna & Farley, 2006).

In short, we find it paradoxical when smart people take disastrous actions. Readers will see in this chapter that this pattern should not be surprising—because there is nothing paradoxical at all in the dissociation between intelligence and rationality. Thus, the developmental trajectories of the latter must be studied in their own right, and this developmental work is summarized in the latter half of this chapter. Our emphasis is on the importance of the development of rational thinking in adolescence, which has been less well studied than other aspects of cognitive competence, such as intelligence.

THE MEANING OF RATIONALITY IN MODERN COGNITIVE SCIENCE

Many philosophers see rationality as one of the most important human values (Nathanson, 1994). As defined in modern cognitive science, rationality is important for a person's well-being because it is a trait that helps us to achieve our goals. This idea is at odds with other characterizations that deem rationality either trivial (little more than the ability to solve textbook logic problems) or in fact antithetical to human fulfillment (as an impairment to an enjoyable emotional life, for instance). However, these ideas about rationality derive from a restricted and mistaken view of rational thought—one not in accord with the study of rationality in modern cognitive science.

Dictionary definitions of rationality tend to be rather unspecific ("the state or quality of being in accord with reason"), and some critics who wish to downplay the importance of rationality have promulgated a caricature that restricts its definition to the ability to do the syllogistic reasoning problems encountered in Philosophy 101.

The meaning of rationality in modern cognitive science is, in contrast, much more robust and important. Cognitive scientists recognize two types of rationality: epistemic and instrumental. *Epistemic rationality* concerns how well beliefs map onto the facts of the world. Epistemic rationality is sometimes called *theoretical rationality* or *evidential rationality* (see Audi, 1993, 2001; Foley, 1987; Harman, 1995; Manktelow, 2004; Over, 2004).

The simplest definition of *instrumental rationality* is: Behaving in the world so that you get exactly what you most want, given the resources (physical and mental) available to you. Somewhat more technically, one could characterize instrumental rationality as the optimization of the individual's goal fulfillment. Economists and cognitive scientists have refined the notion of optimization of goal fulfillment into the technical notion of *expected utility*. The model of rational judgment used by decision scientists is one in which a person chooses options based on which option has the largest expected utility[1] (see Baron, 2008; Dawes, 1998; Hastie & Dawes, 2001; Wu, Zhang, & Gonzalez, 2004).

One of the fundamental advances in the history of modern decision science was the demonstration that if people's preferences follow certain patterns (the so-called axioms of choice—things like transitivity [if A is preferred to B, and B is preferred to C, then A must be preferred to C] and freedom from certain kinds of context effects), then they are behaving as if they are maximizing utility: They are acting to get what they most want (Edwards, 1954; Jeffrey, 1983; Luce & Raiffa, 1957; Savage, 1954; von Neumann & Morgenstern, 1944). This is what makes people's degrees of rationality measurable by the experimental methods of cognitive science. Although it is difficult to assess utility directly, it is much easier to assess whether one of the axioms of rational choice is being violated. This is why the seminal heuristics and biases

---

[1]The principle of maximizing expected value says that the action that a rational person should choose is the one with the highest expected value. Expected value is calculated by taking the objective value of each outcome and multiplying it by the probability of that outcome and then summing those products over all of the possible outcomes. Symbolically, the formula is: Expected Value $= \Sigma\, p_i v_i$; where p_i is the probability of each outcome and v_i is the value of each outcome. The symbol Σ is the summation sign, and simply means "add up all of the terms that follow." The term *utility* refers to subjective value. Thus, the calculation of expected utility involves identical mathematics except that a subjective estimate of utility is substituted for the measure of objective value.

research program[2] inaugurated by Kahneman and Tversky (1972, 1973; Tversky & Kahneman, 1974, 1983) focused on the causes of thinking *errors*.

Rationality has multiple components (Stanovich, 2011), and it is hard to measure the optimal functioning of all of these components. That is, it is hard to specify whether "perfect" rationality has been attained. Researchers have found it much easier to measure whether a particular rational stricture is being violated—that is, whether a person is committing a thinking error—rather than whether their thinking is as good as it can be. This is much like our judgments at a sporting event where, for example, it might be difficult to discern whether a quarterback has put the ball perfectly on the money, but it is not difficult at all to detect a bad throw.

In fact, in many other domains of life this is often the case. Performance errors are much easier to spot than is optimal performance. Essayist Neil Postman (1988) argued, for instance, that educators and other advocates of good thinking might adopt a stance more similar to that of physicians or attorneys. He pointed out that physicians find it hard to define "perfect health," but they are much better at the easier task of spotting disease, so they focus on the latter. Likewise, lawyers are much better at spotting injustice and lack of citizenship than defining "perfect justice" or ideal citizenship. Postman argued that like physicians and attorneys, educators might best focus on instances of poor thinking, which are much easier to identify, instead of trying to define ideal thinking. The literature on the psychology of rationality has followed this logic in that the empirical literature has focused on identifying thinking errors, just as physicians focus on disease. Cognitive biases imply some degree of irrationality, just as failure to display a cognitive bias becomes a measure of rational thought.

A substantial research literature, comprising hundreds of empirical studies conducted over several decades, has firmly established that people's responses sometimes deviate from the performance considered normative on many reasoning tasks. For example, people may assess probabilities incorrectly, test hypotheses inefficiently, violate the axioms of utility theory, or they do not properly calibrate degrees of belief; their choices may be affected by irrelevant context, they may ignore the alternative hypothesis when evaluating data, and they may display numerous other information processing

---

[2]The term *heuristics* refers to why people sometimes make errors in choosing actions and in estimating probabilities—because they use mental shortcuts (heuristics) to solve many problems. Reliance on heuristics introduces systematic biases in actions and probability judgments, for example, when people rely on vivid examples rather than objective statistics to estimate probabilities. These biases can sometimes lead to errors in judgment (e.g., when a vivid stimulus is not very probable). In most instances, however, the use of heuristics is efficacious. The heuristics and biases research tradition focuses on the minority of instances where the use of heuristics leads to errors. It emphasizes that these situations may be a minority of the decisions we make in life, but that they can be extremely important ones (Milkman, Chugh, & Bazerman, 2009; Stanovich, 2009b).

biases (Baron, 2008; Evans, 2007; Gilovich, Griffin, & Kahneman, 2002; Kahneman & Tversky, 2000; Stanovich, 1999, 2004, 2009b). Demonstrating that descriptive accounts of human behavior sometimes diverge from normative models is a main theme of the heuristics and biases research program. The heuristic processes that lead to such errors are often evolutionarily adaptive (Cosmides & Tooby, 1992, 1996; Oaksford & Chater, 2007), but it is important to understand that the evolutionary adaptiveness of subprocesses does not imply that humans, as whole organisms, are rational (de Sousa, 2007; Hurley & Nudds, 2006; Samuels & Stich, 2004; Skyrms, 1996; Stanovich, 2004, 2011; Stanovich & West, 2003; Stich, 1990).

RATIONALITY AND INTELLIGENCE

Intelligence, as measured on many commonly used tests, is often separated into fluid and crystallized components, deriving from the Cattell/Horn/Carroll (CHC) theory of intelligence (Carroll, 1993; Cattell, 1963, 1998; Horn & Cattell, 1967). Sometimes termed the *theory of fluid and crystallized intelligence* (Gf/Gc theory), this theory posits that tests of mental ability tap, in addition to a general factor (g), a small number of broad factors, of which two are dominant (Geary, 2005; Horn & Noll, 1997; Taub & McGrew, 2004). Fluid intelligence (Gf) reflects reasoning abilities operating across of variety of domains—in particular, novel ones. It is measured by tasks of abstract reasoning such as figural analogies, Raven Matrices, and series completion. Crystallized intelligence (Gc) reflects declarative knowledge acquired from acculturated learning experiences. It is measured by vocabulary tasks, verbal comprehension, and general knowledge measures. Ackerman (1996) discussed how the two dominant factors in the CHC theory reflect a long history of considering two aspects of intelligence: intelligence-as-process (Gf) and intelligence-as-knowledge (Gc).

There is a large literature on the CHC theory and on the processing correlates of Gf and Gc (see Duncan et al., 2008; Geary, 2005; Gignac, 2005; Horn & Noll, 1997; Kane & Engle, 2002; McGrew & Woodcock, 2001; Taub & McGrew, 2004). In addition to Gf and Gc, other broad factors at the level termed stratum II are things like memory and learning, auditory perception, and processing speed (for a full account, see Carroll, 1993). However, most of these components are correlated with each other and with g, Gf, and/or Gc. When later in this chapter we discuss correlations between cognitive ability and rational thought, the cognitive ability indicators in the studies discussed will all be indicators of g, Gf, and/or Gc (Frey & Detterman, 2004).

In our theoretical approach to intelligence, our stance has been the standard one in cognitive science: to tie the concept to the actual empirical operationalizations in the relevant literature. In the wider literature on intelligence in education, however, there is a contrary tradition. That contrary tradition leads to the distinction between broad and narrow theories of intelligence (Stanovich, 2009b). Broad theories include aspects of functioning that are captured by the *vernacular* term intelligence (e.g., adaptation to the environment, showing wisdom, displaying creativity) *whether or not* these aspects are actually measured by existing tests of intelligence. Narrow theories of intelligence, like that adopted in our discussion, confine the concept to the set of mental abilities actually tested on extant IQ tests.

In a sense, broad theories of intelligence are intellectually promiscuous in that they use a concept of intelligence that is not tied to existing tests of cognitive functioning. In fact, broad theories of intelligence have implicitly undervalued rational thinking by encompassing such skills under definitions of intelligence. The problem with such a stance is that it ignores the fact that none of the best-known intelligence tests measure rational thinking in any way. Our position is that broad theories of intelligence have been the source of much confusion both within the field and among the general public. They have led to overvaluing what IQ tests can reveal about intellectual functioning.

To think rationally means adopting appropriate goals, taking the appropriate action given one's goals and beliefs, and holding beliefs that are commensurate with available evidence. None of the currently used tests of intelligence assesses any of these functions (Perkins, 1995, 2002; Stanovich, 2002, 2009b; Sternberg, 2003, 2006). Thus, operationally, intelligence and rationality are separate things. However, although tests of intelligence fail to assess rational thinking directly, it could be argued that the processes that are tapped by IQ tests largely overlap with variation in rational thinking ability. If this were true, then measures of intelligence would correlate with measures of rational thinking despite the fact that the latter are not directly assessed on tests of the former. Variation in intelligence has been one of the most studied topics in psychology for many decades (Carroll, 1993; Deary, 2001; Geary, 2005; Lubinski, 2004), and the development of the cognitive abilities related to intelligence is likewise a central topic in developmental science (Anderson, 2005; Bjorklund, 2004; Kail, 2000). In contrast, variation in rational thought among adults has only recently been the focus of research (Bruine de Bruin, Parker, & Fischhoff, 2007; Stanovich & West, 1998c, 2000, 2008b).

Nonetheless, it has become apparent that intelligence and rational thinking skills are so modestly related that the former cannot be reliably used as a proxy for the latter. For example, some tasks in the heuristics and biases literature are related to intelligence, but the correlations are only in the range of .10–.40. For example, Stanovich and West (1997, 1998c, 1998d, 1999, 2000; see also Kokis, Macpherson, Toplak, West, & Stanovich, 2002; Sá, West, & Stanovich, 1999; Toplak, Sorge, Benoit, West, & Stanovich, 2010;

Toplak & Stanovich, 2002; Toplak, West, & Stanovich, in press; West & Stanovich, 2003; West, Toplak, & Stanovich, 2008) found correlations with intelligence to be roughly (in absolute magnitude): .35–.45 for belief bias in syllogistic reasoning, .25–.35 for various probabilistic reasoning tasks, .20–.25 for various covariation detection and hypothesis testing tasks, .25–.35 on informal reasoning tasks, .15–.20 with outcome bias measured within-subjects, .20–.40 with performance in the four-card selection task, .10–.20 with performance in various disjunctive reasoning tasks, .15–.25 with hindsight bias, .25–.30 with denominator neglect, and 05–.20 with various indices of Bayesian reasoning (see Stanovich, West, Toplak, 2011, for sources and examples of each of these paradigms). Other investigators have found relationships of a similar effect size between intelligence and a variety of tasks in the heuristics and biases literature (Bruine de Bruin, Parker, & Fischhoff, 2007; De Neys, 2006; DeShon et al., 1998; Handley et al., 2004; Klaczynski & Lavallee, 2005; Newstead et al., 2004; Parker & Fischhoff, 2005; Peters et al., 2006; Valentine, 1975).

The magnitude of these correlations may be underestimated, of course, because of unreliability of measurement or restriction of range. Our point, however, is not that they are near-zero correlations, or even small correlations, but only that they are so far below unity that a test of intelligence cannot be taken as a proxy for a test of rational thinking skill. For example, reading skill and intelligence can display correlations as high as .60, yet this magnitude of correlation leaves enough room for mismatches between the two that the discrepancies (e.g., low reading ability in the face of high performance on an IQ test) draw an extreme amount of attention from learning disability theorists.[3] Our point with respect to the correlations between intelligence and measures of rational thought is similar. They may be higher than the raw correlations listed in the previous paragraph, but they will end up being estimated at so far below unity that we will not be able to use an IQ test score as an indirect measure of rational thinking. There will be a significant number of discrepancies (e.g., low rational thinking ability in the face of high performance on an IQ test) in any sample, and this discrepant pattern is of great theoretical and practical interest (Stanovich, 2009b, 2011).

Although some of these correlations are no doubt attenuated by restriction of range, there are other reasons to believe that the correlational values

---

[3]It is another question entirely whether educational policy should focus so much on this group of children. There is a substantial body of work indicating that the focus on discrepancy measurement in the domain of reading disability was a mistake. The proximal cause of most cases of reading difficulty—problems in phonological processing—is the same for individuals of high and low IQ (Stanovich, 2000; Stuebing, Barth, Molfese, Weiss, & Fletcher, 2009; Vellutino, Fletcher, Snowling, & Scanlon, 2004). Phonological processing is only modestly correlated with intelligence, so that cases of reading difficulty in the face of high IQ are in no way surprising and do not need a special explanation.

obtained in this research may be *overestimated*. In a commentary on this research on individual differences, Kahneman (2000) pointed out that the correlations observed may well have been inflated because most of the relevant studies used within-subjects designs that contain cues signaling the necessity of overriding automatic processing (Bartels, 2006; Fischhoff, Slovic, & Lichtenstein, 1979; Frisch, 1993; Kahneman & Tversky, 1982). Kahneman (2000) argued that between-subjects tests of the coherence of responses represent a much stricter criterion and perhaps a more appropriate one because "much of life resembles a between-subjects experiment" (p. 682).

Kahneman (2000; see also, Kahneman & Frederick, 2002) conjectured that these less transparent designs would reduce the observed relationships between intelligence and judgmental and decision-making tasks. Much less is known about the relation between cognitive ability and the tendency to make coherent judgments in between-subjects situations. However, in a series of studies, Stanovich and West (2007, 2008a, 2008b) attempted to examine a variety of effects from the heuristics and biases literature to see if intelligence was associated with these biases as they are displayed in between-subjects paradigms. In this series of experiments we found that, to a surprising degree, cognitive ability was independent of the tendency to show a variety of rational thinking biases. In university samples, intelligence was virtually independent of base rate neglect, framing effects, conjunction errors, outcome bias, anchoring effects, preference reversals, omission bias, and myside bias when these effects and biases were measured between subjects (for sources and examples of each of these paradigms, see Stanovich, West, & Toplak, 2011).

Thus, the judgment and decision-making tasks that represent the operational definition of rational thought are neither empirically nor conceptually identifiable with intelligence. Empirically, as just shown, the relationships are modest. Conceptually, we view rationality as a more encompassing construct than intelligence. To be rational, a person must have beliefs well calibrated with reality and must act appropriately on those beliefs to achieve goals. Additionally, in previous publications, we have argued that these aspects of rationality depend on certain thinking dispositions (see Stanovich, 2009a, 2009b, 2011; West, Toplak, & Stanovich, 2008).

No current test of intelligence or cognitive ability attempts to measure directly an aspect of epistemic or instrumental rationality. Neither does any test indirectly assess rational thought by examining any of the thinking dispositions that relate to rationality. For example, although intelligence tests do assess the ability to focus on an immediate goal in the face of distraction, they do not assess at all whether a person has the tendency to develop goals that are rational in the first place. Likewise, intelligence tests are good measures of how well a person can hold beliefs in short-term memory and manipulate those beliefs, but they do not assess at all whether a person has the tendency to *form* beliefs rationally when presented with evidence. And again, similarly, intelligence tests are good measures of how efficiently a person processes information that has been provided, but they do not at all assess whether the person is a *critical assessor* of information as it is gathered in the natural environment.

Substantial empirical evidence indicates that individual differences in thinking dispositions and intelligence are far from perfectly correlated. Many different studies involving thousands of subjects (e.g., Ackerman & Heggestad, 1997; Austin & Deary, 2002; Baron, 1982; Bates & Shieles, 2003; Cacioppo et al., 1996; Eysenck, 1994; Fleischhauer et al., 2010; Goff & Ackerman, 1992; Kanazawa, 2004; Kokis et al., 2002; Noftle & Robins, 2007; Zeidner & Matthews, 2000) have indicated that measures of intelligence display only moderate to weak correlations (usually less than .30) with some thinking dispositions (e.g., actively open-minded thinking, need for cognition) and near-zero correlations with others (e.g., conscientiousness, curiosity, diligence).

Other important evidence supports the conceptual distinction made here between intelligence and rational thinking dispositions. For example, across a variety of tasks from the heuristics and biases literature, it has consistently been found that rational thinking dispositions will predict variance in these tasks after the effects of general intelligence have been controlled (Bruine de Bruin, Parker, & Fischhoff, 2007; Klaczynski, Gordon, & Fauth, 1997; Klaczynski & Lavallee, 2005; Klaczynski & Robinson, 2000; Kokis et al., 2002; Newstead et al., 2004; Macpherson & Stanovich, 2007; Parker & Fischhoff, 2005; Sá & Stanovich, 2001; Stanovich & West, 1997, 1998c, 2000; Toplak, Liu, Macpherson, Toneatto, & Stanovich, 2007; Toplak & Stanovich, 2002; Toplak, West, & Stanovich, in press). Thinking disposition measures tell one about the individual's goals and epistemic values; they also index broad tendencies of pragmatic and epistemic self-regulation at a high level of cognitive control. The empirical studies cited indicate that these different types of cognitive predictors are tapping variance separable from intelligence.

CATEGORIES OF ERROR IN JUDGMENT AND DECISION MAKING

We have demonstrated in the previous section that an intelligence test is not a good proxy for individual differences in judgment and decision making skills. As a result, the developmental trajectories of the latter must be studied in their own right. We trace several such developmental trajectories in this chapter, but our review cannot be exhaustive. There are simply too many thinking errors and biases that have been demonstrated in the judgment and decision-making literature. In fact, a taxonomy of systematic error types is badly needed, and several investigators have made some initial efforts at a classification scheme (e.g., Arkes, 1991; Oreg & Bayazit, 2009; Reyna, Lloyd, & Brainerd, 2003; Shah & Oppenheimer, 2008). We shall use a simplified and abbreviated version of our own taxonomy (Stanovich, 2009a, 2009b, 2011; Stanovich, Toplak, & West, 2008; Stanovich, West, & Toplak, 2011; Toplak et al., 2007) to organize our discussion of developmental trends. Our taxonomy is based around the finding that the human brain has two broad characteristics that make it less than rational. One is a processing problem and one is a content problem, and intelligence provides insufficient inoculation against both.

The processing problem is that we tend to be cognitive misers in our thinking. This has been a major theme throughout the past 40 years of research in the cognitive science of human judgment and decision making (Dawes, 1976; Simon, 1955, 1956; Taylor, 1981; Tversky & Kahneman, 1974). When approaching any problem, our brains have available various computational mechanisms for dealing with the situation. These mechanisms embody a tradeoff, however. The tradeoff is between power and expense. Some mechanisms have great computational power—they can solve a large number of problems and solve them with great accuracy. However, this power comes with a cost. These mechanisms take up a great deal of attention, tend to be slow, tend to interfere with other thoughts and actions we are carrying out, and require great concentration that is often experienced as aversive. In contrast, other brain mechanisms, often termed heuristic processes, are low in computational power but have the advantage that they are low in cost. These mechanisms do not permit fine-grained accuracy, but they are fast-acting, do not interfere with other ongoing cognition, require little concentration, and are not experienced as aversive.

We humans are cognitive misers in our basic tendency to default to heuristic processing mechanisms of low computational expense. Using less computational capacity for one task means that there is more left over for another task if they both must be completed simultaneously. This would seem to be adaptive. Nevertheless, this strong bias to default to the simplest cognitive mechanism—to be a cognitive miser—means that humans are often less than rational. Increasingly, in the modern world we are presented with decisions and problems that require more accurate responses than those generated by heuristic processing. Heuristic processes often provide a quick solution that is a first approximation to an optimal response. But modern technological societies are in fact hostile environments for people reliant on only the most easily computed automatic response. Think of the multimillion-dollar advertising industry that has been designed to exploit just this tendency. Modern society keeps proliferating situations in which shallow processing is not sufficient for maximizing personal happiness—precisely because many structures of market-based societies have been designed explicitly to exploit the tendency toward heuristic processes. Being cognitive misers will seriously impede people from achieving their goals. Many effects in the heuristics and biases literature are the results of the human tendency to default to miserly processing: anchoring biases, framing effects, preference reversals, nondisjunctive reasoning, myside biases, and status quo biases, to name just a few (for a review and descriptions of these paradigms, see Stanovich, 2011; Stanovich et al., 2011).

The second broad reason why humans are less than rational represents a content problem. As described in the previous several paragraphs, rationality often requires that responses based on heuristic processing be overridden and replaced by responses that are more accurately computed. An aspect of human information processing that has been relatively neglected is that the override process is not simply procedural but instead utilizes content, that is, it uses declarative knowledge and strategic rules (linguistically coded strategies). In previous discussions, override has been treated as a somewhat disembodied process. The knowledge bases and strategies that are brought to bear have been given little attention. But in fact problems and gaps in these knowledge structures represent a second major class of reasoning error.

The term *mindware* was coined by Perkins (1995) to refer to the rules, knowledge, procedures, and strategies that a person can retrieve from memory to aid decision making and problem solving. If one is going to trump a heuristic response with conflicting information or a learned rule, one must have previously learned the information or the rule. If, in fact, the relevant mindware is not available because it has not been learned, the result is a thinking error that we have termed a *mindware gap* (Stanovich, 2009b; Stanovich et al., 2008). Mindware gaps can occur in a potentially large set of coherent knowledge bases in the domains of probabilistic reasoning, causal reasoning, logic, and scientific thinking (e.g., the importance of alternative hypotheses), the absence of which could result in irrational thought or behavior.

Mindware problems, in our view, are of two types: mindware gaps and contaminated mindware. Mindware encompasses a variety of declarative knowledge bases as well as some of the more content-laden strategies of rational thought, such as principles of scientific thinking and knowledge of probability. When an override of heuristic processing is necessary but the mindware for a substitute response is not available, then we have a case of a mindware gap. However, the subcategory of contaminated mindware is designed to draw attention to the fact that not all available mindware is helpful, either to goal attainment or to epistemic accuracy. In fact, some acquired mindware can be the direct cause of irrational actions that thwart our goals. Such effects thus define the subcategory of contaminated mindware. For example, one type of contaminated mindware that is discussed in the literature is mindware that contains evaluation-disabling properties (Blackmore,

1999; Dawkins, 1993; Distin, 2005; Dennett, 2006; Lynch, 1996; Stanovich, 2004). Some of the evaluation-disabling properties that help keep some mindware lodged in their hosts are: the promise of punishment if the mindware is questioned, the promise of rewards for unquestioning faith in the mindware, or the thwarting of evaluation attempts by rendering the mindware unfalsifiable.

THE DEVELOPMENTAL TRAJECTORIES OF RATIONAL THINKING SKILLS

The empirical literature on the development of rational thinking is still relatively sparse (see Byrnes, 1998; Jacobs & Klaczynski, 2005; Kokis et al., 2002; Reyna, Estrada, DeMarinis, Myers, Stanisz, & Mills, in press; Reyna, Lloyd, & Brainerd, 2003; Reyna & Rivers, 2008; Stanovich et al., 2008). More specifically, it might be said that the developmental literature is spread widely, but it is thin. We characterize this literature as thin because of the sheer number of different effects and biases that have been studied in the heuristics and biases adult literature (see Arkes, 1991; Baron, 2008; Evans, 1989, 2007, 2008; Gilovich, Griffin, & Kahneman, 2002; Johnson-Laird, 2006; Koehler & Harvey, 2004; Larrick, 2004; Lichtenstein & Slovic, 2006; McFadden, 1999; Nickerson, 2008; Reyna et al., 2003; Stanovich, 2009b, 2010). These tasks and effects represent the field of judgment and decision making in cognitive science. Continuous differences on these tasks and effects, as we previously discussed, define the construct of individual differences in rational thought. Although there have been some initial developmental studies on some of the tasks in the heuristics and biases literature, none of the tasks have been the subject of intense investigation. In this section, we discuss exemplar developmental studies involving many of the different tasks and biases of rational thinking.

A Problem of the Cognitive Miser: Vividness Effects

Affect substitution is a specific form of a more generic trick (attribute substitution) of the cognitive miser discussed by Kahneman and Frederick (2002): the substitution of an easy-to-evaluate characteristic for a harder one, even if the easier one is less accurate. One of the most common processing defaults of the cognitive miser is the tendency to default to vivid presentations of information and to avoid nonsalient presentations of evidence. For example, a picture would be vivid compared to a numerical presentation of evidence (Slovic & Peters, 2006).

In the heuristics and biases literature, a typical problem requires the participant to make an inductive inference in a simulation of a real-life decision.

The information relevant to the decision is conflicting and of two different types. One type of evidence is statistical: either probabilistic or aggregate base-rate information that favors one of the bipolar decisions. The other evidence is a concrete case or vivid personal experience that points in the opposite direction. The classic Volvo versus Saab item (see Fong, Krantz, & Nisbett, 1986, p. 285) provides an example. In this problem, a couple is deciding to buy one of two otherwise equal cars. Consumer surveys, statistics on repair records, and polls of experts favor the Volvo over the Saab. However, a friend reports experiencing a severe mechanical problem with the Volvo he owns. The participant is asked to provide advice to the couple. Preference for the Volvo indicates a tendency to rely on the large-sample information in spite of salient personal testimony. A preference for the Saab indicates reliance on the personal testimony over the opinion of experts and the large-sample information.

Kokis et al. (2002) adapted several problems such as this for children. One problem went as follows: Erica wants to go to a baseball game to try to catch a fly ball. She calls the main office and learns that almost all fly balls have been caught in section 43. Just before she chooses her seats, she learns that her friend Jimmy caught two fly balls last week sitting in section 10. Which section is most likely to give Erica the best chance to catch a fly ball?

(a)   Definitely section 43
(b)   Probably section 43
(c)   Probably section 10
(d)   Definitely section 10

Selection of options *a* or *b* indicates the use of the aggregate base-rate information. Selection of options *c* or *d* indicates that the child is using the vivid information from a friend. Kokis et al. (2002) found a significant developmental trend whereby 13- to 14-year-olds displayed significantly less reliance on the vivid personal information than did a group of 10- to 11-year-olds.

Jacobs and Potenza (1991) found an analogous, and significant, developmental trend in the so-called object condition of their experiment where the problems were similar to those used by Kokis et al. (2002). However, in the so-called social condition of the Jacobs and Potenza study, the developmental trend was in the opposite direction—there was more reliance on the vivid information and less reliance on the more diagnostic statistical information by the *older* children. A consideration of the nature of the social problems reveals why this was the case. Here is an example of a social problem: In Juanita's class, 10 girls are trying out to be cheerleaders and 20 are trying out for the band. Juanita is very popular and very pretty. She is always telling jokes and loves to be around people. Do you think Juanita is trying out to be a cheerleader or for the band? Here the statistical information points in the direction of band, but the personal information points in the direction of cheerleader. But to understand the diagnosticity of the indicant information in this problem, one must have knowledge of a social stereotype (that popular girls are drawn more to cheerleading than to band). Knowledge of this stereotype might well increase with age and thus be less available to the younger children. As a result, there is no conflict between the indicant and the base rate for the younger children.

Thus, the performance in the Jacobs and Potenza (1991) study is less inconsistent with the findings of Kokis et al. (2002) than may be apparent on the surface. The same is true of the social problems in a study by Davidson (1995). Finally, the developmental trend in Kokis et al. and in the object condition of Jacobs and Potenza (1991) is consistent with studies of individual differences of cognitive ability *within* an age group. Reliance on vivid individuating information is *negatively* correlated with cognitive ability (Kokis et al., 2002; Stanovich & West, 1998c, 1998d).

A Problem of the Cognitive Miser: Framing Effects

Framing effects represent the classic example of miserly information processing. For example, in discussing the mechanisms causing framing effects, Kahneman (2003) stated that "the basic principle of framing is the passive acceptance of the formulation given" (p. 703). The frame presented to the subject is taken as focal, and all subsequent thought derives from it rather than from alternative framings because the latter would require more thought. One of the most compelling framing demonstrations is from the early work of Tversky and Kahneman (1981).

Decision 1

Imagine that the United States is preparing for the outbreak of an unusual disease, which is expected to kill 600 people. Two alternative programs to combat the disease have been proposed. Assume that the exact scientific estimates of the consequences of the programs are as follows: If Program A is adopted, 200 people will be saved. If Program B is adopted, there is a one-third probability that 600 people will be saved and a two-thirds probability that no people will be saved. Which of the two programs would you favor, Program A or Program B?

Most people when given this problem prefer Program A—the one that saves 200 lives for sure. There is nothing wrong with this choice taken alone. However, inconsistent responses to another problem define a framing effect:

Decision 2

Imagine that the United States is preparing for the outbreak of an unusual disease, which is expected to kill 600 people. Two alternative programs to combat the disease have been proposed. Assume that the exact scientific estimates of the consequences of the programs are as follows: If Program C is adopted, 400 people will die. If Program D is adopted, there is a one-third probability that nobody will die and a two-thirds probability that 600 people will die. Which of the two programs would you favor, Program C or Program D?

Most people when presented with Decision 2 prefer Program D. Thus, across the two problems, the most popular choices are Program A and Program D. The problem here is that Decision 1 and Decision 2 are really the same decision; they are merely redescriptions of the same situation. Program A and C are the same. That 400 will die in Program C implies that 200 will be saved—precisely the same number saved (200) in Program A. Likewise, the two-thirds chance that 600 will die in Program D is the same two-thirds chance that 600 will die ("no people will be saved") in Program B. Many people show inconsistent preferences, their choice switches depending on the phrasing of the question. This is an example of a problem with very transparent equivalence. When presented with both versions of the problem together, most people agree that the problems are identical and that the alternative phrasing should not have made a difference.

Such a lack of so-called descriptive invariance is a very fundamental violation of some of the simplest strictures of rational thought (see Tversky & Kahneman, 1981, 1986). A theory of why these framing effects occur was presented in the prospect theory of Kahneman and Tversky (1979), which contains the key assumption that the utility function is steeper (in the negative direction) for losses than for gains. This explains why people tend to be more risk averse for gains than for losses (for an alternative explanation, see Kuhberger & Tanner, 2010; Reyna & Brainerd, 1991, 1995; Reyna et al., in press).

The literature on framing effects in adults is vast (see Epley, Mak, & Chen Idson, 2006; Kahneman & Tversky, 1984, 2000; Kuhberger, 1998; Levin, Gaeth, Schreiber, & Lauriola, 2002; Maule & Villejoubert, 2007; Schneider et al., 2005). However, the developmental literature is quite small. Obviously, the complexity of the problems has to be vastly reduced and made appropriate for children. Outcomes in developmental studies become small prizes that the children receive instead of the imaginary deaths or real money used in adult studies. Several investigators have creatively adapted framing paradigms for children, but the results of these experiments have not converged. Levin and colleagues (Levin & Hart, 2003; Levin, Hart, Weller, & Harshman, 2007) found no developmental trend for framing effects. Children (6- to 8-year-olds) were more risk averse for gains than for losses in the manner that prospect theory predicts, but the magnitude of the framing effects that they displayed was the same as that found for adults. Nonnormative framing effects were found for 5-year-olds, 6-year-olds, and 9- to 10-year-olds in Schlottmann and Tring (2005), and in 14.8-year-olds in Chien, Lin, and Worthley (1996). In Schlottmann and Tring (2005), the framing effects were roughly similar in magnitude.

The results of these studies were not completely convergent with those of a study by Reyna and Ellis (1994; see also, Reyna, 1996). The data patterns in the Reyna and Ellis study were complex, however, and very variable over the ages studied. Reyna and Ellis predicted these results based on fuzzy trace theory, building on results with adults. Framing interacted with level of risk and magnitude of reward at certain ages. Briefly though, preschoolers' responses were consistent across frames: they displayed no framing effect. Second graders displayed a small reverse framing effect—they were more risk averse for losses. Fifth graders displayed a small reverse framing effect at the highest reward magnitude and the standard framing effect (more risk seeking for losses) only for lowest reward magnitude (see also Reyna & Farley, 2006).

The results of Levin and colleagues and those of Reyna and Ellis (1994) are consistent in one important respect, however: None of the studies reported evidence of a monotonically decreasing framing effect with age. This lack of developmental trend converges with studies of individual differences within an age group. Framing effects show very small (sometimes zero) correlations with cognitive ability, especially when tested in a between-subjects design (Bruine de Bruin et al., 2007; Parker & Fischhoff, 2005; Stanovich & West, 1998b, 1999; 2008b; Toplak & Stanovich, 2002).

Override Failure: Denominator Neglect

As previously discussed, rationality often requires that responses based on heuristic processing be overridden and replaced by responses that are more accurately computed. But override is a capacity-demanding operation (see Stanovich, 1999, 2009b, 2011; Stanovich & West, 2000, 2008b). Thus, any tendencies toward miserly processing in a situation where override is required will result in a failure to substitute the superior response for the heuristic one. One of several phenomena in the heuristics and biases literature that illustrate the failure of heuristic override is the phenomenon of denominator neglect. Epstein and colleagues (Denes-Raj & Epstein, 1994; Kirkpatrick & Epstein, 1992; Pacini & Epstein, 1999; see also Reyna & Brainerd, 2008) demonstrated that it can result in a startling failure of rational judgment. Adults in several of his experiments were presented with two bowls that each contained clearly identified numbers of jelly beans. In the first were nine white jelly beans and one red jelly bean. In the second were 92 white jelly beans and eight red. A random draw was to be made from one of the two bowls, and if the red jelly bean was picked, the participant would receive a dollar. The participant could choose which bowl to draw from. Although the two bowls clearly represent a 10% and an 8% chance of winning a dollar, a number of subjects chose the 100-bean bowl, thus reducing their chance of winning. The majority did pick the 10% bowl, but a healthy minority (from 30% to 40% of the participants) picked the 8% bowl. Although most of these participants in the minority were aware that the large bowl was statistically a worse bet, that bowl also contained more of the enticing winning beans—the eight red ones. In short, the tendency to respond to the absolute number of winners, for these participants, trumped the formal rule (pick the one with the best percentage of reds) that they knew was the better choice. That many subjects were aware of the poorer probability but failed to resist picking the large bowl is indicated by comments from some of them such as the following: "I picked the one with more red jelly beans because it looked like there were more ways to get a winner, even though I knew there were also more whites, and that the percents were against me" (Denes-Raj & Epstein, 1994, p. 823).

Kokis et al. (2002) found no significant trend for denominator neglect to decrease across their two age groups of 10- to 11-year-olds and 13- to 14-year-olds. However, Kokis et al. did find that cognitive ability was negatively correlated with denominator neglect to a significant degree. They used a paradigm very similar to that of Epstein and colleagues, but Klaczynski (2001b) altered the paradigm in an interesting way, by presenting options with equal probabilities and a response option that reflected the equivalent status of the two options. He had participants select from three alternatives: (a) a jar with one winning ticket out of 10, (b) a jar with 10 winning tickets out of 100, or (c) that it would not matter which jar was picked. Picking alternative b would indicate denominator neglect. Alternative c is the normatively correct response. Only a minority of participants chose the normatively correct response, but the normatively correct response did increase across three groups: early adolescents, middle adolescents, and young adults. In contrast, the majority response—denominator neglect—did not show a developmental trend. Amsel et al. (2008) also used Klaczynski's paradigm and found no developmental increase in the normatively correct responding of 13-year-old middle school students and 23-year-old college students. Thus, even though the number of relevant developmental studies is quite limited, the existing research suggests that, at most, only minimal decline in denominator neglect occurs during adolescence.

Override Failure: Belief Bias

Clearer results have been obtained with another phenomenon caused by the failure of heuristic override: belief bias. Belief bias occurs when judgments of the believability of a conclusion interfere with judgments of logical validity (Evans, Barston, & Pollard, 1983; Evans & Curtis-Holmes, 2005; Evans, Newstead, Allen, & Pollard, 1994). Consider the following syllogism:

Premise 1: All living things need water.
Premise 2: Roses need water.
Therefore: Roses are living things.
Judge the conclusion as either logically valid or invalid.

Premise 1 says that all living things need water, not that all things that need water are living things. So, just because roses need water, it does not follow from Premise 1 that they are living things. However, consider the following syllogism with exactly the same structure:

Premise 1: All insects need oxygen.
Premise 2: Mice need oxygen.
Therefore: Mice are insects.

Here it seems very easy to see that the syllogism is not valid. In both problems, prior knowledge about the nature of the world (that roses are living things and that mice are not insects) is becoming implicated in a type of judgment that is supposed to be independent of content: judgments of logical validity. In the rose problem, prior knowledge was interfering, and in the mice problem prior knowledge was facilitative.

Using syllogistic reasoning problems suitably modified for children, Kokis et al. (2002) found a significant developmental trend in which 13- to 14-year-olds displayed significantly less belief bias than did a group of 10- to 11-year-olds.

A much broader age span was examined by De Neys and Van Gelder (2009), who found a curvilinear developmental trend, whereby a group of 20-year-olds displayed less belief bias than either a group of 12-year-olds or a group of 65+-year-olds. Because fluid cognitive ability is likely to be on the decline for the latter subjects (Baltes, 1987; McArdle, Ferrer-Caja, Hamagami, & Woodcock, 2002), the developmental trends in both Kokis et al. (2002) and De Neys and Van Gelder (2009) are consistent with studies of individual differences within an age group. There, it has been found that belief bias is negatively correlated with cognitive ability (De Neys, 2006; Handley et al., 2004; Sá et al., 1999; Stanovich & West, 1998c).

Override Failure: Prudently Discounting the Future

The tendency toward miserly processing is reflected in the choices often observed in delay discounting tasks, wherein an individual must choose between smaller-earlier and larger-later rewards. People are miserly because they do not expend the effort to inhibit the "gut-level" preference for the earlier reward and wait for the larger, delayed reward. It takes cognitive effort to inhibit the preference for the earlier, smaller reward, and many people are miserly in not being willing to expend this effort.

Delay discounting refers to the decreasing value often placed on a future reward as the length of the delay needed to obtain the future reward increases. There is nothing inherently irrational about valuing an immediate reward more than a slightly greater future reward; indeed, it may sometimes be true that "a bird in the hand is worth two in the bush." However, an extensive literature suggests that many people tend to imprudently discount the value they place on future rewards (e.g., Ainslie, 1975; Herrnstein, 1990; Kirby, 1997). One highly robust finding is that the rate at which rewards are discounted is nicely described by a highly concave function that is steeper for short delays than for long delays—called a *hyperbolic discount function* (Ainslie, 2001; Kirby, 1997).

Although almost everyone displays delay discounting that is consistent with such hyperbolic functions, there are large individual differences in the steepness of the initial portion of the curve. For some people, even relatively brief delays can result in drastic drops in the value placed on future rewards. These individuals may place little value on future rewards and, thus, may be particularly susceptible to making impulsive decisions (Ainslie, 1975, 2001). Kirby, Winston, and Santiesteban (2005) explored this possibility with college students. They estimated hyperbolic discount rates using a willingness-to-pay auction paradigm for real delayed monetary rewards (ranging from 1 to 43 days in delay and from $10 to $20 in monetary rewards). They found that steep discounting of future rewards was negatively correlated with college GPA, even after controlling for SAT scores. This finding suggests that students who steeply discount the value of future rewards may overvalue immediate alternatives to studying now, relative to the future rewards associated with obtaining higher grades later.

Adolescents, particularly young adolescents, are frequently characterized as being exceedingly focused on the present and inadequately valuing the future consequences of their present decisions. Steinberg et al. (2009) used a delay discounting task to explore this characterization with large, representative groups of 10- to 11-, 12- to 13-, 14- to 15-, 16- to 17-, 18- to 21-, 22- to 25-, and 26- to 30-year-olds. For the discounting task, participants indicated their preferences between immediate rewards of various monetary amounts and a delayed reward of $1,000. The length of the delays ranged from 1 day to 1 year. Although delay discounting was observed for each of the seven age groups in the study, participants in the two youngest age groups (ranging from 10 to 13 years old) had significantly higher discount rates than participants in the four oldest age groups (ranging from 16 to 30 years of age). Although the discounting rate for participants in the 14- to 15-year-old group was between those of the younger and older groups, these differences failed to reach a level of significance. Thus, the amount of an immediate reward judged to be of equal value to a future reward of $1,000 was lower for participants 14 years of age and younger than for those 16 years of age and older. No significant developmental trends were found in the discount rates within this older age range. These findings are consistent with those of Green, Fry, and Myerson (1994; see also Green, Myerson, & Ostaszewski, 1999) with 12.1- and 20.3-year-olds. Interestingly, the developmental trend continued—with 67.9-year-olds showing the lowest discounting rate.

These developmental results are consistent with the studies that have examined cognitive ability correlations *within* an age group. A meta-analysis with 24 eligible studies by Shamosh and Gray (2008) reported that higher intelligence was negatively correlated with delay discounting (weighted $r = -.23$). The Steinberg et al. (2009) study discussed above reported a similar negative association between delay discounting and IQ ($r = -.27$). Shamosh et al. (2008) also reported that steeper discounting was associated with lower cognitive ability.

Mindware Gaps: Probabilistic Reasoning

As previously discussed, in addition to miser tendencies, the second category of cognitive errors is represented by mindware problems—both mindware gaps and contaminated mindware (see Stanovich, 2009b, 2011). Mindware gaps are common in the domain of probability knowledge and judgment (see the classic studies by Kahneman & Tversky, 1972, 1973). Conjunction effects represent rational thinking errors that arise because of mindware gaps in the domain of probability. Consider a problem that is famous in the literature of cognitive psychology, the so-called Linda problem (Tversky & Kahneman, 1983):

> Linda is 31 years old, single, outspoken, and very bright. She majored in philosophy. As a student, she was deeply concerned with issues of discrimination and social justice, and also participated in antinuclear demonstrations. Please rank the following statements by their probability, using 1 for the most probable and 8 for the least probable.
> a. Linda is a teacher in an elementary school. ____
> b. Linda works in a bookstore and takes yoga classes. ____
> c. Linda is active in the feminist movement. ____
> d. Linda is a psychiatric social worker. ____
> e. Linda is a member of the League of Women Voters. ____
> f. Linda is a bank teller. ____
> g. Linda is an insurance salesperson. ____
> h. Linda is a bank teller and is active in the feminist movement. ____

Most people make what is called a *conjunction error* on this problem. Because alternative (h) (Linda is a bank teller and is active in the feminist movement) is the conjunction of alternatives (c) and (f) the probability of (h) cannot be higher than that of either (c) (Linda is active in the feminist movement) or (f) (Linda is a bank teller). All feminist bank tellers are also bank tellers, so (h) cannot be more probable than (f)—yet many people in adult studies rate alternative (h) as more probable than (f), thus displaying a conjunction error.

Davidson (1995) reported the counterintuitive finding of a developmental trend of increasing conjunction errors with age. However, the stimuli in this study had the same problem as those in the social condition of the Jacobs and Potenza (1991) study—they depended on the knowledge of a stereotype that might increase with age. For example, one item went as follows:

> Mrs. Hill is not in the best health and she has to wear glasses to see. Her hair is gray and she has wrinkles. She walks kind of hunched over. Do you think that Mrs. Hill is: a waitress in a local restaurant; an old person who has grandchildren and a waitress at a local restaurant; [and so on].

Knowledge of the stereotype might lead children to make a conjunction error, but the knowledge of the stereotype is undoubtedly more extensive among sixth graders (Davidson's oldest group) than among second graders (Davidson's youngest group).

Another way to state the problem with the Davidson (1995) stimuli is to say that the potential of the stimuli to trigger a representativeness judgment is confounded with age. Such stimuli are fine for certain questions, but they are not appropriate stimuli to use when addressing the generic question of whether the propensity to commit a conjunction error with age increases or decreases. Klaczynski (2001a) used stimuli that were less confounded in this manner and found no developmental trend in the number of conjunction errors from early adolescence (mean age, 12.4 years) to middle adolescence (16.3 years).

In contrast to Davidson's findings, a number of studies using stimuli that were less confounded reported modest developmental trends of decreasing conjunction errors between early childhood and late childhood, and more substantial developmental trends of decreasing conjunction error between late childhood and young adulthood (Agnoli, 1991; Fischbein & Schnarch, 1997; Fisk, Bury, & Holden, 2006; Fisk & Slattery, 2005).

A developmental trend in favor of more optimal reasoning by older than younger adolescents has been found in other domains of probabilistic reasoning, including the gambler's fallacy, the law of large numbers, and reliance on the representativeness heuristic for probabilistic judgment (Fischbein & Schnarch, 1997; Klaczynski, 2000, 2001a; Klaczynski & Narasimham, 1998).

For example, Fischbein and Schnarch (1997) examined a variety of probability problems in Israeli 10- to 11-, 12- to 13-, 14- to 15-, and 16- to 17-year-old students, and in college students. None of the students had had instruction in probability. In a "representativeness" problem, students had to decide whether someone who chose the lotto game sequence 1, 2, 3, 4, 5, 6 had a greater, a lesser, or the same chance of winning than someone who chose the sequence 39, 1, 17, 33, 8, 27. Nonconsecutive sequences in general are much more likely than are consecutive sequences. However, any specific sequence, whether consecutive or not, is no more likely than any other. Many students incorrectly chose the nonconsecutive sequence as being the more likely sequence, apparently because of its resemblance to—or intuitive representativeness of—lottery sequences in general. However, a clear developmental trend toward correctly responding was found.

The gambler's fallacy was examined with a coin toss problem that asked the students about the chance of a coin coming up heads a fourth time after having come up heads on the three previous tosses (Fischbein & Schnarch, 1997). Once again, a developmental trend toward normative responding was found. Finally, Fischbein and Schnarch (1997) also examined the conjunction fallacy using a scenario that described a young man who appeared likely to be headed toward a career in medicine. The young man had registered at the university, and the question was whether he was more likely to be a student in the medical school or a student. The three younger groups of students were found to be much more likely to commit the conjunction error than were the two groups of older students. Taken together, these studies indicate a developmental trend of increasing probabilistic knowledge.

Contaminated Mindware: Pseudoscientific and Superstitious Beliefs

The other type of mindware problem that prevents rational thinking is caused by the presence of contaminated mindware. An important category of contaminated mindware is that of pseudoscientific beliefs. From a developmental standpoint, there is no a priori reason to expect many superstitious, paranormal, and pseudoscientific beliefs (e.g., beliefs in alien abduction, astrology, creationism, extrasensory perception, ghosts, quack medical or health claims) to be negatively associated with intellectual growth or intelligence, and many such beliefs undoubtedly are acquired as one ages. A case in point is a shocking claim made by Pat Robertson, elderly televangelist and host of the television's *The 700 Club*, in the face of the horrific Haitian earthquake of 2010. Robertson's claim was that Haiti had been cursed after a pact with the devil—that the people of Haiti had gotten together and sworn a pact with the devil in order to free them from French control (Parker, 2010).

Skepticism about superstitious, pseudoscientific, and paranormal beliefs can be acquired through science and other educational experiences. Preece and Baxter (2000) found that although the levels of superstitious and pseudoscientific beliefs were common, there was nonetheless a steady developmental trend toward increased skepticism about the superstitious and pseudoscientific beliefs in a large sample of 14- to 16-year-old students in England. Preece and Baxter speculated that science education may have contributed to this developmental trend, particularly because the level of skepticism continued to increase from 17- to 18-year-old science students to postgraduate pre-service science teachers. It is perhaps noteworthy, however, that Preece and Baxter intentionally avoided exploring beliefs with religious connotations. It is possible that these types of supernatural phenomena might be little affected by development.

Grimmer and White (1992) looked more directly at the role of specific educational training in a study of a large sample of Australian university students. Medical students showed the highest level of skepticism, science students showed the next highest level, and arts students were the least skeptical. Thus, these two studies reviewed above suggest that science education may play a role in reducing superstitious, pseudoscientific, and paranormal beliefs. However, the empirical data in this area are currently very limited, and considerably more research will be needed before anything can be confidently concluded about the role of development and educational experiences.

Multiply Determined Reasoning Problems

Many thinking errors in the heuristics and biases literature are multiply determined—that is, they result from a combination of miserly processing and mindware problems. One example of such a multiply determined reasoning problem is probably Wason's (1966) four-card selection task. In this task, the participant is told the following:

> Each of the boxes below represents a card lying on a table. Each one of the cards has a letter on one side and a number on the other side. Here is a rule: If a card has a vowel on its letter side, then it has an even number on its number side. As you can see, two of the cards are letter-side up, and two of the cards are number-side up. Your task is to decide which card or cards must be turned over in order to find out whether the rule is true or false. Indicate which cards must be turned over.

The participant chooses from four cards labeled K, A, 8, 5 (corresponding to not-P, P, Q, and not-Q). The correct answer is to pick the A and the 5 (P and not-Q), but the most common answer is to pick the A and 8 (P and Q)—the so-called matching response.

In the four-card selection task, incorrect responses are probably due to a variety of cognitive errors (see Evans, 2007; Klauer, Stahl, & Erdfelder, 2007; Osman & Laming, 2001), some of them reflecting miserly processing and some of them mindware gaps. The much-discussed matching bias (unreflectively picking the elements mentioned in the rule) evident in the task (Evans, 1972, 1998; Evans & Lynch, 1973) is clearly a case of miserly processing. However, it is perhaps also the case that the matching response goes uncorrected because of insufficiently instantiated mindware that embodies the importance of thinking about alternative hypotheses. Developmental and individual-differences studies of the task are consistent, however. Superior performance on the task is associated with development (Klaczynski, 2001a; Overton, Byrnes, & O'Brien, 1985) and with cognitive ability (DeShon, Smith, Chan, & Schmitt, 1998; Stanovich & West, 1998a; Toplak & Stanovich, 2002; Valentine, 1975).

As another example of a multiply determined cognitive bias, consider myside bias. Critical thinking is often thought to entail the ability to decouple prior beliefs and opinions from the evaluation of evidence and arguments (Baltes & Staudinger, 2000; Evans, 2002; Kuhn, 2001; Johnson-Laird, 2006; Perkins, 1995, 2002; Sternberg, 2003). People display myside bias when they evaluate evidence, generate evidence, and test hypotheses in a manner biased toward their own opinions (Greenhoot, Semb, Colombo, & Schreiber, 2004; Klaczynski & Lavallee, 2005; Nussbaum & Kardash, 2005; Perkins, 1995; Sá, Kelley, Ho, & Stanovich, 2005; Stanovich & West, 2007, 2008a; Toplak & Stanovich, 2003; Wolfe & Britt, 2008). Myside bias surely derives in part from the miserly tendency to build the easiest cognitive model: a model from a single perspective—one's own. Contributing additionally, however, might be contaminated mindware that structures our knowledge of the world from an egocentric perspective.

Developmental trends in myside processing have been studied by Klaczynski and colleagues (1997; Klaczynski & Gordon, 1996; Klaczynski, Gordon, & Fauth, 1997; Klaczynski & Lavallee, 2005; Klaczynski & Narasimham, 1998). They presented participants with flawed hypothetical experiments that led to either opinion-consistent or opinion-inconsistent conclusions and evaluated the quality of the reasoning used when the participants critiqued the flaws in the experiments. In these experiments, myside bias effects were also evident; participants found more flaws when the experiment's conclusions were inconsistent than when they were consistent with their opinions and beliefs. However, there was no developmental trend for myside bias to increase or decrease—at least for the early, middle, and late adolescent groups that were the focus of most the Klaczynski lab's research.

The lack of a developmental trend in myside bias in the Klaczynski group's studies is consistent with studies of individual differences within an age group. Across a variety of myside paradigms, there has been little evidence that myside bias is associated with cognitive ability (Klaczynski & Lavallee, 2005; Klaczynski & Robinson, 2000; Macpherson & Stanovich, 2007; Sá, Kelley, Ho, & Stanovich, 2005; Stanovich & West, 2007, 2008a; Toplak & Stanovich, 2003).

OVERALL DEVELOPMENT TRENDS IN RATIONAL THOUGHT

Collectively, the biases discussed in this chapter (and many others in the heuristics and biases literature not covered here) define departures from rationality and hence indirectly index rationality itself. The minimal conclusion to be drawn from the body of developmental work taken as a whole is that children unequivocally do show the biases that have been displayed in the adult literature: vividness effects, framing effects, denominator neglect, belief bias, conjunction errors, myside bias, and so forth.

Beyond this minimal conclusion, however, we must be tentative because of the rather sparse nature of the empirical literature. Very few of the areas covered in this review have been the subject of enough research to establish developmental trends with confidence. This caveat aside, the suggestive trends that are in the literature vary considerably across the various cognitive biases. Across the age ranges studied, there appear to be developmental increases in the avoidance of belief bias, analytic responding in the selection task, probabilistic reasoning, and reliance on statistical information in the face of conflicting personal testimonials. All of these trends are in the direction of increasingly rational thought, at least according to accepted normative standards.

These findings contrast, however, with the trends apparent in developmental studies of myside bias and framing effects. Neither of these biases was attenuated by development (see other such effects in Table 3 of Reyna & Farley, 2006). The lack of developmental decreases in these two biases is interestingly convergent with findings that neither bias displays much of a correlation with intelligence (Stanovich & West, 2007, 2008b). These aspects of rational thought are thus quite independent of cognitive ability, reinforcing the fundamental point with which we opened this chapter: Measures of cognitive ability, as traditionally defined, fail to assess degrees of rationality.

In the case of conjunction errors and contaminated mindware, the literature on developmental trends is simply too inconsistent and sparse to warrant any strong conclusions at this point. One reason that developmental trends in some of these areas might be unclear is that whether or not rational thinking tasks yield a conflict between heuristic and analytic responses is not fixed, but instead is a function of the individual's history of mindware acquisition. Early in development, the relevant mindware will not be present and the heuristic response will be inevitable; no conflict will even be detected. Someone with no training in thinking probabilistically—or, for that matter, logically in terms of subset and superset—may experience no conflict in the Linda problem. As experience with statistical and probabilistic thinking grows, a person will begin to experience more of a conflict because relevant mindware is available for use in the simulation of an alternative response by the analytic system. The final developmental stage in this sequence might well be that the mindware used in analytic simulation becomes so tightly compiled that it is triggered in the manner of a natural heuristic response. Some statistics instructors, for example, become unable to empathize with their students for whom the basic probability axioms are not transparent. The instructor can no longer remember when these axioms were not primary intuitions. This final stage of processing is perhaps captured by developmental models of heuristic versus analytic processing that trace a trajectory in which fluent adult performance looks very heuristic (Brainerd & Reyna, 2001; Ericsson & Charness, 1994; Kahneman & Klein, 2009; Klein, 1998; Reyna, Lloyd, & Brainerd, 2003; Reyna et al., 2005; Shiffrin & Schneider, 1977).

The difficulty of pinning down some of these developmental trends highlights how thin the literature is on children's rational thought. One cannot amalgamate all of the studies reviewed here (as well as others not reviewed) as evidence on a single issue; doing so would misleadingly suggest that the literature is more extensive than it is. Rational thought spans many domains. It encompasses many different thinking dispositions and knowledge domains, each of which has been investigated separately in the adult literature. For example, there is an enormous adult literature on conjunction effects (Fisk, 2004), on framing (Kahneman & Tversky, 2000), on base rate use (Koehler, 1996), and on every one of the myriad effects in the heuristics and biases literature. A parallel effort in each of these domains will be necessary in order to fully understand the development of rational thought.

Understanding the development of rationality will clearly be a tall order. It will be worth the effort, however, not just for scientific reasons. Assumptions about the nature and development of rationality are implicated in judgments of legal responsibility. Reyna and Farley (2006) emphasized how background assumptions about adolescent rationality frame efforts to change adolescent risk behavior. For example, theories that stress adolescent feelings of invulnerability serve to avoid the attribution of irrationality to adolescents who engage in high-risk behavior. If these adolescents have strong feelings of invulnerability, or if they overestimate the probabilities of negative outcomes but weight rewards sufficiently highly, then a consequentialist calculation might well make engaging in high-risk behaviors rational for them.

An alternative approach, one supported by the research in the heuristics and biases tradition, would relax the rationality assumption and conclude instead that some of these adolescent behaviors violate standard rational strictures. Such a stance finds additional motivation from an observation that Reyna and Farley (2006) discussed: Many adolescents making poor choices are alienated from the choices they make. As Reyna and Farley put it, "People who take unhealthy risks often agree that their behavior is irrational, on sober reflection, but they gave in to temptation or were not thinking at the time of the decision, and are worse off for having done so" (p. 35). Instead of the dated economics-like assumption of adolescents as coherent rational actors, modern approaches in decision science highlight the image of a decision maker in conflict (Evans, 2008, 2009; Stanovich, 2004, 2009b, 2011). This comports well with the fact that many adolescents with behavior problems will indeed verbally reject their own behavior. Such a philosophical reorientation could, as Reyna and Farley (2006) demonstrated, have profound implications for how we interpret many findings in the area of adolescent decision making.

REFERENCES

Ackerman, P. L. (1996). A theory of adult development: Process, personality, interests, and knowledge. *Intelligence, 22,* 227–257. doi:10.1016/S0160-2896(96)90016-1

Ackerman, P. L., & Heggestad, E. D. (1997). Intelligence, personality, and interests: Evidence for overlapping traits. *Psychological Bulletin, 121,* 219–245. doi:10.1037/0033-2909.121.2.219

Agnoli, F. (1991). Development of judgmental heuristics and logical reasoning: Training counteracts the representativeness heuristic. *Cognitive Development, 6,* 195–217. doi:10.1016/0885-2014(91)90036-D

Ainslie, G. (1975). Specious reward: A behavioral theory of impulsiveness and impulse control. *Psychological Bulletin, 82,* 463–496. doi:10.1037/h0076860

Ainslie, G. (2001). *Breakdown of will.* Cambridge, England: Cambridge University Press.

Amsel, E., Klaczynski, P. A., Johnston, A., Bench, S., Close, J., Sadler, E., & Walker, R. (2008). A dual-process account of the development of scientific reasoning: The nature and development of metacognitive intercession skills. *Cognitive Development, 23,* 452–471. doi:10.1016/j.cogdev.2008.09.002

Anderson, M. (2005). Marrying intelligence and cognition: A developmental view. In R. J. Sternberg & J. E. Pretz (Eds.), *Cognition and intelligence* (pp. 268–287). New York, NY: Cambridge University Press.

Arkes, H. R. (1991). Costs and benefits of judgment errors: Implications for debiasing. *Psychological Bulletin, 110,* 486–498. doi:10.1037/0033-2909.110.3.486

Audi, R. (1993). *The structure of justification*. New York, NY: Cambridge University Press.

Audi, R. (2001). *The architecture of reason: The structure and substance of rationality*. New York, NY: Oxford University Press.

Austin, E. J., & Deary, I. J. (2002). Personality dispositions. In R. J. Sternberg (Ed.), *Why smart people can be so stupid* (pp. 187–211). New Haven, CT: Yale University Press.

Baltes, P. B. (1987). Theoretical propositions of life-span developmental psychology: On the dynamics between growth and decline. *Developmental Psychology, 23*, 611–626. doi:10.1037/0012-1649.23.5.611

Baltes, P. B., & Staudinger, U. M. (2000). Wisdom: A metaheuristic (pragmatic) to orchestrate mind and virtue toward excellence. *American Psychologist, 55*, 122–136.

Baron, J. (1982). Personality and intelligence. In R. J. Sternberg (Ed.), *Handbook of human intelligence* (pp. 308–351). New York, NY: Cambridge University Press.

Baron, J. (2008). *Thinking and deciding* (4th ed.). New York, NY: Cambridge University Press.

Bartels, D. M. (2006). Proportion dominance: The generality and variability of favouring relative savings over absolute savings. *Organizational Behavior and Human Decision Processes, 100*, 76–95. doi:10.1016/j.obhdp.2005.10.004

Bates, T. C., & Shieles, A. (2003). Crystallized intelligence as a product of speed and drive for experience: The relationship of inspection time and openness to g and Gc. *Intelligence, 31*, 275–287. doi:10.1016/S0160-2896(02)00176-9

Bjorklund, D. F. (2004). *Children's thinking: Cognitive development and individual differences*. Stamford, CT: Wadsworth.

Blackmore, S. (1999). *The meme machine*. New York, NY: Oxford University Press.

Brainerd, C. J., & Reyna, V. F. (2001). Fuzzy-trace theory: Dual processes in memory, reasoning, and cognitive neuroscience. In H. W. Reese & R. Kail (Eds.), *Advances in child development and behavior* (Vol. 28, pp. 41–100). San Diego, CA: Academic Press.

Bruine de Bruin, W., Parker, A. M., & Fischhoff, B. (2007). Individual differences in adult decision-making competence. *Journal of Personality and Social Psychology, 92*, 938–956. doi:10.1037/0022-3514.92.5.938

Byrnes, J. P. (1998). *The nature and development of decision making*. Mahwah, NJ: Erlbaum.

Cacioppo, J. T., Petty, R. E., Feinstein, J., & Jarvis, W. (1996). Dispositional differences in cognitive motivation: The life and times of individuals varying in need for cognition. *Psychological Bulletin, 119*, 197–253. doi:10.1037/0033-2909.119.2.197

Carroll, J. B. (1993). *Human cognitive abilities: A survey of factor-analytic studies*. New York, NY: Cambridge University Press. doi:10.1017/CBO9780511571312

Cattell, R. B. (1963). Theory for fluid and crystallized intelligence: A critical experiment. *Journal of Educational Psychology, 54,* 1–22. doi:10.1037/h0046743

Cattell, R. B. (1998). Where is intelligence? Some answers from the triadic theory. In J. J. McArdle & R. W. Woodcock (Eds.), *Human cognitive abilities in theory and practice* (pp. 29–38). Mahwah, NJ: Erlbaum.

Chien, Y. C., Lin, C., & Worthley, J. (1996). Effect of framing on adolescents' decision making. *Perceptual and Motor Skills, 83,* 811–819.

Cosmides, L., & Tooby, J. (1992). Cognitive adaptations for social exchange. In J. Barkow, L. Cosmides, & J. Tooby (Eds.), *The adapted mind* (pp. 163–228). New York, NY: Oxford University Press.

Cosmides, L., & Tooby, J. (1996). Are humans good intuitive statisticians after all? Rethinking some conclusions from the literature on judgment under uncertainty. *Cognition, 58,* 1–73. doi:10.1016/0010-0277(95)00664-8

Davidson, D. (1995). The representativeness heuristic and the conjunction fallacy effect in children's decision making. *Merrill-Palmer Quarterly, 41,* 328–346.

Dawes, R. M. (1976). Shallow psychology. In J. S. Carroll & J. W. Payne (Eds.), *Cognition and social behavior* (pp. 3–11). Hillsdale, NJ: Erlbaum.

Dawes, R. M. (1998). Behavioral decision making and judgment. In D. T. Gilbert, S. T. Fiske, & G. Lindzey (Eds.), *The handbook of social psychology* (Vol. 1, pp. 497–548). Boston, MA: McGraw-Hill.

Dawkins, R. (1993). Viruses of the mind. In B. Dahlbom (Ed.), *Dennett and his critics* (pp. 13–27). Cambridge, MA: Blackwell.

Deary, I. J. (2001). *Intelligence: A very short introduction.* Oxford, England: Oxford University Press.

Denes-Raj, V., & Epstein, S. (1994). Conflict between intuitive and rational processing: When people behave against their better judgment. *Journal of Personality and Social Psychology, 66,* 819–829. doi:10.1037/0022-3514.66.5.819

De Neys, W. (2006). Dual processing in reasoning—Two systems but one reasoner. *Psychological Science, 17,* 428–433. doi:10.1111/j.1467-9280.2006.01723.x

De Neys, W., & Van Gelder, E. (2009). Logic and belief across the lifespan: The rise and fall of belief inhibition during syllogistic reasoning. *Developmental Science, 12,* 123–130. doi:10.1111/j.1467-7687.2008.00746.x

Dennett, D. C. (2006). From typo to thinko: When evolution graduated to semantic norms. In S. C. Levinson & P. Jaisson (Eds.), *Evolution and culture* (pp. 133–145). Cambridge, MA: MIT Press.

DeShon, R. P., Smith, M. R., Chan, D., & Schmitt, N. (1998). Can racial differences in cognitive test performance be reduced by presenting problems in a social context? *Journal of Applied Psychology, 83,* 438–451. doi:10.1037/0021-9010.83.3.438

de Sousa, R. (2007). *Why think? Evolution and the rational mind.* Oxford, England: Oxford University Press.

Distin, K. (2005). *The selfish meme*. Cambridge, England: Cambridge University Press.

Duncan, J., Parr, A., Woolgar, A., Thompson, R., Bright, P., Cox, S., . . . Nimmo-Smith, I. (2008). Goal neglect and Spearman's g: Competing parts of a complex task. *Journal of Experimental Psychology: General, 137*, 131–148. doi:10.1037/0096-3445.137.1.131

Edwards, W. (1954). The theory of decision making. *Psychological Bulletin, 51*, 380–417. doi:10.1037/h0053870

Epley, N., Mak, D., & Chen Idson, L. (2006). Bonus or rebate? The impact of income framing on spending and saving. *Journal of Behavioral Decision Making, 19*, 213–227. doi:10.1002/bdm.519

Ericsson, K. A., & Charness, N. (1994). Expert performance: Its structure and acquisition. *American Psychologist, 49*, 725–747. doi:10.1037/0003-066X.49.8.725

Evans, J. St. B. T. (1972). Interpretation and matching bias in a reasoning task. *The Quarterly Journal of Experimental Psychology, 24*, 193–199. doi:10.1080/00335557243000067

Evans, J. St. B. T. (1989). *Bias in human reasoning: Causes and consequences*. Hove, England: Erlbaum.

Evans, J. St. B. T. (1998). Matching bias in conditional reasoning: Do we understand it after 25 years? *Thinking & Reasoning, 4*(1), 45–82. doi:10.1080/135467898394247

Evans, J. St. B. T. (2002). The influence of prior belief on scientific thinking. In P. Carruthers, S. Stich, & M. Siegal (Eds.), *The cognitive basis of science* (pp. 193–210). Cambridge, England: Cambridge University Press. doi:10.1017/CBO9780511613517.011

Evans, J. St. B. T. (2007). *Hypothetical thinking: Dual processes in reasoning and judgment*. New York, NY: Psychology Press.

Evans, J. St. B. T. (2008). Dual-processing accounts of reasoning, judgment and social cognition. *Annual Review of Psychology, 59*, 255–278. doi:10.1146/annurev.psych.59.103006.093629

Evans, J. St. B. T. (2009). How many dual-process theories do we need? One, two, or many? In J. Evans & K. Frankish (Eds.), *In two minds: Dual processes and beyond* (pp. 33–54). Oxford, England: Oxford University Press.

Evans, J. St. B. T., Barston, J., & Pollard, P. (1983). On the conflict between logic and belief in syllogistic reasoning. *Memory & Cognition, 11*, 295–306. doi:10.3758/BF03196976

Evans, J. St. B. T., & Curtis-Holmes, J. (2005). Rapid responding increases belief bias: Evidence for the dual-process theory of reasoning. *Thinking & Reasoning, 11*, 382–389. doi:10.1080/13546780542000005

Evans, J. St. B. T., & Lynch, J. S. (1973). Matching bias in the selection task. *British Journal of Psychology, 64*, 391–397. doi:10.1111/j.2044-8295.1973.tb01365.x

Evans, J. St. B. T., Newstead, S., Allen, J., & Pollard, P. (1994). Debiasing by instruction: The case of belief bias. *European Journal of Cognitive Psychology, 6*, 263–285. doi:10.1080/09541449408520148

Eysenck, H. J. (1994). Personality and intelligence: Psychometric and experimental approaches. In R. J. Sternberg & P. Ruzgis (Eds.), *Personality and intelligence* (pp. 3–31). London, England: Cambridge University Press.

Fischbein, E., & Schnarch, D. (1997). The evolution with age of probabilistic, intuitively based misconceptions. *Journal for Research in Mathematics Education, 28,* 96–105. doi:10.2307/749665

Fischhoff, B., Slovic, P., & Lichtenstein, S. (1979). Subjective sensitivity analysis. *Organizational Behavior & Human Performance, 23,* 339–359. doi:10.1016/0030-5073(79)90002-3

Fisk, J. E. (2004). Conjunction fallacy. In R. Pohl (Ed.), *Cognitive illusions: A handbook on fallacies and biases in thinking, judgment and memory* (pp. 23–42). Hove, England: Psychology Press.

Fisk, J. E., Bury, A. S., & Holden, R. (2006). Reasoning about complex probabilistic concepts in childhood. *Scandinavian Journal of Psychology, 47,* 497–504. doi:10.1111/j.1467-9450.2006.00558.x

Fisk, J. E., & Slattery, R. (2005). Reasoning about conjunctive probabilistic concepts in childhood. *Canadian Journal of Experimental Psychology.*

Fleischhauer, M., Enge, S., Brocke, B., Ullrich, J., Strobel, A., & Strobel, A. (2010). Same or different? Clarifying the relationship of need for cognition to personality and intelligence. *Personality and Social Psychology Bulletin, 36,* 82–96. doi:10.1177/0146167209351886

Foley, R. (1987). *The theory of epistemic rationality.* Cambridge, MA: Harvard University Press.

Fong, G. T., Krantz, D. H., & Nisbett, R. E. (1986). The effects of statistical training on thinking about everyday problems. *Cognitive Psychology, 18,* 253–292. doi:10.1016/0010-0285(86)90001-0

Frey, M. C., & Detterman, D. K. (2004). Scholastic assessment or g? The relationship between the Scholastic Assessment Test and general cognitive ability. *Psychological Science, 15,* 373–378. doi:10.1111/j.0956-7976.2004.00687.x

Frisch, D. (1993). Reasons for framing effects. *Organizational Behavior and Human Decision Processes, 54,* 399–429. doi:10.1006/obhd.1993.1017

Geary, D. C. (2005). *The origin of the mind: Evolution of brain, cognition, and general intelligence.* Washington, DC: American Psychological Association. doi:10.1037/10871-000

Gignac, G. E. (2005). Openness to experience, general intelligence and crystallized intelligence: A methodological extension. *Intelligence, 33,* 161–167. doi:10.1016/j.intell.2004.11.001

Gilovich, T., Griffin, D., & Kahneman, D. (Eds.). (2002). *Heuristics and biases: The psychology of intuitive judgment.* New York, NY: Cambridge University Press.

Goff, M., & Ackerman, P. L. (1992). Personality-intelligence relations: Assessment of typical intellectual engagement. *Journal of Educational Psychology, 84,* 537–552. doi:10.1037/0022-0663.84.4.537

Goswami, U. (Ed.). (2004). *Blackwell handbook of childhood cognitive development*. Malden, MA: Blackwell. doi:10.1111/b.9780631218418.2004.x

Green, L., Fry, A. F., & Myerson, J. (1994). Discounting of delayed rewards: A lifespan comparison. *Psychological Science, 5*, 33–36. doi:10.1111/j.1467-9280.1994.tb00610.x

Green, L., Myerson, L., & Ostaszewski, P. (1999). Amount of reward has opposite effects on the discounting of delayed and probabilistic outcomes. *Journal of Experimental Psychology: Learning, Memory, and Cognition, 25*, 418–427. doi:10.1037/0278-7393.25.2.418

Greenhoot, A. F., Semb, G., Colombo, J., & Schreiber, T. (2004). Prior beliefs and methodological concepts in scientific reasoning. *Applied Cognitive Psychology, 18*, 203–221. doi:10.1002/acp.959

Grimmer, M. R., & White, K. D. (1992). Nonconventional beliefs among Australian science and nonscience students. *Journal of Psychology: Interdisciplinary and Applied, 126*, 521–528.

Handley, S. J., Capon, A., Beveridge, M., Dennis, I., & Evans, J. S. B. T. (2004). Working memory, inhibitory control and the development of children's reasoning. *Thinking & Reasoning, 10*, 175–195. doi:10.1080/13546780442000051

Harman, G. (1995). Rationality. In E. E. Smith & D. N. Osherson (Eds.), *Thinking* (Vol. 3, pp. 175–211). Cambridge, MA: MIT Press.

Hastie, R., & Dawes, R. M. (2001). *Rational choice in an uncertain world*. Thousand Oaks, CA: Sage.

Herrnstein, R. J. (1990). Rational choice theory: Necessary but not sufficient. *American Psychologist, 45*, 356–367. doi:10.1037/0003-066X.45.3.356

Horn, J. L., & Cattell, R. B. (1967). Age differences in fluid and crystallized intelligence. *Acta Psychologica, 26*, 107–129. doi:10.1016/0001-6918(67)90011-X

Horn, J. L., & Noll, J. (1997). Human cognitive capabilities: Gf-Gc theory. In D. Flanagan, J. Genshaft, & P. Harrison (Eds.), *Contemporary intellectual assessment: Theories, tests, and issues* (pp. 53–91). New York, NY: Guilford Press.

Hurley, S., & Nudds, M. (2006). The questions of animal rationality: Theory and evidence. In S. Hurley & M. Nudds (Eds.), *Rational animals?* (pp. 1–83). Oxford, England: Oxford University Press.

Jacobs, J. E., & Klaczynski, P. A. (Eds.). (2005). *The development of judgment and decision making in children and adolescents*. Mahwah, NJ: Erlbaum.

Jacobs, J. E., & Potenza, M. (1991). The use of judgment heuristics to make social and object decisions: A developmental perspective. *Child Development, 62*, 166–178.

Jeffrey, R. C. (1983). *The logic of decision* (2nd ed.). Chicago, IL: University of Chicago Press.

Johnson-Laird, P. N. (2006). *How we reason*. Oxford, England: Oxford University Press.

Kahneman, D. (2000). A psychological point of view: Violations of rational rules as a diagnostic of mental processes. *The Behavioral and Brain Sciences, 23,* 681–683. doi:10.1017/S0140525X00403432

Kahneman, D. (2003). A perspective on judgment and choice: Mapping bounded rationality. *American Psychologist, 58,* 697–720. doi:10.1037/0003-066X.58.9.697

Kahneman, D., & Frederick, S. (2002). Representativeness revisited: Attribute substitution in intuitive judgment. In T. Gilovich, D. Griffin, & D. Kahneman (Eds.), *Heuristics and biases: The psychology of intuitive judgment* (pp. 49–81). New York, NY: Cambridge University Press.

Kahneman, D., & Klein, G. (2009). Conditions for intuitive expertise: A failure to disagree. *American Psychologist, 64,* 515–526. doi:10.1037/a0016755

Kahneman, D., & Tversky, A. (1972). Subjective probability: A judgment of representativeness. *Cognitive Psychology, 3,* 430–454. doi:10.1016/0010-0285(72)90016-3

Kahneman, D., & Tversky, A. (1973). On the psychology of prediction. *Psychological Review, 80,* 237–251. doi:10.1037/h0034747

Kahneman, D., & Tversky, A. (1979). Prospect theory: An analysis of decision under risk. *Econometrica, 47,* 263–291.

Kahneman, D., & Tversky, A. (1982). On the study of statistical intuitions. In D. Kahneman, P. Slovic, & A. Tversky (Eds.), *Judgment under uncertainty: Heuristics and biases* (Vol. 11, pp. 493–508). Cambridge, MA: Cambridge University Press.

Kahneman, D., & Tversky, A. (1984). Choices, values, and frames. *American Psychologist, 39,* 341–350. doi:10.1037/0003-066X.39.4.341

Kahneman, D., & Tversky, A. (Eds.). (2000). *Choices, values, and frames.* New York, NY: Cambridge University Press.

Kail, R. (2000). Speed of information processing: Developmental change and links to intelligence. *Journal of School Psychology, 38,* 51–61. doi:10.1016/S0022-4405(99)00036-9

Kanazawa, S. (2004). General intelligence as a domain-specific adaptation. *Psychological Review, 111,* 512–523. doi:10.1037/0033-295X.111.2.512

Kane, M. J., & Engle, R. W. (2002). The role of prefrontal cortex working-memory capacity, executive attention, and general fluid intelligence: An individual-differences perspective. *Psychonomic Bulletin & Review, 9,* 637–671. doi:10.3758/BF03196323

Kirby, K. N. (1997). Bidding on the future: Evidence against normative discounting of delayed rewards. *Journal of Experimental Psychology: General, 126,* 54–70. doi:10.1037/0096-3445.126.1.54

Kirby, K. N., Winston, G. C., & Santiesteban, M. (2005). Impatience and grades: Delay-discount rates correlate negatively with college GPA. *Learning and Individual Differences, 15,* 213–222. doi:10.1016/j.lindif.2005.01.003

Kirkpatrick, L. A., & Epstein, S. (1992). Cognitive-experiential self-theory and sub-jective probability: Evidence for two conceptual systems. *Journal of Personality and Social Psychology, 63,* 534–544. doi:10.1037/0022-3514.63.4.534

Klaczynski, P. A. (2000). Motivated scientific reasoning biases, epistemological beliefs, and theory polarization: A two-process approach to adolescent cognition. *Child Development, 71,* 1347–1366. doi:10.1111/1467-8624.00232

Klaczynski, P. A. (2001a). Analytic and heuristic processing influences on adolescent reasoning and decision making. *Child Development, 72,* 844–861. doi:10.1111/1467-8624.00319

Klaczynski, P. A. (2001b). Framing effects on adolescent task representations, analytic and heuristic processing, and decision making: Implications for the normative-descriptive gap. *Journal of Applied Developmental Psychology, 22,* 289–309. doi:10.1016/S0193-3973(01)00085-5

Klaczynski, P. A., & Gordon, D. H. (1996). Self-serving influences on adolescents' evaluations of belief-relevant evidence. *Journal of Experimental Child Psychology, 62,* 317–339. doi:10.1006/jecp.1996.0033

Klaczynski, P. A., Gordon, D. H., & Fauth, J. (1997). Goal-oriented critical reasoning and individual differences in critical reasoning biases. *Journal of Educational Psychology, 89,* 470–485. doi:10.1037/0022-0663.89.3.470

Klaczynski, P. A., & Lavallee, K. L. (2005). Domain-specific identity, epistemic regulation, and intellectual ability as predictors of belief-based reasoning: A dual-process perspective. *Journal of Experimental Child Psychology, 92,* 1–24.

Klaczynski, P. A., & Narasimham, G. (1998). Development of scientific reasoning biases: Cognitive versus ego-protective explanations. *Developmental Psychology, 34,* 175–187. doi:10.1037/0012-1649.34.1.175

Klaczynski, P. A., & Robinson, B. (2000). Personal theories, intellectual ability, and epistemological beliefs: Adult age differences in everyday reasoning tasks. *Psychology and Aging, 15,* 400–416. doi:10.1037/0882-7974.15.3.400

Klauer, K. C., Stahl, C., & Erdfelder, E. (2007). The abstract selection task: New data and an almost comprehensive model. *Journal of Experimental Psychology: Learning, Memory, and Cognition, 33,* 680–703. doi:10.1037/0278-7393.33.4.680

Klein, G. (1998). *Sources of power: How people make decisions.* Cambridge, MA: MIT Press.

Koehler, D. J., & Harvey, N. (Eds.). (2004). *Blackwell handbook of judgment and decision making.* Oxford, England: Blackwell. doi:10.1002/9780470752937

Koehler, J. J. (1996). The base rate fallacy reconsidered: Descriptive, normative and methodological challenges. *Behavioral and Brain Sciences, 19,* 1–53. doi:10.1017/S0140525X00041157

Kokis, J. V., Macpherson, R., Toplak, M., West, R. F., & Stanovich, K. E. (2002). Heuristic and analytic processing: Age trends and associations with cognitive ability and cognitive styles. *Journal of Experimental Child Psychology, 83,* 26–52. doi:10.1016/S0022-0965(02)00121-2

Kühberger, A. (1998). The influence of framing on risky decisions: A meta-analysis. *Organizational Behavior and Human Decision Processes, 75,* 23–55. doi:10.1006/obhd.1998.2781

Kühberger, A., & Tanner, C. (2010). Risky choice framing: Task versions and a comparison of prospect theory and fuzzy-trace theory. *Journal of Behavioral Decision Making, 23,* 314–329. doi:10.1002/bdm.656

Kuhn, D. (2001). How do people know? *Psychological Science, 12,* 1–8. doi:10.1111/1467-9280.00302

Larrick, R. P. (2004). Debiasing. In D. J. Koehler & N. Harvey (Eds.), *Blackwell handbook of judgment & decision making* (pp. 316–338). Malden, MA: Blackwell. doi:10.1002/9780470752937.ch16

Levin, I. P., Gaeth, G. J., Schreiber, J., & Lauriola, M. (2002). A new look at framing effects: Distribution of effect sizes, individual differences, and independence of types of effects. *Organizational behavior and human decision processes, 88,* 411–429.

Levin, I. P., & Hart, S. S. (2003). Risk preferences in young children: Early evidence of individual differences in reaction to potential gains and losses. *Journal of Behavioral Decision Making, 16,* 397–413.

Levin, I. P., Hart, S. S., Weller, J. A., & Harshman, L. A. (2007). Stability of choices in a risky decision-making task: A 3-year longitudinal study with children and adults. *Journal of Behavioral Decision Making, 20,* 241–252. doi:10.1002/bdm.552

Lichtenstein, S., & Slovic, P. (Eds.). (2006). *The construction of preference.* New York, NY: Cambridge University Press.

Lubinski, D. (2004). Introduction to the special section on cognitive abilities: 100 years after Spearman's (1904) "General Intelligence, Objectively Determined and Measured." *Journal of Personality and Social Psychology, 86,* 96–111. doi:10.1037/0022-3514.86.1.96

Luce, R. D., & Raiffa, H. (1957). *Games and decisions.* New York, NY: Wiley.

Lynch, A. (1996). *Thought contagion.* New York, NY: Basic Books.

MacPherson, R., & Stanovich, K. E. (2007). Cognitive ability, thinking dispositions, and instructional set as predictors of critical thinking. *Learning and Individual Differences, 17,* 115–127. doi:10.1016/j.lindif.2007.05.003

Manktelow, K. I. (2004). Reasoning and rationality: The pure and the practical. In K. I. Manktelow & M. C. Chung (Eds.), *Psychology of reasoning: Theoretical and historical perspectives* (pp. 157–177). Hove, England: Psychology Press.

Markovits, H. (2004). The development of deductive reasoning. In J. P. Leighton & R. J. Sternberg (Eds.), *The nature of reasoning* (pp. 313–338). New York, NY: Cambridge University Press.

Maule, J., & Villejoubert, G. (2007). What lies beneath: Reframing framing effects. *Thinking & Reasoning, 13,* 25–44. doi:10.1080/13546780600872585

McArdle, J. J., Ferrer-Caja, E., Hamagami, F., & Woodcock, R. W. (2002). Comparative longitudinal structural analyses of the growth and decline of multiple intellectual abilities over the life span. *Developmental Psychology, 38,* 115–142. doi:10.1037/0012-1649.38.1.115

McFadden, D. (1999). Rationality for economists? *Journal of Risk and Uncertainty, 19,* 73–105. doi:10.1023/A:1007863007855

McGrew, K. S., & Woodcock, R. W. (2001). *Technical Manual: Woodcock-Johnson III.* Itasca, IL: Riverside.

Milkman, K. L., Chugh, D., & Bazerman, M. H. (2009). How can decision making be improved? *Perspectives on Psychological Science, 4,* 379–383. doi:10.1111/j.1745-6924.2009.01142.x

Nathanson, S. (1994). *The ideal of rationality.* Chicago, IL: Open Court.

Newstead, S. E., Handley, S. J., Harley, C., Wright, H., & Farrelly, D. (2004). Individual differences in deductive reasoning. *Quarterly Journal of Experimental Psychology A, 57,* 33–60.

Nickerson, R. S. (2008). *Aspects of rationality.* New York, NY: Psychology Press.

Noftle, E. E., & Robins, R. W. (2007). Personality predictors of academic outcomes: Big five correlates of GPA and SAT scores. *Journal of Personality and Social Psychology, 93,* 116–130. doi:10.1037/0022-3514.93.1.116

Nussbaum, E. M., & Kardash, C. A. M. (2005). The effects of goal instructions and text on the generation of counterarguments during writing. *Journal of Educational Psychology, 97,* 157–169. doi:10.1037/0022-0663.97.2.157

Oaksford, M., & Chater, N. (2007). *Bayesian rationality: The probabilistic approach to human reasoning.* Oxford, England: Oxford University Press.

Oreg, S., & Bayazit, M. (2009). Prone to bias: Development of a bias taxonomy from an individual differences perspective. *Review of General Psychology, 13,* 175–193. doi:10.1037/a0015656

Osman, M., & Laming, D. (2001). Misinterpretation of conditional statements in Wason's selection task. *Psychological Research, 65,* 128–144. doi:10.1007/s004260000023

Over, D. E. (2004). Rationality and the normative/descriptive distinction. In D. J. Koehler & N. Harvey (Eds.), *Blackwell handbook of judgment and decision making* (pp. 1–18). Malden, MA: Blackwell. doi:10.1002/9780470752937.ch1

Overton, W. F., Byrnes, J. P., & O'Brien, D. P. (1985). Developmental and individual differences in conditional reasoning: The role of contradiction training and cognitive style. *Developmental Psychology, 21,* 692–701. doi:10.1037/0012-1649.21.4.692

Pacini, R., & Epstein, S. (1999). The relation of rational and experiential information processing styles to personality, basic beliefs, and the ratio-bias phenomenon. *Journal of Personality and Social Psychology, 76,* 972–987. doi:10.1037/0022-3514.76.6.972

Parker, A. M., & Fischhoff, B. (2005). Decision-making competence: External validation through an individual differences approach. *Journal of Behavioral Decision Making, 18,* 1–27. doi:10.1002/bdm.481

Parker, K. (2010). Rising above hurtful remarks by Pat Robertson and Limbaugh. *The Washington Post*. Retrieved from http://www.washingtonpost.com/wp-dyn/content/article/2010/01/15/AR2010011502420_pf.html

Perkins, D. N. (1995). *Outsmarting IQ: The emerging science of learnable intelligence*. New York, NY: Free Press.

Perkins, D. N. (2002). The engine of folly. In R. J. Sternberg (Ed.), *Why smart people can be so stupid* (pp. 64–85). New Haven, CT: Yale University Press.

Peters, E., Vastfjall, D., Slovic, P., Mertz, C. K., Mazzocco, K., & Dickert, S. (2006). Numeracy and decision making. *Psychological Science, 17,* 407–413. doi:10.1111/j.1467-9280.2006.01720.x

Postman, N. (1988). *Conscientious objections*. New York, NY: Vintage Books.

Preece, P. F. W., & Baxter, J. H. (2000). Scepticism and gullibility: The superstitious and pseudo-scientific beliefs of secondary school students. *International Journal of Science Education, 22,* 1147–1156. doi:10.1080/09500690050166724

Reyna, V. F. (1996). Conceptions of memory development, with implications for reasoning and decision making. *Annals of Child Development, 12,* 87–118.

Reyna, V. F., Adam, M. B., Poirier, K., LeCroy, C., & Brainerd, C. J. (2005). Risky decision making in childhood and adolescence: A fuzzy-trace theory approach. In J. E. Jacobs & P. A. Klaczynski (Eds.), *The development of judgment and decision making in children and adolescents* (pp. 77–106). Mahwah, NJ: Erlbaum.

Reyna, V. F., & Brainerd, C. J. (1991). Fuzzy-trace theory and framing effects in choice: Gist extraction, truncation, and conversion. *Journal of Behavioral Decision Making, 4,* 249–262. doi:10.1002/bdm.3960040403

Reyna, V. F., & Brainerd, C. J. (1995). Fuzzy-trace theory: An interim synthesis. *Learning and Individual Differences, 7,* 1–75. doi:10.1016/1041-6080(95)90031-4

Reyna, V. F., & Brainerd, C. J. (2008). Numeracy, ratio bias, and denominator neglect in judgments of risk and probability. *Learning and Individual Differences, 18,* 89–107. doi:10.1016/j.lindif.2007.03.011

Reyna, V. F., & Ellis, S. (1994). Fuzzy-trace theory and framing effects in children's risky decision making. *Psychological Science, 5,* 275–279. doi:10.1111/j.1467-9280.1994.tb00625.x

Reyna, V. F., Estrada, S., DeMarinis, J., Myers, R., Stanisz, J., & Mills, B. (in press). Neurobiological and memory models of risky decision making in adolescents versus young adults. *Journal of Experimental Psychology. Learning, Memory, and Cognition.* doi:10.1037/a0023943

Reyna, V. F., & Farley, F. (2006). Risk and rationality in adolescent decision making. *Psychological Science in the Public Interest, 7,* 1–44.

Reyna, V. F., Lloyd, F. J., & Brainerd, C. J. (2003). Memory, development, and rationality: An integrative theory of judgment and decision making. In S. L. Schneider & J. Shanteau (Eds.), *Emerging perspectives on judgment and decision research* (pp. 201–245). New York, NY: Cambridge University Press.

Reyna, V. F., & Rivers, S. E. (2008). Current theories of risk and rational decision making. *Developmental Review, 28,* 1–11. doi:10.1016/j.dr.2008.01.002

Sá, W., Kelley, C., Ho, C., & Stanovich, K. E. (2005). Thinking about personal theories: Individual differences in the coordination of theory and evidence. *Personality and Individual Differences, 38,* 1149–1161. doi:10.1016/j.paid.2004.07.012

Sá, W., & Stanovich, K. E. (2001). The domain specificity and generality of mental contamination: Accuracy and projection in judgments of mental content. *British Journal of Psychology, 92,* 281–302. doi:10.1348/000712601162194

Sá, W., West, R. F., & Stanovich, K. E. (1999). The domain specificity and generality of belief bias: Searching for a generalizable critical thinking skill. *Journal of Educational Psychology, 91,* 497–510. doi:10.1037/0022-0663.91.3.497

Samuels, R., & Stich, S. P. (2004). Rationality and psychology. In A. R. Mele & P. Rawling (Eds.), *The Oxford handbook of rationality* (pp. 279–300). Oxford, England: Oxford University Press.

Savage, L. J. (1954). *The foundations of statistics.* New York, NY: Wiley.

Schlottmann, A., & Tring, J. (2005). How children reason about gains and losses: Framing effects in judgement and choice. *Swiss Journal of Psychology, 64,* 153–171. doi:10.1024/1421-0185.64.3.153

Schneider, S. L., Burke, M. D., Solomonson, A. L., & Laurion, S. K. (2005). Incidental framing effects and associative processes: A study of attribute frames in broadcast news stories. *Journal of Behavioral Decision Making, 18,* 261–280. doi:10.1002/bdm.500

Shah, A. K., & Oppenheimer, D. M. (2008). Heuristics made easy: An effort-reduction framework. *Psychological Bulletin, 134,* 207–222. doi:10.1037/0033-2909.134.2.207

Shamosh, N. A., DeYoung, C. G., Green, A. E., Reis, D. L., Johnson, M. R., Conway, A. R. A., . . . Gray, J. R. (2008). Individual differences in delay discounting relation to intelligence, working memory, and anterior prefrontal cortex. *Psychological Science, 19,* 904–911. doi:10.1111/j.1467-9280.2008.02175.x

Shamosh, N. A., & Gray, J. R. (2008). Delay discounting and intelligence: A meta-analysis. *Intelligence, 36,* 289–305. doi:10.1016/j.intell.2007.09.004

Shiffrin, R. M., & Schneider, W. (1977). Controlled and automatic human information processing: II. Perceptual learning, automatic attending, and a general theory. *Psychological Review, 84,* 127–190. doi:10.1037/0033-295X.84.2.127

Simon, H. A. (1955). A behavioral model of rational choice. *Quarterly Journal of Economics, 69,* 99–118. doi:10.2307/1884852

Simon, H. A. (1956). Rational choice and the structure of the environment. *Psychological Review, 63,* 129–138. doi:10.1037/h0042769

Skyrms, B. (1996). *The evolution of the social contract.* Cambridge, England: Cambridge University Press.

Slovic, P., & Peters, E. (2006). Risk perception and affect. *Current Directions in Psychological Science, 15*, 322–325. doi:10.1111/j.1467-8721.2006.00461.x

Stanovich, K. E. (1993). Dysrationalia: A new specific learning disability. *Journal of Learning Disabilities, 26*, 501–515. doi:10.1177/002221949302600803

Stanovich, K. E. (1999). *Who is rational? Studies of individual differences in reasoning.* Mahwah, NJ: Erlbaum.

Stanovich, K. E. (2000). *Progress in understanding reading: Scientific foundations and new frontiers.* New York, NY: Guilford Press.

Stanovich, K. E. (2002). Rationality, intelligence, and levels of analysis in cognitive science: Is dysrationalia possible? In R. J. Sternberg (Ed.), *Why smart people can be so stupid* (pp. 124–158). New Haven, CT: Yale University Press.

Stanovich, K. E. (2004). *The robot's rebellion: Finding meaning in the age of Darwin.* Chicago, IL: University of Chicago Press.

Stanovich, K. E. (2009a). Distinguishing the reflective, algorithmic, and autonomous minds: Is it time for a tri-process theory? In J. Evans & K. Frankish (Eds.), *In two minds: Dual processes and beyond* (pp. 55–88). Oxford, England: Oxford University Press.

Stanovich, K. E. (2009b). *What IQ tests miss: The psychology of rational thought.* New Haven, CT: Yale University Press.

Stanovich, K. E. (2010). *Decision making and rationality in the modern world.* New York, NY: Oxford University Press.

Stanovich, K. E. (2011). *Rationality and the reflective mind.* New York, NY: Oxford University Press.

Stanovich, K. E., Toplak, M. E., & West, R. F. (2008). The development of rational thought: A taxonomy of heuristics and biases. *Advances in Child Development and Behavior, 36*, 251–285. doi:10.1016/S0065-2407(08)00006-2

Stanovich, K. E., & West, R. F. (1997). Reasoning independently of prior belief and individual differences in actively open-minded thinking. *Journal of Educational Psychology, 89*, 342–357. doi:10.1037/0022-0663.89.2.342

Stanovich, K. E., & West, R. F. (1998a). Cognitive ability and variation in selection task performance. *Thinking & Reasoning, 4*, 193–230. doi:10.1080/13546 7898394139

Stanovich, K. E., & West, R. F. (1998b). Individual differences in framing and conjunction effects. *Thinking & Reasoning, 4*, 289–317. doi:10.1080/13546 7898394094

Stanovich, K. E., & West, R. F. (1998c). Individual differences in rational thought. *Journal of Experimental Psychology: General, 127*, 161–188. doi:10.1037/0096-3445.127.2.161

Stanovich, K. E., & West, R. F. (1998d). Who uses base rates and P(D/~H)? An analysis of individual differences. *Memory & Cognition, 26*, 161–179. doi:10.3758/BF03211379

Stanovich, K. E., & West, R. F. (1999). Discrepancies between normative and descriptive models of decision making and the understanding/acceptance principle. *Cognitive Psychology, 38,* 349–385. doi:10.1006/cogp.1998.0700

Stanovich, K. E., & West, R. F. (2000). Individual differences in reasoning: Implications for the rationality debate? *Behavioral and Brain Sciences, 23,* 645–665. doi:10.1017/S0140525X00003435

Stanovich, K. E., & West, R. F. (2003). Evolutionary versus instrumental goals: How evolutionary psychology misconceives human rationality. In D. E. Over (Ed.), *Evolution and the psychology of thinking: The debate* (pp. 171–230). Hove, England: Psychology Press.

Stanovich, K. E., & West, R. F. (2007). Natural myside bias is independent of cognitive ability. *Thinking & Reasoning, 13,* 225–247. doi:10.1080/1354678 0600780796

Stanovich, K. E., & West, R. F. (2008a). On the failure of intelligence to predict myside bias and one-sided bias. *Thinking & Reasoning, 14,* 129–167. doi:10.1080/ 13546780701679764

Stanovich, K. E., & West, R. F. (2008b). On the relative independence of thinking biases and cognitive ability. *Journal of Personality and Social Psychology, 94,* 672–695. doi:10.1037/0022-3514.94.4.672

Stanovich, K. E., West, R. F., & Toplak, M. E. (2011). Intelligence and rationality. In R. J. Sternberg & S. B. Kaufman (Eds.), *Cambridge handbook of intelligence* (pp. 784–826. New York, NY: Cambridge University Press.

Steinberg, L., Graham, S., O'Brien, L., Woolard, J., Cauffman, E., & Banich, M. (2009). Age differences in future orientation and delay discounting. *Child Development, 80,* 28–44. doi:10.1111/j.1467-8624.2008.01244.x

Sternberg, R. J. (2003). *Wisdom, intelligence, and creativity synthesized.* Cambridge, England: Cambridge University Press. doi:10.1017/CBO9780511509612

Sternberg, R. J. (2006). The Rainbow Project: Enhancing the SAT through assessments of analytical, practical, and creative skills. *Intelligence, 34,* 321–350. doi:10.1016/ j.intell.2006.01.002

Stich, S. P. (1990). *The fragmentation of reason.* Cambridge, MA: MIT Press.

Stuebing, K. K., Barth, A., Molfese, P. J., Weiss, B., & Fletcher, J. M. (2009). IQ is not strongly related to response to reading instruction: A meta-analytic interpretation. *Exceptional Children, 76,* 31–51.

Taub, G. E., & McGrew, K. S. (2004). A confirmatory factor analysis of Cattell-Horn-Carroll theory and cross-age invariance of the Woodcock-Johnson Tests of Cognitive Abilities III. *School Psychology Quarterly, 19,* 72–87. doi:10.1521/ scpq.19.1.72.29409

Taylor, S. E. (1981). The interface of cognitive and social psychology. In J. H. Harvey (Ed.), *Cognition, social behavior, and the environment* (pp. 189–211). Hillsdale, NJ: Erlbaum.

Toplak, M., Liu, E., Macpherson, R., Toneatto, T., & Stanovich, K. E. (2007). The reasoning skills and thinking dispositions of problem gamblers: A dual-process taxonomy. *Journal of Behavioral Decision Making, 20*, 103–124. doi:10.1002/bdm.544

Toplak, M. E., Sorge, G. B., Benoit, A., West, R. F., & Stanovich, K. E. (2010). Decision-making and cognitive abilities: A review of associations between Iowa Gambling Task performance, executive functions, and intelligence. *Clinical Psychology Review, 30*, 562–581. doi:10.1016/j.cpr.2010.04.002

Toplak, M. E., & Stanovich, K. E. (2002). The domain specificity and generality of disjunctive reasoning: Searching for a generalizable critical thinking skill. *Journal of Educational Psychology, 94*, 197–209. doi:10.1037/0022-0663.94.1.197

Toplak, M. E., & Stanovich, K. E. (2003). Associations between myside bias on an informal reasoning task and amount of post-secondary education. *Applied Cognitive Psychology, 17*, 851–860. doi:10.1002/acp.915

Toplak, M. E., West, R. F., & Stanovich, K. E. (in press). The Cognitive Reflection Test as a predictor of performance on heuristics and biases tasks. *Memory & Cognition*. doi:10.3758/s13421-011-0104-1

Tversky, A., & Kahneman, D. (1974, September 27). Judgment under uncertainty: Heuristics and biases. *Science, 185*, 1124–1131. doi:10.1126/science.185.4157.1124

Tversky, A., & Kahneman, D. (1981, January 30). The framing of decisions and the psychology of choice. *Science, 211*, 453–458. doi:10.1126/science.7455683

Tversky, A., & Kahneman, D. (1983). Extensional versus intuitive reasoning: The conjunction fallacy in probability judgment. *Psychological Review, 90*, 293–315. doi:10.1037/0033-295X.90.4.293

Tversky, A., & Kahneman, D. (1986). Rational choice and the framing of decisions. *The Journal of Business, 59*, S251–S278. doi:10.1086/296365

Valentine, E. R. (1975). Performance on two reasoning tasks in relation to intelligence, divergence and interference proneness: Content and context effects in reasoning. *British Journal of Educational Psychology, 45*, 198–205. doi:10.1111/j.2044-8279.1975.tb03244.x

Vellutino, F. R., Fletcher, J. M., Snowling, M., & Scanlon, D. M. (2004). Specific reading disability (dyslexia): What have we learned in the past four decades? *Journal of Child Psychology and Psychiatry, and Allied Disciplines, 45*, 2–40. doi:10.1046/j.0021-9630.2003.00305.x

Von Neumann, J., & Morgenstern, O. (1944). *The theory of games and economic behavior*. Princeton, NJ: Princeton University Press.

Wason, P. C. (1966). Reasoning. In B. Foss (Ed.), *New horizons in psychology* (pp. 135–151). Harmonsworth, England: Penguin.

West, R. F., & Stanovich, K. E. (2003). Is probability matching smart? Associations between probabilistic choices and cognitive ability. *Memory & Cognition, 31*, 243–251.

West, R. F., Toplak, M. E., & Stanovich, K. E. (2008). Heuristics and biases as measures of critical thinking: Associations with cognitive ability and thinking dispositions. *Journal of Educational Psychology, 100,* 930–941. doi:10.1037/a0012842

Wolfe, C. R., & Britt, M. A. (2008). The locus of the myside bias in written argumentation. *Thinking & Reasoning, 14,* 1–27. doi:10.1080/13546780701527674

Wu, G., Zhang, J., & Gonzalez, R. (2004). Decision under risk. In D. J. Koehler & N. Harvey (Eds.), *Blackwell handbook of judgment and decision making* (pp. 399–423). Malden, MA: Blackwell. doi:10.1002/9780470752937.ch20

Zeidner, M., & Matthews, G. (2000). Intelligence and personality. In R. J. Sternberg (Ed.), *Handbook of intelligence* (pp. 581–610). New York, NY: Cambridge University Press.

13

A FUZZY TRACE THEORY OF ADOLESCENT RISK TAKING: BEYOND SELF-CONTROL AND SENSATION SEEKING

CHRISTINA F. CHICK AND VALERIE F. REYNA

Using fuzzy trace theory, we integrate behavioral and neuroscientific evidence in a process model of adolescent risky decision making that emphasizes gist and verbatim thinking, reward sensitivity, and cognitive control. Gist thinking, which increases with age, facilitates recognition of danger and protects against unhealthy risk taking. Adolescents, who rely on verbatim thinking and thus analyze the expected value of a risk, are susceptible to unhealthy risk taking, particularly when reward magnitude is high. Signal in the nucleus accumbens of the brain is proportional to reward magnitude, which is more active in adolescents than in adults during the outcome phase of reward tasks.

Personality traits and motivational factors, such as reward sensitivity and cognitive control, interact with gist and verbatim mental processes during risky decision making. Reward sensitivity magnifies the perceived magnitude of a reward, which interacts with the verbatim calculation of approximate expected value in order to encourage risk taking. However, gist-based thinking supplants magnitude-sensitive verbatim thinking over time, and gist helps to cue values that guard against risk taking, facilitating cognitive control. Prefrontal cortex contributes to cognitive control through better appraisal of decision options and better inhibition with development, consistent with fuzzy trace theory and other neurobiological models.

In sum, developmental differences in the brain are consistent with fuzzy trace theory: The anatomical theme of "less is more," reflecting pruning of gray matter during adolescence, echoes behavioral findings summarized by fuzzy trace theory. Thus, adolescents process fewer, higher quality aspects of information as they approach adulthood, a shift in processing reflected in a more stream-lined, efficient, and interconnected neural network.

Decision making is among the best-characterized topic areas in neuro-science, and risk taking has long been a focus of those interested in decision making (see, e.g., Jacobs & Klaczynski, 2005; Vartanian, Mandel & Duncan, 2011). The stereotypical risky decision maker is the adolescent, spurring special interest in the adolescent brain. Although some adults relish risk, adolescents and young adults are at their lifetime peak of engaging in risk taking, such as binge drinking, reckless driving, or violent crime (Reyna & Rivers, 2008). Adolescents also initiate lifestyle habits, such as smoking, that are major causes of adult morbidity and mortality. Old enough to know better, in principle, but too young to exercise judgment or self-control, the adolescent brain exhibits fascinating paradoxes with socially significant seque-lae. Yet we are only beginning to build process models that explain and predict adolescent risk taking, and few of these models incorporate knowl-edge about the adolescent brain.

In this chapter, we present one such process model, gathering the extant evidence from multiple, independent laboratories. The building blocks of the model come from fuzzy trace theory, a theory of memory, judgment, and deci-sion making and their development across the life span. This theory is inte-grated with neuroscientific evidence, which bears mainly on developmental differences in reward processing (e.g., individual differences in sensation seek-ing; Freeman & Beer, 2010) and executive processes, particularly, inhibition (i.e., self-control; Somerville, Jones, & Casey, 2010; Van Leijenhorst, Moor, et al., 2010). The implication of this integrated account is that factors such as sensation seeking and self-control are not sufficient to account for major findings regarding adolescent risk taking—although they are very important. Research shows that additional factors account for unique variance in risk taking (e.g., Reyna et al., 2011). Therefore, we present an augmented account that includes how decision options are "framed" in the mind of decision mak-ers (their mental representations), the retrieval of social and moral values, and the application of those values in real-world situations.

In what follows, we first introduce fuzzy trace theory and then describe developmental changes in brain anatomy and connectivity, which are con-sistent with predictions made by the theory. These changes set the basis for the functional changes that have been documented in relation to processing of rewards. Similar functional changes are then discussed in terms of valua-tion, a mental process that takes into account not only reward but also the probability of obtaining that reward. Next, we account for the role of emo-tion in risk processing, noting that while emotional impulses may encourage risk taking, aspects of emotion that are incorporated into gist-based intuition can also protect against risk taking.

We continue on to discuss intuition in the context of inhibition, which benefits from developmental increases not only in the ability to suppress impulses but also in the tendency to default to gist-based intuition. In closing the chapter, we bring all of these themes together in summarizing research on the framing effect, which is a case study of the importance of additional factors, beyond reward magnitude and risk probability, in shaping risk preferences. These additional factors, we argue, are gist and verbatim mental representations and the values that are applied to them. We end by summarizing evidence that mental representations, above and beyond reward sensitivity and inhibition, predict much of the variance in adolescents' intentions to engage in real-life risk taking.

FUZZY TRACE THEORY

Fuzzy trace theory is based on memory and decision-making studies indicating that people encode multiple, parallel representations of information that vary in precision from verbatim (a mental representation of the literal stimulus) to gist (a mental representation of the basic meaning of the stimulus; see the summary by Reyna & Brainerd [1995]). *Verbatim* representations are detailed but devoid of meaning; they consist of the surface form of information, such as exact numbers and precise wording. *Gist* representations, in contrast, are high-level in terms of meaning extraction, but they lack the precision and detail of verbatim representations. Gist-based thinking promotes categorical distinctions that can easily be mapped onto values and preferences (Rivers, Reyna, & Mills, 2008). Fuzzy trace theory was inspired by gestalt-theory research on reasoning and by psycholinguistic research on comprehension (Kintsch, 1974). However, gist representations have also been shown to operate beyond the linguistic realm, in modalities such as music, pictures, graphs, numbers, and events (Reyna & Brainerd, 1995). Fuzzy trace theory differs from standard dual process models in assuming that gists are not derived from verbatim traces (e.g., Reyna & Kiernan, 1994). Instead, the two are encoded and retrieved independently and in parallel.

Gist and verbatim representations are not so much discrete categories as anchors of a continuum (Reyna & Brainerd, 1995). Taking representations of numbers as an example, the hierarchy ranges from quantitative differences (e.g., the exact difference between two quantities of money) to ordinal differences (e.g., more money or less money) to nominal or categorical differences (e.g., some money or no money; Reyna & Brainerd, 1991). The level of gist extracted varies with multiple factors, especially the requirements of the task and the developmental level of the extractor. Task requirements affect the level of gist extraction because different response formats require varying levels of precision. The effect of task requirements on the level of gist extraction is called *task calibration* (Reyna, Lloyd, & Brainerd, 2003). *Developmental level* refers to both chronological age and experience; the more experience one has with a given stimulus or situation, the simpler the representation (Reyna, 2008; Reyna & Lloyd, 2006). The preference for fuzzy (gist-based) processing increases with age, because age covaries with experience (Rivers et al., 2008). A long tradition of evidence in the memory, judgment, and decision-making literatures suggests that gist-based (intuitive) thinking is advanced both in ontogenic development and in the development of expertise (Brouwer, 1952; Ericsson & Kintsch, 1995; Reyna, 2008; Simon & Chase, 1973).

Fuzzy trace theory assumes that gist-based decision making consists of three steps (Reyna & Brainerd, 1995), each of which has an effect on risky decision making (Rivers et al., 2008). First, as we have discussed, a decision maker must form a *mental representation* of the situation by extracting both verbatim and gist representations. Gist representations are shaped by stored knowledge and values, which is why fuzzy trace theory emphasizes that development is defined by experience, not merely by chronological age (Reyna & Brainerd, 1995; Reyna & Ellis, 1994). One can form a mental representation of a risky activity without ever having tried it; movies and stories from friends, for example, contribute to the knowledge and beliefs that inform mental representations (Reyna & Farley, 2006).

After forming mental representations, the decision maker must *retrieve* knowledge, values, or reasoning principles that are relevant to her mental representations of the situation. An individual might possess knowledge and values that are relevant to the situation but that, nonetheless, do not influence the decision because they are not cued by the mental representations or are not strongly embedded in the individual's value system (Reyna & Farley, 2006; Rivers et al., 2008). After retrieving relevant values and reasoning principles, the individual must *implement* them in the current situation by choosing a course of action that is consistent with the cued values (Reyna & Brainerd, 1995; Reyna & Farley, 2006; Rivers et al., 2008).

The tendency to use gist versus verbatim processing varies among individuals and over the course of development. In the context of risky decision-making, gist-based operations consist of gleaning the bottom line of a dangerous situation and using this mental representation to cue personal values that protect against risk taking (Mills, Reyna, & Estrada, 2008). Verbatim operations, in contrast, support the calculation of expected value as reward magnitude multiplied by the probability of obtaining the reward (Reyna & Brainerd, 1991; Tversky & Kahneman, 1981). Aside from these cognitive operations, other factors in decision making include reward sensitivity and inhibition, which are relatively stable individual differences, although they also vary with developmental stage. In the verbatim calculation of expected value, reward sensitivity magnifies the perceived magnitude of a reward, and an individual can be more or less sensitive to different classes of reward (e.g., some people have a sweet tooth but are indifferent to alcohol). Thus, verbatim processing encourages risk taking by supporting a focus on the tradeoff between risk and reward and by permitting greater influence of reward sensitivity (Reyna et al., 2011). Both gist-based processing, by facilitating the application of protective values, and trait inhibition (self-control), which helps to manage impulses, guard against risk taking (Reyna & Mills, 2007; for a schematic of this model, see Figure 13.1). However, fuzzy trace theory models inhibition as a third process that is independent of gist and verbatim processing (Reyna & Mills, 2007). We now describe documented changes in brain structure and connectivity, interpreting them in terms of predictions made by fuzzy trace theory.

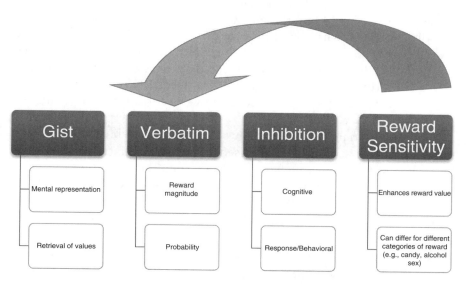

Figure 13.1. Factors in risk taking include mental processes (gist and verbatim) and individual differences (inhibition and reward sensitivity). Gist processes include the formation of mental representations and the retrieval of stored social values. Verbatim processes underlie the calculation of expected value as reward magnitude multiplied by the probability of obtaining the reward. In the verbatim calculation of expected value, reward sensitivity magnifies the subjective reward magnitude (hence the arrow), and an individual can be more or less sensitive to different classes of reward (e.g., some people have a sweet tooth but are indifferent to alcohol). There are generally two classes of inhibition: cognitive, which pertains to thought processes and can be unconscious, and response/behavioral, which pertains to the willful suppression of actions.

DEVELOPMENTAL DIFFERENCES IN BRAIN ANATOMY: LESS IS MORE

During adolescence, two well-documented changes in brain anatomy are consistent with the behavioral evidence that thinking becomes more streamlined—more gist-based—with age. First, following a surge in gray matter production at the beginning of adolescence, weak or unused synapses are pruned over the course of adolescence, resulting in reduced gray matter in both the basal ganglia (Sowell et al., 1999) and the cortex (Giedd et al., 1999; Gogtay et al., 2004; Paus, Keshavan, & Giedd., 2008; Sowell et al., 1999; Toga, Thompson, & Sowell, 2006). Eliminating all but the most important connective pathways is thought to facilitate speed and efficiency of neuronal information transfer (Geier & Luna, 2009; Reyna et al., 2011). To the same end, communication between distal neural networks is facilitated by an increase in myelination, the white matter that insulates synaptic connections in order to increase the speed of information transfer (Huppi & Dubois, 2006; Klingberg, Vaidya, Gabrieli, Moseley, & Hedehus, 1999; Luna & Sweeney, 2004; Mukherjee & McKinstry, 2006). These changes are broadly consistent with the fuzzy trace theory emphasis that "less is more" during cognitive development, but they are hard to reconcile with theories that describe development as increased connections in processing networks (Bjorklund, 2012; cf. Reyna & Brainerd, 1995; for evidence that increased connections can be associated with unhealthy risk taking, see Berns, Moore, & Capra, 2009).

The gains in processing efficiency conferred by myelination and synaptic pruning occur at different rates in sensory versus integration regions of the brain. For example, declines in gray matter begin in the striatum and sensorimotor cortices; gray matter in the visual cortex reaches adult levels during childhood (Huttenlocher, 1990). In contrast, higher level association areas, such as the dorsolateral prefrontal cortex (DLPFC), orbitofrontal cortex (OFC), and lateral temporal cortex, continue to be pruned throughout adolescence (Casey, Jones, & Hare, 2008; Giedd, 2004; Gogtay et al., 2004; Zielinski, Gennatas, Zhou, & Seeley, 2010). Although some connections are pruned, other connections continue to develop, especially longer connections between the prefrontal cortex and parietal and subcortical regions. In parallel with synaptic pruning, myelination continues into young adulthood in association areas of the frontal, temporal, and parietal lobes, whereas lower level processing centers such as the occipital lobe reach adult levels of myelination by early adolescence (Asato, Terwilliger, Woo, & Luna, 2010; Klingberg et al., 1999; Mukherjee & McKinstry, 2006). Higher levels of myelinated connectivity between brain regions have been associated with increased blood-oxygen-level-dependent signal during a visuospatial working-memory task (Olesen, Nagy, Westerberg, & Klingberg, 2003) and with better performance on a go/no-go task (Liston et al., 2005), suggesting a relationship between anatomical and functional development.

This pattern of anatomical development is consistent with the evidence that people come to rely on streamlined gist-based thinking, as opposed to elaborate analytical thinking, during childhood and young adulthood (Reyna, 2008). On the one hand, the increased capacity to integrate information is implied by increased white matter connectivity, suggesting that young people should become better able to tie bits of information together in decision making (e.g., integrating reward magnitudes with levels of risk; Geier & Luna, 2009). Indeed, recruitment of the OFC, an integration region that responds to changes in both reward magnitude and probability, has been associated with overall valuation of decision options (Bechara, Damasio, Tranel, & Damasio, 2005).

On the other hand, the capacity for analysis does not imply the tendency to use it, and elaborate analysis is not beneficial in all situations. To the contrary, adults' tendency to rely on the crudest distinctions sufficient in order to complete a task benefits them in most situations (Reyna & Brainerd, 1995). Experiments indicate that adults (unlike adolescents and children) analyze less, not more, when they make accurate decisions (see the summary by Reyna et al., 2003). For instance, adults operate on bottom-line meanings that they have extracted from problem information, getting the right answers, even when they can no longer remember the details of the problem (Brainerd & Reyna, 1993; Fisher & Chandler, 1991; Hastie & Park, 1986; Reyna & Brainerd, 1995).

Adults' cognitive biases, however, have also been attributed to this reliance on crude or streamlined gist (Reyna, 2008). The increased reliance on gist is demonstrated by age differences in cognitive biases (e.g., for a review, see Reyna & Farley, 2006). Even children are able to trade off reward magnitude against probability, avoiding contextual influences such as how the options are framed (e.g., as wins or losses) and instead making decisions that are consistent with multiplicative trading-off of risk and reward (multiplying yields the expected value; e.g., winning $2 with .50 probability is $4 multiplied by .5 = $1; Reyna & Ellis, 1994). It is adults who are "irrational," displaying cognitive biases such as framing effects; for example, adults treat *getting $3 guaranteed, and then losing $2 with .50 probability* very differently from simply *winning $2 with .50 probability*. This age difference is due to an increased reliance on gist-based categorical processing, as opposed to detailed analytical processing, which is adaptive in most real-life contexts (Reyna & Brainerd, 1995; Reyna & Farley, 2006).

The tendency to default to gist-based thinking increases not only with age but also with expertise. For instance, expert physicians make more accurate diagnoses than do medical students, despite processing fewer aspects of information; this is because, over decades of practice, experts learn to "connect the dots" and find a meaningful relationship among the presenting symptoms

(Lloyd & Reyna, 2009). In this case, less is more because experts focus on the most diagnostic symptoms as opposed to giving equal consideration to scores of facts, most of which are irrelevant to the diagnosis. This gist-based processing, which involves forming crude representations and retrieving relevant gist-based principles to apply to those representations, is fundamentally different from the precise, deliberative analysis that many dual process theorists claim to be the pinnacle of rational thought (see Evans, 2008; Reyna & Brainerd, 1995).

In sum, evidence suggests that decreased gray matter and increased myelination contribute to the efficient integration of information from multiple modalities (Geier & Luna, 2009; Giedd, 2004). This synthesis should facilitate the meaning extraction that has been shown to occur during gist-based processing (Reyna, 1996, 2008). *Gist-based processing* involves manipulating information by forming bottom-line representations and retrieving relevant gist-based principles to apply to those representations; this process differs from computational, deliberative analysis. Although gist-based processing generally is adaptive, it contributes to systematic cognitive biases that increase from youth to adulthood. The parsimonious account of this evidence is that adolescents process fewer, higher quality aspects of information as they approach adulthood, a shift in processing that is reflected in a more streamlined, efficient, and interconnected neural network (Casey, Tottenham, Liston, & Durston, 2005; Geier & Luna, 2009; Reyna et al., 2011; Steinberg, 2008).

NEURAL CORRELATES OF THE ADOLESCENT REWARD RESPONSE

Having just described the overarching anatomical and functional changes that occur during adolescence, we now narrow our focus to the development of reward sensitivity, a trait that is relatively stable within individuals but can vary with developmental stage (Romer, 2010; Steinberg, 2008). According to fuzzy trace theory, mental representations of rewards can emphasize the verbatim information (e.g., six cookies, worth 150 calories each), or the gist information (e.g., a dessert, a treat, cheating on a diet). The difference is that verbatim representations are based on literal aspects of the stimulus, such as the objective magnitude, whereas gist representations are based on the interpretation, or appraisal, of the stimulus, which is rooted in contexts such as one's goals and value systems (Ochsner et al., 2009; Rivers et al., 2008). The concept of reappraisal has been important to recent summaries of emotional self-regulation, which show that one's interpretation (i.e., gist) of a situation can be more important to one's emotion and behavior than are objective facts (McRae et al., 2009; Reyna, 2008).

As a result, the developmental shift toward a default of gist-based processing shapes the way people experience rewards and motivation. For example, reward sensitivity is a trait that makes people more motivated to pursue experiences that they find rewarding (e.g., Steinberg, 2008). Although this trait varies among individuals, there are also individual differences in the salience of particular rewards or classes of rewards. For example, some people have a sweet tooth, while others crave salty snacks. An offer of six cookies is more tempting to someone with a sweet tooth, even if that person has the same level of overall reward sensitivity as does someone who finds sweets less attractive. Whatever their level of reward sensitivity and their preference for different classes of rewards, people can sometimes regulate their appetitive response to a stimulus via mental retraining, or cognitive reappraisal (e.g., Ochsner et al., 2009; Reyna, 2008). For example, an overweight person can shift his or her mental representation of cookies from "a reward at the end of a tough day" to "a sugar high that will make me crash later." The ability to flexibly reinterpret the gist of an appetitive stimulus requires a mature system of gist-based processing, which does not fully develop until adulthood, as a function of knowledge and experience (Reyna & Farley, 2006; Rivers et al., 2008). The main factors in reward processing, including traits (e.g., reward sensitivity and inhibition) and cognitive processes (e.g., gist and verbatim), are summarized in Figure 13.1. Keeping in mind the interplay of traits, such as reward sensitivity, and cognitive processes in reward representation, we now summarize the research documenting developmental changes in reward processing.

The literature on reward processing is broadly consistent with the characterization of adolescents as verbatim-based, analytical information processors who trade off reward and risk. Adolescents have been characterized as unduly sensitive to rewards (Galván et al., 2006; Steinberg, Albert, Cauffman, Banich, Graham, & Woolard, 2008; Van Leijenhorst, Moor, et al., 2010), with the consequence of ignoring or underweighting potential negative outcomes associated with such rewards (i.e., evidence suggests they are less sensitive to punishment; Somerville et al., 2010). Naturally, if rewards loom larger for adolescents than for adults, it will seem as though they are ignoring or underweighting negative consequences associated with such rewards; if rewards loom larger than risks, then teens who trade off rewards and risks will make risky choices (Reyna et al., 2011; Reyna & Farley, 2006).

Although many authors posit a general increase in sensitivity to rewards during adolescence (usually measured via monetarily incentivized tasks, e.g., Galván et al., 2006), some specify increased salience of particular classes of rewards, such as social acceptance, during adolescence (e.g., Chein, Albert, O'Brien, Uckert, & Steinberg, 2010; Steinberg et al., 2008). For instance, in a simulated driving task, Gardner and Steinberg (2005) showed that participants who were in the presence of peers took more risks than did those who were alone, an effect that was larger in adolescents and children than in adults.

In contrast to this hyperresponsiveness hypothesis, there is also evidence that in some contexts, adolescents display less reward sensitivity than do adults (e.g., Bjork, Knutson, Fong, et al., 2004; Bjork, Smith, Chen, & Hommer, 2010). This apparent hyporesponsiveness to reward is proposed to drive adolescents toward extreme behaviors, which offer a higher reward but are often risky, in order to derive adequate pleasure from their environments (Spear, 2000). In fact, there is evidence that adolescents recruit the nucleus accumbens (NAcc, a part of the ventral striatum reward system that is rich in dopaminergic neurons; St. Onge, Chiu, & Floresco, 2010; Wahlstrom, Collins, White, & Luciana, 2010; Wahlstrom, White, & Luciana, 2010) to a lesser extent than do adults in some circumstances but to a greater extent in others (see the discussion that follows).

To resolve this discrepancy, multiple authors (Galván, 2010; Geier & Luna, 2009) have suggested that different temporal phases of reward processing, such as anticipation versus outcome notification, elicit different neural activation patterns in adolescents and adults. Table 13.1 summarizes fMRI studies of risk and reward processing in adolescents. As is evident from these studies, the interaction of age with temporal phase of reward is particularly evident in the NAcc. As a whole, the studies in Table 13.1 suggest that adolescents, relative to adults, have demonstrated less activation in the NAcc during the anticipatory period (that between predictive cue and reward onset) but equal or greater activation during the outcome period (that following reward onset).

In addition to the distinction between anticipation and outcome, multiple other factors have been cited to explain seemingly contradictory results, including different age groups, different baseline comparisons or contrasts, and different learning requirements. Galván (2010) provided a thoughtful discussion of these factors, and aspects of each study relevant to these discrepancies are described in Table 13.1. Remaining attentive to these factors, particularly the anticipatory versus outcome distinction, we discuss two points about reward processing. First, the NAcc has been shown to respond monotonically to increases in reward magnitude in both adults and adolescents, but adolescents are especially sensitive to high magnitudes of reward. Similarly, there is behavioral evidence that adolescents shift and become more analytical when rewards increase in magnitude (Reyna & Ellis, 1994; Reyna et al., 2011). Second, children tend to focus more on positive outcomes (e.g., correct feedback, monetary gains), whereas adults tend to focus more on negative outcomes (e.g., error feedback, monetary losses), with adolescents displaying behavior that falls in between.

TABLE 13.1
Imaging Studies of the Adolescent Reward Response

Authors (year)	Task	Subjects	Timeline	Valences	Results
Bjork, Knutson, Fong, Caggiano, Bennett, & Hommer (2004)	MID • Outcome DOP • Subjects earned rewards or avoided losses by responding to targets following cues predicting rewards (circle), losses (square), or neutral (triangle) • 144 trials (54 gain, 54 loss, 36 neutral)	Adolescents • Ages 12–17, $M = 14.75$ • $N = 12$, 6 female Adults • Ages 21–28, $M = 23.78$ • $N = 12$, 6 females	Anticipation Response Feedback • After each trial	Gain Neutral Loss	During anticipatory but not outcome phase, adults vs. adolescents showed significantly greater right NAcc activation vs. baseline for large-magnitude gain vs. nongain trials. Also significant correlation between age and right NAcc activation for anticipation of high-magnitude gains.
Bjork, Knutson, & Hommer (2008)	MID • Outcome DOP • Subjects earned rewards or avoided losses by responding to targets following cues predicting rewards (circle), losses (square), or neutral (triangle) • 72 trials	Adolescent COA • Ages 12–16, $M = 13.8$ • $N = 13$, 5 female Adolescent controls • Ages 12–16, $M = 13.9$ • $N = 13$, 5 female	Anticipation Response Feedback • After each trial	Gain Neutral Loss	Anticipation of gain elicited activation of left NAcc in controls but right NAcc in COA. During outcome phase of loss vs. loss avoidance trials, controls showed greater activation in right anterior insula. Results otherwise similar to Bjork, Knutson, Fong, et al. (2004) and Bjork, Smith, Chen, & Hommer (2010).

(continues)

TABLE 13.1

Imaging Studies of the Adolescent Reward Response *(Continued)*

Authors (year)	Task	Subjects	Timeline	Valences	Results
Bjork, Smith, Chen & Hommer (2010)	MID • Outcome DOP • Subjects earned rewards or avoided losses by responding to targets following cues predicting rewards (circle), losses (square), or neutral (triangle) • 72 trials	Adolescents • Ages 12–17, $M = 14.8$ • $N = 24$, 12 female Adults • Ages 22–42, $M = 29.3$ • $N = 24$, 12 female	Anticipation Response Feedback • After each trial	Gain Neutral Loss	In anticipation of reward vs. non-incentive and of loss avoidance vs. nonincentive, adolescents had less right NAcc activation than did adults. During reward anticipation, age correlated with net signal change (vs. nonincentive anticipation) in right NAcc. During loss avoidance feedback, misses (losses) vs. hits (avoided losses) showed ACC activation in adults but not in adolescents.
Chein, Albert, O'Brien, Uckert, & Steinberg (2010)	Stoplight Driving Game • Outcome DOP • Subjects drove a virtual car; each trial, they approached a stoplight turning from green to yellow to red • Subjects decided to stop (safe) or proceed through intersection (risky) • Subjects made their decisions either alone or with two friends watching the task and communicating via intercom from an adjacent room	Adolescents • Ages 14–18, $M = 15.7$ • $N = 14$, 8 female Young adults • Ages 19–22, $M = 20.6$ • $N = 14$, 7 female Adults • Ages 24–29, $M = 25.6$ • $N = 12$, 6 females	Anticipation Response Feedback • After each trial	Gain Loss	All age groups performed comparably when alone, but only adolescents took significantly more risks in presence of peers. Sensation seeking, but not impulsivity, predicted risk taking in driving task. VS activation in peer condition correlated negatively with self-reported resistance to peer influence. Only adolescents showed increased VS and OFC activation in peer condition (regardless of decision) and during risky (go) vs. safe (stop) decisions (regardless of peer presence). LOFC activation increased with age regardless of peer presence,

Study	Task/Procedure	Participants		Results
	• Subjects won money by reaching their destination as quickly as possible; risk taking (running the yellow light) resulted in either (a) gain: faster arrival and more money or (b) loss: slower arrival and less money • 80 trials			consistent with behavioral results suggesting that inhibition did not drive age differences in peer-present risk behavior.
Cohen, Asarnow, Sabb, et al. (2010)	Probabilistic Learning • Subjects earned rewards by classifying abstract stimuli with a fluctuating base rate • Reward magnitudes ranged from 1–5 gold coins, each worth 5 cents • 144 trials	Children • Ages 8–12, $M = 10.8$ • $N = 18$, 9 female Adolescents • Ages 14–19, $M = 15.8$ • $N = 16$, 6 female Adults • Ages 25–30, $M = 26.5$ • $N = 11$, 4 female	Response Feedback • After each trial	Gain	Adolescents, but not adults, responded more quickly to large rewards than to small rewards (i.e., adolescents were more behaviorally sensitive to reward magnitude). In the striatum and angular gyrus, activation following positive vs. negative feedback (reward-prediction error) peaked in adolescence. In the medial OFC, activation associated with stimulus onset (probabilistic classification and association of stimulus with reward magnitude) decreased linearly with age.

(continues)

TABLE 13.1

Imaging Studies of the Adolescent Reward Response   *(Continued)*

Authors (year)	Task	Subjects	Timeline	Valences	Results
Crone & van der Molen (2007)	Hungry Donkey Task • Outcome DOP • Modalities: ECG, skin conductance, respiration • Subjects were told to help the hungry donkey by opening the door (A, B, C, or D) they thought concealed the most apples • 2 high-reward doors (4 apples: A & B) • 2 low-reward doors (2 apples: C & D) • 2 frequent-punishment doors (50%: A & C) • 2 infrequent-punishment doors (10%: B & D) • 100 trials	Children • Ages 8–10, $M = 9.5$ • $N = 22$, 12 female Early Adolescents • Ages 12–14, $M = 13.3$ • $N = 29$, 15 female Late adolescents • Ages 16–18, $M = 17.3$ • $N = 30$, 23 female	Response Feedback • After each trial (amount won during trial)	Gain Loss	Overall, age differences in skin conductance level were present during anticipation of response but not during performance feedback. Skin conductance level preceding response was not significantly different from baseline in 8–10- or 12–14-year olds. However, in 16–18-year-olds, skin conductance level increased preceding choices that could result in frequent (but lower magnitude) as opposed to infrequent (but higher magnitude) punishment. There were no significant age group differences in skin conductance or heart rate during performance feedback. In all age groups, skin conductance level was higher after loss feedback than after gain feedback, but only when the loss followed a disadvantageous choice and occurred on a trial with infrequent but higher magnitude punishment. In all age groups, heart rate slowed more after loss than after reward.

Ernst, Nelson, Jazbec, et al. (2005)	Wheel of Fortune • Gambling • Outcome DOP • Colored pie charts depicted 50–50 odds of high reward ($4) or low reward (50 cents) vs. zero reward • Subjects guessed which color the computer would randomly select • Outcome DOP • 54 trials: 18 high-reward, 18 low-reward, and 18 monochromatic control	Adolescents • Ages 17–19, $M = 13.3$ • $N = 16$, 9 females Adults • Ages 20–40, $M = 26.7$ • $N = 14$, 6 females	Response Feedback • After each trial	Gain Gain Omission	Adults, but not adolescents, showed significantly greater amygdala activation for reward omission vs. reward receipt trials. Adolescents, but not adults, showed significantly more activation in left NAcc for reward receipt vs. reward omission. Adults discriminated between win (gain) and no-win (gain omission) in the amygdala, whereas adolescents discriminated in the NAcc. Further, amygdala was more sensitive to reward omission than to reward receipt in adults (but not adolescents), whereas NAcc was more sensitive to reward receipt than to reward omission in adolescents (but not adults).
Eshel, Nelson, Blair, Pine, & Ernst (2006)	Wheel of Fortune • Gambling • Outcome DOP • High risk, high reward: 10:90 (win $4 or win nothing) vs. 90:10 (win 50 cents or win nothing) • Low risk, low reward: 30:70 (win $2 or win nothing) vs. 70:30 (win $1 or win nothing)	Adolescents • Ages 17–19, means not reported (same sample as Ernst et al., 2005) • $N = 16$, genders not reported Adults • Ages 20–40, means not reported	Response Feedback • After each trial (amount won during trial)	Gain Gain Omission	Adults, compared with adolescents, showed greater OFC, VLPFC, and dACC activation when making risky vs. safe monetary choices. Both overall and within the adolescent group, less activation in OFC, VLPFC, and dACC correlated with higher percentage of risky choices.

(continues)

TABLE 13.1
Imaging Studies of the Adolescent Reward Response (Continued)

Authors (year)	Task	Subjects	Timeline	Valences	Results
	• 75 trials: 25 high-risk/reward, 25 low risk/reward, and 25 monochromatic control trials	• $N = 18$, genders not reported			
Galván, Hare, Parra, et al. (2006)	Pirate task • MID • Rule learning • Outcome DOP • 3 cues (pirate cartoons) associated with distinct reward levels (low, medium, high) of unspecified magnitudes • One pirate at a time appeared on left or right side of screen • Subjects indicated whether previous pirate had appeared on left or right side of screen • 90 trials	Children • Ages 7–11, $M = 9.8$ • $N = 16$, 7 female Adolescents • Ages 13–17, $M = 16$ • $N = 13$, 6 female Adults • Ages 23–29, $M = 25$ • $N = 12$, 6 female	Anticipation Response Feedback • After each trial	Gain Gain Omission	Subjects were not warned that each pirate had a characteristic reward level, but reaction times were faster for high-reward pirates, indicating subjects learned the pattern. For reward trials (collapsing across anticipation, response, and outcome phases) compared with baseline fixation cross, magnitude of activation (% MR signal change) in NAcc showed peak in adolescence; magnitude of activation in the OFC showed a linear decrease with age. Extent of activation (number of interpolated voxels) in both NAcc and OFC showed linear decrease with age (i.e., activation is more diffuse in younger participants and becomes more focal with age).

Galván, Hare, Voss, Glover, & Casey (2007)	Pirate task • MID • Rule learning • Outcome DOP • 3 cues (pirate cartoons) associated with distinct reward levels (low, medium, high) of unspecified magnitudes • One pirate at a time appeared on left or right side of screen • Subjects indicated whether previous pirate had appeared on left or right side of screen • 90 trials	Children • Ages 7–11, M = 9.8 • N = 16, 7 female Adolescents • Ages 13–17, M = 16 • N = 13, 6 female adults • Ages 23–29, M = 25 • N = 12, 6 female • Same sample as Galván et al. (2006)	Anticipation Response Feedback • After each trial	Gain Gain Omission	Used Cognitive Appraisal of Risk Activities to assess likelihood of engaging in risky behaviors in next 6 months as well as perceived positive and negative consequences of those risky behaviors. Within-group for adolescents and adults, NAcc activation during reward trials (collapsing across anticipation, response, and outcome phases) vs. baseline fixation cross correlated positively with intentions to engage in risky behavior within 6 months. NAcc activation during reward trials also correlated positively with rating of positive consequences and negatively with rating of negative consequences.
Geier, Terwilliger, Teslovich, Velanova & Luna (2010)	Antisaccade • MID • Outcome DOP • Following a cue indicating whether money could be won on the following trial, subjects were instructed to look away from a yellow dot which appeared at an unpredictable location • 112 trials	Adolescents • Ages 13–17, M = 15.3 • N = 18, 8 female Adults • Ages 18–30, M = 21.7 • N = 16, 10 female	Anticipation Response	Gain Gain Omission Neutral	Adolescents, compared with adults, showed decreased VS activation during incentive cue, but increased activation in VS and control regions while anticipating reward response (saccade inhibition). Adolescents showed reduced recruitment of areas responsible for saccade inhibition in nonreward trials, suggesting that incentives can enhance inhibitory capacity in some cases (e.g., short delay to reward).

(continues)

A FUZZY TRACE THEORY OF ADOLESCENT RISK TAKING   395

TABLE 13.1
Imaging Studies of the Adolescent Reward Response (Continued)

Authors (year)	Task	Subjects	Timeline	Valences	Results
Hare, Tottenham, Galván, Voss, Glover, & Casey (2008)	Emotional go/no-go • Outcome DOP • Subjects viewed successive happy, fearful, or calm faces from 12 individuals, 6 female • Two emotions were featured at a time, one of which (the target) subjects responded to by pressing a button, the other of which required withholding a prepotent response • Targets occurred on 75% of trials • 288 trials	Children • Ages 7–12, $M = 9.1$ • $N = 12$, 5 female Adolescents • Ages 13–18, $M = 16$ • $N = 24$, 10 female Adults • Ages 19–32, $M = 23.9$ • $N = 24$, 14 female	Response	Happy Fearful Calm	Compared with children and adults, adolescents showed a surge in amygdala activation during emotional go/no-go. Subjects higher in trait anxiety showed less amygdala habituation over repeated trials and less functional connectivity between ventral PFC and amygdala. Amygdala habituation was less for fearful than for happy targets in anxious adolescents but not in less anxious adolescents or in adults.
May, Delgado, Dahl, et al. (2004)	Hidden Number Guessing • Outcome DOP • Subjects guessed whether random hidden number < or > 5 • Numbers ranged from 1 to 9 • 2:1 ratio of wins ($1) to losses (50 cents) • 135 trials	Children & adolescents • Ages 9–16, $M = 13.5$ • $N = 12$, 7 female	Response Feedback • After each trial	Gain Gain Omission Neutral Loss	Results did not vary significantly by age. The VS, lateral and medial OFC, ACC, and middle temporal gyrus showed responses that depended on valence (reward vs. loss vs. neutral) and on time course following feedback. The VS showed an earlier peak and more sustained response to reward feedback than to loss feedback. OFC showed a late and transient peak following

Van den Bos, Guroglu, van den Bulk, Rombouts, & Crone (2009)	Probabilistic Learning • Trial-and-error • Outcome DOP • Subjects won rewards or avoided losses by selecting one stimulus from a pair • 2 types of stimulus pairs: AB (A, 80% chance to win; B, 20% chance to win) or CD (C, 70% chance to win; D, 30% chance to win) • A and C were always most advantageous, and left-right order within each pair was randomized • 200 trials	Children • Ages 8–11, no mean reported • N = 18, 9 female Adolescents • Ages 13–16 • N = 27, 13 female Adults • Ages 18–22 • N = 22, 13 female	Response Feedback • After each trial	Gain Neutral Loss	reward feedback but little change during loss feedback. ACC activation was stronger and later for reward than for loss feedback. Middle temporal gyrus showed sustained activation to reward and sustained deactivation to loss. Adults showed more DLPFC, parietal, and ACC activation after negative feedback; children, after positive feedback. This occurred only when subjects chose the less advantageous option (i.e., B or D). The adolescent response was intermediate, resembling children in positive feedback response but resembling adults in negative feedback response.

(continues)

TABLE 13.1

Imaging Studies of the Adolescent Reward Response *(Continued)*

Authors (year)	Task	Subjects	Timeline	Valences	Results
Van Duijvenvoorde, Zanolie, Rombouts, Raijmakers, & Crone (2008)	Rule selection and application • Rule learning • Decision making • Outcome DOP • Subjects selected target from a pair of objects based on prior notification of relevant rule set (color or shape) and feedback from previous trial • 400 trials	Children • Ages 8–9, $M = 8.6$ • $N = 18$, 8 female Early adolescents • Ages 11–13, $M = 11.7$ • $N = 19$, 8 female Adults • Ages 18–25, $M = 22.3$ • $N = 18$, 11 female	Response Feedback • After each trial	Gain Gain Omission Loss	Adults, who were more behaviorally responsive to negative feedback, showed increased DLPFC and superior parietal cortex activation to negative feedback. Children, who were more behaviorally responsive to positive feedback, showed increased DLPFC and superior parietal cortex activation after positive feedback. Young adolescents showed an intermediate pattern. Both adolescents and adults, but not children, showed increased activation in supplementary motor area and ACC following negative feedback.
Van Leijenhorst, Crone, & Bunge (2006)	Cake Gambling • Child-friendly version of Cambridge Gambling Task • Outcome DOP • Subjects earned rewards or avoided losses by guessing which flavor (chocolate or strawberry) the computer would randomly select	Children • Ages 9–12, $M = 11.3$ • $N = 12$, 7 female Adults • Ages 18–26, $M = 21.5$ • $N = 14$, 9 female	Response Feedback • After each trial	Gain Loss	Both age groups showed increased DLPFC and OFC activation during high-risk conditions in the high-risk condition compared with the low-risk condition. Children, but not adults, also showed more activation in medial PFC and ACC during decisions in the high-risk (vs. low-risk) condition. For negative (vs. positive) feedback, both age groups showed increased medial PFC, VLPFC, and LOFC activation. Children had more LOFC activation during negative feedback than did adults.

| Van Leijenhorst, Moor, de Macks, et al. (2010) | • Odds signified by a cake with 9 slices of chocolate and strawberry in various ratios
• Probability varied from high risk (3:6 or 4:5) to low risk (1:8 or 2:7)
• Reward remained constant (1 point for correct guess, −1 point for incorrect guess)
• 162 trials
Cake Gambling
• Child-friendly version of Cambridge Gambling Task
• Outcome DOP
• Ss earned rewards or avoided losses by guessing which flavor (chocolate or strawberry) the computer would randomly select
• Odds signified by a cake with 6 slices of chocolate and strawberry in 4:2 ratio
• Low-risk gamble (4:2) worth 1 euro
• High-risk gamble (2:4) worth 2, 4, 6 or 8 euro
• 84 trials | Children
• Ages 8–10, M = 9.7
• N = 13, 7 female
Early Adolescents
• Ages 12–14, M = 13.4
• N = 15, 8 female
Late Adolescents
• Ages 16–17, M = 17.1
• N = 15, 7 female
Adults
• Ages 19–26, M = 21.6
• N = 15, 7 female | Response Feedback
• After each trial | Gain Loss | Across age groups, high-risk choices resulted in VMPFC activation, and low-risk choices resulted in lateral PFC activation. dACC activation for high risk vs. low risk choices decreased linearly with age. For gain vs. non-gain outcomes following high-risk choices, VMPFC and VS activation peaked in adolescence. |

(continues)

TABLE 13.1

Imaging Studies of the Adolescent Reward Response   *(Continued)*

Authors (year)	Task	Subjects	Timeline	Valences	Results
Van Leijenhorst, Zanolie, van Meel, et al. (2010)	Slot Machine • Outcome DOP • Subjects viewed 3 side-by-side slot machines, which they activated by pressing a button. Pictures of fruit appeared consecutively in 3 possible orders: XYZ, XXY, XXX • Subjects earned 0.05 euro for XXX, zero for the other two orders, and lost 0.1 euro if they failed to press the button • 120 trials	Children • Ages 10–12, M = 11.6 • N = 17, 8 female Adolescents • Ages 14–15, M = 15.0 • N = 18, 10 female Adults • Ages 18–23, M = 20.2 • N = 15, 7 female	Anticipation Feedback • After each trial	Gain Gain Omission Loss	While awaiting an uncertain reward outcome, adolescents showed more anterior insula activation than did young adults. Following notification of reward, VS activation peaked in middle adolescence, compared with young adolescence or young adulthood. Following notification of reward omission, young adults, but not adolescents, showed increased OFC activation.

Note. ACC = anterior cingulate cortex; dACC = dorsal anterior cingulate cortex; DLPFC = dorsolateral prefrontal cortex; DOP = dependent on performance; COA = children of alcoholics; ECG = electrocardiograhy; LOFC = lateral orbitofrontal cortex; MID = monetary incentive delay; MR = magnetic resonance; NAcc = nucleus accumbens; OFC= orbitofrontal cortex; PFC = prefrontal cortex; VMPFC = ventromedial prefrontal cortex; VS = ventral striatum.

The proportional response of the NAcc to increasing monetary rewards has been demonstrated in several tasks, most of which require little skill or learning from participants. For instance, Bjork et al. (2004) used a task in which, by responding to predictive cues, subjects could earn rewards or avoid losses of prespecified magnitudes. They found that, whereas adults and adolescents showed little difference in NAcc activation during notification of gain outcomes, activation in the NAcc during anticipation of responding for $5 gains correlated with both age and ratings of excitement about the $5 gain. Adults showed more activation in the NAcc during anticipation of responding for potential gains than did adolescents.

Bjork and colleagues (2010) did a follow-up study in which they made each trial longer to better detect differences in response to the anticipatory versus the outcome phases. When anticipating responding for reward versus nonincentive trials, adults showed more right NAcc activation than did adolescents, although both groups' NAcc activation was proportional to the magnitude of reward at stake. This result replicated the 2004 study. However, in contrast to the 2004 study, during the outcome phase, adolescents showed more NAcc activation in response to successful outcomes (rewards and avoided losses, compared with losses and rewards that were missed out on) than did adults. Although both groups showed NAcc activation proportional to reward magnitude in the outcome phase, the interaction of outcome with magnitude was higher in adolescents than in adults. Taken together, these two studies by the Bjork group (2004, 2010) suggest that the NAcc is more active in adults than in adolescents during anticipation of responding, but it is more active in adolescents than in adults during notification of reward outcomes, especially for high-magnitude rewards during the outcome phase.

Galván et al. (2006) used a task similar to the one used by Bjork et al. (2004, 2010), in which distinct predictive cues (pirate cartoons) were associated with different magnitudes of reward. During anticipation of responding following cues associated with the highest magnitude reward, adults showed higher NAcc activation than did adolescents. However, after entering their response in high-magnitude reward trials, adolescents showed higher NAcc activation than did adults. During this high-magnitude outcome period, both adolescents and adults showed a proportional increase in NAcc activation with increasing reward magnitude, reflected in faster reaction times as a function of reward magnitude in adults and adolescents but not children. However, adolescents showed improvement in reaction times only in the highest magnitude trials.

Thus, the study by Galván et al. (2006) lends additional support to the findings by Bjork et al. (2004, 2010) of a proportional response to reward magnitude in the NAcc. In addition, like Bjork et al. (2010), Galván et al. (2006) showed that adolescents' outcome-related increase in NAcc activation, relative to adults, occurred only in the highest magnitude reward trials. Adolescents appear to be hypersensitive to rewards only during the outcome phase, and only when the magnitude of the reward is high. In all three studies, however, adults relative to adolescents showed higher NAcc activation during anticipation of responding for potential rewards, demonstrating that adolescents, relative to adults, can be either hypo- or hyperresponsive to rewards, depending on the time phase of the trial and the magnitude of the reward. In the next section, we further refine the characterization of developmental differences in the reward response by discussing tasks involving varying probabilities.

VALUATION: NEURAL CORRELATES OF THE RISK–REWARD TRADEOFF IN ADOLESCENCE

The process of valuation requires integrating information about both the magnitude of the potential reward and the probability of obtaining it (i.e., the risk). Like reward processing, processing of risky information can emphasize verbatim or gist processing. For example, imagine an adolescent asked whether he or she would play Russian roulette to win $6 million (in Russian roulette, players load one bullet into the chamber of a gun, spin the chamber, and fire the gun at their own head; if players survive, they win the money). In a game in which the gun contained six chambers and the prize was $6 million, the expected value of the gamble would be the chance of winning (5/6) multiplied by the reward ($6 million), for an expected value of $5 million. On the one hand, accepting this risk (playing the game) is "rational" in the sense that it has a positive expected value. On the other hand, most adults would insist that the game is intuitively irrational—it is not worth risking one's life, no matter how large the prize. In other words, the meaningful interpretation of this game leads to conclusions very different from those of the "rational" calculation of expected value (Reyna, Adam, Poirier, LeCroy, & Brainerd, 2005). This is an example of the difference between risk-related decisions that are based on verbatim traces (which can account for all of the information yet miss the point) and those based on gist traces (which rely on intuitive interpretations, rather than rote calculations). Without the ability to form a gist representation of a risky scenario, adolescents are in the vulnerable position of knowing the price of everything and the value of nothing.

We have mentioned evidence that verbatim analysis predicts real-life risk taking (Mills et al., 2008; Reyna et al., 2011) and that people shift away from verbatim and toward gist-based thinking as they gain experience with a task or situation (Reyna & Ellis, 1994; Reyna, 2008). The way in which experience contributes to a valenced knowledge store is exemplified in the Iowa

Gambling Task, which has been used (sometimes with adaptations) to assess risk behavior in developmental and clinical populations (Bechara et al., 2005). In this task, through the process of drawing cards from multiple decks with varying payoffs, subjects come to learn which decks are "good" and which ones are "bad," that is, which ones have higher versus lower payoff in the long run. In the beginning stages of the task, when subjects have drawn few cards, there are not enough data to form strong valenced associations with particular decks. As the task progresses, however, subjects amass experience with each deck and learn to make more advantageous decisions based on their cumulative impressions of each deck as "good/bad" or "better/worse."

One might compare adolescence to the period when subjects first begin drawing cards; since adolescents lack experience with many risky decisions, they lack intuition about whether to engage in an activity or to steer clear of it (Reyna & Farley, 2006; Rivers et al., 2008). Worse yet, if an adolescent's limited experience happens to include mostly instances in which no negative outcome occurred, they might generalize from these limited data an impression that the risk associated with that activity is low (whereas there is some evidence that people become risk averse as they gain experience with a particular type of risk; Shiv, Loewenstein, & Bechara, 2005).

Using a modified version of the Iowa Gambling Task (in which participants could opt in or out of each round as opposed to making a forced choice), Cauffman et al. (2010) found that the rate of learning to play increasingly from the advantageous decks over multiple trials peaked in adolescence, whereas the rate of learning to avoid the disadvantageous decks increased linearly with age. Performance on the Iowa Gambling Task in adults has been associated with structural integrity and activation of the ventromedial prefrontal cortex (VMPFC; Bechara et al., 2005; Li, Lu, D'Argembeau, Ng, & Bechara, 2010). The importance of the VMPFC to performance on the Iowa Gambling Task, which requires integration of information about both reward and risk, is consistent with a growing body of evidence that the medial PFC and OFC are central to the process of valuation as the product of magnitude and probability (Rangel & Hare, 2010).

In this section, we have discussed developmental differences in performance and NAcc activation in simple reward tasks. We now add to this discussion by incorporating evidence from tasks in which rewards are delivered on a probabilistic schedule. In tasks involving learning and uncertainty, the NAcc still plays a central role in reward processing, but regions implicated in valuation, such as the medial PFC and OFC, also come into play. To preview, it is clear that many neuroscience researchers studying valuation assume the validity of some form of verbatim-based analytical process of trading off reward and risk, consistent with traditional theories. Therefore, they have not manipulated factors that would necessarily implicate gist as opposed to verbatim processing. Nevertheless, many results, especially developmental differences, cannot be explained without going beyond traditional theories.

For instance, Van Leijenhorst, Zanolie, van Meel, Westenberg, Rombouts, and Crone (2010) used a slot machine task in which subjects used a button press to start each trial and then passively viewed the outcome (three fruits revealed in succession). Only trials in which all three fruits were the same (XXX) resulted in reward. After the second fruit, trials in which there was still a chance to win (XX trials, in which there would be a reward if the third fruit was also an X), compared with trials in which there would be no reward (XY trials), resulted in ventral striatum activation only in the younger two age groups (10–12- and 14–15-year-olds). After the third fruit was revealed, reward trials (XXX) compared with nonreward trials (XYZ) elicited ventral striatum activation only in the adolescent group (14–15-year-olds), results that further emphasized the pattern of increased adolescent response to reward during the outcome phase of trials.

In another task involving uncertainty but not learning, Ernst et al. (2005) used a Wheel of Fortune task in which a pie chart was divided into two colors of equal proportions; subjects guessed which color the computer would randomly select for a reward of either 50 cents or $4. Adolescents, but not adults, showed a correlation between NAcc activation and self-reported happiness following $4 wins compared with 50-cent wins, further evidence that adolescents are particularly sensitive to high-magnitude rewards and that this sensitivity is reflected in NAcc activation during the outcome phase of the task.

Eshel, Nelson, Blair, Pine, and Ernst (2007) used the same task and sample as did Ernst et al. (2005), but they analyzed trials in which the chances of winning were either 90/10 or 70/30. For example, in the higher risk condition, subjects chose which bet they wanted to make: a 10% chance of winning $4 and a 90% chance of winning nothing, or a 90% chance of winning 50 cents and a 10% chance of winning nothing. In the low-risk condition, subjects chose between a 30% chance of winning $2 and a 70% chance of winning nothing, or a 70% chance of winning $1 and a 30% chance of winning nothing. Thus, in both the 90/10 and 70/30 wheel conditions, the riskier option was associated with slightly lower expected value. Adolescents chose the risky option more often than did adults, consistent with the prediction that, although adolescents might roughly calculate expected value, they are more sensitive to reward magnitudes than to risks (e.g., Casey et al., 2008; Reyna & Ellis, 1994; Reyna et al., 2011).

In addition, for adolescents and adults, each participant's total number of risky choices correlated negatively with activation in the OFC/VLPFC (BA 47) during risky compared with safe choices, consistent with the idea that VLPFC could be related to inhibition but raising questions about OFC. This OFC finding is somewhat surprising, given the prediction that medial

PFC and OFC underlie valuation calculations (e.g., see De Martino, Kumaran, Seymour, & Dolan (2006). However, Eshel et al. (2007) reported that because of scanner artifact, signal dropout in the OFC (BA 11) made this region impossible to analyze. Therefore, although the task was well suited for commentary on the valuation process, we cannot draw firm conclusions from this study about developmental differences in valuation regions.

The NAcc and medial PFC are also important in more complicated valuation tasks, such as those requiring learning. Cohen et al. (2010) used a probabilistic learning task in which subjects were told that abstract designs (generated by a computer) were worn on T-shirts by college students and that each abstract design was usually, but not always, associated with a particular college. There were six abstract designs; two were associated with Eastern University 83% of the time, two were associated with Northern University 83% of the time, and two were randomly associated with each university 50% of the time. Three of the abstract designs (one of each type: 83% Eastern, 83% Northern, and random) always earned subjects five gold coins, and the other three always earned one gold coin.

In this study by Cohen et al. (2010), adolescents, but not children or adults, responded more quickly to stimuli associated with larger rewards, reinforcing the evidence of adolescents' preferential attention to high-magnitude rewards. In response to surprise rewards (i.e., positive prediction error), there was a peak in ventral striatum activation in adolescence, in line with the findings previously discussed in which adolescents show hyperreactivity to rewards during the outcome phase. There was also a negative correlation in the medial PFC between age and expected value at stimulus onset (see Rangel & Hare, 2010). If valuation consists of multiplying expected magnitude times the probability of reward, then, based on the decrease in magnitude sensitivity from adolescence to adulthood (e.g., in the NAcc), we would also expect decreased activation in adults compared with adolescents in regions associated with valuation. The results reported by Cohen et al. (2010) confirm this prediction and are also consistent with less verbatim analytical, and more gist-based, processing with age (Reyna et al., 2011).

For further evidence on the role of the medial PFC in risky decision making, Van Leijenhorst, Moor, et al. (2010) used a task that was adapted for children based on the Iowa Gambling Task. In the Cake Gambling Task, participants saw a cake divided into six slices, four magenta and two blue. Although the probabilities were the same on each trial, the magnitudes of the potential rewards varied. The low-risk option was always worth 1 euro, but the high-risk option was worth either 2, 4, 6, or 8 euros. In the most ambiguous condition (the 2-euro condition, in which the expected value of both options was equal), adolescents chose the risky option more often than did adults, consistent with other evidence of a decrease in risk preference with age (Eshel et al., 2007; Reyna & Farley, 2006). However, all participants took more risks in trials in which more money was at stake (i.e., 4- or 8-euro, in which the options had unequal expected value). This is in line with the fuzzy trace theory assumption that both adults and adolescents process both gist and verbatim traces in parallel. Although adults default to gist, they also have access to the verbatim information and can apply it when the gist and verbatim conclusions conflict (Levin, Weller, Pederson, & Harshman, 2007; Reyna & Brainerd, 1995).

In the higher reward trials (those with unequal expected value), although all participants made riskier choices, there was an age-related peak in adolescence in OFC activation for higher risk compared with lower risk choices. In addition, across age groups, people who took more risks overall showed more VMPFC activation during higher risk than lower risk choices. However, people who took fewer risks overall showed lateral OFC and ACC activation during higher risk compared with lower risk choices. This might explain the finding by Eshel et al. (2007) that people who took fewer risks overall showed higher VLPFC activation during risky compared with safe choices (because VLPFC activation is associated with inhibition; Figner et al., 2010). The combined findings of Eshel et al. (2007), Van Leijenhorst, Moor et al. (2010), and others suggest that VLPFC activation may be associated with a decreased preference for risk taking, whereas activation in the ventral medial PFC and medial OFC may be central to valuation and, hence, risk taking driven by magnitude sensitivity. This pattern of findings is consistent with the assumption by fuzzy trace theory, and other developmental theories, that inhibition ability increases with age (Reyna & Rivers, 2008). In addition to reward and risk processing, which is modulated by inhibition, emotion is often cited as a major influence in adolescent behavior, so we now turn to a discussion of the role of emotion in cognition.

THE ROLE OF EMOTION IN RISK TAKING: VALENCE, AROUSAL, AND MEMORY-BASED COGNITION

How Emotions Influence Mental Representation

Much of the neuroimaging literature assumes that adolescent risk taking results from a failure to inhibit emotional impulses (Chein et al., 2010; Dosenbach, Fair, Cohen, Schlaggar, & Petersen, 2008; Somerville et al., 2010; Steinberg, 2008). According to this paradigm, emotion is counterproductive to healthy decisions about risk taking. Fuzzy trace theory takes a more nuanced view of the role of emotion in decision making. According to fuzzy trace theory, emotion is one of many variables that affect gist-based processing at the level of encoding, retrieval, or implementation. Research suggests that the presence of an emotion does not simply make risk taking more or less likely; rather, it affects the process by which a choice is made (Finucone, Peters, & Slovic, 2003; Rivers et al., 2008).

The role of emotion in decision making highlights a key difference between fuzzy trace theory and other dual process models. There are multiple variations on the standard dual process model, but most make the distinction between a fast, automatic, unconscious way of processing information (called System 1 because it is assumed to be ontogenetically and phylogenetically prior or primitive) and a slow, deliberative, conscious, and advanced way of processing (called System 2; Stanovich, 2004; for a helpful review, see Evans, 2008). These categories have also been called impulsive versus reflective (Strack & Deutsch, 2004), reflexive versus reflective (Lieberman, Gaunt, Gilbert, & Trope, 2002), holistic versus analytic (Nisbett, Peng, Choi, & Norenzayan, 2001), heuristic versus analytic (Evans, 2006), and experiential versus rational (Epstein, 1994).

In standard dual process theories, emotion is essentially synonymous with System 1 thinking; it has no role in the more advanced System 2 thinking. As a result, such theories assume that the influence of emotion on decision making is always primitive and usually maladaptive (e.g., when it differs from the conclusion of the analytical System 2; Evans, 2010). In stark contrast, fuzzy trace theory distinguishes emotion from intuition, integrating aspects of emotion into the most advanced form of thinking (i.e., gist-based intuition). Multiple terms are used interchangeably in the literature, but in summarizing the data, we distinguish among the effects of valence, mood states, and arousal.

Valence, a simple and categorical evaluation such as "good/bad" or "approach/avoid," is an essential component of gist. Valenced knowledge contributes to representations of choices; for example, people often go no further than a valence-driven impression to determine whether a choice is risky or safe (Alhakami & Slovic, 1994). This process was well described by Slovic, Peters, Finucane, and MacGregor (2005), who called it consulting the "affect pool" (p. S36). Recall that according to fuzzy trace theory, individuals default to a fuzzy processing preference; thus, unless cued to process information in greater detail, they often operate on such basic characterizations as the categorical "good/bad" and the ordinal "better/worse" (Rivers et al., 2008). According to fuzzy trace theory, among mature decision makers, valence is not simple-minded but is, rather, the product of experience and of the insight that experience brings.

Whereas valence is a property associated with a stimulus, feeling states (or moods) are similarly categorical properties of the individual's internal context that may affect either the content of an encoding or its degree of specificity (Rivers et al., 2008). Moods are well studied; for example, mood congruency research has demonstrated that individuals sometimes use the way they feel to inform their interpretation of a stimulus, even when their feelings are unrelated to the stimulus (Weber & Johnson, 2009). This is especially likely to occur when the stimulus is ambiguous (Schwartz & Clore, 1996). In addition to shaping the impression of a stimulus, mood can influence the degree of specificity with which the impression is encoded (e.g., verbatim, ordinal, categorical; see Rivers et al., 2008). In particular, negative feeling states and dispositions encourage detailed, calculative (verbatim-based) representations of options, whereas positive feeling states and dispositions tend to co-occur with global, relational, flexible, and efficient (gist-based) processing (Fredrickson & Branigan, 2005; Storbeck & Clore, 2005).

Arousal, or physiological activation, is a third aspect of emotion that influences decision making. Arousal seems to facilitate memory for the gist of negatively valenced emotional stimuli, such as pictures of car crashes (Adolphs, Denburg, & Tranel, 2001). Negative emotional arousal has also been shown to facilitate memory for details of the stimulus that are relevant to the emotionally arousing gist (Kensinger, Garoff-Eaton, & Schacter, 2006, 2007). In the above studies by Adolphs, Kensinger, and their colleagues, negative emotional arousal appeared either to have no effect on peripheral details or to reduce memory for them. In addition, damage to the amygdala reduced the enhancement of gist and the neglect of peripheral details, suggesting the importance of the amygdala in mediating the encoding of gist memories for negatively arousing stimuli (Adolphs, Tranel, & Buchanan, 2005).

In these various ways, multiple facets of emotion interact with impressionistic processing and, according to the fuzzy trace theory account, are implicated in gist-based intuition. For example, valence (judging something as good or bad) can be the product of gist thinking, high arousal can disrupt verbatim thinking (which it is sensitive to interference of any kind), and discrete emotions (e.g., anger, fear, or sadness) can color gist-based interpretations of events (Rivers et al., 2008). However, emotion (defined as valence, arousal, mood or discrete emotion) is distinct from gist-based mental representations. The distinction between intuitive thinking and emotional states is a core difference between the gist-based version of intuition posited by fuzzy trace theory and the System 1 version of intuition posited by standard dual process theories. In fuzzy trace theory, intuition (as gist) is the most advanced form of thinking, whereas, in standard dual process theories, intuition (as System 1) is the most primitive.

Arousal, Valence, and Learning in the Neurobiology of Risk Taking

Different aspects of emotion have been implicated in neuroimaging studies of adolescent risk taking. For instance, the desire for social acceptance is often cited as an emotional factor that sways adolescents toward risky behavior (Steinberg, 2008), and adolescents, compared with children and adults, have been found to be disproportionately influenced toward risk taking in a simulated driving task when in the presence of peers (Gardner & Steinberg, 2005). Some have hypothesized that the presence of peers affects risky decision making by increasing arousal (Van Leijenhorst, Moor et al., 2010). In another study from the Steinberg laboratory, Chein et al. (2010) replicated the behavioral effect found by Gardner and Steinberg (2005). In addition, adolescents showed increased OFC and ventral striatum activation during trials when peers were present relative to trials performed alone, and activation in these regions predicted risk taking. This study underscores the interpretation that adolescents process peer acceptance as a reward.

Valence has also emerged as an important factor in distinguishing adolescent from adult reward processing. This seems to be particularly true in valuation tasks that require learning. For example, the task used by Van Duijenvoorde et al. (2008) required concept learning based on rule sets that changed after each consecutive pair of trials. In each trial, subjects viewed a pair of objects that differed on two dimensions: color and shape (e.g., a blue fish and a red truck). A cue preceding the pair of objects signaled which dimension (e.g., color) defined the rule set for that trial. However, subjects had to learn by trial-and-error which value of the dimension (e.g., blue or red) was the correct rule for each pair of trials. The first trial in each pair was labeled a *guess* trial because, although subjects knew which rule set to use (e.g., color), they did not yet know which rule within the set (e.g., red) to apply. Based on feedback from the guess trial, subjects had all the information necessary to choose the correct object in the *repetition* trial, which immediately followed the guess trial. For example, if the rule set was shape, and the guess trial stimuli were a blue fish and a red truck, a subject might arbitrarily pick the truck. If the feedback indicated that the choice was incorrect, the subject would know to choose the fish on the next trial. A new rule set was established after each pair of guess and repetition trials; no information was carried over from one pair of trials to another.

Learning, defined as the improvement from guess to repetition within each pair of trials, increased linearly with age. However, the age groups showed different sensitivity to positive versus negative feedback. In particular, all subjects showed slower reaction times and decreased accuracy for negative compared with positive feedback, but this effect was largest in children. Negative feedback elicited activation in the DLPFC and superior cortex in adults; it also elicited activation in the presupplementary motor area/ACC in both adults in adolescents. Whereas adults showed DLPFC and superior parietal activation in response to negative feedback, children interestingly showed activation in these same regions in response to positive feedback. Thus, children may rely on positive feedback, perhaps overrelying on it, whereas adults may be better able to incorporate both positive and negative feedback in order to calibrate performance (and inhibit responses). Adolescents show intermediate patterns of behavior and brain activation. In sum, it appears that the DLPFC and superior parietal cortex were active during goal-related concept learning, and the fact that these areas were active for opposite contrasts in children and adults could reflect differential reliance on positively versus negatively valenced information in the two age groups.

Whereas the task used by Van Duijvenvoorde et al. (2008) required concept learning over the course of a pair of trials, that used by Van den Bos, Guroglu, Van den Bulk, Rombouts, & Crone (2009) required probabilistic learning that continued over the entire experiment. Van den Bos et al. (2009) presented subjects with a pair of objects, one of which was always more likely to yield a reward. In one type of pair (AB), stimuli from category A resulted in rewards 80% of the time and were always paired with stimuli from category B, which resulted in rewards 20% of the time. In the second pair (CD), stimuli from category C resulted in rewards 70% of the time and were always paired with stimuli from category D, which resulted in rewards 30% of the time. Thus, the more profitable choice was always A or C. Stimuli consisted of everyday objects such as a jacket, book, or bicycle.

Age differences in recruitment of DLPFC and ACC were very similar to those reported by Van Duijvenvoorde et al. (2008). That is, adults and adolescents showed DLPFC and dorsal ACC activation following unexpected negative feedback (i.e., negative feedback following choices that were more likely to result in reward, such as A and C), but children and adolescents showed DLPFC activation following unexpected positive feedback (i.e., positive feedback following choices that were less likely to result in reward, such as B and D). In addition, children and adolescents showed dorsal ACC activation in response to predictable positive feedback (i.e., positive feedback following choices that were more likely to result in reward, such as A or C).

These results reinforce the emerging interpretation that adults are guided more by negative feedback, whereas children are guided more by positive feedback. These studies suggest that the DLPFC is instrumental in modifying behavior based on each age group's sensitivity to outcomes of different valence. Adolescents show an intermediate pattern, sharing DLPFC and dorsal ACC activation with adults for negative feedback and with children for positive feedback. The DLPFC and ACC have been implicated in multiple executive processes (including inhibition), and we now further examine age differences in the recruitment of these and other regions during the implementation of cognitive control.

MATURATION OF THE NEURAL SYSTEMS SUPPORTING COGNITIVE CONTROL

In many ways, the development of cognitive control goes hand in glove with the development of mature processing of risk, reward, and emotion. Fuzzy trace theory predicts that over the course of development, cognitive control is aided not only by gains in the ability to inhibit impulses but also by selective attention to the most relevant information, which is extracted in the form of gist-based mental representations (Reyna & Brainerd, 1995; see also Gorfein & MacLeod, 2007). For example, imagine a teenager faced with the opportunity to have unprotected sex. Cuing the gist principle "better safe than sorry" or "better to not hurt my partner" would help the adolescent to avoid risk by affirming a personal value rather than merely suppressing an impulse. Such gist-based representations are protective against risky impulses and therefore reduce the need for top-down inhibition, although the ability to inhibit impulses also increases with age (Mills et al., 2008; Reyna et al., 2011).

Accordingly, there is some evidence that brain regions associated with top-down inhibition are, under moderate to low task demands, less active in adulthood than during adolescence. For example, when matched for performance on a sustained-attention-to-response task, adolescents required more activation in frontal, parietal, and medial regions than did adults (Braet, Johnson, Tobin, et al., 2009). Adolescents also recruited the DLPFC to a greater extent than did adults for equated performance on working memory tasks (Luna et al., 2008; Scherf, Sweeney, & Luna, 2006). This is likely to reflect improved interference resolution over the course of development (Geier & Luna, 2009; Reyna & Mills, 2007).

Adults, compared with adolescents, rely on more focal activation to support cognitive control. For example, people achieve adult levels of performance on an antisaccade task by mid-adolescence (Luna, Garver, Urban, Lazar, & Sweeney, 2004), but adolescents and adults use different neural circuitries to achieve the same level of performance (Durston et al., 2006; Geier & Luna, 2009). In one study, children relied on local connections (e.g., within the parietal cortex) to perform antisaccade trials, whereas adults recruited regions such as the inferior frontal gyrus, medial frontal gyrus, and anterior cingulate cortex (ACC), which are implicated in collaborative functions such as goal maintenance, attentional control, and response inhibition (Hwang, Velanova, & Luna, 2010).

In addition to being more efficient and focal, control circuitry is also more interconnected in adults than in adolescents (Geier & Luna, 2009). For instance, Hwang et al. (2010) found not only that prefrontal recruitment increased with age but also that adults showed the strongest functional and effective connectivity between prefrontal regions and downstream regions such as the thalamus and cerebellum. Not only the number of distal connections, but also their strength, increased with age. This coincided with an age-related decrease in local connections, such as those within the parietal cortex (Hwang et al., 2010). Similarly, in a functional connectivity study of ACC development, Kelly et al. (2009) found that, although activation within the ACC became more focal with age, it also occurred in greater synchronization with activation in distal brain regions, reflecting more integrated processing. In summarizing the evidence for the importance of integrative processing in cognitive control, Luna and Sweeney (2004) argued that "cognitive control of behavior results from the reciprocal interactions among different regions of the brain, such as through periods of synchronized activity, instead of a hierarchical transformation of information" (p. 305).

This characterization is consistent with the fuzzy trace theory assumption that gist-based processing increases with age, supplanting magnitude-sensitive verbatim thinking and augmenting the efficiency of top-down cognitive control (Reyna et al., 2011). Although gist-based thinking does not eliminate temptation, it does help to guard against it (Mills et al., 2008). Gist representations are robust to many forms of processing interference from distractions such as peer pressure and the desire for immediate gratification (Reyna, 2008). The increased focalization required for gist-based thinking is likely to result from synaptic pruning, longer connections, and increased myelination, all of which support the tendency to process less (but better) information. Meanwhile, cuing relevant values and principles from memory requires increased connectivity among focalized activations, an effect that has also been attributed to increases in myelinated distal connections (Asato et al., 2010).

In short, the developmental trajectory of the reward response (which is to process information categorically or qualitatively instead of numerically) occurs in cooperation with the developmental trajectory of cognitive control (which is to augment top-down inhibition with gist-based processing, resulting in improved focus on signal as opposed to noise; Egner & Hirsch, 2005). While age-related increases in top-down inhibition (Hwang et al., 2010; Steinberg et al., 2008; Reyna et al., 2011) support developmental gains in cognitive control (Barbalat, Domenech, Vernet, & Fourneret, 2010; Hare et al., 2009; Hwang et al., 2010), they do not fully account for adolescent risk taking (Reyna et al., 2011). Rather, the most developmentally advanced form of cognitive control is to default to simple processing of risk and reward information, which, along with increased coordination of top-down inhibitory circuits, is facilitated by focal but integrated neural networks.

THE FRAMING EFFECT

Given that adolescent risk taking is usually attributed to a combination of reward sensitivity and risk tolerance, the framing task is ideal for studying adolescent risk behavior because it allows both of these variables to be orthogonally varied. The framing effect, first studied by Tversky and Kahneman (1981), is a classic demonstration of irrationality because subjects' preferences for numerically equivalent options change reliably based on superficial details of how the options are presented. In such problems, a scenario is described and two options, one sure (e.g., wining a certain amount) and one risky (e.g., a chance of either getting a higher amount or getting nothing), are presented. Although each question has a sure and a risky option, the options can be framed as gains (e.g., money won, lives saved) or as losses (e.g., money, lives lost). Both the sure and the risky option are presented in a given question, and each question has either gain or loss options, but not both. Crucially, both gains and losses have the same net outcomes in framing tasks. Thus, the rational behavior (in the economists' sense) would be indifference to frame over the course of multiple questions. However, adults consistently favor the sure option in the gain frame and the risky option in the loss frame (Tversky & Kahneman, 1986). This effect holds within subjects, violating the axiom of descriptive invariance (according to which an individual's preferences should be consistent across different conditions; Kahneman, 2003).

The robustness of framing effects has been demonstrated in many replications under different conditions (e.g., with problems about both lives and money, in different languages and countries), and different theories have been offered to explain the mechanism (Reyna & Brainerd, 1991; for a review, see Kuhberger & Tanner, 2010). Prospect theory, for example, explains the pattern via psychophysical discounting of gains (rewards) and losses. According to prospect theory, a loss (e.g., of $200) subjectively "feels" larger than does a gain of the same magnitude.

In classic framing problems, subjects are given an endowment relative to which the loss is really a net gain. So, in this example, a subject who is given $600 and then loses $200 of it feels worse off than does a subject who is simply given $400, even though both subjects receive a net gain that is identical in magnitude. The endowment of $600, according to prospect theory, is ignored, and people focus on the loss of $200 (Kahneman, 2003). Thus, according to prospect theory, the inconsistent preferences demonstrated by framing problems are due to distinguishing between gains versus losses psychologically (in combination with psychophysical distortions).

Whereas prospect theory attributes framing effects to precise (though distorted) calculations, fuzzy trace theory predicts exactly the opposite—that framing occurs when people process options categorically (i.e., based on gist representations) rather than quantitatively (i.e., based on verbatim representations). For example, in the gain frame, the options boil down to winning some for sure versus a chance of winning some and a chance of winning nothing. Although the amounts to win differ in the sure and risky options (so that the expected value is equal), the difference between some and none is categorical. Because "some" for sure is preferable to "some or none," adults choose the sure option in order to avoid the possibility of winning nothing. Likewise, in the loss frame, the options boil down to losing some for sure versus a chance of losing some and a chance of losing nothing. People choose the risky option because it offers the possibility of losing nothing. Thus, according to fuzzy trace theory, framing effects are driven by the zero complement in the risky option (i.e., the chance of winning or losing nothing). This directly contradicts prospect theory and other variants of expected utility theory, which assume that the zero complement makes no difference to the choice because it does not change the valuation (Reyna & Ellis, 1994). In a review, Kuhberger and Tanner (2010) directly compared the predictions of prospect theory with those of fuzzy trace theory and found that the latter accounted better for the evidence in multiple variations of the problem.

Although most adults display the standard framing behavior (preferring the sure option in the gain frame and the risky option in the loss frame), adolescents often show the opposite preference (preferring the risky option in the gain frame and the sure option in the loss frame), a pattern of preferences called *reverse framing*, especially when reward magnitudes are large (Reyna & Ellis, 1994; Reyna et al., 2011). According to fuzzy trace theory, reverse framing is explained by verbatim processing; in which choices are ultimately determined by one of the quantitative dimensions, reward (as opposed to risk, the other dimension), although both risk and reward are processed. Verbatim-based thinking promotes the trading off of risks and rewards. Fuzzy trace theory predicts that reverse framing occurs when subjects make their choice based on the difference in potential rewards between the sure option and the gamble. Because expected value is constrained to be equal across the sure and risky options, the higher magnitude gain is always found in the gamble (and the smaller magnitude loss is always found in the sure thing). More prizes can be won in the gamble option, and fewer prizes can be lost in the sure option, and for those who are hypersensitive to reward magnitude, this results in the reversal of standard framing behavior: risk avoidance in the loss frame and risk seeking in the gain frame, consistent with developmental predictions of fuzzy trace theory that adolescents process quantitative differences (Reyna et al., 2011).

Neural Correlates of Framing in Adults

To date, two studies have examined the neural correlates of framing effects in adults (none has used the task with adolescents or children). De Martino et al. (2006) found increased bilateral amygdala activation when young adults' choices were consistent with, rather than counter to, the standard framing effect. Although the amygdala was more active during choices consistent with the standard framing pattern (vs. counter-frame choices), the intensity of this activation did not predict the frequency with which each subject showed the framing effect over the course of the entire experiment. When subjects chose counter to the standard framing effect (the reverse of the previous analysis), De Martino et al. found increased activation in the anterior cingulate and dorsolateral prefrontal cortices compared to standard framing choices. However, like the amygdala, these regions did not predict the frequency with which each subject showed the framing effect. Instead, activation in the orbital medial prefrontal cortex (OMPFC) and ventral medial prefrontal cortex (VMPFC) during frame-consistent choices, compared with counter-frame choices, predicted a decreased tendency to show the framing effect.

The OMPFC processes many aspects of reward information, many of them computational (e.g., integrating magnitude and probability with subjective value; Rangel, Camerer, & Montague, 2008). The OFC has been implicated in a network that, together with the basolateral amygdala, ventral striatum, and DLPFC, is thought to encode learning and action planning pertaining to rewards (Rangel et al., 2008). De Martino et al. (2006) suggested that the OMPFC contributes to resistance to framing biases by incorporating emotional and numerical information. As De Martino et al. suggested, a relative emphasis on emotional valence as opposed to calculation, corresponding to increased amygdala activation, appears to drive framing behavior.

Consistent with this interpretation, Roiser et al. (2009) provided further evidence about the interactions among the amygdala, ACC, and OFC. They found that individuals homozygous for the short allele of the serotonin transporter polymorphism (5HTT-LPR), which has been associated with amygdala hyperreactivity, were more susceptible to the framing effect and had increased amygdala activation, compared to the homozygous-long group, during choices made in accordance with frame. To the contrary, individuals homozygous for the long allele of the polymorphism, which has been associated with better top-down regulation of amygdala function, were less behaviorally susceptible to the framing effect, and they displayed increased ACC activation as well as increased connectivity between ACC and amygdala during choices made counter to frame. Regardless of genotype, individuals who were less susceptible to the framing effect (i.e., those who were indifferent; this adult sample did not include any reverse framers) showed increased activation in the OFC during choices made counter to frame. Roiser and colleagues took these findings to support a model like that suggested by De Martino et al. (2006), in which amygdala activation drives framing, and activation in conflict detection and quantitative integration regions, such as the ACC and OFC, is associated with attenuated framing.

Adolescent Framing and Its Relationship to Real-Life Behavior

The distinction between calculative and categorical processing lends itself to a critical test of fuzzy trace theory. If, as predicted, the developmental trend is a shift from reliance on quantitative (verbatim-based) thinking to reliance on qualitative (gist-based) thinking, then experiments should yield predictable developmental differences in framing behavior. In particular, children, who rely preferentially on verbatim thinking, should show diminished framing effects because they multiplicatively trade off risk and reward and hence are roughly indifferent between options of equal expected value (Reyna & Ellis, 1994). Adults, who rely on gist processing as a default, should display standard framing effects because framing effects rely on simple, valence-based processing. In addition, children and adolescents should be more likely than adults to display reverse framing, which is driven by verbatim processing (i.e., quantitative differences).

Reyna and Ellis (1994) compared framing behavior in children and young adolescents and reported results consistent with these fuzzy trace theory predictions (see also Reyna et al., 2011; Reyna & Farley, 2006). Although there is evidence that adolescents display a pattern of gist-verbatim processing that is intermediate between that of children and that of adults, until recently, there was no evidence about adolescent framing preferences and their relationship to personality traits and real-life risk taking (see also Mills et al., 2008). Reyna et al. (2011) conducted the first study comparing the framing tendencies of adolescents (ages 14–17) with those of young adults (ages 18–22). The stimuli, including a spinner, were the same as those used by Reyna and Ellis (1994) except for the type of reward (superballs for children in Reyna & Ellis, 1994; money for adolescents and adults in Reyna et al., 2011).

Reyna et al. (2011) found not only that adolescents displayed a distinctive pattern of preferences in the framing task—reverse framing—but also that framing behavior predicted real-life sexual risk taking. This is an important finding because the framing effect can now be included in the set of laboratory tasks that predict real-life risk-taking behavior in adolescents (Bechara et al., 2005; Galván et al., 2006, 2007; Parker & Fischhoff, 2005). Although adults and adolescents were equally sensitive to level of risk (choosing the sure option more often as the level of risk increased), adolescents showed reverse framing when the potential rewards were largest (i.e., when the difference between sure and risky outcome was greatest). This is consistent with multiple fMRI and behavioral studies of risk and reward, which, as we have discussed, suggest that age differences in reward processing are particularly evident for rewards of high magnitude. These findings also validate two fuzzy trace theory predictions: (a) that reverse framing is driven by sensitivity to the magnitude of reward and (b) that adolescents are more likely to use verbatim processing, which allows for distinctions based on magnitude, and hence are more likely to show reverse framing.

The data reported by Reyna et al. (2011) were also consistent with prior findings that reward sensitivity increases curvilinearly with age, peaking in adolescence (Casey, Getz, & Galván, 2008; Steinberg et al., 2008). Reyna et al. (2011) next used factor analyses to test whether gist versus verbatim thinking was merely a proxy measure for traits such as reward sensitivity and inhibitory capacity, or whether the gist-verbatim distinction accounted for unique variance in framing behavior.

In a factor analysis with orthogonal rotation, measures of gist and verbatim attitudes toward risk loaded on separate factors from each other and from sensation seeking and inhibition. As predicted by fuzzy trace theory, verbatim thinking loaded on the same factor as reverse framing. Sensation seeking and behavioral activation loaded together on a factor separate from age and behavioral inhibition, which loaded together. It was interesting that total number of gambling choices, independent of frame, loaded on its own factor, separately from reverse framing. This latter pattern of responses is not simply more risk taking but reflects calculated risk taking, as for high-magnitude rewards, and sometimes risk avoidance, as for losses. Crucially, gist and verbatim thinking (which loaded on separate factors) did not load with any of the trait measures (e.g., behavioral inhibition, behavioral activation, sensation seeking), suggesting that cognitive processing accounts for unique variance in decisions based on risk and reward.

When the five factors (gist, verbatim/reverse framing, age/BIS, SS/BAS, and total risk taking) from the principal components analysis were put into a regression with intentions to have sex (and, in other analyses, risk-taking behavior) as the outcome variable, gist processing consistently predicted a reduction in risk intentions and risky behaviors. The gist factor, which varied negatively with intentions to have sex, also accounted for the most variance (i.e., more gist processing predicted less risk taking). Verbatim processing, including reverse framing in the laboratory task, was associated with increased risk taking in real-life measures. In a separate regression with cumulative number of sexual partners as the outcome variable, the gist factor predicted fewer partners, but the verbatim/reverse framing factor predicted more partners (again underscoring the result that cognitive processing style predicts real-life risk taking). These data were consistent with the fuzzy trace theory predictions that gist-based thinking is protective against sexual risk taking and that verbatim-based thinking (as displayed in reverse framing) encourages risk taking in real life. Moreover, gist-based thinking was a better predictor of risky behavior than was either sensation seeking or inhibition, although these were also related to risk taking.

SUMMARY AND CONCLUSIONS

In this chapter, we have highlighted multiple points of intersection among the memory, decision-making, and neuroimaging literatures on the topic of adolescent risk taking, emphasizing the deleterious influence of risk-reward tradeoffs, especially for potentially catastrophic outcomes, and the benefits of age-related increases in gist-based processing. Over the course of development, brain structure and function benefit from streamlining of synapses, increased interconnectivity among distal brain regions, and increased myelination of these distal connections (hence faster transmission of signals; Luna & Sweeney, 2004). The anatomical theme of "less is more" echoes behavioral findings summarized by fuzzy trace theory (Reyna & Brainerd, 1995). Specifically, the later neural maturation of high-level integration regions, relative to low-level perception regions, parallels the cognitive development of the preference for gist-based processing. This preference confers a tendency to extract meaningful summaries of information and to "connect the dots" in order to make decisions that are consistent with one's values and with the bottom-line meaning of a situation (Reyna, 2008).

Reward sensitivity, which can augment the verbatim representation of reward magnitudes (Figure 13.1), is a relatively stable individual difference that nonetheless varies over the course of development (Reyna et al., 2011; Romer, 2010; Steinberg et al., 2008). The development of reward sensitivity is curvilinear, such that the neural response to rewards peaks in adolescence. However, this pattern depends on the time course of reward processing (i.e., reward anticipation versus reward delivery), as adolescents and adults show differing patterns of neural response during these two phases (see summaries by Galván, 2010; and Geier & Luna, 2009; as well as Table 13.1). However, these conclusions are based on a handful of studies, which use different tasks, and critical tests of alternative explanations should be conducted (e.g., the stimuli used in some studies may be more motivationally salient than the stimuli used in other studies).

Although many authors have described emotional impulses as the driving force in adolescent risk taking (Chein et al., 2010; Steinberg, 2008), the contributions of emotion, reward sensitivity, and impulsivity (the inability to inhibit or to defer gratification) to decision making are conceptually and empirically distinct (Reyna et al., 2011; Reyna & Rivers, 2008). Each of the multiple facets of emotion, including valence, arousal, and feeling states, modifies cognition in a complex way. As a result, the influence of emotion is not always bad, and the influence of analysis is not always good. Instead, these cognitive and emotional processes combine with the effects of reward sensitivity and inhibition during risky decision-making (Reyna et al., 2011).

Although the capacity for reliable top-down inhibition increases linearly with age (Casey et al., 2008; Cauffman et al., 2010; Reyna et al., 2011; Steinberg, 2008), so does the ability to focus on target information and to map this information onto personal values that protect against risk taking (Mills et al., 2008; Reyna et al., 2011). Thus, the development of a reliance on gist-based thinking augments concomitant gains in the ability to suppress impulses (Reyna et al., 2011). The framing effect, which has long been used to study the trade-off between risk and reward, offers insight into the developmental shift from verbatim analysis to gist-based, impressionistic reasoning. For example, reverse framing—an effect rarely found in adulthood but more common in adolescence—reflects verbatim analysis of rewards and was associated with real-life risk taking. Researchers have integrated memory, neuroscience, and decision-making approaches in studying the framing effect, reflecting an increasing recognition that, to paraphrase Weber and Johnson (2009, p. 54), the brain that decides is the same brain that learns and remembers.

REFERENCES

Adolphs, R., Denburg, N. L., & Tranel, D. (2001). The amygdala's role in long-term declarative memory for gist and detail. *Behavioral Neuroscience, 115,* 983–992. doi:10.1037/0735-7044.115.5.983

Adolphs, R., Tranel, D., & Buchanan, T. W. (2005). Amygdala damage impairs emotional memory for gist but not details of complex stimuli. *Nature Neuroscience,* 8, 512–518. doi:10.1038/nn1413

Asato, M. R., Terwilliger, R., Woo, J., & Luna, B. (2010). White matter development in adolescence: A DTI study. *Cerebral Cortex, 20,* 2122–2131. doi:10.1093/cercor/bhp282

Barbalat, G., Domenech, P., Vernet, M., & Fourneret, P. (2010). Risk-taking in adolescence: A neuroeconomics approach. *L'Encephale-Revue de Psychiatrie Clinique Biologique et Therapeutique, 36,* 147–154. doi:10.1016/j.encep.2009.06.004

Bechara, A., Damasio, H., Tranel, D., & Damasio, A. R. (2005). The Iowa Gambling Task and the somatic marker hypothesis: Some questions and answers. *Trends in Cognitive Sciences, 9,* 159–162. doi:10.1016/j.tics.2005.02.002

Berns, G. S., Moore, S., & Capra, C. M. (2009). Adolescent engagement in dangerous behaviors is associated with increased white matter maturity of frontal cortex. *PLoS ONE, 4*(8), 12. doi:e677310.1371/journal.pone.0006773

Bjork, J. M., Knutson, B., Fong, G. W., Caggiano, D. M., Bennett, S. M., & Hommer, D. W. (2004). Incentive-elicited brain activation in adolescents: Similarities and differences from young adults. *The Journal of Neuroscience, 24,* 1793–1802. doi:10.1523/JNEUROSCI.4862-03.2004

Bjork, J. M., Knutson, B., & Hommer, D. W. (2008). Incentive-elicited striatal activation in adolescent children of alcoholics. *Addiction, 103,* 1308–1319. doi:10.1111/j.1360-0443.2008.02250.x

Bjork, J. M., Smith, A. R., Chen, G., & Hommer, D. W. (2010). Adolescents, adults and rewards: Comparing motivational neurocircuitry recruitment using fMRI. *PLoS ONE, 5*(7), 14. doi:e1144010.1371/journal.pone.0011440

Bjorklund, D. F. (2012). *Children's thinking: Cognitive development and individual differences* (5th ed.). Belmont, CA: Wadsworth.

Braet, W., Johnson, K. A., Tobin, C. T., Acheson, R., Bellgrove, M. A., Robertson, I. H., & Garavan, H. (2009). Functional developmental changes underlying response inhibition and error-detection processes. *Neuropsychologia, 47,* 3143–3151. doi:10.1016/j.neuropsychologia.2009.07.018

Brainerd, C. J., & Reyna, V. F. (1992a). Explaining memory-free reasoning. *Psychological Science, 3,* 332–339. doi:10.1111/j.1467-9280.1992.tb00042.x

Brainerd, C. J., & Reyna, V. F. (1992b). The memory independence effect: What do the data show? What do the theories claim? *Developmental Review, 12,* 164–186. doi:10.1016/0273-2297(92)90007-O

Brainerd, C. J., & Reyna, V. F. (1993). Memory independence and memory interference in cognitive development. *Psychological Review, 100*(1), 42–67. doi:10.1037/0033-295X.100.1.42

Brouwer, L. E. J. (1952). Historical background, principles and methods of intuitionism. *South African Journal of Science, 49,* 139–146.

Casey, B. J., Galván, A., & Hare, T. A. (2005). Changes in cerebral functional organization during cognitive development. *Current Opinion in Neurobiology, 15,* 239–244. doi:10.1016/j.conb.2005.03.012

Casey, B. J., Getz, S., & Galván, A. (2008). The adolescent brain. *Developmental Review, 28*(1), 62–77. doi:10.1016/j.dr.2007.08.003

Casey, B. J., Jones, R. M., & Hare, T. A. (2008). The adolescent brain. *Annals of the New York Academy of Sciences, 1124,* 111–126. doi:10.1196/annals.1440.010

Casey, B. J., Tottenham, N., Liston, C., & Durston, S. (2005). Imaging the developing brain: What have learned about cognitive development? *Trends in Cognitive Sciences, 9,* 104–110. doi:10.1016/j.tics.2005.01.011

Cauffman, E., Shulman, E. P., Steinberg, L., Claus, E., Banich, M. T., Graham, S., & Woolard, J. (2010). Age differences in affective decision making as indexed by performance on the Iowa Gambling Task. *Developmental Psychology, 46,* 193–207. doi:10.1037/a0016128

Chein, J., Albert, D., O'Brien, L., Uckert, K., & Steinberg, L. (2011). Peers increase adolescent risk taking by enhancing activity in the brain's reward circuitry. *Developmental Science, 14,* F1–F10. doi:10.1111/j.1467-7687.2010.01035.x

Cohen, J. R., Asarnow, R. F., Sabb, F. W., Bilder, R. M., Bookheimer, S. Y., Knowlton, B. J., & Poldrack, R. A. (2010). A unique adolescent response to reward prediction errors. *Nature Neuroscience, 13,* 669–671. doi:10.1038/nn.2558

Crone, E. A., & van der Molen, M. W. (2007). Development of decision-making in school-aged children and adolescents: Evidence from heart rate and skin conductance analysis. *Child Development, 78,* 1288–1301. doi:10.1111/j.1467-8624.2007.01066.x

De Martino, B., Kumaran, D., Seymour, B., & Dolan, R. J. (2006, August 4). Frames, biases, and rational decision-making in the human brain. *Science, 313,* 684–687. doi:10.1126/science.1128356

Dosenbach, N. U. F., Fair, D. A., Cohen, A. L., Schlaggar, B. L., & Petersen, S. E. (2008). A dual-networks architecture of top-down control. *Trends in Cognitive Sciences, 12,* 99–105. doi:10.1016/j.tics.2008.01.001

Durston, S., Davidson, M. C., Tottenham, N., Galván, A., Spicer, J., Fossella, J. A., & Casey, B. J. (2006). A shift from diffuse to focal cortical activity with development. *Developmental Science, 9,* 1–8. doi:10.1111/j.1467-7687.2005.00454.x

Egner, T., & Hirsch, J. (2005). Cognitive control mechanisms resolve conflict through cortical amplification of task-relevant information. *Nature Neuroscience, 8,* 1784–1790. doi:10.1038/nn1594

Epstein, S. (1994). Integration of the cognitive and psychodynamic unconscious. *American Psychologist, 49,* 709–724. doi:10.1037/0003-066X.49.8.709

Ericsson, K. A., & Kintsch, W. (1995). Long-term working memory. *Psychological Review, 102,* 211–245. doi:10.1037/0033-295X.102.2.211

Ernst, M., Nelson, E. E., Jazbec, S., McClure, E. B., Monk, C. S., Leibenluft, E., . . . Pine, D. S. (2005). Amygdala and nucleus accumbens in response to receipt and omission of gains in adults and adolescents. *NeuroImage, 25,* 1279–1291. doi:10.1016/j.neuroimage.2004.12.038

Eshel, N., Nelson, E. E., Blair, R. J., Pine, D. S., & Ernst, M. (2007). Neural substrates of choice selection in adults and adolescents: Development of the ventrolateral prefrontal and anterior cingulate cortices. *Neuropsychologia, 45,* 1270–1279. doi:10.1016/j.neuropsychologia.2006.10.004

Evans, J. S. T. (2006). The heuristic-analytic theory of reasoning: Extension and evaluation. *Psychonomic Bulletin & Review, 13,* 378–395. doi:10.3758/BF03193858

Evans, J. S. T. (2008). Dual-processing accounts of reasoning, judgment, and social cognition. *Annual Review of Psychology, 59,* 255–278. doi:10.1146/annurev.psych.59.103006.093629

Evans, J. S. T. (2010). Intuition and reasoning: A dual-process perspective. *Psychological Inquiry, 21*, 313–326. doi:10.1080/1047840X.2010.521057

Figner, B., Knoch, D., Johnson, E. J., Krosch, A. R., Lisanby, S. H., Fehr, E., & Weber, E. U. (2010). Lateral prefrontal cortex and self-control in intertemporal choice. *Nature Neuroscience, 13*, 538–539. doi:10.1038/nn.2516

Finucane, M. L., Peters, E., & Slovic, P. (2003). Judgment and decision making: The dance of affect and reason. In S. L. Schneider & J. Shanteau (Eds.), *Emerging perspectives on decision research* (pp. 327–364). New York, NY: Cambridge University Press.

Fisher, R. P., & Chandler, C. C. (1991). Independence between recalling interevent relations and specific events. *Journal of Experimental Psychology: Learning, Memory, and Cognition, 17*, 722–733. doi:10.1037/0278-7393.17.4.722

Fredrickson, B. L., & Branigan, C. (2005). Positive emotions broaden the scope of attention and thought-action repertoires. *Cognition and Emotion, 19*, 313–332. doi:10.1080/02699930441000238

Freeman, H. D., & Beer, J. S. (2010). Frontal lobe activation mediates the relation between sensation seeking and cortisol increases. *Journal of Personality, 78*, 1497–1528. doi:10.1111/j.1467-6494.2010.00659.x

Galván, A. (2010). Adolescent development of the reward system. *Frontiers in Human Neuroscience, 4*(6), 1–9. doi:610.3389/neuro.09.006.2010

Galván, A., Hare, T. A., Parra, C. E., Penn, J., Voss, H., Glover, G., & Casey, B. J. (2006). Earlier development of the accumbens relative to orbitofrontal cortex might underlie risk taking behavior in adolescents. *The Journal of Neuroscience, 26*, 6885–6892. doi:10.1523/JNEUROSCI.1062-06.2006

Gardner, M., & Steinberg, L. (2005). Peer influence on risk taking, risk preference, and risky decision making in adolescence and adulthood: An experimental study. *Developmental Psychology, 41*, 625–635. doi:10.1037/0012-1649.41.4.625

Geier, C., & Luna, B. (2009). The maturation of incentive processing and cognitive control. *Pharmacology, Biochemistry, and Behavior, 93*, 212–221. doi:10.1016/j.pbb.2009.01.021

Geier, C. F., Terwilliger, R., Teslovich, T., Velanova, K., & Luna, B. (2010). Immaturities in reward processing and its influence on inhibitory control in adolescence. *Cerebral Cortex, 20*, 1613–1629. doi:10.1093/cercor/bhp225

Giedd, J. N. (2004). Structural magnetic resonance imaging of the adolescent brain. *Annals of the New York Academy of Sciences, 102*, 77–85. doi:10.1196/annals.1308.009

Giedd, J. N., Blumenthal, J., Jeffries, N. O., Castellanos, F. X., Liu, H., Zijdenbos, A., . . . Rapoport, J. L. (1999). Brain development during childhood and adolescence: a longitudinal MRI study. *Nature Neuroscience, 2*, 861–863. doi:10.1038/13158

Gogtay, N., Giedd, J. N., Lusk, L., Hayashi, K. M., Greenstein, D., Vaituzis, A. C., . . . Thompson, P. M. (2004). Dynamic mapping of human cortical development during childhood through early adulthood. *Proceedings of the National Academy* of Sciences of the United States of America, 101, 8174–8179. doi:10.1073/pnas.0402680101

Gorfein, D. S., & MacLeod, C. M. (Eds.), Inhibition in cognition. Washington, DC: American Psychological Association. doi:10.1037/11587-000

Hare, T. A., Camerer, C. F., & Rangel, A. (2009, May 1). Self-control in decision-making involves modulation of the mPFC valuation system. Science, 324, 646–648. doi:10.1126/science.1168450

Hare, T. A., Tottenham, N., Galván, A., Voss, H. U., Glover, G. H., & Casey, B. J. (2008). Biological substrates of emotional reactivity and regulation in adolescence during an emotional go-nogo task. Biological Psychiatry, 63, 927–934. doi:10.1016/j.biopsych.2008.03.015

Hastie, R., & Park, B. (1986). The relationship between memory and judgment depends on whether the judgment task is memory-based or online. Psychological Review, 93, 258–268. doi:10.1037/0033-295X.93.3.258

Hüppi, P. S., & Dubois, J. (2006). Diffusion tensor imaging of brain development. Seminars in Fetal & Neonatal Medicine, 11, 489–497. doi:10.1016/j.siny.2006.07.006

Huttenlocher, P. R. (1990). Morphometric study of human cerebral cortex development. Neuropsychologia, 28, 517–527. doi:10.1016/0028-3932(90)90031-I

Hwang, K., Velanova, K., & Luna, B. (2010). Strengthening of top-down frontal cognitive control networks underlying the development of inhibitory control: A functional magnetic resonance imaging effective connectivity study. The Journal of Neuroscience, 30, 15535–15545. doi:10.1523/JNEUROSCI.2825-10.2010

Jacobs, J., & Klaczynski, P. (2005). The development of children's and adolescents' judgment and decision-making. Mahwah, NJ: Erlbaum.

Kahneman, D. (2003). A perspective on judgment and choice: Mapping bounded rationality. American Psychologist, 58, 697–720. doi:10.1037/003-006X.58.9.697

Kelly, A. M. C., Di Martino, A., Uddin, L. Q., Shehzad, Z., Gee, D. G., Reiss, P. T., . . . Milham, M. P. (2009). Development of anterior cingulate functional connectivity from late childhood to early adulthood. Cerebral Cortex, 19, 640–657. doi:10.1093/cercor/bhn117

Kensinger, E. A., Garoff-Eaton, R. J., & Schacter, D. L. (2006). Memory for specific visual details can be enhanced by negative arousing content. Journal of Memory and Language, 54, 99–112. doi:10.1016/j.jml.2005.05.005

Kensinger, E. A., Garoff-Eaton, R. J., & Schacter, D. L. (2007). Effects of emotion on memory specificity: Memory trade-offs elicited by negative visually arousing stimuli. Journal of Memory and Language, 56, 575–591. doi:10.1016/j.jml.2006.05.004

Kintsch, W. (1974). The representation of meaning in memory. Hillsdale, NJ: Erlbaum.

Klingberg, T., Vaidya, C. J., Gabrieli, J. D. E., Moseley, M. E., & Hedehus, M. (1999). Myelination and organization of the frontal white matter in children: A diffusion tensor MRI study. NeuroReport, 10, 2817–2821. doi:10.1097/00001756-199909090-00022

Kuhberger, A., & Tanner, C. (2010). Risky choice framing: Task versions and a comparison of prospect theory and fuzzy-trace theory. *Journal of Behavioral Decision Making, 23,* 314–329. doi:10.1002/bdm.656

Levin, I. P., Weller, J. A., Pederson, A. A., & Harshman, L. A. (2007). Age-related differences in adaptive decision making: Sensitivity to expected value in risky choice. *Judgment and Decision Making, 2,* 225–233.

Li, X. R., Lu, Z. L., D'Argembeau, A., Ng, M., & Bechara, A. (2010). The Iowa gambling task in fMRI images. *Human Brain Mapping, 31,* 410–423. doi:10.1002/hbm.20875

Lieberman, M. D., Gaunt, R., Gilbert, D. T., & Trope, Y. (2002). Reflection and reflexion: A social cognitive neuroscience approach to attributional inference. *Advances in Experimental Social Psychology, 34,* 199–249. doi:10.1016/S0065-2601(02)80006-5

Liston, C., Watts, R., Tottenham, N., Davidson, M. C., Niogi, S., Ulug, A. M., & Casey, B. J. (2005). Frontostriatal microstructure modulates efficient recruitment of cognitive control. *Cerebral Cortex, 16,* 553–560. doi:10.1093/cercor/bhj003

Lloyd, F. J., & Reyna, V. F. (2009). Clinical gist and medical education: Connecting the dots. *JAMA, 302,* 1332–1333. doi:10.1001/jama.2009.1383

Luna, B., Garver, K. E., Urban, T. A., Lazar, N. A., & Sweeney, J. A. (2004). Maturation of cognitive processes from late childhood to adulthood. *Child Development, 75,* 1357–1372. doi:10.1111/j.1467-8624.2004.00745.x

Luna, B., & Sweeney, J. A. (2004). The emergence of collaborative brain function: fMRI studies of the development of response inhibition. *Annals of the New York Academy of Sciences, 1021,* 296–309. doi:10.1196/annals.1308.035

Luna, B., Velanova, K., & Geier, C. F. (2008). Development of eye-movement control. *Brain and Cognition, 68,* 293–308. doi:10.1016/j.vandc.200808.019

May, J. C., Delgado, M. R., Dahl, R. E., Stenger, V. A., Ryan, N. D., Fiez, J. A., & Carter, C. S. (2004). Event-related functional magnetic resonance imaging of reward-related brain circuitry in children and adolescents. *Biological Psychiatry, 55,* 359–366. doi:10.1016/j.biopsych.2003.11.008

McRae, K., Hughes, B., Chopra, S., Gabrieli, J., Gross, J., & Ochsner, K. (2010). The neural bases of distraction and reappraisal. *Journal of Cognitive Neuroscience, 22,* 248–262. doi:10.1162/jocn.2009.21243

Mills, B., Reyna, V. F., & Estrada, S. (2008). Explaining contradictory relations between risk perception and risk taking. *Psychological Science, 19,* 429–433. doi:10.1111/j.1467-9280.2008.02104.x

Mukherjee, P., & McKinstry, R. C. (2006). Diffusion tensor imaging and tractography of human brain development. *Neuroimaging Clinics of North America, 16*(1), 19–43. doi:10.1016/j.nic.2005.11.004

Nisbett, R. E., Peng, K. P., Choi, I., & Norenzayan, A. (2001). Culture and systems of thought: Holistic versus analytic cognition. *Psychological Review, 108,* 291–310. doi:10.1037/0033-295X.108.2.291

Ochsner, K. N., Ray, R. R., Hughes, B. L., McRae, K., Cooper, J. C., Weber, J., . . . Gross, J. J. (2009). Bottom-up and top-down processes in emotion generation: Common and distinct neural mechanisms. *Psychological Science, 20,* 1322–1331. doi:10.1111/j.1467-9280.2009.02459.x

Olesen, P. J., Nagy, Z., Westerberg, H., & Klingberg, T. (2003). Combined analysis of DTI and fMRI data reveals a joint maturation of white and grey matter in a fronto-parietal network. *Cognitive Brain Research, 18*(1), 48–57. doi:10.1016/j.cogbrainres.2003.09.003

Paus, T., Keshavan, M., & Giedd, J. N. (2008). Why do many psychiatric disorders emerge during adolescence? *Nature Reviews Neuroscience, 9,* 947–957. doi:10.1038/nrn2513

Rangel, A., Camerer, C., & Montague, P. R. (2008). A framework for studying the neurobiology of value-based decision making. *Nature Reviews Neuroscience, 9,* 545–556. doi:10.1038/nrn2357

Rangel, R., & Hare, T. (2010). Neural computations associated with goal-directed choice. *Current Opinion in Neurobiology, 20,* 262–270. doi:10.1016/j.conb.2010.03.001

Reyna, V. F. (1996). Conceptions of memory development, with implications for reasoning and decision making. *Annals of Child Development, 12,* 87–118.

Reyna, V. F. (2008). A theory of medical decision making and health: Fuzzy-trace theory. *Medical Decision Making, 28,* 850–865. doi:10.1177/0272989X08327066

Reyna, V. F., Adam, M. B., Poirier, K., LeCroy, C. W., & Brainerd, C. J. (2005). Risky decision-making in childhood and adolescence: A fuzzy-trace theory approach. In J. Jacobs & P. Klaczynski (Eds.), *The development of children's and adolescents' judgment and decision-making* (pp. 77–106). Mahwah, NJ: Erlbaum.

Reyna, V. F., & Brainerd, C. J. (1991). Fuzzy-trace theory and framing effects in choice: Gist extraction, truncation, and conversion. *Journal of Behavioral Decision Making, 4,* 249–262. doi:10.1002/bdm.3960040403

Reyna, V. F., & Brainerd, C. J. (1995). Fuzzy-trace theory: An interim synthesis. *Learning and Individual Differences, 7*(1), 1–75. doi:10.1016/1041-6080(95)90031-4

Reyna, V. F., & Ellis, S. C. (1994). Fuzzy-trace theory and framing effects in children's risky decision making. *Psychological Science, 5,* 275–279. doi:10.1111/j.1467-9280.1994.tb00625.x

Reyna, V. F., Estrada, S. M., DeMarinis, J. A., Myers, R. M., Stanisz, J. M., & Mills, B. A. (2011). Neurobiological and memory models of risky decision making in adolescents versus young adults. *Journal of Experimental Psychology: Learning, Memory, and Cognition.* Advance online publication. doi:10.1037/a0023943

Reyna, V. F., & Farley, F. (2006). Risk and rationality in adolescent decision making: Implications for theory, practice, and public policy. *Psychological Science in the Public Interest, 7,* 1–44. doi:10.1111/j.1529-1006.2006.00026.x

Reyna, V. F., & Kiernan, B. (1994). Development of gist versus verbatim memory in sentence recognition: Effects of lexical familiarity, semantic content, encoding instructions, and retention interval. *Developmental Psychology, 30,* 178–191. doi:10.1037/0012-1649.30.2.178

Reyna, V. F. & Lloyd, F. J. (2006). Physician decision making and cardiac risk: Effects of knowledge, risk perception, risk tolerance, and fuzzy processing. *Journal of Experimental Psychology: Applied, 12,* 179–195. doi:10.1037/1076-898X.12.3.179

Reyna, V. F., Lloyd, F. J., & Brainerd, C. J. (2003). Memory, development, and rationality: An integrative theory of judgment and decision making. In S. L. Schneider & J. Shanteau (Eds.), *Emerging perspectives on judgment and decision research* (pp. 201–245). New York: Cambridge University Press.

Reyna, V. F., & Mills, B. A. (2007). Interference processes in fuzzy-trace theory: Aging, Alzheimer's disease, and development. In D. Gorfein & C. MacLeod (Eds.), *Inhibition in cognition* (pp. 185–210). Washington, DC: American Psychological Association. doi:10.1037/11587-000

Reyna, V. F., & Rivers, S. E. (2008). Current theories of risk and rational decision making. *Developmental Review, 28*(1), 1–11. doi:10.1016/j.dr.2008.01.002

Rivers, S. E., Reyna, V. F., & Mills, B. (2008). Risk taking under the influence: A fuzzy-trace theory of emotion in adolescence. *Developmental Review, 28*(1), 107–144. doi:10.1016/j.dr.2007.11.002

Roiser, J. P., de Martino, B., Tan, G. C. Y., Kumaran, D., Seymour, B., Wood, N. W., & Dolan, R. J. (2009). A genetically mediated bias in decision making driven by failure of amygdala control. *The Journal of Neuroscience, 29,* 5985–5991. doi:10.1523/JNEUROSCI.0407-09.2009

Romer, D. (2010). Adolescent risk taking, impulsivity, and brain development: Implications for prevention. *Developmental Psychobiology, 52,* 263–276. doi:10.1002/dev.20442

Scherf, K. S., Sweeney, J. A., & Luna, B. (2006). Brain basis of developmental change in visuospatial working memory. *Journal of Cognitive Neuroscience, 18,* 1045–1058. doi:10.1162/jocn.2006.18.7.1045

Schwartz, N., & Clore, G. L. (1996). Feelings as phenomenal experiences. In E. T. Higgins & A. W. Kruglanski (Eds.), *Social psychology: Handbook of basic principles* (pp. 433–465). New York, NY: Guilford.

Shiv, B., Loewenstein, G., & Bechara, A. (2005). The dark side of emotion in decision-making: When individuals with decreased emotional reactions make more advantageous decisions. *Cognitive Brain Research, 23*(1), 85–92. doi:10.1016/j.cogbrainres.2005.01.006

Simon, H. A., & Chase, W. G. (1973). Skill in chess. *American Scientist, 61,* 394–403.

Slovic, P., Peters, E., Finucane, M. L., & MacGregor, D. G. (2005). Affect, risk, and decision making. *Health Psychology, 24,* S35–S40. doi:10.1037/0278-6133.24.4.S35

Somerville, L. H., Jones, R. M., & Casey, B. J. (2010). A time of change: Behavioral and neural correlates of adolescent sensitivity to appetitive and aversive environmental cues. *Brain and Cognition, 72*(1), 124–133. doi:10.1016/j.bandc.2009.07.003

Sowell, E. R., Thompson, P. M., Holmes, C. J., Jernigan, T. L., & Toga, A. W. (1999). In vivo evidence for post-adolescent brain maturation in frontal and striatal regions. *Nature Neuroscience, 2,* 859–861. doi:10.1038/13154

Spear, L. P. (2000). The adolescent brain and age-related behavioral manifestations. *Neuroscience and Biobehavioral Reviews, 24,* 417–463. doi:10.1016/S0149-7634(00)00014-2

Stanovich, K. E. (2004). Balance in psychological research: The dual process perspective. *The Behavioral and Brain Sciences, 27,* 357–358. doi:10.1017/S0140525X0453008X

Steinberg, L. (2008). A social neuroscience perspective on adolescent risk-taking. *Developmental Review, 28*(1), 78–106. doi:10.1016/j.dr.2007.08.002

Steinberg, L., Albert, D., Cauffman, E., Banich, M., Graham, S., & Woolard, J. (2008). Age differences in sensation seeking and impulsivity as indexed by behavior and self-report: Evidence for a dual systems model. *Developmental Psychology, 44,* 1764–1778. doi:10.1037/a0012955

St. Onge, J. R., Chiu, Y. C., & Floresco, S. B. (2010). Differential effects of dopaminergic manipulations on risky choice. *Psychopharmacology, 211,* 209–221. doi:10.1007/s00213-010-1883-y

Storbeck, J., & Clore, G. L. (2005). With sadness comes accuracy; with happiness, false memory: Mood and the false memory effect. *Psychological Science, 16,* 785–791. doi:10.1111/j.1467-9280.2005.01615.x

Strack, F., & Deutsch, R. (2004). Reflective and impulsive determinants of social behavior. *Personality and Social Psychology Review, 8,* 220–247. doi:10.1207/s15327957pspr0803_1

Toga, A. W., Thompson, P. M., & Sowell, E. R. (2006). Mapping brain maturation. *Trends in Neurosciences, 29,* 148–159. doi:10.1016/j.tins.2006.01.007

Tversky, A., & Kahneman, D. (1981, January 30). The framing of decisions and the psychology of choice. *Science, 211,* 453–458. doi:10.1126/science.7455683

Tversky, A., & Kahneman, D. (1986). Rational choice and the framing of decisions. *The Journal of Business, 59,* S251–S278. doi:10.1086/296365

Van den Bos, W., Guroglu, B., van den Bulk, B. G., Rombouts, S., & Crone, E. A. (2009). Better than expected or as bad as you thought? The neurocognitive development of probabilistic feedback processing. *Frontiers in Human Neuroscience, 3,* 1–11. doi:10.3389/neuro.09.052.2009

Van Duijvenvoorde, A. C. K., Jansen, B. R. J., Visser, I., & Huizenga, H. M. (2010). Affective and cognitive decision-making in adolescents. *Developmental Neuropsychology, 35,* 539–554. doi:10.1080/87565641.2010.494749

Van Duijvenvoorde, A. C. K., Zanolie, K., Rombouts, S., Raijmakers, M. E. J., & Crone, E. A. (2008). Evaluating the negative or valuing the positive? Neural mechanisms supporting feedback-based learning across development. *The Journal of Neuroscience, 28,* 9495–9503. doi:10.1523/JNEUROSCI.1485-08.2008

Van Leijenhorst, L., Crone, E. A., & Bunge, S. A. (2006). Neural correlates of developmental differences in risk estimation and feedback processing. *Neuropsychologia, 44,* 2158–2170. doi:10.1016/j.neuropsychologia.2006.02.002

Van Leijenhorst, L., Moor, B. G., Op de Macks, Z. A. O., Rombouts, S., Westenberg, P. M., & Crone, E. A. (2010). Adolescent risky decision-making: Neurocognitive development of reward and control regions. *NeuroImage, 51,* 345–355. doi:10.1016/j.neuroimage.2010.02.038

Van Leijenhorst, L., Westenberg, P. M., & Crone, E. A. (2008). A developmental study of risky decisions on the cake gambling task: Age and gender analyses of probability estimation and reward evaluation. *Developmental Neuropsychology, 33,* 179–196. doi:10.1080/87565640701884287

Van Leijenhorst, L., Zanolie, K., Van Meel, C. S., Westenberg, P. M., Rombouts, S., & Crone, E. A. (2010). What motivates the adolescent? Brain regions mediating reward sensitivity across adolescence. *Cerebral Cortex, 20*(1), 61–69. doi:10.1093/cercor/bhp078

Vartanian, O., Mandel, D. R., & Duncan, M. (2011). Money or life: Behavioral and neural context effects on choice under uncertainty. *Journal of Neuroscience, Psychology, and Economics, 4*(1), 25–36. doi:10.1037/a0021241

Wahlstrom, D., Collins, P., White, T., & Luciana, M. (2010). Developmental changes in dopamine neurotransmission in adolescence: Behavioral implications and issues in assessment. *Brain and Cognition, 72*(1), 146–159. doi:10.1016/j.bandc.2009.10.013

Wahlstrom, D., White, T., & Luciana, M. (2010). Neurobehavioral evidence for changes in dopamine system activity during adolescence. *Neuroscience and Biobehavioral Reviews, 34,* 631–648. doi:10.1016/j.neubiorev.2009.12.007

Weber, E. U., & Johnson, E. J. (2009). Mindful judgment and decision making. *Annual Review of Psychology, 60,* 53–85. doi:10.1146/annurev.psych.60.110707.163633

Zielinski, B. A., Gennatas, E. D., Zhou, J. A., & Seeley, W. W. (2010). Network-level structural covariance in the developing brain. *Proceedings of the National Academy of Sciences, USA, 107,* 18191–18196. doi:10.1073/pnas.1003109107

V

EPILOGUE

14

PARADOXES OF THE ADOLESCENT BRAIN IN COGNITION, EMOTION, AND RATIONALITY

VALERIE F. REYNA AND MICHAEL R. DOUGHERTY

It was the best of times, it was the worst of times; it was the age of wisdom, it was the age of foolishness.

—Charles Dickens, *A Tale of Two Cities*

Are youth at the height of their rational faculties, as would be inferred from their basic cognitive skills, or are they the quintessential example of irrational beings? In adolescence and young adulthood, the cognitive skills assumed to underlie educational and economic success are at a lifetime peak. Yet educational achievement (as assessed through international comparisons of test performance) is lower for high school students than for elementary or middle schoolers (Reyna & Brainerd, 2007). Moreover, the application of these mental faculties to real life seems woefully inadequate. Instead of learning from experience, reasoning about risks, and making sound decisions, youth often make unhealthy and unsafe choices. The striking contrast between advanced reasoning and poor reasoning, expressed in the quotation from Dickens's *A Tale of Two Cities*, might be represented as *A Tale of Two Brains*. This contradiction is a major motivation for this volume on the adolescent brain.

Is this contradiction explained by a disequilibrium between emotional and cognitive development (Institute of Medicine and the National Research Council, 2010)? Specifically, do the passions (i.e., the reward system in the brain) develop earlier and become heightened during adolescence, with cognitive control (and self-control) maturing later? The dual process explanation for unhealthy risk taking harkens back to Sigmund Freud's primary versus secondary processes, a distinction that has been elaborated in modern theories of the self (e.g., the cognitive experiential self theory; Epstein, 1994). Although an imbalance between dual systems during adolescence has long been assumed, research on behavior and brain development that would test this assumption has been lacking. As reviewed in this volume, animal models and human neuroimaging research have only recently emerged as major sources of evidence for "dueling" dual systems during adolescence through young adulthood.

However, the evidence is not nearly as simple as the familiar behavioral dual process accounts would suggest. Brain mechanisms appear to involve systems of interacting networks, rather than isolated regions of primitive reptilian or limbic brain versus the modern neocortex (e.g., Casey, Jones, & Hare, 2008). Youth are not oblivious to risks; they often overestimate them and their own mortality (e.g., Borowsky, Ireland, & Resnick, 2009). Their reasoning has been shown to be almost hyperrational: Risky behavior seems to result not only from impulse and emotion but also from "rational" analysis and deliberation (Chick & Reyna, Chapter 13, this volume; Reyna & Farley, 2006). Across problem behaviors, risky behaviors are typically predictable from perceptions of risks and benefits, at odds with the idea that such risk taking involves losing control in the presence of emotion (but see Schneider & Caffray, Chapter 11, this volume, for effects of emotion on risky behaviors).

It appears counterintuitive that for youth more so than for adults, the mathematical operations of expected value (i.e., multiplicatively integrating risks and rewards) roughly characterize real-life decision making. (Expected-value, or, similarly, expected-utility, calculations underlie traditional economic characterizations of decision making, too.) Although a rational calculus of expected value and other computational abilities may be related to decision making, there is no need to claim that such computation is conscious. These expected-value operations and other similar inverse relations (e.g., computing area from length and width, computing torque from weight and distance) are studied explicitly in classroom reasoning and problem solving. However, mathematics or quantitative reasoning in the classroom need not be altogether conscious, either. Indeed, there is evidence that linguistically mediated computations are mediated by inferior parietal regions, but online computations are mediated by the intraparietal sulcus—and the links between explicitly learned versus intuitively estimated numerical cognition are not yet clear (Feigenson, Dehaene, & Spelke, 2004).

Computation in the classroom and in everyday life share another similarity: As Ashcraft and Rudig (Chapter 9, this volume) demonstrated, emotion (i.e., anxiety) compromises computation in the classroom, as it compromises clear thinking in social contexts. The labile emotionality of adolescence, then, may interfere with reasoning in the classroom and in real life, offering another explanation for the disparity between cognitive competence and educational performance (as well as with real-life decision making). That is, the intellectual competence of the adolescent may be held hostage by emotional reactivity. As Casey, Jones, and Hare (2008) concluded, "When a poor decision is made in an emotional context, the adolescent may know better, but the salience of the emotional context biases his or her behavior in [the] opposite direction of the optimal action" (p. 7).

Empirically, there are no rigid boundaries between emotion and higher cognition, despite our Cartesian assumptions to the contrary. Education involves the entire individual, emotionally and cognitively. Conversely, coping with real life involves emotion and cognition; learning, reasoning, and deciding help young people make sense of and adapt to challenges in real life. Naturally, higher cognition does not operate identically in social and educational contexts, but there are significant elements of overlap. As the example of expected value demonstrates, but also in a larger sense, brain development and higher cognition are relevant to behavior inside and outside of the classroom.

Similarly, in both social and educational contexts, intelligence has been related to the quality of reasoning and decision making. In Chapter 12 of this volume, Stanovich et al. made a startling claim that challenges the traditional argument that intelligence is the evolutionary engine of rational adaptation. Instead, they argued that intelligence and rationality are not the same construct, offering an alternative explanation for their apparent dissociation in adolescence. In other words, adolescents could be both highly intelligent and highly irrational because these are different dimensions of higher cognition. By irrational, we do not mean psychotic; rather, we refer to the possible combination of high intelligence accompanied by a lack of judgment or good sense, which seems to characterize adolescence. What is missing, as Chick and Reyna (Chapter 13, this volume) explained, is the ability to draw from experience-based intuition in order to understand the meaning of the odds in context; in short, to think about risks in terms of gists, as opposed to calculating outcomes based on verbatim details.

Another major motivation for this volume is the significance of this developmental period. Understanding the developing brain at the threshold of adulthood is important for many reasons. The period from adolescence through young adulthood is full of promise for many young people. Those who graduate high school and attend college, emerging without addictions or mental health problems, are launched on a positive trajectory. Others fail at school, get in trouble, and form unhealthy habits, such as smoking, eating unhealthy foods, and engaging in other risky behaviors. Mathematics is a particular academic challenge during this period, and algebra has been singled out as the Waterloo of many students' academic careers (National Mathematics Panel,

2008). In school and out, behavioral patterns that are initiated in adolescence and young adulthood ramify across the life span.

To be sure, even seemingly successful youth can have addiction and serious mental health problems. Even academic stars are addicted to cigarettes, alcohol, or various other substances. Further, as our developmental colleagues would be quick to point out, pathways are not necessarily linear. Development continues after youth, addictions are overcome, and lives can be reclaimed. Change can occur in a downward direction, too. Successful youth can subsequently develop debilitating behavioral and psychological problems.

Nevertheless, as decades of prevention research have shown, problem behaviors stick together (Institute of Medicine and the National Research Council, 2010). Those who excel in school are less likely to experience premature pregnancy or the juvenile justice system. Conversely, youth who avoid premature pregnancy, alcohol and drug abuse, and the justice system have better academic outcomes and, hence, better lifetime success. As the chapters in this volume illustrate, the skills of life and of the classroom are not disjoint. Higher cognition, which encompasses learning, reasoning, and decision making, is important in both the domain of formal education and in everyday life. As chapters in this volume suggest, placing young children on a steep developmental trajectory may be essential for helping them overcome the many challenges they will face as adolescents and young adults. Cognitive, academic, and self-control skills acquired by adolescence will likely have downstream impacts on individuals' academic achievement as well as their ability to resist risky but seemingly rewarding behaviors.

Despite the intellectual puzzles posed by adolescent cognition, along with its educational and ultimately economic significance, much less is known about it than is known about cognition in childhood or old age. Until recently, adolescence and young adulthood were widely viewed as a period of developmental stasis. However, as the chapters in this volume delineate, the brain is developing appreciably during this period (e.g., Giedd et al., Chapter 1; Galván, Chapter 10). As Confrey explained in Chapter 6, the most fundamental concepts about fractions are not well understood in young adulthood (see also Reyna, Nelson, Han, & Dieckmann, 2009). Deductive arguments and proofs are also elusive, but apparently continue to develop in young adulthood (Knuth et al., Chapter 7, this volume). As McRae, Khalkali, and Hare illustrated in Chapter 2 of this volume, the basic semantic organization of concepts is also still evolving in adolescence. Abstract analogues are more useful for reasoning and problem solving much earlier—in childhood—than once thought (Kaminski & Sloutsky, Chapter 3), and yet concrete analogues remain helpful in adolescence (Blair & Schwartz, Chapter 4). Nevertheless, formal mental operations are not achieved in adolescence, as once believed, and are beyond the reach of many adults. The notion of cognitive stasis, that cognitive development is complete by adolescence, is no longer tenable. Far from being set in stone, the evidence suggests that higher cognition can be changed during this period. Chapman, Gamino, and Mudar (Chapter 5) showed that instructing students, even those with learning disabilities, in extracting the bottom-line gist (or meaning) from educational materials can result in improvements in achievement scores.

In fact, as Atkins, Bunting, Bolger and Dougherty spelled out in Chapter 8 of this volume, this cognitive malleability extends from youth to adulthood. One crucial implication of this result, especially if it continues to replicate across knowledge domains, is that investments to improve higher cognition in youth are not wasted. Although early childhood intervention remains a good idea for many problems, it is unlikely to be directly helpful in teaching algebra or reducing unhealthy drinking. Indeed, programs delivered too early are unsuccessful when target behaviors are not yet relevant developmentally. Moreover, the acquisition of general cognitive skills, such as working memory and inhibitory control, provide scaffolding upon which other, more specialized academic and life skills rely. Skills, knowledge, beliefs, and attitudes are not irretrievably hardened prior to young adulthood. More fundamentally, the way we acquire and apply these cognitive assets continues to change. That is, the evidence suggests that the way young people learn, reason, and decide *changes* and *can be changed*. An important consideration, however, is to identify those individuals who are most at risk for falling behind academically or engaging in risky behavior, so that interventions aimed at accelerating the development of important cognitive and emotional skills target those most in need and are designed within the appropriate sociocultural context. Indeed, the one-size-fits-all approach to inducing positive change is bound to fail, whether it be an educational, cognitive, or clinical intervention.

Contrary to conventional wisdom, then, cognitive development occurs from adolescence to adulthood: The tendency to spontaneously "connect the dots" of meaning grows during this period (Brainerd, Reyna, & Howe, 2009; McRae, Khalkhali, & Hare, Chapter 2, this volume). Emotions run higher and inhibition is lower, relative to adulthood. The massive pruning of gray matter and growth in connectivity in the brain, as Giedd et al. (Chapter 1) and Galván (Chapter 10) described, underscore the changes occurring in this period once viewed as uneventful.

In order to foster positive changes during this period of life, however, educational, cognitive, and brain scientists must be able to communicate with one another. Currently, they often do not seem to speak the same language. Hence, another purpose of this volume is to begin to build a dialogue between disparate groups of scholars. The changes in the brain described in this volume are relevant to educational and health outcomes, as well as to neuroscience research. To a surprising degree, our concerns are common. This volume represents an initial step toward a framework for interdisciplinary collaboration and change.

REFERENCES

Borowsky, I. W., Ireland, M., & Resnick, M. D. (2009). Health status and behavioral outcomes for youth who anticipate a high likelihood of early death. *Pediatrics, 124*(1), e81–e88. doi:10.1542/peds.2008-3425

Brainerd, C. J., Reyna, V. F., & Howe, M. L. (2009). Trichotomous processes in early memory development, aging, and neurocognitive impairment: A unified theory. *Psychological Review, 116*, 783–832. doi:10.1037/a0016963

Casey, B. J., Jones, R. M., & Hare, T. A. (2008). The adolescent brain. *Annals of the New York Academy of Sciences, 1124*, 111–126. doi:10.1196/annals.1440.010

Epstein, S. (1994). Integration of the cognitive and psychodynamic unconscious. *American Psychologist, 49*, 709–724. doi:10.1037/0003-066X.49.8.709

Feigenson, L., Dehaene, S., & Spelke, E. (2004). Core systems of number. *Trends in Cognitive Sciences, 8*, 307–314. doi:10.1016/j.tics.2004.05.002

Institute of Medicine and the National Research Council. (2010). *The science of adolescent risk-taking. Workshop summary.* Committee on the Science of Adolescence. Washington, DC: The National Academies Press.

Reyna, V. F., & Brainerd, C. J. (2007). The importance of mathematics in health and human judgment: Numeracy, risk communication, and medical decision making. *Learning and Individual Differences, 17*, 147–159. doi:10.1016/j.lindif.2007.03.010

Reyna, V. F., & Farley, F. (2006). Risk and rationality in adolescent decision-making: Implications for theory, practice, and public policy. *Psychological Science in the Public Interest, 7*(1), 1–44.

Reyna, V. F., Nelson, W., Han, P., & Dieckmann, N. F. (2009). How numeracy influences risk comprehension and medical decision making. *Psychological Bulletin, 135*, 943–973. doi:10.1037/a0017327

U.S. Department of Education, National Mathematics Advisory Panel (2008). *Foundations for success: The final report of the National Mathematics Advisory Panel.* Retrieved from http://www2.ed.gov/about/bdscomm/list/mathpanel/report/final-report.pdf

INDEX

Emotion
in academic achievement, 432–433
in adolescent paradox, 280
anticipated and anticipatory, 298n1
in higher order cognitive
processes, 433
and mathematics learning, 244
in risk taking, 406–411
Emotional development, 431–432
Emotional states, 294
Empirical support
inductive, 205
as inductive, 190
for justifications, 188–189
in learning trajectories, 157
Empiricist perspective, 195
Endophenotypes, 28
Energetic activities, 323
Engagement, 75
Engle, R. W., 215
Enviromental factors
and genetic factors, 24–26
in intelligence, 213
Epistemic rationality, 339, 344
Epstein, S., 352–353
Equipartitioning, 157
defined, 161
diagnostic assessment of, 171–178
learning trajectories of, 161–166
as learning trajectory, 165–171
reversal of, 168
Ernst, M., 277, 279, 393–394, 404
Error(s)
conjunction, 357, 361–362
heuristic processing in, 339–340
systematic, 159
of thinking, 340
Eshel, N., 279, 393–394, 404–406
Event-related potentials (ERPs),
131–132
Evidence, 184, 189, 192–193
Evidence-based protocols, 144
Evidential rationality, 339
Executive control system, 228
Executive function, 219
Exercise, 299–325
Expected utility, 339
Expected value, 383, 402, 404, 414, 432
See also Valuation
Experience
in developmental level, 382

in health-related behaviors, 317–325
in health-related decision making,
297–298
previous, 299–325
with risky decisions, 403
Expertise, gist-based thinking with,
385–386
Extrinsic motivation, 248
Eysenck, M. W., 253–254

Facilitative effects, 48–50
Fact learning, 124–129, 133–139, 145
Fair sharing, 165
False memory paradigm, 52–55
Families, 322
Farley, F., 294, 298, 324, 362, 363
Featural and Unitary Semantic System
model, 51
Featural relations, 46
Feature production norms, 47
Feedback, 105–109, 410
Feelings, risk as, 317–318
Feeling states, 318, 407–408
Females
brain size of, 18
cerebellum size in, 20
differences from males, 26–27
gray matter volume in, 22
Ferrand, L., 49–50
Ferretti, T. R., 57, 58
Finucane, M. L., 293, 413
Fischbein, E., 358
Fischler, I., 44
5HTT-LPR (serotonin transporter
polymorphism), 415–416
Fluid and crystallized intelligence,
theory of, 341
Fluid intelligence, 341
Fluid intelligence (Gf), 5, 213n1
Flynn, J. R., 213
Flynn effect, 213
Fong, G. W., 389
Formal operational stage, 4, 129
Fractions, 160
learning trajectories of, 164
learning trajectories with, 164
Framing
of decision options, 380, 413–418
neuroimaging of, 415–416
reverse, 414

intelligence in, 433
of mathematics, 167–168
Socialization, 271–272
Socioeconomic status, 322
Somerville, L. H., 273
Sorting, 196–203
Spiderkid, 106–108
Splitting, 161, 168–169
Spreading activation networks, 52
Stamford, J. A., 275
Standard dual process model, 381,
407–408
Standardized tests, 124, 137–138
Stanovich, K. E., 293, 344
State anxiety, 254
Steele, C. M., 255
Steinberg, L., 355–356, 405
STEM (science, technology, engineering,
and mathematics), 196–203
Stereotypes, 258
Stereotype threat, 255–256
Stevenson, H. W., 247
Stimulus onset asynchronies (SOA),
49–50
Strategic attention, 127
Strategic gist reasoning, 123–145
assessment of, 132–137
cognitive training in, 138–140
defined, 127
and higher order cognitive processes,
124–126
in learning efficiency, 126–129,
144–145
mitigating stall in, 138–140
neurocognitive delay in, 137–138
in strategic memory and reasoning
training, 140–143
Strategic memory and reasoning
training (SMART), 140–143
Strategies, 159, 170
Streamlined gist, 385
Strength, 306–317
Striatal system, 268, 272–278
Structural alignment, 73–74, 81–85
Structural equation modeling (SEM), 25
Structure
interpretation of, 72–73
relational, 81–85, 87, 109–112
of working memory, 215–216

Structures, mathematical. *See*
Mathematical structures
Stylianides, A., 184
Subcortical gray matter, 23–24
Subcortical limbic regions, 269–270
Subordinate, 46
Substantia nigra (SN), 274
Subtraction, 163
Summarization, 133–140
Superficial/surface features
of concrete learning materials,
113–115, 118
with mathematical concepts, 71–73
salience of, 85–87
Superordinate categories, 41, 46
Superstitious beliefs, 358–359
Supply-mismatch model, 223
Support, empirical, 157
Surface features. *See* Superficial/surface
features
Sustained-attention-to-response
task, 411
Sweeney, J. A., 412
Symbolic learning materials
and concrete learning materials, 96,
99–103, 117–119
as decontextualized, 75–76
for new mathematical structures,
109–112
Symbols, 69–70
Symmetry, 73
Synaptic pruning, 384
Synchronization, among activity in
different brain regions, 412
Synonyms, 46
Synthesis
of abstract material, 145
of dopamine, 275
of meaning, 139–140
in strategic gist reasoning, 126–129
Systematic errors, 159

Takeuchi, H., 221
A Tale of Two Cities (C. Dickens), 431
Tallal, P., 225
Tanner, C., 414
Task calibration, 382
Task switching, 216–217
TBI (traumatic brain injury),
133–135, 138

ABOUT THE EDITORS

Valerie F. Reyna, PhD, is codirector, Center for Behavioral Economics and Decision Research, and professor of human development, psychology, cognitive science, and neuroscience (IMAGINE Program), at Cornell University. Dr. Reyna is a developer of fuzzy trace theory, an influential model of memory and decision making that has been widely applied in law, medicine, and public health, as well as in neuroscience. A leader in using memory principles and mathematical models to explain judgment and decision making, she helped initiate what is now a burgeoning area of research on developmental differences in judgment and decision making. Her recent work has focused on neuroeconomics; aging, neurocognitive impairment, and genetic risk factors (e.g., in Alzheimer's disease); rationality and risky decision making, particularly risk taking in adolescence; and neuroimaging models of framing and decision making. She has also extended fuzzy trace theory to risk perception, numeracy, and medical decision making by both physicians and patients. She is the past president of the Society for Judgment and Decision Making, and she currently serves on scientific panels of the National Academy of Sciences, National Institutes of Health, and National Science Foundation. Dr. Reyna is an elected Fellow of the American Association for the

Advancement of Science, the Association for Psychological Science, and four divisions of the American Psychological Association.

Sandra B. Chapman, PhD, is the founder and chief director of the Center for BrainHealth, Behavioral and Brain Sciences, and Dee Wyly Distinguished Professor, The University of Texas at Dallas. Dr. Chapman's research as a cognitive neuroscientist, spanning 25 years, is devoted to better understanding how to maximize higher order reasoning, critical thinking, and innovation across the life span, and how to protect and heal cognitive brain function from brain injuries and diseases. Dr. Chapman is actively involved in public policy to address brain health and to discover ways to maximize cognitive brain function from youth through adulthood. Her research reveals that the middle school years represent a pivotal window for developing reasoning skills. Her team has developed ways to measure and advance these skills to address the growing decline in teen reasoning capacity through administering evidenced-based cognitive training programs. Dr. Chapman coined the term Brainomics© to represent the economics of brain power— our greatest economic asset and cost burden—developed at school and in the workplace, for better or worse. With more than 125 publications and 30 funded research grants, her research spans the age spectrum from studies that establish ways to advance teen reasoning to protocols that enhance cognitive brain function into late life.

Michael R. Dougherty, PhD, is an associate professor of psychology, Program in Neuroscience and Cognitive Science, University of Maryland. Dr. Dougherty's work focuses on the fundamental bases of judgment and decision making, cognitive plasticity, the emergence of cognitive ability, and how these capacities interrelate. His research spans such topics as human factors, limitations of attention and working memory, memory search and retrieval, and hypothesis generation and probability judgment. This research involves an integrative approach that implements mathematical and computational modeling, behavioral experiments, and eye-tracking methodologies. His recent work applies neuroimaging techniques to understanding cognitive adaptation and retraining, collaborating with members of the Neuroscience and Cognitive Science Program. Dr. Dougherty also collaborates with researchers at the University of Maryland Center for Advanced Study of Language on projects related to improving language comprehension and cognitive ability. He has received numerous scientific awards, including the Hillel Einhorn New Investigator Award from the Society for Judgment and Decision Making, and the early investigator CAREER award from the National Science Foundation.

Jere Confrey, PhD, is the Joseph D. Moore Distinguished Professor of Mathematics Education at North Carolina State University and a senior scholar at the William and Ida Friday Institute for Educational Innovation. Dr. Confrey is building diagnostic assessments of rational number reasoning using a learning trajectories approach. She is a member of the Validation Committee for the Common Core State Standards, and was vice chairman of the Mathematics Sciences Education Board, National Academy of Sciences (1998–2004). She chaired the National Research Council (NRC) Committee that produced *On Evaluating Curricular Effectiveness*, and she was a coauthor of the NRC's *Scientific Research in Education*. She was also a cofounder of the UTEACH Program at the University of Texas in Austin, the largest secondary teacher education program for mathematics and science teachers at a research university. She was the founder of the SummerMath program for young women at Mount Holyoke College and cofounder of SummerMath for Teachers Program. She coauthored the software Function Probe, Graph N Glyphs and sets of interactive diagrams. She has served as vice-president of the International Group for the Psychology of Mathematics Education; chair of the Special Interest Group—Research in Mathematics Education; on the editorial boards of the *Journal for Research in Mathematics Education, International Journal for Computers in Mathematics Learning,* and *Cognition and Instruction;* and on the Research Committee of the National Council of Teachers of Mathematics. Dr. Confrey has taught school at the elementary, secondary, and postsecondary levels.